DRAMA
for Students

DRAMA
for Students

**Presenting Analysis, Context, and Criticism on
Commonly Studied Dramas**

Volume 10

Michael L. LaBlanc, Editor

GALE GROUP

*Detroit
New York
San Francisco
London
Boston
Woodbridge, CT*

National Advisory Board

Drama for Students

Staff

Series Editors: Michael L. LaBlanc.

Contributing Editors: Elizabeth Bellalouna, Anne Marie Hacht, Ira Mark Milne, Jennifer Smith.

Managing Editor: Dwayne Hayes.

Research: Victoria B. Cariappa, *Research Team Manager.* Maureen Eremic, Barb McNeil, Cheryl Warnock, *Research Specialists.* Andy Malonis, *Technical Training Specialist.* Barbara Leevy, Tamara Nott, Tracie A. Richardson, Robert Whaley, *Research Associates.* Scott Floyd, Nicodemus Ford, Sarah Genik, Timothy Lehnerer, *Research Assistants.*

Permissions: Maria Franklin, *Permissions Manager.* Margaret A. Chamberlain, Edna Hedblad, *Permissions Specialists.* Erin Bealmear, Shalice Shah-Caldwell, Sarah Tomasek, *Permissions Associates.* Debra Freitas, Julie Juengling, Mark Plaza, *Permissions Assistants.*

Manufacturing: Mary Beth Trimper, *Manager, Composition and Electronic Prepress.* Evi Seoud, *Assistant Manager, Composition Purchasing and Electronic Prepress.* Stacy Melson, *Buyer.*

Imaging and Multimedia Content Team: Randy Bassett, *Image Database Supervisor.* Robert Duncan, Dan Newell, *Imaging Specialists.* Pamela A. Reed, *Imaging Coordinator.* Dean Dauphinais, Robyn V. Young, *Senior Image Editors.* Kelly A. Quin, *Image Editor.*

Product Design Team: Kenn Zorn, *Product Design Manager.* Pamela A. E. Galbreath, *Senior Art Director.* Michael Logusz, *Graphic Artist.*

Copyright Notice

Table of Contents

GUEST FOREWORD
  "The Study of Drama"
  by Carole L. Hamilton ix

INTRODUCTION xi

LITERARY CHRONOLOGY xv

ACKNOWLEDGMENTS xvii

CONTRIBUTORS xxi

THE BALCONY
  Jean Genet   1

BLOOD WEDDING
  Federico García Lorca 20

DEATH AND THE KING'S HORSEMAN
  Wole Soyinka 49

THE KENTUCKY CYCLE
  Robert Schenkkan 82

LYSISTRATA
  Aristophanes 104

THE MEMORANDUM
  Vaclav Havel 123

ONCE IN A LIFETIME
  George S. Kaufman and Moss Hart . . 145

RING AROUND THE MOON
  Jean Anouilh 166

SEVEN AGAINST THEBES
Aeschylus 183

SIZWE BANSI IS DEAD
Athol Fugard 220

THE THREE SISTERS
Anton Chekhov 247

TINY ALICE
Edward Albee 281

VOLPONE
Ben(jamin) Jonson 307

THE WILD DUCK
Henrik Ibsen 346

GLOSSARY OF LITERARY TERMS 377

CUMULATIVE AUTHOR/TITLE INDEX . 411

NATIONALITY/ETHNICITY INDEX . . . 415

SUBJECT/THEME INDEX 419

The Study of Drama

We study drama in order to learn what meaning others have made of life, to comprehend what it takes to produce a work of art, and to glean some understanding of ourselves. Drama produces in a separate, aesthetic world, a moment of being for the audience to experience, while maintaining the detachment of a reflective observer.

Drama is a representational art, a visible and audible narrative presenting virtual, fictional characters within a virtual, fictional universe. Dramatic realizations may pretend to approximate reality or else stubbornly defy, distort, and deform reality into an artistic statement. From this separate universe that is obviously not ''real life'' we expect a valid reflection upon reality, yet drama never is mistaken for reality—the methods of theater are integral to its form and meaning. Theater is art, and art's appeal lies in its ability both to approximate life and to depart from it. By presenting its distorted version of life to our consciousness, art gives us a new perspective and appreciation of reality. Although, to some extent, all aesthetic experiences perform this service, theater does it most effectively by creating a separate, cohesive universe that freely acknowledges its status as an art form.

And what is the purpose of the aesthetic universe of drama? The potential answers to such a question are nearly as many and varied as there are plays written, performed, and enjoyed. Dramatic texts can be problems posed, answers asserted, or moments portrayed. Dramas (tragedies as well as comedies) may serve strictly ''to ease the anguish of a torturing hour'' (as stated in William Shakespeare's *A Midsummer Night's Dream*)—to divert and entertain—or aspire to move the viewer to action with social issues. Whether to entertain or to instruct, affirm or influence, pacify or shock, dramatic art wraps us in the spell of its imaginary world for the length of the work and then dispenses us back to the real world, entertained, purged, as Aristotle said, of pity and fear, and edified—or at least weary enough to sleep peacefully.

It is commonly thought that theater, being an art of performance, must be experienced—that is, seen—in order to be appreciated fully. However, to view a production of a dramatic text is to be limited to a single interpretation of that text—all other interpretations are for the moment closed off, inaccessible. In the process of producing a play, the director, stage designer, and performers interpret and transform the script into a work of art that always departs in some measure from the author's original conception. Novelist and critic Umberto Eco, in his *The Role of the Reader: Explorations in the Semiotics of Texts,* explained, ''In short, we can say that every performance offers us a complete and satisfying version of the work, but at the same time makes it incomplete for us, because it cannot simultaneously give all the other artistic solutions which the work may admit.''

Thus Laurence Olivier's coldly formal and neurotic film presentation of Shakespeare's *Hamlet* (in which he played the title character as well as directed) shows marked differences from subsequent adaptations. While Olivier's Hamlet is clearly entangled in a Freudian relationship with his mother, Gertrude, he would be incapable of shushing her with the impassioned kiss that Mel Gibson's mercurial Hamlet (in director Franco Zeffirelli's 1990 film) does. Although each of the performances rings true to Shakespeare's text, each is also a mutually exclusive work of art. Also important to consider are the time periods in which each of these films were produced: Olivier made his film in 1948, a time in which overt references to sexuality (especially incest) were frowned upon. Gibson and Zeffirelli made their film in a culture more relaxed and comfortable with these issues. Just as actors and directors can influence the presentation of drama, so too can the time period of the production affect what the audience will see.

A play script is an open text from which an infinity of specific realizations may be derived. Dramatic scripts that are more open to interpretive creativity (such as those of Ntozake Shange and Tomson Highway) actually require the creative improvisation of the production troupe in order to complete the text. Even the most prescriptive scripts (those of Neil Simon, Lillian Hellman, and Robert Bolt, for example), can never fully control the actualization of live performance, and circumstantial events, including the attitude and receptivity of the audience, make every performance a unique event. Thus, while it is important to view a production of a dramatic piece, if one wants to understand a drama fully it is equally important to read the original dramatic text.

The reader of a dramatic text or script is not limited by either the specific interpretation of a given production or by the unstoppable action of a moving spectacle. The reader of a dramatic text may discover the nuances of the play's language, structure, and events at their own pace. Yet studied alone, the author's blueprint for artistic production does not tell the whole story of a play's life and significance. One also needs to assess the play's critical reviews to discover how it resonated to cultural themes at the time of its debut and how the shifting tides of cultural interest have revised its interpretation and impact on audiences. And to do this, one needs to know a little about the culture of the times which produced the play as well as the author who penned it.

Drama for Students supplies this material in a useful compendium for the student of dramatic theater. Covering a range of dramatic works that span from the fifth century B.C. to the 1990s, this book focuses on significant theatrical works whose themes and form transcend the uncertainty of dramatic fads. These are plays that have proven to be both memorable and teachable. *Drama for Students* seeks to enhance appreciation of these dramatic texts by providing scholarly materials written with the secondary and college/university student in mind. It provides for each play a concise summary of the plot and characters as well as a detailed explanation of its themes and techniques. In addition, background material on the historical context of the play, its critical reception, and the author's life help the student to understand the work's position in the chronicle of dramatic history. For each play entry a new work of scholarly criticism is also included, as well as segments of other significant critical works for handy reference. A thorough bibliography provides a starting point for further research.

These inaugural two volumes offer comprehensive educational resources for students of drama. *Drama for Students* is a vital book for dramatic interpretation and a valuable addition to any reference library.

Source: Eco, Umberto, *The Role of the Reader: Explorations in the Semiotics of Texts,* Indiana University Press, 1979.

Carole L. Hamilton
Author and Instructor of English
Cary Academy
Cary, North Carolina

Introduction

Purpose of Drama for Students

The purpose of *Drama for Students* (*DfS*) is to provide readers with a guide to understanding, enjoying, and studying dramas by giving them easy access to information about the work. Part of Gale's ''For Students'' literature line, *DfS* is specifically designed to meet the curricular needs of high school and undergraduate college students and their teachers, as well as the interests of general readers and researchers considering specific plays. While each volume contains entries on ''classic'' dramas frequently studied in classrooms, there are also entries containing hard-to-find information on contemporary plays, including works by multicultural, international, and women playwrights.

The information covered in each entry includes an introduction to the play and the work's author; a plot summary, to help readers unravel and understand the events in a drama; descriptions of important characters, including explanation of a given character's role in the drama as well as discussion about that character's relationship to other characters in the play; analysis of important themes in the drama; and an explanation of important literary techniques and movements as they are demonstrated in the play.

In addition to this material, which helps the readers analyze the play itself, students are also provided with important information on the literary and historical background informing each work.

This includes a historical context essay, a box comparing the time or place the drama was written to modern Western culture, a critical overview essay, and excerpts from critical essays on the play. A unique feature of *DfS* is a specially commissioned overview essay on each drama by an academic expert, targeted toward the student reader.

To further aid the student in studying and enjoying each play, information on media adaptations is provided, as well as reading suggestions for works of fiction and nonfiction on similar themes and topics. Classroom aids include ideas for research papers and lists of critical sources that provide additional material on each drama.

Selection Criteria

The titles for each volume of *DfS* were selected by surveying numerous sources on teaching literature and analyzing course curricula for various school districts. Some of the sources surveyed included: literature anthologies; *Reading Lists for College-Bound Students: The Books Most Recommended by America's Top Colleges;* textbooks on teaching dramas; a College Board survey of plays commonly studied in high schools; a National Council of Teachers of English (NCTE) survey of plays commonly studied in high schools; St. James Press's *International Dictionary of Theatre;* and Arthur Applebee's 1993 study *Literature in the Secondary School: Studies of Curriculum and Instruction in the United States.*

Input was also solicited from our expert advisory board (both experienced educators specializing in English), as well as educators from various areas. From these discussions, it was determined that each volume should have a mix of "classic" dramas (those works commonly taught in literature classes) and contemporary dramas for which information is often hard to find. Because of the interest in expanding the canon of literature, an emphasis was also placed on including works by international, multicultural, and women playwrights. Our advisory board members—current high school teachers—helped pare down the list for each volume. If a work was not selected for the present volume, it was often noted as a possibility for a future volume. As always, the editor welcomes suggestions for titles to be included in future volumes.

How Each Entry Is Organized

Each entry, or chapter, in *DfS* focuses on one play. Each entry heading lists the full name of the play, the author's name, and the date of the play's first production or publication. The following elements are contained in each entry:

- **Introduction:** a brief overview of the drama which provides information about its first appearance, its literary standing, any controversies surrounding the work, and major conflicts or themes within the work.

- **Author Biography:** this section includes basic facts about the author's life, and focuses on events and times in the author's life that inspired the drama in question.

- **Plot Summary:** a description of the major events in the play, with interpretation of how these events help articulate the play's themes. Subheads demarcate the plays' various acts or scenes.

- **Characters:** an alphabetical listing of major characters in the play. Each character name is followed by a brief to an extensive description of the character's role in the plays, as well as discussion of the character's actions, relationships, and possible motivation.

  Characters are listed alphabetically by last name. If a character is unnamed—for instance, the Stage Manager in *Our Town*—the character is listed as "The Stage Manager" and alphabetized as "Stage Manager." If a character's first name is the only one given, the name will appear alphabetically by the name.

Variant names are also included for each character. Thus, the nickname "Babe" would head the listing for a character in *Crimes of the Heart,* but below that listing would be her less-mentioned married name "Rebecca Botrelle."

- **Themes:** a thorough overview of how the major topics, themes, and issues are addressed within the play. Each theme discussed appears in a separate subhead, and is easily accessed through the boldface entries in the Subject/Theme Index.

- **Style:** this section addresses important style elements of the drama, such as setting, point of view, and narration; important literary devices used, such as imagery, foreshadowing, symbolism; and, if applicable, genres to which the work might have belonged, such as Gothicism or Romanticism. Literary terms are explained within the entry, but can also be found in the Glossary.

- **Historical and Cultural Context:** This section outlines the social, political, and cultural climate *in which the author lived and the play was created.* This section may include descriptions of related historical events, pertinent aspects of daily life in the culture, and the artistic and literary sensibilities of the time in which the work was written. If the play is a historical work, information regarding the time in which the play is set is also included. Each section is broken down with helpful subheads.

- **Critical Overview:** this section provides background on the critical reputation of the play, including bannings or any other public controversies surrounding the work. For older plays, this section includes a history of how the drama was first received and how perceptions of it may have changed over the years; for more recent plays, direct quotes from early reviews may also be included.

- **For Further Study:** an alphabetical list of other critical sources which may prove useful for the student. Includes full bibliographical information and a brief annotation.

- **Sources:** an alphabetical list of critical material quoted in the entry, with full bibliographical information.

- **Criticism:** an essay commissioned by *DfS* which specifically deals with the play and is written specifically for the student audience, as well as excerpts from previously published criticism on the work.

In addition, each entry contains the following highlighted sections, set separate from the main text:

- **Media Adaptations:** a list of important film and television adaptations of the play, including source information. The list may also include such variations on the work as audio recordings, musical adaptations, and other stage interpretations.

- **Compare and Contrast Box:** an ''at-a-glance'' comparison of the cultural and historical differences between the author's time and culture and late twentieth-century Western culture. This box includes pertinent parallels between the major scientific, political, and cultural movements of the time or place the drama was written, the time or place the play was set (if a historical work), and modern Western culture. Works written after the mid-1970s may not have this box.

- **What Do I Read Next?:** a list of works that might complement the featured play or serve as a contrast to it. This includes works by the same author and others, works of fiction and nonfiction, and works from various genres, cultures, and eras.

- **Study Questions:** a list of potential study questions or research topics dealing with the play. This section includes questions related to other disciplines the student may be studying, such as American history, world history, science, math, government, business, geography, economics, psychology, etc.

Other Features

DfS includes ''The Study of Drama,'' a foreword by Carole Hamilton, an educator and author who specializes in dramatic works. This essay examines the basis for drama in societies and what drives people to study such work. Hamilton also discusses how *Drama for Students* can help teachers show students how to enrich their own reading/viewing experiences.

A Cumulative Author/Title Index lists the authors and titles covered in each volume of the *DfS* series.

A Cumulative Nationality/Ethnicity Index breaks down the authors and titles covered in each volume of the *DfS* series by nationality and ethnicity.

A Subject/Theme Index, specific to each volume, provides easy reference for users who may be studying a particular subject or theme rather than a single work. Significant subjects from events to broad themes are included, and the entries pointing to the specific theme discussions in each entry are indicated in **boldface.**

Each entry has several illustrations, including photos of the author, stills from stage productions, and stills from film adaptations.

Citing Drama for Students

When writing papers, students who quote directly from any volume of *Drama for Students* may use the following general forms. These examples are based on MLA style; teachers may request that students adhere to a different style, so the following examples may be adapted as needed.

When citing text from *DfS* that is not attributed to a particular author (i.e., the Themes, Style, Historical Context sections, etc.), the following format should be used in the bibliography section:

''Our Town,'' *Drama for Students.* Ed. David Galens and Lynn Spampinato. Vol. 1. Farmington Hills: Gale, 1997. 8–9.

When quoting the specially commissioned essay from *DfS* (usually the first piece under the ''Criticism'' subhead), the following format should be used:

Fiero, John. Essay on ''Twilight: Los Angeles, 1992.'' *Drama for Students.* Ed. David Galens and Lynn Spampinato. Vol. 1. Farmington Hills: Gale, 1997. 8–9.

When quoting a journal or newspaper essay that is reprinted in a volume of *DfS,* the following form may be used:

Rich, Frank. ''Theatre: A Mamet Play, 'Glengarry Glen Ross'.'' *New York Theatre Critics' Review* Vol. 45, No. 4 (March 5, 1984), 5–7; excerpted and reprinted in *Drama for Students,* Vol. 1, ed. David Galens and Lynn Spampinato (Farmington Hills: Gale, 1997), pp. 61–64.

When quoting material reprinted from a book that appears in a volume of *DfS,* the following form may be used:

Kerr, Walter. ''The Miracle Worker,'' in *The Theatre in Spite of Itself* (Simon & Schuster, 1963, 255–57; excerpted and reprinted in *Drama for Students,* Vol. 1, ed. Dave Galens and Lynn Spampinato (Farmington Hills: Gale, 1997), pp. 59–61.

We Welcome Your Suggestions

The editor of *Drama for Students* welcomes your comments and ideas. Readers who wish to suggest dramas to appear in future volumes, or who have other suggestions, are cordially invited to contact the editor. You may contact the editor via

E-mail at: **michael.lablanc@galegroup.com.** Or
write to the editor at:

Editor, *Drama for Students*
The Gale Group
27500 Drake Rd.
Farmington Hills, MI 48331-3535

Literary Chronology

525 B.C.: Aeschylus is born, probably in Eleusis, just outside Athens, Greece.

467 B.C.: Aeschylus writes *Seven Against Thebes*.

456 B.C.: Aeschylus dies.

450 B.C.: Aristophanes is born in Greece.

411 B.C.: Aristophanes writes *Lysistrata*.

385 B.C.: Aristophanes dies.

1572: Ben Jonson is born near London, England.

1606: Ben Jonson writes *Volpone*.

1637: Ben Jonson dies nine years after suffering a debilitating stroke.

1828: Henrik Ibsen is born in a small town in Norway.

1860: Anton Chekhov is born in Taganrog, a provincial town in the Ukraine area of Russia.

1884: Henrik Ibsen writes *The Wild Duck*.

1889: George S. Kaufman is born in Pittsburgh, Pennsylvania, on November 16.

1898: Federico García Lorca is born on June 5 in the small Spanish town of Fuente Vaqueros, near the city of Granada.

1901: The Moscow Art Theatre produces Anton Chekhov's *The Three Sisters*.

1904: Moss Hart is born in the Bronx, New York, on October 24.

1904: Anton Chekhov dies of tuberculosis in Yalta.

1906: Henrik Ibsen dies following a series of strokes.

1910: Jean Genet is born in Paris, France on December 19.

1910: Jean Anouilh is born in Bordeaux in the southwest of France.

1928: Edward Albee is born in Virginia. He is adopted by Reed and Frances Albee two weeks after his birth.

1930: Moss Hart and George S. Kaufman finish writing *Once in a Lifetime*.

1932: Athol Fugard is born in Middleburg, Cape Province, South Africa, on June 11.

1933: Federico García Lorca writes *Blood Wedding*.

1934: Akinwande Oluwole Soyinka is born in Ijebu Isara, near Akeokuta in western Nigeria, on July 13.

1936: Federico García Lorca is arrested by Spanish fascists near Granada on August 16 and shot to death on either August 18 or 19.

1936: Vaclav Havel is born in Prague, Czechoslovakia, on October 5.

1937: Moss Hart and George S. Kaufman win a Pulitzer Prize for their screenplay *You Can't Take It With You*.

1947: Jean Anouilh writes *Ring Around the Moon*.

1949: Jean Anouilh receives the Grand Prize of French Cinema.

1953: Robert Schenkkan is born.

1956: Jean Genet writes *The Balcony*.

1957: Jean Anouilh wins the New York Drama Critics Award and the French Drama Critics Award.

1961: George S. Kaufman dies of a heart attack in New York City on June 2.

1961: Moss Hart dies on December 20.

1961: Edward Albee wins the Vernon Rice Memorial Award for *The Zoo Story*, which he completed in three weeks.

1964: Edward Albee writes *Tiny Alice*.

1965: Vaclav Havel writes *The Memorandum*.

1966: Edward Albee wins his first Pulitzer Prize for *A Delicate Balance*.

1972: Athol Fugard writes *Sizwe Bansi is Dead*.

1975: Wole Soyinka writes *Death and the King's Horseman*.

1975: Edward Albee wins his second Pulitzer Prize for *Seascape*.

1986: Jean Genet dies of throat cancer on April 15.

1986: Wole Soyinka becomes the first African writer to win the Nobel Prize for Literature.

1987: Jean Anouilh dies in Switzerland.

1989: Vaclav Havel is elected President of Czechoslovakia.

1991: Robert Schenkkan completes *The Kentucky Cycle*.

1991: Edward Albee wins his third Pulitzer Prize for *Three Tall Women*.

1992: Robert Schenkkan's *The Kentucky Cycle* is awarded the Pulitzer Prize for Best Drama.

1993: Vaclav Havel is elected President of the Czech Republic.

Acknowledgments

The editors wish to thank the copyright holders of the excerpted criticism included in this volume and the permissions managers of many book and magazine publishing companies for assisting us in securing reproduction rights. We are also grateful to the staffs of the Detroit Public Library, the Library of Congress, the University of Detroit Mercy Library, Wayne State University Purdy/Kresge Library Complex, and the University of Michigan Libraries for making their resources available to us. Following is a list of the copyright holders who have granted us permission to reproduce material in this volume of *Drama for Students (DfS)*. Every effort has been made to trace copyright, but if omissions have been made, please let us know.

COPYRIGHTED MATERIALS IN *DfS*, VOLUME 10, WERE REPRODUCED FROM THE FOLLOWING PERIODICALS:

American Theatre, v. 15, July-August, 1998; v. 15, December, 1998. Copyright © 1998 Theatre Communication Group. Both reproduced by permission.—*Bulletin of the New York Public Library*, v. 73, 1969. Reproduced by permission.—*Cahiers Élisabéthains*, April, 1985 for "The Progress of Trickster in Ben Jonson's Volpone" by Don Beecher. All rights reserved. Reproduced by permission of the publisher and the author.—*The Classical Quarterly*, v. 45, January-June, 1995 for "Aristophanes, 'Lysistrata' 231" by W.G. Forrest. Copyright © Oxford University Press 1995. Repro-

duced by permission of the publisher and the author.—*College Literature*, v. 19, October-February, 1992. Copyright © 1992 by West Chester University. Reproduced by permission.—*Commonweal*, v. 124, March, 1997. Copyright © 1997 Commonweal Foundation. Reproduced by permission.—*Comparative Drama*, v. 30, Spring, 1996. © copyright 1996, by the Editors of *Comparative Drama*. Reproduced by permission.—*Cross Currents*, Dobbs Ferry, v. 42, Summer, 1990. Copyright 1990 by Association for Religion and intellectual Life. Inc. Reprinted by permission of the publisher.—*The Drama Review*, v. 14, 1970 for "LeRoi Jones' 'Slave Ship'" by Stefan Brecht. Copyright © 1970, *The Drama Review*. Reproduced by permission of the publisher and the author.—*The Economist*, v. 344, November, 1997. Copyright 1997 The Economist Newspaper Ltd. All right reserved. Reproduced by permission. Further reproduction prohibited. www.economist.com—*English Studies*, v. 71, June, 1990. © 1990, Swets & Zeitlinger. Reproduced by permission.—*Maclean's Magazine*, v. 106, June, 1993. © 1993 by *Maclean's Magazine*. Reproduced by permission.—*Modern Drama*, v. 7, May, 1964; v. 10, February, 1968; v. 11, 1968; September, 1976; September, 1987; Fall, 1995. Copyright © 1964, 1968, 1976, 1987, 1995, University of Toronto, Graduate Centre for Study of Drama. All reproduced by permission.—*Modern Language Quarterly*, v. XXIV, March, 1963. © 1963 University of Washington. Reproduced by permission of Duke University Press.—*The Nation*, New York, v. 178, May 29, 1954; v. 257, December, 1993. Copyright 1954, © 1993 *The Nation* magazine/ The Nation Company, Inc. Both reproduced by permission.—*The New Republic*, v. 194, April, 1986; v. 203, July, 1990; v. 209, November, 1993. © 1986, 1990, 1993 The New Republic, Inc. All reproduced by permission of *The New Republic*.—*New York* Magazine, v. 26, November 29, 1993. Copyright © 1993 K-III Magazine Corporation. All rights reserved. Reproduced with the permission of *New York* Magazine.—*The New York Times*, June 16, 1978. Copyright © 1978 by The New York Times Company. Reproduced by permission.—*Performing Arts Journal*, January, 1994. Copyright © John Hopkins University Press 1994. Reproduced by permission of The Johns Hopkins University Press.—*Race & Class*, v. XXI, 1980. Reproduced by permission.—*Renaissance Papers*, 1978. Reproduced by permission.—*Research in African Literatures*, v. 24, Spring, 1993; v. 25, Spring, 1994. Copyright © Indiana University Press 1993, 1994. Both reproduced by permission.—*SEL Studies in English Literature*, 1500–1900, v. 19, 1979. © 1979 William Marsh Rice University. Reproduced by permission of The Johns Hopkins University Press.—*The Theatre Annual*, v. 23, 1967. Reproduced by permission.—*Tulane Drama Review*, v. 11, Spring, 1967. Copyright © 1967, *Tulane Drama Review*. Reproduced by permission of MIT Press, Cambridge, Massachusetts.—*Twentieth Century Literature*, v. 39, Winter, 1993. Copyright 1993, Hofstra University Press. Reproduced by permission.—*U.S. News & World Report*, v. 115, September, 1993. Copyright © 1993, by U.S. News & World Report, Inc. All rights reserved. Reproduced by permission.—*Variety*, v. 374, May, 1998; v. 371, June, 1998. Copyright © 1998 Cahners Publishing Company. Both reproduced by permission.

COPYRIGHTED MATERIALS IN *DfS*, VOLUME 10, WERE REPRODUCED FROM THE FOLLOWING BOOKS:

Bristow, Eugene K. From "Circles, Triads, and Parity in 'The Three Sisters'" in *Checkhov's Great Plays*. Edited by Jean-Pierre Barricelli. New York University Press, 1981. Reproduced by permission.—Cantu, Roberto. For "Understanding Federico Garcia Lorca's 'Bodas de Sangre/Blood Wedding.' From Dramatic Text to Theatrical Performance." Los Angeles Bilingual Foundation of the Arts, 1999. Reproduced by permission of the author.—Chametzky, Jules. From *From Hester Street to Hollywood: The Jewish American Stage and Screen*. Indiana University Press, 1983. Copyright © 1983 by Indiana University Press. Reproduced by permission.—Grossvogel, David I. From *Four Playwrights and a Postscript*. Cornell University Press, 1962. Copyright © 1962 by Cornell University. Reproduced by permission.—Kramer, Karl D. From "'Three Sisters,' or Taking a Chance on Love" in *Checkhov's Great Plays*. Edited by Jean-Pierre Barricelli. New York University Press, 1981. Reproduced by permission.—Porter, David H. From *Only Connect: Three Studies in Greek Tragedy*. University Press of America, 1987. Copyright © 1987 by University Press of America, Inc. All rights reserved. Reproduced by permission.—Stark, John. From "Camping Out: 'Tiny Alice' and Susan Sontag" in *Critical Essays on Edward Albee*. Edited by Philip C. Kolin and J. Madison Davis. G.K. Hall & Co., 1986. Reproduced by permission of The Gale Group.—Thalmann, William G. From *Dramatic Art in Aeschylus's Seven Against Thebes*. Yale University Press, 1978. Copyright © 1978 by Yale University. All rights reserved. Reproduced by permission.—Valgemae, Mardi. From "Albee's Great God Alice" in *Critical Essays on Edward Albee*. Edited by Philip C. Kolin and J. Madison Davis. G.K. Hall & Co., 1986. Reproduced by permission of The Gale Group.—Zeitlin, Froma I. From *Under the Sign of the Shield: Semiotics and Aeschylus' Seven Against Thebes*. Edizioni dell'Ateneo, s.p.a., 1982. 1982 © Copyright by Edizioni dell'Ateneo, s.p.a. Reproduced by permission.

PHOTOGRAPHS AND ILLUSTRATIONS APPEARING IN *DfS*, VOLUME 10, WERE RECEIVED FROM THE FOLLOWING SOURCES:

Act I from a Moscow Art Theater production of "The Seagull" by Anton Chekhov, 1905, photograph. From Konstantin Stanislavsky: Selected Works, compiled by Oksana Korneva. Raduga Publishers, Moscow, 1984.—Act III of a Moscow Art Theater production of "The Seagull" by Chekhov (with Stanislavsky, Lilina, and Roksanova), 1905, photograph. From Konstantin Stanislavsky: Selected Works, compiled by Oksana Korneva. Raduga Publishers, Moscow, 1984.—Anouilh, Jean (wearing plaid blazer, glasses with round lenses), 1971, photograph. AP/Wide World Photos. Reproduced by permission.—Aristophanes (body turned to his right), print. Archive Photos, Inc. Reproduced by permission.—Ashcroft, Peggy, as Irena, with Gwen Ffrangcon Davies, as Olga, a scene from John

Gielgud's theatrical version of Anton Chekhov's play, "The Three Sisters," the Queen's Theatre, photograph. The Kobal Collection. Reproduced by permission.—Buero Vallejo (pipe in mouth, wearing tweed suit), Madrid, Spain, 1986, photograph. AP/Wide World Photos. Reproduced by permission.—Characters from the film version of Anton Chekhov's play, "The Three Sisters," photograph. The Kobal Collection. Reproduced by permission.—Chekhov, Anton, with the Moscow Art theatre troupe, reading his play "The Seagull," 1899, Moscow, photograph. Austrian Archives/Corbis. Reproduced by permission.—David Warner and Irene Worth in Edward Albee's "Tiny Alice" © Donald Cooper/Photostage. Reproduced by permission.—Falk, Peter, Shelley Winters, a scene from the film version of Jean Genet's play, "The Balcony," photograph. The Kobal Collection. Reproduced by permission.—From a theatre production of Robert Schenkkan's "The Kentucky Cycle," Directed by Nina LeNoir, Scene Design by W. J. Langley, Jr., Costume design by Susan L. Hayes at Meyer Jacobs Theatre, Bradley University, 1997/98 Season, scene 'Fire in the Hole,' 1920, Howsen County, Kentucky with the company, photograph by Duane Zehr. BRADLEY UNIVERSITY THEATRE. Reproduced by permission.—From a theatre production of Robert Schenkkan's "The Kentucky Cycle," Directed by Nina LeNoir, Scene Design by W. J. Langley, Jr., Costume design by Susan L. Hayes at Meyer Jacobs Theatre, Bradley University, 1997/98 Season, scene 'Ties That Bind,' 1819, The Rowen Homestead with Shaun O'Keefe as Ezekiel Rowen, Isaiah E. Brooms as Jessie Biggs and Stephen Clark as Zachariah Rowen, photograph by Duane Zehr. BRADLEY UNIVERSITY THEATRE. Reproduced by permission.—From a theatre production of "The Memorandum" by Vaclav Havel, Directed by Rick Jones at The University of Kansas Theatre, October, 1996 with (l-r) Jennette Selig as Deputy Director Ballas, Jefferson R. Bachura as Stroll, Head of the Translation Center and Jamie Johnson as Chariman Helena, Stroll is reading a letter to Ballas and Helena, photograph. The University of Kansas Theatre. Reproduced by permission.—From a theatre production of "The Memorandum" by Vaclav Havel, Directed by Rick Jones at The University of Kansas Theatre, October, 1996 with (l-r) Steve Willingham as Pillar/Column, Lawrence Eric Davis as Gross, Managing Director, Jennette Selig as Deputy Director Ballas, and Kari Wahlgren as Hana, Secretary to the Managing Director, Pillar/Column is standing with his arms raised while the others look on, photograph. The University of Kansas Theatre. Reproduced by permission.—Fugard, Athol, photograph. AP/Wide World Photos. Reproduced by permission.—Genet, Jean, photograph. Archive Photos, Inc. Reproduced by permission.—Havel, Vaclav, photograph. Reuters/Corbis-Bettmann. Reproduced by permission. —James, Geraldine in the theatrical production of Aristophanes' "Lysistrata," the Old Vic Theatre, photograph. © Donald Cooper/Photostage. Reproduced by permission.—Kaufman, George and Moss Hart, photograph. AP/Wide World Photos. Reproduced by permission.—Kingsley, Ben (with unidentified man and Paul Scofield) in "Volpone," photograph. © Donald Cooper/PHOTOSTAGE. Reproduced by permission.—Lorca, Federico Garcia (left arm on armrest of chair, right hand in lap), photograph. Archive Photos/Popperfoto. Reproduced by permission.—McAuliffe, Nichola, as Erdal, scene from theatrical production of "The Wild Duck," the Phoenix Theatre, photograph. © Donald Cooper/Photostage. Reproduced by permission.—Ntshona, Winston (with John Kani) in play "Sizwe Banzi Is Dead," photograph by William L. Smith Published by Solters/Roskin, Inc. Museum of the City of New York/Archive Photos. Reproduced by permission.—Ntshona Winston (with John Kani) in the play "Sizwe Banzi Is Dead," photograph by William L. Smith. Published by Solters/Roskin, Inc. Museum of the City of New York/Archive Photos. Reproduced by permission.—Oakie, Jack, with unidentified woman, a scene from "Once in a Lifetime," photograph. The Kobal Collection. Reproduced by permission.—Playbill title page insert for production of the play "Spike Heels" by Theresa Rebeck, directed by Michael Greif, at the Second Stage Theatre, New York. PLAYBILL (r) is a registered trademark of Playbill Incorporated, N.Y.C. All rights reserved. Reproduced by permission.—Scene from the Moscow Art Theater production of "The Seagull" by Chekhov (man sleeping in wheelchair), 1898, photograph. From Stanislavsky: My Life in the Theatre, Academia, 1936, Soviet Union.—Schenkkan, Robert, photograph. Robert Schenkkan. Reproduced by permission.—Soyinka, Wole, photograph. Archive Photos, Inc./Trappe. Reproduced by permission.—"The Wild Duck," photograph. © Donald Cooper/Photostage. Reproduced by permission.

Contributors

Cynthia Bily: Bily teaches writing and literature at Adrian College in Adrian, MI, and writes for various educational publishers. Entry on *Death and the King's Horseman*. Original essay on *Death and the King's Horseman*.

Liz Brent: Brent has a Ph.D. in American Culture, specializing in cinema studies, from the University of Michigan. She is a freelance writer and teacher of courses in American cinema. Original essays on *Once in a Lifetime* and *Ring around the Moon*.

Roberto Cantú: Cantú is a professor at California State University, Los Angeles. Original essay on *Blood Wedding*.

Carol Dell'Amico Dell'Amico is a Ph.D. candidate in the Program of Literatures in English at Rutgers, The State University of New Jersey. Entry on *Blood Wedding*. Original essay on *Blood Wedding*.

David J. Kelly: Kelly is a professor of English at College of Lake County, IL. Entry on *The Three Sisters*. Original essay on *The Three Sisters*.

Rena Korb: Korb has a master's degree in English literature and creative writing, and has written for a wide variety of educational publishers. Entries on *Tiny Alice* and *The Wild Duck*. Original essays on *Tiny Alice* and *The Wild Duck*.

Sheri Metzger: Metzger is a freelance writer and Ph.D., Albuquerque, NM. Entries on *Lysistrata*, *Seven against Thebes*, and *Volpone*. Original essays on *Lysistrata*, *Seven against Thebes*, and *Volpone*.

Annette Petrusso: Petrusso is a freelance author and screenwriter from Austin, TX. Entries on *The Balcony*, *The Memorandum*, *Once in a Lifetime*, and *Sizwe Banzi Is Dead*. Original essays on *The Balcony*, *The Memorandum*, *Once in a Lifetime*, and *Sizwe Banzi Is Dead*.

Daniela Presley: Presley is an M.A. specializing in Germanic Languages and Literature. Original essay on *Lysistrata*.

Michael Rex: Rex is an adjunct professor at the University of Detroit-Mercy, MI. Entry on *The Kentucky Cycle*. Original essays on *The Kentucky Cycle* and *Lysistrata*.

Chris Semansky: Semansky holds a Ph.D. in English from Stony Brook University, and teaches writing and literature at Portland Community College in Portland, OR. His collection of poems *Death, But at a Good Price* received the Nicholas Roerich Poetry Prize for 1991 and was published by Story Line Press and the Nicholas Roerich Museum. Semansky's most recent collection, *Blindsided*, has been published by 26 Books of Portland, OR. Entry on *Ring around the Moon*. Original essay on *Ring around the Moon*.

The Balcony

JEAN GENET

1956

Jean Genet's *The Balcony* (*Le Balcon* in original French) is considered by many to be the one of his masterpieces, though it was written after he said he would give up writing plays altogether. *The Balcony* was his first commercially successful play. Like many of Genet's works, the play was inspired by Genet's contempt for society and obsession with topics such as sex, prostitution, politics, and revolution. Set inside a brothel where common men play men of power in their sexual fantasies, *The Balcony* reflects on the emptiness of societal roles. Reality and illusion feed off each other in the difficult play. Dreams may make reality tolerable, but when they come true, as when the customers are forced to live the roles they play, it is not as satisfying.

The Balcony was first published in 1956, and was first produced in London on April 22, 1957, at the Arts Theatre Club. Genet did not like the production because it was done in a way that was too tasteful and realistic. His protests led to his banishment from the theater during the production. The play made its American debut in March 1960 at the Circle in the Square Theater, in New York City. There *The Balcony* ran for 672 performances and won an Obie Award for Genet. It was generally well received, though some critics thought it was hard to understand because of its complexity and reliance on illusion. The first French performance of *The Balcony* took place in May 1960. Since these initial performances, the play has been produced on a regular basis. As Donald Malcolm of the *New*

Yorker wrote, "M. Genet's vision of society is both perverse and private, and his play is a species of Grand Guignol—arresting, horrific, and trivial."

AUTHOR BIOGRAPHY

Genet was born on December 19, 1910, in Paris, France. He was the illegitimate son of Gabrielle Genet, a prostitute, and an unknown father. He was abandoned at birth, and did not discover the name of his mother until he was twenty-one years old. Genet spent his early years in a state-run orphanage, before being sent to the country to live with foster parents at the age of seven. Caught stealing from the purse of his foster mother, Genet was labeled a thief. He embraced the label, and any subsequent accusations of criminal activity. By the time Genet was a teenager, he was a confirmed juvenile delinquent, and confined to a reform school.

When Genet was twenty-one years old, he ran away and signed up for the French Foreign Legion. He deserted the military in short order, and spent the next ten years wandering Europe—including Nazi Germany—committing crimes. He continued to steal, as well as work as a male prostitute, pimp, and smuggler. Genet was arrested, imprisoned, and expelled from several countries.

When Genet returned to France during the German occupation in 1941, he was jailed for theft. It was while he was in prison that he began writing. Genet garnered the attention of Jean Cocteau, a leading French writer and artist, for his poem "Under the Sentence of Death." The piece was written about another prisoner who was being executed for murder. Genet's poetry was collected and published in 1948 under the title *Poemes.*

Still a prisoner, Genet began work on a novel. His first pages were confiscated and burned, but Genet began again. The book, *Lady of Flowers,* was published in 1942 and made Genet a literary sensation. Genet wrote several more novels over the course of his life, including *The Miracle of the Rose* (1946) and *The Thief's Journal* (1948). Many of his novels had an autobiographical element and concerned the seamier side of life.

In the mid-1940s, Genet turned to writing plays. The first two, *Deathwatch* and *The Maids,* were also about criminals. When *The Maids*—based on a true

story of murdering sisters—was produced in 1947, Genet received some acclaim. Despite his success as a writer, Genet had not given up his life of crime. He was again convicted of theft, and it was only through a petition signed by France's leading writers and artists that he avoided a life sentence in prison.

Genet wrote his most celebrated and commercially successful plays in the late 1950s: *The Balcony* (1956) and *The Blacks* (1957). Both black comedies played well in Europe and the United States. In 1960, Genet wrote *The Screens,* which was not produced until the late 1960s in France. *The Screens* was ambitious: a five hour epic, a cast of at least forty was needed to perform it.

Towards the end of his life, Genet also wrote nonfiction, though he produced nothing in his final decade. Genet died of throat cancer on April 15, 1986. Upon his death, he was celebrated as one of the most important and colorful figures in twentieth-century French literature.

PLOT SUMMARY

Scene I

The Balcony opens in a brothel, The Grand Balcony, that caters to the fantasies of its male clientele. Irma, the owner of the whorehouse, is arguing with a customer over a fee. He is dressed as a bishop, and is only interested in the revolution that is going on outside and the truthfulness of the sins the woman who serviced him has confessed to. Irma tries to hurry him, but he will not be rushed. He enjoys his role and continues to play it. He does not leave despite the fact that his safety is at risk outside.

Scene II

Inside a room in the brothel, a client plays out a fantasy as a Judge. His whore plays a thief who is about to be executed by the executioner, played by a male employee of the establishment named Arthur. The Judge also relishes his role-play. Every outside noise, however, upsets him. He worries about the revolution, sharing the latest information with the other two. When he returns to his role, he can enjoy it too much, scaring the woman. Mostly, the Judge is the one who is humiliated by the other two for his pleasure.

Scene III

In another room, Irma arranges the setting for the liking of a client who plays a General. Though he is concerned about his safety, he is equally obsessed about the details of his fantasy, and wants them followed to the letter. The General's whore is nearly naked and acts like his horse.

Scene IV

Another client acts out his fantasy as a tramp. He looks at his reflection in three mirrors, and is very happy when his whore hands him a wig with fleas to wear. Sounds of machine gun fire are heard in the background.

Scene V

Inside Irma's room, she is going over accounts with her bookkeeper Carmen, who used to be one of her whores. Irma worries that her lover, George, who is also the Chief of Police, has not shown up yet. She notices that Carmen has changed recently. Carmen tells her she is not happy. She did not like the rules that Irma set up for the women that work at the brothel. They cannot talk about what they do or laugh. Carmen also misses her daughter.

While they talk, Irma checks in on her clients via a device similar to a closed-circuit monitoring system. Irma is rather callous towards Carmen's feelings. She only cares about her business and her material possessions. Carmen tries to explain her problems with the roles she has been required to play, but Irma does really care. She is preoccupied by the revolution going on outside, and the imminent appearance of George.

Irma attempts to appease Carmen by offering her a role as Saint Theresa for a nice client. Carmen is flattered, but only sees the futility of their work. Irma talks proudly about the power of her "house of illusions" and tells Carmen that she is one of the best of her employees. Sounds of fighting between the rebels and the army grow louder. Irma worries about what will happen if the rebels win. She wants Carmen to die with her, but Carmen only wants to flee and find her daughter.

Carmen reports about the other girls to Irma. Irma asks particularly about Chantal, who left the brothel to join the rebellion. Irma worries that her brothel is being watched. Their conversation is interrupted by Arthur, who plays the Executioner. His work is finished, and he wants money to pay for silk shirts he has ordered. Irma says she will give him funds if he goes and looks for George at his

Jean Genet

headquarters. She also wants to know what is going on in the streets. Arthur goes, despite his fears.

Just after Arthur leaves, the George (Chief of Police) shows up. George reports that the palace is surrounded and the Queen is in hiding. He is ambivalent about that situation because he is more concerned about the fantasies being acted out in the whorehouse. He wants to know if anyone has wanted to imitate him. He becomes angry when the answer is negative, though Irma tries to soothe his ego. George vows to prove his worth as a leader and keep killing so that clients will want to be the Chief of Police in their fantasy.

Irma confides to George her fears about the rebellion and what the rebels might do to her studio. He assures her that he has taken every precaution. Irma passes on information obtained from Chantal, who apparently has left the brothel for the rebellion. Irma reveals that her former plumber, Roger, is a rebel, and he and Chantal took off together. Arthur finally returns, and reports about the increasing violence outside. His speech is interrupted by a bullet entering from the outside that kills him.

Scene VI

Near the Grand Balcony, Chantal and Roger express their love for each other among the rebels.

Roger is a bit jealous that Chantal has become a female symbol of the rebellion. Several men want to remove her from Roger to use when the revolution takes the palace. Chantal is enthusiastic, but Roger is more reluctant. She goes, despite his pleas to stay.

Scene VII

Inside the brothel, Irma, George, and Carmen are gathered in the Funeral Studio, with the corpse of Arthur. Everything and everyone is in tatters, except the Court Envoy who is unharmed. Explosions rock the building. The Envoy is enigmatic in his description of the Royal Court, most of whom are dead or injured, including the Queen. The Envoy wants Irma to play the Queen for the populace so that they will feel safer and remain loyal. George is jealous that Irma might be above him, even if she is just playing a role. Irma accepts it.

Scene VIII

Irma appears at the balcony of the brothel, accompanied by the clients who played the General, the Bishop and the Judge, as well as George. Chantal appears and is shot by an assassin.

Scene IX

In Irma's room inside the brothel, the Bishop, the Judge and the General met. They talk about having to live their roles, and their recent public appearances. Photographers are present to take their pictures for posterity. The three men do not know how to act like their roles for the photographs. The Envoy and Irma, who is still playing the Queen, enter. The Envoy questions the men on their official decisions. Irma asks the kind of questions a queen would ask of her men.

George comes in. He wants to appear in the form of a phallus to impress the masses. The men continue to take their roles too seriously, and believe they have more power than George does. Irma and George try to put them in their place. They talk of Chantal who has been made a martyr for their cause. Irma, as the Queen, is still jealous, though she, too, is worshipped. Their ruminations over their future are interrupted by the entrance of Carmen.

Carmen reports that a man has come to the brothel, and he wants to play the role of the Chief of Police. George is ecstatic. They all go to the Mausoleum Studio, which was specifically designed for George. Roger, the plumber, has donned the outfit. After saving a slave (played by the man who was the beggar), the Chief's praises are sung. When his

fantasy has been fulfilled, Roger will not leave. Instead, he castrates himself.

Irma is upset at the damage Roger's act does to her brothel. George decides to spend eternity in the tomb that has been constructed for him. He locks himself inside, as machine gun fire starts again. Irma dismisses the men who played that Bishop, Judge, and General. Even the Envoy leaves. Irma has Carmen lock up and she vows to start all over again at a later time.

CHARACTERS

Arthur

Arthur (also known as The Executioner) works at the whorehouse, playing the Executioner and other roles in the male clientele's fantasy. Irma was forced to hire him by George, the Chief of Police. Though she was reluctant at first, she came to rely on him. Arthur cares solely about his own interests and money. He goes to find George for Irma, only because she will give him money for silk shirts he has ordered. Arthur survives the rebellion in the street, only to be shot dead by a stray bullet when he returns to the Grand Balcony. He is laid out in the Funeral Studio inside the brothel.

The Bishop

The Bishop is one of the clients at the Grand Balcony. He is not actually a bishop, but a customer who plays one in his fantasy. As a client, he is rather fussy, concerned that the details of his fantasy are perfect and that he will survive in the streets after he leaves. Later, when Irma plays the Queen at the Envoy's request to hold onto the loyalty of the people, the Bishop plays his role for real for a short time. He enjoys the power that comes with it, though he is totally unprepared. He is dismissed by Irma when the Chief of Police decides to entomb himself and the revolution heats up again.

Carmen

Carmen is Irma's most loyal and favorite employee. At one time, Carmen worked as a whore in the brothel, but now only keeps the books and assists in preparing the studios for the clients' fantasies. Carmen realizes the futility of the fantasies and can no longer do it, though Irma offers her a choice assignment. Carmen has a daughter who lives in the country. She desperately wants to see and be with her child, but she cannot. Carmen stays at the Grand Balcony to the end, even after it is bombed and the Chief of Police locks himself in his tomb. She regards this place as her lot in life.

Chantal

Chantal worked as a whore at the Grand Balcony at one time. She left the brothel with Roger to join the rebellion. Chantal and Roger became lovers. In scene six, it is revealed that she has become a symbol of the rebellion. Though Roger does not want her to go, Chantal is chosen to represent the revolution and goes with some men to be present when the Royal Palace falls. Later, Chantal is assassinated at the Grand Balcony when Irma makes her appearances as the Queen on the brothel's balcony. In death, Chantal is made to be a martyred saint for Irma as Queen.

Chief of Police

The Chief of Police (also known as George) is Irma's lover and protector. Rather self-centered, his primary focus is increasing his own power and importance. He does arrange to ensure the safety of the Grand Balcony. But he is upset through most of the play because no one who has come to the brothel has wanted to play him. George regards this as the ultimate symbol of his prestige in the eyes of the world. He has Irma build him a tomb, a preeminent symbol of honor for the kind of conqueror he aspires to be.

George does play a key role in putting down the rebellion, though he is annoyed that Irma, as the Queen, has a higher place than him. He is even more peeved that the men who play the Judge, the General, and the Bishop take their roles too seriously when they are forced to play them in real life as well. All these people cut into his ''more real'' power. After Roger comes in and asks to play the Chief of Police, George is satisfied, even though Roger castrates himself at the end. He decides to be locked in his tomb for 2,000 years, as the revolution begins again.

The Court Envoy

A hard-to-understand character, the Envoy appears in Scene Seven enigmatically describing the situation in the Royal Palace. It finally becomes clear that the Queen is dead, and the Envoy con-

MEDIA ADAPTATIONS

- *The Balcony* was adapted as a film in 1963. This version was produced by Lewis M. Allen, Ben Marlow, and Joseph Strick, and directed by Strick. It starred Shelley Winters as Irma.

vinces Irma to take on that role as a symbol the people can rally around. When Irma plays the Queen, the Envoy makes certain that court etiquette is followed as much as possible. After the Chief of Police entombs himself, the Envoy accepts that this act is over and leaves.

The Executioner
See Arthur

The General

The General is one of the clients at the Grand Balcony. He is not really a general, but a customer who plays one in the fantasy he acts out. As a client, the General tries to take charge, but he is very self-involved and pompous. Later, when Irma plays the Queen at the Envoy's request, the General plays his role for real for a short time. He enjoys the power that comes with it, and tries (and fails) to act like a general should. He is dismissed by Irma when the Chief of Police decides to entomb himself and the revolution heats up again.

George
See Chief of Police

Irma

Irma (also known as The Queen) owns and runs the brothel, The Grand Balcony. She is first and foremost a businesswoman, concerned with keeping costs down while making customers happy. Irma is rather callous towards the feelings of her employees, as long as they are in fine physical form for their work. Her favorite employee is Carmen, who used to be a whore but now only does book-keeping and handles details. Carmen is a source of information and reliable ally for Irma.

Irma becomes increasingly worried about the bloody revolution that is going on in the streets. She is worried that it will affect her business, if not shut her down entirely. Her protector and lover, George, the Chief of Police, promises to protect her and her business, but employees are killed and the Grand Balcony is damaged.

Because the Queen is dead, the Court Envoy calls on Irma to play the Queen to appease the masses. She takes on the role, and some of her clients continue to play their lofty roles. Though this seems to quell the rebellion temporarily, the revolution flares up again. After the Chief of Police decides to lock himself up in his tomb, Irma realizes this role is over and closes up the brothel, and will start it up again later.

The Judge

The Judge is one of the clients at the Grand Balcony. He is not actually a judge, but a customer who plays one in his fantasy. As a client, the Judge is very into his role—to the point that he scares the whore who plays the thief—though the revolution-related events outside clutter his conscience. Later, when Irma plays the Queen, the Judge plays his role for real for a short time. He enjoys the power that comes with it, though he is flustered and unsure of himself. He is dismissed by Irma when the Chief of Police decides to entomb himself and the revolution heats up again.

The Queen

See Irma

Roger

Roger was employed at the Grand Balcony as a plumber at one time. He became involved with Chantal, and is now part of the revolution. Though he supports that cause, he does not want Chantal to be the greater symbol of the rebellion. After she is assassinated and the revolution quelled (at least temporarily), Roger appears at the Grand Balcony. He wants to play the Chief of Police in his fantasy. He does so, but clumsily. He does not understand how he should act. When the fantasy is deemed over by Carmen, Roger refuses to end it and leave. He wants the destiny of the Chief of Police and himself

to be intertwined. Roger castrates himself and is dragged out by Carmen.

THEMES

Illusion and Reality

The primary theme in *The Balcony* is the tension between the illusions that rule inside the brothel and the intrusion of reality that rules on the outside. Common men pay money to live out their fantasies in The Grand Balcony. They primarily choose to be men in power (a judge, a bishop, a general), though some who are rich chose to be poor (a tramp). Details are important to these men: their costumes must be perfectly realistic for their fantasies to be enjoyed. Irma, the brothel owner, is concerned that everything meets their specifications, but within reasonable costs.

Irma goes to great lengths to keep reality out of The Grand Balcony. The walls and windows are somewhat soundproof, though the sounds of the revolution that is going on in the streets cannot be fully excised. The exclusion of the outside world is reinforced by the number of mirrors and screens that emphasize the illusion created for the customers. Eventually, though, the reality of the revolution marches into the brothel and takes it over. When the Queen and the Royal Palace are taken over, some of Irma's clients are compelled by the Court Envoy to play their roles for real, while she plays the Queen. This is to keep the status quo in tact in the face of the rebellion, and works for a short time. But the desire for illusion conflicts with the realism of reality, and the experience is not satisfying for everyone concerned. For Genet, illusion is superior to reality, though the latter is necessary for illusion to exist.

Death

An undercurrent of death permeates *The Balcony*. Though only two minor characters (Chantal and Arthur) actually die in the course of the play, death is used as a symbol of immortality. Irma's clients often discuss its power. Chantal, a former prostitutes who leaves The Grand Balcony to join the rebellion with her lover, is chosen as a figurehead or symbol for the revolution, and she is assassinated on the balcony at the brothel. Upon her death, she is co-opted by the side of the royals and made a symbol of martyrdom for their side. Arthur's death is by a stray bullet, though inside the brothel proper. He is laid out in the funeral room there.

Death is used slightly differently in *The Balcony* for the Chief of Police, George. He becomes upset during the course of the play when he learns that no one has asked to play him in their fantasy. He believes that when one is imitated, one becomes immortal. His memory and importance will live on because his role has become part of the canon. After the first man has chosen to play him—Roger in scene nine—George descends into the mausoleum that has been built for him by Irma. He intends to spend 2,000 years there. The mausoleum and the fact that customers will pay to play him are symbols of his greatness in life and death.

Value of Rituals and Symbols

Throughout *The Balcony,* rituals and symbols are depicted as both important and perverted representations of values. The clients of The Grand Balcony brothel insist that the rituals and symbols of the people they are depicting in their fantasies (judge, general, etc.) are as realistic as possible. In this sense, rituals and symbols are respected. Irma spends money to insure that these things are as accurate as possible. Rituals and symbols provide the realism needed to insure that illusion has substance.

When the Queen and the Royal Court are presumed dead, Irma and the clients who play the Judge, the General, and the Bishop assume these roles. They become symbols for the masses to rally around and believe in, yet they do not really know how to be these people. When photographs are taken of the Bishop, for example, he has no idea how he should really act. He finds the role too demanding, as do the others. Here, rituals and symbols are more empty and meaningless. They are used as a tool to manipulate people into remaining loyal to the royal side. When divorced from their fantasy element and forced into more realistic uses, rituals and symbols become perverted.

STYLE

Setting

The Balcony is an absurdist play set in no specific time or place. Nearly all of the action of the play takes place inside The Grand Balcony, a brothel that serves the fantasies of its male clientele. The brothel has different rooms, or studios, that are set up to fulfill these fantasies. The studios shown in

TOPICS FOR FURTHER STUDY

- Research the theories of Antonin Artaud and the Theater of Cruelty. Analyze *The Balcony* in this context.

- Compare and contrast *The Balcony* with Jean-Paul Sartre's play *No Exit* (1943). Especially focus on the characters of Irma in *The Balcony* and Inez in *No Exit*. How do the two women try to control their situation?

- Do sociological and psychological research into women who become prostitutes. Why do women like Carmen chose to stay at the brothel instead of going to find their daughters? Is the portrayal of prostitution in *The Balcony* accurate?

The Balcony include the Funeral Studio, where Arthur is laid out after his death, and the Mausoleum studio, which was specially built for the Chief of Police and those who wish to act as him in a fantasy. Irma also has her own room, with a video monitoring system so she can supervise action in the other rooms. Scene eight takes place on a balcony attached to the Grand Balcony. The only action that takes place outside of the Grand Balcony is scene six, which occurs in a public square held by the rebels. It is within viewing distance of the brothel.

Props, Costumes, and Scenic Decor

Key to the construction and themes of *The Balcony* are the props, costumes, and scenic decor, especially, the mirrors. To fulfill the fantasies of the clients and emphasize the illusionary element of the play, these costumes and other props must be as realistic as possible. Irma complains of the cost of creating such detail, but later, when she is pressed into service to play the Queen for the public and her clients assume their fantasy roles as well, they seem to have been accepted as the real thing. The studios shown in *The Balcony* include the Funeral Studio, where Arthur is laid out after his death. Props, costumes, and mirrors underscore the tension between illusion and reality in the play.

Play-within-a-Play

In the course of *The Balcony,* there are several smaller playlets that are acted out. These are the fantasies of the clients, with the men directing the course by their words and actions. The man who plays the Bishop had his whore confess her sins to him. The client who assumes the role of the Judge has his prostitute play a thief who must confess to her crimes and be struck by an executioner. After much pompous talk, the Judge is forced to crawl by the executioner. The General has his woman act like a horse, and rides her to what he hopes will be his heroic death.

Many such minidramas take place within the Grand Balcony, all monitored by Irma. The most important play-within-a-play occurs in scene nine, when Roger asks to assume the role of the Chief of Police. As the chief, a hero, Roger is exalted by a male slave, who is one of many who has worked on his tomb. When the fantasy is deemed over, Roger refuses to leave and give up the illusion of power. He wants his destiny to merge with that of the chief, but when he is refused, he castrates himself. Such playlets emphasize the illusionary nature of the play, and, in a bigger sense, reality.

Addressing the Audience

At the end of *The Balcony,* after the revolution starts up again and the Chief of Police descends into his mausoleum to live for 2000 years, Irma and Carmen clean up the tattered brothel. As she does so, Irma breaks the illusion of the play and says a few lines directly to the audience. She promises to rebuild her house of illusions, but also tells her listeners that what they will find in their home is even more false than what they found here. Genet attacks bourgeois social values, pointing out how fake he believes they really are.

HISTORICAL CONTEXT

In the mid- to late-1950s, France was still recovering from World War II. During the much of the war, the country was occupied by Nazi Germany. While there were those who collaborated with the Germans—including the Vichy government, which ruled France under the direction of the Germans—an underground movement also existed. The French Resistance worked against the Germans. Under these conditions, France suffered greatly—politically, socially, and economically.

After the end of World War II, France returned to freedom and held free elections. When the so-called Fourth Republic came into existence in 1946, immense political change took place. The prewar government was rejected, in favor of parties that leaned to the left. Though the structure of the government remained generally the same, there were some reforms and the French people were more invigorated. By the mid-1950s, economic recovery came into its own, soon becoming the biggest economic boom in Europe. Despite inflation problems, France's stature had increased in Europe and throughout the world.

One area that France had been playing a leading role in for many years was culture. The Existentialism of Jean-Paul Sartre and Albert Camus came into vogue in the postwar period. Simone de Beauvoir was a leading novelist and philosopher, publishing *Les Mandarins* in 1954. In France, a new type of novel emerged in the mid-1950s, nontraditional in forms and ideas and philosophical in nature. Theater had been subsidized by the French government in the provinces since the late 1940s. Absurdism came to the fore at this time, with Eugene Ionesco and Samuel Beckett being two of the best playwrights in this genre. There was also a new movement in poetry, the so-called poetry of resistance.

France did have political problems, primarily related to their colonial holdings in Algeria and Vietnam. The situation in Vietnam had been heating for many years, and would get worse. Fighting in Vietnam began in 1946, with the advent of a nationalist movement headed by communist Ho Chi Minh. In 1954, the country was divided into north and south parts, as a temporary measure to end conflict. However, this eventually led to the Vietnam War, which would engulf much of world through the mid-1970s, when the communists won. France itself got out of the Vietnam War in the mid-1960s.

Another French colony was even more problematic. Algeria, located in North Africa, was a bigger and more immediate threat. In 1954, Algerian nationalists began rebelling against their French colonial overlords. Within four years, nearly 500,000 French soldiers had been sent there to keep the motherland's hold on Algeria. The situation in Algeria led to two other North African colonies of France getting their freedom in 1956, Tunisia and Morocco.

COMPARE
&
CONTRAST

- **1956:** A nationalist movement has been tearing apart the French colony of Algeria for two years. France has sent a significant number of troops there to hold on to the colony and quell the rebellion.

  Today: Algeria has been a free, independent country since 1962, but has suffered economic crises in the late 1980s and 1990s.

- **1956:** France is a center of the intellectual world, with leading philosophers such as Jean Paul Sartre and Simone de Beauvoir internationally recognized for their writing.

  Today: France's stature in the intellectual community is greatly diminished. No French writer has come close to making the same impact Sartre and the like made in the 1940s and 1950s.

- **1956:** France had a number of colonial holdings, including the troubled Algeria. Many countries, like Algeria, wanted their freedom from the motherland.

  Today: France has few remaining colonial holdings.

- **1956:** Television is just coming into its own as an entertainment medium. Video security does not really exist as a viable business.

  Today: Television can be found in nearly every home in the United States. Video security is commonly found in many places of business. With the advent of the cheap, portable web camera, images can be recorded and seen over the Internet, any time, any where.

The Fourth Republic fell in 1958, primarily because of the situation in Algeria. That year, Charles de Gaulle, a French war hero and political leader, came back into power in the so-called Fifth Republic. Again, the face of the French political landscape changed. By the early 1960s, war with Algeria ended. Most of France's colonies in Africa, including Algeria, achieved self-rule within a few years. For the moment, France was involved in no real conflicts.

CRITICAL OVERVIEW

Though *The Balcony* was Genet's first commercially successful play, the playwright was intensely critical of its first production in London in 1957. Genet believed it was not true to his text; that it was too ordinary and small, whereas his text called for big, theatrical, and bawdy. Martin Esslin, in his book *The Theatre of the Absurd,* called it "a brave attempt in a small theatre and with modest means."

Genet was never happy with way the play was produced.

When *The Balcony* debuted in New York City in March 1960, critics were mixed in their reactions. While many believed that they were viewing a play with deep meaning and implications, they were somewhat confused by its complexities. As Brooks Atkinson of the *New York Times* wrote, "It would take a committee of alienists to define all the abnormalities contained in this witches' cauldron, and a committee of logicians to clarify the meanings. But anyone can see that M. Genet is a powerful writer."

Correctly guessing that *The Balcony* would have a long run in New York (it ended up being 672 performances at the Circle in the Square Theatre), Donald Malcolm of the *New Yorker* argued that the play "satisfies to a degree hitherto unknown our contemporary dramatic appetite for violence, perversion, and squalor . . . [T]hese qualities emerge, in the most natural way imaginable, from the story." But Malcolm did not believe that Genet's commentary on every day society was completely correct.

Peter Falk and Shelley Winters in a scene from the 1963 film adaptation of The Balcony.

He pointed out that judges, for example, did not wield the kind of power that he claimed.

Others, including *New Republic* critic Robert Brustein, saw Genet's social commentary as relevant, deep and complicated. He wrote ''Fashioned by a genius of criminality and revolt, the play is absolutely stunning in its twists and turns of thought, and (despite occasional thefts from [Ugo] Betti, [Jean] Cocteau, and the Surrealists) highly original in its use of the stage. In its interpretation of history, it is both provocative and scandalous.'' *New York Times* critic Atkinson also commented on the play's

symbolic complexities, calling them ''a riddle wrapped in an enigma'' and noting that ''Everything means more than the author or the characters say.''

Harold Clurman of *The Nation* generally concurred with Brustein and Atkinson's assessment of *The Balcony*'s complexities, but attributed them to Genet being more than an playwright. In Clurman's estimation, Genet was an artist. Clurman wrote ''*The Balcony* has its obscurities—no explanatory gloss will elucidate its every metaphorical twist— but in this it resembles every true work of art; true art always retains a certain elusiveness because the emanations of the artist's unconscious project beyond the control of his will.''

Other critics also saw *The Balcony* as more than just a play. Lionel Abel in a 1960 article in the *Partisan Review* believed that with *The Balcony* Genet wrote an excellent example of a metaplay. Abel argued that ''[I]n a way Genet shares the weakness of his revolutionaries in *The Balcony;* he too would like to create something other than the kind of play he can make so magnificently; this master of the metaplay would like to create tragedy.''

Scholars began analyzing *The Balcony* from the beginning. Many compared it to other writers or theatrical movements (for example, the Marquis de Sade and Greek traditions), giving Genet's work a context. One such scholar, Rima Drell Reck, argued in her 1962 article in *Yale French Studies* ''Jean Genet deliberately and drastically creates plays which revolve about ritual and theatrical illusions designed at once to suggest the Attic theatre and point out the distance between it and our own age.''

Over the years, *The Balcony* continued to be performed and analyzed. Commentators often focused on the play's shortcomings, many of which were the same as those criticized in 1960. For example, in Esslin's book *The Theatre of the Absurd,* written in 1980, he noted its unevenness and lack of a coherent plot. Esslin wrote, ''in *The Balcony* Genet is faced with the need to provide a plot structure that will furnish the rationale for his mock-liturgy and mock-ceremonial. And he has not quite succeeded in integrating plot and ritual.''

CRITICISM

Annette Petruso

Annette Petruso is a freelance author and screenwriter in Austin, TX. In the following essay, Petruso explores the complex depiction of women in The Balcony.

Of Jean Genet's *The Balcony,* Robert Brustein noted in the *New Republic* that ''Genet is less interested in the titillations of pornography than its philosophical implications; and the erotic scenes are merely a prologue to his theaticalized version of society, of life, and of history.'' Though *The Balcony* is absurdist, it is revealing in its contradictions about women and their place in the world. Genet's

version of women's role in society is complex and paradoxical, as it was in the reality of his time and still is today. This essay explores these contradictions and the powerful role women play in *The Balcony.*

There are three major female characters: Irma, who runs and owns the brothel, the Grand Illusion; Carmen, Irma's bookkeeper and former whore; and Chantal, another former whore in the brothel. There are also other various brothel prostitutes, who act the fantasies with the clientele. An interesting aspect of the play is that the actual implications of sex are minimal in the play. The prostitution at the Grand Illusion seems to be more about acting out men's power fantasies than the actual sex act. This ever-shifting balance of power between men and women is a key to interpreting the role women play in *The Grand Balcony.*

On the surface, the women that are the least powerful seem to be the actual whores who service the Grand Illusion's clients. There are several specifically depicted in the play and a few others talked about, only three of which are discussed here. Each of these three women plays a role for a male customer. The variety of roles reflect a spectrum of power. It is also important to note that the women work for another woman, Irma, who is discussed later in the essay.

In scene one, the prostitute has just played the role of a sinner who has confessed to a client who plays a Bishop and received his blessing. The Bishop is concerned with her honesty: he wants her sins to be real so that he has the power of forgiveness. She tells him what he wants to hear, though he knows the sins are probably not true. The women are there to help him believe he has power. Though subservient, the prostitute does have his vulnerabilities under her control. The possibility exists that she could hurt him. However, she is paid to be positive, and she does not do anything to really ruin the illusions he paid for.

Another whore plays a thief who is appearing before a judge in scene two. Also part of the fantasy is an executioner, played by a male employee of the brothel, Arthur. This scene contains a more overt power tug of war. The Judge is subservient at one moment—wanting to lick her foot—then domineering the next. She is new to the brothel, and does her best to support the reality he wants to create. He wants to be both a hero and a man who decides the fate of a woman. The Judge asks the executioner to hit her hard, so that he can intervene. Yet by the end

WHAT DO I READ NEXT?

- *The Blacks (Les Nègres)* is a play by Genet that was first published in 1958. In the play, there is also tension between the status quo and a rebellion. Here, the rebels, black actors, mock white colonial society and, to some degree, win some measure of revenge.

- *The Visit*, a play by Friedrich Durrenmatt that was first performed in 1960, concerns topics similar to *The Balcony*. The anti-capitalist play focuses on a woman who runs a brothel.

- *Our Lady of the Flowers (Notre-Dame-des-Fleurs)* is a novel published by Genet in 1943. It concerns the importance of criminal activity in society and its rituals.

- *Tonight We Improvise* is a play written by Luigi Pirandello in 1932. Here actors play roles in the play as well as in the play-within-the-play. The audience must play an active role, at least mentally, to separate the illusions.

- *The Chairs* is an absurdist play written by Eugene Ionesco in 1952. The very theatrical play concerns a couple whose world is constructed around a illusion, not reality.

---

of the scene, she is humiliating him again, making him crawl. As in the first scene, the woman plays what she is paid for, though she has a measure of control over how the Judge feels about himself. She could easily ruin his illusion of power.

In scene three, the whore does not even get to be human. She is a horse for a General, who rides her to his death and certain glory. Throughout the scene, he refers to her as if she is a horse and he is in complete command of her. Like the Judge, he also wants to be a hero. When he hears another woman scream, he wants to save her, but the demands of his fantasy take all his attention. Yet even the woman who plays the horse has some measure over power. She is the one who brings the general's uniform in and dresses him in it. She directs the flow of his fantasy. Though all three of these women appear to be objectified by these men, they do have power over them. They ultimately run their fantasies. Without them, there would be no fantasies.

One woman who lives a fantasy for herself in the course of *The Balcony* is Chantal. She has recently left the brothel with Roger, the plumber, and joined the rebellion that is going on outside. Chantal has much power. First, Roger is in love with her and would do anything for her. Chantal's feelings for him are not as specific, giving her the upper

hand in that relationship. With his reluctant consent, she leaves him and his unit to become a symbol and figurehead leader for the rebellion at large. As a whore, she was used to playing the role of a symbol and cannot resist playing it on a bigger scale.

Chantal becomes a rallying point for the movement. Chantal's power in this sense is short-lived. She is assassinated (perhaps by the Bishop) when she visits the balcony of the Grand Balcony, where Irma has taken on the role of the queen. When Chantal is killed, the power of her image is further increased. She is co-opted by the other side and made into a saint. It is as if what Chantal stood for is both pure and sinful, a contradiction commonly ascribed to women. She could not live a long life as both a woman and a symbol because she might hold too much "real" power. By being killed, she (and her illusion) could be controlled.

Carmen is one of the only whores to see the problems with playing roles. She no longer plays subservient roles in the clientele's fantasies, and is now the bookkeeper to Irma, the brothel owner and manager. No specific reason is given for Carmen's choice, though she often played the Immaculate Mother. It seems that Carmen wants to play a real life role: as mother to her young daughter who lives in a nursery in the country. In an attempt to control

Carmen, Irma emphasizes that such a role does not really exist for her. Carmen already accepts this by herself. She realizes that she has chosen her fate and will not leave the "house of illusions." Reality will probably be worse, if not deadly. It is as if Genet is emphasizing that society believes that a woman's place is in the home, even it is a brothel.

But this idea is turned on its head by Irma, the ultimate contradiction of women's roles and power. The Grand Illusion is *her's* in most every way. Irma controls how long fantasies are. She tells the Bishop in scene one that they are only two hours long, and gets peeved when he wants more. She oversees the purchasing of the costumes and props, makes sure the details are to her client's liking, but arguing points when she feels she is correct. She puts off their complaints about the rebellion that is going on outside, appeasing the rebels but only to a point.

Irma also controls her workers. Carmen criticizes the fact that they always have to be serious. They cannot smile with clients, or have any hints of love because it would ruin the illusion that they are trying to create to keep the men happy. Irma will not let them talk about their work once it is done. She responds to Carmen's criticisms by trying to further control her, and warning her not to cross her. Irma is rather cruel and callous, and will not compromise to make her employees happier in their work.

The only thing that Irma does care about is money and her jewels, though she does not perform in any of the fantasies to further her business. She worries about protection and management and the like. In this sense, she is very masculine. She even has a male body to rely on. Her former lover and current business partner the Chief of Police forced her to hire Arthur, the man who plays the executioner. At one point, Irma describes Arthur to George, the Chief of Police, in these terms: "I'm his man and he relies on me, but I need that rugged shop-window dummy hanging on to my skirts. He's my body, as it were, but set beside me." However, Arthur is killed soon after she says this.

Therein lies the biggest contradiction about Irma. Though she is obviously in charge, she relies on the protection and support of the Chief of Police. Irma worries when he does not show up on time, and does much to feed his ego and his illusion of power. Yet, like Chantal, she also becomes a public symbol of power, greater in many ways than even George. When the Queen becomes incapacitated, Irma is asked by the Court Envoy to take her place, a physical symbol for the people to rally around.

> THE PROSTITUTION AT THE GRAND ILLUSION SEEMS TO BE MORE ABOUT ACTING OUT MEN'S POWER FANTASIES THAN THE ACTUAL SEX ACT."

Though George is momentarily jealous because she would be above him, he accepts her decision to play the role because it might benefit him. Irma succeeds for a short time, though her power is undermined by the three customers who take on the real roles of Bishop, Judge, and General, and by the resumption of the rebellion. Irma's role as queen is short-lived, but she survives her moments as a symbol intact and stronger. If nothing else, Irma is a survivor.

In *The Balcony,* women often seem in power. A Queen runs their unnamed land. But she seems to be nothing more than a replaceable figurehead. Chantal plays the same role for the rebels. The whores play seemingly interchangeable roles for their clients. Even Irma, strong and powerful as she may be, is, in many ways, no more than the brothel's figurehead for the Chief of Police. Women have no real control in Genet's play. Like everything else in *The Balcony,* it is a (profitable) illusion.

Source: Annette Petruso, in an essay for *Drama for Students,* Gale, 2001.

Albert Bermel

In this excerpt from "Society as a Brothel: Genet's Satire in 'The Balcony,'" Bermel explores the implementation of imagination to portray satire.

Genet's plays, like Pirandello's, have become a treasure house for the rococo critical imagination. As the visitor basks in the heady atmosphere—the mirrors, the screens, masks, grandiose costumes and *cothurni,* the role-playing, verbal efflorescence, and paradoxes—he burbles about the undecipherable nature of levels, dimensions, contexts, multiple images, loci, ritualism, and infinities of reflections. . . .

Genet takes for granted [in *The Balcony* the] confusion between sexual and social obsessions. In

> " A PLAY CAN SHOW US, MORE CLEARLY THAN A SCRUTINY OF LIFE CAN, WHAT LIFE IS REALLY ABOUT. IT CAN REVEAL KINKS AND SHAMS FOR WHAT THEY ARE. IT CAN DO A SORTING JOB, BRING LIFE INTO FOCUS. IT CAN MAKE US LAUGH AT THESE CHARACTERS . . . UNTIL WE REALIZE THAT WE ARE LAUGHING AT OURSELVES."

the brothel's studios the devotees abandon themselves to sexual consecration; the house of pleasure is a house of worship. In it each man finds a contrary, double satisfaction: he acquires a feeling of potency from the clothes and the role he puts on; at the same time he abases himself in that role. Or rather, he abases the role and its clothing in order that it may serve his sexual satisfaction. There is then an element of masochism in each of the aberrants' personalities. . . .

From the first Genet intermingles sexual and religious ceremonies. Scene One sets the tone by introducing us to the Bishop in a studio set that represents a sacristy. He wears robes of exaggerated size so that he looks larger than human, like a principal in a Greek tragedy. . . .

Now, although we are led to believe that this Bishop is played by a gas man, we never see the gas man, only the Bishop. There may be a gas man in the story but there is none in the action; and if a gas man in Bishop's apparel differs dramatically from a bishop in bishop's apparel, Genet declines to show us the difference; if we insist that this is a gas man *metaphorically* wearing a bishop's mask, that mask then has the same lineaments as the face behind it—or else it is transparent—or else it is not a mask any longer but has become a face. . . .

[The other patrons of the brothel] seem to don roles the way some tribesmen assume charms, as a plea to heaven for virility and safety. But Genet shows us only the roles. These roles *are* the characters. . . .

In [Pirandello's] *Six Characters in Search of an Author,* the six characters are actually in search of an audience. An author may dream up the Father, but it takes a spectator to recognize him as that character. . . .

Genet introduces something like this reciprocity into the action of *The Balcony.* To be the Bishop, the character needs an "opposite," a penitent, somebody who will confess to him and whose sins he will absolve, somebody who will certify him as the Bishop. . . . But if the function of the opposites is to take the kinkies seriously and attribute roles to them, the girls seem unable to take themselves seriously *as opposites.* They keep breaking out of their parts and virtually winking at the audience: in the Judge's scene the Executioner does "exchange a wink with the Thief." These girls are never anything but whores.

Later in the play the opposites become dispensable. When the Envoy asks the kinkies to drive through the city in a coach as the "real" Bishop, Attorney-General, and General, they feel nervous about abandoning their brothel scenarios and translating themselves from private images in Irma's studios into public images in the world at large. . . . When their public performance begins, the only doubt that arises is whether they will sustain their parts convincingly or look like kinkies.

At this point, in the absence of the brothel girls, the task of being a collective "opposite" or role-confirmer falls to the general public. We do not see this public, but we do learn subsequently that it accepted the Bishop, Judge, and General for real, without question. Possibly the public was blinded by the "gold and glitter" that surrounded the dignitaries. In any event, it responded favorably; it threw flowers and cheers at them; it even blew them kisses. And why not? We, the other "general public," have already attributed these roles to the kinkies; to us they have *become what they pretended to be.* . . .

Irma is another case in point. The Envoy asks her to stand in for the missing queen. . . . Irma is not impersonating the queen, but extending her own personality. She is playing *herself,* and the Envoy, who later says she made a first-rate queen, functions as her opposite. As though to underscore this conclusion, at a certain point in the text Genet drops her name and starts calling her the Queen; it is the most natural thing in the world for this procuress to assume royalty.

What does Genet mean by this demonstration? That life is all pretext, appearances, theatre? I think he is driving us toward a narrower, sharper, and more satirical conclusion: bishops, judges, and generals are kinkies; queens are procuresses; opposites (the public) who take these figures at their dressed-up value and serve them are whores: revolutionary slogans and symbols (Chantal) are whore-mongering.

Genet likens this state of affairs to the performance of a play. But Irma's much-quoted final speech, which compares her brothel with a theatre, has been frequently misunderstood:

> In a little while, I'll have to start all over again . . . put all the lights on again . . . dress up. . . . (*A cock crows*) Dress up . . . ah, the disguises! Distribute roles again . . . assume my own. . . . (*She stops in the middle of the stage, facing the audience.*) . . . Prepare yours . . . judges, generals, bishops, chamberlains, rebels who allow the revolt to congeal, I'm going to prepare my costumes and studios for tomorrow . . . You must now go home, where everything—you can be quite sure— will be even falser than here. . . .

She is not saying that life is less ''real'' than Genet's theatre (or her brothel) is. To claim this on his behalf would be to deprive the play of its application to life. She is insisting that there are more disguises and pretense in life than in the theatre, and that in life the disguises are harder to discern. A play can show us, more clearly than a scrutiny of life can, what life is really about. It can reveal kinks and shams for what they are. It can do a sorting job, bring life into focus. It can make us laugh at these characters . . . until we realize that we are laughing at ourselves. For if we have accepted what the play says, we are the people who make bishops, judges, and generals out of kinkies, and queens out of whore-mistresses.

Most of the criticism of *The Balcony* fastens on to other aspects of it, in particular the rituals, disguises, and mirrors, which are constantly held up as prima-facie evidence of Genet's contempt for reality: his masks beneath masks, reflections within reflections, screens behind screens, and other infinite recessions. . . .

What is a ritual? It is a prearranged ceremony. A church service is a ritual; so is a public parade. They go according to form, according to plan. There are no serious hitches, no divergences from the timetable or program. If a horse in a parade kicks an onlooker or if one of the ceremonial figures passes out, that part of the ritual resembles theatre. But ritual is the opposite of theatre, just as the girl who plays the Penitent is the opposite of the Bishop. She

defines him, and ritual defines theatre; it marks one of theatre's boundaries by being what theatre is not: predictable, self-contained, formal. . . .

[The screens, disguises and mirrors] are part of a device that Genet uses theatrically, not ritualistically. And far from telling us that nothing is real, they tell us that in the brothel, as in the playhouse, everything is adaptable. . . .

Irma thoughtfully provides a mirror for each studio. The Bishop gazes into his and is smitten with his image. . . . Up to now he has not tasted the power of being a bishop; he uses the image in the mirror for erotic stimulation, yet even as he does he appeases his power-lust by profaning the robes and ''destroying'' their ''function.''

The Judge, too, has a mirror available to him, but does not use it. Instead he looks at beefy Arthur, the male whore, and talks lovingly to him as though to an idealized version of himself, heavy wtih tangible musculature. . . .

The mirror in the General's studio has the same purpose again. Admiring his image in it, the General sees shining back at him an historical validation: he is the hero of Austerlitz, Napoleon vanquishing the Austrians. . . . As in the two previous scenes, the kinky loves his image in the mirror because what he sees there is *himself transfigured*.

As an element in the stage design, the mirrors have a further purpose, suspense. Each one is angled to reflect to the audience part of Irma's room. We will not see that room until Scene Five, but the mirrors forecast it. They alert us to Irma's omnipresence as the brothel's grandmistress, and they hint at the immensity of the premises. . . .

By reflecting the studios and Irma's room to each other, they enlarge the brothel and unify the scenes. They also enlarge the studios: mirrors make a room look artificially bigger.

Genet's language serves as another means of enlargement and ratification. The Bishop says, ''We must use words that magnify.'' And most of the characters do. Their speeches move effortlessly out of conversation and into clusters and imagery. Genet sometimes handles images the way a writer like Shaw handles logic, with comic hyperbole. By exalting the dialogue, raising it beyond simple meanings, he frees it from the constraints of everyday banter and attains a language that can cope with complicated states of consciousness.

The brothel ... seems to resemble a vast, rotating movie lot with the sound stages distributed around the hub of Irma's office. Genet does not provide a full list of the studios, but if we visualize each one as a miniature of some activity outside the theatre and brothel, the brothel is a miniature of society as a whole. The mirrors in each scene reflect the world to itself. . . .

As a satire of society, *The Balcony* laughs at men in authority as they seek for images of themselves that they can love. It laughs more bitterly at men without authority who defer to those images (attribute them) and even worship them. Both groups are taking part in a game. X names himself a judge or bishop or general. He drapes himself in an awesome outfit, grows confident from the feeling of being dressed up and from the sight of his magnified reflection, and so enlarges himself artificially in the eyes of other men. His old self or personality fades away.

These games are what gives the play its unity of tone, games such as I'll-be-bishop-and-you-be-penitent. But they are games played in earnest; games propelled by desperate intentions; games that are liable, because of their peculiarities, to invoke the unexpected; games of life and death.

Now, games are play and the gerund *playing* has two principal meanings: it means enjoyment, as in a house of pleasure; it also means mimesis. . . . The Bishop begins by masturbating or ''playing'' with himself; he ends by wishing to play with other men's lives, to move them about like pieces: ''Instead of blessing and blessing and blessing until I've had my fill, I'm going to sign decrees and appoint priests.'' . . .

Theatre, as an arena for games, plays by heightening its effects. In his playhouse-brothel Genet takes this heightening to a personal extreme. He pours into his drama a sumptuous language, bulks out his conceptually big characters with padded costumes; and seizes other theatrical opportunities, such as keeping visible that token of the post-Renaissance, indoor theatre, the chandelier.

As part of the heightening procedure he plants contradictions in the characters' desires: they feel pulled between playing games of sex (the mastery of themselves) and games of authority (the mastery of others). Genet marries the contradictions, without trying to resolve them, in an ingenious way: he implies that power over oneself and power over others can be achieved simultaneously by playing games of death.

In the early scenes he seems to show us the brothel as a theatricalization of life, of real life, with a real bishop, judge, and general giving rein to their all-too-real kinks in order to live at the top of their bent. But there are plenty of hints that death is a more attractive game for them to play than life is. . . .

At last it is the turn of the gaudiest character in *The Balcony* to play the game of death. He is the Police Chief, Georges by name, the ultimate provenience of power in the state. . . .

Genet's exquisite irony intensifies. Georges decides that his ideal memorial, his death-in-life, would be for somebody to impersonate him in the brothel. While the impersonator mimics him, he will mimic death by disappearing to ''wait out the regulation two thousand years,'' the equivalent of the Christian era. The two millennia will sanctify him, much as the Church (the Bishop), the Law (the Judge), and the Military (the General) have been sanctified by the two millennia since the death of Christ and the decline of Rome. He will, we assume, mimic resurrection too when he feels like it, and re-emerge as top dog in the state. . . .

Fortunately for Georges, Roger the defeated revolutionary comes into the brothel expressly to impersonate him. No sooner is he inside a studio (which is got up to look like a mausoleum) than Roger is awarded his ''opposite,'' a slave, to attribute to him the role of Police Chief. But Roger is still secretly a rebel. And in him the revolution twitches its final, futile defiance.

He ends his scenario by making ''the gesture of castrating himself.'' With this gesture he hopes to mutilate the image of the Police Chief as a man of power. . . . For the purposes of the play, he is dead. And his gesture has gone awry. Trying to discredit Georges, he has succeeded only in becoming Georges' opposite, an impotent, and in confirming Georges. . . .

Georges, Genet's most savage portrait in the play, is so unmanned that he cannot play out his own fantasies. He must wait until somebody does the job for him by proxy—anybody, no matter who, an avowed revolutionary if necessary—just so long as he does not get hurt. Now he can go into his two-thousand-year hibernation. A studio has been prepared. It is a mocked-up replica of a tremendous piece of architecture still in the planning stage. It incorporates law courts, opera houses, railroad stations, pagodas, monuments. . . . But this edifice is no less than a magnification of the brothel, right down to the mirrors. Like the brothel, a floating balcony, it will "sail in the sky" on top of its mountains. Here Georges's image will live on with its wound, while he plays the game of death in a brothel mausoleum. The image will evoke the images we retain of other symbolically castrated heroes: the shorn Samson, the blinded Oedipus, Philoctetes and his rotting foot, Christ crucified.

A magnified image in a magnified brothel. So much, says Genet, for your saints and heroes. . . .

Source: Albert Bermel, "Society as a Brothel: Genet's Satire in 'The Balcony,'" in *Modern Drama,* September, 1976, pp. 265–80.

David I. Grossvogel

In this excerpt, David I. Grossvogel relates "The Balcony" to "a house of illusions."

The balcony [in Genet's dramas] is a stage upon Genet's stage, a place of sumptuousness, triumph, and make-believe.

The Balcony is a conscious stage from the first. . . . But this stage is also . . . "the most artful, yet the most decent house of illusions." A house of illusions is the traditional French name for a brothel, a place for the creation and enjoyment of intimate fancies. . . . No problem, says Genet, should be resolved in the imaginary realm, especially since the dramatic solution is an indistinct part of the closed social structure. It is rather the play that should bring its reality to the spectator. And so Genet has placed a mirror on the right-hand wall of his set which reflects an unmade bed that would be, if this stage room had a normal extension, in the midst of the orchestra's spectators. The playgoer does not enter into *The Balcony* with impunity— once the curtain is up, he *is in* a bawdyhouse.

But he is also in the theater. The set *appears* to represent "a sacristy," formed by three folding screens of blood-red cloth: The sacristy is where the priest puts on the holy vestments, the alchemist's kitchen (in *The Maids,* the scullery was referred to as the sacristy). Note that the setting merely appears to represent; this is a stage, not the real thing. The spectator must not attempt to fool himself; if he makes of this a real sacristy, it loses its virtues of staginess and mystery, and the wellspring of ritual turns into a dressing room. It is made of folded screens [a later play is called *Folding Screens*], those tenuous walls that are suggestion, not sub-

> THE STAGE OF GENET IS MORE IMPORTANT THAN THE SPECTATOR SINCE IT REQUIRES A SPECIFIC SPECTATOR AND, BARRING THAT, A SPECTATOR DISGUISED."

stance. And finally, the set is blood red, the color of the sacrificial and the sexual acts—the sacred ritual of death and rebirth as life, or as beauty, according to its moment. . . .

[There are in *The Balcony*] moments of illusion . . . for the private enjoyment of certain people on stage who are not so very different from the spectator—that participant watching the proceedings from behind a peephole that has the full dimensions of the proscenium. The half-naked girls in the sadistic sex play are exhibited to the spectator as well as to the actor in his role as brothel customer—bishop, judge, general, and so on. The world which these create in the stage privacy of their own mind is just as much the spectator's; the objective stimuli are the same.

To this dimension which incriminates him, the spectator is asked to add another for which the evidence is less explicit: it is that of the revolution [taking place outside the brothel], echoed in the gunfire and the concerns of the principals on stage. The contaminated spectator participates immediately in only one level of the actor's reality, for the actor on stage plays a role concerned with events other than merely those of the brothel. . . .

[Genet] contrasts with the sealed world of the Balcony the world of the revolutionaries. These are by definition the ones who don't play; they are . . . the reality of their action. The brothel is their symbolic enemy since its life principle—esthetic distance that separates the performer from his act— would be their death; for them, "hand-to-hand fighting eliminates distance." These priests of factuality are solemn. The danger to their revolution does not come from want of strength; it comes from lack of purity. The moment their solemnity is in doubt, the moment their action takes on the appearance of a game, they will find themselves defeated even in victory, having merely replaced the old order by another image of itself. Theirs is the struggle of the purposeful against the purposeless; when they have won, they will *organize* their freedom and their relaxation, their festivities and their ritual. Their greatest victory has been won not in the streets but through conversion: one of the revolutionary leaders, Roger, has brought over to their side a prostitute from the Balcony—the singer Chantal. And it is out of that victory that defeat will spread to the revolutionary camp. Chantal becomes the illusion which even the revolutionaries now require in the fire of action, the myth—a symbol singing on the barricades. The revolutionary image must die, confused with the image of that against which it was directed, in order for the revolution to succeed. . . .

The Balcony is largely an expository play, a commentary upon the nature of reality and illusion and upon the function of the stage. *The Blacks* . . . is the play based on that theory. . . . In *The Blacks,* Genet demands a public of whites. He is insistent upon this to the extent of asking for at least one ceremonial white spectator if the play were performed for an audience of blacks, in which case the entire performance would be addressed to that single figure. Lacking even that single sacrifice, the blacks would have to wear white masks. "And if the blacks refuse the masks, then a dummy will have to be used." Thus the magic object has now moved beyond the footlights into the hitherto privileged realm of the spectator. This play forces implementation of Genet's admonition: "Let no problem be resolved in the imaginary world."

The stage of Genet is more important than the spectator since it requires a specific spectator and, barring that, a spectator disguised. (If the stage should have to settle for a dummy white, Genet will have succeeded in inverting completely the order of things: the performers will then be playing for only themselves.) The play is first of all a game, a diversion whose full meaning will be made clear later on; on stage, it is a performance put on by blacks for the benefit of other blacks dressed and masked as whites. It will be, as conceived by blacks, a definition of blacks by whites for the benefit of an exclusively white audience. Its paraphernalia will be the customary flowers and a coffin, the sacred objects in a ritual concerned with beauty and death.

Genet begins this act of play by eliminating the stage. The curtain does not come up mechanically, but is drawn—the human hand, portent of human mystery, replaces the machine. Thereafter, Genet adds the aspect of reality that ultimately defiles the mystery of the figureheads in *The Balcony* by

making the reality of their first vision dependent upon the vision of someone else: these blacks are played by Negroes. At this level of reality, the spectator cannot detach himself from the stage. . . .

Having stated the primacy of the stage-as-reality, Genet proceeds to subvert that reality in order to make of the stage the place of magic and mystery which it must also be if it is to sustain a genuine ritual; something is going on somewhere beyond this stage—an emissary occasionally breaks into the play with news from a world alien to the one of the play. The pseudo-whites on the dais are obviously actors, and not very good ones. Those who are below, performing for them, although they are ostensibly actors and spectators in a yet unspecified ritual are likewise learning their parts as actors and spectators. On each of these levels, the actual reality is being transformed into an artifact—something which will acquire a dimension other than that of its immediacy as existence.

The "whites" upstairs have come to witness the ritual murder of one of their number. The "organizer," who is a central performer in every one of Genet's plays, is a black by the name of Archibald, and he begins the ritual. This is built around a catafalque on center stage which supposedly contains the remains of a white savagely murdered by the blacks. The play is defined by Archibald as ritual: tonight again, the play goes on, the scene is to be enacted once again. The theater is asserting its own reality; these blacks are *ideas* of blacks—white pictures interpreted by the blacks themselves. Although they are Negroes, they now exist at their own level of the stage. In addition to being the generic reprobates, the outcasts that people each of Genet's stages, they are the shoeshine blacks, bad-smelling, lustful, murderous, childish—and, withal, exotic symbols because of these nonwhite attributes and because of their physical power and beauty. The whites are similarly mental images, though less complex. They are the black's notion of white authority. . . .

These "whites" try to see themselves as a necessary radiance; they are the born masters whose being legislates and justifies. The blacks, in addition to their own definition of themselves, are able to legitimate their personal feelings by this view of the "whites": their "black" hatred, their desire to possess and kill, rape, and obliterate those who need not justify their own rule over them, returns the stage gradually to the reality of that which encompasses even the stage. Genet is transferring to these blacks the prerogatives of the criminals, the per-verts, and the inverts of his plays and novels. They are automatic forces attempting to become more consciously and more hugely *themselves,* in order to "deserve [the whites'] reprobation . . ."*. . . .

The ritualistic killing . . . (for what is in the coffin is of little importance, "an old horse will do, or a dog or a doll"), that symbolic gesture, must thus not only destroy an individual, aiming at the destruction of a historical moment, but also the mask which that individual wears—the black hatred worn by the white. . . .

This grisly tribal dance of passion and murder is suddenly broken short by Genet; the esthetic and voodoo object is cast aside. News comes from the outside which all the blacks gather about to hear, including those on the dais who remove their false white faces. . . . [An emissary announces that a] congress has elected the one who is on his way to organize the fight: "Our aim is not only to corrode and dissolve the idea they'd like us to have of them, we must also fight them in their actual persons, in their flesh and blood." The Negroes on stage were real as "blacks," not as actors in their various roles. Now Genet actualizes even the roles which they were playing. Not only were the blacks representing to the symbolic whites on the dais the metaphor of an off-stage reality, but it turns out that the real plot is being performed beyond the theater. Blacks are rising the world over . . . , while these blacks on stage were providing a screen with their ritualistic actions . . . , with whites drowsing in the illusion of a play as blacks rise to action before their sinking figures. . . .

This drama is fraudulent. The white spectator (any spectator) who has seen *The Blacks,* or any play by Genet, has been deceived. He has seen a conjurer, or what Sartre calls an elegant ballet which is the orchestration of those interreflecting mirrors. At the moment of his most intense percep-tion, that which he derives from the human revela-tion of the magical object, he has been concerned with only a small part of man, the part giving the illusion status as an essential human perplexity. But the human perplexity is far more complex. Man does not live by any single anguish—nor, inciden-tally, by the raptures of an esthetic experience. . . . [A] single fiber, however vibrant, does not de-fine man. . . .

Source: David I. Grossvogel, "'Jean Genet: The Difficulty of Defining' and 'Postscript,'" in *Four Playwrights and a Postscript,* Cornell University Press, 1962, pp. 135–74, 175–99

SOURCES

Abel, Lionel, "Metatheater," in *Partisan Review,* Spring, 1960, pp. 324-30.

Atkinson, Brooks, review of *The Balcony,* in *The New York Times,* March 20, 1960, section 2, p. 1.

———, "Work by Genet Opens at Circle in Square," in *The New York Times,* March 4, 1960, p. 21.

Brustein, Robert, "The Brothel and the Western World," in *The New Republic,* March 28, 1960, pp. 21-22.

Clurman, Harold, review of *The Balcony,* in *The Nation,* March 26, 1960, pp. 282-83.

Esslin, Martin, *The Theatre of the Absurd,* Penguin Books, 1980, pp. 215-23.

Genet, Jean, *The Balcony,* Grove Press, 1966.

Malcolm, Donald, "Now Go Home," in *The New Yorker,* March 12, 1960, pp. 117-19.

Reck, Rima Drell, "Appearance and Reality in Genet's *Le Balcon,*" in *Yale French Studies,* Spring-Summer, 1962, pp. 20-25.

FURTHER READING

Jacobsen, Josephine, and William R. Mueller, *Ionesco and Genet: Playwrights of Silence,* Hill & Wang, 1968.
    This study of absurdist theater focuses on the plays and themes of Genet and Eugene Ionesco.

Sartre, Jean-Paul, and Bernard Fechtman, trans., *Saint Genet: Actor and Martyr,* Pantheon Books, 1963.
    This biography, by one of France's leading intellectu-als and friend of Genet, created and perpetuated many of the myths about Genet's life. This book allegedly gave Genet writers block for several years.

Thody, Philip, *Jean Genet: A Study of His Novels and Plays,* Stein and Day, 1968.
    This book is a critical work which includes commen-tary on Genet's life and frequent themes in his works, as well as extensive criticism of each of his major plays and novels.

White, Edmund, *Genet: A Biography,* Alfred A. Knopf, 1993.
    This in-depth biography of Genet tries to separate the fact from the myths that Genet and others created about himself.

Blood Wedding

FEDERICO GARCÍA LORCA

1933

Blood Wedding, completed in 1932, premiered in Madrid in 1933. Its popular success was such that Lorca was able to support himself from proceeds stemming from his writing for the first time. Its success also demonstrates the degree to which large Spanish audiences, by 1933, were highly receptive to the innovations in theater and literature that had been developing since the turn of the century. The play incorporates song, chant, poetry, music, and rhythm, and its action and sets are highly symbolic and stylized. These nonrealistic and antinaturalistic techniques capitalized on drama as a live event. As opposed to a play whose actions and sets seemed exactly like things in everyday life, Lorca's audience witnessed the stage exploited for all of its sensate and dramatic potentialities.

While some argue that the play treats certain universal themes, others disagree with this point of view, seeing it instead as a veiled criticism of certain sectors of Spanish society. On the surface, *Blood Wedding* is a tragedy that plays out the conflict between individual wishes and societal decrees and laws. It is a tragedy insofar as two of the central characters, Leonardo and the Bride, were once in love, but due to unknown impediments, were never married. Their tragedy is the tragedy of love missed. In the meantime, Leonardo has married another and the Bride is betrothed and about to be married herself. The thought of a definitive loss of his first love to another man drives Leonardo to

instigate the major event of the play, which is the lovers' flight on the very day that the Bride marries.

For those critics who view the play within its historical context, Lorca's theme is based in the rigid laws of the lovers' community, which decree that Leonardo must die for his transgression. That is, the terrible vengeance enacted against Leonardo is seen to represent extremism, intolerance, and inflexibility. These charges of inflexibility were understood to be leveled against those persons who were resistant to social and cultural change during an era when such change was largely inevitable.

AUTHOR BIOGRAPHY

Federico García Lorca was born on June 5, 1898, in the small town of Fuente Vaqueros, near the city of Granada, in Spain. He grew up in comfortable and pleasant circumstances, cultivating his tastes and talents for music (piano) and writing. By 1909 his family had moved to Granada, and by 1914 Lorca was enrolled in the University of Granada studying the liberal arts and law. He published a first book of collected articles and essays in 1918.

This first book whetted Lorca's appetite for more ambitious literary forays. In 1919, Lorca moved to the Residence of University Students in Madrid, where he believed he would encounter and benefit from a greater concentration of cultural activity than Granada, at the time, could offer. In Madrid, Lorca became acquainted with and established close, lifelong associations with Salvador Dalí, the surrealist artist, and Manuel de Falla, the orchestral composer, amongst others.

While Lorca wrote some dramatic pieces in his early writing years, he began his literary career most notably as a poet. However, while he was writing this poetry, he was also involved in a theatrical group of which he was the director. It was in the late 1920s that Lorca began to concentrate on drama. His famous trilogy of rural plays, of which *Blood Wedding* is one, was written between 1933-1936. Two of them were also staged during these years. (This trilogy includes *Yerma* and *The House of Bernarda Alba*.)

Lorca's short life was busy and full. He wrote a great deal, he was feted and admired, and he traveled extensively (for example, to the United States, Cuba, and South America). While Lorca's public life is well documented, biographers are less certain about precise details concerning Lorca's private life. The reason for this is that Lorca was gay, and the frank disclosure of such a fact during his time would have substantially endangered his career and social position.

Lorca was assassinated in 1936 just outside of Granada. The Spain of the early 1930s was a country uneasily negotiating the shift from monarchical, parliamentary traditionalism to full democracy and cultural liberalism. The political and social situation in Spain was as beleaguered and chaotic as that which characterized European politics and society, in general, at the time. The continent as a whole was struggling with the effects of lingering post-WW I economic depression as well as the rise of fascism in Italy, Germany, and Spain. The fascist army general Francisco Franco was gaining support in Spain, primarily from those who feared substantive change in either cultural or political terms. It was supporters of right-wing leaders such as Franco who saw Lorca and others as threats to the traditionalism and dictatorial society and law they wished to impose upon the Spanish nation. Lorca was arrested on August 16, 1936, and shot on either August 18th or 19th.

PLOT SUMMARY

Act I

The play opens in the home of the Mother and Bridegroom. It is learned that her husband and other son met violent ends, presumably in a feud. They also discuss the son's upcoming betrothal and marriage, until he leaves for work at his vineyard. A neighbor woman arrives and provides information concerning the Bride and her family. She confirms the mother's suspicions regarding the Bride having had an earlier love, and it turns out that this love, Leonardo, is from the family whose members are responsible for the deaths of her husband and son. The second scene takes place at Leonardo's house. Leonardo's wife and mother-in-law are rocking a baby to sleep. Leonardo's wife asks him why his horse is always tired these days; she says he has been seen "on the far side of the plains," which is where the Bride lives. Leonardo denies that he has been riding in that vicinity, and the subject of conversation shifts to the upcoming marriage of the Bride and Bridegroom. The third and final scene of Act I takes place at the Bride's home. The mother of the Bridegroom and the father of the Bride formal-

Federico Garcia Lorca

ize the match, each praising the worthiness of their offspring. The Bride is demure and reticent in company, but once alone with the Servant she expresses her true frame of mind, which is impatient and frustrated. The Servant asks her if she heard a horse at the house the night before, and the Bride says no. But, at this point, a horse is heard and both see that it carries Leonardo.

Act II

Act II takes place at the Bride's house on the day of the wedding. Young girls and others appear singing and chanting wedding songs. Leonardo and his wife and mother-in-law are the first guests to arrive, and soon Leonardo and the Bride are speaking heatedly. He declaims against her marriage, their continued separation, and the disaster of their never having married. She replies that she is marrying to finally bury the past and the memory of him. By the second scene of Act II the guests have returned from the marriage ceremony. The wedding celebration is set to begin. In the midst of a large gathering, the mother and father speak of Leonardo, noting his family's reputation for violence. Soon, the overwhelmed Bride announces her wish to rest for a time. When the Bridegroom goes to find her a bit later, she is nowhere to be found. It is discovered that the lovers have fled. A party with the Bride-

groom at its head is formed to seek out the lovers and exact revenge for their transgression.

Act III

Act III takes place mostly in a forest. This is as far as the lovers have managed to flee by the time the party catches up with them. Three woodcutters open the scene, commenting on the terrible events. Death and the Moon also appear in this scene, both looking forward to what will be, inevitably, somebody's death. Death, as a beggar woman, points the way to the lovers for the Bridegroom. In the meantime, the Bride encourages Leonardo to escape without her, as their horse is unable to carry them both. She knows that they will try to kill him. He refuses to leave her. With the stage directions having indicated the lovers' exit and the Moon's entrance, two shrieks are heard. At the sound of the second shriek, Death appears and moves to center stage with her back to the audience. She spreads out her arms such that a great cape unfurls. This impressive sight ends the second scene of Act III. The final scene of the play opens with two girls winding a skein of red wool. Confusion reigns with various characters appearing and asking for definitive news about the hunt for the lovers. Finally, the Mother is apprised of the terrible truth; her last son is dead at the hands of Leonardo. Leonardo is also dead. The Bride appears, dejected, asking for death. The Mother barely registers her presence as she announces her final descent into inconsolable pain and suffering.

CHARACTERS

Beggar Woman
See Death, Old Woman

Bride
The Bride is the last of the major protagonists to be introduced in the play's first act. The order in which the major characters are introduced—first the Bridegroom and Mother, then Leonardo, and then the Bride—could indicate their degree of social power and instrumentality. Unlike Leonardo, for example, who has the freedom and mobility to instigate the action and tragedy, the Bride is a character who must wait at home for things to happen to her. The first thing that happens to her is that her hand in marriage is asked for. Her behavior

during the betrothal meeting and her conversations with the Servant show her frustration over her lot and her relative disinterest in the Bridegroom. She will marry only to drive out the memory of Leonardo. However, she believes that she will one day come to love her husband, even if it is with a love less passionate than the love she has for Leonardo. In joining Leonardo in flight from the community, the Bride knows that she and her lover are doomed. Clearly, she is as passionate as he, and this rebellion and expression of her repressed desires is a release.

Bridegroom

Of the major characters in the play, the Bridegroom is perhaps the least compelling. Unlike Leonardo, the Bride, and the Mother, he is devoid of struggle and deep emotion. He is, rather, a straightforward and content young man. He works hard, he obeys his parents, and looks forward to his connection with the Bride with all the confidence of a groom who is convinced that he is making an excellent match.

Death

Death (also known as Beggar Woman and Old Woman) as a beggar woman is an outsider to the play's community who does not bother herself with the community's pain. On the contrary, she seems to enjoy the proceedings, and as Death she thirsts after every life with which she comes into contact. Her bloodthirstiness and emotional coldness suggest how death is thought of by mere mortals, who view its inevitability and demands as anathema to human wishes and hopes.

Father

The Father can be aligned with the Bridegroom and contrasted to the doubting and suspicious Mother. Like the Bridegroom, this patriarch is wholly oblivious to the fact that anything exists in his world to disturb its smooth workings. He seems convinced of his daughter's willingness to marry, and he seems to have wholly forgotten her earlier passion for Leonardo, if indeed he was ever aware of it at all. He does not notice, as does the Servant, that Leonardo is visiting his daughter. He thinks, instead, of how the ensuing match will enhance the already solid stature of the two families.

First Woodcutter

Like the young girls in the play, the Woodcutters function like a chorus, that is, characters who

MEDIA ADAPTATIONS

- *Blood Wedding* was adapted into a film in 1981. The film, directed by Carlos Saura, tells the story through a stylized form of flamenco dance (a flamenco troupe was used in the film). The film is in Spanish, but subtitled versions are available in the United States.

are peripheral to the main action but who comment on it. The woodcutters are appropriate characters with which to open the last act of the play. As men who cut down living trees, they foreshadow the deaths of the two young men. The First Woodcutter, like the Second Woodcutter, seems to sympathize with the lovers' passion and transgression. ''You have to follow the path of your blood,'' he says of the lovers' rebellion.

Leonardo

Leonardo is the only character in Lorca's play who has a proper name. The other characters are designated according to their societal position or role. This indication of individuality suggests how he is the protagonist who disturbs the smooth social workings of his community. He asserts his own will against the rules of the community and brings tragedy upon all of the families to which he belongs or to which he is dramatically connected. He is driven by deep passion, as his furious travels by horse to and from the Bride's house demonstrate. Leonardo's fateful decision to deny the bonds of matrimony in favor of his abiding desire for the Bride occurs only when the Bride is certain to be married to another. This suggests the manner in which Leonardo's actions are motivated by possessiveness. As long as the Bride belongs to no other, Leonardo can tolerate their separation. While Leonardo's motivations are in certain respects selfish or possessive, and while he brings pain and suffering upon a number of persons, the play nevertheless generates a great deal of sympathy for his and the Bride's actions. The ''doubleness'' of Leonardo's character, that is, its attractiveness and its faults, suggests how there is a fine line between righteously asserting personal will and wrongful antisocial behavior.

Moon

The Moon (also known as Young Woodcutter) is personified and made into a character just as Death is. It appears as a young woodcutter with a white face. Like Death, the Moon appears to look forward to the culmination of events, the bloody conclusion to the hunt for the fleeing lovers. The Moon enters the final act of the play craving tragedy as if tragedy were needed in order for its own life to be sustained. This suggests how tragedy is an unavoidable part of life; it is as likely as the moon in the sky. The Moon, accordingly, offers to flood the land brightly with its light so that the lovers will have no place to hide.

Mother

The Mother is the strongest presence in Lorca's play. She senses and expresses the likelihood of the imminent tragedy, and she discourses freely on how things should be as opposed to how they often turn out. As a wife, mother, and widow who has trod the path of social respectability and duty, she has accrued the considerable social power available to women in her society. This power is clearly substantial even if it is less instrumental than that of men. For example, her influence over her son amounts to almost total control, and in this way women's indirect power over what happens outside of the home is evinced. Much is made of her stoic suffering in the play (suffering that occurs due to the deaths of loved ones). On the one had, her acceptance of life's freak injustices and her decision to suffer quietly is noble and supports the reader's sense of her considerable strength of character. However, insofar as her limited access to public life keeps her ignorant of the histories of the Bride and Leonardo, and insofar as she is alert and willing to dispense orders and advice, she might very well have been able to prevent this latest tragedy if she were not so closely tied to the private space of the home. As the play's references to the lives of married women suggest, women in this society are unduly kept from public affairs and spaces. The Mother's stoicism takes on a different meaning when these particular factors are considered. Clearly, the Mother embraces and supports the widely opposed roles given to men and women and the curtailing of her considerable powers that this entails. In this respect, her stoicism and sense of duty is like quietism, or the passive acceptance of things that can or should be changed.

Mother-in-Law

Leonardo's Mother-in-Law is known as a woman who was scorned by her husband. Her daughter is soon to suffer the same plight. This generational repetition creates a sense of inevitability in regards to these women's situation. It is as if there will always be those who are scorned. Indeed, the Mother-in-Law and Wife prepare for the Wife's imminent humiliation with a minimum of agitated bitterness and a maximum of sorrow and acceptance. The Mother-in-Law is companion and support to her daughter.

Neighbor

The Neighbor Woman provides important information for the audience; information that neither the Mother nor the Bridegroom can know if events are to have proceeded as far as they have when the play opens. Thus, a family outsider must appear in order for this information to be presented. The neighbor's conversation with the Mother in the first act apprises the audience of the Bride's past connection with Leonardo, such that it also comes out that Leonardo is of the dreaded Félix family, members of which are responsible for the deaths of the Mother's husband and son. This information establishes, from the play's start, a sense of foreboding and imminent tragedy.

Old Woman

See Death, Beggar Woman

Second Woodcutter

The Second Woodcutter joins the First Woodcutter in sympathy for the fleeing lovers, saying that the community "ought to let them go." He vacillates as to the success of the lovers' escape attempt, saying at one moment that one never escapes payment for a transgression ("But blood that sees the light of day is drunk up by the earth."), and at another that they might just be able to avoid punishment ("There are many clouds and it would be easy for the moon not to come out").

Servant

The Bride's Servant is, in contrast to the Father, quite aware of what is happening in the Bride's house. Her exchanges with the Bride bring out the Bride's true feelings and frustrations. Throughout the play, the Servant attempts to rein in the Bride's feelings by instilling calm and caution in the young woman. Thus, for all of her enthusiastic participation in the wedding events, it is sensed that she is aware that things are not as they seem. She makes every effort to protect the Bride from herself and from Leonardo, begging Leonardo, at one point, to let the young woman alone: "Don't you come near her again."

Third Woodcutter

The Third Woodcutter is the least sympathetic to the lovers of the three, and he is no way convinced that they will succeed in escaping. His first words are: "They'll find them." His succeeding comments are equally blunt. For example, he states that "they'll kill them," and that when the "moon comes out they'll see them." Like Death as the beggar woman, he seems to look forward to a gruesome end to events.

Wife

Leonardo's Wife is clearly wronged by her husband's and the Bride's actions. Yet, there is little sympathy felt for this character. Her failure to win substantive sympathy is partly, at least, due to the degree to which she accepts, indeed almost expects, her fate. Yet, her passivity is crucial for the overall sense of the play. Through this character the manner in which these women are largely dependent upon the actions of men for their happiness is made clear. Her passivity is a necessary feature for a play, which contains strong criticism regarding the lesser social freedoms of women at the time. Her passivity is therefore a symptom of a society in which women learn early and well, and better than men, how to curb their desires and wants.

Young Girls

Individual, paired, or groups of young girls appear at various points in *Blood Wedding*. Their function is usually to lyrically accompany or comment on action; like the woodcutters, then, they are like a chorus. For example, on the day of the wedding, girls enter and exit singing or chanting wedding songs and verses. This accompaniment helps to create the appropriate stately but festive wedding atmosphere. At the end of the play, two girls open the final scene winding a skein a red wool, which reminds the audience of blood. They sing of death but, later, they clearly do not have specific information about the wedding, the hunt, at its outcome. As characters within the events of the play, their actions and knowledge are realistic, but when they serve as figures who comment on action, they might be drawn outside of events so that they can be all-knowing commentators.

Young Men

The young men serve as counterparts to the young girls during the wedding scenes. These youths' function to represent the future of all young men just as the young girls exemplify the future of all young women. Interacting as they do on a wedding day, the play suggests how both the girls and these boys will, one day, marry themselves. Together, the young men and girls contribute to a sense of the unceasing cycles of life, in which marriage occurs as routinely as does birth and death.

Young Woodcutter
See The Moon

THEMES

Death

There are two ways the theme of death is developed in this play. First, there is death as the end, and the enemy, of mortal life. Death as an inevitable end that must be accepted is developed through the character of the Mother, who often laments the deaths of loved ones, while stoically enduring these painful losses nevertheless. There is more to this first theme of death than death's inevitability, however. The passionate bond of the lovers gives shape to another aspect. Their bond represents human life in general as being characterized by our connections to others. Death, therefore, kills not only our physical body, it also puts an end to that which makes us human. In claiming a person's life, Death sunders human bonds. Lorca introduces and develops this of death in the actions of his characters. For example, it is learned at the play's outset that the Mother's husband and one son were violently killed. One way the Mother mourns these events is by pointing to the fact that the killers reside seemingly content in jail. Not only do the killers escape real punishment, but she, the wholly innocent one, is the one being punished by having been deprived of her loved ones, and they, the loved ones, are being punished by having been deprived of their share of life. Death does not simply end life, it is anathema to it by destroying precious connections. Hence the play's characterization of death as a cruel and cold beggar woman who acts as the

TOPICS FOR FURTHER STUDY

- Research the Symbolist movement in literature. Which elements of Lorca's play suggest symbolist influences?

- Metaphors, similes, and symbols are words in a literary work which refer to other things. Using *Blood Wedding* as your sample text, demonstrate the difference between these three literary devices. How, for example, does a symbol function substantially differently than metaphors and similes?

- Compare and contrast the role of the chorus in a Greek tragedy you have read and in *Blood Wedding*.

- Explore the role of setting in Lorca's play.

- Examine the rise of fascism in the 1930s in Europe. How do historians account for the popularity of leaders such as Hitler, Mussolini, and Franco? What were these leaders' governing political convictions?

- Research the international battalions of the Spanish Civil War, especially the Abraham Lincoln brigade from the United States.

- Research the drama project, La barraca, of which Lorca was artistic director. What were the aims of the project?

---

lovers' ''enemy'' by revealing their whereabouts to the hunters.

If death is anathema to life, then being deprived of a full life is like death-in-life. The theme of death-in-life is generally most closely associated with the female characters, although it is also closely associated with Leonardo and the Bride, in particular. It is linked to Leonardo and the Bride since, to them, not to be able to love each other is not to live fully. Hence, at the end of the play, both would prefer death than endure the death-in-life of separation. As the First Woodcutter says, ''Better dead with the blood drained away than alive with it rotting.'' In terms of the female characters, the theme of death-in-life takes on broader connotations. Women as beings whose lives occur behind ''thick walls'' is underscored throughout the play. For example, at one point in the play, the Mother asks the Bride: ''Do you know what it is to be married, child?'' The Bride says she does but the Mother emphasizes her point anyway: ''A man, some children, and a wall two yards thick for everything else.'' Their lives, in the private realm of the home, is like life within a thick-walled coffin. It is a death-in-life because these exaggerated limits on women's social roles prevents them from pursuing all of the joys and varieties life has to offer. The men come and go; but the women are mostly at home. While the women are depicted as having many responsibilities and solid social stature, they are nevertheless firmly excluded from deciding how the community is run and what its rules, laws, and traditions will be. The stark separation of male and female spheres no longer seems like fairly divided work when the differing nature of the work is considered. If women cannot contribute to making the rules, then the rules might not accommodate their needs. If their needs are not accommodated then they cannot live fully and must live a death-in-life.

The Individual versus Society

The theme of the individual versus society is central to *Blood Wedding*. Leonardo and the Bride find their respective social positions intolerable and rebel against their fates. They break the bonds of marriage and destroy the equilibrium of the community. The way the characters are named in Lorca's play reveals a great deal about how the playwright conceives this problem. With the exception of Leonardo, who instigates the disequilibrium, none of the characters are given proper names. Rather, they are designated according to their societal position or role. The Bride, therefore, is on her way to become a Wife or a Mother. The Bridegroom, besides being a son, is on his way to become a Husband or a Father. What this suggests is the manner in which, in some deep sense, there are no real individuals in societies, insofar as individualism entails total self-determination. In other words, to live in harmony with other humans, human beings in fact conform to a limited number of roles and possibilities that accord with the rules and agreements of social living and life. Hence, it is only Leonardo, who contests these rules, who can be individualized by being given a proper name. The play's development of this problem gives credence to those critics who see the play as a criticism of sectors of Spanish society unwilling to countenance change. These views will ring true as long as there is a need for persons to assert themselves against their society when its institutions or laws do not allow for the reasonable happiness and creativity of its members. Since the play generates sympathy for the passion of the lovers, it can be seen to generate sympathy for the forces of change.

STYLE

Setting

Lorca's stage directions indicate settings that are simple, stark, and highly symbolic. The play opens within the house of the Bridegroom in a room that is painted yellow. The Bridegroom will be associated with yellow throughout the play. This color symbolizes his wealth, since gold is yellow, and his vigor, since yellow is the color of wheat, from which bread, the food of life, comes. It also symbolizes his eventual death, since yellow is the color of his lips when he is dead at the play's end. Leonardo's and the Bride's homes, however, are characterized by the color pink, a variant on red which is the color of passion and of vibrant life (or blood). They are, certainly, the characters who are the most passionate in the drama. The final scene takes place in a stark white dwelling, as if to suggest a place bleached of life and hope. The stage directions say that the room's white lineaments should resemble the architecture of a church. A church is the place where the rituals of birth and death are routinely commemorated; hence, it is an appropriate place for the mother to learn of her last son's demise and to accept her future drained of happiness. In contrast to these dwellings, is the forest to which the lovers flee. The forest has long been that

setting in literature where society's rules mutate, change, break down, or no longer apply. It is a wild place, beyond human-made, communal order. These lovers, clearly, cannot be together within their community, and so their only recourse is to attempt to escape its bounds. Their true home, in some sense, therefore, is this forest.

Modernism

The movement in the arts known as Modernism was an international, metropolitan set of movements. Impressionism and Dadaism in the arts, stream-of-consciousness techniques in the novel, and atonality in music are some of its central artistic movements and forms. It was announced very vigorously by Picasso's strange Cubist paintings, for example, that instead of painting people how they seemed in real life, painted them with three eyes, two heads (or one head seen from different perspectives), and so forth. Other modernist movements were Symbolism and Surrealism, to which Lorca was close. Lorca's play is a modernist play. Like Picasso's paintings, it departs from realism, or the highly naturalistic and realistic sets, plots, and action that dominate European and Spanish theater in the decades immediately preceding this set of movements. Lorca's modernism entails the attempt to return the ''drama'' to drama by making the theatrical event into a feast for the senses and the deepest emotions. The stark settings, the chanting, and the songs and music all contribute to an event which is designed to move an audience through all of the visual, aural, and dramatic means available to the dramatist.

Chorus

A chorus in a play is made up of a group of commentators, chanters, or singers not directly involved in the play's action. The chorus's role is either to comment on the action, to present the views of the community regarding the events, or, simply, to lyrically accompany action. Choruses of all of these types were common in Classical-age Greek plays. Lorca's play adapts from this tradition. A single girl, or a pair or groups of young girls, for example, will enter and circulate at various points, singing or chanting songs and commentary. In the final scene of the play, two young girls sing about how brief mortal life is and what might have happened at the wedding. Their contribution is primarily a lyrical accompaniment to the action, as the mother waits in fear to hear about the fate of her son.

COMPARE
&
CONTRAST

- **1930s:** The socialist government funds art projects aimed at including the rural peasantry and provincial audiences. Lorca founds a touring theatrical group, La barraca, which presents classic Spanish theater to rural audiences. It is run mostly by university students during their summers and breaks.

  Today: While the Spanish dictator's regime was characterized by the strict policing and censorship of art, post-Franco Spanish governments demonstrate generous governmental support and funding for the arts.

- **1930s:** Despite pockets of industrialization and modernization, Spain is still a country steeped in classism and gender bifurcation. It is also still attempting to hold on to the last of its imperial and colonial holdings. Its poorest classes, moreover, are still a landless, rural peasantry.

Today: A middle-class predominates and Spain has earned the curious distinction of having the lowest birth rate in Europe. Spanish economists predict that the nation will need large numbers of foreign workers in the coming decades to sustain its economy.

- **1940s:** Francisco Franco's allies, Adolf Hitler and Benito Mussolini, are defeated in WW II. Spain is isolated as a nation.

  Today: Spain, along with most European countries, makes up the European Economic Community (EEC). A common European currency, which is circulating in all of the participating countries, alongside each country's national currency, will completely replace the national currencies in 2001.

HISTORICAL CONTEXT

A Nation Divided

Spain entered the twentieth century as a constitutional monarchy. The Spanish populace, however, had little faith in this regime as the country was hampered by persistent and grave economic instability. Clearly, a change in the political and economic order of things was necessary. Widely opposed forces vied for contention. In various parts of the country, where industrialization had taken place, workers determined to ensure their proper treatment and compensation and to enhance their social status. These groups were eager to see a left-wing, socialist government take the reins of Spain. These groups were forward-looking in cultural terms. A society still imbued with classist notions, for example, was not a society able to accommodate a new working and middle class made up of former peasants who would no longer tolerate the old class hierarchy. This old hierarchy heavily favored the aristocracy and educated classes. These new social

groups were also staunchly antimonarchical, and they were also secular in view. To the opposing groups of Spaniards, these forces of change represented a drastic and fearful break from centuries of tradition, whether in social, cultural, or political terms. These other groups wished to maintain a traditional class structure, the succession of kings and queens, and the Catholic Church as a centrally shaping social and educational force. Lorca was on the side of change. His relations with the left-wing government voted into power in 1931 were cordial. Its Minister of Education, Fernando de los Ríos, funded the theater project of which Lorca was artistic director (the project was called La barraca).

The Democratic Republic versus The Dictatorship

The political scene in Spain was highly changeable during the late 1920s and early 1930s. A left-wing government, elected in 1931, was voted in again in 1936 after a brief return to a right-wing government in between. But Spain seemed determined to change, to try to negotiate the difficulties of modifying political and cultural institutions shaped for centuries by attitudes and beliefs no longer viable. This effort was effectively halted, however, as one of the leaders of Spain's traditionalist factions staged a coup d'état, or overthrow of the government, in 1936. This army general, Francisco Franco, was funded by fellow European nationalist and fascist leaders Adolf Hitler and Benito Mussolini. A bloody three-year civil war ensued, with the forces of Franco finally winning. As Lorca was clearly aligned with the forces of change, he was an obvious political target at the time. He declared his solidarity with workers and the republic on a number of public occasions. His murder was an act of terror, designed to quell the spirit of those who contested Franco's right to claim power by force instead of by election. The Civil War attracted a number of foreigners, both men and women alike, sympathetic to the Republic. In democratic regimes around the world, the Republican effort would come to be known as "The Good Fight."

CRITICAL OVERVIEW

When *Blood Wedding* premiered in Madrid in 1933, Lorca was a celebrated poet. He had not yet had a major theatrical success. *Blood Wedding* changed this. On opening night, the Teatro Beatriz in Madrid was filled to capacity, and in the audience were Spain's leading intellectuals, artists, and critics. The play was an outstanding success. It was interrupted numerous times by extended applause, and the playwright was compelled to emerge twice during its course to take a bow for the wildly appreciative audience. The play was translated into English and staged in New York, in 1935, as *Bitter Oleander*. It made its way fairly quickly to France and Russia, as well. It found its greatest foreign audiences, however, in the Latin American countries, in Argentina in particular. Lorca traveled to the Argentine capital, Buenos Aires, in 1933, where he, his lectures and his plays were most favorably received.

Blood Wedding is certainly the most enduringly popular of Lorca's plays. It has long been considered to represent the maturing of Lorca's dramatic talent, along with the other plays of what is known as the "rural trilogy." *Blood Wedding* was the first of trilogy to be written, with *Yerma* following, and *The House of Bernarda Alba* completing the cycle.

Candelas Newton, in *Understanding García Lorca,* sums up this long-standing critical opinion: "The so-called rural trilogy ... has been traditionally appraised as the culmination of Lorca's dramatic production. Of the three rural tragedies, the last one written, *The House of Bernarda Alba,* is considered to represent the culmination of his talents, in that he relies less on poetry and poetic interludes to create his effects." These plays are seen to represent the maturing of Lorca's talents in the sense that before these three plays, he had written a number of more experimental pieces of drama. These shorter, experimental pieces do not make up all of his dramatic work before *Blood Wedding,* but they do characterize it. However, as Newton also points out, recent scholarly work is revising this traditional view of Lorca's work and career. The experimental pieces are now being reconsidered: "Regarding the more experimental plays, Lorca himself claimed them as his true voice. Although theater at the time may have been unprepared for such a different dramatic orientation as those plays represent, they are presently achieving increasing recognition in critical studies and stage performance."

The critical literature on Lorca's work is vast, and approaches to *Blood Wedding* are various. However, all of these studies, in some way, examine and analyze the formal and thematic elements of the work. Formal approaches explore Lorca's dramatic techniques, such as his incorporation of chant, song, and poetry. According to Gwynne Edwards in *Dramatists in Perspective: Spanish Theater in the Twentieth Century,* Lorca's "fondness for [the] integration of different art forms" stems from his reverence for Symbolist theater. This Symbolist movement, along with Surrealism, Edwards states, are the contemporaneous modernist movements to which Lorca was closest (many of his experimental works are surrealistic). Other critics, such as Herbert Ramsden in his book *Bodas de Sangre,* mine the rich field of imagery and symbolism in Lorca's play. Ramsden, as do many other critics, points out that Lorca is, above all, a poet "of the concrete." "Thus," says Ramsden, "instead of referring to death as an abstraction, García Lorca evokes a death scene." Lorca's characters do not talk about death, rather, their words conjure up the very vision of one dead. Or, death appears in the play as an actual character. This avoidance of abstraction and this reliance on the concrete, highly visual image, is part of what Lorca derives from the Symbolist poets and dramatists he so avidly read. Other studies of *Blood Wedding* focus on the play's various themes, such

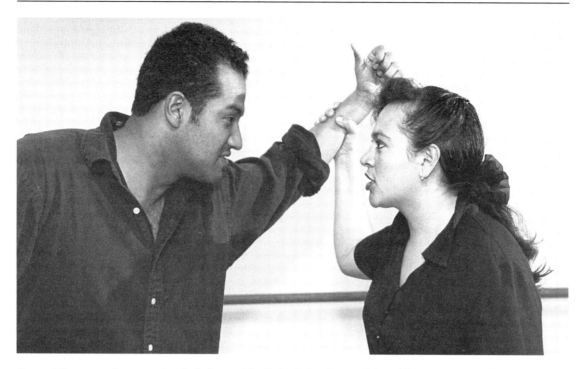

Juan Maza, as Leonardo, fighting with Grisel Ayala, as his wife, in a scene from Blood Wedding, *performed at California State University, Los Angeles.*

as passion, fate, or death. Gwynne Edward's book, *Lorca: The Theater Beneath the Sand,* contains a lengthy chapter on the drama's major themes.

Other approaches to *Blood Wedding* focus on its literary antecedents and influences, whether in Greek tragedy, classical Spanish theater, or contemporaneous developments in theater. These studies often remark on Lorca's reputation as a thoroughly Spanish poet and dramatist, in the sense that his style and subject matter seem to draw heavily from indigenous traditions and mores. These studies, however, must reconcile Lorca's closeness to broad European trends in the arts. In the introduction to *Lorca: A Collection of Critical Essays,* Manuel Duran captures this doubleness: "Symbol of Spain and of all thing Spanish, compared to Lope de Vega by Damson Alonso because of his direct and profound understanding of the popular idiom, acclaimed outside Spain and in his own country as the embodiment of the Spanish spirit, he nevertheless could state a few days before his death he was "a brother of all men" and that he detested the Spaniard who was only a Spaniard." Lorca's art, thus, is seen to fuse the "popular idiom" and contemporaneous developments in the arts. According to Duran, Lorca's "task was to assimilate [the new] movements with-

out destroying the Spanish tradition, or rather to assimilate them in a way that would allow this tradition to make itself felt again, to acquire a new vitality."

Most critics also draw links between Lorca's political sympathies and the play's subject matter. Spain was not, during the 1920s and 1930s, a country in which a citizen did not know his or her political mind. Lorca, in this respect, was staunchly on the side of Republicanism, and deeply committed to policies which would improve the lot of the country's poorest citizens. Lorca's adoption of the "popular idiom," and of folklore and legend, takes on a political significance in this light. It announces his belief that the culture which arises from a country's people is as rich as any culture produced by an educated elite.

CRITICISM

Carol Dell'Amico

Carol Dell'Amico is a Ph.D. candidate in the Program of Literatures in English at Rutgers, The State University of New Jersey. In the following

WHAT DO I READ NEXT?

- *Lament for the Death of a Bullfighter and Other Poems* (1962). A short volume of selected poems, translated and introduced by A.L. Lloyd.

- *The House of Bernarda Alba* (1936) is the final play of Lorca's so-called "rural trilogy"; it was completed in the last year of his life. It was first staged in 1945, in Buenos Aires. Bernarda Alba is a stern matriarch whose household stifles the lives and desires of her children.

- *Antigone* (late 440s B.C.E.), by the Greek dramatist Sophocles, concerns the tragedy of Antigone who acts against royal decree in order to fulfill funeral rites for her brother. She is condemned to death for her actions.

- *Romeo and Juliet* (1595) is William Shakespeare's most enduring play of love and passion. The lovers of the drama's title meet their deaths in an attempt to escape the nets of a family feud, which would otherwise keep them apart.

- *A Street Car Named Desire* (1947), by the U.S. playwright Tennessee Williams, is a drama of elemental passions in which a vibrant couple is set against the febrile decline of an unstable heroine.

---

essay, Dell'Amico examines how Garcia Lorca's story celebrates commuity, social life and living, at the same time that it points to the necessity of rebellion in situations where social laws and mores are oppressive or unduly limiting. Carol Dell'Amico teaches English at Rutgers, the state university of New Jersey.

One of Federico García Lorca's most notable features is how his protagonists are named. With the exception of Leonardo, the characters are designated according to their societal position or role; hence, there is a Mother, a Father, a Bridegroom, and so forth. This particular practice of naming *deindividualizes* his protagonists. They are made to seem less important as individuals than as social beings. This technique suggests that the play advocates the appropriateness and inevitability of communal, social life. Yet, troubling the stability of this theme is the naming of the Bride's lover, Leonardo. In choosing to individualize a single character in this way, the play advances the possibility that social customs, and the conformity they require, might be a problem. Clearly, the reader is to sympathize with Leonardo's rebellion and the lovers' desire to be together. The play thus poses the following questions: Is it ever appropriate to break social laws? Are such acts always destructive and antisocial? This essay examines these problems of social life and an individual's transgression of social mores.

The play's simultaneous celebration and criticism of social life and conformity finds expression in its presentation of two different types of communality, one that is rendered in an attractive light, and another that seems ominous or oppressive. The first type is a development of human sociality as part of what is beautiful about life on earth, and the other type points to a variety of social conformity that is like ethical quietism, or the refusal to stand up to laws and beliefs that are repressive or oppressive.

The idea that human life is governed by certain perennial institutionalized routines that are wondrous, simply because they define an unchanging aspect of human life, is consistently developed throughout the play. For example, in including only a single "Mother" character, a single "Father" character, and a single "Mother-in-law" character, and so on, the play likens the broad community within the play to a single family. The family, whether in its extended or more limited, contemporary guises and arrangements, is still and always has been a universal human institution. It is an institution in which each member is supposed to be succored and protected by the others. Likening the

> IF SUCH REBELLION BRINGS ABOUT TRAGEDY WITHIN A COMMUNITY, THIS IS UNDERSTOOD TO OCCUR ONLY BECAUSE A COMMUNITY HAS DEVELOPED IN WAYS THAT THWART THE OTHERWISE REASONABLE INCLINATIONS OF ITS MEMBERS."

play's society to a family thus suggests its naturalness, inevitability, and the manner in which social life is designed to ensure the well-being of each of its members. Individuals wither, left to their own, lonely devices, the play suggests, and a person is only healthy and happy when he or she is a part of different communities and groups.

This idea of the wondrousness of human sociality is also imparted by the play's theme of social life as that which is utterly natural in an organic sense, as natural as the growing of trees or the falling of rain. This sense of the naturalness of human interdependence is effected through the drama's linking of humans to things in nature, in conjunction with its focus on the community's closeness to the land. For instance, the Mother refers to her (now dead) husband as a "carnation," and to this husband and a son together as "beautiful flowers." In another of her expressions, men in general are linked to, indeed considered indistinguishable from, "wheat": "Men, men; wheat, wheat," she says. These simple and earthy metaphors for human beings gain full significance once they are considered against the play's rural backdrop. The community's wealth and stability derive, clearly, from the agricultural potential of the land. This land the men work diligently. A small plot of land not owned by either of these families permanently divides the properties belonging to the families of the Bride and Bridegroom, who should never have married. This detail suggests that even the land, or the earth itself, decrees that the union should not take place. If it were meant to take place, then their properties would not be divided. The play, in this way, imparts the sense that the rhythms, bounties, and terrain of the earth itself determine the rhythm and shape of these peoples' lives. Since

their lives reflect the very structures of the earth, and since metaphors consistently render the characters indistinguishable form things springing from the earth (flowers, wheat), the play succeeds in suggesting that this community gains its salient and central traditions based on the authority of the universe itself. The community and how it lives are utterly natural events; human community is as beautiful and inevitable as carnations or wheat. While communal social life clearly is sanctioned and celebrated by the play, other elements point to the necessity of rebelling against social roles and rules. If such rebellion brings about tragedy within a community, this is understood to occur only because a community has developed in ways that thwart the otherwise reasonable inclinations of its members. This idea comes about through the story of the lovers, the Bride and Leonardo.

The circumstances that pertain to the original relationship between the lovers are shrouded in mystery. It is never known why the Bride and Leonardo never married. Regardless, what is significant about the action of the play is that the Bride and Leonardo desire each other above all others, and find themselves enchained in arrangements neither can tolerate. Leonardo's dismissive behavior towards his wife, and his mother-in-law's history, tell the reader a great deal about such arrangements. Like her mother before her, Leonardo's wife is a scorned woman, a woman never truly loved by her husband: "One thing I do know. I'm already cast off by you. But I have a son. And another coming. And so it goes. My mother's fate was the same." Both Leonardo's wife and her mother, then, endure marriages and lives in which they must suffer a certain degree of humiliation and frustration. Unloved and not being able to love, they are nevertheless bound within marriages they cannot escape. As frustrating as Leonardo's wife's situation is, so is the Bride's, before she escapes and enjoys, however briefly, some satisfaction of her true desires. When the Mother and Bridegroom leave her house after the betrothal meeting, she expresses her sense of her intolerable social limitations to the Servant. When the Servant playfully asks to see the Bride's betrothal presents, the young woman cannot bring herself to be obliging. It is clear that the thought of her impending marriage is torture. Her mood is foul, and so she shakes off the Servant's kind hands violently. Her violence is so extreme that the woman exclaims over her strength: "You're stronger than a man." To this, the Bride replies: "Haven't I done a man's work? I wish I were.'' For this young woman to wish she were a man suggests the problematic extent of her social limitations, limitations which derive from her status and gender. As an unmarried young woman, she can in no way consider leaving her father's house to seek, for instance, forgetfulness in a new life in some town or city far away. She is bound by the rules of decency to remain in her childhood home until she moves to the home of a husband. There is never to be any independence for her; she always must be under the close protection of a man. Related to these limitations are the indignities suffered by Leonardo's wife in a world in which flight from the bonds of marriage, or separation or divorce, are unthinkable and profoundly shameful acts. This gallery of thwarted female characters tells the story of Catholic Spain in Lorca's time. Divorce was simply not an option; it was not legal.

The depth of the lovers' passion for each other suggests the degree to which it is an authentic problem, and not merely unthinking or selfish willfulness of a destructive or antisocial nature. The lovers are like the famous Shakespearean literary pair, Romeo and Juliet. Their rebellion, like Romeo and Juliet's, is the sincere rebellion of individuals who must step outside of their socially designated roles and assert their individual wills. Romeo and Juliet's rebellion teaches their respective families the folly of their continued mutual hatred. The particular rebellion recounted in Lorca's play, however, signified to many of Lorca's audiences the playwright's criticism of socially conservative Spain. His conservative detractors saw in his presentation of the Bride's sullenness and depression an implicit feminist plea to allow women to become more independent. They saw in his treatment of the passive and downtrodden wife of Leonardo a plea for divorce legislation. These conservative groups in Spanish society were outraged by such intimations of change, and this outrage fueled, in part, the events that led to Lorca's murder by right-wing sympathizers in 1936.

Meditation on social living and individuality suggests that while the play celebrates the fact of each person's dependence and indebtedness to others and to shared rules, these obligations can only be demanded by a society whose rules are just. Thus, if Leonardo is given a proper name, and in this way is set apart from his community, he is set apart and acts in order to effect the greater social good. *Blood Wedding* reminds its readers that while social living is natural, it is still made up of laws, mores, and regulations that are made and shaped by human beings. When these laws become oppressive, they must be contested so that they will be changed.

Source: Carol Dell'Amico, in an essay for *Drama for Students,* Gale, 2001.

Roberto Cantú

Roberto Cantú is a Professor at California State University, Los Angeles. In the following essay he examines the structure of The Blood Wedding *with regard to its formal aspects associated with tragedy of the Spanish Golden Age.*

Originally set in southern Spain, *Bodas de sangre/Blood Wedding* (1933) dramatizes a bride's ambivalence between a marriage sanctioned by society because it promises upward mobility, and the inward calling of a true love bound by the forces of fate. Lorca scholars have interpreted the play's theme of a love triangle as an allegory of Spain's modernization and the cultural crisis manifested prior to the Spanish Civil War (1936-1939), ominously anticipated in this drama of family murders and forbidden love. Viewed from a different perspective, the play's mythical cluster represented by the Moon, a Horse, and Death, unveils a symbolic dimension of madness, lustful passion, and the price paid when social conventions and family interests are not obeyed. Scholarly interpretations aside, you will note that the title of Lorca's drama plays on the ironic meaning of ''blood weddings,'' on the one hand as a violent aftermath (i.e., the death of the bridegroom after the wedding) and, on the other, as the *true* ''blood'' marriage in the play, namely: that between the bride and Leonardo. After their elopement, the Moon declares: ''You must follow your heart. They did well to run away. They had been lying to each other. But in the end, blood was stronger!'' *Blood Wedding* is thus structured according to formal aspects associated with tragedy of the Spanish Golden Age and classically manifested in a protagonist's difficult and often destructive choice, followed by a change from ignorance to self-knowledge.

Margarita Galban's adaptation divides the play in two acts (as opposed to the original three), and allows Death and the Moon to intervene throughout the play, consequently intensifying the sequential and conflicting elements of the plot while creating a tragic subtext written in the language of maternal premonitions, symbolic pagan features and sacramental allusions. For instance, the opening scene

VIEWED FROM A DIFFERENT PERSPECTIVE, THE PLAY'S MYTHICAL CLUSTER REPRESENTED BY THE MOON, A HORSE, AND DEATH, UNVEILS A SYMBOLIC DIMENSION OF MADNESS, LUSTFUL PASSION, AND THE PRICE PAID WHEN SOCIAL CONVENTIONS AND FAMILY INTERESTS ARE NOT OBEYED. SCHOLARLY INTERPRETATIONS ASIDE, YOU WILL NOTE THAT"

begins with the bridegroom leaving home to work in the vineyard, considering grapes as sufficient breakfast; a reference to a work knife elicits in the mother a series of associations with violent weapons and the memories of two murders: her husband and her first-born son. The mother's language of mourning conjoins her erotic memories; when referring to her dead husband, she states: "To me he smelled like carnations, and I enjoyed him only three short years. How can it be that something as small as a pistol or a knife can destroy a man who is like a bull? I'll never be quiet." Later she will tell her son about his grandfather: "That's good stock, good blood! Your grandfather left a son on every corner. That I like—men that are men, wheat that is wheat." The theme of grapes and wine-central to the ancient worship of Dionysus and to Christ's Passion-thus frame a story of Nature's fertility and of man's alienation, hence the tendency towards self-destruction and misguided affections.

Desirous to change the subject, the son reminds his mother about his fiancée and his forthcoming marriage; the mother, not one to be discouraged, feels a stronger premonition: "every time I mention her, I feel as if I'd been struck on the forehead with a rock." Reassured by her son that his fiancée is a good person in spite of having been in love with a previous boyfriend ("Girls have to look carefully at who they are going to marry," he argues), the mother reluctantly accepts to ask for the girl on his son's behalf. In the second scene, the mother learns

through a neighbor that the fiancee's past boyfriend—Leonardo Felix, now married to the fiancee's cousin—belongs to the family who killed her husband and first-born son. A dramatic pattern of doubles begins to surface with the theme of unhappy marriages: the fiancee's mother is said to have been beautiful, but not in love with her husband, hence the tacit connection to her daughter's fate. In subsequent scenes, Leonardo's growing detachment from his wife will find expression in the obsessive galloping to and from the future bride's home. In acts that mirror each other, Leonardo denies his nocturnal wanderings when asked by his wife, while the former girlfriend also insists in denying Leonardo's nightly visits. But by the end of the first act, both Leonardo and the bride admit to the fatality of their attraction. From this point in the drama, a series of fast-paced actions will reveal that the mother's premonitions were justified.

At the core of the unhappiness is family wealth. Indeed, the only available ladder to social climbing in this pastoral setting appears to be a "good" marriage. You will note, for instance, that the play sketches a triple-tiered agrarian hierarchy composed of landed gentry whose domains include fertile vineyards (e.g., the mother and the bridegroom); secondly, there are small ranchers who own sterile plains (e.g., the father, the bride); lastly, the landless peasantry (e.g., Leonardo Felix) are found at the bottom of the economic hierarchy. Once grasped, this problematic generates a story that unfolds as follows: although in love with Leonardo, the bride soon looks to the play's bridegroom as a better suitor because of his economic standing (he has recently enlarged his inheritance with yet more vineyards). In addition, we learn that bride and bridegroom have been in courtship for three years, and that Leonardo married the bride's cousin two years back, consequently there is an overlapping year that suggests a period of ambivalence and contradictions in the soul of the bride. Should she marry into poverty or into wealth? On the morning of her wedding, Leonardo addresses the bride and, oblivious to the situation, speaks reproachfully: "Tell me, what have I ever been to you? Look back and refresh your memory! Two oxen and a tumbledown hut are almost nothing. That's what hurts."

And yet it is more than just poverty that afflicts Leonardo, for he represents the stereotype of the "impractical" Gypsy who wastes his life on errands and illusions. When asked by the bridegroom why they don't buy land, Leonardo's wife responds: "We don't have any money. And the way things are going. . .[Leonardo] likes to move around too much. He goes from one thing to another. He's very restless." But this restlessness is also felt by the bride, who approaches the altar with last-minute doubts. It is at this point, as well, that Lorca's dramatic art effectively sketches the onset of complications and obstacles that Leonardo and the bride must face and resolve. Since the choice rests on the protagonist, the moral trajectory of the play is thus embodied in the bride who must choose between two men. And her choice will cause destruction but, in the process, will also resolve the play's major conflict: marry for love or for wealth. Unexpectedly, the bride undergoes two weddings, one traditional, and the second by elopement-with both resulting in the violent death of her two suitors. When Leonardo's wife discovers the elopement, major changes occur in three characters: the bridegroom, the mother, and the bride. The first two characters change from peace-loving social stereotypes (as has often been observed, only Leonardo has a first name) into revenge-seeking characters who are moved by a sense of honor. On the other hand, the bride—far from offending her audience with a husband's betrayal-soon reaches tragic proportions, first through the nature of her frailty (her own tragic flaw) and, secondly, because her subsequent suffering far exceeds the expected punishment. She is both a virgin and a widow on the day of her wedding, which also coincides with the day of her twenty-second birthday.

Let's recall that the play opens with Death singing a brief "overture," with references to the Moon in a language of contradiction: the Moon "lewdly, purely" "bares her breasts of solid steel," followed by references to Spain's Gypsies and to a Moon-gazing child. The poetic diction of this overture gives expression to an ambivalent motherhood that borders on transgression (lewd, but pure), and contextualizes the inner exile symbolized by the Gypsies, thus challenging our understanding of the play's Romantic theme, namely: the cosmic madness and the lust that consume lovers when Fate binds their destinies. Next to the language of motherhood that strongly characterizes Lorca's *Yerma* (1934), and to the despair that leads to suicide in the play *La casa de Bernarda Alba* (1936), *Blood Wedding* has instances of rhetorical expressions that construct a female sexuality and eroticism that are not necessarily limited to motherhood nor to an eagerness to leave an oppressive maternal house-

hold. When Leonardo appears on the morning of the wedding, the bride admits the profundity of her attraction: "I can't listen to you! I can't listen to your voice! It's as if I drank a bottle of anisette and fell asleep on a quilt of roses. And it draws me under, and I know I'm drowning, but I follow."

This attraction, governed by Fate, constitutes the heroine's moral flaw and the cause of her widowhood. The conclusion of the play discloses how importantly dramatic are the mother and the bride, for both mourn the men they loved. And although the mother's role continues to be fundamental to the play's success (and brilliantly acted by Margarita Lamas), as a character she will be overshadowed by the bride, thanks to the courage and honesty of her appeal. In an unexpected turn, Lorca transcends the sexual and erotic levels so as to reach the moral plane that best fits a tragedy. In a moment of dramatic eloquence and convincing dialogue, the mother and bride confront each other; admittedly, we are left with the impression that the latter wins the argument. Again, the moral victory is made with a language that the mother understands: the language of desire voiced in the condition of widowhood: "Because I ran away with another man, I ran away! You would have gone, too! I was a woman consumed by fire, covered with open sores inside and out, and your son was a little bit of water from whom I hoped for children, land, health! But the other was a dark river filled with branches that brought close to me the whisper of its rushes and its murmuring song . . .Your son was what I wanted, and I have not deceived him. But the arm of the other dragged me-like the surge of the sea, like a mule butting me with his head-and would have dragged me always, always, always! Even if I were old and all the sons of your son held me by the hair!"

The resolution of the conflict in *Bodas de sangre* ends all complications and closes with an irony: in the opening scene, the mother tells her son that she wishes he had been born a girl. At the conclusion of the play, the mother mourns the death of her son, but has gained a daughter: the daughter-in-law. Listen to the concluding lines and you will hear the same song in the lips of the mother and bride-at this point easily understood as a leitmotiv that opens and closes the play—speaking against weapons that cut lives before their time.

Source: Roberto Cantú, in an essay for *Drama for Students,* Gale, 2001.

Gema Sandoval (on floor), Angela Jiménez, and Margarita Stocker (far right) star in California State University's 1999 production of Blood Wedding.

Mona Molarsky

In the following essay, Molarsky provides an overview of the countries that performed Lorca's plays for his 100th birthday commemoration.

A spate of international productions serve up the passionate depths of Garcia Lorca's plays.

Three days before opening night, New York's Gramercy Park Theater is dark inside. It's so black you have to feel your way down the aisle. Then a soft, dream-like spot appears upstage left and gradually brightens.

"A little more, just a little more!" calls director Rene Buch from the depths of the balcony. "Yes. Perfect. Que bonita!" he laughs, shifting into Spanish. A young man walks downstage, draped in white chiffon. "Do you like it, Flor?" he asks Buch, doing a slow turn. "No. No quiero! It looks like Carole Lombard," Buch complains to the costume designer. In a minute she's up on stage, snipping and pinning the fabric.

Tonight is the pre-dress rehearsal for a long-overdue New York premiere. Written in 1930 by Spanish poet and playwright Federico Garcia Lorca, *El Publico* has had to wait almost 70 years to get

produced in the same city where it was conceived. Dubbed by Lorca his "impossible theatre" because of its technical difficulties and then-taboo theme—homosexual love—*El Publico* "disappeared" after Lorca's 1936 execution by Fascists during the Spanish Civil War. When it reemerged, 20 years later, the play stayed unperformed for another whole decade. *El Publico* has since been published, translated and performed numerous times, but never—until now, that is—in New York. This year, to honor the 100th anniversary of Lorca's birth, Buch, and the company of which he is artistic director, Repertorio Espanol, is producing the still-subversive play.

Lorca has been a mainstay at Repertorio, which over the last 30 years has produced all his major works, including *Blood Wedding, Yerma* and *The House of Bernarda Alba,* his three tragedies set in the Spanish countryside. Staging *El Publico* is clearly an act of love for the company—and a way for it to be judged in the international arena during Lorca's centennial year.

Throughout the world, from Buenos Aires to Tokyo, theatre groups are mounting tributes to the playwright, who was born in on June 5, 1898, in Granada. Every one of his 15 plays is currently in production somewhere—including Madrid, Brussels, Havana, Cairo, Lyon, Moscow and New York, among other cities. Even his lesser-known plays—the comedies, tragicomedies, puppet shows, and "experimental" works like *El Publico*—are finally getting the attention they deserve.

This year, Spain alone is hosting a vast array of events to commemorate Lorca, who remained censored there from the Civil War until Franco's death in 1975. There are festivals, poetry readings, dance performances, concerts, exhibitions and lectures dedicated to Lorca, offering the chance to see unusual productions like Lorca's short, experimental piece *Buster Keaton's Bike Ride in Barcelona.* In the spirit of La Barraca, Lorca's traveling theatre group that brought classics to the poor during the early '30s, several companies are now touring rural Spain. An unprecedented number of puppet productions are scheduled, too. Lorca was fond of puppetry and wrote several puppet plays, including *The Billyclub Puppets* and *The Puppet Play of Don Cristobal.*

Lorca's work has long been venerated in the Spanish-speaking world. As Buch puts it, "When he published his poems, *The Gypsy Ballads,* in 1928, he became a torero, a bullfighter. Everyone in Spain knew his poems and quoted them." At this time, as Lorca was being hailed "the people's poet," he was also working on various experimental theatre projects, plans for a traveling puppet troupe and an avant-garde magazine. His friends and artistic collaborators included painter Salvador Dali, filmmaker Luis Bunuel and composer Manuel de Falla. In 1930, Picasso designed the costumes for Lorca's comedy *The Shoemaker's Prodigious Wife,* which premiered in Madrid with Spanish star Margarita Xirgu in the lead role. By 1933, when he arrived in Buenos Aires, where *Blood Wedding* was a hit, Lorca had become a celebrity in Latin America as well. He remains beloved there to this day.

But Lorca in translation is another matter entirely. In 1935, the same year that *Waiting for Lefty* catapulted Clifford Odets to fame, *Blood Wedding* opened at New York's Neighborhood Playhouse to bemused reviews. What could Americans make of a play that included among its characters the Moon, personified as a woodcutter, and Death as a beggar? Plain-talking actors from the land of Jimmy Stewart found themselves speaking lines like "with a knife/ with a tiny knife/that barely fits the hand/but that slides in clean/through the astonished flesh."

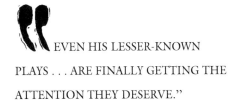

EVEN HIS LESSER-KNOWN PLAYS . . . ARE FINALLY GETTING THE ATTENTION THEY DESERVE."

In the six decades since, Lorca has never become a staple of the American theatre, but south of our border and in much of Europe, he's mentioned in the same breath as Synge, Brecht, Pirandello and Genet. Some American directors have been frightened off by supposedly difficult works like *El Publico,* and translation problems have dogged his plays. One critic, reviewing Ted Hughes's version of *Blood Wedding* in London two years ago, said, "Its poetry—at once flinty and florid—is damnably hard to make work in English."

But Lorca's troubled relationship with Anglos involves more than just language. The author, whose American visit in 1929 compelled him to write *Poet in New York,* a book containing poems like "Landscape of the Vomiting Multitudes," has an emotional temperature many on these shores find unnerving. Once famous for declaiming his writings at the drop of a hat, Lorca is vibrantly theatrical and emotional to the core. What might read like "The Surrealist Manifesto" on paper reveals a potently visceral force on stage.

That much was clear when I returned to Repettorio on opening night. From the first moment when veteran actor Ricardo Barber made his entrance down the center aisle, the house was spellbound. A ghostly light, the sound of whispers and wind blowing-little in the way of costumes or sets was necessary. Director Buch had stripped *El Publico* down to its essentials—actors on a stage, engaged in wild, intense, free-flowing dialogue. The play, like so much of Lorca, attacks the conventions of theatre and gender, arguing for a more flexible, profound reality. Early on, two men fall into a lover's quarrel:

A: If I turned into a cloud?

B: I'd turn into an eye.

A: If I turned into caca?

B: I'd turn into a fly.

A: If I turned into an apple?

B: I'd turn into a kiss.

A: If I turned into a breast?

B: I'd turn into a white sheet.

A: And if I turned into a moonfish?

B: I'd turn into a knife.

Actors Edward Nurquez-Bon and Chaz Mena batted the images back and forth as if they were so many humorous little insults. Their grace and inimitable timing had the audience roaring. Deep in this modernist text, Repertorio Espanol has located Lorca's soul, subversive and passionate as ever.

Source: Mona Molarsky, ''A Feast of Lorca,'' in *American Theatre,* Vol. 15, No. 6, July–August, 1998, p. 52.

R. A. Zimbardo

In the following essay, Zimbardo analyzes the symbolic imagery and its relationship to the characters.

Lorca's *Blood Wedding* enjoys a curiously paradoxical fame. Critics are unanimous in praising it, both as an expression of Lorca's best mode, his ''Andalusian vision'' and as one of the finest products of that twentieth century movement in drama which tries to find new roots in the elemental soil. Yet the praise itself is damning, for we have been led to think of Lorca's plays as ''peasant drama,'' so Spanish in their symbolism as to be incomprehensible beyond the locale which inspired them. For example, in the judgment of Angel del Rio, *Blood Wedding* ''may very well miss becoming a world classic because of its local color and the fact that its action seems limited and appears to lack real spiritual content . . . a great deal of its atmosphere can be communicated only to a Spanish-speaking public steeped in Spanish artistic traditions.'' This perception of the play not only confines it to the Spanish speaking world, but suggests that its atmosphere is its crucial ingredient. Elemental emotion, or atmosphere, is thought to constitute the very meaning of *Blood Wedding.* ''Sensuality, hatred, love and tragic destiny bringing with it a bloody and violent death are the central themes of this play.'' Moreover, the confusion of the atmosphere with theme, unfortunately suggesting melodrama, extends even to close critical interpretation. Campbell, for example, in discussing the lullaby of Act I asserts in one breath that it is evocative and meaningless: ''though it means little enough, yet [it] suggests . . . terror and tragedy,'' or again, ''In spite of its lack of meaning, this 'nonsense rhyme' creates the same ominous atmosphere as the nonsense of Edgar in *Lear.*'' Our response to *Blood Wedding* is generally to praise its elemental power and then refuse to take it seriously.

Lorca's drama is not ''peasant drama'' if we mean to imply by that description either parochiality or mindless simplicity. It is elemental in the way ancient drama is elemental; its symbolism operates in much the same way as that of Aeschylus. Although Lorca reaches for his imagery into the depths of Spanish consciousness, the images emerge beyond Spanishness as symbols universal in the Western tradition. The bull as a symbol of fertility, or the moon as a symbol of the changing aspects of the life-force (now a wedding moon, now a moon of death) are, after all Greek and, beyond Greek, universal. Moreover, powerful as Lorca's imagery is, it does not exist for its own sake. Its function is not sensational; it is not ''delightful gibberish.'' Rather it operates within the most formal of dramatic structures to figure the archetypal pattern of tragedy, or, to be more precise of ur-tragedy, for Lorca is in this play shaping the elemental conflict in human nature out of which the vision of tragedy arises. *Blood Wedding* is not merely about a wedding but about the wedding in the blood of the antagonistic forces that together compromise the paradoxical human condition. The play envisions this war in the blood on many levels. It is the conflict between physical nature, in whose hands man is merely an instrument for creating new life, and individual will, which asserts the value of itself. It is the antagonism between the tribal self and the individual self. And ultimately it is the cosmic struggle between community of the species, which insures endless life, and individuation, which insures endless death. The theme of this play is not its atmosphere, but its ritual enactment of the wedding in man's blood of his divided human nature. It structures a vision of the fractured whole that Lorca once suggested in the image of a pomegranate:

> The pomegranate is the pre-history
> Of our own blood. So gashed apart
> Its bitter globe reveals the mystery
> Both of a skull and of a heart. . .
> Cancion Oriental

The governing metaphor of *Blood Wedding* is an extended allusion to a ritual enactment that, like the play itself, is elemental in Spanish consciousness but reaches beyond nationality toward archetype: the bull fight. The mother tells the Bridegroom that he, like his father before him, is a bull-man, and she calls the Felix family matadors. The wedding of the Bride and Bridegroom arises, as the handmaidens sing, ''like a bull,'' a bull that is destined to be destroyed by the matador, Leonardo. If we pursue this figure we find that it leads to the central thematic pattern of the play. The bull, here as in ancient thought, embodies the principle of natural order. It symbolizes human fertility *within* a natural cycle of fertility. Those characters who are associated with the bull have no individual identity. They *are* that which their position within the cycle of fertility demands—''the Mother,'' ''the Son,'' ''the Bride's father.'' The matadors, on the other hand, do have individual identity; they are the Felix family, their name expressing the irony of their destinies. Leonardo Felix, still more precisely identified, is the matador, a solitary figure who is the antagonist of the natural order, or the individuating principle in human consciousness. At the moment of truth the matador confronts nature, challenges it with his singularity, defines his man-ness in resisting, rather than in cooperating with it. Yet his very individuation contains death. Like the bull fight to which it alludes, Lorca's play imitates the elemental conflict in man's nature.

The design of the play is tri-partite; its structure rests on the three points that define the arc of life; the promise of birth, the fulfillment of sexuality and the limitation of death. The opening movement is dominated by the tribal theme. It promises the rebirth of nature in the movement toward the wedding. It looks toward the union of the Bride and Bridegroom within the communion of nature. The zenith of the arc, the center of the play's structure, is the wedding feast itself. Here two men contend for the Bride, a vessel that contains the potentiality both for life and death. The Bridegroom offers her the fulfillment of her tribal destiny, peace and fertility within nature. Leonardo offers separation from the tribe and the fulfillment of her individual destiny, an individuation that contains death. If we consider this configuration mythically we find that the Bride has associations with the triple goddess in her aspect of ''the divine maiden'' who embraces the whole of the life force and who is therefore potentially both the giver and destroyer of life. The twin males who vie for her are the summer king—the Bridegroom descendant of bulls—and the winter king—Leonardo, the horse whose hooves are frozen. The goddess in turn cooperates with one against the other. The last movement which completes the design of the play and the arc it traces is the ritual sacrifices, the triumph of death over life, of winter over summer, of barrenness over fertility.

Act I, the movement toward the wedding, or rebith in union, shapes the tribal theme. Interestingly, its structure expresses tribal truth, for scenes 1and 3 (dominated by the Mother and the Bride's father who hope for renewal of life in the land and in

> ''. . . POWERFUL AS LORCA'S IMAGERY IS, IT DOES NOT EXIST FOR ITS OWN SAKE. ITS FUNCTION IS NOT SENSATIONAL; IT IS NOT 'DELIGHTFUL GIBBERISH.'''

human beings) surround Scene 2 (which is dominated by Leonardo). In this first movement the tribe contains, or embraces, the urge toward separation. The play begins, as the arc begins, with the Mother. Her son, the Bridegroom, has been born from the union of the Earth mother and the rain god themselves. The Mother cannot differentiate human nature from all of nature. She is Demeter herself, a stalk of wheat the sign of her power. In the past, the time of her own fertility, she looked only to her husband, who was a planter of trees.

> Your father, he used to take me. That's the way with men of good stock; good blood. Your grandfather left a son in every corner. That's what I like. Men, men; wheat, wheat.

In the present she lives only in her son and the hope of renewal in his fertility.

Half of the Bride's nature descends from this same drive toward fertility. Her father, like the bridegroom's mother, urges the communion of nature and looks to the renewal of life in his daughter.

> FATHER: If we could just take twenty teams of oxen and move your vineyards over here, and put them down on that hillside, how happy I'd be!
>
> MOTHER: But why?
>
> FATHER: What's mine is hers and what's yours is his. That's why. Just to see it all together. How beautiful it is to bring things together.

The time of his fertility, like that of the Mother's, was cut short. He too was undone by the death-dealing Felix family, but death came to him in the barren lovelessness of his wife and his land.

> BRIDEGROOM: This is the wasteland.
>
> MOTHER: Your father would have covered it with trees.
>
> BRIDEGROOM: Without water?
>
> MOTHER: He would have found some. In the three years we were married he planted ten cherry trees. Those three walnut trees by the mill, a whole vineyard

and a plant called Jupiter which had scarlet flowers—
but it dried up.

The Bride's father was prevented from being
such a planter of trees by the resistance of the soil,
the matter in which he had to work.

FATHER: When I was young this land didn't even
grow hemp. We've had to punish it, even weep over it,
to make it give us anything useful.

As resistant as his barren earth, was his frozen
wife, a Felix who "didn't love her husband" and
who also had to be tortured to bring forth anything
useful. The Bride carries within her the twin nature,
her mother's barren, resistant Felix blood, as well as
her father's will to bring life.

Act I, Scene 2, contained in the center of a
promise for life, centers on Leonardo Felix. As the
bridegroom and his father are bulls, Leonardo is the
"snow-wounded" horse, more specifically the horse
who "won't drink from the stream." The bridegroom's father watered the land and drew forth its
life, and the bride's father wept over it to pierce its
barrenness, but Leonardo *refuses* to drink from the
stream of life, the stream of birth, begetting, death
and rebirth. In *Mañana* Lorca says of water,

For some good reason Jesus
Realized himself in water
For some good reason Venus
In its breast was engendered.

The stream of life for Leonardo are his wife and
son, the tribal promise of immortality, but he turns
away from them in pursuit of personal passion. He
is Felix because he wants his own happiness, his
own desire and it is this that threatens communion,
the harmony in nature that the bridegroom promises. The ballad of the horse, which Campbell says
is meaningless, contains the whole idea of Leonardo,
the principle of individuation so crucial to the
theme. The horse is wounded by winter, the death of
nature; his hooves and mane are frozen because he
will not be reborn in the stream of life. Moreover we
are made to understand why he cannot drink: "deep
in his eyes stuck a silvery dagger." Leonardo, the
horse, cannot look outward to the harmonious whole;
he can only look inward to the self. The horse must
die in his own blood because he will not be reborn in
the stream of life.

In Act II, the climax of the play, as it is the
zenith of the arc that the play describes, the "wedding," or warring, in the blood, is presented
emblematically. Here summer and winter, life and
death, contend for the possession of nature. The
forces of life, represented by the bride's father and
the bridegroom's mother, urge the triumph of the

Bridegroom. They look to the fertility of man ("My
daughter is wide-hipped and your son is strong")
within the fertility of nature, for they are concerned
with the work of promoting life.

This land needs hands that aren't hired. There's a
battle to be waged against weeds, the thistles, the big
rocks that come from one doesn't know where. And
those hands have to be the owner's, who chastises and
dominates, who makes the seeds grow. Lots of sons
are needed.

The Bridegroom promises not only the vertical
union of man with nature but the horizontal union of
man with man. His heritage is the whole network of
the tribe.

MOTHER: Whole branches of families came.

BRIDEGROOM: People who never went out of
the house.

MOTHER: Your father sowed well and now you're
reaping it.

The wedding guests come from the seacoast as
well as the land. Their dancing which, as the stage
directions tell us, should form "an animated crossing of figures," is the dance of life. They are the
intricate pattern of life which man tries to set as a
bulwark against the dissolution, death and chaos
that constantly threaten him. It is under the subjec-
tion of this tribal order that the Bridegroom tries to
bring the Bride. But, as the Bride says, "The step is
a very hard one to take," for it consists in submitting self to the race, dissolving into the network of
the tribe, and working in the service of the life force
rather than the service of individual need.

The Bride chooses instead to follow the winter
king, Leonardo. As the Bridegroom, the Father and
the Mother represent one force in human nature,
that which impels the human being to dissolve
himself in the life of the race and thereby find a kind
of immortality, Leonardo represents the other, equally
strong force in human life, that which demands the
satisfaction of the selfish passions which, because
they turn a man's eyes inward, are isolating. This
isolated, defined self, by the very nature of its
individuation, must suffer dissolution. The first step
that Leonardo and the Bride take toward realizing
their desires is isolation; they cut themselves off
from the tribe and thereby prepare for the third and
last phase of the ritual, sacrificial death.

In contrast to the Bridegroom and his father, the
planters of seed, whose presence opens Act I, Act III
is opened by the woodcutters, the destroyers of
nature's life. Moreover the moon has changed from
the new moon, associated with the labor of childbirth, to the full moon, the moon of death that brings

the cycle to its end. As the moon has changed its face, so has the tribe. In this aspect the tribe no longer promotes life but hunts it down.

FIRST YOUTH: This is a hunt.

BRIDEGROOM: A hunt. The greatest hunt there is.

The Bridegroom no longer promises peace and fertility in the tribe; he has become the armed might of the tribe that must hunt down and kill the deviant. The Mother, before the promoter of life, pants for the blood of Leonardo and the Bride. It is she who turns the tribe into avenging Furies.

> Two groups. There are two groups here. My family and yours. Everyone set out from here. Shake the dust from your heels. We'll go help my son. For he has his family: his cousins from the sea, and all those who came from inland. Out of here! On all roads. The hour of blood has come again. . . . After them! After them!

The communal order must kill the deviant because his singularity threatens the whole; it fights one-ness because one-ness must lead to death. The third phase of the ritual is the casting out of the pharmakos. In casting out, hunting down and slaying Leonardo, the community is casting out and destroying individuating passion, the human impulse that threatens tribal harmony.

The climax of Act III, Scene 1, is a strange stychomythia between Leonardo and the Bride. The stage directions tell us that the scene must be played with violence and great sensuality. The relation between Leonardo and the Bride is not a union, rather it is a most intense conflict. Passion, because it grows out of the need of the self, is the antithesis of the union that the Bridegroom offered. Individual passion is ambiguous; it weds pleasure with pain. It consumes that which it enlivens. The Bride is driven by her passion toward Leonardo but her passion does not nourish, it would rather destroy him.

> LEONARDO: And whose were the hands/strapped spurs to my boots?
>
> BRIDE: The same hands, these that are yours but which when they see you would like to break the blue branches and sunder the purl of your veins. I love you! I love you! But leave me for if I were able to kill you I'd wrap you round in a shroud.

The Bride does not want life ("neither bed nor food") from Leonardo. He is the demand for the satisfaction of passion, of self. He is the object of her sensuality, for sense serves the individuated self. Only reason is able to abstract the conception of a communal order to which self must be subjected.

The final scene of the play, like the lullaby of Act I, presents the theme emblematically. It is opened by little girls, the Fates, who wind the red wool of man's life.

> FIRST GIRL: Wool, red wool, what would
>   you make?
> SECOND GIRL: . . . At four o'clock born,
> At ten o'clock dead.
> A thread from this wool yarn,
> A chain 'round your feet
> A knot that will tighten
> The bitter white wreath.

And they sing of the "dirty sand" that is "over the golden flower." The cycle has come its full course; all human order falls to ruin, all natural life ends in death. The end of the arc, like its beginning, is dominated by the presence of the Mother-goddess, but here she assumes the form of the Mater Dolorosa. She has come to the final isolation, and ironically, she has been freed from her life-promoting work and worry. She is left in the confines of herself: "The earth and I. My grief and I. And these four walls." She has no function, for the Mother, deprived of young, loses identity.

The Bride in this last phase of the play is nature locked in the grip of winter. She takes pride in her barrenness: "they can bury me without a single man ever having seen himself in the whiteness of my breasts." Having denied the Bridegroom, the chance to bring forth life, for Leonardo, personal desire which is self-love, the Bride is snow-bound in her own whiteness, a barren virgin. Her virginity is unimportant to the Mother for the chance for life to be renewed in her is gone. The mourning Demeter can finally only bless the cycle of life which she has embodied.

> But what does your good name matter to me? What does your death matter to me? . . . Blessed be the wheat stalks because my sons are under them; blessed be the rain, because it wets the face of the dead. Blessed be God who stretches us out together to rest.

Source: R. A. Zimbardo, "The Mythic Pattern in Lorca's *Blood Wedding*," in *Modern Drama*, Vol. 10, No. 4, February, 1968, p. 364.

Eva K. Touster

In the following essay, Touster discusses the concept of "modern poetic drama" through a variety of styles.

Lorca has been widely praised for the achievement in *Blood Wedding* of a tragic form the distinctive features of which are the fusion of lyric and dramatic impulses; the skillful integration of a musical pattern in the drama's structural design; the thematic relevance of songs, stage effects, and recurrent images—in short, for the assimilation of the Spanish folk and classical traditions in a poetic drama that is modern, sophisticated, and authentic. But some questions remain to puzzle the reader, especially the reader of an English version of the play: How does *Blood Wedding* fit our current concept of poetic drama? In what sense is the organization of the play musical? What is the function of the lyrics in the development of action and theme? Is there a comprehensive structure of imagery defining the tonality and modulations of the play, and supporting themes perhaps resting upon and therefore nearer to the surface of the text than those more profound echoes of vegetation gods and human sacrifice which the archetypal symbols of the play suggest? The following essay is an attempt to explore some aspects of these questions.

Our concept of modern poetic drama has been formed largely on the theory and practice of Yeats and Eliot, yet no one has been willing to call either Yeats or Eliot a dramatist of the first rank. The consensus seems to be, as Francis Fergusson implies, that Yeats is "cultish" and Eliot "middle-brow ersatz." But either label would be inaccurate if applied to Lorca. It is true that his range is limited, even that he speaks primarily to a Spanish audience, but, as Fergusson says, "he writes the poetry of the theater as our poets would like to do." Yeats, Eliot, and Lorca are all fundamentally lyric poets working toward the drama. In their use of myth, ritual, and symbol they cut across the barriers of national cultures, but only Lorca has cut across intellectual class lines to appeal to both the naive and the sophisticated in his own culture (as Shakespeare did in his day). Perhaps in the modern world this could happen only in Spain, where class lines are not drawn on the basis of speech habits.

What is the source of this appeal? Perhaps it is "poetic drama." Although Eliot is far from being satisfied with his own plays—and I suspect that he would not be satisfied with Lorca's—there are some features of *Blood Wedding* that should please him. Not, certainly, the medium. Eliot is opposed to a mixture of verse and prose unless, as in Shakespeare, the author wishes to produce a jolt, to "transport the audience violently from one plane of reality to another." But Lorca has come near achieving that "ideal toward which poetic drama should strive": the expression of a range of sensibility not possible to prose drama (the kind of feeling almost but not quite conveyed in the plays of Chekhov and Synge). In Eliot's terms the ideal poetic drama would be "a design of human action and of words,

such as to present the two aspects of dramatic and of musical order . . . without losing that contact with the ordinary everyday world with which drama must come to terms. . . ." The real problem, then, for the writer of poetic drama is not versification, but the resolution in a single work of two principles: that of decorum (a synthesis of incidents, character, and theme) and that of associative rhythm, which may be more verbal than metrical. In his essay on "The Music of Poetry" Eliot makes the point that a musical design can be observed in several of the plays of Shakespeare, "a music of imagery as well as sound." In *Blood Wedding* Lorca has created such a design without violating the principle of decorum which underlies dramatic action. And he has remained sufficiently close to the world in which the audience lives so that the poetry is acceptable on the stage.

Although the plot was suggested by a newspaper account of an incident that occurred in Almería, the play is as far removed from the realism that characterizes folk drama as it is from the urbanity of Eliot's own dramatic dialogues. Its highly stylized medium conveys authentic folk emotion; and if its lyrical passages do not reproduce the speech rhythms of the Spanish folk, its images "come from the speech people of the Andalusian countryside use in emotional moments, describing their passions and half-comprehended thoughts in ageless, occult metaphors, as though in magic formulas." It is this quality in *Blood Wedding* that brings it close to being Eliot's ideal poetic drama. And it is this quality rather than the versification that is preserved in the English text of the play.

It is worth noting that Lorca called *Blood Wedding* simply a tragedy, whereas he designated *Yerma* "a tragic poem." The labels might have been reversed. I say this because, although both plays conform to Kenneth Burke's description of the tragic rhythm (from purpose to passion to perception), it is in *Blood Wedding* rather than in *Yerma* that the theme is embodied in the play not primarily by the logic of character, but by the rhythm of its imagery. *Blood Wedding* is indeed a tragic poem, a meditation on life and death in which the characters (all are nameless except Leonardo) are victims of a collective and inevitable destiny. Leonardo and the Bridegroom meet violent death, but the Mother is the real incarnation of the tragedy. She is the most vital person of the play, the chief interpreter of the human situation as well as the chief victim of the tragic circumstances. If it is the Bridegroom who affirms the "purpose" and

Leonardo and the Bride who supply the "passion," it is the Mother who furnishes the "perception" of the play. And she speaks for all women frustrated in their love and haunted by the fear of extinction. The response to *Blood Wedding* is, as Northrop Frye asserts the response to all tragedy properly is, "this must be" rather than "what is the cause?" It has already been observed that in *Blood Wedding* "a knife can be drama's final reason." Here, as in Greek tragedy, the event is of first importance; the explanation—other than in Fate or Destiny—is secondary.

The generic affinity of *Blood Wedding* with Greek drama is a valuable directive and illuminates as many features of the play as does the comparison generally made with the dramas of Lope de Vega and Calderon. The ceremonial and spectacular content as well as the lyric chorus are conventions of Greek drama recognizable in *Blood Wedding* however they have been adapted to a contemporary situation and theme. Lorca's "hero" is scarcely a dying god, although associations with the autumn fertility ritual enhance the play and place it in the larger context of literature dealing with fecundity and death as reconcilable opposites in a natural process. But the impact of *Blood Wedding* is felt not so much in the sacrifice of the flower of manhood to Mother Earth as it is in the grief of the women and the ambivalence of its tragic motifs. For all its violence and Fate, the play modulates to an elegiac conclusion. When the reconciliation with death comes, it is the submission of the Mother to the nature of things—and it is religious. But the meaning of the play is more than the Mother's experience of the tragic event. It inheres in universal symbols the significance of which the Mother only half perceives. If the play does not rise to the triumphant conclusion of traditional elegy, it becomes less starkly tragic in the explicitly Christian dirge with which it closes.

In the development of the theme of death and the other themes related to it—honor, passion, pride—the lyrical passages are of the utmost significance. There are lyrics of several kinds (the lullaby, the prothalamion, the love-duet, the choral ode, the dirge) and the range of emotion they express is as great as their several kinds suggest. But they are not isolated or incidental poems; they are linked to each other and to the prose of the play in a comprehensive scheme of images that includes the whole world of nature and contemplates human life from the cradle to the grave as part of a unitive life-death experience. To use the metaphors suggested by the play,

> ITS HIGHLY STYLIZED MEDIUM CONVEYS AUTHENTIC FOLK EMOTION; AND IF ITS LYRICAL PASSAGES DO NOT REPRODUCE THE SPEECH RHYTHMS OF THE SPANISH FOLK, ITS IMAGES 'COME FROM THE SPEECH PEOPLE OF THE ANDALUSIAN COUNTRYSIDE USE IN EMOTIONAL MOMENTS, DESCRIBING THEIR PASSIONS AND HALF-COMPREHENDED THOUGHTS IN AGELESS, OCCULT METAPHORS, AS THOUGH IN MAGIC FORMULAS.'"

the grave becomes not only the marriage bed, the wedding sheet now the winding sheet; it becomes the cradle as well, where all mothers' sons may sleep in peace. (Near the end of the play, the Mother, mourning her dead son, says: "And of my dreams I'll make a cold ivory dove that will carry camellias of white frost to the graveyard. But no; not graveyard, not graveyard: the couch of earth, the bed that shelters them and rocks them in the sky"—an ironic reminder of the lullaby in Act I and the second of the marriage songs in Act II.)

The imagery throughout is that of the Earth itself, of the fundamental categories of existence: the knife and associated images from the mineral kingdom (the silver dagger stuck in the horse's eyes, the pins from the bridal wreath, the glass splinters stuck in the tongue of the Bride, the nails, the metal chain, the frost and snow, the Moon, the ashes); from the vegetable kingdom the flowers, weeds, wheat, bread with which the fathers and sons of men are identified (Man is a "mirror of the earth"); and from the animal kingdom the man himself, inseparable from his horse; the woman associated with the serpent; the birds. The supreme image of the play is blood, with its analogue and opposite water. Both blood and water are ambivalent symbols, as are many of the images of the play that connote both life and death (the knife and the

Moon, male and female symbols of fertility as well as of coldness and death; the serpent, a symbol of fertility and of treachery; the bird—the luminous dove associated with the Bridegroom, traditional Catholic symbol of the Holy Spirit, divine instrument of fecundation, and the "great bird with immense wings" that is Death).

This ambivalent imagery presents the life-death opposition as a process in which the polar extremes appear as a single experience. In the moment of most intense life man is aware of his doom, and in death he becomes an instrument of life. Although most of the images of decay and death are drawn from the mineral kingdom as those connoting life are drawn from the vegetable and animal kingdoms, the categories of being are merged in many metaphors that identify or associate plant, animal, and mineral (as knife with snake and fish, man with water, flower, and ashes). Honig has noticed in Lorca's imagery this "compulsion of one element or quality of nature to become another and to throw off its own inevitable form to live vicariously in one of its own choosing."

Such shifts of identity are eminently "poetic," for the linking of antagonistic "worlds" is fundamental in all metaphoric expression. And they are eminently fitting in a play which shows man's experience of life to be one with his experience of death and man himself to be one with Nature. But the unity of man with external nature does not diminish his integrity as man, and man's awareness of death only clarifies and intensifies his longing for life (Passion and Pride). The imagery of *Blood Wedding* is sufficient evidence that Lorca was master of an important unifying principle in a work of art. As Frye has lucidly put it, "All poetry . . . proceeds as though all poetic images were contained within a single universal body. Identity is the opposite of similarity or likeness, and total identity is not uniformity, but a unity of various things."

As the blood-water opposition forms the nucleus of the symbolism of life-death, it becomes the focal image of the related themes of honor, pride, and passion. Good blood in the sense of one's family heritage means not only men who produce many sons, it means men of honor. The Mother refers to the Bridegroom's family as men of "good stock; good blood. Your grandfather left a son on every corner. That's what I like. Men, men; wheat, wheat." And later when the Bride's Father says of Leonardo, "He's not of good blood," the Mother replies: "What blood would you expect him to have? His whole family's blood. It comes down from his great-grandfather, who started in killing, and it goes on down through the whole breed of knife wielding and false smiling men." It is interesting that here in the Mother's single-minded remarks about Leonardo's heritage the ambivalence of blood is apparent to the reader—in the allusion first to the begetting and then to the destroying of life. This technique of symbolic suggestion, which produces in the reader a response to the symbol beyond that of the character speaking is one which Lorca uses consistently and with increasing subtlety throughout the play. It is most effective in references to fertility symbols such as blood, the knife, and the serpent.

From the Mother's point of view the heritage of the Bride is also suspect. What could be hoped from a girl who, as her Father said, resembled her mother "in every way"? For the Bride's mother "didn't love her husband" although "her face glowed like a saint." The "dishonorable" passion of the lovers is expressed in references to blood and water. Leonardo is "hot-blooded"; he is described by the Bride as "a dark river," and the Bride herself had been too indecent to throw herself into the water: "decent women throw themselves into the water; not that one." Here water is both purifying and destructive. The reference to Leonardo as "a dark river" links the themes of passion, honor, and life-death. The connection is very clear if one reads the whole speech of the Bride, in which she refers to the fatal force of the dark river in contrast to the "little bit of water [the Bridegroom] from which [she] hoped for children. . . ."

The themes of honor and passion are similarly linked with that of life-death in many passages in which recurrent images of water and blood are the unifying principle, as, for example, in the passage just cited when the Mother says, "There are two groups here. My family and yours. . . . The hour of blood has come" and in the scene by the arroyo where the blood is spilled and "two great torrents are still at last." The Woodcutters anticipate the spilled blood and link it with the tainted passion of the lovers.

SECOND WOODCUTTER. You have to follow your passion. . . .

FIRST WOODCUTTER. They were deceiving themselves but at last the blood was stronger.

THIRD WOODCUTTER. Blood!

FIRST WOODCUTTER. You have to follow the path of your blood.

SECOND WOODCUTTER. But blood that sees the light of day is drunk up by the earth.

FIRST WOODCUTTER. What of it? Better dead with the blood drained away than alive with it rotting.

Here again the association of blood with both life and death is clear. The forest "wedding" of the lovers is the first blood wedding; the second (the death of the men) is inherent in the first. The concept of "tainted nature" ("the fault is the earth's"), the emphasis on chastity, even the suggestion of purification by water and blood are as much a part of the play's cultural Christianity as the serpent and the dove and the "sweet nails / cross adored / sweet name / of Christ our Lord." And they focus a dimension of the imagery fully as rich as that of its pre-Christian sub-structure.

The imagery of Earth, then—of Earth as the plenum of existence—reconciles opposites and thus strengthens the ambivalent force of *blood* in respect to honor, passion, and the life-death continuum. Viewed from the perspective of their imagery, the lyrics function as a matrix of thematic development. They focus the dominant images, which recur somewhat in the manner of a complicated tapestry or an intricately wrought mosaic, and control the tone of the play. They function, in short, both visually and aurally and give to *Blood Wedding* some of the effects of both painting and music. Stage settings and color symbolism also contribute to these effects. But much of the pleasure of reading the play as opposed to witnessing it on the stage comes from perceiving the marvelous organization of its imagery. It is the pattern of image, symbol, and motif that constitutes the "musical structure" of the play, and it is chiefly the lyrics that give it movement and variety. A conscious awareness of the complexity of this structure is the reward of a close reading of the text, as a grasp of the subtleties of the sonata form results from analysis of the score.

With respect to the episodes the three acts of *Blood Wedding* might be called Betrothal, Wedding, and Blood Wedding (Death—which is a "wedding," hence the promise of life— *and* a "wedding "which is Death and hence the frustration of life). The lyric movement begins in Scene Two with the Lullaby of "the big horse who didn't like water." This scene, which has sometimes been regarded as an interlude, not only occupies a key position in the sequence of incidents in Act I, it also prefigures the central event and the dominant images of the entire play. The Lullaby, rendered antiphonally by Leonardo's Wife and the Mother-in-law, introduces the blood-water opposition, recalls the (phallic)

knife (now a "silvery dagger") which entered the play in Scene One, and anticipates the entry of Leonardo's horse, whose hoof-beats are heard as Act I comes to a close. Hence the song is a preparation for the "blood wedding" of Act III in both senses of the term.

That the horse in the Lullaby is to be identified with Leonardo's horse and his wounds with the fate of Leonardo is indicated by the action accompanying the song. In the midst of the singing Leonardo enters, and the Wife and Mother-in-law begin to question him about his horse. It becomes obvious that Leonardo has been riding his horse out to the mountainous wasteland where the Bride lives. There is talk of the approaching wedding and the Wife's jealousy flares up when she is reminded that the Bride was once a sweetheart of Leonardo's. When, after her quarrel with Leonardo, the Wife resumes the Lullaby, she moves "as though dreaming" and her weeping increases to the end of the song. In view of Leonardo's unsuccessful effort to resist his passion for his former sweetheart and the Wife's sense of being abandoned after she and Leonardo discuss the coming wedding, certain lines in the Lullaby take on new possibilities of meaning: "Go away to the mountains . . . that's where your mare is" and, after Leonardo leaves, the Wife's variation of the refrain from "The horse won't drink from the stream" to "the horse is drinking from the stream."

The tone of the Lullaby is portentous, foretelling the fatal wounds and the grief to come. And the "black water," the "snow wound," the "silvery dagger," and the singing stream itself are echoed in subsequent references to Leonardo's fate. In the love-duet between Leonardo and the Bride, for example, Leonardo says, "But I was riding a horse / and the horse went straight to your door. / And the silver pins of your wedding / turned my red blood black." Later the Beggar Woman refers to the teeth of the dead men as "two fistfulls of hard-frozen snow" and the Bride calls Leonardo "a dark river, choked with brush, that brought near me the undertone of its rushes and its whispered song." Compare the words of the Lullaby: "The water was black there/ under the branches. / When it reached the bridge/ it stopped and it sang."

In Act II the songs (one in each scene) are prothalamia sung by the Bride's servant and the wedding guests. They are part of the two phases of the nuptials introduced into the action: the ceremony of preparing the Bride for the church and the festivities preceding the entry of the Bride and

Groom into the bridal chamber. Both lyrics employ the now familiar imagery of flower, branch, and stream and both make visible another thread of imagery that is to become increasingly prominent as the themes of pride and passion move toward their ultimate resolution in the theme of death. It is the imagery of fire. As water is both life-giving and life-destroying, so fire is symbolic of life as well as of death. The marriage songs are ambivalent both in imagery and tone, the irony of each poem increasing as the action moves toward the climactic elopement of the Bride and Leonardo at the end of Act II.

In the first poem the Bridegroom is a "flower of gold" and the Bride is a "mountain flower" whose bridal wreath is to be borne along by "all the rivers of the world." The poem is linked to the Lullaby by the contrasts of motif and tone. Note the recurring "Go to sleep" (*Duermete*) of the Lullaby and the "Awake" (*Despierte*) of the "wedding shout." ("Like a bull the wedding is rising here!") The bull, an ancient symbol of fertility, is to the Spanish mind one of the chief means of the contemplation of death. And here there is a dark undertone. The design of the entire scene, including the stage effects, is a kind of counterpoint of light and dark. As the scene opens it is night. The Bride and her servant are dressed in "white petticoats . . . and sleeveless white bodice." They talk of the wedding and the Bride hurls her orange blossom wreath away, saying that "a chill wind cuts through [her] heart." The servant begins the wedding song, but it is interrupted by Leonardo (as the Lullaby is interrupted in Act I). In spite of her desire to forget Leonardo, the Bride acknowledges the power he has over her. ("It pulls me along and I know I'm drowning—but I go on down.") As Leonardo goes out, daylight comes and the guests arrive, singing of the "white wreath," the "white bride," and the "maiden white":

> As you set out from your home
> and to the church go,
> remember you leave shining
> with a star's glow.

But the Bride herself is "dark" and she appears wearing a black wedding dress. The "star's glow" which was to accompany the Bride to church stimulates only bitterness from Leonardo's Wife ("I left my house like that too.") and later when she announces the elopement of the lovers she ironically echoes the imagery of the marriage song: "They've run away! They've run away! She and Leonardo. On the horse. With their arms around each other, they rode off like a shooting star." In Act III the star

imagery is given further development, but the immediate consequence of the elopement is expressed, at the end of Act II, in images of blood and water: "Decent women throw themselves in water; not that one. . . . The hour of blood has come again. Two groups! You with yours and I with mine."

Ironically, the blood has been a part of the wedding festivities. It is introduced in the second lyric of Act II, a soliloquy of the servant. This lyric also anticipates the blood, water, and fire imagery of Act III:

> the wheel was a-turning
> and the water was flowing,
> for the wedding night comes. . . .
> Elegant girl . . .
> Hold your shirts close in
> under the Bridegroom's wing
> and never leave your house,
> for the Bridegroom is a firebrand
> and the fields wait for the whisper
> of spurting blood.

When the Mother enters, she unconsciously echoes the language of the song as she voices her obsession with blood spilled on the ground: "A fountain that spurts for a minute, but costs us years." The reference to the Bridegroom's breast as a firebrand prepares for the Woodcutter's seeing the Bridegroom set out "like a raging star. His face the color of ashes"—an especially meaningful description that captures the ambivalence of fire. The "raging star" and the "shooting star" link the two men metaphorically as they are linked in the play's action, in their passion for the Bride and in their death. Leonardo tells the Bride that his proud effort to quell his desire for her only served to "bring down the fire" and later the Bride and Leonardo exclaim about the "lamenting fire" that "sweeps upward" in their heads. She tells Leonardo that she is "seared" by his beauty, and he answers her, prophetically associating himself with the Bridegroom in death: "The same tiny flame will kill two wheat heads together." The fire is associated with the theme of honor as well as with the themes of passion and death, for the Bride is willing to submit to the test of fire to prove to the Mother that she is chaste. ("Clean, clean as a new-born little girl. And strong enough to prove it to you. Light the fire. Let's stick our hands in; you for your son, I, for my body. *You'll* draw yours out first.")

The lyric impulse of the play culminates in Act III, where the themes of honor and passion are absorbed in the theme of death that paradoxically is life. The play's double perspective on death is suggested in the dual manifestation of Death. In one image Death is an Old Woman demanding "a crust of bread" (and thus echoing both the exclamation of the Mother, "Men, men; wheat, wheat," and the description in the Skein Song of the thread of Destiny "Running, running, running / and finally to come to stick in the knife / to take back the bread"). In another image Death is the white-faced Moon longing for life and seeking in the death of the men "a heart," the "crest of the fire," and "red blood" for his cheeks. Death as an aged person is a familiar figure in literature (one thinks of Chaucer's caitiff). The Moon is one of the "concrete things which speak of death to Spanish minds" mentioned by Lorca in a lecture given in Cuba in 1930. In the same listing he includes the chopping knife and the clasp knife. In *Blood Wedding* both the knife and the Moon are agents of Death as well as sexual symbols, male and female ("The Moon sets a knife abandoned in the air"), but the Moon is also identified with Death, as the chant of the Woodcutters indicates: first, "O rising moon! . . . O lonely moon! . . . O evil moon! . . . O sorrowing moon! . . . ," and then, after the Moon's song, "O rising Death! . . . O lonely Death! . . . O sad Death! . . . O evil Death!" As an agent of Death the Moon will "light up the horse/ with a fever bright as diamonds," will "light up the waistcoat" so that the "knives will know the path." In this cluster of images the wind assists the Moon, "blowing hard with a double edge." The linking of wind with the knife has been made earlier by the Bride ("A chill wind cuts through my heart.") and by the Mother ("Men are like the wind. They're forced to handle weapons."). It is interesting that the blood which the knife produces is now associated with the knife itself in a curious metaphor that recalls the "serpent knife" of the opening scene. The Moon says: "But let them be a long time a-dying. So the blood / will slide its delicate hissing between my fingers." In a sense it is man's blood that betrays him—his heritage. Woman, too, is involved in the treachery. "You snake!" cries the Mother to the Bride when she sees her after the knife has done its work.

The dialogue of the lovers in the forest prior to the bloody wedding of the men to the Earth is a kind of love-death for the Bride too. She longs for actual death with her lover. ("It's fitting that I should die here / with water over my feet / with thorns upon my head. And fitting the leaves should mourn me / a woman lost and virgin.") And after her emergence from the forest she is in a sense dead, since she had followed the lover instead of the Bridegroom—the lover who, she acknowledges, "sent me against

hundreds of birds who got in my way and left white frost on my wounds, my wounds of a poor withered woman, a girl caressed by fire." In another sense, of course, she is alive only when she is with Leonardo. The *birds-frost-fire* sequence constitutes an especially rich cluster of the symbols of life and death fused in a manner characteristic of Lorca. The imagery of the love-duet recalls that of the Lullaby and brings to a climax the identification of the animate and inanimate worlds.

The final scene is a recapitulation of this imagery of Earth and a lyric epilogue which contemplates man's destiny. Death, which is ordained for every man ("Over the golden flower, dirty sand . . . an armful of shrivelled flowers . . . a fading voice beyond the mountains now. . .a heap of snow. . . .") is at last found to be a "fitting" end. And though the flesh must be violated (it remains "astonished" as the knife penetrates cleanly to the "dark root of a scream"), the Earth is kind: "Blesséd be the wheat stalks, because my sons are under them; blesséd be the rain, because it wets the face of the dead. Blesséd be God, who stretches us out together to rest." This is the Mother's reconciliation to Death, the final insight of the play. The Skein Song and the Dirge are choral odes which juxtapose the pagan and Christian attitudes toward death implicit in the symbols of the play. If the pre-Christian concept appears to dominate the imagery, it is significant for a complete reading of *Blood Wedding* that the final scene takes place in a simple dwelling that "should have the monumental feeling of a church" and that the closing invocation to the "sweet name of Christ our Lord" ("May the cross protect both the quick and the dead") mitigates the tragedy. Without becoming explicitly doctrinal, the Christianity of the play points to the recognition of Death as a paradox and is thus an appropriate context for the development of Lorca's major theme. The Dirge finally establishes the tone of the play and completes the pattern of image, symbol, and motif by which Lorca has conveyed his meaning.

Source: Eva K. Touster, "Thematic Patterns in Lorca's Blood Wedding," in *Modern Drama,* Vol. 7, No. 1, May, 1964, p. 16.

SOURCES

Barnstone, Willis, *Six Masters of the Spanish Sonnet,* Southern Illinois University, 1993.

Duran, Manuel, ''Introduction,'' in *Lorca: A Collection of Critical Essays,* Prentice Hall, Inc., 1962.

Edwards, Gwynne, *Dramatists in Perspective: Spanish Theater in the Twentieth Century,* St. Martin's Press, 1985.

———, *Lorca: The Theater Beneath the Sand,* Marion Books, 1980.

Garcia Lorca, Federico, *Bodas de sangre,* ''Introducción'' de Fernando Lazaro Carreter, Edición Colección Austral, 1971.

———, *Blood Wedding,* translated by Langston Hughes and W.S. Merwin, Theatre Communications Group, 1994.

Garcia Lorca, Francisco, *In the Green Morning: Memories of Federico,* translated by Christopher Maurer, New Directions, 1986.

Morris, Cyril Brian, ed., *Cuando yo me muera: Essays in Memory of Federico Garcia Lorca,* University Press of America, 1988.

Newton, Candelas, *Understanding Federico García Lorca,* University of South Carolina Press, 1995.

Ramsden, Herbert, *Bodas de Sangre,* Manchester University Press, 1980.

Senz de la Calzada, Luis, *La Barraca,* Revista de Occidente, 1976.

Smith, Paul Julian, *The Theatre of Garcia Lorca: Text, Performance, Psychoanalysis,* Revista de Occidente, 1976.

FURTHER READING

Eisenberg, Daniel, ''A Chronology of Lorca's Visit to New York and Cuba,'' in *The Kentucky Romance Quarterly,* 24 (1975): 233-50.
An excellent accompaniment for the student studying Lorca's *Poet in New York* poetry collection.

Gerould, Daniel, *Doubles, Dreamers, and Demons: An International Collection of Symbolist Drama,* Performing Arts Journal Publications, 1985.
A collection of symbolist plays for the student wishing to examine the forms and types of symbolist drama. This collection includes an introduction by Gerould.

Gibson, Ian, *The Assassination of Federico García Lorca,* Penguin Books, 1983.
An exploration of the circumstances leading up to and surrounding Lorca's political murder, by a writer who has published extensively on the author (Gibson has written a well-known biography on Lorca).

Jackson, Gabriel, *The Spanish Republic and the Civil War 1931–1939,* Princeton University Press, 1966.
A history of the turbulent 1930s in Spain.

Stainton, Leslie, *Lorca: A Dream of Life,* Farrar, Straus and Giroux, 1999.
The most recent biography of Lorca to be published in English.

Death and the King's Horseman

WOLE SOYINKA

1975

Death and the King's Horseman is considered by many to be among the best of Wole Soyinka's plays, which number more than a dozen. In awarding Soyinka the Nobel Prize for Literature in 1986, the Swedish Academy drew special attention to *Death and the King's Horseman* and *Dance of the Forests* (1960) as evidence of his talent for combining Yoruban and European culture into a unique kind of poetic drama.

Death and the King's Horseman play tells the story of Elesin, the king's horseman, who is expected to commit ritual suicide following the death of the king, but who is distracted from his duty. The story is based on a historical event. In 1946, a royal horseman named Elesin was prevented from committing ritual suicide by the British colonial powers. Soyinka alters the historical facts, placing the responsibility for Elesin's failure squarely on Elesin's shoulders, so that he might focus on the theme of duty rather than of colonialism.

The play is well known in the United States, frequently anthologized in textbooks as an example of African drama for students and teachers who are increasingly curious about the literature of other parts of the world. Because of its mingling of Western and Yoruban elements, and because of the universality of its theme of cultural responsibility, *Death and the King's Horseman* is seen as a good introduction to African thought and tradition. While it is frequently read, however, the play is seldom

performed outside of Africa. Soyinka himself has directed important American productions, in Chicago in 1976 and at Lincoln Center in New York in 1987, but these productions were more admired than loved. Although respected by critics, Soyinka's plays are challenging for Westerners to perform and to understand, and they have not been popular successes.

AUTHOR BIOGRAPHY

Akinwande Oluwole Soyinka was born in Ijebu Isara, near Akeokuta in western Nigeria, on July 13, 1934. His parents, who were from different Yoruba-speaking ethnic groups, were Christians, but other relatives observed African beliefs and deities. Nigeria was at the time a colony of Great Britain. Soyinka grew up, therefore, with exposure to both Yoruban and Western culture. At twenty he left Nigeria to attend the University of Leeds in England, a university with a strong drama program. After graduation he joined London's Royal Court Theatre as a script-reader and then as a writer, and produced his first play, *The Swamp Dwellers,* there in 1959.

The next year Nigeria gained independence. Soyinka returned to his homeland, where the Arts Theatre in Ibadan had begun presenting plays by Nigerian playwrights, on Nigerian themes, for Nigerian audiences. Soyinka traveled throughout Nigeria, absorbing all he could of the Yoruba people's rich oral literature, graphic art, dance, and pageantry. He created plays incorporating traditional Yoruban dance, music, and proverbs with political messages about the need for Nigerians to break free from the influences of Western culture. His third play, *A Dance of the Forests* (1960), is typical of Soyinka's early work in several ways: it deals with conflicts between African and colonial values, it is written in English but includes Yoruban materials, and its first productions featured Soyinka as author, producer, director, and performer.

Independent Nigeria has been a troubled country, headed by greedy and corrupt leaders. In 1965, Soyinka was arrested for criticizing the government over the radio, but he was acquitted. In 1967 he criticized the government in print, and was arrested again. This time he was held prisoner without charges for more than two years, spending fifteen

months in solitary confinement. After his prison experiences, his work became more political and more strident. In many of his newer plays, he turned his critical gaze away from British colonialism and toward corrupt African leaders. Other plays, including *Death and the King's Horseman* (1975), examine weaknesses in Nigerian society as a whole, caused by individuals forgetting their traditions, their culture, and their duty to themselves and to each other.

Soyinka has written more than a dozen plays, as well as poetry, criticism, and an autobiography. In 1986 he became the first African writer to win the Nobel Prize for Literature. The award increased his international stature and widened the audience for his political messages. Within Nigeria, Soyinka is a well-known intellectual and political activist, speaking and writing against government corruption. The government has made its displeasure clear, and Soyinka lived in the United States for a few years during the late 1990s after being accused of treason. "Some people think the Nobel Prize makes you bulletproof," he said in an interview with Ciugu Mwagiru. "I never had that illusion."

PLOT SUMMARY

Act I

As *Death and the King's Horseman* opens, Elesin Oba walks through a Nigerian village market at the close of the business day. He is followed by an entourage of drummers and praise-singers, and as he makes his way through the market he talks with the praise-singer Olohun-iyo about "the other side" and about the importance of "this day of all days." Apparently, Elesin Oba is enjoying his last day on earth; at night he will go to join his "great forebears." The women abandon their work of putting away the goods from their stalls and come to flirt with Elesin, who is obviously a great favorite and well known for his sexual prowess and his many conquests.

Much of the dialogue is written in rhythmic free verse. Elesin dances, and chants the story of the Not-I bird, a bird who fails to fulfill his duty. In an exchange with the crowd, laced with Yoruba proverbs, Elesin promises that when the time comes to fulfill his duty he will not delay. Led by Iyaloja, the mother of the market, the women dress Elesin in their richest cloths and dance around him. Suddenly he is distracted by the sight of a beautiful woman whom he has never seen before. Although she is already engaged to someone else, Elesin demands that he be allowed to take her to bed before he dies. Because Elesin is at the threshold between life and death, he cannot be refused. Iyaloja warns him not to be deterred from his duty, and not to bring trouble on the people who will remain. Then, as the other women prepare the young woman to be Elesin's bride, Iyaloja leaves to prepare the bridal bed.

Act II

This act occurs during the same evening, at the home of the district officer, Simon Pilkings, a British officer stationed in the British colony of Nigeria. Simon and his wife, Jane, are listening to a tango, dancing in the shadows. Amusa, a Nigerian working for the British as a native administration policeman, arrives and is horrified to see that Simon and Jane are dressed in the clothing traditionally worn for the *egungun* ceremony, costumes sacred to members of a local religious cult. Simon has confiscated the robes from the cult leaders, and he and Jane plan to wear them to win a prize for best costume at a fancy-dress ball the British are holding that night. Although Amusa is a Muslim and not a part of the cult, he respects the clothes and will not speak to Simon until he has removed them.

Amusa and the house-servant Joseph explain that Elesin will commit ritual suicide that night. The *alafin* or king of Elesin's people died one month before, but has not yet been buried. According to ''native law and custom'' Elesin, as the king's chief horseman, must kill himself that night so the king will not be alone. Simon and Jane discuss the foolishness of native belief, and remember proudly that Simon helped Elesin's oldest son, Olunde, leave the village to attend medical school in England, against his father's wishes. Simon also reveals a surprise: the prince of England will be at the ball. Although Simon does not care personally what happens to Elesin, he cannot afford to have any trouble while the prince is visiting his district. To prevent Elesin's death, Simon orders him arrested.

Act III

The third Act returns to the market, where one of the stalls has been converted into a wedding chamber. Amusa and two constables are attempting to arrest Elesin, but the women stand around them hurling insults, claiming that working for the white

Wole Soyinka

man has cost Amusa his manhood. The women grab the men's hats and batons, do a mocking imitation of British officers, and send the men away.

Elesin emerges from the wedding chamber, and shows Iyaloja the stained cloth that proves that the bride was a virgin. As he makes plans for his final moments on earth, he listens to the sound of the ritual drumming; he can tell that the king's horse and dog have already been killed, and that soon it will be his turn to die. As he listens to the drums, he falls into a state of semi-hypnosis, and begins his passage to the next world. He dances, his limbs becoming heavier and heavier, as the praise-singer calls out to him, wishing Elesin could stay.

Act IV

The fourth Act opens at the home of the resident, the British chief officer, as the prince enters the ballroom accompanied by an orchestra playing ''Rule Britannia.'' The prince admires Simon and Jane's *egungun* attire, then joins the dancing. Alerted by Amusa, Simon and the resident have a whispered conference in the hallway. Simon tells his superior about the ''strange custom'' that Elesin will be prevented from carrying out, and the men agree that there must be no trouble while the prince is visiting. Realizing that it is midnight, Simon leaves hurriedly for the marketplace, leaving Jane to enjoy the rest of the ball.

As soon as Simon is gone, Elesin's son Olunde steps from the shadows to speak with Jane. He gently rebukes her for wearing the sacred *egungun* garments for a trivial purpose. He thinks the British are disrespectful people, but praises the courage British men have shown in fighting the Second World War, which is raging in Europe but almost unnoticed in Nigeria. Olunde needs to speak with Simon, and asks for Jane's help in finding him. Word reached Olunde in England that the king has died, and Olunde knows that on this night he will be called as oldest son to bury his father. He also knows that Simon will try to prevent Elesin's suicide, and he wants to stop Simon from making this mistake. He tries to explain to Jane that the tradition is sacred, and that it holds the universe on course even if she and Simon cannot understand it. He can calmly accept his father's death, because he knows it is necessary.

Simon returns, and Olunde thanks him for not interfering. But there is a commotion outside, and Olunde hears Elesin's voice. Elesin is alive, shouting accusations at the white men who have brought him shame. Against all propriety, the father and son see each other, something they are forbidden to do once the king is dead. Disgusted by Elesin's failure, Olunde says, "I have no father" and walks away.

Act V

The final Act is set in Elesin's prison cell. Simon comments on the peaceful night, but Elesin corrects him, telling him that because the ritual has not been enacted the world will never know peace again. Simon cannot understand the importance of Elesin's failure, and rejects any suggestion that something is amiss. The two discuss Olunde's fate. Simon is sure that Olunde will return to England to continue his studies. Elesin is proud that his son, who had seemed to reject his own culture, was man enough to reject him. Iyaloja comes to Elesin, reminding him of her earlier warning. She knows that Elesin, not Simon, is at fault for not carrying out his suicide, because he allowed himself to be distracted by the young woman, and Elesin accepts the blame. Iyaloja reveals that she has brought "a burden": the body of Olunde, who has killed himself in his father's place. When he sees his son, Elesin manages to strangle himself with his chains. The bride does her wifely duty, closing Elesin's eyes with dirt, then leaves with Iyaloja, who coun-

sels her, "Now forget the dead, forget even the living. Turn your mind only to the unborn."

CHARACTERS

Amusa

Amusa is a sergeant in the native administration police, a black African working for the white British colonialists. His position is a difficult one: he is not trusted by Simon Pilkings, his superior, because Simon cannot conceive of an African as being intelligent or honest, and he is no longer trusted by the villagers because he works with the whites to enforce "the laws of strangers." Amusa was converted to Christianity two years before the play begins, but he still feels profound respect for native beliefs. He will not speak with Simon so long as Simon is wearing the *egungun* garments, but Amusa does not hesitate to follow Simon's orders and arrest Elesin to prevent his suicide.

Bride

The Bride does not speak at all during the play. Already engaged to Iyaloja's son, the Bride is seen by Elesin and taken to bed by him; no one asks for her consent. When Elesin is arrested she sits silently beside him, and upon his death she closes his eyes in fulfillment of her wifely duty.

Iyaloja

Iyaloja is the Mother of the market, the spokesperson and leader of the women of the village. She is the voice of wisdom in the play, the one who can see beyond Elesin's charms to the danger he represents when he swerves from his responsibility. When Elesin asks for the young woman as his Bride, Iyaloja has no choice but to hand her over, even though the young woman is engaged to Iyaloja's own son. Iyaloja knows the power of the forces of the universe, and she understands that refusing the request of a man who is "already touched by the waiting fingers of our departed" will "set this world adrift." But she warns Elesin not to leave a cursed seed behind him, and she reminds him of her warning when she brings Olunde's body to Elesin's cell.

Elesin Oba

Elesin Oba, a man of "enormous vitality," was the chief horseman of the dead king. As the king's companion, Elesin enjoyed a luxurious life of rich food and fine clothing, the rewards of a man of his position. He enjoyed that life, and now that the king has been dead for a month and is ready for burial Elesin is expected to complete the horseman's duty and commit ritual suicide. The play opens on the evening of Elesin's last day of life; at midnight he will die. He says repeatedly that he is ready to give his life, and he knows the importance of fulfilling his responsibility. But Elesin, well known for his many sexual conquests, sees a young woman of great beauty and demands that he be allowed to take her to bed before he dies. Just after leaving the wedding chamber, Elesin begins his passage into the next world, and dances in a hypnotic dream-like trance. But when Simon's men come to arrest Elesin, he cannot summon the strength to resist them and continue through the transitional state into the next world. Instead, he lives, and brings shame to himself and chaos to the world.

Olohun-iyo

See The Praise-Singer

Jane Pilkings

Jane is the wife of Simon Pilkings, the British district officer. Although she shares most of Simon's superior attitudes, she is, in Olunde's words, "somewhat more understanding" than her husband. Unlike Simon, she can sense that Simon has offended Amusa and Joseph (the house servant), although she agrees with Simon that the native customs and beliefs are "horrible." She has no active role in the main events of the play, but serves as a sounding board for Simon as he thinks things through.

Simon Pilkings

Simon is the district officer, charged with maintaining order in the one district of the British colony of Nigeria. He has no interest in learning about the Africans and their culture. He and his wife Jane socialize only with other Europeans, who have tried to transplant as much of their own food, clothing, and manners as they can to maintain their own style of life in a foreign country. Simon is sure of himself and of his way of life, and easily dismisses anything he does not understand. When he learns that Elesin intends to commit suicide on the night of the prince's visit to the district, Simon uses his authority to stop Elesin not because he values Elesin, but because he does not want any commotion to disrupt a fancy-

MEDIA ADAPTATIONS

- *Death and the King's Horseman* has not been filmed or recorded.

dress ball and the prince's visit. Ironically, the steps Simon takes to ensure peace in the village actually help bring about chaos in the universe. Because he does not care to understand Yoruba belief, his actions do more harm than good.

Praise-Singer

The Praise-Singer (also known as Olohun-iyo) accompanies Elesin on his last journey, singing and chanting. He is devoted to Elesin, and sees into the darkest corners of his heart. Almost like a conscience, he voices Elesin's hesitations and questions about his passage into the next world. As Elesin enters his trance to begin the transition, the Praise-Singer monitors his progress. He can sense Elesin moving away from him, and calls him back in a ritual, repetitive chant. Once Elesin is arrested and brought to his cell, the Praise-Singer is not seen nor heard again.

THEMES

Life Cycle

Like many African cultures, the Yoruba have a fundamental belief that life is a continuum. The dead are not forgotten; the ancestors are honored and cherished as guides and companions. The not-yet-born are also cherished, and new babies may in fact be ancestors returning to physical life. The most highly charged moments in the life cycle are the moments of transition from one type of existence to the next that is, the passage into the physical world during birth and the passage into death. Elesin's responsibility as king's horseman is to enact the

TOPICS FOR FURTHER STUDY

- Research the involvement of African nations in World War II. Where on the African continent were battles fought? Which nations were involved in the fighting? Does it seem reasonable that the characters in *Death and the King's Horseman* would be largely oblivious to the war? How accurate and appropriate is the term "world war"?

- The British used to have a proud saying: "The sun never sets on the British Empire." Using research and a map of the world, identify the parts of the world that were under British rule in the early 1940s, when *Death and the King's Horseman* takes place. Then identify the parts of the world under British rule in 1975, when the play was written. Where does the British Empire reach today?

- Soyinka was raised as a Christian, but his parents were also Yoruba. What evidence of this rich combination of influences is found in *Death and the King's Horseman*

- Find audio recordings of the kinds of music that are heard in this play: a tango, a Viennese waltz, the song "Rule Britannia," and indigenous Yoruba music. How does each type of music reflect the culture that produced it?

- Research masquerade rituals performed in West Africa, paying special attention to the traditional clothing, masks, and other objects associated with these ceremonies. How are they alike and unlike the ceremonies performed in your own religious or ethnic practice?

transition from life into death in a ritual manner, to remind the entire community through his death that life is a continuum.

The idea of death is found throughout the play. Elesin and the women of the village are preparing for his death. The clothing that the Pilkingses wear to the ball has been taken away from a group performing the *egungun* celebration, a ritual in which men dress as the ancestors and mingle with the living. The masqueraders take the ritual seriously, as a reminder that the ancestors are always present, and even the Muslim Amusa has respect for the stolen garments. Simon and Jane, however, cannot understand the calm acceptance of death demonstrated by the Yoruba or the respect shown for the ancestors. They perform a mocking imitation of the *egungun* ceremony, they try to prevent Elesin from dying, and they find Olunde "callous" and "unfeeling" because he does not mourn his father's death.

As a person in transition, Elesin has special powers and special rights. His request for the Bride, although unexpected, must be granted, because "the claims of one whose foot is on the threshold of their abode surpasses even the claims of blood." Iyaloja realizes that the child born of Elesin and the Bride will be extraordinary, "neither of this world nor of the next. Nor of the one behind us. As if the timelessness of the ancestor world and the unborn have joined spirits."

Elesin, of course, does not complete his transition. Olunde dies in his place and Elesin, seeing the chaos demonstrated by the father and son reversing roles, kills himself. Simon and Jane are horrified, but Iyaloja and the Bride are placid and accepting. Iyaloja rebukes Simon for his panic, and the Bride "walks calmly into the cell" to close Elesin's eyes in the appropriate, ritual manner. The last line of the play, spoken to the Bride by Iyaloja, repeats the idea of the continuum of life: "Now forget the dead, forget even the living. Turn your mind only to the unborn."

Culture Clash

Westerners who come to *Death and the King's Horseman* without much knowledge about Yoruba culture and belief are apt to focus on the theme of the clash of cultures. Clearly, two cultures, Yoruba and British, are uneasily occupying the same geographic space, although their emotional and spiritual worlds could not be further apart. During Acts 2 and 4, for example, the British listen to a tango and orchestral music, while the sound of African drumming is continually heard in the background. Both communities call their members together during the same evening: The British hold a fancy-dress ball with the prince in attendance, and the Yoruba gather for the ritual suicide of the king's richly robed horseman and the burial of the king and his entourage. Although the differences are interesting to observe, the two communities do not enrich each other, but remain apart.

Simon and Jane Pilkings do not understand the beliefs of the Africans, and they dismiss what they do not understand as "nonsense," and as "barbaric" and "horrible custom." They see no harm in wearing the sacred *egungun* garments to a costume party and mocking the ceremonial dance, even after Amusa and Olunde point out the disrespect in their actions. Elesin's sense of tradition is so important to him that he is willing to die for it. By contrast, Simon's Christianity seems to mean little to Simon, who mocks Joseph for his devout faith in "that holy water nonsense." Nevertheless, this man of little faith feels qualified to label Elesin an "old pagan." Simon does not understand or respect Elesin's culture, and he uses his authority to interfere only because he does not want to be embarrassed while the prince is visiting.

It is tempting, therefore, to see Simon as the cause of Elesin's not fulfilling his duty, to see the clash of cultures as the force that moves the universe off its course. But in an Author's Note that accompanies the play, Soyinka indicates his displeasure with this reading, which he calls "facile." For Soyinka, Simon's inability to understand is clearly present, but the focus of the play is on what happens to the universe when duty goes unfulfilled. Simon is simply an instrument or a "catalytic incident merely." Those who understand Yoruba belief can easily see the metaphysical confrontation in the play. For most Westerners, however, the recognizable conflict is between two religions, two races, two communities, and two cultures.

Duty and Responsibility

When Elesin heads toward death, he is repaying a debt. All his life he has enjoyed the company of the king, the finest clothes, "the choicest of the season's harvest." He has always known that he would follow the king in death, and as a man of honor he claims that he is eager for death and "will not delay." He knows his responsibility, and he accepts it. However, he is distracted at the end by the richness of the physical world. Rather than letting go of the world he draws it to him more closely, demanding finer clothing and one last sexual encounter.

His distraction proves his downfall. The ritual suicide is delayed while Elesin takes his new bride to bed, and the delay is enough time for Simon to have him arrested. The failure is Elesin's not Simon's, though Elesin tries to put the blame on the "alien race." Iyaloja rejects this interpretation. If Elesin were strong enough in spirit, Simon could not keep him from his duty. Elesin is surrounded by others who fulfill their responsibilities: Iyaloja gives her son's bride-to-be to Elesin, Olunde travels all the way from England to bury his father and dies in his father's place, the bride closes her dead husband's eyes. Only Elesin fails, and the cost of his failure is high.

STYLE

Setting

Death and the King's Horseman takes place in the Nigerian town of Oyo in approximately 1943 or 1944. Nigeria became a colony of Great Britain in the nineteenth century, and into the 1940s British officers kept order and protected a small group of white Europeans who lived in the country. The white expatriates and the black Africans, members of the Yoruba people, inhabited parallel worlds, each group attempting to maintain its own traditional way of life.

The market is the center of the community, where people gather to socialize, to trade, to celebrate and to perform rituals, and it is here that Elesin comes as his last day draws to a close. The Western-style homes of the district officer and the resident are set apart from the village, but close enough that the sounds of the ceremonial drumming can be still be heard. The two communities, each holding a special event on the night of the play's action, do not mingle. No whites are present at the ceremony

COMPARE & CONTRAST

- **1940s:** Nigeria is a colony of Great Britain, governed by a white British minority bureaucracy.

  1963: Nigeria becomes an independent republic, with Nnamdi Azikiwe as first president.

  1975: A military coup brings General Olusegun Obasanjo to power. He is Nigeria's third military dictator since 1966.

  1999: The latest in a series of military rulers, General Abdulsalami Abubakar, assumes power and invites Soyinka back from a four-year exile. The general pledges to bring Nigeria out of its long period of oppression at the hands of corrupt military rulers.

- **1967:** Soyinka begins a prison term of more than two years for criticizing the Nigerian government. He will serve fifteen months in solitary confinement.

  1974: Nobel-prize-winning author Aleksandr Solzhenitsyn is stripped of his Soviet citizenship and forced into exile. Writer Es'kia Mphahalele is living in exile from South Africa, after being arrested for protesting apartheid. Soyinka accepts a position as a visiting lecturer at Cambridge University in England.

  2000: Solzhenitsyn, his citizenship restored, again lives in Russia. Mphahlele and Soyinka live in their home countries, where they are honored as intellectuals and political activists.

- **1970s:** African writing is not much taught in European or American schools, and is not widely read or understood outside Africa. When Soyinka is invited to be a visiting lecturer at Cambridge

University, he is invited to talk about not literature, but about anthropology.

  1986: Soyinka becomes the first African writer to be awarded the Nobel Prize for Literature. It is both an acknowledgment of his importance to world literature and an opportunity to attract even more readers around the world.

  2000: High schools and colleges routinely offer courses in World Literature, and these courses increasingly include African and other so-called Third World literatures. Soyinka's plays, including *Death and the King's Horseman*, are frequently included in textbooks.

- **1953:** In the nation's first official census, 43 percent of Nigerians report themselves as Muslims; 22 percent label themselves Christians; 34 percent are recorded as followers of ancestral religions.

  1999: Fewer Nigerians now practice traditional religions. Approximately 50 percent are Muslims, 40 percent are Christian, and only 10 percent adhere to ancestral beliefs.

- **1945:** Few opportunities for higher education are available for blacks in Nigeria. Formal education consists mostly of missionary schools, and does not extend beyond the secondary level.

  2000: Nigeria has an extensive system of public schools as well as many religious schools. There are several universities, and a few medical schools affiliated with teaching hospitals. Nigerians pursuing medical careers need not go abroad for their education.

---

marking Elesin's passage, and the only blacks at the fancy-dress ball are servants.

Tragedy

In its structure, *Death and the King's Horseman* appears to be based on the tragedy. The tragedy

is an ancient form of drama in which an important person passes through a series of events and choices, resulting in a great catastrophe. Tragedies have been written all around the world over thousands of years, to examine the dignity of humans and their greatest strengths and weaknesses. According to the ancient Greeks, tragedy filled the audience with fear and pity, and so helped a community deal psychologically with these emotions. The structure of a tragedy may be generally divided into several distinct parts: an introduction in which the characters, setting and situation are established; the complication or rising action, during which an opposing force is introduced; the climax or turning point; the falling action, or another focusing on the opposing forces; and the catastrophe, or the unhappy conclusion.

Death and the King's Horseman has in fact been built on this pattern. Act 1 introduces Elesin and his duty; Act 2 introduces an opposing force in the figure of Simon Pilkings, who plans to prevent Elesin's suicide; Act 3 ends with the climax of Elesin in transition, apparently only moments away from the central action, his death; Act 4 shifts the focus back to Simon Pilkings, and ends with the revelation that Elesin's suicide has been prevented; Act 5 contains Elesin's musings on the disorder brought about by his failure, and presents the deaths of Olunde and Elesin.

Foreshadowing

When a play or story includes early clues to what will happen later, the writing is said to include foreshadowing. In *Death and the King's Horseman* there are several hints in Act 1 that Elesin will not carry through with his plan to commit suicide. As Elesin and the Praise- Singer enter the market, for example, Elesin comments on the attractiveness of the women there. The Praise-Singer agrees, but warns, ''The hands of women also weaken the unwary.'' This warning creates in the audience's mind the possibility of failure, even danger. When Elesin promises that he will be faithful and join his forbears, the Praise-Singer replies, ''In their time the world was never tilted from its groove, it shall not be in yours.'' Again, the possibility of failure is presented, as it will be several more times by the Praise-Singer and the women of the market as they assure each other that Elesin will not fail.

Elesin himself speaks eagerly about his determination to complete his duty. He dances and chants a long tale of the ''Not-I bird,'' a bird who flew away when ''Death came calling.'' Several critics have pointed out that Elesin seems here to be protesting too much. Why does he repeatedly assure the crowd that he will ''not delay''? Why does he keep raising the specter of failure on what should be a glorious day of celebration? The foreshadowing helps prepare the audience for what will happen,

prolonging and intensifying the experience of watching Elesin confront and then turn away from his duty.

Ritual

Death and the King's Horseman is set firmly in Yorubaland, and the metaphysical issues spring from Yoruba belief. However, as Nigeria and the rest of the world move ''forward,'' the world becomes more homogenous and Western, and ancient beliefs and customs are lost. Soyinka writes in the Author's Note of the play's ''threnodic essence,'' or the play's mourning the loss of tradition. With Elesin and Olunde both dead, the tradition of the king's horseman cannot continue, because it depends on the job of chief horseman being passed down from father to son. With Elesin's failure, an important ritual has been lost.

On stage, the play both celebrates and mourns ritual. Unlike the plays of William Shakespeare, which contain almost no stage directions, *Death and the King's Horseman* includes several lengthy passages in which the playwright describes what the actors are doing in addition to speaking their lines. Frequently, these stage directions describe elements of music, dance, and costume that are specific to Yoruba ritual. For example, Elesin parades into the market with an entourage of drummers and praise-singers, and the beginning of the play before a line is spoken—is a reenactment of part of the ritual of the horseman's last day. The stage directions also mandate that Elesin dance, accompanied by drumming, as he chants the story of the ''Not-I bird''; that the *alari*-cloth the women drape him with be bright red and that they dance around him; that Simon and Jane dance the tango, and that they perform a sacrilegious imitation of the *egungun* ceremony; that Elesin dances his way into a trance; and so on. These scenes are rich with sound and color, and most of them are not discussed by the characters. They form a separate layer of understanding, unavailable to those who merely read the printed script. In addition to the themes and ideas portrayed by the words the actors speak, the audience of a performance also witnesses a series of rituals enacted on stage as they used to be enacted in village markets.

HISTORICAL CONTEXT

A Nation in Turmoil

When Soyinka wrote *Death and the King's Horseman* in 1974 he was living in exile from

Nigeria, lecturing at Churchill College of Cambridge University in England. The preceding years had been difficult for Nigeria, and for Soyinka personally. In 1967, the southeastern area of Nigeria declared itself the independent Republic of Biafra, and a civil war erupted. The causes of the conflict were complex: the secessionists were mostly from the Ibo tribe, and believed that the Nigerian government favored the Hausa tribe; many in the southeast were Christian, while those in the north were predominantly Muslim; oil was being produced in the region, and there was disagreement about how the revenues would be distributed.

Soyinka believed that the government policies toward Biafra were unjust, and he said as much in letters to the editors of national publications. Soyinka was arrested in 1967 and held without charges for two years and two months. For fifteen of those months, he was in solitary confinement. While he was in prison, the war continued, and the Biafrans were pushed to a smaller and smaller area of land. Shortly after Soyinka was released from prison in 1969, the war was over and Biafra had been completely wiped out. It was the first modern war between African blacks, and it left over one million people dead and many more homeless and starving. The Nigerian economy was in ruins; although profits from oil skyrocketed, most of the money was divided up between corrupt Nigerian military rulers and European oil companies, while the average Nigerian was unemployed and underfed.

After these experiences, Soyinka directed the University of Ibadan's Theatre Arts Department for a short time, and then lived mostly outside Nigeria for five years. He traveled throughout Europe and the United States, teaching, writing, and directing, and he spent two years as an editor in Ghana. According to many critics, his attention shifted after his imprisonment. Whereas previously he had written about the negative effects of the colonial powers on the colonized, he now addressed weakness and corruption wherever he found it. In particular, he was concerned with exploring the ways in which Africans treated each other unjustly, and the ways in which his own community had betrayed itself. *Death and the King's Horseman* is a play that reflects this later vision, as Soyinka himself insists in his Author's Note.

African Literature

African writers during the second half of the twentieth century faced a dilemma. Most of the traditional African forms of literature were based on oral traditional and ritual performance, and these ancient forms were becoming less and less familiar even to the local people. On the other hand, more widely popular genres like the novel and dramatic forms like the classical tragedy were based on European structures and philosophies, and did not always seem to fit African themes and beliefs. Language was also an issue: a play written in the local language would obviously capture the atmosphere and the spirit of a people better than the same story told in English, but the audience for such a play would be very limited.

Most of the African writers who are now considered major international figures traveled, taught, and produced important work in Europe and the United States, and they created works that combined European influences with African materials. With each new work they attempted to define what was ''African'' about African literature. Soyinka and others wrote eloquent essays in which they explored the place of Africa in world literature, and tried to determine how an African writer should make sense of various influences. Ngugi wa Thiong'o of Kenya, after several successful publications, decided to stop writing in English; since 1977 he has written his novels and plays in Gikuyu, but encouraged their publication in translation. Soyinka's works are written in English, but retain the original Yoruba for quoting certain proverbs, as in *Death and the King's Horseman*. However, in 1994 Akin Isola produced a translation of the play into Yoruba, as part of a new movement of Yoruba literature, a translation Soyinka endorsed.

CRITICAL OVERVIEW

Death and the King's Horseman has been recognized from the beginning as an important work, but its critical reputation has been somewhat different in Nigeria than in Europe and the United States. Westerners have almost universally praised the play, and the Swedish Academy drew special attention to it in awarding Soyinka the 1986 Nobel Prize for Literature. Within Nigeria and within the community of Africans on the political left, however, some critics have quarreled with the play's political messages.

A central question answered differently by various critics and reviewers is the question of theme. What is the play about? Reviewers of performances of the play have tended to see the theme as the clash of cultures, focusing on the inability of the Pilkingses to understand Elesin and his responsibility. This is also how most audiences of performances have interpreted the play, as might be expected since most Western theater-goers do not bring much knowledge of Yoruba culture with them. In her study of the 1987 Lincoln Center production in New York, which Soyinka himself directed, Kacke Gotrick points out that even with Soyinka's Author's Note being reprinted in the *Playbill* and with Soyinka shaping every facet of the staging, some critics ''nonetheless understood a cultural clash to be the central theme.'' Gotrick observes, as others have, that ''Since Soyinka's drama relies on the Yoruba world-view, the interpreter's degree of knowledge of this world-view becomes decisive for his or her interpretation.'' The culture clash is also the theme analyzed by most Westerners who read the play, including high school and college students, as they also bring little knowledge of Yoruba to their reading experience.

Writers of scholarly articles and books, who have generally had the opportunity and the responsibility to learn more about Soyinka and about Yoruba cosmology, have been more likely to understand Soyinka's insistence that the clash of cultures is less important than the metaphysical examination of duty and ritual, and the representation of transition, a stage of the life cycle that connects the unborn, the living, and the dead. The theme of unfulfilled duty is explored in Derek Wright's *Wole Soyinka Revisited*. Wright examines the differences in plot between Soyinka's play and the historical events on which it is based, and points out Soyinka's own insistence that Simon Pilkings is only a catalyst. The emphasis is on the ritual that is not completed: ''Elesin's failure to die, and so keep faith with his ancestors, spells the death of the ancestral past and the betrayal of the entire community of humans and spirits existing over the whole of time.''

In his *Wole Soyinka: An Introduction to his Writing,* Obu Maduakor focuses on transition, the term Soyinka uses in the Author's Note. Maduakor describes Soyinka's cosmology, and concludes that ''Elesin's bride represents the world of the living; the seed implanted in her womb is a visitor from the world of the unborn. The dead Alafin, the 'King' of the play, has gone to the world of the dead, and Elesin himself is a creature of the twilight world of passage.'' Maduakor also traces Elesin's story, and demonstrates how it parallels the passage of Ogun,

one of the Yoruba deities, through preparation, ritual death, and rebirth.

A major focus of criticism of *Death and the King's Horseman* has been providing assistance to readers who are not familiar with Yoruba culture. Much of the published criticism of the play offers little more than close reading, supported by helpful background information about the traditional role of the Praise-Singer, or the market, or the *egungun* ritual. An excellent example of this type of material is Bimpe Aboyade's *Wole Soyinka and Yoruba Oral Tradition* in *Death and the King's Horseman,* in which the writer explains the Yoruba oral traditions of the poets of the *egungun,* the hunters and the talking drum, and the aura of the ancestral masque. These cultural analyses are invaluable for Western readers or for African readers who are unfamiliar with Yoruba tradition.

Death and the King's Horseman has not been without detractors. Several critics have commented on the anachronistic situation presented by the play, observing that by the 1940s the failure of the king's horseman to commit ritual suicide would not have rocked the community. Some have found it difficult to accept that the European-educated Olunde would participate in the ritual. Other critics, particularly those in Nigeria, have written that Soyinka has romanticized the Yoruba, presenting them as more unified and tradition-bound than they are. African Marxist critics find that in emphasizing the cultural and religious differences between the British and the Yoruba, the play ignores essential class differences within Nigeria. Underlying much of the negative criticism is a sense that Soyinka's drama, influenced as it is by his study of drama around the world and also by study of Nigeria oral tradition, is simply not ''African'' enough. The universality that makes his plays so respected in Europe and North America is a sign, for some, that Soyinka has in many ways betrayed his own culture.

CRITICISM

Cynthia A. Bily

Bily teaches English at Adrian College in Adrian, Michigan. In the following essay she discusses the roles of women in Death and the King's Horseman.

Wole Soyinka's *Death and the King's Horseman* tells the story of a man who fails to fulfill a

WHAT DO I READ NEXT?

- *The Lion and the Jewel* (1963) is one of Soyinka's earliest plays, and one of the first to be performed in Africa. More humorous than *Death and the King's Horseman*, it depicts a clash of cultures through the story of a confrontation between a schoolteacher and the village chief. As the two men try to win the hand of a beautiful woman, they argue the values of tradition and modernity.

- *Ake: The Years of Childhood* (1981) is Soyinka's second volume of memoir. Chosen by the *New York Times* as one of the twelve best books of 1982, it describes the first ten years of his life. Although Soyinka was something of a prodigy, beginning school at age three and becoming a teacher at ten, his gentle self-mocking humor makes the book delightful rather than self-serving.

- *The Handbook of Yoruba Religious Concepts* (1994) by Baba Ifa Karade presents clear and simple explanations of Yoruba beliefs and ceremonies. The presentation is not meant to win converts, but rather to strip away some of the mystery and make the traditions accessible to those who would wish to practice them or just to understand them. Karade also demonstrates similarities and differences between Yoruba and other spiritual beliefs.

- *The Palm-Wine Drinkard* (1953) by Amos Tutuola is a novel of a devoted West African drinker who undergoes a series of imaginative adventures. Tutuola built this humorous and dreamlike story out of traditional Yoruba folktales.

- *Things Fall Apart* (1958) is the first and most widely read novel by Nigerian writer Chinua Achebe, Through the story of Okonkwo, a member of the Ibo tribe, it depicts the changes in village life brought about when colonialism and Christianity intrud. Okonkwo is a complex character, not a simple victim of colonialism; his downfall comes both from forces within and from without.

- *Hamlet, Prince of Denmark*, a play written in approximately 1601 by William Shakespeare, is one of the most famous tragedies ever written. Prince Hamlet is the son of the king, who has just been murdered by Hamlet's uncle. The dead king urges Hamlet to revenge his death. Hamlet proves incapable of fulfilling his duty to the dead king, bringing chaos and death to himself and many of those close to him.

---

responsibility. When Elesin, the king's chief horseman, does not complete his ritual suicide so that he can accompany his dead king to the world of the ancestors, he breaks a thread of continuity that has for generations connected the worlds of the unborn, the living, and the dead. The connecting thread in this case is based on patriarchy: the kingship passes down from father to son, and so does the position of king's horseman. Olunde, as eldest son, knows as soon as he receives word of the king's death that his own father will die a month later and Olunde will be required to properly bury his father and then step into his role. When Olunde dies before his father, and leaves no son of his own, the thread is broken, and the ritual can no longer be performed.

Death and the King's Horseman focuses on a man's world, and a man's responsibility, and women are incidental to its central ritual. The role of women in this play can be problematic for Western readers who have become attuned to Western-based forms of feminism, and who are practiced at unearthing belittling treatments of women in literature written by men. As a white Christian woman from the American Midwest, I would not presume to judge Yoruba culture, or to analyze Yoruba women under a Western lens. I do think, however, that a close look at the women characters in *Death and the King's Horseman* can reveal different ways of thinking about power and influence and responsibility.

To be sure, there are moments in *Death and the King's Horseman* that make a Western feminist cringe. As the play opens, Elesin comes strutting into the market bragging about his many sexual conquests. The Praise-Singer fondly remembers the time the horseman was caught with his sister-in-law and claimed, ''but I was only prostrating myself to her as becomes a grateful in-law.'' Later in the same Act, Elesin becomes distracted, ''his attention is caught by an *object* off-stage'' (italics mine). That ''object'' is soon revealed to be a young woman, the bride, whose body Elesin praises piece by piece. In Act 3, Elesin emerges from the wedding chamber with the stained cloth that proves that the bride was a virgin when he took her and that she has not dishonored him. Clearly the rules are different for men and for women. When Elesin is in his cell for the last Act and Jane Pilkings tries to make him see her husband's motives, Elesin is pointedly rude and dismissive: ''That is my wife sitting down there. You notice how still and silent she sits? My business is with your husband.''

A reader must not stop here, however. It is true that Elesin has an important position in a male world, and that he does not see women as important influences on that position. But in fact, the women in the play tend to be wiser and stronger, and they appear to be closer to the spirit world and less bound to the material world, than the men.

As Mother of the market, Iyaloja is the leader of the women, and even Elesin pays respect to her. She can see more deeply than Elesin can. She is the one who recognizes that the child of the union between Elesin and the bride will be ''the elusive being of passage.'' (Elesin has no high moral or spiritual purpose in asking for the bride. He simply wants sex.) Iyaloja is also the one who sees the danger in Elesin's request, and she warns him to be careful: ''be sure the seed you leave . . . attracts no curse.'' Of course, Elesin does not listen to her, just as he refuses to hear Jane Pilkings. Only in the last Act is he forced to admit, ''I more than deserve your scorn.''

In every pairing of a woman and her ''equal'' in stature, the woman emerges as the wiser. Iyaloja, the highest-ranking woman, is wiser than Elesin, the king's horseman. The market women easily make fools of Amusa and the two constables and run them off, although the police officers come bearing batons and authority. Of the two Pilkingses, Jane is

> WOMEN CHARACTERS IN
> *DEATH AND THE KING'S HORSEMAN*
> MAY BE SUBSERVIENT TO MEN, BUT
> THEY ARE STRONG, AND THEY ARE
> THE ONLY HOPE FOR THE FUTURE.''

much more observant and sensitive than Simon, although she is not able ultimately to understand the Yoruba people she lives among.

It is Jane who is able to sense and understand that Amusa's discomfort at seeing the *egungun* garments misused is genuine, and she encourages Simon to remove the clothing. Jane does not, however, ultimately respect Amusa's feelings and she carries out her plan to dance mockingly in the robes at the fancy dress ball. Similarly, she realizes that Simon has offended Joseph by making fun of holy water. Again, she does not respect the Roman Catholic faith, but she can sense Joseph's feelings and she has something to gain by bowing to them. She does not want Joseph to remain angry because, as she tells Simon, ''He's going to hand in his notice tomorrow, you mark my word.''

Unlike his father, Olunde is willing to talk with Jane. He acknowledges her limitations when he finds her wearing the *egungun* mask, and tells her, ''I discovered that you have no respect for what you do not understand.'' But of the two Pilkingses, he prefers to speak with Jane: ''I need your help Mrs. Pilkings. I've always found you somewhat more understanding than your husband.'' Jane does not understand Olunde's reaction to his father's death, and she calls him ''callous'' and a ''savage.'' But while Simon assumes he understands the Africans under his supervision and has no wish to learn more, Jane feels deeply the limits of her understanding. She begs Olunde to teach her: ''Your calm acceptance for instance, can you explain that? It was so unnatural. I don't understand it at all. I feel a need to understand all I can.'' She continues, ''I feel it has to do with the many things we don't really grasp about your people.''

Elesin betrays his people by failing to fulfill his ritual responsibility. He is turned away from his duty by the relatively trivial distractions of rich robes and a pretty face. By contrast, two female characters in the play are shown to recognize their responsibility and to fulfill it completely, even when the path is a difficult one. Iyaloja, for example, is asked to give up the woman who is engaged to her own son so that Elesin may enjoy a few last moments of pleasure. She is at first displeased with the request, and the other women encourage her to speak up, but she refuses to deny Elesin what he wants. The responsibility to meet the ancestors is Elesin's, but Iyaloja knows that her responsibility is to help him, and she will not "burden him with knowledge that will sour his wish and lay regrets on the last moments of his mind."

The repetition of Yoruba proverbial language shows that Iyaloja's decision is just as significant as Elesin's. At the beginning of Act 1 the Praise-singer honors Elesin for his commitment to his duty, reminding him that "the world was never tilted from its groove, it shall not be in yours," and "Our world was never wrenched from its true course." Breaking faith with the ancestors is a catastrophic failure. The same language is used by Iyaloja when the other women encourage her to refuse Elesin's request for the young woman: "don't set this world adrift in your own time; would you rather it was my hand whose sacrilege wrenched it loose?" Both Elesin and Iyaloja are free to act, but the wrong action will have grave consequences. Elesin recognized Iyaloja's hesitation, and scolds her for it, but she quickly sees the importance of the sacrifice and is, in the words of the stage directions, is "completely reconciled."

The bride, too, has a duty, and she sees it through. The bride does not speak a word throughout the play, so her thoughts and feelings are not examined. We have no way of knowing whether she loved Iyaloja's son, the man she was to have married, or what personal benefit she might look forward to in marrying a man whom she had never met, and who would be dead a few minutes after the marriage was consummated. The stage directions give no hint about her reaction to Elesin's "proposal," no description of joy or of protest. Elesin's face "glows with pleasure" when the Bride comes to him, but what does her face look like? Regardless, she does what she is supposed to do: she marries Elesin and has intercourse with him.

The bride emerges from the wedding chamber and stands "shyly" by her husband's side as he instructs her how to close his eyes after he is dead. When he is imprisoned, she sits quietly outside his cell, "her eyes perpetually to the ground." Even when Elesin blames her for "sapping" his will, she does not protest. As Elesin proudly points out to Jane Pilkings, the bride knows her place. When Elesin is dead, she "walks calmly into the cell and closes Elesin's eyes. She then pours some earth over each eyelid and comes out again." What has it cost her to give herself to this man who saw her for a moment and wanted her? What will it cost her now to bear his child? The silent woman does not reveal any emotion; she sees her duty, and she performs it.

Women characters in *Death and the King's Horseman* may be subservient to men, but they are strong, and they are the only hope for the future. By the end of the play, the men have made a mess of things. Elesin and Olunde are dead, and Simon will have some explaining to do in the morning. The opening image of the play is of Elesin and his entourage parading into the market in a loud and colorful celebration of male power. The play ends with Iyaloja admonishing the bride, "Now forget the dead, forget even the living. Turn your mind only to the unborn." Their eyes squarely on motherhood and the future, Iyaloja and the bride walk off stage, accompanied by the sound of women's voices.

Source: Cynthia A. Bily, in an essay for *Drama for Students*, Gale, 2001.

Wole Ogundele

In this essay, Ogundele argues that the actions of Elesin represent the "form and functioning state of his culture."

In the "Author's Note" to his play *Death and the King's Horseman* (1975), Wole Soyinka, while instructing the play's future producer on its correct stage interpretation, incidentally also describes the kind of tragedy he has written: its "threnodic essence," he says, is largely the metaphysical confrontation "contained in the human vehicle which is Elesin and the universe of the Yoruba mind. . . ." This description does more than guide the producer: its terms (metaphysical confrontation, human vehicle, universe of the Yoruba mind) suggest that the experience enacted is fundamentally that of the ritual.

Death and the King's Horseman (*DKH*) is of course about the acting out of a people's collective religious emotions and desires at a crucial moment in its politico-cultural history, all framed and structured in a ritual. It is also about the disruption of that ritual by its chief celebrant who is motivated by his own private feelings that are not in conflict with the public ones, ones that in fact derive from that same occasion. With its emphasis on the use of the human body—through dance, music, songs, and chants, a reported sexual act, and two deaths—to complement dialogue that expresses those feelings, values, and beliefs, the play's subject is also textured by aesthetic rituals. To these we may still add the playwright's statement in an interview with Chuck Mike that *DKH* is the second in his "trilogy of transition." All these internal and external evidences fully support any categorizing of the play as a ritual drama.

This certainly is how Alain Severac reads it in his essay "Soyinka's Tragedies: From Ritual to Drama." In that essay, however, Severac argues that "the drama [of *DKH*] remains separate from the ritual" because, in his opinion, it does not complete the third movement of the tripartite "pattern of tragic conflict (challenge of transitional abyss; disintegration; achievement of new order) as suggested by Soyinka." Because of this perceived non-completion of the tripartite movement, Severac judges the play to be deficient in its service to (its) society.

I agree that in his theoretical and speculative essays on African (Yoruba) worldview, Soyinka discovers the tripartite pattern of tragic conflict in the myths and rituals of Yoruba deities (most especially in that of Ogun) and gives each stage equal stress. But then, the essays are on the traditional myths, belief systems, and ethics of the people, as well as the religious rites that validate them. Those rites are also performed during sacred periods when the priests are incarnations of the deities. Yet no matter how extensively they use ritual elements or how closely they approximate rituals, Soyinka's plays are actually about mortals acting in secular time. The myths and rites, plus the values and beliefs they express, are present in the plays, possibly as defenses against reality, but more certainly as ideals by which the reality that is their primary concern is measured (and of which it is seen to fall short). The priest who, while incarnating a god, acts out all the stages of the tragic conflict in full view of his people is serving them: he is reinforcing the sacred dimension of their collective life and also giving therapy. But the (secular) dramatist who uses his plays to question the creeds is also serving: by showing why a new order cannot yet follow the plunge into the abyss and the disintegration stages, he is nudging his society towards self-scrutiny, change, and self-liberation.

> THIS ESSAY . . . SEEKS TO DEMONSTRATE THAT THE PLAY IS A FULL-FLEDGED, AUTONOMOUS, SECULAR TRAGEDY AND THAT, BEING SO, IT INTERROGATES THE CULTURAL VALUES AND ETHICS WHICH MAKE ITS ACTION POSSIBLE, IN THE PROCESS REVEALING THOSE CULTURAL PREMISES TO BE GRAVELY FLAWED."

This essay, however, is not a rejoinder to Severac's, nor does it seek to justify *DKH* as a full-fledged ritual drama; rather, it seeks to demonstrate that the play is a full-fledged, autonomous, secular tragedy and that, being so, it interrogates the cultural values and ethics which make its action possible, in the process revealing those cultural premises to be gravely flawed. *DKH* may be a play of metaphysical confrontation, but that confrontation is firmly grounded in historical fact, not in myth. As such, an historical approach to how it questions the culture as well as how it reveals the contradictions in the ethics of that culture at that point in time is useful. There are other reasons for this approach. The play is possibly Soyinka's most historical one so far: its protagonist is based on a real figure and his equally factual action; the Second World War background and the real visit of the Prince to Nigeria during that war are necessary to its plot; written within five years of the Nigerian Civil War, a parallel between olokun esin's behavior in Oyo in 1946 and the lifestyle of the nation's leadership during and immediately after that war could have suggested itself to the poet's mind. . . .

Although this approach is fraught with the danger of intentional fallacy, it at least relates the play, in a general way, to contemporary political culture in Africa; it also allows us to see the fictional ritual as ambivalent and problematic, just as the real one had become in Oyo by 1946. A ritual can serve to affirm the status quo or be used to question it; but a religio-political and state ritual, such as was to be re-enacted in Oyo in 1946, is not likely to be available for the latter purpose. A dramatist working as a free, creating agent can, however, appropriate and use it to express his own dissentient vision: he can appear to be going along with the ideals and values embodied in the ritual while, underneath, he is actually exposing its inadequacies and making it condemn itself. The resultant play may or may not have a tragic plot, but it can hardly do without the dramatic weapon of irony. *DKH* is such a play, and in it ritual functions more technically than symbolically to create meaning.

We may now return to Soyinka's description of the play's tragic essence and to its constituents: metaphysical confrontation, the universe of the Yoruba mind which places the (historical) world of the living at the center; and the human vehicle Elesin. In other words, here are present all three crucial ingredients of tragedy: a cosmic order and man's place in it; the individual's relation to his society and his place in it; the individual in relation to himself All genres of drama deal with the second element and may or may not touch on the other two; it will be a poor tragedy that does not explore the third, or in which the first is neither implicit nor explicit, in one form or another.

Except in the scene (off-stage) where he goes in to consummate his marriage, Elesin on the stage is perpetually surrounded by crowds, a visual feature which emphasizes the centrality of his relation to society and his place in it—as an individual as well as a man whose personality is defined by his social identity. It is, therefore, perhaps better to base our analysis on the latter two elements.

Oral history tells us that originally, the olokun esin (Master of the Horse) did not have to die along with his king for any reason at all, political or metaphysical. The first olokun esin to die did so willingly. The reason, the oral historians say, was that that particular olokun esin and the king were uncommonly close friends. Such was the friendship that the olokun esin enjoyed all the rights and privileges that the king himself had, plus all the good things of life available in the empire. When the king died, this particular olokun esin thought that the only way to demonstrate his love and loyalty to his friend, the dead king, was to die, too. Thus was established the political custom in which a man had all the social rights, privileges, and power of a king without the necessary political and moral restraints of that state.

True history or not, we can detect behind this picturesque story the bold outlines of the warrior

ethic in a heroic age. The heroic society gives to the hero the best in life: all the wealth, prosperity, and freedom to satisfy all his desires; in return, he willingly pays with his life on the battlefield. By dying in war so that his community can survive, he fulfills his obligation totally. Such death is, therefore, part of his social life, a fulfillment of his own side of the bargain. As long as the heroic society lasts, such an ethic is only paradoxical; once the society goes, its retention becomes an intolerable contradiction: the community lavishly sustains a man only to ask him to die willingly at a moment's notice.

The Oyo empire collapsed and, with it, the heroic society and culture. The military responsibilities of the olokun esin dwindled, finally to be rendered a mere honorific office by colonial conquest. Of the many ways in which colonialism brought about cultural alienation, one is especially relevant here. The colonial religion preached an alternative cosmic order in which ritual self-immolation on behalf of society is neither desirable nor necessary. With the power of this new cosmic order manifested in its victorious political power that was evident to everybody, the spiritual mooring of the colonized was no longer secure: absolute conviction in the old ways was no longer possible. That the old cultural values and norms could not support fully the emergent psychology no doubt played a part in the decision of the historical olokun esin not to die in 1946.

Precisely because the obligation to die was now no longer a military but spiritual affair, the two aspects of the warrior ethics, which had hitherto been complementary, were now discrete entities. The rights and privileges attached to the office might still be embraced—but the reciprocal obligation recoiled from. The colonial presence made this possible—even without the physical intervention of any district officer. Furthermore, the life abundant still enjoyed by olokun esin now made self-immolation a most unattractive prospect, posthumous honor notwithstanding. The warrior ethic had degenerated into opportunism. In building the action of *DKH* around the 1946 cultural fiasco in the Oyo community, Soyinka was exploring how that degeneration came about and why.

A conventional reading of the play would blame Elesin alone for his failure to die. This is to view the play purely as a ritual performance in which the celebrant-protagonist allowed his attention to be fatally diverted. This in fact is how Iyaloja interprets the failure; but then, she is the spokesperson of the injured party. Rather, the play as a whole is more concerned with the inevitability of that failure—plus its causes and effects—than with finding a villain. This reading of the play as tragic drama therefore shows that Elesin's character and action up to the point when he should have died and his inability to die are consistent with each other, and that this consistency is a revelation of the ambiguities and shortcomings of his culture at this point in history. He is as much an effect of that culture as he is a cause of its smashing ''on boulders of the great void.'' With all the above in mind, we may go on to examine Elesin's moral and social behavior and relationships.

For a play so thematically complex and profound, *DKH* has a surprisingly simple structure. But regarding the characterization of Elesin, this simple structure has to be followed twice: once forward, then backward. Act I establishes firmly his heroic character and social identity; by the longer second half of Act III, his marriage is already consummated and he embarks on his journey through the metaphysical abyss, a liminal figure. But then he surfaces again completely human at the end of Act IV, and we have to trace the causes of his failure back into the character established earlier. However, the forward movement first.

Acts I and II are justly famous for their dramatic power and extraordinary poetic impact, much of which are concentrated on the character and characterization of Elesin. From the moment he enters as ''a man of enormous vitality'' who ''speaks, dances and sings with that infectious enjoyment of life. . .,'' we are in the presence of a character of epic proportions. Elesin's vitality is not just enormous, it is elemental. His life has been totally dedicated to the fulfillment of all sensual desires and appetites. In all his hedonistic life, Elesin has known only happiness, or anger, but never moral doubt. His acceptance of life as he met it is complete, passionate, impulsive. The life he leads is as dynamic as it is flamboyant and theatrical, for he can express himself completely in words and deeds. Power, joy, triumph rule his life—and death. This last he is now embracing as triumphantly as he has lived:

> My rein is loosened.
> I am master of my Fate. When the hour comes
> Watch me dance along the narrowing path
> Glazed by the soles of my great precursors.
> My soul is eager. I shall not turn aside.

His passage through the market is the crowning, valedictory performance of that theatrical life; his death is a consummation of his power.

These are the constituents of Elesin's public character; they do not, however, explain fully either the heroic bluster with which he enters the market or the adulatory reception he gets from the women. That explanation lies in the social-metaphysical ambience of the culture: Elesin, too, ''died'' the day his king died; the remaining thirty days left for him are just the preparatory period for his burial. Thus, although still corporeally here, his body is assumed to be already in the liminal state, half-possessing the metaphysical authority and potency of a redoubtable ancestor. His life is already complete, his person in the process of being transformed into the passage that connects this world and the next; all that remains now is for him to let his soul pass through.

That remaining action will prove his heroic will-power and mastery over culture and nature (death) and have beneficial effects on the world he is leaving behind. Thus, although it involves dying, it is an action that calls for celebration. To this extent, the ritual action conforms with Soyinka's description of ritual tragedy in Yoruba cosmology as set out in his essays.

But Elesin delays, postpones, this ''happy tragic action'' by first having a wedding. If now we read the play in the secular, questioning spirit in which it is written and therefore choose to define an action as tragic owing to its (ironic) effects on the protagonist's subsequent fortunes (plus the moral quality of heroic suffering attendant on those plunging fortunes) as well as on the society, we find its tragic action (and error) lies in Elesin's postponement of a death for a wedding, not in his inability to die. The failure to die comes as a consequence of his decision to have a wedding—and consummate it—before his metaphysical transition. That decision in turn shows that his mind and body are still firmly rooted in this world; the white man has nothing whatsoever to do with it; and it is perfectly in character. We may now proceed to examine more closely how Elesin's character leads him to take this fateful decision and action; in this, we follow Aristotle's Poetics, read in conjunction with his Ethics.

Elesin's character so far reveals that he has all the virtues necessary for happiness; but as Aristotle noted, virtues alone do not make for happiness—virtues have to be exercised in action for that to come about. But every action is a risk because it does not depend on our virtues alone: other circumstances, including hitherto unsuspected traits in our own makeup, may conjoin and take the action out of control. Once the action has been initiated, these other forces are set in motion and can produce totally unwanted effects. Thus, tragedy results, turning what was formerly a virtue into a defect. Elesin's sexual prowess, which all along has made him a hero among women, is, for lack of propriety, exercised once too often. With this, the moral complexion of his character changes: what before was heroic self-assertiveness now becomes irresponsible self-indulgence, with catastrophic consequences for all. His character explains the act, but nothing whatsoever justifies it, least of all the occasion. His rationalization of it (that he is shedding an excessive load ''that may benefit the living'') convinces no one; rather, the act is the culmination of his life-long habit of sensualizing the essentially spiritual destiny he was born to serve. The compulsive possession of the girl is, in other words, a matter of private lust and exercise of power by a man who has always had his way. But although lust and power are now selfishly exercised, they no doubt are approved of by the ethos of the culture, one of whose cardinal values is the pleasure-principle.

That ethos (I am using Clifford Geertz's definition: ''the tone, character, and quality of. . . life, its moral and aesthetic style and mood'') explains why the grim ritual about to take place is turned into a frolicsome occasion. It in turn explains Elesin's act of hamartia. At the beginning, Elesin enters the market ''pursued by his drummers and praise-singers.'' Borne aloft by the combined intoxicants of music, dance, spell-binding chants, and admiring women, Elesin's passage, which should have been a progression in inward withdrawal, gathers more and more momentum in aggressiveness. The momentum might have seen him through the combat with death, for which he needs all his heroic energy; but it is deflected into breaking a hymen. Having wasted much of his ''vital flow'' in this enterprise, it is not surprising that the reserve is insufficient for the main battle shortly afterwards. From now on, disasters follow in ever greater magnitude; an action started as a ritual performance to secure the world in its metaphysical moorings completes itself in tipping that world over into the void. The ethical and dramatic processes by which this happens is complex but can be outlined. In effect, what Elesin attempts to do is to reconstruct and reinvent the ritual by adding the marriage to it and thereby inscribe his own personality into its processes. And has has been noted, that personality is essentially a

sensual one—one that is perpetually seeking to aestheticize the ethical and the spiritual. In this, he is aided by his knowledge of the nature of Yoruba public ceremonies: their flexibility which allows for personal intervention and improvisation so that a bold man can ''dance'' at the edge of propriety. In such an ethically fluid situation, only the outcome of such ''playing'' with the festival process and turning it into a spectacle of personal power display can determine whether the boundaries have been transgressed.

This may have been impossible for his spectators to judge, but it is not for the readers of the play: we know that Elesin's motives for improvising on and reconstructing the ritual are morally suspect. Now, as is implicit in Aristotle, initiating an action is one thing, guaranteeing its successful eventual outcome quite another. The risk is greater because the purity of motive for an action cannot in itself ensure its success. So in drama, the failure of an action whose initial motivation was morally suspect reduces the tragic stature of the actor, for it makes us feel somewhat that the punishment is well deserved. Elesin therefore suffers from the delusion of his own invincibility. He thinks that he is totally free to invent the rules as he goes along, still arriving at the appointed end. He also assumes that his power to control things—including his power of self-control—is limitless. He has forgotten, or neglected, the fact that rituals have taboos. Observance of such taboos, especially ones that have to do with the sensual appetites, gives the power of mastery over the self and other forces; to break the taboos, however, is not only to frustrate the desired end, but also positively to invite disaster.

Yet to ask how Elesin came under the delusion of total power and freedom, to the point where he wreaks so much havoc on himself and his community, is to implicate that community as well as its ethos which sanctions certain forms of morally ambiguous action in its leaders. If Elesin is guilty of self-indulgence, the community indulged him. When Iyaloja confronts a disgraced and humiliated Elesin, she lashes out: ''We called you leader and oh, how you led us on.'' Her tone here should be a mixture of anger and regret, for the leading on is mutual. Earlier (Act I), when Elesin's predatory and indiscriminate sexuality is praised, the women chorus ''Ba-a-a-ba O!'' in ecstatic admiration. In other words, this behavior is expected of him—and encouraged. It is characteristic of his class and sanctioned by the ethos of his culture, both of which he is product and, because of his exalted position, producer. When he makes his impulsive demand for the girl, the women do not judge that demand improper; they protest only that the girl is betrothed. Ultimately they reason that the union is honorable, desirable even, considering the end that they hope it would serve. The contrived marriage therefore has its source in the ethics and metaphysics of the culture. The action is equivocal, but the ethical preference for satiation over abstinence leads all into mistaking an egotistic demand for an altruistic gesture. Elesin's action is not the private sin of betrayal that Iyaloja later makes it out to be, but a collective error resulting from the interplay of character, the pressure of the occasion, and the ethical values of the culture. The error reveals that the ethical values are now gravely flawed.

We may account for this negative state of affairs by going back to the warrior ethic. As outlined earlier, the ethic operates in a heroic society that needs to send out its men to die in its defense. As the warriors become a special class, their special privileges and status become part of the social definition of that class, even in times of peace. In the post-empire, post-heroic Oyo society, the military obligation became transformed into a politico-religious one performed by the olokun esin alone. This change in character and significance of the warlord's obligation also implies that more spiritual than physical resources are needed. In other words, a ritual suicide requires the dousing of the fires of desire and withdrawal from the world (though not its denial). The ritual that Elesin is called upon to go through is oriented to the other world and therefore requires strictly controlled and austere actions; yet his progress through the market—a metaphor for his journey through life so far—is nothing but spontaneous and sensual, a warrior-rake's progress, not an ascetic's. The ascetic's telos has thus been superimposed on and mixed with the warrior's lifestyle. Having spent all his life as a sensualist, he is now asked to spiritualize his body plus all its appetites. His tragic error and subsequent inability to die are therefore inevitable. And the failure suddenly reveals that, in the culture, not only has a wide gulf separated the religious from the ethical and both from the political, but also that all three are set one against the other. Thus, Elesin's having his way with the girl and over Iyaloja's feeble protest is a victory for the culture's political order (subjugation of women), achieved at the expense of its spirituality. And because it lacks any spirituality, the act is banal. At this point in its history, it has squeezed out much of the spiritual

predisposition conducive to a strategic renunciation of the world.

If his charmed audience in the market could have listened more attentively, it would have detected the melancholy undertone of longing and regret in Elesin's very sensuous description of the sensual life he has lived:

> The world is not a constant honey-pot.
> Where I found little I made do with little.
> Where there was plenty I gorged myself.
> We shared the choicest of the season's
> Harvest of yams. How my friend would read
> Desire in my eyes before I knew the cause

However rare, however precious, it was mine. Put simply, Elesin overdramatizes his eagerness to go in order to hide his reluctance—even from himself. Pilkings might be a bungling do-gooder, but he perceives this underlying psychological truth about the culture when he reminds Elesin of the saying among his people:

> The elder grimly approaches heaven and you ask
>   him to bear your
> greetings yonder; do you really think he makes the
>   journey willingly?

Which truth Elesin himself admits to his unfortunate bride a few moments later. . . .

Related to the reluctance to let go of the honey-pot that Elesin's life has been is another cultural contradiction dramatized in the play: the true position of women. Iyaloja's towering role easily blinds us to women's essentially inferior position in the culture. In spite of her, or even with her active connivance, Elesin's relationship with the women shows a distorted application of the warrior ethic. In the heroic society the warrior is the protector of his community's women, but the ravisher of those of enemy communities. In the absence of that enemy community, Elesin lays siege on the chastity of the women of his own community. He rationalizes his demand for the girl, and after a few tense, awkward moments, Iyaloja is persuaded. The political meaning of her consent is simply that it is not Elesin but the girl who is being sacrificed so that their (Elesin and Iyaloja's) world may stay on its ancient course. Literally, the act violates the girl's purity; symbolically, it violates the ethical sanctity and pure form of the ritual and of the culture behind it. We are not sure that Iyaloja fully realizes this even in her moment of discovery, revealed later in the great speech on Elesin's betrayal of sacred trust. This speech can be read ironically, the irony being the playwright's on Iyaloja. A pointer to this is that she has nothing to say to the girl, who, incidentally, remains voiceless throughout—and nameless: she is denied this least of personal/social identities. In the name of the metaphysical destiny and the political status quo, both ride rough-shod over an individual's happiness and integrity, because the culture says that that individual herself is expendable. Iyaloja's consent to Elesin's demand is a betrayal of her son and it comments on the reality of the society-individual relationship in the culture. But more significantly, it is part of the youth-senescence conflict in the play.

Youth-senescence conflict is recurrent in Soyinka's drama, taking different forms: father-son (or their surrogates); conservative authority–rebellious youth, etc. These conflicts usually end up in either a stalemate or a defeat of youth, or in general anarchy. Soyinka's criticism has not yet paid much attention to this motif and its wider psycho-social meanings and dimensions. This is not the place for that, however. Suffice it to remark here that in *DKH* the displacement of the girl's fiancée and usurpation of his role by tyrannical senescence is avenged with devastating tragic irony later, and with more catastrophic consequences for the community: Olunde displaces his own father and usurps his role where it matters most to the culture (the two halves of this compound irony, one occurring near the beginning and the other close to the end, also provide poetic justice and aesthetic balance in the play). He does more: he takes revenge on behalf of the young man (and all young men) who has been dispossessed of his fiancée. Olunde's act completely destroys Elesin's masculinity, heroic stature, and status: all of his manhood and therefore occupation.

This analysis has so far concentrated on the internal workings of the culture—and therefore on the internal logic of the tragic action of the play. Where does the external (colonial) factor come in then, if at all? It is true that the District Officer intervenes to "stop" Elesin; but as the author, the play, and this analysis so far all insist, that intervention is superfluous. It does no more than provide Elesin with a lame—and soon discarded—excuse. The colonial factor does not come in directly. But since the internal workings of its own culture provide an opposite and alternative metaphysics, ethics, and worldview, the colonial presence in the vicinity alone is enough to undermine the self-confidence of the native culture and expose the limited power of its symbols. In the play, the metaphysical power of the native culture is symbolized in the egungun cult, its political power represented by the Elesin lineage. (At death, Elesin too,

of course, becomes an ancestor to be incarnated in the egungun.)

There are two parallel sequences of action going on in the play: one at the market place, the other at the District Officer's bungalow (later moved to the Residency). But instead of keeping the sequences apart until the climax, the playwright juxtaposes an event in one sequence with one in the other, so that the two otherwise unrelated events can provide reverse mirror images of one another. At any rate, this effect is produced in the sudden transition of scenes between Acts I and II. In Act I we have the great celebrative affirmation of the power of the metaphysical/political universe of the native culture; Act II goes straight into showing that the Pilkingses have turned the dress of the dreaded egungun cult into a mere fancy-dress. Surely Soyinka intends to show more than another instance of desecration here: the juxtaposition is an implicit and objective comment on the limitations of the metaphysical power which that cult symbolizes, Amusa's terror notwithstanding. Indeed, considered within the strict ironic objectivity of the play, Pilkings is right to be disappointed in Amusa's continued belief in "any mumbo-jumbo." After all, Amusa himself had helped arrest the cult leaders—with impunity. In addition to incarnating the dead, the egungun cult also performed judicial functions; the colonial police is the new egungun cult—the representatives of the new power—in fancy dress:

RESIDENT . . . Hey, didn't we give them some
　　colourful fez hats with all those wavy
　　things, yes, pink tassels. . . .

The old egungun was arrested by the new with impunity, and Pilkings, the leader of the new cult, further undermines its metaphysical power when he assimilates its symbol into his own secular culture. And, most ironic of all, all these parallel and mutually contradictory actions have in common the element of transformation. Of course, the old culture avenges itself by having the new egungun (i.e., the Native Authority Police) desecrated in turn in the market, but there is no doubt where greater damage has been done.

The questioning and undermining of the potency and self-confidence of the one culture by mere presence of the other is also there in the tangle between Elesin and Pilkings over Olunde. What is important here is not that Olunde escapes to England, but that Pilkings wins with impunity—just as he wears the egungun dress with impunity. The point is not lost on Joseph:

Oh no, master is white man. And good christian.
Black man juju can't touch master.

The conflict itself plus its long-term outcome also constitute a complete tragic irony that is the complementary opposite of the other self-contained unit of the usurpation motif noted earlier. Pilkings's victory at first threatens to put an end to the great symbolic action of ritual suicide which the Elesin lineage must carry on. But when Olunde suddenly returns and willingly takes his reluctant father's place, that victory appears only temporary. Olunde's suicide may have redeemed family honor and racial pride, demonstrated the pristine strength of the heroic ethic, and thwarted Pilkings's design of making a fine doctor of him, but it makes the latter's victory total and permanent: there is no living son to initiate into the secret power of the lineage. With his death the ritual bridge that links the world with those of the unborn and the dead is cut at both ends.

But perhaps the playwright's deliberate selection and arrangement of events to portray the culture ironically is most evident in the Prince's visit, which ''just happens'' to be on the night Elesin is ''committing death.'' In the chronology of events in the play, the masque at the Residency and Elesin's passage through the metaphysical abyss are taking place simultaneously. However, although separated in space, the two events are brought together—for comparison and contrast—in the impromptu debate between Olunde and Jane Pilkings. This debate is so subtle and economical in the way in reveals Olunde's character, so complex in its relation to all that comes before and after, that this writer considers it crucial to any deep understanding of the play.

After four years in England, Olunde returns expecting only to see—and bury—his father's body. But we have to understand why a man who escaped from the ''fatal'' clutch of tradition and who is being educated for higher things in the metropole should still acknowledge the claim of tradition; his character, too, has to be further established, in preparation for his resolute act later on. Hence the impromptu debate. In it Olunde manages to reveal what he has learned from British conduct in the war: moral courage on the part of a leadership that can unhesitatingly sacrifice itself on behalf of society when that society's survival is at risk. This was exemplified recently in the action of the captain of the warship, and right now in the Prince's visit. Olunde's witnessing of these acts of moral and physical courage in the British leadership has strengthened his belief in the rightness of what his father has to do. But Olunde has been away for four

years and has also been disowned by his father. He is, in other words, an exile. It is from this position that he finds the intellectual conviction to perform the act which his father, a complete insider, is unable to do. His act shows tremendous will-power and even proves the pristine, if residual, strength of the culture's worldview. But its conviction is part-intellectual and part-derived from outside; to that extent it lacks the spontaneous purity and intuited certainty with which Elesin should have performed it.

The debate also further reveals the essential aspect of Olunde's character that has troubled the Pilkingses, and which his resolute act later confirms. Strong-willed, austere, introspective and deep, he shows traits of self-renunciation and asceticism which are more suitable for the great task of the Elesin lineage. In this regard, his being the polar opposite of (and therefore foil to) his father is further ironic commentary on the state of the culture: in its present actuality, such spiritual qualities, like the girl's purity, are wasted. The colonial factor, then, serves in the play no more than as a historical mirror which reflects the moribund and impotent state of the native ethics at this time in history.

In conclusion, the argument of this essay may be summarized as follows: The drama of *DKH* centers on Elesin's actions and the conditions which make them possible, all of which together constitute the actual form and functioning state of his culture at that point in time. The irreconcilable contradictions between its different cardinal ideals, and between those ideals and reality, have become so strong that they overwhelm and destroy the major ritual that symbolizes and guarantees its political power. In fiction, if not in reality, tragedy is often the form in which such a situation plays itself out. After the exhaustion, the way is clear for a new beginning. Thus, paradoxically enough, it is Elesin's ritual-negating actions, and not Olunde's salvaging gesture, which make possible that new beginning. This essential function of tragedy tells us that Soyinka, above everything else, is in this play most concerned with the need for a new ethical beginning more appropriate for the new historical and social circumstances. This is the symbolic import and message of the new life taking root in the innocent girl's womb. That child is Elesin's. So, then, in more ways than one, Elesin is in truth ''the human vehicle'' of ''the metaphysical confrontation'' that is necessary for the renewal of ''the universe of the Yoruba mind.''

Source: Wole Ogundele, "'Death and the King's Horse-man': A poet's quarrel with his culture," in *Research in African Literatures,* Vol. 25, No. 1, Spring, 1994, p 47.

Adebayo Williams

In the following essay, Williams uses the concept of the political unconscious in its examination of the political function of rituals.

In feudal societies, ritual was part of the cultural dominant. In other words, ritual was part of a complex and insidious apparatus of cultural and political reproduction employed by the dominant groups. It is to be expected, given the superannuation of the feudal mode of production in Western societies, that the phenomenon of ritual itself would have lost much of its power and social efficacy. There is a sense in which this development cannot be divorced from the gains of the Enlightenment and the triumph of rationality. From the eighteenth century, scientific reasoning seemed to have gained ascendancy over the imaginative apprehension of reality. This ascendancy, which also reflected the triumph of the bourgeois world-view in Europe (along with its radical impatience for ancient myths and rituals) received perhaps its classic formulation from Karl Marx. According to him, "all mythology overcomes and dominates and shapes the forces of nature in and through the imagination, hence it disappears as soon as man gains mastery over the forces of nature"....

Yet this notwithstanding, it is also obvious that within the context of post-colonial cultural politics, the entire concept of ritual has become a casualty of linguistic imperialism—a Eurocentric, unilinear notion of historical development which negates the other by a forcible evacuation of its space. Thus, in the industrial and scientific age, ritual has acquired the pejorative connotation of a meaningless exercise, a mundane routine. But if any meaningful intellectual encounter between Western societies and the emergent post-colonial cultures of the Third World is to take place, such "emptied" spaces must be recontested with a view to directing people's attention to this profoundly subtle hegemonic assault. To do this is to problematize the very concept of ritual. The first step in this process would be to return ritual to its sacred origins, that is, to see it as an aspect of symbolic thinking which Mircea Eliade regards as sharing the same substance with human existence. Ritual, then, in the words of Ake Hulkrantz, is a "fixed, usually solemn behaviour that is repeated in certain situations. Anthropologists like to call the latter 'crisis situations,' but there is not always any crisis involved. It would be better to speak of sacred situations in Durkheim's spirit"....

For people in pre-industrial societies, rituals served as a vehicle for reestablishing contact with the ontological essence of the tribe. On the sacred nature of rituals, Eliade is again invaluable when he notes that "rituals are given sanctification and rationalization in a culture by being referred to supposedly divine prototypes. Rituals periodically reconfirm the sacredness of their origins and reestablish 'sacred' (as opposed to 'profane') time for the community performing the rituals"....

As can be seen from this line of argument, rituals are expressions of human needs and desires; they are also instrumental in satisfying such needs and desires. Since human needs are varied, there will be several prototypes of rituals to take care of them. Whatever the form ritual might take, it is clear that human sacrifice is its most severe and extreme form. Several rationales have been advanced to explain the phenomenon of human sacrifice. They range from the need for a reactualization of direct relations between a people and their god to a drive towards the seasonal regeneration of sacred forces. Although the precise function of this undeniably harsh ritual might vary from place to place, it too is a function of social needs.

Many African writers have had recourse to ritual in refuting assumptions about Western cultural superiority. In Chinua Achebe's *Things Fall Apart,* for example, the suicide of Okonkwo is part of a complex ritual of atonement and reassertion of the collective will. In *Arrow of God,* the main crisis is triggered by the imminent repudiation of the sacred ritual of yam-eating. On another level, there is an ideological simulation of ritual suicide in the fate that befalls Clarence, the protagonist in Camara Laye's *The Radiance of the King* and in the horrific mutilations that abound in Yambo Ouologuem's *Bound to Violence.* All these episodes constitute nothing less than the deployment of ritual in a desperate cultural offensive. The mythicization of historical events and prominent figures by some African writers is part of this renewed attempt to discover an authentic African heritage.

But of all these writers, none has been more consistent and unapologetic in the enlistment of ritual for ideological purposes than Wole Soyinka. Soyinka is, by critical consensus, a writer of forbidding depth and complexity. A substantial part of this complexity derives from his deep communion with the cultural paradigms of his people, the Yoruba:

their mores, their myths, and above all their rituals. In an insightful appraisal of Soyinka's work, Stanley Macebuh has noted that "for him 'history' has not been so much a record of human action as a demonstration of the manner in which social behaviour so often symbolizes a sometimes voluntary, sometimes unwilling obedience to the subliminal impulse of the ancestral memory." It is not surprising, then, that ritual should play such a crucial role both as an ideological strategy and as a formal category in most of Soyinka's works. A random sample is instructive: the death of Eman, the protagonist of *The Strong Breed;* the killing of the Old Man in *Madmen and Specialists;* the sacrifice of Pentheus in his adaptation of Euripides's *The Bacchae;* the mental and physical destruction of Sekoni in *The Interpreters;* and the annihilation of the Professor in *The Road.* All of these incidents have strong ritualistic overtones.

I have analyzed the political implications of Soyinka's penchant for the mythic resolution of actual contradictions as well as the shortcomings of the historicist opposition to this position (Williams "Mythic Imagination"). It is in *Death and the King's Horseman* that we find Soyinka's most explicit deployment of ritual both as an organizing principle and as a surgical instrument for prizing open a people's collective consciousness at a crucial moment of their historical development. The crisis in the play stems from an acute political and psychological threat to the ritual of human sacrifice. This is indeed a critical moment of history, and since the play is a refraction of an actual historical event, it is bound to provide the playwright with an appropriate forum for seminal reflections on a communal impasse. Yet it is important to unravel the deeper ideological necessity behind the ritual in *Death and the King's Horseman,* that is, the actual collective "narrative" of which it is socially symbolic or, to employ the terminology of structural linguistics, the communal "langue" behind the author's "parole." To do this is to inquire into the political reality of the "political unconscious" behind both the social text itself and the playwright's textualization of it in his play.

The idea of a political unconscious as a corollary for the collective consciousness is not a new one. Its hazy outlines can be glimpsed in the works of Sigmund Freud and Carl Jung. In fact, Freud's concept of repression (i.e., the specific mechanism by means of which individuals and societies alike suppress hostile and intolerable truths as a strategy for containing or postponing confrontations with

> " . . . IT IS ALSO OBVIOUS THAT WITHIN THE CONTEXT OF POST-COLONIAL CULTURAL POLITICS, THE ENTIRE CONCEPT OF RITUAL HAS BECOME A CASUALTY OF LINGUISTIC IMPERIALISM—A EUROCENTRIC, UNILINEAR NOTION OF HISTORICAL DEVELOPMENT WHICH NEGATES THE OTHER BY A FORCIBLE EVACUATION OF ITS SPACE."

reality) actually foreshadows the theory of the political unconscious.

The political unconscious is inseparable from a theory of culture, for culture, being the material, intellectual, and spiritual totality of a people's way of life, normally sets the pace and the terms for whatever passes into the realm of the political unconscious. But culture itself is always an unstable totality mediated by a whole range of countervailing forces. In a diachronic sense, these forces are often hostile accretions from an earlier cultural mode or developments within the society whose sheer incompatibility with the dominant order might be symptomatic of newer modes struggling to come into existence. Raymond Williams has described these forces as the residual and the emergent.

But the diachronic analysis does not exhaust the possibilities of the countervailing forces. Existing synchronically with the dominant order are tendencies that portend fractures within this order. By virtue of the fact that it is often a reaction to urgent existential dilemmas, the political unconscious is clearly involved with these synchronic forces. Although it is tempting to see the political unconscious as one more instrument for furthering the hegemonic ambitions of the dominant classes, this is not necessarily the case, because the political unconscious has a utopian dimension, enabling it to serve social needs that transcend class barriers. A particular ritual might well serve the political interests of the dominant class, but it can at the same time serve the psychological needs of the dominated class, and in a situation of revolutionary rupture within society, it is possible for the psychological to prevail over the political.

It has been suggested that Freud himself was prevented by a combination of historical and ideological circumstances from realizing the true significance of his great discovery and from pressing it to its logical conclusion. Imprisoned within the self-legitimizing snares of a stable and relatively prosperous bourgeois society, denied the beneficial insight of a major historical rupture within his society, Freud was content with transferring political and social unease to psychological categories. In other words, Freud himself was a victim of the political unconscious.

In recent times, the most accomplished theorist of the political unconscious is Fredric Jameson, the influential American Marxist scholar. Drawing sustenance from disparate sources including Levi-Strauss, Freud, Foucault, Greimas, Lyotard, and Althusser, Jameson's *The Political Unconscious: Narrative as a Socially Symbolic Act* makes a rigorous case for an overtly political interpretation of all works of art. His thesis is that, since narrative is nothing but a specific mechanism through which the collective consciousness (as expressed through the "parole" of the artist) represses harsh historical contradictions, the overriding task of criticism is to confront the political unconscious of the narrative with the Real.

Two important points emerge from Jameson's approach to the problem. First, he ascribes a collective function to narrative. Appropriating Wittgenstein's seminal insight into the social nature of language, he posits that we cannot imagine a story or indeed its narrator without at the same time imagining the society from which both of them spring. Second, in a direct polemical riposte to conventional Marxists, Jameson avers that the repression of uncomfortable truths is not just a function of the hegemonic classes in human societies, but that it is also adopted by the oppressed as a strategy for survival. In an interesting gloss on this point, William Dowling notes that "for Jameson as a Marxist this is not, of course, some dark, paranoid fantasy: it is the nightmare of history itself as men and women have always lived it, a nightmare that must be repressed as a condition of psychological survival not only by the master but also by the slave, not only by the bourgeoisie but also by the proletariat"....

Jameson's indebtedness to Levi-Strauss's "The Structural Analysis of Myth" is obvious. In his study of the facial decorations of the Caduveo Indians, Levi-Strauss advances the thesis that the cultural artifact is nothing but the symbolic resolution of a real contradiction, a strategy for containing on the imaginary plane an intolerable concrete dilemma—in this case, the contradictions inherent in a rigidly hierarchical society. Equally obvious is Jameson's indebtedness to Althusser's celebrated definition of ideology as "the imaginary representation of the subject's relationship to his or her real conditions of existence"....

For Althusser as for Jameson, ideology is not the monstrous concoction of oppressive classes in oppressive societies; it is a trans-historical and supra-class phenomenon. Ideology is "not just mystification (that is, something that obscures the real relations of things in the world) but essential mystification; one could not imagine a human society without it." Althusser's original insight into the dynamics of ideology and Jameson's judicious appropriation of it, constitute a mortal blow to what the latter, in a different context, has dismissed as the "luxury of old-fashioned ideological critique." Taken together, Althusser and Jameson can be seen to have opened up new frontiers for radical aesthetics and for the possibility of profoundly subtle and sophisticated analyses of an author and his text's insertion within what Althusser has described as the "interpellation"....

The political unconscious, then, is the realm of collective day-dreaming or mass fantasy. It is hardly a simple affair, since it involves active struggles on the psychological and political planes. Indeed, it becomes extremely problematic when it involves artistic refractions of what lies within the political unconscious. An artist's relationship with his or her society is often complex, more so if the artist is as politically aware, as culturally conscious, and as intellectually combative as Soyinka.

Jameson's cautionary note is instructive. For him, "daydreaming and wish-fulfilling fantasy are by no means a simple operation, available at any time or place for the taking of a thought. Rather, they involve mechanisms whose inspection may have something further to tell us about the otherwise inconceivable link between desire and history"....

To be sure, Jameson is not without his critics. Some accuse him of confusion and eclectic opportunism both in his theorization of the concept of the political unconscious and in his application of it.

According to some of his critics, he often relapses into a theological Marxism by treating arguable hypotheses as "apodictic categories." Robert Kantor and Joel Weinsheimer make the same point. In perhaps the most sustained statement of these objections, Brom Anderson charges Jameson with "a profoundly apolitical millenarianism." Such objections notwithstanding, the theory of the political unconscious remains a powerful weapon for plotting the dynamics between the surface characteristics of a work of art and its deeper ideological structure.

Within Soyinka's corpus, *Death and the King's Horseman* has achieved the status of a classic. Critics with a formalist bias have hailed its superb characterization, its haunting beauty, and above all its lyrical grandeur, although an oppositional critic such as Biodun Jeyifo has objected to the lyrical beauty of the play on the ideological ground that it seduces us into accepting what he considers to be Soyinka's reactionary worldview in the play. Kyalo Mativo has even gone so far as to observe that "when great form is not in service of great content, it is fraud." I have addressed these objections elsewhere ("Marxian Epistemology" and "Marxism"), but whatever the case might be, even the objections reinforce the consensus view that the play is possibly the most intensely poetic of all Soyinka's dramatic writings.

Written during a period of exile and existential anguish, the play derives its powerful dynamics from Soyinka's first attempt to grapple directly on the creative level with the "colonial question"—a question that obsessed his literary peers on the continent for over two decades. The playwright's contemptuous dismissal of "hidebound chronologues" notwithstanding, *Death and the King's Horseman* is the creative equivalent of a return of the repressed. In this play, Soyinka manages to capture the power and glory of the ancient Yoruba state in its dying moment. At the same time, he poses a serious intellectual challenge to those who would deny a conquered people their unique mode of apprehending and making sense of reality.

Death and the King's Horseman represents an attempt to confront on a creative level the arrogance and cultural chauvinism of Western imperialism. Soyinka himself has taken umbrage at the "reductionist tendency" that views the dramatic tension in his play as having arisen from "a clash of cultures." According to him, this "prejudicial label. . . presupposes a potential equality in every

given situation of the alien culture and the indigenous, on the actual soil of the latter" ("Author's Note"). The bitterly polemical tone of this rebuttal illustrates the extent to which Soyinka's threnodic temperament is affronted by mundane cultural equations. Yet by exploring the sacred terror of ritual suicide within the context of the cynicism and cultural dessications of the colonialists, Soyinka is engaged in nothing less than a sublime cultural battle. By counterposing the notion of honor in the ancient Yoruba kingdom (as seen in the tragic career of its principal custodian of culture) against the cynical presumptions and calculations of the colonial officials, Soyinka exposes the absurdity inherent in all assumptions of cultural superiority.

Death and the King's Horseman opens with a grand panorama of the Yoruba market place. Here, Soyinka deploys all his artistic power to paint a picture of grandeur and vitality. According to an old Yoruba saying, "The world is a market place; heaven is home." Apart from its obvious economic importance, the market occupies a signal cultural, political, and spiritual position in the Yoruba cosmos. First, it is a site of political and cultural ferment. Second, it doubles as that numinous zone in which the distinction between the world of the dead and that of the living is abolished. The ancient Yoruba saying captures this crucial contiguity. In most Yoruba towns, the evening market is regarded as the most important, and before the advent of electricity, it was a most eerie sight indeed. Moreover, the market serves as a barometer for the spiritual and psychic health of the community. The most important communal rites are carried out there. It was therefore a stroke of genius to focus on the market place at the beginning of the play. But even here there is a profound irony, for what is going on between the indigenous culture and the alien culture runs counter to the natural logic of the market—a forum for buying and selling. We are confronted with the bizarre phenomenon of a culture that insists upon forcing its hardware on another culture without making a commensurate purchase in return.

The crisis in the play is thus predicated on what is known in economics as a trade imbalance or as a trade deficit between the conqueror's culture and that of the conquered. The praise-singer, in a moving dialogue with Elesin, captures the angst and spiritual anguish of his people:

> Our world was never wrenched from
> Its true course. . . . [I]f that world leaves
> its course and smashes on the boulders
> of great void, whose world will

give us shelter?

Behind the unease and anguish of this intensely poetic lamentation lie the sympathies of the playwright himself. His very choice of images, "wrench," "boulders," and "void" betrays a starkly apocalyptic mood.

Against this turbulent background one must situate the vexatious dynamics that transform Elesin, an otherwise minor cultural functionary of the ruling class, into a world-historic role as the deliverer of his people. Precisely because his suicide is supposed to compel respect for the integrity and inviolability of a besieged culture, Elesin's routine function takes on a major historical and political burden. For the people, the success or failure of the ritual therefore becomes a matter of life and death. Here is the classic example of a particular ritual that, under historical pressure, transcends its original cultural signification to assume a greater political and spiritual significance.

Yet, if historical circumstances compel a particular ritual to serve purposes more complex than its original ones, how can the same circumstances transform a minor figure into a major historical personage? Indeed, the reverse is often the case. Karl Marx's brilliant comparison of the two Bonapartes comes to mind: "[The French] have not only a caricature of the old Napoleon, they have the old Napoleon himself, caricatured as he must appear in the middle of the nineteenth century." In an interesting gloss on this passage, Terry Eagleton observes: "Bonaparte is not just a parody of Napoleon; he is Napoleon parodying himself. He is the real thing dressed up as false, not just the false thing tricked out as real. What is in question now is not a regressive caricature but a caricaturing regression". . . .

So it is with Elesin. And this is the source of the collective and individual tragedy in *Death and the King's Horseman*. Elesin's consciousness has been shaped by the dialectic of his material and political circumstances. If he appears weak, vacillating, self-pitying, self-dramatizing, and self-indulgent, it is because the old Empire has exhausted itself. If he is cynically preoccupied with pleasure and the spoils of office, if he is skeptical about the credibility of his destiny, his attitude is not unrelated to the fact that the hegemony of the empire had long ago been fissured by internal contradictions as well as by the antagonistic logic supplied by the conquering invaders. As evident in the play, the crumbling empire has already been thoroughly infiltrated by the "other"

empire and its various fetishes of political authority and cultural power: batons, bands, balls, cells, gramophones, etc. In a rather resentful categorization of the opulence of the Residency, Soyinka comes close to the truth when he describes it as being "redolent of the tawdry decadence of a far-flung but key imperial frontier". . . .

In its dying moment, the empire can only produce an Elesin, a pathetic but ultimately subversive caricature of his illustrious forebears. In the light of this insight, it is difficult to agree with Jeyifo when he asserts that "the play never really dramatises either the force of Elesin's personality or the inevitability of his action." In actuality, there is no force to dramatize; it is absent from Elesin's personality. It is paradoxical that a Marxist critic should slip into the bourgeois notion that history and literature are no more than the study of the acts of great men. A genuinely materialist aesthetics must not be fixated on great personalities; on the contrary, it must strive to relocate personalities within the social and historical forces which engendered them in the first instance. The character of Elesin is an acute reflection of these forces at play.

In this context, it would be utopian to expect him, a critically misendowed man, to surmount the overwhelming historical and social forces ranged against him. To expect such an act is to expect the impossible. That the playwright fails to recognize this fact demonstrates the extent to which his own imagination has been colored by the lingering efficacy of the ideological apparatus of the old Yoruba state. Indeed, in an attempt to resist the mundane forces of concrete history, Soyinka is compelled to look beyond Elesin to his son, Olunde, who is perhaps the most sensitively drawn character in the play. He is the ideological spokesman for the playwright, who is obviously in profound sympathy with the young man's aspirations. Olunde's material and historical circumstances are quite different from his father's. He is armed with immense personal courage and conviction; and his considerable intellect has been honed by a sustained contact with the alien culture in all its contradictions and foibles. He is therefore a perfect match and counterfoil to the arrogance and chauvinism of the colonial administrators. As he tells Mrs. Pilkings: "You forget that I have now spent four years among your people. I discovered that you have no respect for what you do not understand." In another cutting riposte, he exclaims with bitter irony, "You believe that everything which appears to make sense was learnt from you". . . .

Consumed by his contempt and hatred for the hypocrisy and cant of Western civilization, bewildered by his father's lack of honor, Olunde chooses suicide as a means of redeeming the honor of his society and of expiating what must have seemed to him as his father's abominable cowardice and treachery. But rather than alleviating the burden of the people, Olunde's suicide only compounds their misery. The praise-singer again captures this moment of historic stress:

> What the end will be, we are not
> gods to tell. But this young shoot has
> poured its sap into the parent stalk,
> and we know this is not the way
> of life. Our world is tumbling in
> the void of strangers.

Yet despite the enormous integrity of Olunde's self-sacrifice, it is difficult to identify the point at which his role as a cultural hero ends and where his role as the rearguard defender of a backward-looking political order prevails. But Soyinka does not leave us in doubt as to his conviction that, if suicide is the ultimate option available to Africa's revolutionary intelligentsia in the struggle for a cultural revalidation of the continent, it must be embraced without flinching.

This position engenders profound ideological difficulties. To start with, it lays itself open to the charge of promoting a cult of romantic suicide. To leftwing critics, Olunde, by terminating his own life, has succumbed to the whims of a reactionary culture and a flagrantly feudalistic ethos. Indeed, for critics of this persuasion, there might be something paradoxically progressive in Elesin's refusal to honor his oath. Jeyifo is precise and uncompromising on this point. According to him, "The notion of honour (and integrity and dignity) for which Soyinka provides a metaphysical rationalisation rests on the patriarchal, feudalist code of the ancient Oyo kingdom, a code built on class entrenchment and class consolidation". . . .

It is necessary at this point to probe further, to "problematize" these various antithetical positions. The first step towards accomplishing this goal will be to counterpose Jameson's doctrine of the political unconscious against Jeyifo's instrumentalist Marxist objection to Soyinka's ideological thrust. As it is, the Elesin ritual is a projection of a people's collective consciousness. Elesin's suicide is designed to facilitate the smooth transition of the departing king from the world of the living to the world of the dead. Even for departing royalties, solitude might be a terrifying prospect in what

Soyinka himself often somberly refers to as the "the abyss of transition." As the Iyaloja, the unwavering matriarch of culture and tradition, explains:

> He knows the meaning of a king's passage;
> he was not born yesterday. He knows
> the peril to the race when our dead
> father who goes as intermediary,
> waits and waits and knows he is
> betrayed. . . . He knows he has condemned our
> king to wander in
> the void of evil with beings who are enemies
> of life. . . .

In Yoruba culture, a king never "dies." A king wandering "in the void" is therefore an abomination, a serious threat to life and communal well-being. Thus, insofar as Elesin's suicide is conceived to usher the departed king into his new kingdom, it is a crucial ritual of continuity, well-being, and hope; hence, the collective anxiety about the dire consequences of its abortion. Yet as Jameson has contended, a political unconscious always coexists uneasily with even the most apparently innocent manifestations of a people's collective consciousness. The question then becomes: What is the political unconscious behind Elesin's ritual and Soyinka's fabulization of it? In other words, what is the historical contradiction for which the Elesin ritual is supposed to be a symbolic resolution?

On one level, the ritual suicide of Elesin is supposed to take the sting out of the trauma of death by enacting the drama of a privileged carrier who willingly undertakes the journey to the unknown. This act in itself might serve to assuage the people's collective anxiety about being forsaken as a result of the departure of the father of the "tribe." On another level, the ritual might well signify a symbolic conquest of death itself. For in the absence of viable oppositional forces in the community, Death becomes the distinguished scourge and ultimate terror of the ruling class: unconquerable, unanswerable, firm, unsmiling.

The Elesin ritual, then, magically transforms death into an ally of the rulers. In death, the power and grandeur of the rulers remain. The transition of individual kings is thus immaterial: the kingdom remains unassailable. Erich Auerbach regards the poetry of Homer as performing analogous functions for the ancient Greek aristocracy. According to him: ". . . rather than an impression of historical change, Homer evokes the illusion of an unchanging society, a basically stable order, in comparison with which the succession of individuals and changes in personal fortunes appear unimportant." Similarly, the Elesin ritual is designed to reconcile the people of the ancient Oyo empire to the supremacy, invincibility, and divine nature of what is essentially a feudal society. It is a socially symbolic act insofar as it negotiates the painful reality of death for the ruling class. Hence, the ritual suicide is one of those insidious strategies of survival and containment that Althusser has characterized as an ideological apparatus of the state. It is the political unconscious behind the Elesin ritual in *Death and the King's Horseman.*

Seen from this perspective, Jeyifo's objection is not without merit. *Death and the King's Horseman* does provide metaphysical rationalization for a patriarchal and feudalist code. The play's complicity with this order is obvious in the sense that the playwright accepts the ritual as a communal necessity. But it is not just the dominant classes that fear death. The terror of death is a common denominator in all societies; it is therefore a supra-class phenomenon. Returning to Althusser's definition of ideology, this particular maneuver of the ruling class is an essential mystification, ultimately beneficial to the entire society.

It is this utopian dimension of the Elesin ritual that Soyinka's leftwing critics have failed to comprehend. While recognizing the power and urgency of negative hermeneutics within the Marxist critical enterprise, Jameson argues that the ultimate task of Marxist criticism is to restore the utopian dimension to the work of art, that is, to view the work of art as an expression of some ultimate collective urge while not overlooking ''the narrower limits of class privilege which informs its more immediate ideological vocation.'' Jameson's conclusion bears quoting at length:

> Such a view dictates an enlarged perspective for
>   any Marxist analysis of culture,
> which can no longer be content with its
>   demystifying vocation to
> unmask and to demonstrate the ways in which a
>   cultural artifact fulfils a
> specific ideological mission, in legitimating a
>   given power structure. . . but
> [which] must also seek through and beyond this
>   demonstration of the
> instrumental function of a given cultural object, to
>   project its simultaneously
> utopian power as the symbolic affirmation of a
>   specific historical and
> class form of collectivity.

Jameson's theory has nothing to do with Durkheim's conservative notion of religious and ritual practice as a symbolic affirmation of unity in all collective entities. The failure of Durkheim's

theory stems from its fixation on the utopian impulse, a fixation that overlooks the division of all societies into dominant and dominated groups. The obverse of this inadequate approach is any criticism that simply rewrites or allegorizes a work of art in terms of Marx's insight into history as an arena of conflicts between opposing classes.

In the final analysis, what Soyinka accomplished in *Death and the King's Horseman* was to counterpose the dominant culture of the ancient Oyo kingdom against the equally hegemonic culture of the white invaders. His strategy is a brilliant, decolonizing venture. In an age characterized by new forms of cultural domination that result from the economic marginalization of the third world, such an approach might well represent a more pressing project than analyzing the class content of indigenous cultures. In a perceptive critique of Jeyifo's position on *Death and the King's Horseman,* Gareth Griffins and David Moody conclude:

> The issue here is less the correctness of Soyinka's
>   choice of subject or of the
> revolutionary character of the ''class'' of his
>   protagonists than the project
> which the choice of subject and protagonist serve.
>   It seems to us that
> Soyinka's is a profoundly de-colonising project,
>   and that Jeyifo has lost
> sight of this in his demand that an alternative
>   (although not actually
> opposed) project be undertaken by African writ-
>   ers. . . . However, the route
> forward in Nigeria, as in all post-colonial societies,
>   is in part through a
> preservation of what Soyinka has called ''self-
>   apprehension.''. . .

In *Death and the King's Horseman,* then, the playwright is an unabashed horseman (''Elesin'' in the Yoruba language) of a besieged culture, fighting a desperate battle against the cultural ''other.'' In such turbulent circumstances, he could not direct his gaze at the inequities of the traditional hierarchy, lest his resolve be weakened; neither could he bring himself to recognize that the culture he was defending had already succumbed to the alienating necessity of history, lest the rationale for mustering a stiff resistance disappear. This conflict is the political unconscious of the writer himself, and it shows its classic manifestation—Soyinka's prefatory protestations notwithstanding—in this imaginary resolution of a concrete cultural dilemma.

By the same token, his radical critics are also complicit horsemen of the cultural and post-colonial ''other.'' For by insisting on the decadent and oppressive nature of the indigenous culture, they are in ideological collusion with that genetic evolutionism and naively unilinear historicism that seeks to justify the cultural, economic, and political atrocities of colonialism as the inevitable consequence of historical "progress." This is the corollary of the teleological fallacy which regards any capitalist formation as an automatic advancement on all indigenous economic formations. It is the cardinal sin of the founding father of Marxism himself. That Karl Marx, despite his initial unease, eventually made his peace with a flagrantly bourgeois notion of historical development shows the extent to which his own sensibility was steeped in the ideological constellations of the nascent capitalist age.

Eagleton has defined succinctly Marx's epistemological impasse. According to him, "In his effort to theorize historical continuities Marx finds the evolutionist problematic closest to hand, but it is clear that it will not do. For you do not escape a naively unilinear historicism merely by reversing its direction." This lapse of consciousness in all its smug Eurocentric complacency demonstrates how all master narratives, including Marxism, are dogged by a political unconscious which derives from the logic of their own insertion into the historical process. It is the urgent task of all genuinely revolutionary post-colonial discourses to smuggle themselves into this gap in colonial narratives with a view to exploding their internal contradictions. *Death and the King's Horseman* fulfils this historic obligation. Whatever its complicity with the indigenous ruling class might be, the importance of Soyinka's classic for a viable postcolonial cultural and political praxis lies in this achievement.

Source: Adebayo Williams, "Ritual and the political unconscious: the case of 'Death and the King's Horseman,'" in *Research in African Literatures,* Vol. 24, no. 1, Spring, 1993, p. 67.

Tanure Ojaide

In the following essay, Ojaide discusses the problems of teaching an African play to English students.

Set in the colonial era (1946), written by Nigerian Wole Soyinka when a fellow at Cambridge, England in the early 1970s, and published in 1975, *Death and the King's Horseman* is not typical of works written in Africa in the 1970s, which generally deal with sociopolitical protest against government corruption. It is more like works of the late 1950s and early 1960s, which express cultural conflict between the African and European (Western) worlds.

Teaching *Death and the King's Horseman* at the University of Maiduguri in Nigeria before teaching it at both Whitman College in Walla Walla, Washington and The University of North Carolina at Charlotte, I have had the opportunity of exposing the play to a diverse student population. Ironically African literary works are classified in the West as postcolonial, but never construed so by African writers and their primary audience of Africans. In Maiduguri, as I expect in other African universities, the postcolonial discourse invented by critics in the Western academy has not caught up with teachers of African literature. African critics of African literature in Africa and some more nationalistic ones abroad speak of "post-independence African literature" instead of the postcolonial. A Nigerian poet and scholar teaching in the United States, I favor the "post-independence" classification, which emphasizes the people's responsibilities to themselves over the never-ending "postcolonial," which seems paternalistic by comparison. Writers in Africa have moved from putting blame for their fate on colonialists to taking their fate in their own hands, a sort of self-criticism.

The focus of this note is to articulate my experience of teaching *Death and the King's Horseman* at both Whitman College and The University of North Carolina at Charlotte, to bring out problems of the teacher and students, which are sometimes symbiotic, and share strategies and techniques I adopted to make the play accessible. In my experience, racial, cultural, feminist, and ideological tendencies, among others, tend to condition student responses to the play.

I have encountered two types of responses in my teaching of *Death and the King's Horseman* in America, whose academy, with others in the West, has been promoting postcoloniality. These problems are both general and specific. General problems have to do with the reception of any African literary work in America, and the specific relates to *Death and the King's Horseman* as a text.

The first general problem concerns teaching an African play in English to students used to the Euro-American literary tradition. I complicated issues in both colleges by calling Wole Soyinka "our W. S.," which reminded students of the English "W. S.," William Shakespeare. In the spring 1992 class, mainly of sophomores and seniors, a British female student and the remaining American students saw

> "IN MY EXPERIENCE, RACIAL, CULTURAL, FEMINIST, AND IDEOLOGICAL TENDENCIES, AMONG OTHERS, TEND TO CONDITION STUDENT RESPONSES TO THE PLAY."

everything in the light of Shakespeare, the touchstone of English drama. My strategy was to show Soyinka as having a double heritage of African and Western dramatic traditions. I had to explain that Soyinka is very familiar with classical Greek drama and that he studied at Leeds under the famous Shakespearean scholar Wilson Knight, who became his mentor. But in addition, the African drama in traditional terms integrates music, poetry, and dance with conventional aspects of festival or ritual. I made the students aware of Greek, Shakespearean, and modern concepts of tragedy and had to approach *Death and the King's Horseman* from the angle they understood, while showing how the play is different in being African. The tragedy in the play has on one level to do with a son superseding his father in doing his duty; this involves Olunde dying in the place of his father to save his family from disgrace. In traditional African culture, a son buries his father, not the other way around. Elesin's son dies before him. So he symbolically eats leftovers, and will have to ride through dung to the afterworld. That is his tragic failure. Seeing this, students are able to extend their knowledge of concepts of tragedy.

The second general problem I have to tackle in *Death and the King's Horseman* concerns language. Soyinka has his own indigenous African language, Yoruba, before English. A Yoruba writing in English poses problems to the American reader because of what Abiola Irele calls "the problematic relation . . . between an African work in a European language and the established conventions of Western literature." While Soyinka is able to blend Yoruba thoughts into English effortlessly, students have problems with the indigenous background of his voice. Familiar with African language systems and proverbs, I have to decode the language of the play for the students. I explain the nature and function of ritual language and the significance of proverbs in African sociocultural discourse. This

language issue directly leads to problems and strategies specific to *Death and the King's Horseman* as a unique text.

A white student at The University of North Carolina at Charlotte asked: "Is it okay to commit wrong acts in the name of tradition?" This question, illustrative of students' initial ignorance of other cultures, shows the difficulty of teaching a "postcolonial" non-Western text to American students. Students ask: "What are praise-singers?" They do not know how to pronounce the names of characters. In both Whitman College and The University of North Carolina at Charlotte the students unanimously found Act 1 difficult. A black female student at Charlotte has expressed this difficulty succinctly: "I felt thrown into the midst of a cultural event, knowing absolutely nothing." The ritualistic language poses a difficulty to the students for the first time. The symbolism of the market, which is central to the play, is not discerned when it should be, nor is that of the egungun costume.

Students need background materials about the Yoruba people and/or traditional Africa—especially the place of traditional religion in the lives of the people—to give them a gradual induction into the world of the Old Oyo Kingdom in which the play is set. (Showing a feature film on African culture can help with this.) The living and the dead in traditional Africa are closely related, and the social set-up in Africa is such that the community takes precedence over the individual: the sacrifice of an individual for the harmony of the group is traditional in many areas. A brief historical survey of Old Oyo, British colonization of Nigeria and other parts of Africa with its "Indirect Rule" system, and World War II will also be helpful, as students will then be in a position not only to know the cultural background but also the historical setting of the play. After all, modern African literature directly reflects African history. Once students know the sanctity of the egungun cult and its costume, it will be easier for them to understand the colonialist insensitivity to African culture as displayed by the wearing of the cultic dress by the District Officer and his wife, the Pilkings.

The cultural dimension of the play raises both general and specific problems. How will American students grasp the full meaning of an African play which has so much to do with culture? Soyinka chooses the mystical mode in *Death and the King's Horseman.* To American students reading the play, he seems to be talking a mystical language to a secular people not used to the African sense of religious ritual. My strategy at Charlotte in two different African literature courses, after my experience at Whitman College, is to explain the mystical nature of African life. Without doing this, the mystical focus of the dramatist on the ''numinous passage'' and ''transition'' will be lost on students, black and white, male and female.

Olunde killing himself in place of his father is not a total surprise to the African reader as it is to the Euro-American. Like the Pilkings, my students tend to believe that Olunde as a medical student who has been educated abroad would not kill himself, in fact, would not support the customary practice of the king's horseman ritually killing himself so as to accompany his master-king to the spirit world. However, if students are exposed to the Yoruba world-view, as I have been through study and living with them, they would understand that Olunde would not abandon his culture for any other one. Generally, the Yoruba are absorptive and borrow from other cultures what can strengthen theirs. Olunde's stay in England and his medical training only convinced him more about his father's responsibility of self-sacrifice. His experience of war casualties in English hospitals, the captains' self-sacrifice, and the British Prince's braving the seas in war time for a ''showing-the-flag tour of colonial possessions'' reinforce his faith in his culture and people. He has to perform the ultimate sacrifice for his family honor and the harmony of the Oyo State.

The culture conflict in the play evokes racism in the United States. The play has consistently specially appealed to Southern African-American students. When the play is taught in a Colloquium course that includes John Edgar Wideman's *Fever,* black students are thrilled by Olunde's intelligence and high self-esteem. They like Olunde, a black man, who is more than a match for Jane Pilkings, who had at first appeared condescending to him. The students relish Olunde's statements to Jane that ''I discovered that you have no respect for what you do not understand.'' The racist remarks of both Simon Pilkings and his aide-de-camp remind African-Americans of racism in America. A white colleague, Dr. Susan Gardner, with whom I co-taught a course that included *Death and the King's Horseman,* complained of the stereotypical way the British characters are portrayed. I agreed with her and the students, but explained that Simon Pilkings is portrayed as a typical district officer rather than as an individual. Jane is more individualized. The cultural and racist concerns bring out

different perspectives that are valid readers' responses to the text.

A feminist or women-oriented dimension is strongly brought out in the play, so that gender matters very much in determining responses. My female students, black and white, like the market women's teasing of Amusa. Black female students relate Amusa to Uncle Tom and feel he deserves his humiliation. The entire class (and female students in particular) are ecstatic at the girls' mimicking of the English accent and mannerisms. Women generally, black and white, like Iyaloja who seems to be in command of events, especially at the end when she chastises Elesin for failing to perform his duty. Her dominant character is also borne out by her forbidding Mr. Pilkings from closing dead Elesin's eyes and asking the Bride to do it.

Identification makes students respond to the play in their own ways. The part in Act 4 where Olunde talks with Jane Pilkings elicits this. The exchange especially appeals to black students, male and female, with a nationalistic inclination. It is as if Olunde, an educated African confronting Western imperialism, is speaking for them as African-Americans who have been dominated by whites. There is also the appeal to African-American women of a black male, Olunde, who is not only intelligent, ''sharp'' and ''smart,'' but also talks of his family honor. Seeing in him an ideal of a black male who is not easy to come by in America, they talk passionately of him.

Similarly, black and white women students prefer Jane to her husband Simon Pilkings. It seems they see in her the humane and sensitive aspects of womanhood that are lacking in Simon. In both instances, there is solidarity on the basis of race and gender. Black and white male students have not shown any liking for Simon Pilkings, who is portrayed as symbolic of the colonial administrator rather than just a male character.

The most difficult and perhaps debatable aspect of the play in my teaching at both Walla Walla and Charlotte for some three years is that many students cannot understand why Iyaloja, the market women, the Praise Singer, Olunde, and others blame Elesin for not doing his duty when already arrested. I link this problem to notions of tragedy and time in cultural perspectives. To many students, Elesin goes very far in the trance and has no way of killing himself once arrested. I counter this argument with: ''But he kills himself in spite of chains when he really wants to!'' In other words, earlier he hadn't the will to die because of his attachment to material things—market, fine clothes, and a young woman. To understand the play as a tragedy, I impress it on my students that Elesin's failure is not refusing to die, but not dying at the appropriate moment. It is a ritual and there is a time for everything. However, Elesin delays and provides the opportunity for his arrest and the excuse not to die. Interestingly, white students sympathize with Elesin, saying it is difficult for any human being willingly to take his or her life. Black students tend to feel that Elesin knows from the beginning what his position as the King's Horseman entails, and that since he has enjoyed the privileges of the position he should, as the custom demands, perform his duty properly. Students tend to defend or condemn Elesin.

I have adopted a part-seminar part-lecture strategy of teaching the text, which encourages students' questioning and my own as well. In lecture I may explain, for instance, that African time follows the rhythm of nature, like the moon, and is not precise as Western Swiss-watch time. Still, frequent inquiry as to why we should blame Elesin for not dying after being arrested, since the ritual was disrupted by Amusa and his fellow police, has led me to look more critically at the passage of time in this play whose classical structure entails a unity of time. It appears to me that there is a structural problem about the time that Elesin is supposed to die. There is a gap that the content of the play as it stands does not fill. While drums tell when Elesin is supposed to die, a time that the position of the moon is expected to manifest, and Olunde knows, there is the question as to whether Elesin was already arrested or not at that crucial time. Soyinka might have deliberately made it vague for suspense or unconsciously to leave gray areas in this play of the "numinous passage," but it constitutes a problem for readers.

At both Whitman College and The University of North Carolina at Charlotte, Soyinka's *Death and the King's Horseman,* resurrects the American experience in the students. After all, every reader responds to a text based on prior experience. As I explained earlier, training in the Western critical canon makes my students compare Soyinka with Shakespeare. What I find most interesting is that many of my students who are black, Southern, and raised in an evangelical atmosphere compare Elesin to Christ and Martin Luther King, Jr. to understand the meaning of sacrifice.

Teaching Soyinka's *Death and the King's Horseman* especially here in the South, I have developed

strategies and techniques that will alert my students to other dimensions of interpretation and understanding from which their culture alone would have excluded them. Their inquisitive questions and exchanges with me and among themselves have also widened my perspectives of the book as an African literary classic. Directing the students' response to the text from what they are already familiar with helps them to comprehend it fully. While my personal background as a Nigerian would help, I do not recommend an essentialist approach, but feel any teacher with some effort can make the play an enjoyable learning experience for students.

Source: Tanure Ojaide, ''Teaching Wole Soyinka's 'Death and the King's Horseman' to American college students,'' in *College Literature,* Vol., 19, No. 3, October–February, 1992, p. 210.

SOURCES

Gotrick, Kacke, ''Soyinka and *Death and the King's Horseman,* or How Does Our Knowledge or Lack of Knowledge of Yoruba Culture Affect Our Interpretation?,'' in *Signs and Signals: Popular Culture in Africa,* edited by Raoul Granqvis, University of Umea, 1990, pp. 137, 139.

Maduakor, Obi, *Wole Soyinka: An Introduction to His Writing,* Garland, 1986, p. 273.

Mwagiru, Ciugu, ''A Crusader's Return,'' in *World Press Review,* Vol. 46, no. 2, February 1999, p. 35.

Wright, Derek, *Wole Soyinka Revisited,* Twayne, 1993, p. 73.

FURTHER READING

Aboyade, Bimpe, *Wole Soyinka and Yoruba Oral Tradition,* in *Death and the King's Horseman,* Fountain Publications, 1994.
   A brief examination of the importance of oral tradition in Nigerian culture, and as a source for the play. Aboyade, himself a Yoruban, describes the *egungun* celebration, explains the role of the praise-singer, and considers the way in which Elesin and his people would understand honor.

Durosimi Jones, Eldred, *The Writing of Wole Soyinka,* 3d ed., Heinemann, 1988.
   The first edition of this volume, issued in 1973, was part of the Twayne World Authors Series, and for many years was considered the best book-length study of Soyinka. The third edition is still strong on the early years and early works, and on Soyinka's

incorporation of Christian and Yoruba elements, but the discussions of later plays, including *Death and the King's Horseman,* are brief.

Gibbs, James, ed., *Critical Perspectives on Wole Soyinka,* Three Continents Press, 1980.

A collection of critical essays on Soyinka's plays, poetry, memoir and criticism from a variety of perspectives. The book is now somewhat dated, and many of these essays may be difficult for the general reader, but the essays are consistently insightful and the collection is thorough.

Gotrick, Kacke, ''Soyinka and *Death and the King's Horseman,* or How Does Our Knowledge or Lack of Knowledge of Yoruba Culture Affect Our Interpretation?,'' in *Signs and Signals: Popular Culture in Africa,* edited by Raoul Granqvist, University of Umea, 1990, pp. 137-148.

Gotrick delineates the two major interpretations of the play as Elesin's failure or as a clash of cultures and concludes that readers and viewers are likely to choose an interpretation based on their level of ''Yoruba competence.'' The analysis is based on the 1987 New York production, and the article includes three photographs from that production.

Levy, Patricia, *Nigeria,* Marshall Cavendish, 1996.

Part of the Cultures of the World series, this volume is intended for middle school and high school students. Accessible but substantial, it gives an objective overview of Nigeria's history and geography, and explores the religions, languages, arts and festivals of the major ethnic groups. The many colored pictures illustrate dramatically the ways in which Nigeria is like and unlike North America.

Maduakor, Obi, *Wole Soyinka: An Introduction to His Writing,* Garland, 1986.

This volume is intended to make Soyinka more accessible to Western students by explaining the playwright's world view, his use of mythology, and his use of language. Maduakor analyzes *Death and the King's Horseman* as a play about transition from one spiritual world to another, paralleling the passage of the hero-god Ogun.

Wright, Derek, *Wole Soyinka Revisited,* Twayne, 1993.

An excellent introduction to Soyinka's life and work, with an emphasis on Yoruban traditions and themes as they inform Soyinka's writing. Wright's discussion of *Death and the King's Horseman* focuses on the changes Soyinka made to the actual historical events, demonstrating how these changes reinforce the themes of interrupted ritual and substitution.

The Kentucky Cycle

ROBERT SCHENKKAN

1992

When he first conceived the idea of *The Kentucky Cycle,* Robert Schenkkan never believed that it would grow into a history making, award winning, epic drama of Americana. He began the work in 1984 after a trip through rural eastern Kentucky as a wedding present to his wife, Mary Anne. The play grew as Schenkkan researched more about the region and his desire to say something about how modern America thinks of and rethinks its past and what that history means. *The Kentucky Cycle* won a grant from the Kennedy Center Fund for New American Plays, which allowed Schenkkan to complete the cycle by fall of 1991 when it premiered at Intiman Theatre in Seattle. The 1992 Pulitzer Prize for Best Drama propelled *The Kentucky Cycle* to New York, where it opened to mixed reviews. Schenkkan captures the essence of America's past and its fears and translates them into a work that many critics see as the best theater in the last two decades of American drama.

The Kentucky Cycle is a series of nine plays that spans over 200 years of American history in a small portion of eastern Kentucky. Although the features are local, the issues raised in the play are universally American and draw on the very best and the very worst in America's history. The plays explore violence as a part of American life—whether that violence is racial, gender-based, or environmental—and how each generation deals with and works through the American tendency to use force first and ask questions later.

AUTHOR BIOGRAPHY

Born in 1953, Robert Schenkkan wrote the *The Kentucky Cycle* after a trip to the Appalachian mountains in the early 1980s. There he was impressed by the rugged beauty of nature and the utter devastation that strip-mining had brought to the landscape. Schenkkan was also struck by the great divide between rich and poor in such a compact area as eastern Kentucky. He says that he began writing *The Kentucky Cycle* in 1984 as a wedding present to his wife. The cycle of plays grew into a tale about "America from its "discovery" by Europeans to its rediscovery" in the 1960s.

Schenkkan originally began his career as an actor, appearing in films with Christian Slater and episodes of *Star Trek: The Next Generation,* but he soon discovered his talents for writing and scripting. His plays have won multiple awards and critical acclaim. He won the Julie Harris/Beverly Hills Theatre Guild Award in 1989 for *Heaven on Earth,* the LA Weekly's Critic's Choice Award for *Tachinoki,* and a "Best of Fringe" Award at the Edinburgh Festival for *The Survivalist.* Schenkkan has also written screenplays for Oliver Stone, Denzel Washington, and Ron Howard.

The Kentucky Cycle won Schenkkan the largest grant ever presented by the Kennedy Center for New American Plays and broke box-office records when it premiered in Seattle in 1991. In 1992, he made history when *The Kentucky Cycle* won the Pulitzer Prize for Best Drama, the first time a play had won the Pulitzer without having first played on Broadway. After the Pulitzer Prize, *The Kentucky Cycle* was also nominated for Tony, Drama Desk, and Outer Critics Circle awards.

The Kentucky Cycle has become more than just a series of plays for its author. Schenkkan sees this work as a metaphor for how America works. It has also become his statement on the functioning of the American Dream. He originally envisioned one or two plays, four at the most, but as he wrote the story got bigger and bigger until it was a full seven hours long, with nine plays, spanning over 200 years. Schenkkan wanted his epic play cycle to reflect the beauty, the reality, and the brutality of modern American life.

Robert Schenkkan

PLOT SUMMARY

Part One

The first part of *The Kentucky Cycle* contains five plays: *Masters of the Trade (1775), The Courtship of Morning Star (1776), The Homecoming (1792), Ties that Bind (1819),* and *God's Great Supper (1861).* These plays explore the motives of violence and revenge, all in the name of family and land.

Masters of the Trade concerns Michael Rowen and how he comes to acquire the land in the first place. Michael is an Irish immigrant whose family has been killed in a Cherokee attack in eastern Kentucky prior to the American Revolution. Michael expresses no real remorse for his wife and daughter, but rather sees their deaths as an opportunity. He finds the man who sold the Cherokee their guns and he and his accomplice, Sam, kill the man. The shots bring the Cherokee warriors, who do not trust Michael, but decide to trade with him. Michael then kills Sam to show that he, Michael, can be trusted as the one to kill the man who killed their friend, Earl Tod. Michael trades the guns, powder, and shot that the Cherokee want for the land that he wants. However, Michael is not a good man. Not only has he killed two men, but the blankets that he gives the Cherokee are infected with smallpox. Michael knows that the disease will wipe out the tribe.

The Courtship of Morning Star, the second play in the cycle, concerns Michael's marriage to a Cherokee girl, Morning Star. She is one of the few survivors of Michael's smallpox plague and she knows that he is the one who has decimated her tribe. He has kidnapped her because he needs a woman to complete his plan. He needs children. Michael is brutal in his rape and treatment of Morning Star. He gives her no choice but to live with him and bear his children. When she tries to escape, he catches her and cuts her Achilles tendon. He does this so that she will never be able to run away from him again. Michael continues to threaten her. He tells her that their first child MUST be a boy or he will kill the child. Morning Star's fear and loathing for this man become clear in her speeches during her pregnancy. She mourns for her family and fears for herself. The play ends as Morning Star sings to her son and Michael expresses his fear of the child.

The Homecoming picks up the story sixteen years later as Patrick Rowen tries to make sense of his life and of his fear of both his parents. Patrick is in love with Rebecca Talbert, daughter of a neighboring farmer, Joe, but both families oppose the match. Michael is too jealous of his son and Joe just does not like the Rowens. Morning Star convinces Patrick that Michael intends to disinherit him and the only way Patrick can secure his claim to the land is to kill his father. After a trading trip, Michael returns to his home with a female slave. All successful farmers in the South had slaves and Michael was determined to be a success. Patrick stabs his father while the man is bathing in front of his mother, the slave, and, unfortunately, Rebecca and her father, Joe. However, this is exactly what Morning Star planned. She wanted to get rid of Michael and her son, but Patrick's violence was too strong for her. He killed Joe, the only man she had ever loved, and threatened to kill Morning Star as well. Neither the slave, Sallie, nor Rebecca, whom he would rape and ''marry'' could help her. Patrick drinks a toast to his ''wedding'' over his father's dead body.

Fourth in the cycle of plays is *Ties that Bind.* This play takes place in 1819, over twenty years later. Rebecca has died in childbirth with the second of two sons, and Patrick never remarried. Zeke and Zach have grown up with Sallie acting as mother and her son as brother. They are vaguely aware of an approaching disaster, but the true depth of Morning Star's revenge becomes obvious slowly. Patrick is heavily in debt and the bank is foreclosing on his loans. The justice of the peace comes to Patrick's farm, armed to the teeth, and sets out the terms of his bankruptcy. An unidentified man holds all the loans on Patrick's land and slowly, piece by piece he forces Patrick to give up everything, including Sallie and her son, Jessie. Even the news that Jessie is Patrick's half brother does not stop him. Finally, with nothing left, Patrick begs the stranger for mercy. Only then does Jeremiah Talbert reveal himself and Morning Star appears as well. Patrick realizes that they have tricked him and his family out of everything they own and his anger burns deep. However, there is nothing he can do about it at the moment. Zach, disgusted by his father's selling of his own flesh and blood, leaves and is never heard from again. Patrick survives, nursing his hatred and vengeance.

The last play in Part One is *God's Great Supper.* This play is the climax and focal point for all the other plays. Patrick has aged to a drooling old man and his son, Zeke, and grandson, Jed, are bent on revenge against the Talberts. Jed pretends to befriend the young Randall Talbert, Jeremiah's grandson, thus alienating his own family. Jed, of course, is only doing this to please his father and his hatred of the Talberts runs just as deep as the other members of his family. Jed volunteers for Richard Talbert's unit in the Civil War and kills Talbert by pushing him off the boat after they have escaped from the enemy. Jed joins a group of outlaws for a while before he comes home to oversee the murder of Randall and the rapes of his two sisters. The Talbert family home is destroyed and Jed claims the land back as his birthright. There is no one left to oppose him.

Part Two

Part Two of *The Kentucky Cycle* has the remaining four plays: *Tall Tales (1885), Fire in the Hole (1920), Whose Side are You On? (1954),* and *The War on Poverty (1975).* All four of these plays deal with coal mining and its affects on the people of eastern Kentucky.

The first play of Part Two, *Tall Tales* narrates how Jed Rowen finally lost the land that his ancestors had fought and died over. Jed is now middle aged with a young daughter, lots of land, very little money, and less sense. His family is isolated and his wife and daughter dream of far away places and luxuries that they simply cannot afford. A story-teller, JT Wells, arrives at the Rowen farm and starts to spin his magic. Although he claims to be from the area, he says he has lived in New York City, New Orleans, and other exotic places. Mary Anne, Jed's daughter, and Lallie, his wife, are mesmerized by JT's hypnotic tales. The only one who is not happy is Tommy Jackson, who is in love with Mary Anne and thinks that the stranger is there to steal her heart. In reality, he is there to steal her land. By fake ''hard'' bargaining, JT convinces Jed to sell, not only the mineral rights, but his entire farm for $1 per acre. This does not sit well with Lallie and she tries to convince him not to sell even a rock of his place. Jed, however, will not listen to a woman's advice and sells his property thinking he has made a great deal. Though the land was actually worth millions, Jed sells everything that he and his ancestors had built for $170. In a fit of remorse, JT tries to tell Mary Anne what the deed really means, but she cannot comprehend that other people would be so sneaky. Tommy attacks and kills JT; and Jed, again refusing to listen to a woman, stands by his signa-ture. Mary Anne's favorite tree is the first thing the mining company cuts down.

Fire in the Hole and *Whose Side are You On?* make up the core of Schenkkan's cycle of Amer-ica's rise and fall. These two plays deal with the conditions in eastern Kentucky after the mining companies take over and the workers' attempts at unionization. Mary Anne Rowen and Tommy Jack-son are married and she has watched five of her six sons die of the typhoid that hits the area with horrible regularity. The mining company literally owns the entire town; there is no other employment. Tommy and Mary Anne cannot even pay for the medicine to heal their last child, Joshua. Where Mary Anne's father had once owned the entire valley, she and her family are reduced to renting a house from the company, buying food at the com-pany store, and loading ten tons of coal a day, six days a week. The miners are not even paid in money, but given company script good only at the company store. A stranger, Abe Steinman, arrives on the scene and attempts to organize the miners. He pays for Joshua's medicine, thus winning Mary Anne's eternal gratitude and devotion. Tommy, however, is not so easily swayed. He does agree to help Abe organize the workers and even arranges to buy guns from Cassius Biggs, his cousin (although neither admit to being related). But at the last

moment, Tommy panics and tells the mine owners everything. Abe and the other organizers are killed, setting off a chain of angry events. Mary Anne blames Tommy and he is dragged off and killed by other miners. She takes back her maiden name and forms the union that Tommy was afraid would destroy their lives. As with all such labor organiza-tions, the blessings are mixed.

Schenkkan portrays these mixed blessings in the eighth play *Whose Side are You On?*. Joshua has become the president of the local chapter of the United Mine Workers Union and quite a skillful politician. He lacks the idealism of his son, Scotty, preferring instead, a jaded realism. He allows major safety violations to go uncorrected because James Talbert Winston, the owner of the mine, threatens to shut the operation down completely if he does not. James, Franklin Biggs, and Joshua play with the numbers of layoffs, severance packages, and wages without any real concern that they are playing with people's lives. Scotty has problems with his father's callous attitude and refuses to play along with his game. Joshua and James's corner-cutting on safety causes a cave-in at the mine and Scotty is killed. Even in the face of his personal tragedy, Joshua plays the part James wants him to and he passes the cave-in off as a mere accident, not something that was preventable. The play ends as Scott Rowen's name is read as one of the victims.

The final play in *The Kentucky Cycle* , is called *The War on Poverty.* It takes place twenty-one years after Scotty's death. The mining company has gone bankrupt and there is nothing left of either the company, the union, or the community. Joshua, James, and Franklin are wandering out on the land that was supposed to become the county hospital and was originally the Rowen homestead. Although Joshua does not know it, he feels a connection to the land and he is not ready to give up as the other two men are. They discover the mummified remains of a child, wrapped in bead embroidered buckskin, that was unearthed by a pair of scavengers. The audi-ence realizes that this is the body of Morning Star's girl child that Michael had killed in 1782. While James and Franklin want to take the buckskin back to town to sell, Joshua suddenly feels the need to rebury the child. He threatens his friends with his rifle and they put the body down. Joshua feels his connection to the land and celebrates the beauty of the Kentucky landscape by howling with a lone wolf nearby.

CHARACTERS

Franklin Biggs

Franklin Biggs is a black man, descended from Sallie Biggs, Michael Rowen's slave. He "controls" the African-American population in Howsen County. He makes deals with both Joshua and James, neither of whom seems to really like him, but he does not care. He gets what he wants for his community. He is a successful business man, who can deliver the "black vote" and can influence his community to go along with whatever Blue Star Mining wants. Franklin also lacks any connection to the land and does not share in Joshua's joy at seeing the wolf.

Sallie Biggs

Sallie Biggs is the slave Michael Rowen brings home just before Patrick kills him. She is pregnant with Michael's son, but she does not tell anyone who the father is until Patrick tries to sell the boy to pay off debts. She begs Patrick not to sell her son, but he does anyway. Her descendants lead the civil rights struggle in the latter parts of the cycle.

Tommy Jackson

Tommy is Mary Anne's husband. He has been in love with her for most of his life. He took a mining job when all the farm land was sold to the Blue Star Mine. He works hard and tries to help with the unionizing effort, but gets frightened at the end. He sells out his fellow organizers and Mary Anne publicly rejects him and he is killed by a group of angry strikers.

Morning Star

Morning Star is Michael Rowen's Cherokee wife. He kidnaps her from her tribe, rapes her, and treats her badly. After she attempts to escape, he cuts the tendons in her leg so that she will always limp. Morning Star becomes resigned to her fate; she teaches her son, Patrick, to hate and fear his father. She finally convinces Patrick to kill his father so that she can finally be free to live with her lover, Joe Talbert. When Patrick kills Joe as well, Morning Star is devastated, but swears revenge. Years later, she forces her son and grandsons to forfeit their land to Talbert's heir. While Morning Star may love her son, she never forgets that he is his father's child, nor what his father did to her and her people. Nor does she forgive.

Ezekiel Rowen

As Patrick Rowen's direct heir, Zeke (also known as Ezekiel) inherits not only his father's bloodlust, but also his grandfather's as well. Zeke becomes a minister bent on revenging for his family against the Talberts. He devises a plan to kill all the male Talberts, including ten-year-old Randall, and destroy the two daughters (through rape and torture) so that there will be no one to stop the Rowens from reclaiming the land. Unlike his brother, Zeke does not see anything wrong with Patrick selling his own half-brother, nor in threatening Randall, nor anything wrong with a minister planning rapes and murders.

Jed Rowen

Jed Rowen carries on the family tradition of lying and murder when he kills Richard Talbert and then oversees the murder of Randall Talbert and the rapes of his sisters, Rose Anne and Julia Anne. Jed reclaims the Rowen land but proves to be just as unlucky as his grandfather was. He sells the mineral rights to his land for a dollar an acre when it is worth $15,000 to $20,000 per acre.

Joshua Rowen

Joshua Rowen, along with James Talbert Winston, and Franklin Biggs, is one of the major characters in the last part of *The Kentucky Cycle*. He is, unlike the rest of his ancestors, an honorable man. He is president of the local miners' union and tries to balance what is good for the individual members and the overall industry. He agrees to allow the mine to keep operating even though it is not safe and his son, Scotty, is killed in a cave-in. Joshua feels a connection with the land, raped and neglected as it is, which the other characters do not feel. He is connected to the land in a way that not even Michael or Morning Star were. He feels the land's pain and rejoices in the opportunity to save it at the end of the cycle. He discovers the body of Patrick's sister, buried 200 years before and forces the other men to return the mummified body to the earth. Joshua ends the cycle in the sheer joy of the wilderness as he watches a wolf run across the ridge.

Mary Anne Rowen

Mary Anne is Jed's daughter. She is almost destroyed when the mining companies come in and cut down her trees and rip the guts out of her mountains. In a final defeat, she marries a local boy,

Tommy Jackson, and watches as all of her sons die of typhoid. Abe Steinman encourages Mary Anne to think about a miners' union. After his arrest and Tommy's betrayal of the cause, Mary Anne rejects her husband, takes back her maiden name, and leads the fight for a union in the mines. She becomes a mythical figure who inspires future generations of miners and their families.

Michael Rowen

Michael Rowen is the founder of the Rowen family and the main character in the first two plays. He also establishes the moral tone of the plays. He is a thief, a liar, and a murderer. As the cycle opens, Michael kills Earl Tod, the Scottish trapper who trades with the Cherokee in the area. He then kills his accomplice, Sam, to prove his "trustworthiness" to the Cherokee. Michael's bloodshed continues as he infects the Cherokee with smallpox and kidnaps a young Cherokee woman, Morning Star and makes her his wife. He continues to threaten her and even kills the girl child that she has after giving birth to a son. The violence, rage, and murder within Michael get passed down to all of his descendants, so Michael is the key character to understanding the other characters in the play.

Patrick Rowen

Patrick Rowen is Morning Star and Michael's son. Their other child, a girl, is killed by Michael when she is born. Patrick never forgot that action and hates his father for it. He also fears his father. He feels victimized by everyone around him: his father, his mother, his love, Rebecca, and her father, Joe Talbert. He kills his father, Rebecca's father, forces his mother to flee for her life, and rapes Rebecca in a watered-down version of his own parents' "marriage." When Morning Star returns years later, she witnesses Patrick selling everything to an unnamed stranger who owns the mortgage on his property. Patrick even sells his own half-brother, Jessie Biggs. His own son, Zach, cannot stand Patrick's actions and flees. Unlike his father, Patrick lives to be an ancient man who drools and fantasizes about revenge.

Zachariah Rowen

Zachariah (also known as Zach) Rowen is Patrick's youngest son. He sees no difference between himself, his brother, and Jessie Biggs, the son of his family's slave, Sallie. When he finds out that Jessie is actually Patrick's half-brother, he pleads

MEDIA ADAPTATIONS

- In 1995, Robert Schenkkan sold the film rights to *The Kentucky Cycle* to Kevin Costner and his HBO production partners. While Schenkkan was hired to rework the plays as a film or mini-series script, Costner has postponed production indefinitely. He does claim that he wants to do a film version of *The Kentucky Cycle*, but not until he can devote the proper attention to it.

- *The Kentucky Cycle* has been performed at various theaters all over the country between 1992–1996, particularly at college drama departments and civic theater groups.

with his father not to sell him, and when Patrick does, Zach leaves the farm never to be heard from again. Zach represents the Rowens' conscience and without him they descend into moral depravity.

Abe Steinman

Abe Steinman is a union organizer who decides that The Blue Star Mine, built on what used to be the Rowen land, is ripe for unionizing. He is successful in getting the miners' wives and some of the miners to join him, but they are betrayed by Tommy and he is killed.

Jeremiah Talbert

This is Joe Talbert's son, who returns to get revenge against Patrick. Aided by Morning Star and the legal system, Jeremiah forces Patrick to sell him everything he has and forces him to become a sharecropper on his own land.

Richard Talbert

Richard Talbert is Jeremiah Talbert's son and so owns the land that was formerly Patrick's land. Zeke and his son, Jed, plan their revenge and begin with Richard. Jed joins Richard's Civil War company and kills Richard in the middle of a battle.

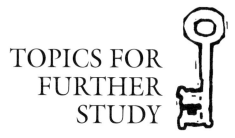

TOPICS FOR FURTHER STUDY

- Research the European settlement of Kentucky during the late eighteenth century. Compare the historical accounts to the events in the first two plays in *The Kentucky Cycle*.

- How does strip-mining work? Why would strip-mining and the condition of mine workers in the 1920s cause them to want to unionize?

- How do the Rowens, specifically Michael, Patrick, Jed, and Mary Anne, display the ideas of the American Dream?

- After researching the environmental damage done by strip-mining, explain why Joshua feels the joy he does when he sees the wolf at the end of *The Kentucky Cycle*.

- How do the women in the plays react to the violent natures of the men in their lives? What makes the difference between the women of the earlier plays, Morning Star, Rebecca, and Joleen, and Mary Anne in Part II?

James Talbert Winston

James is the owner of Blue Star Mine, descendant of Jeremiah Talbert, and an emotionless capitalist. He does not care about the safety of his workers, but only his profit margin. When the cave-in kills over twenty miners, including Joshua Rowen's son, James cannot really apologize because it is his fault. However, he and Joshua and Franklin Biggs become friends as the movers and shakers of Howsen County. He digs up the body of Patrick Rowen's sister and wants to sell the beautifully beaded baby quilt Morning Star had made for her doomed infant. At the end of the cycle, he realizes that mining is a dead profession, but he cannot see any value to the land nor can he feel any connection to this place. He, like Franklin, looks on as Joshua yells with the wolf, thinking he has gone crazy.

Zach

See Zachariah Rowen

Zeke

See Ezekiel Rowen

THEMES

Violence

Violence looms large in the text of *The Kentucky Cycle*. Every play contains physical and emotional violence, or the threat of that violence. Schenkkan wants to explore the role of violence in the shaping of American history. Michael Rowen murdered, stole, and raped his way to a family legacy. That legacy was continued with Patrick's violence, Jed's murdering the Talbert men, and finally the way the Blue Star Mining Company raped the earth and the lives of its workers. Violence becomes an inescapable part of American life in these plays, although Schenkkan suggests that when violence is used to protect the land, as when Joshua threatens to shoot James and Franklin, or for benefit of others, as was the case with the unionizing miners, it can be productive. However, in most respects, violence simply breeds more violence and revenge in an almost never-ending cycle.

The American Dream

The idea of the American Dream, a land where anyone can come from nothing and become someone, is a powerful theme in American literature. All of the characters in the first half of Schenkkan's cycle want the American Dream, but they rarely find it. Michael Rowen is killed by his own son before he can realize his dream of "owning" all the mountains, while both Patrick and Jed see their portion of the dream legally stolen out from under them. Yet, through it all, the dream remains alive, as it does in real life when it is battered by reality. The characters in the second part of the cycle have all given up, except for Mary Anne and Scotty. Mary Anne is able to forge a better life for her son, but Scotty's idealism dies at the hands of his father's cynicism.

Rewriting American History

In one of his speaking tours after winning the Pulitzer Prize, Schenkkan suggested that this cycle of plays is the American history that remains unwritten, a cultural "dirty little secret." In this sense, *The Kentucky Cycle* is a mirror for America and its blood-spattered past. No one likes to think about how the settlers moved the native peoples out of the way. It was done through murder and disease. No one wants to think about slavery or the treatment of women, or the way some Americans swindled other Americans out of their homes and farms. Yet everyone likes the stories of the wild frontier, brave mountain men living by their wits, gun in hand. Everyone likes to hear the rags to riches story of successful Americans like John Paul Getty and Andrew Carnegie, but no one talks about the workers who were underpaid, underfed, and overworked as the means for these men to attain the wealth they did. Schenkkan wants his audiences to realize exactly how much pain, heartache, sorrow, and bloodshed went into making the America of today.

Personal Integrity versus Greed

The characters in *The Kentucky Cycle* have problems with personal integrity. Except for Mary Anne and Scotty, virtually all of them place personal greed above morality. Michael does not care that he killed dozens of people as long as he has his land and family. Morning Star does not care about her child except to see him broken and begging, Patrick, Zeke, and Jed live only for revenge and murder, while Joshua thinks only about the art of the deal. The only character who succeeds is Mary Anne, because she puts the needs of her community above her personal needs. Scotty tries, but gets caught in his father's lies and pays the ultimate price. Joshua is redeemed by his connection to the land and the ghost of his ancestor when he refuses to give into the greed consuming James and Franklin. Ultimately, Schenkkan seems to be saying that personal integrity is more successful and rewarding than greed can ever be.

STYLE

Classical Greek Structure

Schenkkan uses a traditional plot structure, borrowed from classical Greek tragedy, which combines climactic structure on the level of the individual plays with episodic structure for the entire cycle of plays. Each play focuses on individual characters, involving them in a series of ever-greater complications and bringing them to a startling climax. Together these plays function as a series of episodes in the entwined family histories of the Rowens and the Talberts. Each family is bound up in the fate of the others, yet each generations follows the path of the previous ones. The Talberts are generally always in control while the Rowens are always fighting to reclaim something that they had stolen in the first place. Like the chorus of a Greek tragedy, the Biggses live on the fringes of the action, providing both labor and an audience for the feud between the Talberts and the Rowens. The use of classical Greek tragic elements includes the character flaws that run through all the major characters: violence and greed. The long hard fall of the Rowens from land owners to sharecroppers to day laborers is also a familiar trait of Classical Greek Tragedy.

Setting and Set Design

Since this cycle of plays takes place over 200 years and involves over thirty characters, setting and set design are major elements in how the play is put together. Throughout the entire cycle, the physical setting does not change except for a few scenes where the action is not on the thirty-nine acres Michael Rowen originally bought from the Cherokee. The stage directions are purposefully spare since Schenkkan is not aiming for realism, but rather for mood. In the preface to the plays, he suggests a large box of dirt to represent the land with the actors adding tombstones as the plays progress. He suggests that excessive properties (props) and costuming will get in the way of the message, and should be minimized as much as possible. The sparsity of the stage and set design helps to focus attention on the words of each character.

Dramatic Irony and Cycling

The characters in *The Kentucky Cycle* are caught in a never-ending circle of murder, betrayal, and revenge. Schenkkan uses the repetition of situation and events to build dramatic irony and tension. The struggle seems pointless since the next generation is just going to do the exact same thing that the previous generation did. However, this cycling builds the dramatic irony to its highest point in *The War on Poverty*. In this play, the audience knows, although Joshua does not, that he is standing on the land of his forefathers and that the found body is that of Patrick's sister killed so long ago by her own father. Here is the irony. All Michael, Patrick, Zeke, Jed, and Mary Anne ever wanted was to carry on the family name, but they were completely cut off from their strength, the land. Yet, Joshua, whose only child is dead, and with whom the Rowen line will die out, realizes his connection to the land and his responsibility toward it. This last member of a dying family rejoices in the sight of a wolf in the wild. Wolves were supposed to be extinct in most of the United States in 1975, save for Wisconsin, Minnesota, and North Dakota. The cycle of life, like *The Kentucky Cycle* itself comes full circle and the play ends were it began: a futureless individual in the wilderness.

HISTORICAL CONTEXT

There is a greater difference than is often thought between the mid to late 1980s and early 1990s, on the one hand, and the later 1990s, on the other. The 1980s saw the creation of huge personal wealth for some; but this was contrasted with the widespread problems of unemployment, homelessness, and lack of universal healthcare, as well as the expansion of the national debt to grotesque proportions. To many, the Reagan-Bush era in American politics seemed meaner than those of the 1970s; the policies of "trickle-down economics" and bankrupting the Soviet-bloc countries seemed harsh and expensive. Cast against this political background, there was a growing "green" or environmental movement pushing for stricter enforcement of air pollution laws, automobile exhaust emissions standards, and awareness of the devastating effects of strip-mining and coal burning factories on the environment.

By the late 1980s, America was again involved in foreign wars that did not seem to serve any real American interests or obligations. The economy was in recession, federal money for social programs was being used to make interest payments on the national debt, and people were ready for a change and a new beginning. Issues like race relations, women's rights, and the state of the environment became less urgent, not because they were solved, but because people got tired of talking and thinking about them. In this atmosphere, Robert Schenkkan wrote *The Kentucky Cycle* as a way to force people to reexamine these issues.

This cycle of plays specifically took on the issues that were dying in the late 1980s and early 1990s. Schenkkan wanted to force people to explore treatment of and attitudes towards women, African-Americans, and the poor in America. He wanted to exploit the righteous anger many people felt at seeing the destruction of the Appalachian mountains by strip-mining and turn it into action to reclaim the land for the people of the area. He wanted people to recognize the inherent violence in our history, in an America based on conquest and blood rather than community and cooperation.

CRITICAL OVERVIEW

The production of a piece as large and grand as *The Kentucky Cycle* can hardly be met without both praise and disdain. While it has won many awards, including the Kennedy Center New American Plays Award, the Critics' Choice Award and the Pulitzer Prize, Schenkkan's work has not been heralded by all. Many critics doubt its value and some saw it as being the death of American theater. However, most reviewers found it powerful in its message, sparse in its presentation, and humbling in its catharses.

The early reviews were the best. The reviews in Seattle, at its premiere, and Arizona were stunning. Theatre Week called the production marvelous and brutally honest in its depiction of American history. The California reviews were just as good. *The Kentucky Cycle* started to run into critical problems when Schenkkan decided to take the play to Broadway after winning the Pulitzer Prize. Many New York theater critics found the plays boring, too long, and too unsophisticated for the New York audience. As it turned out, *The Kentucky Cycle* performed well in New York, although not as well as Schenkkan had hoped. The plays' popularity did get a boost from Stacey Keach's appearance on *Good Morning America* as he was starring in the plays at the time.

Many critics felt that the lack of stage design and the use of actors for multiple roles detracted from the cycle's power and dramatic force. New York critics, basking in the age of Andrew Lloyd Webber's lush productions like *Cats, Jesus Christ Superstar,* and *Phantom of the Opera* seemed disappointed in Schenkkan's ideas of dialogue-inspired drama instead of set-driven spectacle. They wanted a costume piece, but he wanted to talk about America. Schenkkan intended for a group of about ten to twelve actors to play all the roles, thus putting the burden of dramatic production on their skills and on the audience's "willing suspension of disbelief." However, many New York critics found this burden to be too heavy, and panned the plays. In regional theaters and touring shows, *The Kentucky Cycle* fared better, and struck a chord with most of its audiences.

Academic criticism has been relatively sparse. Both Marianthe Colakis and Charles Edward Lynch take Schenkkan to task for his approach to language and violence in the cycle, while Lynch criticizes the playwright more harshly for what he sees as an insult to the people of Appalachia. Harold Dixon, an enthusiastic supporter of Schenkkan and *The Ken-*

COMPARE
&
CONTRAST

- **1700s–1800s:** Women do not have any rights under the law. Women can be raped by their husbands, have no rights to the property or money they may have earned, and their children belong to their husbands.

  1920: The 19th Amendment to the U.S. Constitution gives women the right to vote in local, county, state, and federal elections.

  Today: While women today still earn less than their male counterparts for equal work, the gap is narrowing and laws against sexual harassment and gender discrimination are being enforced.

- **1700s:** Slavery is common in the early years of the United States. Kentucky is a "slave state," but it does not secede from the Union during the Civil War. Owners routinely father children by their female slaves and consider those offspring slaves as well. Families are often broken up and sold to different people, especially as punishment for misbehavior.

  1960s: Lead by men like Martin Luther King, Jr. and Malcolm X, and women like Fannie Mae Johnson and Rosa Parks, African-Americans demand an equal share in the glory and goods that is America during the Civil Rights Movement. Although both King and Malcolm X are assassinated, their desire for unity and harmony among the races live on.

  Today: Relations between the white and black peoples of the United States are better in some ways, but still do not approach the color-blind society that King envisioned. African-Americans are financially better off now than in the 1960s, but they still earn less than whites, have less access to health care, and are more likely to smoke and abuse alcohol.

- **1700s–1800s:** Land is seen as a possession and a never-ending resource. After the Revolution, settlers are encouraged to move west in order to stake America's claim to the land, to drive out the native population, and turn the country into farmland.

1900s: The idea of an endless frontier becomes part of the American Myth. The Homestead Act of 1882 and the purchase of Alaska from Russia in the 1870s help fuel the western expansion and the illogical and wasteful use of land. When the Census Board closed the frontier in 1890, Americans had to find new ones. Hawaii is conquered in 1892; her last queen arrested, tried, and executed by an American court. Alaska becomes the "New Frontier" with the gold rushes of the 1900s and 1910s. American culture does not believe in conserving or protecting land or its ecosystems.

Today: The environment is an important political issue. April 22 is celebrated as Earth Day and most major cities have recycling programs to reduce waste going to landfills. Politicians in Washington are reexamining the ways land is used in the western states in an attempt to improve the health of the environment. Major spills and chemical leaks are also being cleaned up.

- **1700s–1800s:** In a young America, particularly in its frontier, violence is just a part of life. Native peoples are often hostile (with good reason) as are other settlers when supplies ran low. Men and women both learn to shoot and defend themselves.

  1800s–1900s: While violence has not changed, the type of violence has. It is no longer customary for civilized people to carry firearms. Violence becomes more socialized and more civilized.

  Today: Violence ranks as the most pressing social problem in the United States. However, violent crimes have been on the decrease since 1992, with the murder rate by firearms falling fastest. Most major cities have restricted gun ownership, require trigger locks on new guns, and outlawed guns for children. While the number of real guns has fallen across the country, the level of real and pretend violence is just as much a part of our national identity as it was in 1775.

A scene from the second play (Fire in the Hole) *of part II of Schenkkan's* The Kentucky Cycle, *performed at Bradley University's Meyer Jacobs Theatre in 1997.*

tucky Cycle, understands the reluctance of people in Kentucky to embrace the play: "the characters are ignorant, their speech is rough. But this play is not meant to put down Kentucky. Rather, it's a play about America that happens to be told through the particularities of the Bluegrass State." Jim Stoll, another supportive critic, states that "*The Kentucky Cycle* is exciting, compelling and memorable. The critics who say it is not worthy of its Pulitzer Prize become irrelevant once the lights dim. Whatever else it is, it's a damn good show."

Whatever the critics say, in performance *The Kentucky Cycle* moves its audiences. Some find it boring, guilty of regional stereotyping, and silly; and some find it wrenching, an important milestone in modern American culture, and inspirational; but most audiences say that the six hours the complete cycle takes is well worth it.

CRITICISM

Michael Rex
Rex has a Ph.D and specializes in literature, poetry, and drama. In the following essay he ex-plores the intersection between gender and violence in Robert Schenkkan's series of plays.

Robert Schenkkan's *The Kentucky Cycle* has been called one of the best examples of unwritten American history; the stuff Americans do not like to talk about. Violence, racism, and domestic abuse are America's dirty little secrets. The West was the great Frontier, our "Manifest Destiny," but how often do Americans truly look at what "moving West" meant? The lands beyond the Eastern sea-board were already populated and America's ex-pansion meant that these peoples must be displaced. Schenkkan suggests that this primary displacement of the native peoples tainted the West and the American identity. *The Kentucky Cycle* shows that violence, particularly men's violence, has become an inherent part of American life and history. The characters of Michael, Jed, and Mary Anne Rowen clearly show that male-dominated thinking and action causes the rise in the level of violence and the degeneration of the American Dream.

Michael Rowen is a bad man from the very beginning of the cycle. *The Kentucky Cycle* opens shortly after the Cherokee have massacred a white

WHAT DO I READ NEXT?

- Aeschylus's classic trilogy, *The Oresteia*, traces the events leading up to the Trojan War and Clytemnestra's revenge on her husband for the murder of their daughter. The other two plays deal with the outcome of Agamemnon's death at the hands of his wife and Clytemnestra's death at the hands of their son, Orestes. A smash hit since 458 B.C.E., *The Oresteia* has influenced the development of tragic drama ever since.

- *Medea*, Euripides's fourth-century B.C.E. blood tragedy explores the impact of characters caught in a cycle of revenge and murder. Much like Morning Star has Patrick kill Michael and then has Jeremiah punish him, Medea kills her children to punish her unfaithful husband, Jason. Everyone in the play gets caught up in the web of bloodshed and murder and they all pay for their crimes, save Medea who is carried off to safety in a snake-drawn chariot.

- Arthur Miller's classic 1952 play, *The Crucible*, also explores a dark chapter in American history—the Salem Witch Trials of 1692. Miller uses this setting to explore concepts of justice, evil, and mass hysteria while giving his audience a glimpse into how good people ended up hanging nineteen of their own. The ideas of violence inherent in the American identity are also present in Miller's play.

- In 1959 Lorraine Hansberry produced her award-winning play, *A Raisin in the Sun*, a bittersweet story about hope and hard work in an African-

American family. It became an instant classic and forever changed American theater. Hansberry broke all the stereotypes and presented African-Americans as real people with hopes, dreams, desires, and problems. The play does have a happy ending, another rare element in American drama of the 1950s and early 1960s.

- *Centennial*, James Michener's mammoth mid-1970s novel of the American West, peopled with Native Americans, European trappers, and American settlers, treats much of the same territory as Schenkkan does. Michener's prose is denser and geared more toward story-telling without all the moral allegory in *The Kentucky Cycle*.

- *Flyin' West*, by Pearl Cleage (1992), much like *The Crucible* and *A Raisin in the Sun* uses a historical setting to explore contemporary issues of family, domestic violence, and racism. Cleage sets her story in the all black Kansas town of Nichodemus and shows just how far a group of women will go to protect themselves, their loved ones, and their way of life.

- Theresa Rebeck's 1992 *Spike Heels* takes on modern day ideas about gender class, sex, and violence with a wit and humor rarely seen in contemporary theater. Georgie, the heroine, is torn between the lover who would be "good" for her and the man who wants her. In many ways, *Spike Heels* is a modern version of George Bernard Shaw's *Pygmalion*, only a lot funnier.

---

settlement. Michael finds Earl Tod, the man who sold the guns to the Cherokee and plays the innocent survivor in order to get information out of Tod. Michael shows no remorse for the deaths of his wife and children nor for the other settlers. Instead, he sees this as an opportunity to stake his claim to the land. This is Michael's first mistake. In the world that Schenkkan creates, land cannot be "owned." It simply exists. Michael violates the land by the

means he uses to obtain it. He kills Tod and then kills his young accomplice, Sam, without thought or remorse. Michael's purchase comes with the shedding of blood. Even the Cherokee are not safe from Michael's evil. Although he makes a deal with them for guns, lead, and gun powder in exchange for land, Michael cannot deal honestly with them. The blankets that he gives them are infected with smallpox. As the title of the first play suggests, Michael is a

MICHAEL IS DISGUSTED BY THE FACT THAT MORNING STAR'S BREASTS BLEED AS SHE FEEDS THE BABY; MILK AND BLOOD TOGETHER ARE WHAT MAKES HIM A ROWEN."

"master of the trade" of death, evil, and the double cross.

Michael's evil becomes more focused in the next two plays, *The Courtship of Morning Star* and *The Homecoming.* Both of these plays expose Michael's hatred and fear of women and his own mortality. Michael is evil and Schenkkan goes to great lengths to portray that evil as a fundamental part of the American character. Michael realizes that all of his work will be for nothing if he does not have children to establish his legacy. However, he does not have the time, energy, or character to convince any woman to live with him. In a macho feat, he kidnaps a young Cherokee girl whose tribe has been practically destroyed by Michael's "gift" of smallpox. She tries to escape, but Michael is determined. He does not ask her if she wants to be with him; he makes her his property through rape and torture. After her first escape attempt, he cuts the tendons in her leg to keep her from being able to run. Michael is such a disgusting creature that he knows that no woman would want to be around him, much less have children for him, without force.

Michael insists that a family and children are what he wants from Morning Star, but his violence and evil dominate even in this aspect of his life. He threatens Morning Star that if her first child is not a boy, he will kill the child. Here, Schenkkan is displaying Michael's utter ignorance of biology; most people today know that the man determines the sex of the child, not the woman. Yet even when Patrick is born, Michael cannot bring himself to touch the child, much less love him. Michael is disgusted by the fact that Morning Star's breasts bleed as she feeds the baby; milk and blood together are what makes him a Rowen. However, Michael is afraid of his son, afraid of what having a child and growing older means. Violence can only rule while the tyrant is strong and young enough to physically

enforce his/her rule. This fear becomes manifest in *The Homecoming.*

The Homecoming is pivotal in the development of violence because it shows that the violence crosses both gender and generation lines. Patrick seems like a much better man than his father. There is a hint that he cares for Rebecca Talbert and that he will reject the evil ways of his father. However, Morning Star's hatred for her husband and Michael's own evil character force Patrick to behave exactly like him. Michael returns from town with an African slave. Again, Michael could not get a woman to be with him voluntarily; he has to capture or to buy them. Michael, reenforced by Morning Star's earlier conversations with her son, pushes Patrick beyond his breaking point, by calling him a half-breed and hinting that he, Patrick, will never inherit Michael's land. In an almost instant replay of how his father got his land and wife in the first place, Patrick stabs Michael, shoots Rebecca's father, forces her into the house where he will rape and marry her, and banishes Morning Star. Michael can die because Patrick has become just as evil and violent as he was.

The violence in the Rowens continues to flow through the generations. Patrick's evil matches that of his father when he sells Jessie Biggs, his own half-brother. The violence seems to skip a generation only because Zeke does not have the opportunity to wield it as his father and son do. However, Zeke's violence is possibly more dangerous. He has tainted his son, Jed with a lust for vengeance and a taste for blood. Jed's violence is less obvious that either of his ancestors. He is devious and pretends to be a trusted friend and companion. He seems to like Randall Talbert, the ten-year-old son of Richard Talbert. Randall worships Jed as only a young boy can worship his hero. Yet, Jed is part of an evil plot to destroy the Talbert family. The Rowens, drenched in blood and violence, see nothing wrong with murdering the Talbert men and raping the Talbert women. Again, violence has become a way of life, integral to the functioning of society.

The depths of Jed's evil only become apparent after he has joined Richard Talbert's regiment. While Richard is going to fight for honor and the Southern way of life (things unworthy of protecting anyway), Jed could care less. He is only waiting for an opportunity to kill Richard. Unlike Michael, Patrick, and even Zeke, who are open about their hatred, violence, and anger, Jed pretends to be Richard's friend. He saves Richard in a battle only to push him off the boat as they cross the a river escaping from the enemy. Richard, fool that he was, never realized nor suspected that a product of such violence could be violent himself. Jed carries on this mission when he rides with the outlaws and returns home to oversee the destruction of the Talberts. Without remorse or even hesitation, he kills Randall, and rapes both of his sisters. The cycle of violence has come full circle. The Rowens once again are in possession of the land, which they got through blood, violence, and murder.

One of the most interesting aspects about *The Kentucky Cycle* is the intersection between violence and gender. The Rowens, in Part One, are all men. The only Rowen daughter, born to Morning Star, was killed by Michael, only a few days after her birth. Schenkkan seems to be chastising American society for the way it has raised boys. Boys and men, in this cycle of plays, are violent, bloodthirsty, murdering thugs who cannot get enough of whatever it is, be it money, land, or women.

The only Rowen woman born to the family and allowed to live is Mary Anne, Jed's daughter. Schenkkan states in his "Author's Note" that Mary Anne is based on and named after his own wife. She is also the only admirable, good character in the entire cycle. All the other characters, even the other women, are evil or, at least, manipulative. Mary Anne, on the other hand, seems pure of heart and genuine. She first appears in *Tall Tales* as both a heart-broken adult and a wide-eyed girl of fourteen. As a young girl, full of hope and love, Mary Anne dreams of a future and far-off places. She is the first character who seems to love the land for itself, not to own or for what it can produce, but just for itself. The loving description she gives of Spring in the opening of *Tall Tales* displays more than just a foreshadowing of what is lost to strip-mining. It gives the audience an insight into Mary Anne's soul. Here is a character without the bloodlust and violence that has tainted her family. She does, however, have a touch of greed about her.

Mary Anne wants something different than what her community can offer. She wants to see London, Paris, New York, and New Orleans. She wants to experience life and love and joy so badly that she does not realize that she has all of that right at home. Even after JT Wells has tricked her father into selling his land for a tiny fraction of what it was worth, Mary Anne believes in the myth JT has spun at the dinner table. She, pure of heart and without the violence that taints her family and society,

cannot conceive of people so mean and devious as the mining companies JT represents. In the end, that innocent trust costs her all that she held dear. Schenkkan seems to be saying that murder, bloodshed, and vengeful violence are not the answer to survival, but neither is wide-eyed, trusting innocence.

Mary Anne is shocked out of her innocence by the actions of the mining companies and the presence of one man, Abe Steinman. Mary Anne had been trapped in the life of a miner's wife, watching her husband kill himself in the mine, watching her children die of typhoid, watching her mountains die from rape and exposure, and her community collapse under the weight of suffering. She feels helpless and defeated. Then Abe comes. Abe arrives to organize a union among the miners. Mary Anne latches onto the idea of community, working together rather than separately. This idea inspires Mary Anne, fuels her, and allows her to overthrow the legacy of blood and murder in her family. Although there is violence associated with the Union and its efforts, Schenkkan suggests that this kind of violence is necessary to prevent the soul-destroying violence of corporate greed. Mary Anne is successful in establishing a union that is supposed to fight for the community and provide what the people need in terms of education, health care, and social healing. Mary Anne, because she is female and because she has rejected the vengeful bloody violence inherent in the American identity comes closer than any other character to catching and holding her dreams.

Violence, whether for good or ill, is a part of America's heritage and history. *The Kentucky Cycle* exploits this tendency in Americans, showing that violence can be useful, as in the character of Mary Anne. However, violence in the name of personal or corporate greed, murder, or domination is never anything but evil. All Americans, women and men, are susceptible to the taint of violence that seems inherent in our very national character.

Source: Michael Rex, in an essay for *Drama for Students*, Gale, 2001.

David Kaufman

In the following review, Kauffman presents "The Kentucky Cycle" negatively through its lack of themes.

A decade after MTV confirmed that the American attention span has been reduced to approximately two and a half minutes, it's more than a little ironic that playwrights are offering endurance tests in lieu of dramas. Less than a year after the highly praised Part I of Tony Kushner's epic *Angels in America* opened on Broadway, Robert Schenkkan's Pulitzer Prize-winning *The Kentucky Cycle* has finally arrived on the Great White Way. Consuming six hours of playing time evenly divided two discrete seatings (as compared to the roughly seven hours of *Angels in America*), *The Kentucky Cycle* is more an event than a play. Its commercial success will depend on how many people are willing to invest $85 or $100 for seats to prove that their power of concentration is greater than that of their neighbors. But what, ultimately, is there to concentrate on?

Like so many other plays and performance pieces that have emerged in the aftermath of the Jesse Helms-N.E.A. imbroglio over the past few years, *The Kentucky Cycle* may be relentlessly politically correct but it's also dramatically wrong, even vacant. Set in eastern Kentucky and spanning 200 years in American history beginning in 1775, Schenkkan's cycle of nine one-act "plays" focuses primarily on one family line as it sets out to debunk the myth of the American frontier, among other things. For the scope of its ambitions, the media have been invoking everyone from Aeschylus and Wagner to Shakespeare, in a misguided effort of accommodate Schenkkan's achievement.

One might find more natural comparisons to Eugene O'Neill and August Wilson for their similar efforts to capture a sprawling history of this violent and materialistic continent through a marathon cycle of plays. Though O'Neill wrote only two of his intended nine-play cycle (*A Touch of the Poet* and the unfinished *More Stately Mansions*), and one might quibble about the relative merits of the different plays in Wilson's ongoing oeuvre (having thus far engendered *Ma Rainey's Black Bottom, Fences, Joe Turner's Come and Gone, The Piano Lesson* and *Two Trains Running*), both of these playwrights point to the principal weakness in Schenkkan's scheme. Not only does Schenkkan lack the poetry that they sometimes achieve, but the nature of his aspiration pales in comparison with their more epic undertakings.

Ironically, in spite of its imposing length, *The Kentucky Cycle* (at the Royale Theatre) proves too brief to develop any of its seventy-odd characters or to sustain any of its themes in anything other than bromidic ways. It's a matter of ambition masquerading as art. But it's precisely the kind of ambition

that a television-saturated culture can latch on to and promote simply for its gargantuan body.

Rather than joining the ranks of great playwrights who have endeavored to portray the human dilemma over a vast period of generations, Schenkkan owes his real inspiration of TV miniseries, by now generic, with their bite-sized morals and vestpocket characters engulfed by byzantine plots of mammoth proportions. It's not a six-hour attention span that Schenkkan is catering to (or banking on) but a thirty-minute one, which is more or les what each "play" in the cycle requires to be performed. The only things missing from the enterprise are commercial breaks.

On its own limited, soap-opera terms, *The Kentucky Cycle* does make for superb and efficient storytelling. It provides lurid melodrama, suspense and violence at practically every turn, to the point where it becomes ludicrously predictable as one generation of the Rowen family bleeds into the next. The first of Schenkkan's long line of evil protagonists is Michael Rowen, an Irish indentured servant. In the opening "play" (in any other context, this twenty-minute scenario would be referred to as a prologue or a scene), called "Masters of the Trade," Michael tracks down Earl Tod, a Scottish trapper who smuggles guns to the Cherokees. Both Michael and his young sidekick Sam have lost family members in a recent Indian massacre, and they're seeking revenge. But moments after Sam kills Tod, it's Michael himself who offers gunpowder to the Indians to save his own skin. To further appease the Cherokees who considered Tod their friend, Michael brutally stabs Sam. "What kind of animal are you?" ask the Cherokees. "A necessary animal," responds Michael.

By offering to supply them with more rifles, Michael secures a promise from the Cherokees that he can live on the land, although in the first of many obviously portentous lines, they warn him that the land is "cursed" and "dark and bloody." Just to indemnify himself against betrayal, Michael gives the Indians blankets contaminated with smallpox.

In such obvious fashion does Schenkkan load the villainous deck not only against Michael Rowen but against all his offspring. Presented as a paradigm of the American frontiersman—and, as we shall see, not only of his descendants but of all Americans except female Americans, African-Americans and Native Americans—Michael Rowen sets the stage for the greed and backstabbing vengeance that will follow over successive generations, taking us up to 1975. But what really emerges in the first of Schenkkan's nine-part cycle is a formula for reductive dramatic tactics and revisionist history, puerile devices that ultimately undercut consideration of any of his more meaningful themes.

To make his primary cardboard villain more villainous still, Schenkkan retains Michael Rowen as a character in the next two "plays." In "The Courtship of Morning Star," set in 1776, or a year after the opening, Michael goes about the messy business of taming his Cherokee wife, Morning Star: first by chaining her to him while they sleep at night, and finally by cutting a tendon in her leg to prevent her from ever running away. Michael tells Morning Star that he wants her to bear him children, but he admonishes that he will murder any female offspring, since they're of no use in him—a heinous deed he eventually commits.

"The Homecoming," set sixteen years later, focuses on Michael's son Patrick, who is being wooed by Rebecca Talbert. Patrick intends to marry Rebecca for her father's land, which he covets and which adjoins the Rowen property he expects to inherit. But after learning from his mother that his hateful father won't bequeath the family land, Patrick—shades of Marrat!—brutally stabs him while he's bathing. His mother encourages the murder so she can pursue her love affair with Joe Talbert, Rebecca's father. But in one of many melodramatic eavesdropping developments, Joe and Rebecca were offstage, in the ostensible bushes, where they observed Patrick's patricide. And when Joe threatens to turn Patrick over to the authorities, Patrick has no recourse but to kill him as well, in the process banishing his mother from the family homestead.

From Michael to Patrick, the apple hasn't fallen far from the tree, like father like son, and the child is father to the man. The superficial mortality and greetingcard mentality that mark the first third of *The Kentucky Cycle* become the basic roots of the remainig six "plays." In "Ties That Bind," set in 1819, the Talberts legally recover the land from the Rowens vow to get it back, and do so forty-two years later (in "God's Great Supper") by killing off much of the Talbert clan in the midst of the Civil War.

Between the Rowens and the Talberts, the cycle quickly becomes more than a little reminiscent of old Devil Anse and the Hatfield-McCoy feud, as the eras roll by and the plays pile on. Even more ludicrous is the token introduction of a black family line, which commences with a woman slave Michael Rowen brings back from Louisville but re-

> IRONICALLY, IN SPITE OF ITS IMPOSING LENGTH, *THE KENTUCKY CYCLE* (AT THE ROYALE THEATRE) PROVES TOO BRIEF TO DEVELOP ANY OF ITS SEVENTY-ODD CHARACTERS OR TO SUSTAIN ANY OF ITS THEMES IN ANYTHING OTHER THAN BROMIDIC WAYS."

mains in the subservient background throughout the entire cycle.

In 1890, the Rowens sell the mineral rights to their recovered property to "those Standard Oil people." By 1920, they're forming a union to combat poor working conditions in a coal mine run by, of all people, the Talberts. But even as the plays become longer and more detailed, somehow it all becomes murkier and harder to keep track of who's a Talbert, who's a Rowen, much less to care. By 1954, the coal workers' union is contending with infighting and under-the-table deals. Joshua Rowen, president of the local chapter, loses his son Scott in a mining accident that could have been avoided had he not cooperated with management by overlooking certain safety violations.

Though this particular development is straight out of Arthur Miller's *All My Sons,* it's not Joshua's guilt as much as Schenkkan's apparent reluctance to end pessimistically that permits this final Rowen character to break with the past. We're given to understand that the pattern of greed, vengeance and bloodshed that ruled in these here parts for 200 years is suddenly, and inexplicably, erased. Joshua discovers the corpse of the infantt girl murdered by his great-great-great grandfather, Michael, and returns it to its proper burial site. There are other symbols, of course, such as a pocket-watch that gets passed down from generation to generation and connects these playlets more handily than the script does; or a giant oak tree on the Rowen homestead that is cut down by the mining concerns.

According to Schenkkan, it was only after his cycle of plays grew that he began to realize it transcended the history of eastern Kentucky to be ''about America. It had become an unintended exploration of the process of 'myth making': that alchemy of wish fulfillment and political expediency by which history is collected and altered and revised, by which events become stories, and stories become folklore, and folklore becomes myth. Ultimately, I realized that the play was about American mythology.''

In an author's note to the script of *The Kentucky Cycle,* Schenkkan proceeds to discuss the Myth of the Frontier, which he further subdivides into the Myth of Abundance and the Myth of Escape. The first he uses to point out ''our ruin on a great scale,'' our rape of natural resources. The second has led to an avoidance of our past and a loss of identity. ''Without the past, what is there to connect us to the present?'' asks Schenkkan rhetorically. ''If actions don't have consequences, how can there be a mortality? Individuals who display such a cavalier attitude toward their own lives are currently diagnosed as 'sociopaths'; but what do you call a society that functions that way?''

This is all to be applauded even as it suggests a simplistic glimpse of grave and complicated issues. Though many of the cycle's plot twists resemble those in Greek tragedy and Shakespeare's revenge plays, what's missing is subtlety and depth to flesh out the characters' motives. To be at all effective, the cycle must rely on the resources of the staging and the energies of its overworked, twenty-one-member ensemble.

As conceived by the author in collaboration with the director Warner Shook, the spartan scenic elements are geared to emphasize the theatricality of the event. When they aren't part of the action on stage, the actors can be seen sitting on the sidelines, bearing ''witness'' to what transpires like so many members of a Greek chorus. With exposed scaffolding, a rear brick wall and little more than costumes to indicate the specific period, it all becomes a throwback to Thornton Wilder. (*The Kentucky Cycle* is essentially an *Our Town* gone wrong, which is yet another manifestation of Schenkkan's revisionist look at history.) The sweep and the movement of the ensemble are more directly borrowed from *Nicholas Nickleby.* But Shook never derives the ingenious moments of magic and felicity that Trevor Nunn obtained in his staging of that marathon Dickens classic a decade ago.

Stacy Keach, the one ''name'' in the cast who joined *The Kentucky Cycle* company last summer in time for its run at the Kennedy Center prior to

Broadway, is imposing as various Rowen patriarchs. And Scott MacDonald is particularly effective as a number of Rowen sons. Lillian Garrett-Groag and Jeanne Paulsen stand out as a few of the Rowen wives and matriarchs, who are women and therefore noble victims in keeping with Schenkkan's sophomoric scheme. But the players have all they can do to differentiate the many characters they portray, let alone rise above the cliches they embody.

Despite the ensemble's efforts, there is more drama—and mystery, for that matter—in how this work managed to come to Broadway than there is in the cycle itself. Much has been made of the fact that it's the most expensive nonmusical in theatrical history. But because it's essentially two plays, its $250 million price tag should be halved for a more accurate assessment. There's been even more brouhaha over its being the first play to win the Pulitzer Prize for Drama before playing in New York. This isn't exactly true either, however, since Wilson's *The Piano Lesson* won the Pulitzer technically before it opened on Broadway a few years ago.

But even if *The Kentucky Cycle* set a precedent by winning the Pulitzer in 1992, or a good year and a half before it arrived on Broadway, it's more telling that such an occurrence became a pattern when *Angels in America* won this past season, also before opening on Broadway (indeed, even before Kushner finished writing the second half of his marathon work). It's all rather indicative of pressure on the Pulitzer committee to honor the regional theater movement, which has grown dramatically in the past decade. Without the kind of momentum and advance publicity the Pulitzer bestows, it's doubtful that a play like *The Kentucky Cycle* would make it to Broadway at all. But to mention that *Why Marry?, Beyond the Horizon, Icebound,* and *Hell-Bent Fer Heaven* were four of the first six plays to win a Pulitzer is to throw into question the ultimate value of the prize in the first place.

The phenomenon that is *The Kentucky Cycle* is even more revealing in terms of cultural competition between the West and East Coasts, if not the different sensibilities they seem to represent. Perhaps predictably, what wowed them in Seattle and Los Angeles, where *The Kentucky Cycle* was nutured, is being less warmly welcomed in New York. But in this case, it isn't just a matter of ''Your play's not good enough for us.'' It's rather that the theatricalization of what amounts to a TV miniseries was more apt to have an appeal and be mistaken for ''art'' in Los Angeles than it was in New York. And the poor folk in the middle of the country, let's say Kentucky, may be forgiven for not knowing who to believe anymore. Or what to watch.

Source: David Kaufman, ''The Kentucky Cycle,'' (review) in *The Nation,* Vol. 257, No. 20, December 13, 1993, p. 740.

Robert Brustein

In the following essay, Brustein explores the study of American materialism despite the play's several limitations.

Robert Schenkkan's Pulitzer Prize-winning *The Kentucky Cycle,* now stopping at the Kennedy Center's Eisenhower Theater in Washington before it goes to Broadway, is in nine acts and two parts, consuming about six hours of playing time. Aside from any values it might have as a work of the imagination, The *Kentucky Cycle* is yet another sign that American dramatists are beginning to fashion their plays into protracted journeys at the very moment when audiences are apparently losing patience with sitting in the theater at all.

Marathon plays, of course, have been a commonplace of dramatic literature since *The Oresteia.* One thinks of Marlowe's two-part *Tamburlaine,* Goethe's two-part *Faust,* Ibsen's *Brand* and *Peer Gynt,* Strindberg's trilogy *The Road to Damascus* and Shaw's ''metabiological *Pentateuch*'' *Back to Methuselah,* among others, all of which attempted to endow the drama with something approaching epic form. But until the last few years, there was little evidence that American dramatists had a similar appetite for theatrical giantism, apart from Eugene O'Neill, whose monumental works culminated in a projected nine-play cycle about American materialism.

O'Neill's cycle was left unfinished (*A Touch of the Poet* and an early draft of *More Stately Mansions* are the only surviving remnants), but there have recently been a number of American efforts to achieve O'Neillian scope, among them Preston Jones's *The Texas Trilogy,* Tony Kushner's *Angels in America* and Robert Wilson's early large-scale extravaganzas (one of which took seven days to perform). Now comes *The Kentucky Cycle,* designed to be precisely what O'Neill originally envisioned—an epic study of American materialism as seen through the prism of family life.

Whatever one thinks of Schenkkan's achievement, one has to admire his nerve. *The Kentucky*

Bradley University's 1997 production of The Kentucky Cycle, *featuring Shaun O'Keefe as Ezekiel Rowen, Isaiah E. Brooms as Jessie Biggs, and Stephen Clark as Zachariah Rowen. This scene from* Ties that Bind *depicts the recurring violence in Schenkkan's play, as Jessie chokes a member of the Rowen family.*

Cycle is a construct of domestic plays endowed with the dimensions of a national saga. In the program, Schenkkan provides a genealogical chart to help us follow the extended progress of three different families tied to each other by marriage and hatred. Beginning with the Indian wars of 1775, the play ranges through 200 years of American life, touching on the Civil War, the unionization of coal miners in the 1920s, the compromises of the umw in the 1950s and the aftermath of the Korean War in 1954, finally ending in 1975 with an epilogue devoted to tying up the strands of plot and theme. Although the references to recorded history are often muted, and the canvas is geographically narrow, it is clearly the author's intention to provide a general historical overview of this continent through the device of familial events.

Schenkkan's central theme is the despoilation of the American landscape by greed and rapine. There are virtually no heroes in this work, only

"ASIDE FROM ANY VALUES IT
MIGHT HAVE AS A WORK OF THE
IMAGINATION, THE *KENTUCKY
CYCLE* IS YET ANOTHER SIGN THAT
AMERICAN DRAMATISTS ARE
BEGINNING TO FASHION THEIR
PLAYS INTO PROTRACTED JOURNEYS
AT THE VERY MOMENT WHEN
AUDIENCES ARE APPARENTLY
LOSING PATIENCE WITH SITTING IN
THE THEATER AT ALL."

plunderers and their victims. The one pure element, aside from a few black characters, is the land itself, and that is gradually reduced to mud and rubble. To reinforce this point, most of the action takes place in Howsen County, in the Cumberland district of eastern Kentucky, marked by a thick forest and a magnificent oak tree that serves as the central symbol. Neither the forest nor the oak survives the ravages of rapacious men. The property belongs to the Rowen family after its patriarch Michael procures it from the Cherokees in exchange for guns (though the Indians believe that "no one owns this land, it cannot be given"). It is entirely consistent with Rowen family behavior throughout the next 200 years that Michael also trades the Indians contaminated blankets that will infect most of the tribe with small pox.

Although Schenkkan's Indians are not exactly noble savages, they are contrasted with the white man in a manner clearly influenced by the racial assumptions of the movie Dances with Wolves. (There is even a howling wolf to begin and end the play.) "Here the savage was taught his lessons in perfidy by masters of the trade," reads the epigraph by Harry Caudill, whose *Night Comes to the Cumberlands* was the inspiration for Schenkkan's research. The Cherokees stick to their bargains; the settlers are invariably mean and treacherous. Treachery, in fact, is almost a leitmotif of the play, and its repeated reversal device is an offer of friendship followed by an abrupt and savage murder. Rowen

even betrays his own wife, an Indian woman named Morning Star, first by cutting her tendon to prevent her departure, then by killing their infant daughter and finally by fathering a child on a slave girl he bought at an auction (thus initiating a related black family line). He is rewarded in kind when his half-breed son, Patrick, stabs him to death in a tub.

The only vaguely moral figure in this murderous family is Patrick's grandson, Jed, but even he is involved in a series of grisly actions. After the Talbert family, a rival clan though also related by blood, has reduced the Rowens to sharecroppers on their own property, the Rowens take delayed revenge by slaughtering all but the Talbert womenfolk. Jed joins Quantrill's raiders during the Civil War and participates in a scurvy ambush of Union soldiers.

After the war, Jed makes the mistake of selling mining rights to his recovered land for a dollar an acre, and Standard Oil, strip-mining for coal, creates a sulfurous scene of havoc and pillage that more than compensates for the sins of the family. The unionization of the coal miners is marked by similar acts of treachery. Mary Ann Rowen's husband, Tommy, characteristically betrays a friendly union agitator who is gunned down by the owners. When their son, Joshua, eventually becomes the president of the district union, he betrays his own local by compromising on safety standards. In the inevitable catastrophe, his own son is killed. The play ends with Joshua recovering a 200-year-old infant corpse, wrapped in buckskin, which happens to be the murdered baby daughter of his ancestor Michael.

As my synopsis might suggest, this remorseless depiction of the white settler's duplicity and meanness eventually grows tiring, even to a spectator with no particular illusions about the benevolence of human nature. Occasionally a character, usually a woman, will detach herself from the contemptible crowd to express a decent emotion. But for the most part, everyone acts like a survivalist, sacrificing friend and foe alike for the sake of personal gain. It's as if only Snopeses inhabited Yoknapatawpha County. There is no sentiment in this play, but, curiously, Schenkkan's endless parade of base-hearted men eventually becomes a reverse form of sentimentality. One leaves the theater persuaded of the human capacity for evil but also confirmed in one's own virtue.

Where the author excels is in his storytelling. Despite its length, the play is never boring, and despite its growing predictability, it is often engrossing. The scene in the first part called ''Ties That Bind,'' in which Patrick Rowen is dispossessed of his land by a venal judge and a vengeful neighbor, is a subtle portrait of relentless retribution, as satisfying as a morality play. Even here, however, where a suspenseful plot carries the action forward, one wishes for language that would deepen it. Schenkkan's dialogue is never less than serviceable, and his hillbilly dialect usually sounds authentic. What is missing is the poetry that could plumb emotions beyond vengeance and hatred.

In short, for all its ambitions, *The Kentucky Cycle* rarely escapes melodrama, and its panoramic sweep suggests that it would be most comfortable as an epic film or a television miniseries. I don't say this patronizingly, only as a way of suggesting that its limitations might be better disguised by authentic locations and rural landscapes. Schenkkan's laudable desire to universalize his theme is often trivialized by domestic twosomes involved in table arguments. And the importance he attaches to the land as a central symbol is not reinforced very well by a set composed of wood platforms and steel pipes.

Given these limitations, Michael Olich's abstract scene design is very flexible, and Warner Shook's direction is a model of fluidity and economy. The twelve-member cast, supported by an eight-member chorus that acts as townfolk, scene changers and silent witnesses, transforms into a variety of characters with considerable authority. Stacy Keach, playing a medley of black-hearted Rowen characters, gives his most ferocious performance since *Macbird.* Jeanne Paulsen displays towering strength in a number of matriarchal roles. And Gregory Itzin, Randy Oglesby, John Aylward, Jacob (Tuck) Milligan, and Ronald Hippe create a range of colorful Kentuckians, making Howsen County seem a lot more populated than it really is.

So, with all my cavils, and with no small doubts about how it will fare in the commercial theater, I wish this epic well on its journey to New York. Evolved by a system of resident theaters, it is a testimony to the creative health that sometimes manages to flourish there, against all odds.

Source: Robert Brustein ''The Kentucky Cycle,'' (review) in *The New Republic,* Vol. 209, No. 18, November 1, 1993, p. 28.

Miriam Horn

In this review, Horn portrays ''The Kentucky Cycle'' as a mythological study in the American past.

Arriving in Kentucky's Cumberland hills in 1775, the patriarch of the Rowen clan kidnaps for himself a Cherokee bride. When she proves unwilling and tries to escape, he lames her by slashing her tendons. Fifteen years later, this resourceful pioneer coos to his captive bride his sweet memories of their ''courtin' days.''

Such distortions of memory—both personal and historical—are at the core of *The Kentucky Cycle,* the Pulitzer Prize-winning 6-hour drama that opened last week at Washington's Kennedy Center before heading to Broadway this fall. Encompassing 200 years and nearly 100 characters, the play is not only a darkly revisionist view of American history but a meditation on the process by which history is constructed, varnished and mythologized. In playwright Robert Schenkkan's vision, the proud frontier myth is itself the source of much of America's social and environmental decay. His cycle of nine one-act plays—seen over the course of two evenings—demands of audiences a less romantic confrontation with their past. Depending on sensibilities, the controversial drama is either a thrillingly theatrical study in historiography or yet another politically correct slander against the American past.

The genesis of the play came more than a decade ago, during Schenkkan's own chance encounter with America's first frontier. On a trip with a friend to the ''hollers'' of Appalachia, in a one-room shack with a dirt floor where an unemployed teenage couple were struggling to raise two small children, Schenkkan discovered the ''smell of poverty—as though you had taken a corn-shuck mattress, soaked it in piss, covered it with garbage and coal and set it on fire.'' Even more disturbing was his visit to the gleaming mansion nearby, where a coal mine owner scorned the playwright's pity for the ''lazy welfare queens.''

The desire to understand the ''unacknowledged relationship'' between such extremes of wealth and poverty led Schenkkan to the searing accounts of Appalachian history by Kentucky legislator Harry Caudill and, eventually, to the creation of the two great rival clans whose enduring blood feud provides the spine of Schenkkan's cycle. It is through the prism of these families—the rich land-owning Talberts and the poor laboring Rowens as well as the Biggs family, descended from Michael Rowen's slaves—that Schenkkan traces America's two centuries of history. To their few hundred acres of ''dark and bloody land'' come the Indian wars and the Civil War, coal mines, company towns, strikes,

" ENCOMPASSING 200 YEARS AND NEARLY 100 CHARACTERS, THE PLAY IS NOT ONLY A DARKLY REVISIONIST VIEW OF AMERICAN HISTORY BUT A MEDITATION ON THE PROCESS BY WHICH HISTORY IS CONSTRUCTED, VARNISHED AND MYTHOLOGIZED."

corrupt unions and, finally, shattered war veterans and abandoned, alcoholic wives.

Just as important as the history is the way that history is transformed over time. Neighbors murder one another's children and poison one another's land; their greed prevails over even the laws of kin. But as quickly as crimes are committed, they are also forgotten, masked with patriotic cant or the preaching of hellfire and the righteous vengeance of God. "There ain't no truth," says the sweet-talking con man who swindles the Rowens out of the mineral rights to their land. "All there is is stories."

Debunking myths. Stories, Schenkkan believes, can be a dangerous thing, the denial of the past as destructive for a nation as it is for a human being. In his own life, Schenkkan has struggled to accept the loss of his stillborn first child, despite the urgings of friends that he "be quiet and move on." From that experience he learned the hazards of "misguided forgetting" and was propelled toward the extraordinarily ambitious task of exposing stories that obscure painful memories and whitewash heinous deeds. Three cherished myths are particular targets of his angry debunking. The myth of wholesome pioneer life and the white man's civilizing influence on the savage falls in the blaze of cold knives and hot lead that rips through this saga. The violence in today's urban streets is not some aberration, Schenkkan insists, but a manifestation of an enduring American tradition. The myth of abundance, of the inexhaustible bounty of the land, also crumples as the small piece of Kentucky these families covet and kill for is finally skinned and bled dry.

Above all, Schenkkan assails the myth of escape—the idea that what one did in the past doesn't matter, that a man can endlessly reinvent himself and begin anew. The villains of this saga are those who forget too easily. Michael Rowen won his land by giving smallpox-infected blankets to the Cherokee, but just one generation later his descendants boast of the Treaty Oak where their grandfather purchased his land. "If there's no connection between the past and the present, then actions don't have consequences," says Schenkkan. "And if actions don't have consequences, morality is impossible."

The play's austere production reflects its desire for a direct, unembellished encounter with the past. On a rough-hewn stage, where bare scaffolding and light racks serve as everything from mine tunnels to river barges, the tale unfolds in the simplest story-theater style. Those actors not in a scene sit visibly on the sidelines, like ancestors and descendants watching their families' crimes unfold. At times a banjo or guitar chimes in, being plucked in a Cherokee lullaby or Baptist hymn. Yet for all its plainness, the epic sustains an emotional intensity sometimes difficult to endure. Reminiscent of a dime-store Western, full of outsize characters and adventure, it also has a high, almost classical tone, with incantatory language, allusions to the Bible and Greek tragedy, operatic leitmotifs and a heavily laden symbolism.

Signs of success. By most measures, *The Kentucky Cycle* is already an enormous success. At its run last year at the Mark Taper Forum it won five Los Angeles Drama Critics Circle Awards and broke box office records. At $2.5 million, it will be the most expensive nonmusical ever to come to Broadway. And, in what seems an inevitable move, it is currently being made into a miniseries for Home Box Office.

But some critics have damned the drama as "politically correct," with attitudes, in the words of the *Chicago Tribune,* "that seem more formulaic than deeply felt."

University of Kentucky English professor Gurney Norman calls it "L'il Abner with fancy literary pretensions." With its "quaint, violent, brutish, generally lowdown and sorry" hillbillies, he says, it "serves everyone who feels that they are hip to Schenkkan's little urban sophisticated ultraliberal agenda."

Schenkkan remains unmoved by such criticisms. His play is not remotely a documentary, he points out, but "a work of art, in an honorable American tradition of plays about families and their emotional and psychological legacies.'' He has no more tolerance than his critics for the politically correct inclination ''to impose contemporary concerns over historical events.'' Nor is he interested, he insists, in assigning blame. Even Michael Rowen, the vile white European male settler who abuses women, Indians and slaves, is treated with generous compassion by the playwright. Still, Schenkkan rejects the ''libel'' that to be critical of history is to be unpatriotic.

He is also more hopeful than despairing, convinced that damage acknowledged is damage that can be undone. *The Kentucky Cycle* is less a eulogy for the nation than it is massive group therapy. As Harry Caudill once wrote: ''The Cumberlands are a great many things, but most of all, a warning.''

''The problems of the Cumberland are not simply political or economic or social; they lie somewhere in the bewildering maelstrom of corrupting legacies that has trapped the people and the region in recurring cycles in a poverty that is as much spiritual as physical.''—Robert Schenkkan

Source: Miriam Horn, ''The Kentucky Cycle,'' (review) in *U.S. News & World Report,* Vol. 115, No. 11, September 20, 1993, p. 72.

SOURCES

Colakis, Marianthe, ''Aeschlyean Elements in Robert Schenkkan's *The Kentucky Cycle,*'' in *Text-and-Presentation,* Vol. 16, 1995, pp. 19–23.

Colby, Douglas, review of *The Kentucky Cycle,* in *The Spectator,* Vol. 27, November, 1993, p. 60.

Lahr, John, review of *The Kentucky Cycle,* in *The New Yorker,* December 6, 1993, pp. 213–18.

Lynch, Charles Edward, ''Breaking *The Kentucky Cycle:* A Native's Struggle with Language and Identity,'' in *The Southern Quarterly,* Vol. 32, No. 4, 1994, pp. 141–48.

Regan, Margaret, ''Arizona Repertory Theatre Stages Robert Schenkkan's *The Kentucky Cycle,*'' in *The Tucson Weekly,* Vol. 5, November, 1995.

Schenkkan, Robert, ''Author's Note,'' in *The Kentucky Cycle,* Plume, 1993, pp. 329–334.

Simon, John, review of *The Kentucky Cycle,* in *New York,* November 29, 1993, p. 79.

Stoll, Jim, ''*Cycle* Delivers on Kentucky Story,'' Kernel Press, 1996.

FURTHER READING

Caudill, Harry, *Night Comes to the Cumberlands, a Biography of a Depressed Area,* Little Brown, 1963.
  This work is a sociological study of the Cumberland Plateau, full of rich characters, violence, and courage. The study reads in a theatrical style and deals with many of the same issues expressed in *The Kentucky Cycle.*

Evans, Greg, '''Cycle' Rolls into Broadway's Red Sea,'' in *Varitey,* December 20, 1993, pp. 55–58.
  Robert Schenkkan's two-part *The Kentucky Cycle* is expected to join a growing group of straight plays with losses that once were the sole province of expensive musicals. The play grossed only $170,951 of a potential $349,299 on Broadway for the week ending December 5, 1993.

Mason, Bobbie Ann, ''Recycling Kentucky,'' in *The New Yorker,* November 1, 1993, pp. 52–60.
  In ''The Kentucky Cycle,'' Robert Schenkkan set out to redress the exploitation of Eastern Kentucky, but some Kentuckians wish he hadn't. One criticism of the play is that it portrays the victims as bringing about their own downfall.

McCarthy, Cormac, *The Stonemason: A Play in Five Acts,* Ecco Press, 1994.
  McCarthy's play explores the effects of racism, sexism, and daily life on a family of African-Americans in Louisville, Kentucky in modern times.

Morris, Rebecca, *The Kentucky Cycle,* in *The London Times,* January, 1994, p. 64.
  The set design for the New York City production of *The Kentucky Cycle* at the Royale Theater is discussed. Set designer Michael Olich thinks of his work as more of a scenic installation than a traditional set.

Lysistrata

ARISTOPHANES

411 B.C.

Lysistrata is often produced in contemporary thea-tre. Modern audiences enjoy the sexuality and hu-mor in Aristophanes' work, and they enjoy what appears as modern feminism and the depiction of strong women. Comedies were very popular pres-entations during the Greek festivals, and there is no reason to think that *Lysistrata* was not immensely popular. At the time of the play's initial production, Athens and Sparta had been at war for twenty years, and this play would have offered one of the few opportunities to laugh at war. The idea that Lysistrata could unite women to end the war would have set up the audience for a traditional battle between the sexes. However, there are also serious ideas to be found in Lysistrata's speeches. She reminds the audiences of the many men who have died during the Peloponnesian War, and the Chorus of Old Men emphasizes that there are no young men to take up their position. Aristophanes uses a woman to bring peace, but in doing so, he is pointing out to men that they have failed in their efforts to settle the war. With the failure of men, women are the only re-maining hope for peace. There is no record that Aristophanes received any awards for *Lysistrata,* but the play's popularity in modern productions points to its probable success on stage. In 1930, *Lysistrata* enjoyed a successful revival in New York City, which lasted for several months. It has in-spired an opera, *Lysistrata and the War,* which was written in the early 1960s and first performed by the Wayne State University opera workshop, as a pro-

test to the Vietnam War. The theme of war and women's efforts to invoke love as a replacement for war works as well in the twenty first century as they did in the late fifth century B.C.

AUTHOR BIOGRAPHY

Little is known of Aristophanes, except that his father, who was from Athens, may have been a property owner. When Aristophanes was born, Athens was at its most glorious, both culturally and politically. Born at about 450 B.C., Aristophanes was a young man when the Peloponnesian war was fought between Athens and Sparta. This war (431-401 B.C.) provided some of the historical framework for Aristophanes' comedies. Athen's loss in this war affected Aristophanes, and in response, he used comedy to ridicule the political order responsible for the war and the city's loss. Aristophanes' sympathy with the aristocratic landowners and condemnation of the rulers of Athens makes him appear more revolutionary than many of his cohorts. Aristophanes is associated with the Old Comedy, or *comoedia prisca,* which is earthy and irreverent and willing to attack prominent people.

Aristophanes' comedies are the only ones to have survived from this period. Of the forty-four comedies he wrote, eleven have survived. The Athenian festival of Dionysis was the first festival, in 486 B.C., to officially include comedy. Aristophanes entered the festival and won three first prizes, which was less than either of his rivals, Cratinus and Eupolis. The themes of Aristophanes' eleven surviving comedies reflect the poet's dissatisfaction with the government of Athens. Aristophanes wrote many of his plays during the war between Athens and Sparta. The works that have survived include *Acharnians,* 425 B.C.; *Knight,* 424 B.C.; *Clouds,* 423 B.C. (revised c. 418 B.C.); and *Wasps,* 422 B.C. Other surviving plays include *Peace,* 421 B.C.; *Birds,* 414 B.C.; *Lysistrata,* 411 B.C.; *Thesmophoriazusae (Women Keeping the Festival of the Thesmophoriae),* 411 B.C.; and *Frogs,* 405 B.C. The remainder of Aristophanes' extant work includes *Ecclesiazusae (Assemblywomen* or *Women in Parliament*), 392 B.C.; and *Plutus (Wealth),* 388 B.C. A number of other plays have been lost. Three of these comedies—*Lysistrata, Thesmophoriazusae,* and *Ecclesiazusae*—depict women as the moving force in human society. After his death, Aristophanes' popularity ceased, and he was not rediscovered until the Renaissance, and it was not until modern times that Aristophanes reentered the Western literary canon. In the Byzantine world, however, Aristophanes always held the rank of a major author: he was assiduously copied, studied, and appreciated by scholars.

PLOT SUMMARY

The play opens with Lysistrata pacing back and forth as she waits for the other women to arrive. She is impatient and tells her neighbor, Calonice, that women have a reputation for sly trickery, but when they are needed for something important, they lie in bed instead of rushing to meet. Lysistrata tells her neighbor that the safety of all of Greece lies with the actions of the women of Greece. Soon, all the women arrive, and Lysistrata tells them of her plan to end the war between Athens and Sparta. But first the group enters into some ribald joking about their figures and about sex. Lysistrata asks the women if they would not rather their husbands were home instead of fighting elsewhere. When the women reply in the affirmative, Lysistrata relates a plan to have all the women deny their husbands and lovers their sexual favors until the men vow to stop fighting and end the war. The women are difficult to convince, but eventually they agree to the plan. Lysistrata also tells the women that if they are beaten, they may give in, since sex that results from violence will not please the men. Finally, all the women join Lysistrata in taking an oath to withhold sex from their mates.

With Lampito returning to Sparta to secure the agreement of the Spartan women, Lysistrata and the women who remain with her make plans to join the women who have seized the Acropolis and its treasury. Within moments, a group of old men arrive, planning to set the base of the Acropolis on fire and force the women out. The old men complain that the women they have nourished all these years have turned against them and seized a sacred shrine. But while the men are busy with their smoking logs, the women enter, carrying pitchers of water, which they will pour over the fires that the men have set. The old men and old women trade insults, but the women will not back down, and they empty their water over the heads of the old men. When the magistrate arrives, he tells the men that the women's behavior is the result of the men spoiling their women, treating them with gentleness when they do

Aristophanes

not deserve to be cherished. The magistrate orders that the men force open the doors, but he moves to a safe distance to watch.

When the doors are forced open, Lysistrata emerges. The magistrate orders her arrested, but the policeman is too intimidated by Lysistrata to arrest her. The other women join Lysistrata in defying the policemen, who are too cowed to follow the magistrate's orders to seize the women. The magistrate responds to the women's actions with a claim that they shall never lose to women, and the newly brave police attack the women, but they are soon beaten off and in retreat. When there is calm again, Lysistrata explains that the women have seized the Acropolis to keep men from using the money to make war and to keep dishonest officials from stealing the money. The women say they can administer the money, since they are used to administering the household money. Lysistrata also tells the magistrate that the women have been patient while the men mucked up the war and refused to listen to any advice, but now, the women have decided to take action, since there are few men left in Greece. When the magistrate continues to protest, the women dress him in women's clothing, and then they explain that they will approach the problems of state in the same way that they approach the carding of wool. When the magis-

trate continues to insult the women, the women dress him as a corpse, and the man runs away. Left to continue the argument, the old men and old women turn to insults again. The old women meet each of the men's insults with rebuttals of their own. They remind the men that women bear children, but men make no contribution. The shouting and insults eventually turns to physical fighting, as both sides strip off their tunics and set upon each other.

Although there is no division of scene, it is understood that an interval of five days has passed since the previous action, and Lysistrata is now dealing with a possible mutiny. Many of the women are deserting and going to the men. Lysistrata tries to convince the women that the men are also miserable sleeping alone, and she pulls out an oracle from the gods telling the women they will win. The women are convinced, and the rebellion is soon ended, as they return to the Acropolis. A group of old men and old women soon enter singing, and Lysistrata calls their attention to a man, who is approaching. Cinesias is mad with passion, and in great pain and distress, since he misses his wife, Myrrhine. But she refuses to abandon her oath and join him, until the men stop the war. Through a succession of maneuvers, Myrrhine teases Cinesias until he is exasperated, and then she leaves him and returns inside. The chorus of old men sympathize with Cinesias, but it is not sympathy that he wants; he is now quite angry. Within moments a magistrate from Athens arrives and is joined by a herald from Sparta. Both are suffering from the women's absence, as are men everywhere. The two agree that something must be done, and the herald returns to Sparta with instructions to return with someone who can arrange a truce. While everyone awaits the peace envoy, the women seek to soothe the men. When the ambassadors arrive, Lysistrata is sent for, and the negotiations begin. But when it appears that neither group can reach an agreement, the men are invited inside to feast. The men's desire for their wives increases with the wine, and soon the treaty is signed, and both men and women leave for their homes.

CHARACTERS

Calonice

Calonice (also called Cleonice) is a friend of Lysistrata, but she is at first reluctant to make the sacrifices that Lysistrata asks. Calonice is earthy and funny, especially in voicing her lust for her husband. She becomes one of Lysistrata's strongest supporters, but not without having first been browbeaten by Lysistrata.

Child

Cinesias brings his infant son to the siege in an attempt to convince Myrrhine to return home.

Chorus of Old Men

The chorus of old men leads an assault on the Acropolis. They try to burn the women out by setting fire to the base of the building. When action fails them, the old men engage in a war of words with the old women, who have seized the treasury. The old men are offended by the women's desire to control the treasury, but they are ineffective against the strength of the women.

Chorus of Old Women

The old women prove a formidable force, easily defending the Acropolis against the old men's attack. They pour water on the men, when they attempt to set a fire, and they prove themselves wittier and more effective in a war of words with the old men. The old women point out that men only pass useless laws that lead to disorder.

Cinesias

Cinesias is Myrrhine's husband. He suffers from unfulfilled lust and begs his wife to forget her oath and return to his bed.

Cleonice

See Calonice

Lampito

Lampito is a Spartan woman who agrees with Lysistrata and who helps to bring about peace between the two enemies. She is athletic and bold, and demonstrates that she is also loyal and resourceful. Lampito provides the Spartan equivalent to the Athenian Lysistrata.

Lysistrata

Lysistrata is an idealistic young woman who wants to bring a stop to the war. She decides that the most effective way to get the men to stop fighting is

MEDIA ADAPTATIONS

- There are no filmed adaptations of this play. However, *Lysistrata*, was adapted as an opera in 1963–1967, to be performed by the Wayne State University opera workshop. There is a 90-minute cassette of the music available from Greenwich Publishers in Saskatchewan, Canada.

to deny them sex. She brings all the other women together and with some help from Lampito, convinces all the women to join in her in this plan. Lysistrata is smart and funny, a heroine with good analytical abilities, who is easy to admire. She helps the old women defend the Acropolis, thus controlling the treasury and preventing any more money being spent on war. When it appears that many of the women cannot hold out any longer, Lysistrata finds a prophecy that convinces the women to stick with the plan. She displays intelligence and the ability to be creative and convincing. When it appears that the peace talks between Athens and Sparta will end without an agreement, Lysistrata devises additional means to convince the men to find a peaceful solution.

Magistrate

The magistrate attempts to convince the women to return home, threatening them with silly and demeaning punishments. His attempts to disband the women fail, and his effectual control over the women illustrates how Aristophanes views the ineffectual government. This character is the target of Aristophanes' ridicule of the governing system and represents the foolishness of the leaders.

Myrrhine

Myrrhine is one of Lysistrata's strongest supporters and a willing captain in her service. When her husband tries to convince her to leave, Myrrhine denies him sexual favors and teases her husband with what he is missing. Her support of Lysistrata's scheme shifts the balance of power and marks the beginning of the men's defeat.

Spartan Envoys

It is the Spartan envoys who finally agree to a peace.

Spartan Herald

The Spartan herald is one of the men suffering without a woman.

THEMES

Obedience

One of the most ''shocking'' aspects of the women's actions is their disobedience to men. When the men arrive with logs and the intention of burning out the women, they tell the audience that they are shocked that the women they have nourished, and through implication spoiled, have turned on the men. In short, the women of Athens are no longer obedient to the men of Athens. Moreover, the women are willing to trade insults and even to fight, if necessary. This behavior contradicts the expected demeanor of the women. The magistrate, who represents the legal and conventional expectations of women, finds that he has no control. The women first dress him in women's garb and then in the clothing of a corpse. The women have abandoned their traditional roles as obedient wives and daughters, and assumed a position of power.

Sex

It is sex that permits the women to seize control. The men are held captive to their carnal desires and are unable to deal with the women as they had previously. Sex is both the women's weapon and their prize to withhold. Sex gives the women a power they would not ordinarily hold; and with the simple banding together of the women, the desire for sex leads the men to capitulate. One of the women, Myrrhine, uses her sexuality to tease her husband, and to assert her power over him. Near the end of the play, as Lysistrata tries to negotiate a peace, she uses sex to motivate the men, by parading a nude representation of reconciliation in front of the sex-deprived males. When this maneuver fails

to work, Lysistrata plies the men with wine, in a ironic reversal of the traditional male effort to seduce a woman. When the men begin drinking they become even more desperate for sex, and finally agree to a truce.

Strength and Weakness

Lysistrata correctly identifies the men's weakness and uses their weakness to create a truce. The women in this play are depicted as strong and brave. They willingly stand up to the old men and to the magistrate. They refuse to be intimidated or frightened from their oath. Instead, the women readily defend their choice and the Acropolis. They understand that a war cannot be fought without money, and that if for some reason the oath to withhold sex fails to work, they will have another tool with which to bargain. Where sex proves to be the women's strength, it is also the men's weakness, since they will promise anything to have sex.

War and Peace

It is war that has devastated Athens. The chorus is made up of old men because there are no young men left. Those who have not been killed in the war, now in its twentieth year, are off at war. The women remain behind and must manage children and property with little assistance. Young women have no one to wed. Lysistrata says that when men return from war, even the old ones can find wives. But once their time has passed, young women will never find a husband. This is one of the injustices of war, the abandonment of the women. The Peloponnesian War provides the background for this comedy, but the subject, the tragedy that this war brought to Athens, illustrates that war victimizes everyone.

STYLE

Audience

The people for whom a drama is performed. Authors usually write with an audience in mind. Aristophanes writes for an audience interested in drama as entertainment, but this is also an audience that would expect the playwright to include important lessons about life. In this case, the lesson is about an effective society and government that allows a war to continue after so many years. This comedy uses satire and humor to suggest to the audience that the men in power have not been effective in dealing with the war.

Character

A person in a dramatic work. The actions of each character are what constitute the story. Character can also include the idea of a particular individual's morality. Characters can range from simple stereotypical figures to more complex multifaceted ones. Characters may also be defined by personality traits, such as the rogue or the damsel in distress. *Characterization* is the process of creating a life-like person from an author's imagination. To accomplish this the author provides the character with personality traits that help define who he will be and how he will behave in a given situation. As is usually the case in Greek drama, the character's names in *Lysistrata* suggest their function. Lysistrata's name means "she who disbands the army."

Chorus

In ancient Greek drama, a chorus consisted of a group of actors who interpreted and commented on the play's action and themes, most often singing or chanting their lines. Initially the chorus had an important role in drama, as it does in *Lysistrata,* but over time its purpose was diminished, and as a result, the chorus became little more than commentary between acts. Modern theatre rarely uses a chorus.

Drama

A drama is often defined as any work designed to be presented on the stage. It consists of a story, of actors portraying characters, and of action. Historically, drama has consisted of tragedy, comedy, religious pageant, and spectacle. In modern usage, drama explores serious topics and themes but does not achieve the same level as tragedy. *Lysistrata* is traditional Greek drama. Just as drama educates and warns, comedy can provide important lessons for men about how they govern. The laughter of the audience makes comedy a safer forum for criticism of the governing body.

Genre

Genres are a way of categorizing literature. Genre is a French term that means "kind" or

TOPICS FOR FURTHER STUDY

- How does the comedy in Lysistrata differ from the comedy of one of William Shakespeare's comedies, such as *Taming of the Shrew*?

- Consider the ways in which *Lysistrata* attacks Athenian society and discuss the effectiveness of ridicule and irony in changing political decisions. Would such satire be effective in attacking politicians today? Or do modern politicians simply ignore satire?

- How are the men's attitudes toward women depicted in this play, and how do the women respond to the men's attack? Who do you think demonstrates the stronger position?

- Research the war between Sparta and Athens. Does Aristophanes' attack on Athenian society reflect the uselessness of this war? That is, is the playwright correct in having Lysistrata point out that both Sparta and Athens would be better off uniting to fight a common enemy?

"type." Genre can refer to both the category of literature such as tragedy, comedy, epic, poetry, or pastoral. It can also include modern forms of literature such as drama novels, or short stories. This term can also refer to types of literature such as mystery, science fiction, comedy, or romance. *Lysistrata* is a Greek comedy, in this case an Old Comedy, which refers to earthy and humorous sexuality.

Farce

Much of the action and most of the dialogue in this play is farcical, filled with nonsense and exaggeration. The action of the play is suppose to be divided over a period of five days, with the women organizing and seizing the Acropolis, and the meeting between Athenian and Spartan ambassadors occurring five days later. Periods of time are never exactly noted, but the time lapse is certainly not long enough to account for the state of misery that the men portray. The emphasis in the play is on their physical discomfort and the obvious signs of that discomfort. The humor is ribald and lewd, with risque references to just what it is that the women are denying the men.

Plot

This term refers to the pattern of events. Generally plots have a beginning, a middle, and a conclusion, but they may also sometimes be a series of episodes connected together. Basically, the plot provides the author with the means to explore primary themes. Students are often confused between the two terms; but themes explore ideas, and plots simply relate what happens in a very obvious manner. Thus the plot of *Lysistrata* is how women decide to withhold sex to force the men to stop the war. But the theme is how ineffective men have been in bringing an end to a war that has lasted twenty years and which will last another seven years.

Scene

Traditionally, a scene is a subdivision of an act and consists of continuous action of a time and place. However, Aristophanes is not using acts, and so the action, is contained in one scene, covering an unspecified period of time, perhaps a few days at most.

Setting

The time, place, and culture in which the action of the play takes place is called the setting. The elements of setting may include geographic location, physical or mental environments, prevailing cultural attitudes, or the historical time in which the action takes place. The primary location for *Lysistrata* is Athens. The action spans a space of several days; five days is suggested in the text.

HISTORICAL CONTEXT

The Peloponnesian War was in its twentieth year when Aristophanes wrote *Lysistrata*. Athens and Sparta had been long-standing enemies, but they had finally negotiated an uneasy peace in 445 B.C. When Athens wanted to extend its empire, the uneasy peace was broken, and war erupted. When the war began in 431 B.C., Greece was not a country

as we know it today. Instead it was a collection of small, rival city-states, located both on the mainland and on the surrounding islands. The war began after Sparta demanded certain concessions of Athens, and the Athenian leader Pericles convinced the Athenians to refuse, and instead, go to war. There was a short truce after ten years of fighting, when it appeared that the war was deadlocked between the two city-states; but soon the war resumed. Initially Athens seemed to be winning; in spite of having lost many people to the plague, they were winning some battles and appeared to be stronger than their enemy, Sparta. Sparta even suggested peace, which Athens rejected. But soon, the war changed, with Sparta in the stronger position. Athens had a stronger navy than Sparta, and the Athenian forces commanded the seas, but when the battle shifted, Sparta emerged as the stronger force. A major shift in the war occurred when Athens attempted to invade Sicily. This unsuccessful attack led to serious losses at land and at sea. These losses made Athens more vulnerable to Sparta's land forces, which had always been stronger than those of Athens. In addition, Athens' navy, which had always been its strongest force, had been destroyed in the ill-fated invasion of Sicily. Although Athens' navy was later rebuilt, it was eventually destroyed again by Sparta. By 405 B.C., the war was over and Athens had lost, having suffered near ruin. When Lysistrata reminds the audience of the terrible losses that the city has endured, everyone in the audience would have recognized the truth of her words. The chorus in *Lysistrata* is made up of old men because there are no young men remaining. Lysistrata laments the shortage of men because there are no grooms for the young women who seek husbands. The war, which has lasted twenty long years, shows no sign of ending, when Aristophanes is staging his play. The war will end in another seven years, but only after the Athenians are starved into surrendering.

The end of the war was a major defeat for Athens, one from which it could not recover. A peace agreement was signed in 404 B.C., and Sparta imposed severe penalties on Athens. In addition to surrendering almost all of their remaining ships, Athens was also forced to tear down the city walls, and adhere to the same foreign policy as Sparta. The Peloponnesian War was a catastrophe for Athens, leading to the destruction of her empire. The city continued to exist as a center for culture and wealth, but its political strength was never the same. The city treasury, which Lysistrata and the old women hoped to preserve, was laid waste by a war that

COMPARE
&
CONTRAST

- **c. 411 B.C.:** The democracy of Athens is overthrown by extremists, who are in open negotiation with Sparta. These extremists are soon overthrown, and the Athenian navy defeats the Spartan navy a few months later.

  Today: Greece is a united country at this time, with no city-state attempting to seize control over the country.

- **c. 411 B.C.:** The war between Sparta and Athens has continued for twenty years. The Peloponnesian War will end in 404 B.C., with Athens' defeat.

  Today: Greece, which has been dominated by military coups and turmoil with neighboring Turkey since the end of World War II, is no longer considered a dominant military force.

- **c. 411 B.C.:** In 429 B.C., a plague killed one third, and perhaps as many as two thirds of the population of Athens. Because of this plague, many Athenians ceased to believe in their gods, and much of the population fell into drunkenness, gluttony, and licentiousness. The effect of this change can be seen in the drama, *Lysistrata*, in which there is little mention of the gods-as there had been in many earlier Greek dramas.

  Today: Medicine has helped to identify the cause of disease, and most modern populations no longer blame the gods for the plague. But occasionally, as was the case with the initial discovery of AIDS, a segment of the population will attribute the victims' disease to a punishment of god and a judgment on behavior.

- **c. 411 B.C.:** The annual drama prizes at the Dionysus competition continue to draw the most talented dramatists. The prizes are sought after, and even in the midst of war, the leading dramatists of the period continue to challenge one another for prizes and recognition as the greatest playwright.

  Today: Drama competition continues with prizes for film and theatre eagerly sought each spring. Winners of the Best Film at the Academy Awards or the Best Play at the Critic Circle Awards are assured of accolades and monetary rewards that will ease the production of subsequent work.

- **c. 411 B.C.:** 25–35 percent of the population of Greece are slaves, many of whom work in the silver mines.

  Today: Slavery has long since ended, but Greece is now dealing with severe poverty and a shrinking economic base.

lasted twenty-seven years. The government of Athens changed, as well. There were many political murders, most at the hands of the committee of thirty that Sparta placed in control of Athens' government.

CRITICAL OVERVIEW

By 411 B.C., the Peloponnesian War had lasted twenty years, and Athens was in a state of turmoil. The plague of a few years earlier had decimated the population, killing anywhere from one-third to two-thirds of the people. At the time of the initial presentation of Aristophanes' *Lysistrata*, probably in January of 411 B.C., the political atmosphere of Athens was one of unrest. Within months, extremists would overthrow the democracy of Athens, and engage in open negotiations with Sparta. Although these extremists would soon be overthrown, their initial success indicates how unstable the atmosphere of Athens was at the time. But those events were still six months away at the time of Aristophanes' play, and there were other events that revealed how difficult life had become for Athenians. Athens had only recently suffered a significant and disastrous military loss in the attempted invasion of Sicily. With the destruction of their navy, the importation of food became a pressing concern for Athens, and serious food shortages and hunger were the result. Although there are many comedic moments in *Lysistrata,* there are many serious moments, such as when Lysistrata tells the magistrate that many of Athens' young men had died, and so, many of the city's young women will never have the chance to marry and have families. Lysistrata's actions will end the war, something that men had not been able to do in the past twenty years. Aristophanes gives important lines to his heroine, a woman, to point out to the audience just how inept their government had become. The Greek audience knew of women's weaknesses, but Lysistrata's strengths illustrate that one weak women can accomplish what men cannot. In Aristophanes' play, women are strong, and they are a force that can end a war.

Since there are no records of how this play was received, and since Aristophanes won no prize for its writing, it is difficult to reconstruct how the audience reacted to this depiction of women as heroic. However, it is possible to examine how well *Lysistrata* has endured by focusing on the play as source material for modern productions. It should not be surprising, given its antiwar motif and the depiction of women as strong movers of social change, that Lysistrata's story has continued to be a popular play in modern productions. Although *Lysistrata* was originally produced as musical comedy, most modern productions either eliminate the music or severely reduce its presence. Although there have been many productions of Aristophanes' play during the past one hundred years, there are two New York productions that offer contrasting views of this play's applicability to modern life. In 1930, *Lysistrata* enjoyed a successful and commercially profitable run on the New York stage. In an evaluation of the reviews from the period, critic Clive Barnes quotes 1930 reviews as pronouncing the play ''a smash.'' Some of these earlier Broadway critics noted that this Greek comedy contained set designs that offered a ''rich-hued, towering Acropolis,'' and that the actors helped to make the play ''a delectable desert for Broadway palates.'' Subsequent productions have not fared so well, with a 1959 Broadway production earning mostly negative reviews. Among the reviewers, none were enthusiastic, but most simply found this new production of *Lysistrata* either dated or offensive. Robert Coleman described the play as ''a bit shopworn,'' while John McClain labeled the play, ''tasteless and revolting.'' Much of McClain's ire was directed toward an attempt to modernize the play through revealing costumes and an emphasis on eroticism.

Aristophanes' audience was committed to the theatre, which was not a daily or even weekly occurrence. The festivals during which the plays were presented demanded something more from an audience than that which modern audiences are prepared to give. Since plays were only presented during the festivals, perhaps a couple of times in a year, Greek audiences arrived early and stayed late. Audiences sat on stone benches from sunrise to sunset, and in the large theatre at Dionysus, seventeen thousand, mostly men, sat to listen to the words of Sophocles, Aristophanes, Euripides, Aeschylus, and others. It would be difficult for today's audience to grasp the excitement that greeted *Lysistrata* when it first appeared on stage, and this is made more difficult in an atmosphere where theatre is readily available every day.

CRITICISM

Sheri E. Metzger

Metzger has a Ph.D., and specializes in literature and drama at The University of New Mexico, where she is a Lecturer in the English Department and an Adjunct Professor in the University Honors Program. In the following essay, she discusses Aristophanes' depiction of women and suggests that this depiction of women in Lysistrata *misinforms the audience about the public forums available to women in 5th-century B.C. Greece.*

The premise of *Lysistrata* is easy to understand: if men will not fix the mess they have made, then women must fix it for them. Aristophanes' comedy provides women with a strong incentive to, and an even stronger means to, create peace. The men of Athens have waged war for twenty years, and there appears to be no end to the war, in the foreseeable future. One woman, Lysistrata, decides that if men cannot end the war, women must do so, and so, she calls the women of Athens and a representative of Sparta together to form an alliance. This alliance of women will use the one bit of power that they possess—their sexuality—to control men. This plotting on behalf of the women is inspired, since men and religion most often criticize women for using

A 1993 production of Lysistrata, *performed at London's Old Vic Theatre.*

their sexuality as a way to maneuver men into abdicating control. In this play, Aristophanes takes this criticism of women and turns a traditionally negative view into a positive depiction of women. Or does he? It is worth considering this depiction of women in two ways. The first approach to evaluating Aristophanes' portrayal of women is to examine the way in which men are depicted, but in this case, men have little to say about war. But the second, more illuminating examination is to compare the women of *Lysistrata* to fifth century Athenian women. It is this last inquiry that demonstrates how little strength Lysistrata and her cohorts really depict in this play.

On the surface, *Lysistrata* appears to endorse women as strong, decisive members of their society. After all, the Peloponnesian War is in its twentieth year, and men have not been able to bring the carnage to an end. Indeed, the war has brought unrelenting tragedy to Athens. In the previous twenty years, Athenians have endured a devastating plague, the depletion of their treasury, and a humiliating and tragic loss in the attempted invasion of Sicily. Their navy, once a source of great pride and strength, has been destroyed. To add to the overall feelings of despondency, the citizens of Athens are virtually prisoners in their city, forced to witness from within

their walls how badly the war has been going. But Aristophanes' play never attributes the exact blame for all this mess, just that nothing is being done to resolve it. The author never suggests that it is men who have failed to end the war. But in placing the potential for resolving the conflict in the hands of women, he does imply that it is men who are responsible for the general feeling of disappointment that all the people are feeling. The implication is clear: women will do what men have not—end the war. But although Aristophanes fails to condemn men, women are also left without any genuine endorsement. Moreover, men frequently attack the women, painting them as deceptive (lines 671-679), lustful (lines 130-137), and without merit (lines 369, 399-420). Actually, there is little said of women, either by women or by men, that is complimentary. Women do bring an end to the war, but in doing so, they reinforce traditional Greek constructs of women's lives.

Virgina Woolf observed in 1929 that women in fiction have an authority and voice that they lacked in real life. This is especially true for *Lysistrata,* in which the title character appears strong and brave, or as Woolf suggests, ''a person of the utmost importance . . . heroic and mean . . . as great as a man, some think even greater.'' But this is only a

WHAT DO I READ NEXT?

- *Thesmophoriazusae*, also by Aristophanes, was produced in 411 B.C. Like *Lysistrata*, this play also depicts women as an important force in society.

- *Peace*, also by Aristophanes (421 B.C.), addresses the problem of war, with a stronger presence by the gods of Mt. Olympus.

- *Four Plays by Aristophanes: The Clouds, The Birds, Lysistrata, The Frogs*, is a compilation of four of Aristophanes' plays. This New American Library paperback (1984) is an easy and inexpensive way to become acquainted with this author.

- The Penn Greek Drama Series, *Aristophanes, 2: Wasps, Lysistrata, Frogs, The Sexual Congress*, (1999) provides a scholarly translation of four of Aristophanes' plays.

- William Shakespeare's, *The Taming of the Shrew* (1592), offers a romantic examination at the war between men and women.

- Menander, a later Greek playwright, also wrote comedy, including, *Samia* (c. 300 B.C.), a romantic comedy about confused identities. Menander represents the new Comedy, but only fragments of his plays are available.

---

fictional construct, and not the reality for women in ancient Greece. Thus as Woolf points out, women in literature exist in an imaginary, fictional world, where they are important, but in the real world, women are completely insignificant. In ancient Greece, women were not in control of their sexuality, and few men would have been willing to abdicate their desires to those of women. In the real Greek world, women were property, purchased through marriage or purchased through prostitution, but always, they were subordinate to men. In an examination of the sexual hierarchy present in 5th-century B.C. Greek life, Brian Arkin suggests that the way people behave sexually in a culture, is determined by what society finds acceptable. To illustrate, he notes that in ancient Greek culture, society was ''organized to meet the needs of the adult male citizen,'' who dominated the way society functioned. This meant that males were in control of sexual expression, and as Arkin notes, ''sex acts [were] not mutual,'' since ''in masculine discourse sex is something that you do to somebody.'' To extrapolate from Arkin's work an application to Aristophanes' play, means that Lysistrata's actions had no basis in reality. To put it briefly, women did not deny men sexual favors. Aristophanes' audience would not see Lysistrata's actions as anything but broad farce or entertaining slapstick. Since women were routinely excluded from Greek society, and men, in general, had a low opinion of women's intelligence, there would have been no reason for Lysistrata to attempt reason; sex was the only weapon that Aristophanes could give her. But in giving her this weapon, he makes her choices, and those of the women who join her, laughable. Clearly that was his intention, but he might also have hoped to point out that men, who did have an authority denied to women, should be ashamed of their inaction, especially when faced by a fictional woman's attempt to bring peace. Arkin is also concerned, as was Woolf, that women lacked an authentic voice on the stage:

> Greek men effectively silenced women by speaking for them on those occasions when men chose to address significant words to each other in public, in the drama, and they required the silence of women in public in order to make themselves heard and impersonate without impediment.

Women lacked a forum to speak out against the war, but Aristophanes could give voice to his own outrage by appropriating a woman's voice. Thus Greek women *appeared* to have an authority that they lacked in their own lives. In a sense, they were denied existence in their society twice, once by the cultural and societal rules that made males dominant, and once by the theatre, that usurped their lives, so that the playwright might give voice to his own agenda. On stage, Lysistrata might enter the world of men and conquer that world, but this could not ever happen in reality, as Arkin mentions. Women might grow tired of the deaths of their men, but they would never publicly protest the war.

There was only one forum available to women, where they might publicly comment on the war, and that was at the graves of their husbands, sons, and brothers. Women were expected to grieve properly, both as a sign of love and obedience to the men in their lives, but also, as a signal that they supported their society, and by extension, their government. This determination of proper grieving was so important, that the Athenian general, Pericles, spoke of this obligation at the first of the public funerals held after the Peloponnesian War began in 431 B.C., in which he addressed his comments to the women who had come to mourn. The historian, Thucydides, reported that Pericles told the women:

> If I must recall something about the excellence of those women who will now be widows, I will point out everything with brief advice. Great is the glory for you not to become worse than your innate nature, and hers is the great reputation whose fame, whether for excellence or blame, is spread among the males.

Thus, Pericles admonishes the women to grieve properly, but to remember that in their grief, they still must support their city's efforts to win the war. In an analysis of these lines, William Blake Tyrrell suggests that Pericles "was trying to fashion in the context of a funeral and mourning the dead the kind of women he needed for success." At the start of another long war, the women of Athens must have been worried about the effect war would have on their homes and marriages. Women in ancient Greece had a prescribed formula for mourning, which required that women give voice to their anguish. Women may be opposed to the war, but they could not voice that opposition, nor could they choose to protest silently. Tyrrell notes that "silence among women over the dead would be the worst of calamities." Women would be criticized if they did not mourn properly, but Tyrrell suggests that Pericles' words were not just intended for the widows who had come together to bury their husbands at this first funeral; instead, they were intended for the women, who would be called upon to repeat this ceremony over the course of many years of war. Mourning was women's work, and so it was appropriate that Aristophanes should have a woman grow tired of this work. Lysistrata tells the audience that there have been too many deaths, too many young men

> THE IMPLICATION IS CLEAR:
> WOMEN WILL DO WHAT MEN HAVE
> NOT—END THE WAR. BUT
> ALTHOUGH ARISTOPHANES FAILS TO
> CONDEMN MEN, WOMEN ARE ALSO
> LEFT WITHOUT ANY GENUINE
> ENDORSEMENT."

lying dead from this war. Her lament at all this death is the only recourse open to her. In expressing her grief, Lysistrata does come closest to depicting the real Greek woman of 5th-century B.C. Athens. In contrast, the women's lament at their sexual deprivation is little more than male fantasy. There is little in *Lysistrata* that tells the audience of women's lives; but, then, Aristophanes' audience would have little interest in listening to what women had to say. To get the audience's attention, the playwright needed to make the audience laugh at the war, and there is little about twenty years of war that can elicit humor. The bawdiness of sexual humor entertains the male audience, even if it creates a fiction of women's lives.

Source: Sheri E. Metzger, in an essay for *Drama For Students,* Gale, 2001.

Michael Rex

Michael Rex has a Ph.D. specializing in literature, poetry, and drama. In this essay he explores the ideology of Lysistrata's sexuality and how translators can affect this sexuality.

Without argument, Lysistrata is a play about sex. However, the attitudes of the translators often get mixed up in how the play expresses the sexuality of the title character. As an image of a traditional Greek woman, Lysistrata would not have behaved in the manner that she did because, according to history and respectable male philosophers, respectable Greek women did not engage in sexual activity. More recent studies, like Merlin Stone's *When God Was a Woman,* Pauline Schmitt's *A History of Women: From Ancient Goddesses to Christian Saints,* and Elaine Fantham's *Women in the Classical World* suggest that women had more control and took more of an active part in their lives, especially their sex lives. The play, while written by a man, with all male actors (although the musicians and choruses included women), and performed for a mostly male audience, was written for the yearly festival of Demeter, the Greek Goddess of agriculture, whose rites and religious services, especially those performed by women, are under explored and rather hazy. What we have left is the play. However, how the play is translated affects the way the audience and the actors interact with the play's title character. In five versions, the translator's attitudes toward Lysistrata's sexuality alter the way the audience sees the play's message about power, sex, and war.

In the last twelve years, two major new translations of Lysistrata have reintroduced the comedy to college and community theaters as well as classrooms. Both claim that "new" translations are needed to cut through the prudery of the 19th-century versions and the older American versions which seem to have problems with sex. Nicholas Rudall published his translation in 1991 and Alan Sommerstein published his in 1987. Both translators claim to be correcting a popular translation from the 1960s, the Donald Sutherland translation of 1961.

Sutherland's depiction of Lysistrata is not so concerned with sex, but with how comedy works. Sutherland suggests that comedy is very immediate and does not translate well over cultures. The use of proper names and the overwhelming local references that made the play funny to its first audiences gets lost on modern audiences even with large numbers of footnotes. For this reason, Sutherland suggests that power, sex, and war become much more important as the carriers of the comedy. Power and war go hand in hand for Sutherland and he goes to great lengths to suggest that these elements are subordinated to men's sexual desire when that desire goes unfulfilled by the women traditionally responsible for that fulfillment. Sutherland also tries to shift the focus of the comedy from the sexual to the social by giving the Spartans an American Southern accent and the Athenians a more Mid-Western speech pattern.

In terms of sex, Sutherland seems reluctant to mention the idea at all. Sex, sexual intercourse, reproduction, or screwing are not words used in Sutherland's translation. Lysistrata could as easily be talking about cooking or cleaning house. In fact, Sutherland makes the Greek men more concerned

about losing control over the money and having to do their own grocery shopping than whether or not they are getting sex. This treatment of sex in interesting, given that Sutherland was writing in the "sexually liberated" 1960s with a tone as repressed as a good Victorian.

It was this type of prudery that Alan Sommerstein and Nicholas Rudall argue against in their translations of Lysistrata. Sommerstein's translation, for Penguin Books, is full of sexual puns, contemporary jokes, people, and places. His translation oozes sex and he comes right out and uses all of the common words for the male and female anatomy as well as "vulgar" names for the sex act. Sommerstein argues that Lysistrata and the Greek women represent all women in their desire to control their own bodies and influence the course of political and social events. He also suggests that Lysistrata was more egalitarian in her movement including respectable women, whores, temple women, and slaves so as to cut off the supply of sexual release altogether. The women are portrayed as active sex partners, desiring sex in ways not traditional thought possible for Greek women. Sommerstein also plays down the money and the idea of fighting to emphasize the sexual elements of the play and the women's enjoyment of the men's discomfort. His translation suggest a solidarity among women that is lacking in other translations of the play.

While Nicholas Rudall reacts against the sexlessness of Sutherland's translation, he does not embrace the wholesale sexual freedom that Sommerstein suggests. Rudall is much more philosophical in his translation. He sees the play as much more about the fundamental biological differences in how the sexes see and use power. In his translation, peace, community and compromise are female attributes while war and destruction are "male phallic aberration[s]." He insists that the women withholding sex are respectable Greek *married* women. The idea that these women are married seems very important for Rudall and his interpretation of Aristophanes. Lysistrata and her comrades are not just refusing to have sex to stop a war; they are refusing to produce sons to be ground up as cannon fodder. Rudall removes sex from the physical realm and imbues it with spiritual and social power. However, Rudall's actual words tend to undermine his high-mindedness. Lysistrata talks about wanting to "get laid" and the "hardness" of her man's nights, while the men talk to their penises in stage directions.

Rudall may argue that the women are fighting on a philosophical plane and using sex (or lack there of) as a way to make a political point, but in modern performances, Lysistrata dwells much more with sexual politics than spiritual ones. Two recent college performances illustrate this point. The first, produced by Maureen McIntyre at Sam Houston State University in 1990, used a chorus of nude male student actors (over the objections of local ministers) with clothed female actors as a way to argue against the overwhelming display of female nudity in American media while men are covered. In fact, most of the male actors in that production were nude or relatively so. This production argued for the power of women through the use of sex in a feminist manner which many men find uncomfortable.

The 2000 production of Lysistrata by Karen Sheriden at Oakland University developed along similar lines. While none of the actors were naked, the sexual politics still took prescience over the philosophical ones. The production used modern rock music and portrayed Lysistrata and her comrades as the Spice Girls, thus arguing for ''Girl Power'' and the right of women to make their own decisions about their bodies, their lives, and their futures. The poster for the production had a young man lying on the ground, shielding his face with his hand while Lysistrata, in a pair of six inch open toed sandals, stood over him, her foot on his chest. Again, the sexual politics are obvious. The male body is to be viewed as an object rather than the female body, as tradition would have it. All the picture shows of the woman is a foot and a bit of calf. Under the picture are the words, ''Give Peace a Chance,'' yet the picture suggests that a different kind of war will be waged. Both of these productions, and most recent ones, as well, attempt to make men the ''object of the gaze.'' In other words, making men sexual objects for women in the same way men have made women into sexual objects. This ideology of sexuality differs greatly from the ideology expressed in most modern translations of the play.

Most translations of Lysistrata are still done by men as scholarly exercises to get tenure at some American college or university. Therefore, they must justify producing a new version of one of the most translated plays in the English language. Each translator argues for the idea of peace over war, the harmony of feminine community, and the noise of

> SO WHILE THE TRANSLATORS ARGUE OVER PHILOSOPHICAL IDEAS, THE DIRECTORS WHO EMPHASIZE THE SEX SEEM TO BE GETTING CLOSER TO WHAT ARISTOPHANES ACTUALLY INTENDED.''

phallic power, yet they all ignore the power of Lysistrata's character and her control of her sexuality. She is in control at all times. She is the first and the most steadfast of the women, going without sex for months, and forcing the peace treaty on all the delegations. Even without the shift in the gaze that modern, female directors give the play, Lysistrata's use of sex shows that more is at stake than most readers realize at first glance. Aristophanes seems to be arguing for women's control over their own bodies and lives in a way that fits into the religious festival of the play's first performance. His striking characterization of Lysistrata as a woman who claims the right to control when and with whom she will sleep threatens the establishment in ways that any other subject simply cannot do. So while the translators argue over philosophical ideas, the directors who emphasize the sex seem to be getting closer to what Aristophanes actually intended.

Translators, directors, and playwrights can never truly free themselves from the cultures in which they live. Lysistrata attempts to address the unequal nature of sexual relationships in Greece through power politics because the idea of sexual politics had not been articulated yet. Modern translators, generally men, have tried to gloss over the problems of sexuality in the play, arguing about the higher motives of the playwright and his culture, while ignoring the glaring problems of sexual relationships between men and women in that culture and in their own. However, Lysistrata is still a play much more about sex and its politics than it is a play about power and peace.

Source: Michael Rex, in an essay for *Drama for Students,* Gale, 2001.

Daniela Presley

Presley is an M.A. specializing in Germanic Languages and Literature. In this essay she discusses the function of the chorus in Lysistrata.

Perhaps the element of ancient Greek drama and comedy that is most difficult for the modern reader to visualize is the chorus. We know that the chorus sang and danced, but unfortunately the original music and dance movements have not survived. Comedic choruses usually consisted of twenty-four men wearing elaborate masks, costumes, and especially important in Lysistrata, exaggerated phalluses. There are two semi-choruses in Lysistrata, probably consisting of twelve performers each: a chorus of old war veterans and the other of old or middle-aged women. The choral members probably partnered up with a member of the opposing chorus and acted out the lines as they spoke or sang them. Each chorus would also have a leader who spoke or sang lines solo. At other times the whole chorus would perform lines in unison. Because so little is known of the actual movements of Greek choruses, modern directors of ancient Greek comedy are left a lot of room for individual interpretation.

The semi-choruses in Lysistrata play an essential role in the comedy. For one thing, they serve as a dramatic device that accelerates the time of the main action. While the choruses are bickering on stage, days pass for Lysistrata and the other women inside the Acropolis. But the choruses' main function is to react to and expand on the themes established by the main actors. The three main interactions that the semi-choruses have with each other mirror Lysistrata's plot as it moves from problem to conflict to resolution.

The premise of Lysistrata is well known. An Athenian woman, Lysistrata, proposes a sex strike to force the men to stop waging war. The Spartan and Athenian women have no problem uniting for a common cause, which forces their men to unite in their commonality as men. Lysistrata's plan shifts the conflict from Athenian versus Spartan to man versus woman. The chorus will dramatize this conflict to comedic affect by depicting the relationship between men and women as a war. Lysistrata's plan also redirects the human drive for death and destruction into the drive for birth and creativity. She calls on the power of Aphrodite to ''breathe down over our breasts and thighs / an attraction both melting and mighty'' so that men will only raise ''their cudgels of passion.'' The men will therefore exchange their spears and arrows for ''weapons'' of love, that is, their penises. The actions of the chorus will show that the human impulse to make war and the desire to make love actually come from the same urge. As Anna Lydia Motto and John R. Clark explain, in Lysistrata ''[e]pic heroism is humbled in the dust, for the psychological implications of this dramatic fiction are that male aggressiveness, realized in its penchant for swordsmanship, is nothing more than the sexual urge run wild.''

The chorus makes its first appearance after the problem of the play has been established and the main characters have left the stage. At this point, the Chorus of Old Men enters, joined a few moments later by the Chorus of Old Women. The old men labor to carry logs up to the Acropolis in order to start a fire to force the women out. In a play abounding with blatant phallic references, it is easy to suggest that the logs represent the phallus. The old men's struggle with the logs is a humorous reminder of their waning virility. They try to light a fire but only produce smoke; they have difficulty igniting flames, just as they have difficulty igniting their sexual ability. The Chorus of Women sneaks up behind the old men, ambushing them at the top of the Acropolis with jugs of water. The women dump water on the feeble flames that the men have managed to kindle, dampening what little virility the old men were able to muster.

This sexual metaphor of engulfing female wetness (water) that smothers male virility (fire) is framed by the parody of war that the two choruses enact. After each chorus sings its introductory song, they exchange violent threats and insults. The men compare their defense of the Acropolis now to their defense of it in a military siege one hundred years ago. The Spartan enemy has been exchanged for a female one. Now, however, the old men are reduced to ordering around pots of coal: ''These are your orders, Colonel Pot,'' says one member of the male chorus. The women call on the warrior goddess, Athena, to help them carry water in their battle. The choruses exchange taunts like rival armies, the women daring the men to try physical violence on them. The women do not back off when the men reply in kind; instead they threaten that they will ''chew your lungs out and your innards and your eyes.'' The themes of war and sex also combine in the old men's attempt to take back the Acropolis as a violent parody of sexual intercourse itself. They attempt to penetrate the citadel by force with logs and fire. But as Lysistrata said earlier, ''they'll never bring against us threats or fire enough to force open the gates, except upon our terms.'' In the spirit of sexual double meaning that abounds in the play, the "gates" that she speaks of are the gates of the Acropolis as well as the entrance to the vagina.

The sight of the Chorus of Old Men laboring to carry logs and pots of coal also emphasizes the threat that war poses to the fertility and growth of the Athenian city-state. The Chorus of Old Women calls the men "tombs" and jokes that the men carry the fire for their own cremations. Then the women playfully call them "bridegrooms." Death and marriage are combined in the war-torn state. The death-making impulse of war overrides the life-producing impulse, resulting in a waste of fertility. Thousands of young and healthy men have died in the Peloponnesian war, and women produce sons only to sacrifice them to the war machine. Furthermore, the war takes men away from their procreative duties. Lysistrata speaks of the cruelness of this absence to young women when she says that "the season of woman is very short," and it is hard to find a husband for a woman once she is beyond childbearing years.

The second major exchange between the two semi-choruses occurs after the debate between Lysistrata and the Commissioner. The main characters again leave the stage to the chorus who continues the theme of the debate: whether women should be allowed a voice in governmental matters. The men express paranoid theories of conspiracy and treachery. Since the women seized the Acropolis and took over the male tools of power housed inside, money and the means of communicating with the gods, the normal possession of power has turned upside down. The women's chorus argues that they should be allowed a voice in government: "I've a share in this economy, for I contribute men," they say. The old men, on the other hand, contribute nothing. They simply receive their military pensions and drain the resources of the state.

The rational debate soon breaks down. The Chorus of Old Men throws off their cloaks so that the women can smell their masculinity. "Every man with both his balls must make ready-take our shirts off, for a man must reek of male outright," they declare. The men, threatened by the women's boast of fertility, must give physical evidence of their own virility. The women respond by throwing off their own cloaks to release the smells of their bodies. "No woman smells ranker!" they boast. The choruses challenge each other with their bodies' smells, just as animals do to mark territory and signal aggression. Such a use of smell is also often a

> ... THE CHORUSES' MAIN FUNCTION IS TO REACT TO AND EXPAND ON THE THEMES ESTABLISHED BY THE MAIN ACTORS. THE THREE MAIN INTERACTIONS THAT THE SEMI-CHORUSES HAVE WITH EACH OTHER MIRROR LYSISTRATA'S PLOT AS IT MOVES FROM PROBLEM TO CONFLICT TO RESOLUTION."

signal of sexual receptivity among mating animals. In this way, the themes of sex and territorial aggression (war) are again combined. Furthermore, the women threaten, "Say an unkind word, / I'll pursue you till you drop, / as the beetle did the bird." This line requires a footnote to reveal its full meaning. As Jeffery Henderson observes, "The old women allude to midwifery, a usual occupation of their age-group, and to a fable in which the lowly beetle avenge the loss of its young by breaking the eagle's eggs (here metaphorical for testicles)." Henderson's translation of the line reads, "Just give us a chance / to pull down your pants/ and deliver your balls by caesarian," which poses women's birth-giving power as a threat to male virility.

The final choral dialogue occurs near the end of the play, after the comic scene between Myrrhina and Cinesias. This scene underscores what is taken for granted in Lysistrata's plan: marriage and heterosexual relations therein are essential to the stability of the state. The chorus will pick up on the love exhibited by Myrrhina and Cinesias and carry this spirit of partnership to its happy conclusion. The men begin the choral exchange with now familiar invectives against women, but then the women begin to show nurturing by slipping the cloaks back on the men and dislodging painful bugs from their eyes. The men respond warmly and conclude that the old proverb is right: "There's no living with the bitches and, without them, even less." The chorus has introduced here the final theme of reconciliation, and in that spirit, it says it is not going to do what was traditional for Greek comedy. Usually at this point, the chorus would sing songs that made fun of prominent men in the audience. Instead, they sing an invitation to a banquet for the next night. The Chorus of Old Men regains their virility and is able to participate heartily in the dancing and singing that will follow. As Lois Spatz writes, ''As is to be expected, the victory of Lysistrata's plan will bring about the defeat of old age. When these choruses lay aside their enmity, they will gain youthful vigor and sexual desire as well as peace.''

At Lysistrata's conclusion, the fractured chorus has become a harmonious whole, just as Spartan and Athenian, and man and woman have reunited in partnership and love. The chorus plays an indispensable role in dramatizing this transition from enmity to friendship, while offering much comedic support along the way.

Source: Daniela Presley, in an essay for *Drama for Students,* Gale, 2001.

W.G. Forrest

In the following essay, Forrest illustrates the similarity between the principles being held by Leaina and Lysistrata.

In his admirable commentary, Jeffrey Henderson notes the significance of posture and of physical setting. He does not remark that the statue of Leaina near to which Lysistrata and Kalonike are standing on the Akropolis was intimately tied to the obscure story of the later years in the Athenian tyranny. With minor variations of detail or colour the story was that Leaina, a hetaira beloved of Harmodios or Aristogeiton, had been tortured by Hippias after the murder of Hipparchos but, brave girl, had preferred to die than say yes, or indeed say anything. She bit out her tongue. The Athenians set up a bronze lioness, the work of Amphikrates, to commemorate her martyrdom. . . .

It is towards this crouching figure that Lysistrata raises her hand as she asks her sorority to swear 'I shall not squat like a lioness [Greek text omitted!. . . .]'. On what would the audience have expected that particular lioness to squat? On a cheese-grater? Hardly. On a tyrant, surely, or even more precisely, on a tyrant-slayer. An able actor would have had no trouble with a minor clash of stress or tone. A very alert auditor might have picked up an earlier suggestion of sex and politics at vv.59/60. But even the dumbest would be alive to an issue that had been tickling his fancy and his fears for nearly four years now.

Thucydides' petulant outburst at 6.53 owes much to his arrogance and something, no doubt, to his family tradition but the fact of popular panic was real enough and behind it lay two anxieties that were always lurking in Athenian minds, tyranny and Sparta; to give body to the former there was Alkibiades who, like another Olympic victor in the past, might have been thought to be 'growing his hair long with a view to tyranny.' By spring 411 the panic had subsided, *Lysistrata* is a confident play, but there was talk of Alkibiades' return, of being 'democrats with a difference,' and the Spartans were at Dekeleia. Sensitivity was there to be rekindled.

The events of 514–510 offered a perfect maze from which to tease out vice or virtue according to taste and purpose. Who freed Athens? The blameless young heroes, Harmodios and Aristogeiton, or the Alkmeonidai with the Spartans? Were the young heroes blameless or just erotically miffed? Were the Alkmeonidai supported by Apollo's will or Apollo's venality? Thucydides is better evidence for the existence of the arguments than for the facts behind them. But whatever the facts there was something here for every taste, intrigue in high places, violence, sex in many shapes. Small wonder that with Spartan alliance as part of his plot and the Akropolis as his setting, Aristophanes should exploit what lay to hand. The hint at 59/60 and the firm allusion at 231 are followed by a stream of titbits about tyrants, tyrannicides, Alkmeonidai and Spartans not forgetting a makeweight in Athens' aid to Sparta at 1137–48. All natural enough.

There may, however, be more to it. Between *Lysistrata* and earlier plays I sense a shift, both qualitative and quantitative, in allusions to Athens' past. Contrast the vagueness of the old men in *Acharnians* or *Wasps* with the precision, however unreliable, here. I renew a suggestion made in *GRBS* 10 (1969), that some work of 'scholarship' had come to Aristophanes' attention and that that work might have been part of what later became Hellanikos' Atthis. For me, following Jacoby, Hellanikos was in the Athenian democratic tradition; Sparta always needed foreign aid; Athens could solve its own problems. Hence Kimon's glorious mission to Messenia (1137ff.; contrast Thuc. 1.102), hence emphasis on the tyrannicides at the expense of Sparta and the Alkmeonids: 231 (I believe), 621, 630ff., 665ff. (perhaps); contrast Hdt. 5.55–65, Thuc. 6.53ff. Other Aristophanic oddities, notably the curious role of the old men at Leipsydrion, could be welded into a Hellanikan story, but it would scarcely be profitable to create it.

Better to conclude with a sort of parallel. The role of the monarchy in this country has been discussed for some time; recent activities of the royal family occasioned rumour and more debate; it was the appearance of Andrew Morton's book which added a pretence of scholarly accuracy. Hellanikos could well have given a lecture or two on Hippias, Aristogeiton—and Leaina, the girl who kissed but would not tell.

Source: W.G. Forrest, ''Aristophanes, 'Lysistrata' 231,'' in *The Classical Quarterly,* Vol. 45, No. 1, Jan–June, 1995, p. 240.

SOURCES

Aristophanes, *Lysistrata*, edited by Jeffrey Henderson, The Focus Classical Library, 1992.

Arkins, Brian, ''Sexuality in Fifth-Century Athens,'' in *Classics Ireland,* University College, 1994.

Barnes, Clive, compilation of reviews of the 1930 production of *Lysistrata,* in *New York Times Directory of the Theatre,* Arno Press, 1973.

Coleman, Robert, review of *Lysistrata,* in *Daily Mirror,* November 25, 1959.

McCain, John, review of *Lysistrata,* in *Journal American,* November, 15, 1959.

Motto, Anna Lydia, and John R. Clark, ''Lysistrata: Overview,'' in *Reference Guide to World Literature,* 2nd ed., edited by Lesley Henderson, St. James Press, 1995.

Tyrrell, William Blake, and Larry J. Bennett, ''Pericles' Muting of Women's Voices in Thuc. 2.45.2,'' paper delivered at the Kentucky Foreign Language Conference, 1999.

Woolf, Virginia, ''A Room of One's Own: Shakespeare's Sister,'' in *The Lexington Reader,* D.C. Heath & Co., 1987, pp. 50-60, originally published in 1929.

FURTHER READING

Bowie, A. M., *Aristophanes: Myth, Ritual, and Comedy,* Cambridge University Press, 1996.
   This book uses the techniques of cultural anthropology to compare Aristophanes' plays with Greek myths and rituals. This book also attempts to reconstruct the probable reaction of the audience to these plays.

MacDowell, Douglas M., *Aristophanes and Athens: An Introduction to the Plays,* Oxford University Press, 1995.
   This book provides information about the political background of Aristophanes' plays and is very helpful

> WITH MINOR VARIATIONS OF DETAIL OR COLOUR THE STORY WAS THAT LEAINA, A HETAIRA BELOVED OF HARMODIOS OR ARISTOGEITON, HAD BEEN TORTURED BY HIPPIAS AFTER THE MURDER OF HIPPARCHOS BUT, BRAVE GIRL, HAD PREFERRED TO DIE THAN SAY YES, OR INDEED SAY ANYTHING."

to new readers or audiences, who might lack an understanding of the political and social forces behind this writer's work.

Rehm, Rush, *Greek Tragic Theatre,* Routledge, 1994.
   This book is helpful to readers who want to understand how Greek tragedy works. This author looks at performances of several plays and encourages readers to consider the context in which the plays were performed.

Strauss, Barry S., *Fathers and Sons in Athens: Ideology and Society in the Era of the Peloponnesian War,* Princeton University Press, 1993.
   This text examines how social upheaval, especially during time of war, affects the family, especially the relationship between father and son. Strauss also draws connections between the problems that faced Athenian families and the dynamics of modern families.

Thucydides, *History of the Peloponnesian War,* Penguin Classics, 1986.
   Thucydides' great history of the war between Sparta and Athens remains one of the great histories of all time.

Walton, J. Michael, *Living Greek Theatre,* Greenwood, 1987.
   This text focuses on the staging and performance of Greek theatre. The author attempts to integrate classical and modern theatre, while providing a great deal of information about a number of the most important plays from the classical Greek period.

Wise, Jennifer, *Dionynsus Writes: The Invention of Theatre in Ancient Greece,* Cornell University Press, 1998.
   The author discusses the relationship between literature and theatre by examining the influences of a newly emerging literary world on drama. This text also provides some interesting ideas about the role of the oral tradition on theatre.

Zelenak, Michael X., *Gender and Politics in Greek Tragedy,* Peter Lang, 1998.

    This book offers some insight into the status of women in Greek culture and theatre and provides interesting analysis of many women characters from Greek drama.

The Memorandum

VACLAV HAVEL

1965

The Memorandum (*Vyrozumení*) is one of the best known and most popular plays by Czechoslovakia's (later the Czech Republic's) best known playwrights, Vaclav Havel. Inspired by the absurdities of life in Eastern Europe under Communism, Havel began writing the satirical play as early as 1960. Rewritten many times over the next few years, *The Memorandum* became the second of Havel's plays produced at Prague's Theatre of the Balustrade, where he was then literary manager. The play made its American debut in 1968 at the Shakespeare Festival's Public Theatre. This production of *The Memorandum* won an Obie Award for best foreign play. *The Memorandum* was first produced in London in 1977, and has been revived regularly around the world.

Like much of Havel's writing, *The Memorandum* is political, at least implicitly. The play concerns the tribulations of Josef Gross, the managing director of an organization encumbered by a bureaucracy that is out of control. The introduction of an artificial language, Ptydepe, is supposed to streamline office communications, but only makes it worse. Havel's satire is full of irony about the kind of jobs created by communism as well as the constant surveillance by office spies. Though Havel's vision was informed by his observations, many critics have noted that the office politics depicted can be found around the world. The importance of conformity to keep one's job is seen as relatively common. As Michael Billington of *The Guardian* wrote, ''The play may have grown out of experi-

ence of Czech communism; its application, however, is universal.''

AUTHOR BIOGRAPHY

Vaclav Havel was born in Prague, Czechoslovakia, on October 5, 1936, the son of Vaclav M. and Bozena (nee Vavreckova) Havel. His family was wealthy and well-connected in the arts and business. Havel's father was a restaurateur and real estate developer. In 1948, the Communists took over Czechoslovakia and the Havels's property was taken away. Havel was denied a high school education. He got around this by working as a lab technician at a school for five years. This allowed him to attend night school, from which he graduated in 1954. Involved in Prague's literary scene, Havel was already writing, primarily poetry and essays.

After a two-year stint in the Czechoslovakian army, where he founded a theater company, Havel got a job as a stagehand at a theater in Prague, the Divadlo ABC (ABC Theater). The following year Havel took the same job at the Balustrade. His dedication led to bigger roles within the theater. He aspired to be a playwright, and helped others write plays. Havel got his first solo play produuced at Balustrade in 1963, *The Garden*. This was followed by *The Memorandum* in 1965. By 1968, he was the theater's resident playwright.

That year, a new repressive regime, headed by Gustav Husak, came into power in Czechoslovakia. Havel became a human rights activist. His activities lead to the banning of his works in 1969, a ban that lasted for the next twenty years. While continuing his political activities, Havel continued to write and work in theater, though plays dwindled in quantity and, and, some would say, quality, by the mid-1970s. His financial situation was so dire that he had to work in a brewery to support himself and his wife Olga.

In the late 1970s, Havel was arrested and convicted several times for his human rights protests. In 1979, he was sentenced to hard labor. He served time until 1983, when pneumonia forced his release. Letters he wrote to his wife from jail were later compiled in a book *Letters to Olga* (1988).

After his release, Havel continued to protest. He was again arrested and jailed for nine months in 1989. That year, however, as a consequence of the so-called Velvet Revolution, the Czech communist regime collapsed. By the end of the year, Havel was elected president of Czechoslovakia. Though the adjustment to the presidency was difficult, Havel was internationally acclaimed and reelected president again the following year.

Considering his lack of political experience and the many difficulties he faced, Havel succeeded well as president. One significant problem for Havel was the rise of Slovak nationalism. (Czechs and Slovaks had been forced to share a country for many years.) The Slovak Republic was formally created in 1992, the same year Havel resigned his presidency. The following year, he was elected President of the Czech Republic. Despite a bout with lung cancer in 1995, in which half of one of his lungs was removed, and some hints of political scandal, Havel remained in power at the beginning of the twenty-first century.

PLOT SUMMARY

Scene I

The Memorandum opens in the office of Josef Gross, the managing director of an office. He is reading his mail when he comes across an important memorandum written in what seems like an incomprehensible language. His secretary, Hana, informs him that it is written in Ptydepe, a new language that is supposed to be more efficient for communication. Gross learns that his deputy director, Jan Ballas, has ordered its introduction without his knowledge. Gross asks him to cancel its introduction, and while Ballas agrees at first, he later convinces Gross that the use of Ptydepe would be best for everyone. This is endemic of the growing power struggle between Gross and Ballas. While Gross wants to work on a humanist principle, Ballas is ready for a conflict and believes he has everyone in the organization on his side.

Scene II

In the classroom where Ptydepe is being taught, the teacher, Lear, explains the background of the language to four clerks/students. The language is supposed to be more reliable because it is more redundant.

Scene III

Gross takes the memo to the Ptydepe Translation center. He meets with Otto Stroll, the head of the section, in hopes someone will translate the memo. Stroll tells him that he needs authorization, and that those who work in the center are not experts in the language. Gross must get authorization from Alex Savant, the Graduate Ptydepist. Stroll and Savant go to lunch, while Gross waits, talking to others including the secretary, Maria. When they return, Savant tells Gross he cannot give him the authorization. He must get it from Helena, the chairman.

A birthday party is going on next door, to which all but Gross go to. He is left alone with classified materials, though Helena tells him that he will be watched by the staff watcher, George. George watches everything in these offices through cracks in the wall. When Maria returns, Gross asks her to translate the memo for him. She will not risk her job. Gross is verbally abused by George when he asks for a cigarette, and returns to his office.

Scene IV
In Gross's office, Ballas, accompanied by his ever present but always silent associate Ferdinand Pillar, awaits. Gross still insists that Ptydepe be eliminated from the workplace. Ballas tries to black-mail him into submission on this point. Gross finally agrees to sign an order allowing the introduction of the language. Ballas then insists that he become the managing director, and Gross the deputy. Gross sees the logic in this move and steps down.

Scene V
In the Ptydepe classroom, Lear continues to lecture on the background of the language. Gross interrupts, asking him to translate the memo. Lear agrees, but only if Gross shows genuine interest in the class. Lear drills the students on specifics of the language. Gross gets frustrated and leaves.

Scene VI
Gross returns to the Translation center, where most of the employees are still at the birthday party. As the employees start to return, Gross tries to get Helena to give him authorization to get the memo translated. Helena will give it to him, but only if he has not yet received a memo in Ptydepe. Gross asks her to translate the memo, but she will not. Gross becomes frustrated as it proves impossible to get the memorandum translated according to the paradoxical rules set out. Gross's outburst is heard by Ballas and Pillar, who have snuck in behind him. Ballas fires Gross, and hires George, the staff watcher, as his new deputy. Gross is to report the next day to tidy up the details of his firing.

Vaclav Havel

Scene VII
The next day, Ballas and Pillar come to work. Ballas chides Pillar for not learning Ptydepe. When Hana appears, Ballas is appalled to learn she has stopped taking Ptydepe classes because they were too hard. Even Ballas has stopped taking the classes, though he claims it is because of the demands of work. It seems only Lear and those who work in the Translation center know the language. Ballas is also annoyed that Pillar keeps leaving with members of the Translation center staff. When Gross enters for a third time, Ballas offers him the position of staff watcher. Gross takes it. Hana reports that everyone, except Ballas, is unhappy with Ptydepe. Ballas does not like this news.

Scene VIII
In the Ptydepe classroom, Lear is now teaching only one student, Thumb. He explains interjections to Thumb. Lear is disappointed by Thumb's progress in learning the language. Lear throws Thumb out of class for holding up the other students.

Scene IX
In the Translation center, Maria reports for work. Gross scares her when he compliments her clothes through the chink in the wall used by the

staff watcher. Maria tells him that she had found a job for him in the theater. After she leaves, Ballas appears and questions Gross on what he has observed, especially about the staff's reception to Ptydepe. Ballas asks those who work in the translation center about their work. The translation work is slow and Ptydepe is taking on emotional overtones, which is not supposed to happen. Ballas asks Helena if the language is not doing what it should, and she confirms that is so.

Ballas gives Gross the Deputy Directorship again, and demotes George back to staff watcher. Ballas wants Gross to help him get to where they were originally: enthusiastic about the use of the language. After Gross leaves, Ballas further questions the staff of the Translation center. He learns about the paradoxical situation concerning authorizations of translation of documents. Helena, Stroll, and Savant accuse him of thinking up this vicious circle of bureaucracy. Ballas gives orders that should clarify the situation, and has them translated into a document for him. It is a protest that makes him look bad, making Ballas even more angry. He leaves.

Gross appears in the office again, startling Maria. Gross is self-critical about his previous actions. His insight moves Maria, and she offers to translate his memo for him. It praises him for being a good managing director and humane decision maker. It also agrees that Ptydepe is not good for the organization. After Gross leaves, George informs Maria that he heard the whole exchange.

Scene X

Gross returns to the managing director's office, and reclaims his job. He tells Ballas that his tenure is over and that Ptydepe will have to be removed. Ballas agrees with him and graciously steps aside. While Gross intended that Ballas be fired, Ballas blackmails him so that he can remain deputy director. Gross wants them both to resign, but realizing the futility of such a move, allows Ballas to have his way. The translation center staff appears, demanding to know who insisted they work with Ptydepe. When it becomes obvious that Ballas is accusing Pillar, he finally speaks and declares his support for natural speech before exiting. A man, Column, appears at the back door, and quickly replaces Pillar.

Scene XI

In the Ptydepe classroom, Lear is lecturing to his four original students on the problems with Ptydepe. He reveals that the office will use a new artificial language: Chorukor. It is based on similarity of words.

Scene XII

In the translation center, most of the staff is at another party. Gross bursts in, angry that another artificial language will be used. Ballas criticizes him for not being with the program. After Ballas leaves, Maria tells Gross that she is upset because George overheard her translating the memorandum. She was fired by Ballas, and asks Gross to overturn his decision. Gross declines, telling her to work with the theater in the job she found for him. Maria is invigorated by his words, and leaves.

CHARACTERS

Jan Ballas

Jan Ballas is the deputy director of the organization, under managing director Josef Gross. With silent constant companion Ferdinand Pillar (later replaced by Mr. Column), Ballas undermines the authority of his superior. Ballas is cold and calculating, always trying to increase his power. It is Ballas who orders the introduction of Ptydepe, and overrules Gross's objections by blackmail. Such moves get Ballas the managing directorship. However, once he is in the position of power, Pillar begins to betray him and Ballas grows paranoid. Ballas also gets stuck in the bureaucratic mire surrounding the translation of documents in Ptydepe. After Gross forces his way back into his original job, Ballas again survives because of his calculated earlier move. Gross would have him leave entirely, but Ballas's blackmail gets him the deputy directorship back.

Mr. Column

Mr. Column replaces Pillar as Ballas's constant companion and silent supporter in scene 10 after Pillar's outburst.

George

George is the staff watcher for the office. He sits in the space between the offices and watches everyone's actions. George can interact with staff members via a chink in the wall. When Gross is fired by Ballas, George is temporarily hired as deputy director. Gross temporarily becomes the staff watcher for a while as well. When Gross becomes managing director again, George returns to the staff watcher position. It is he who catches Maria translating the memorandum for Gross, leading to her termination as an employee.

Josef Gross

Josef Gross is the central character in *The Memorandum.* He is the managing director for the organization, though his power seems limited and is often challenged. Gross receives a memorandum written in a new artificial language, Ptydepe, and becomes frustrated when he cannot get the document translated due to organizational bureaucracy and staff indifference. Gross's power is also undermined by his deputy director, Ballas. Ballas ordered the introduction of the language without Gross's knowledge. Gross agrees to step down to the deputy position, and then is fired because of Ballas. Gross later retakes the managing directorship after he convinces Maria to translate the memorandum for him. The memorandum praises Gross's human touch in the office. At the end of the play, Gross will not reconsider Ballas's firing of Maria, letting her lose her job though she helped him regain his. Gross's power is firmly entrenched.

Hana

Hana is the secretary to the managing director. She does little actual work. Hana spends most of her time brushing her hair and running to the shops to get food items. She does provide Gross, and later Ballas, with information on occasion, but does not do much else.

Helena

Helena works in the translation center as a chairman of something unspecified. Like Stroll and Savant, Helena is an indifferent part of the bureaucracy. She follows the rules and goes along with what will allow her to keep her job. Helena is often concerned with sending Maria to get food items, as well attending birthday parties and flirting with her co-workers. She refuses to help Gross translate his memorandum.

Mark Lear

Mark Lear is the Ptydepe teacher in the Ptydepe classroom. He goes on and on about the background of the language in an attempt to teach it to his clerk-students. While he offers to translate Gross's memorandum for him as a classroom exercise if Gross shows himself to be a sincere student. Lear believes that Gross fails to, and refuses to translate the document.

Maria

Maria is the secretary in the translation center. She is often sent on errands to get food items by Helena. While Maria wants to hold on to her job, she is more sympathetic and human than most other characters. When Gross loses his job, she arranges for him to work at a theater company. Though Gross does not take the job, this gesture is a prime example of her generosity. Empathetic of Gross's situation, Maria finally translates the memorandum for him, though it is against the rules and George, the staff watcher, overhears. After he regains his post as managing director, Gross declines to overturn Ballas's firing of Maria for translating the document. Heartened by Gross's ''nice'' words of encouragement, Maria happily leaves the organization.

Ferdinand Pillar

Ferdinand Pillar is the silent constant companion of Ballas. They seem to be co-conspirators, with Pillar being Ballas's loyal employee. After Ballas gets the managing directorship, Pillar leaves with various employees of the translation center in what seems like scheme to undermine Ballas. This seeming betrayal unnerves Ballas. After Gross regains the managing director position, and Ballas is about to reveal Pillar's treachery concerning Ptydepe's fall from grace, the silent man speaks for the first time in support of natural human speech. Pillar then leaves and does not return. Mr. Column replaces him as Ballas's silent partner.

Alex Savant

Alex Savant is the graduate Ptydepist, part of the translation office. Like Stroll and Helena, Savant is an indifferent part of the bureaucracy. He follows the rules and goes along with what is best for his continued employment. He likes to eat lunch, go to office parties, and talk about women. Savant refuses to translate Gross's memorandum without the proper authorization. Savant often speaks in Ptydepe, but at one point admits that no one knows the language really well.

Otto Stroll

Otto Stroll is the head of the organization's translation center. Like Savant and Helena, he is an indifferent bureaucrat, who follows the rules and goes along with what is best for his survival in the office. Stroll does nothing to help Gross's efforts to get the memorandum translated, save relating the regulations involved. He also will not share his cigars with Gross. Stroll is more concerned with eating lunch, going to office birthday parties, and talking about women.

Peter Thumb

Peter Thumb is the eager clerk/student in Lear's language classroom. Thumb constantly asks questions, and at one point, gets thrown out of the class for interfering with the education of the other students. By that time, he is the last one left. Thumb is not particularly bright, but very enthusiastic.

THEMES

Absurdity

The Memorandum is a play full of absurdities, most related to Gross's problematic memorandum. The language that the memorandum is written is at the core of the absurdity. Ptydepe is an artificial language that is supposed to be more efficient for office communication. Yet the language is cumbersome, repetitive, and hard to learn. Only a few at the office actually know it. The absurdity grows as Gross tries to get the memorandum translated. A catch-22 of bureaucracy prevents anyone in the organization's translation center from actually translating the document for him. Anyone who receives a memo in Ptydepe can only get a Ptydepe text translated after the memorandum has been translated, an absurd paradox. A similarly contradictory circle exists in getting authorization for the translation from the bureaucrats. Gross tries to get around this situation by going to Lear's Ptydepe class to get the memorandum translated. But he is thrown out of the class for being doubtful about the language, closing another means of getting the document translated. In the end, Gross gets the memorandum translated by Maria. She only does it out of pity for him, and ends up losing her job in the process. The play's absurdities are Havel's comment on the economic structure of life under communism in Czechoslovakia and the rest of the Eastern Bloc, where everyone was employed but the jobs were often meaningless.

Betrayal and Deception

Several characters in *The Memorandum* engage in betrayal and deception, adding to the absurdity of the play. Ballas continually works to undermine his superior, Gross, betraying and deceiving him at every turn. Ballas uses the fact that Gross brought the bank endorsement rubber stamp home to do work as blackmail to get him to sign one document. Ballas also does not tell Gross that he ordered the introduction of Ptydepe straight out in the beginning, behind Gross's back. Ballas also ordered the introduction of a translation center, moved the accounts department to the basement, and instructed all staff member, save Gross, to take Ptydepe classes, bypassing Gross entirely. Ballas blackmails him again, getting him to sign a supplementary order for the introduction of Ptydepe. This is used in another blackmail scheme of Ballas's. All of Ballas's deceptions pay off in the end, to some degree. Though he gains, then loses, the managing directorship, he uses the advantage gained by his numerous betrayals to keep his job when Gross wants to get rid of him.

Other characters engage in similar betrayals and deceptions. Pillar conspires with those in the translation center against Ballas, before Ballas accuses Pillar of being against Ptydepe from the beginning. Everyone's actions are monitored by George, the staff watcher, who does his work from an office located between the walls of everyone else's work space. It is George's observations that leads to Gross's only major deception of the play. George catches Maria translating Gross's memorandum, and reports the action to Ballas. Ballas orders her firing, and Gross does not overturn it, despite the fact that her translation led to his regaining the managing director's job. Betrayal and deception are a fundamental part of the life depicted in *The Memorandum*. The bureaucracy seems to function on it.

Individual versus Machine

Gross is a man caught in the wheels of the bureaucratic machine. No matter what he does, he cannot escape its teeth. If it is not Ballas and Pillar using the details of bureaucratic paperwork to manipulate Gross into doing their will, the demands of getting approval so that the translation center will translate his memorandum ensnare him. For a time, Gross loses his job, until Pillar begins to conspire against Ballas. Ballas also becomes caught in the bureaucratic machine, and is as frustrated as Gross.

The only way that Gross can succeed in his goal to get the memorandum is to go outside of the machine. Maria, the translation center secretary, finally feels sorry for him and does the translation. The memorandum praises Gross for his human touch as a bureaucrat. This tiny rebellion against the machine leads to Maria's firing, but Gross will not save her job. He sends her off with human-like words of support. His position relatively secure,

Gross seems to accept that he is a cog in the machine at the end of *The Memorandum*.

STYLE

Setting

An absurdist play, *The Memorandum* takes place in a group of offices in Havel's contemporary place and time. That is, Czechoslovakia in the mid-1960s, when the country was under the rule of Soviet-aligned communists. Under this system, everyone was employed in jobs that were sometimes meaningless and redundant. Each of the three offices is essentially the same, with the furniture arranged differently. Unseen at the conjunction of the offices is the space of the staff watcher, George. His job is to spy on everyone else and make sure they are following the rules. This setting emphasizes oppressive atmosphere and the uniformity of attitudes among those who work in the offices.

Language

At the center of *The Memorandum* is an artificial language, Ptydepe. This language is supposed to be more efficient and accurate than common vernacular in office communications. Lear tells his students that Ptydepe is scientific, rational, and precise, yet difficult, complex, and redundant. Words in Ptydepe are so long, they must be broken up into subwords. Common words, however, are the shortest of all. Only a few in the office even understand a little Ptydepe, and most drop out of the language classes because it was too hard to learn. Even Stroll, the head of the translation center, says that while they are in charge of translating documents, they are "no experts." Thus, translations, like the one that Gross so desperately seeks, are hard to come by.

Thus in the play, language is used as means of control. Since there are a limited number of speakers/translators and authorization for translations are hard to come by, power is held by those who know Ptydepe. This is Gross's central problem. Ptydepe is used all around, but he has no idea what is being said. Though he is managing director for most of the play, he does not have much real authority. Also, when Maria breaks the rules and translates Gross's memorandum for him, she ends up losing her job, for the breach of the rules concerning language is unacceptable. Though Ptydepe's flaws are seen by

TOPICS FOR FURTHER STUDY

- Research how artificial languages are created and function. Discuss Ptydepe, the artificial language in *The Memorandum*, in these terms.

- Research the economic implications of Soviet-style communism on Eastern Europe. Why did this economic system create such an expansive bureaucracy? What were the psychological effects on the people who worked?

- Research the ideas behind the Theater of the Absurd, perhaps through the writings of Albert Camus or Martin Esslin. Is *The Memorandum* a true example of Absurdist theater? Discus your theory in detail.

- Compare and contrast Maria, the secretary in *The Memorandum* with her counterpart in Havel's earlier play, *The Garden Party*. How does Havel depict these women? How do they react to their similar situations?

the end of the play, another artificial language will take its place: Chorukor.

Repetition

There is a certain amount of repetition in the action and dialogue of *The Memorandum,* which underscores the endless circle of redundancy of this office life. Conversations are repeated, nearly word for word, over and over again. For example, the managing director's secretary, Hana, constantly asks to leave to get a specific item at the store. She needs to fetch milk first, then the rolls, and so on each of the two days of the play. Hana also tells her superior that he will like the lunch they are serving that day. Similarly, every correct answer Thumb gets in Lear's Ptydepe class provokes this response from the teacher: "Correct, Mr. Thumb. You get an A." There is a birthday party for a co-worker each day in the office adjacent to the translation center. As Ballas works against Gross in scenes 1-6, Pillar works against Ballas in scenes 7-11. When Gross explodes his frustrations at the bureaucratic catch-

22 that is the translation center in scene 6, Ballas expresses nearly the same sentiments in scene 9. Though Ptydepe is the first artificial language that fails, it is not the last. Chuorukor will take its place. All these parallels show how unchanging the organization is at its core; only the topic of controversy varies.

HISTORICAL CONTEXT

In the mid-1960s, Czechoslovakia was part of the Warsaw Treaty Organization (also known as the Warsaw Pact). That is, the country was part of the Eastern Bloc, behind the Iron Curtain. Czechoslovakia was a communist country essentially controlled by the Soviet Union. The political regime that was in power in Czechoslovakia was somewhat repressive, though the situation would grow worse in 1968. To understand the situation in 1965, the country's history during and after World War II.

Just prior to and during World War II, the country was split apart by Nazi Germany. Slovakian nationalism became strong, as it would again in the mid-1990s, and Czechoslovakia was torn apart. For their part, independent Czech patriots were put in concentration camps. During the war, Czechs suffered greatly. After World War II ended, Czechoslovakia was liberated by the Soviet Union. Though many in Czechoslovakia called for American intervention, none was given. The country always identified more with the West than the East, but this history did not change the situation.

Initially, Czechoslovakia had a noncommunist president, though it was under the control of the Soviets. Communism soon pervaded the country, and by 1948, Czechoslovakia was firmly communist. New Soviet leader Josef Stalin imposed the Soviet system on Czechoslovakia. Former capitalists, like Havel's family, were stripped of their holdings, as were churches. All who disagreed with him were 'purged.'

By the mid-1960s, the Soviet economic model was firmly entrenched, and Czechoslovakia was dependent on the rest of the Soviet block. However, this had created serious economic problems for Czechoslovakia, led by president Antonin Novotny. The standard of living was low, compared to what Czechs were used to, though it was comparable to

other Eastern Bloc countries. The agriculture industry was in shatters. The market was based on the premise that anything produced could be sold, though this was not true. Membership in and loyalty to the communist party guaranteed a person a better job, even if he or she was not qualified for it. Everyone who wanted a job was employed.

Faced with this faltering economic situation, reform measures were proposed in 1964 and 1965 that would have created a mixed economy. More private businesses would be allowed. Incentives would be offered for success. Prices, credit, and interest would interplay. More foreign trade would be allowed. Though initially approved, none of these reforms were actually implemented. Still, industry grew a little in 1965, but overall the economy would suffer for many years.

Despite this kind of communist control, before the 1968 crackdown, Czechoslovakia had something of an unrepressed intellectual and cultural life in the early and mid-1960s. There was more contact between Czechoslovakia and Western Europe. Films were being produced and seen outside of the country. Novels and plays described life under communism. There was some censorship, but writers, like Havel, still protested against those in power and promoted reform.

In 1968, however, Novotny was ousted by pressure brought by students and writers. He was soon replaced by a hard-line Soviet supporter, Gustav Husak, who took a strong stand against such agitators. Writers such as novelist Milan Kundera were driven out of the country. Czechoslovakia was more repressed than ever, and while writers such as Havel continued to protest for many years, it was not 1989 that Czechoslovakia emerged as a free country.

CRITICAL OVERVIEW

Since *The Memorandum* made its debut in the United States in 1968, it has received near universal praise. Critics commented on the play's depth and cleverness, noting that while Havel was depicting life in communist-controlled Czechoslovakia, his themes were relevant to life in the west as well. An unnamed critic in *Time* writes, ''no audience need live in a Communist country to feel the tickle of

COMPARE
&
CONTRAST

- **1965:** Czechoslovakia is a whole country, as it has been for most of the time since its creation in 1918.

  Today: The country has been split in two for many years. The rise of Slovak nationalism after the Velvet Revolution led to the creation of two new countries: Slovakia and the Czech Republic.

- **1965:** Czechoslovakia is a communist country, controlled by the Soviet Union as part of the Warsaw Pact.

  Today: The Czech Republic and Slovakia are free, independent nations. Havel is the president of the Czech Republic, as he has been since 1993. Previously, he was president of Czechoslovakia from 1989 to 1992. Havel was the first noncommunist president since the 1940s.

- **1965:** Under the Soviet economic model, everyone has a job, but the standard of living is low in Czechoslovakia.

  Today: Unemployment is higher, but the standard of living is also higher, in the new free market economy of the Czech Republic and Slovakia.

- **1965:** Those in power, primarily the Communists, have restrictions on what can be written. Censorship, while not as harsh as at other times in Czechoslovakian history, still exists.

  Today: There is no overt censorship on creative endeavors in the Czech Republic.

Havel's barbs—it is enough to have experienced alienation in the midst of a scientific, computerized society. His main target is the mechanization of human beings.''

Other American critics were surprised by the humanity of the play, often found in the details. Writing in the *New Yorker* Edith Oliver argues that ''There are more than a few hints that the play, for all its high jinks [sic] in execution, is meant to be a tract about the power of the system to crush all the humanity and courage from a decent man, but I must say that its incidental scenes and small human touches are more enlightening as a picture of life in Czechoslovakia than its abstract whole.'' Along similar lines, Clive Barnes of the *New York Times* believes that ''Gross's unavailing struggle against the tendrils of bureaucracy are very amusing but also—and this is where Mr. Havel is particularly successful—strangely touching. You really feel for the weak and vacillating Gross and for the little office girl who by helping him loses her own job.''

Robert Hatch of *The Nation* is also among those who believe that Havel successfully balances depth with humor in *The Memorandum*. He writes, ''Mr. Havel entertains himself, and his audience, with some speculation as to what usually lies behind the more passionate ideological disputes. Chiefly, he finds, it is a matter of whose initials will validate a chit—a dominance too loosely guarded by those who enjoy it and hungered for with exaggerated appetite by those who do not.''

The Memorandum was produced regularly over the years, including a London, England production in 1977. However, when the play was revived in London at the Orange Tree Theater in 1995, some critics believed the plays was showing its age. Absurdism was no longer in vogue, though the play's universality was still seen by as relevant by some. Many critics qualified their praise.

For example, while Jeremy Kingston of *The Times* wrote that ''Havel writes amusing scenes in which this ghastly tongue [Ptydepe] is being taught . . . but the play's real meat is the endless circling by Gross around the building, becoming ever deeper entangled in the deceit and betrayal.'' Later in his review, Kingston argued that ''Shortly before

A scene from the 1996 University of Kansas Theatre production of The Memorandum, *featuring (from left to right) Jennette Selig as Jan Ballas, Jefferson R. Bachura as Otto Stroll, and Jamie Johnson as Helena.*

the half-way mark the play is becalmed in repetition, and some of the Absurdist baggage has not worn well.''

Similarly, Michael Billington of *The Guardian* believes that ''What is impressive is how many targets Havel manages to hit in the course of the play.'' But Billington also writes that ''Havel's concern with symmetry makes it hard for him to end the work when he should. But his writing also has a blithe playfulness.''

Other London critics were more enthusiastic. Sarah Hemming of *Financial Times* echoes reviews of the 1968 New York production when she wrote ''It is a funny and very clever play, and its revival . . . reveals it to be just as pointed as at its premiere. The portrayal of an unwieldy bureaucracy, whose only purpose seems to be self-perpetuation, will strike many people as familiar.'' She only chides Havel's play by saying it ''can be verbose and over-intellectual.'' Lucy Hughes-Hallet of *Plays & Players* makes a point similar to Hemming's. She writes, ''The plot is circular, or rather caucus race-shaped, in that everyone ends up exactly where they started in the hierarchy of the firm, but the Ptydepe affair

shakes things up enough to reveal both the funny and the sinister side of excessive bureaucracy.''

CRITICISM

Annette Petruso

Annette Petruso is a freelance author and screenwriter in Austin, TX. In the following essay, Petruso considers the odd ending to The Memorandum, *discussing critical interpretations and giving an in-depth analysis of the characters involved.*

One element of Vaclav Havel's satirical absurdist play *The Memorandum* has been the subject of much critical discussion: the ending. Its tone does not seem to fit the rest of the play. At the end, Josef Gross—the managing director whose effort to get a memorandum translated from Ptydepe is constantly stymied—will not help Maria, the translation center secretary, get her job back. She is fired because she translated the document for him, though it was against the rules, and was caught by the staff watcher

WHAT
DO I READ
NEXT?

- *The Trial*, a book by Franz Kafka, published in 1925. It also concerns the trials and tribulations of a man, Josef K., caught up in the system.

- *1984*, a novel by George Orwell, published in 1949. The work describes a futuristic society in which everyone is monitored and controlled by an overwhelming bureaucracy.

- *Audience*, a play by Havel written in 1975. It also concerns the oppression of bureaucracy.

- *Metamorphosis*, a novel by Franz Kafka, published in 1915. This is a book that also focuses on a man trapped in an impossible situation.

- *Animal Farm: A Fairy Story*, is a novella by George Orwell that was published in 1945. It also concerns bullying, structure, and power, and shares some repetitive qualities with *The Memorandum*.

(office spy), George. Instead Gross sends her on her way with a long speech in which he basically tells her that he cannot risk his job by saving her's. He also tells her that she could easily get a job in the theater, one that she previously arranged for him. After a few compliments, Gross tells her that he must go to lunch. Collecting her things, Maria says ''Nobody ever talked to me so nicely before.''

Over the years, critics and scholars have had varying interpretations of this ending. Many saw it as a manifestation of Gross's inadequacies. In 1968, the unnamed critic in *Time* believed the events of the play had ''so depersonalized'' Gross that he could not risk helping her. The same year, Clive Barnes of the *New York Times* calls Gross ''weak and vacillating,'' blaming him entirely for Maria's job loss. Scholar Robert Skloot also put the fault on Gross. In 1993, he wrote in the *Kenyan Review* that ''That Maria remains 'happy' because 'nobody ever talked to me so nicely before' does not excuse Gross's avoidance of moral action nor his failure to reciprocate Maria's genuine expression of love toward him.''

Others saw the ending as reflecting more on Maria and her qualities. In 1994, *The Times*' Jeremy Kingston believes that truth has not been served by the ending. He speculates that she might be happy because she is going to be part of the theater, like Havel was at the time, though there is no real indication that this job is even open to her. Scholar

Jude R. Meche, writing in *Modern Drama* in 1997, believes that Maria emerges as the stronger character. ''Maria's willingness to risk termination in translating the memorandum does nothing to condemn Gross; her willingness only testifies to her courage and sympathy for a fellow human being in need. Gross condemns himself . . . [and] excus[es] himself from this debt with a wave of self-important rhetoric.''

While all of these arguments have at least some validity, I believe the ending of *The Memorandum* is the most revealing moment of the play. It is the culmination of attitudes, subtly expressed through details and innuendoes that are often secondary to the main action. This essay looks in depth at the motivations, attitudes, and building of the characters of Gross and Maria, then at how the ending validates these characterizations.

As the *New York Times*' Barnes suggests, Gross shows himself to be a weak man, from the very beginning of *The Memorandum*. Admittedly, he is in a tough situation. Gross is the managing director of the unnamed organization, and his power does not seem that great. He is constantly undermined by his deputy director, Jan Ballas. It is Ballas who orders the introduction of the artificial language Ptydepe, demands that all the staff take classes in it, and moves the accounts department to the basement so a Ptydepe translation center can be set up in its place. Gross does not find this out from Ballas, but from Hana, his secretary. Gross even has to ask her, prompted by the receipt of a memorandum written in an unknown language. Everyone else in the organization has been informed about the introduction of Ptydepe. Gross always seems one step behind and rather dense.

Thus, even when Gross is managing director (the situation changes throughout the play, and he allows himself to be demoted to deputy director, loses his job, and then is rehired by Ballas as the office spy known as the staff watcher, promoted to deputy director again before reclaiming his original position), Ballas is firmly in control because he knows how to play on Gross's weaknesses. Ballas uses information he has on Gross to keep him in line and prod him into signing incriminating documents. Gross never tries to turn the tables on Ballas, but bows to his demands and cowers at every opportunity. Most revealing is a statement made by Gross in scene 1. He tells Ballas, and his ever-present silent companion and coconspirator Mr. Pillar, that "I don't mind taking risks, but I'm not a gambler."

Gross's only possible weapon against Ballas is the memorandum in Ptydepe. But the tangled, contradictory bureaucracy works against him as he tries to get it translated. Those who are in charge at the translation center—Dr. Alex Savant, a supposed expert in Ptydepe; Otto Stroll, the department head; and Helena, its chairman—follow the arcane rules that make it nearly impossible for Gross to get his memorandum put into vernacular. They also treat Gross with disrespect. Though he is the managing director, then deputy director, they walk in and out of the room and worry about food-related issues during scenes three and six, not finishing their

explanations about why they cannot help him. These three from the translation center definitely respect Ballas, however. When Gross becomes completely frustrated with them and verbally berates them in scene six, they will not sit down when he orders them to because Ballas and Pillar are in the room behind him. Only when Ballas tells them to sit down, do they do so.

The only person in the whole organization who seems to have any real respect for Gross is Maria. She gets little herself. Maria, the translation center secretary, is treated like a slave and an object by her three immediate superiors. As Lucy Hughs-Hallet of *Plays [and] Players* points out, Maria is "the only character in this whole play about work who is ever actually seen to do any work (and even then her job consists mainly of doing her superiors' shopping)." From her first introduction in scene three, she is constantly doing their bidding—running to the store for onions, cantaloupes, milk, limes, chocolate and coffee; ironing Helena's slip; and so on—as well as typing reports and doing other typical secretarial work. Stoll and Savant also objectify her. When she leaves on an errand, Savant says to Stroll "Sexy little thing, isn't she?" Maria does not seem bitter or angry by this treatment. She does her job more than adequately.

Into this world comes Gross. Maria is never seen outside of the translation center; Gross always comes to her. From the beginning, Gross tries to take advantage of her. There is a box of cigars in her work area that belongs to Stroll. She will not give him one because they are counted and she would get in trouble. This angers him slightly. At the end of the same scene, Gross tries to get Maria to translate the memorandum for him. Again, she says she must follow the rules and cannot. Gross tries to flatter her into doing what he wants. He says her name is "pretty" then presses her to translate it again. She declines again. Maria is a nice, polite person, but her continued employment is obviously of value to her.

By scene six, Gross's supposed affections for Maria have been noticed. Savant and Stroll tease him for calling her "sweetheart," as the staff watcher George has told them. Gross continues to be humiliated by these supposed inferiors, as Maria is kept running around by them. But Maria witnesses the moment at the end of the scene when Ballas fires Gross. Her fundamental goodness kicks in and she finds a job for Gross outside the organization in her brother's theater group. But Gross is rehired by

Ballas as staff watcher in the face of a mutiny against him by Pillar. In scene nine, Gross continues to compliment her, calling her ''kind'' and complimenting her new hat. By the end of the scene, Gross has been promoted back to deputy director, and invites her to visit him in his office some time.

It is at this moment that Maria finally reveals her hand. Gross is about to leave, and Maria holds on to him for a few last moments. Maria says that ''I believe that if one doesn't give way, truth must always come out in the end.'' He admits his faults ''always hesitant, always full of doubts'' among others, and promises to do better as a person. He will do ''real deeds'' and speak ''fewer clever words.'' Gross's supposed honesty compels Maria to offer to break the rules for him: she will translate it. The memorandum supports the position he has had all along about Ptydepe, supporting him by saying that ''you have been conscientious and responsible in the directing of your organization'' and giving him their ''full confidence.'' Before Maria admits her feelings for him, Gross says to her ''I promise you that this time I shall not give way to anything or anybody, even at the risk of my position.'' After Gross leaves, however, George tells her that he heard her break the rules.

By the end of the play, nothing has really changed for Gross. All his ''moral'' words and empty rhetoric return him to the status quo at the beginning of the play. He is still merely the managing director at the mercy of Ballas. In scene ten, the moment when Gross should triumph, he cannot even get Ballas fired. Ballas turns the tables on him yet again. Another artificial language, Chorukor, is also being introduced. In scene 12, the last scene of the play, Maria asks Gross to intercede on her behalf because Ballas has fired her for translating the memo. Maria has asked nothing from anyone over the course of *The Memorandum*. She has done her job and even helped Gross. Her actions led to Gross regaining the managing directorship.

Gross refuses to reverse the decision, citing his conflict with Ballas among the reasons why he cannot save her job. This is in direct contrast to what he has declared moments before. From the beginning, Gross has proved weak and ineffectual, and it results in Maria losing her livelihood. Gross tries to sweeten the moment by reminding her that she is still young and that she could work for her brother in his theater group. He tells her that she should still ''trust in people'' and ''keep smiling!'' The final insult is when Gross excuses himself from the room by saying he has to eat lunch. Throughout the play, everyone has been treating him with disrespect by putting food, drink, and smokes, before him, and he does the same thing to Maria. She is the only person he has any real power over.

Maria's line (''Nobody ever talked to me so nicely before.'') and her happy exit are both ironic and honest. She really has not been treated so well before. Gross actually paid attention to her, took a few moments to talk to her when no one else did, even if it was with a secondary agenda on his part. Gross's lack of intervention also means that Maria is free of this bureaucratic hell. *The Times*' Kingston and Gross seem to believe that she can now work with her brother's theater group—though if she had wanted to do that, it seems she would already be working there. Gross's weakness is his greatest strength for Maria at the end. He let his savior martyr herself for him, and Maria has been liberated. She has options in life no one in that organization seems to have. But, knowing the fickle nature of those employed in *The Memorandum,* Maria could still return to her job. It does not seem clear how any of them could live without her because no one else does any work. At least Maria is free for the moment, a moment longer than the rest of them.

Source: Annette Petruso, in an essay for *Drama for Students,* Gale, 2001.

Stanislaw Baranczak

In the following essay, Baranczak discusses the various character techniques used throughout The Memorandum.

''SIX ONE-ACT PLAYS BY SIX WORLD LEADERS'' was what a recent *New Yorker* cartoon envisaged as a canopy advertisement above the door to an off-Broadway theater. The wit is in the arithmetic. The number six suspends the joke precisely between the actual state of affairs and the realm of the improbable. Had the sign said, ''TWO ONE-ACT PLAYS BY TWO WORLD LEADERS,'' we would not laugh, because the estimate would be too realistic. Had it said ''TEN ONE-ACT PLAYS BY TEN WORLD LEADERS,'' we would not laugh, because the estimate would be too fantastic. But six, why not?

Not long ago, there was just one world leader whose resume included a few plays actually written by him and performed on stage (though their production anywhere near Broadway seems a rather

> WHAT THESE CHARACTERS SHARE IS A POSITION IN SOCIETY. ALL OF THEM CAN BE ROUGHLY DEFINED AS DISSIDENTS IN A TOTALITARIAN STATE, OR AT LEAST . . . JAMMED COGWHEELS IN THE OTHERWISE SMOOTHLY FUNCTIONING MACHINE OF A POWERFUL INSTITUTION."

remote possibility). Now there are two: the pope has been joined by the president of Czechoslovakia. Who's next? Hasn't a recent article published in a Solidarity newspaper proposed Leszek Kolakowski for the presidency of Poland? Kolakowski, let's not forget, is the author not just of works of philosophy, but also of a comedy he wrote in his spare time. The trend seems to be on the rise. You don't have to be royalty to collect royalties; being the president of a small nation will suffice.

Our amusement at the sight of a playwright becoming his country's president speaks volumes about the declining standards in the West's political life. What's so strange about the election of an outstanding writer from Bohemia? Is it any more consistent with the natural order of things if a much less outstanding golf player from Indiana gets elected to do the same? Weren't Lincoln and Churchill gifted writers? Wouldn't we all be slightly better off if our leaders knew how to select a proper word, put together a precise sentence, plant a stirring idea in a well-constructed paragraph?

Admittedly, even though there might be some truth in the tired Shelley line (you know, the one about poets being the unacknowledged legislators of the world), things get a little complicated when a poet, or a playwright, becomes acknowledged as a legislator, a minister, or a president. First of all, the sort of parliament or government he serves is not entirely inconsequential. The sad case of the talented poet Ernesto Cardenal, who lent support to Daniel Ortega's regime by accepting the position of its minister of culture, is just one example of the incompatibility between literature's natural thirst for freedom and despotism's natural desire to suppress freedom. That is a conflict in which something has to give, and all too often it has been the writer's conscience that has given.

Moreover, history provides us with a hair-raising number of examples of humanity's worst enemies, from Nero to Hitler, Goebbels, Stalin, and Mao, who considered themselves, at least before their ascent to power but sometimes also a long time after it, artists or writers. A failed artist or a graphomaniac seems to be particularly good material for the making of a ruthless oppressor; he need only apply his crude aesthetic principle of mechanical symmetry to the unruly and formless human mass.

And even if the political system is a democratic one, and the "acknowledged legislator" or leader happens to be an artist or a writer wise enough to be profoundly aware of human diversity, his success in the world of politics is far from assured. As a writer, his chief strength—the force that made him a legislator, "however unacknowledged," in the first place—was his steadfast rejection of compromise. As a politician, however, he soon finds out that politics in a democratic society is nothing but the art of compromise.

If it so happened one day that destiny wanted the first president of post-Communist Czechoslovakia to be a writer, what kind of writer should he ideally be? Let us imagine a group of Czechoslovak citizens gathered secretly in a private apartment in the middle of 1989, taking refuge from their depressing reality by discussing this preposterous question, a question as thoroughly outlandish to them as the seashore that Shakespeare gave Bohemia in *A Winter's Tale.* Any answer would certainly have included the reverse of the qualities we have just mentioned.

First, the literary president should be a writer with an extraordinarily strong moral backbone, someone whose life, like his work, has been dedicated to searching for the untraversable borderline between good and evil; someone, therefore, who would be able to bring the spirit of ethics into his country's national and international politics. Second, the literary president should be a good writer, endowed with the sense of measure and balance that in the sphere of aesthetics is called good taste or artistic skill, and in the sphere of politics translates into a pluralistic tolerance for the natural diversity of people and their opinions. A playwright—someone who shows the world through dialogue—would be a particularly well-qualified candidate: the spectacle of conflicting human perspectives forms the lifeblood of his art.

And third, the literary president should be a writer blessed with a tremendous sense of humor, preferably of the self-mocking, ironic, absurdist sort. For it is only with such a sense of humor that a writer-turned-president would be able to think seriously of making his nation ascend from the depths of the totalitarian absurd toward a more or less rational social organization, while at the same time never taking himself and the miracle of his own ascension too seriously. In short, the ideal president of Czecholslovakia that our depressed friends would have likely dreamed up is this: a genuinely good playwright with a genuinely strong set of moral convictions balanced by a genuine sense of pluralistic tolerance and a genuine sense of humor.

In the middle of 1989, there happened to be one living and breathing candidate who matched this impossibly exacting description. His name was Vaclav Havel.

The real test of a man is not how well he plays the role he has invented for himself, but how well he plays the role that destiny assigned to him." This is how Havel himself, quoting the dictum of his friend and mentor, the late philosopher Jan Patocka, reflects on all the twists of fate that made him first Czechoslovakia's most vilified dissident and then its most venerated president. The issue of the "role" (a fitting term in the mouth of a playwright) is crucial in Havel's philosophical system. What he means by that is the responsibility that man, "thrown into the world," accepts by relating his life to the Absolute Horizon of transcendence (which is defined by Havel, who is reluctant to resort to the vocabulary of theology, as the "Memory of Being").

This kind of outlook, in Havel's case, owes as much to the inspiration drawn from the works of existentialists and phenomenologists as to the inspiration provided by life. *Letters to Olga,* Havel's most detailed and extensive exposition of his philosophy of existence, was written, symbolically enough, in a prison cell—a place to which his "role" consistently led him. It was a place that he converted, ironically, into a stage on which to play, even more eloquently, the same role he had played outside the prison walls. Letters to Olga focused on the final outcome of a life, on its complete philosophy. The life that produced this outcome has now, in turn, become the focus of *Disturbing the Peace,* a highly engaging autobiographical sketch in the form of a book-length interview. This much-needed book

explains how the events of the unbelievable fall of 1989 can be seen as an almost inevitable phase in Havel's lifelong "role," which was both "assigned to him" by destiny and "invented" by himself.

The facts of Havel's life were more or less known in the West even before 1989, mostly thanks to the publicity generated by his trials and his prison sentences. Havel's life was marked by absurd paradoxes early. Born in 1936 into the wealthy family of a civil engineer, he was suddenly a social pariah—the child of a class enemy—in 1948, when Czechoslovakia turned Communist. He was denied access to a higher education, worked for a while as a laboratory technician, and went through a two-year military service. Throughout that ordeal, he wrote (his first article was published in 1955), and made his presence known in public appearances, such as his speech at an official symposium of young writers in 1956, shockingly critical of the official hierarchy of literary values.

From 1959 on, his life was inextricably linked to theater. He joined Prague's unorthodox Theater on the Balustrade, initially as a stage hand, and ended up as its literary adviser. *Garden Party,* his first play, premiered in 1963. In 1965 he joined the editorial staff of the monthly Tvar, a tribune of rebellious young writers.

Those were heady times of growing ferment and hope, but change was yet to come. Tvar was soon closed down by its own editors, unable to continue publishing under the watchful eye of the Party. Between 1956 and 1968, Havel used consecutive congresses of the Czechoslovak Writers' Association as forums for his increasingly critical speeches, but his ideas were staunchly resisted by the well-entrenched camp of Communist writers. In March 1968 he helped establish the Circle of Independent Writers, thus creating a cultural alternative of major importance. Meanwhile his next plays had their Czech and Western premieres, and his name became internationally known.

Havel became even better known after the Prague Spring and the Soviet invasion, when he emerged one of the most eloquent champions of human rights in Husak's police state. His participation in actions of protest and his own analyses of the social apathy induced by Brezhnev's Czechoslovak puppets (such as his famous "Letter to Dr. Gustav Husak," which was written in 1975) brought down on him increasingly vicious personal attacks in the official media as well as unrelenting police harassment. On January 1, 1977, Havel joined Patocka and Jiri Hajek as a spokesman for the Charter 77 movement. The rest is a story of interrogations, investigations, detentions, provocations, searches, house arrests, buggings, prosecutor's charges, trials, jail sentences, labor camps, prison hospitals, and, amid all this turmoil, more writing.

As we all know, this particular story has a happy ending, the impeccable symmetry of which—the nation's most persecuted writer turns overnight into the nation's president—looks downright suspicious. Were Havel's life a novel, it might be the most naive piece of literary kitsch in the twentieth century. A clear-headed observer of the world's ways knows that there is no such neat example of virtue miraculously rewarded in real life. Is Havel's life a fairy tale, a dream? The honest and the brave, after all, are supposed to get beaten to death by unknown assailants, to disappear without trace, to be found in the trunk of an abandoned car with bullets in their heads. Havel's triumph is so unequivocally well deserved that it looks utterly outlandish.

And no wonder: this particular writer, again, is a walking paradox. This is true not merely of the course of his life, but also of his inner nature. Havel's role seems to have been delineated from the very beginning of his public and literary activity by his mind's preoccupation with two seemingly incompatible inclinations. His works and his actions reflect, on the one hand, a strong sense of moral order and of the need for justice, and on the other, a good-natured tolerance mixed with an absurd, zany sense of humor. An episode mentioned in *Disturbing the Peace* nicely illustrates the constant coexistence of these two inclinations. At one point early in Husak's rule, Havel took part in a general assembly of the governing boards of the unions of writers and artists, which feared—not without foundation, it soon turned out—that their forcible dissolution was imminent. Havel was included in a three-member committee charged with drafting a strong statement to protest, and to try to deflect, the blow:

> Unfortunately, I was also expected to participate in the opening of a show of paintings by a friend of mine in the Spalena Gallery, on Spalena Street, not far away. I wasn't going to give a serious speech—there were art historians for that—just take part in a little program of verses and songs. This was the dadaist wish of my friend, who loved the way I sang patriotic songs out of tune and gave impassioned recitations from our national literary classics at parties. And so, pretending that I had to go to the bathroom, I fled from the task of writing the historic manifesto and I ran to the gallery opening, where I sang and recited to a

shocked audience, then rushed back to the film club to write the final paragraph.

Havel proceeds to note "something symbolic in this accidental juxtaposition." It illustrates, he suggests, certain fusions of a more general scope: the way the Czechs' sense—and more generally, the Central Europeans' sense—of misery about their existence is wed to a "sense of irony and self-deprecation." "Don't these two things somehow belong essentially together?" asks Havel. "Don't they condition each other?" The Central European writer's taste for the absurd, for dark humor, produces in him the saving art of maintaining constant distance" from the world while never completely disengaging from it. Paradoxically, it is exactly the art of distance that allows you to see your subject from up close. As Havel puts it, "The outlines of genuine meaning can only be perceive bottom of absurdity."

In truth, the episode says more about Havel himself than about Central European culture. The distinguishing feature of his life and his art seems to be the nearly perfect balance between the seriousness of his moral imperatives and the boundlessness of his self-irony. That irony is not just his mind's innate inclination. It also stems from his recognition that his own vision of the truth—no matter how scrupulously precise he tries to make it, no matter how much he is himself sure of its accuracy—is still only one of many individual human truths.

It is by now quite obvious how much this balance of moral strength without fanaticism and pluralistic tolerance without relativism has affected Havel's progress along his political path. It is perhaps less clear how this same balance is reflected in his art. There just as in Havel's politics, the equilibrium of opposites keeps the forces in check, so that the extreme manifestations of each can cancel the other out.

An artist of Havel's sort is truly himself when he submits to his moral impulses, when his work originates from his fundamental objection to the world's injustice. But if that were all it took, the art might easily lapse into dogmatic and self-righteous didacticism, the work would be noble yet tedious moral instruction. Another condition, clearly, must be met. In the arts, the moralist needs to have a sense of humor.

This is not as easy as it sounds. A sense of humor is shorthand for many abilities, from the power to understand others' positions and motivations to the willingness to take oneself with a grain of salt. Only this kind of humor can save the artist from the chronic stiffness of his moral backbone, a disease that is quite common among artists in oppressed societies. It is a disease with which you can live, but not, for instance, dance: you can hold yourself impressively erect, but be too rigid for unrestrained expression. Of course, if the backbone suffers from permanent softening (an even more common affliction), if all that remains is the relativism and the absurdist sense of humor, the effects are even more frightening: when left to himself and to his choreographies, the artist may display much flexibility, but also yield easily to the slightest pressure. That is why Havel the playwright cannot really be squeezed into either of the two familiar drawers, "Theater of the Absurd" or "Protest Theater." He is too embedded in a stable bedrock of moral principles to fit into the first, and he is too irreverent and self-ironic to fit into the second. More precisely, his plays fall into two different categories, one stemming from the tradition of political theater, the other suggesting some superficial affinities with the Theater of the Absurd. The first category is represented by more or less realistic works such as the series of three one-act "Vanek plays," inaugurated in 1975 by the famed *Audience. Largo Desolato,* one of Havel's relatively recent creations, also belongs here. In plays of this sort, realism takes a deep whiff of grotesque exaggeration, but there is no doubt, particularly in the Vanek trilogy, that the action takes place in Husak's Czechoslovakia and that the characters' behavior is motivated by circumstances of that time and that place. (Unfortunately, the English version of *Largo Desolato,* otherwise excellently done by Tom Stoppard, obliterates this Czechoslovakian specificity by Anglicizing the names.)

The other category, which includes *The Memorandum* and *Temptation,* is represented by plays, usually of greater length and based on more developed plots, that are parabolic rather than realistic. Sometimes they border on anti-utopian fantasy. Instead of a realistic setting, the typical drama revolves around a fictitious institution such as the Orwellian office in *The Memorandum,* complete with watchmen hidden in the hollow walls to keep an eye on employees through special cracks, and the scientific institute at war with society's "irrational tendencies" in *Temptation.* What goes beyond realism, actually, is not so much the setting as the plot's starting device: the introduction of Ptydepe, the artificial language for interoffice communication, in *The Memorandum* and the bureaucratic forms of

idolatry of rational science" that produce the Faustian rebellion of the protagonist in *Temptation.*

The difference between Havel's two types of plays, however, is one of degree. Both deal with essentially the same issues; the parabolic differs from the realistic perhaps only in that the grotesque and the absurd are turned up a notch. But the grotesque and the absurd are intrinsically present even in the most "realistic" of Havel's plays. In the strictly realistic *Audience,* a play that utilizes Havel's own firsthand experience of work at the Trutnov brewery, a socialist workplace that re-educates its employees by making them submit regular reports on themselves to the secret police cannot help but seem like a profoundly aberrant institution. And it is no less so than the imaginary office in *The Memorandum* that forces its employees to learn a special language, one that would help them produce more precise memos if its utter precision not make it impossible to use. The only difference is that *Audience* could really have happened in Husak's Czechoslovakia, while something not so blatantly idiotic as *The Messenger,* but something similar in spirit, could perhaps have happened there.

Another striking similarity between Havel's "realistic" and "parabolic" plays lies in their protagonists, fact, it would only be a slight oversimplification to say that whatever sort of play Havel writes, a single protagonist by the name of Ferdinand Vanek always pops up at the center of its plot. The now legendary figure of Vanek appeared first in *Audience* (to my mind, still the most perfectly executed accomplishment of Havel's wit), to reappear in his next two one-act plays, *Unveiling* and *Protest.* At the same time, the underground success of *Audience* gave rise to a one-of-a-kind literary phenomenon: a constellation of plays employing the same protagonist but written by different authors. ("The Vanek plays" in that broader sense include pieces written by Pavel Kohout, Payel Landorsky, and Jiri Dienstbier, and they are all reprinted in UBC Press's handy collection.) But Leopold Nettles of *Largo Desolato* is also, to a large extent, another incarnation of Vanek, and Vanek-like characters spur the dramatic action in Havel's "parabolic" plays as well.

What these characters share is a position in society. All of them can be roughly defined as dissidents in a totalitarian state, or at least (as in the cases of Josef Gross in *The Memorandum* and Dr. Foustka in *Temptation*) jammed cogwheels in the otherwise smoothly functioning machine of a powerful institution. This position entails a number of consequences. The most crucial is that the Vanek-like character represents, obviously, a political and moral minority. He is one of the last Mohicans of common sense, truthfulness, and human decency in a society that has laboriously adopted, in lieu of those simple principles, a Darwinian methodology of survival. Blind obedience to authority, thoughtless concentration on necessities of everyday life, and deep-seated distrust of any protester or reformer are the chief precepts of this methodology. Thus Vanek is by no means a valiant knight in shining armor or a modern Robin Hood whom the wretched of the earth look up to. Despite all the words of cautious support and solidarity that some of his acquaintances occasionally dare whisper into his ear, Vanek is hated and despised. Hated, because he is "disturbing the peace" of pacified minds; despised, because he is—cannot help being—a loser. The forces that he opposes are too powerful; he will certainly be crushed in the foreseeable future.

Hence the central paradox of Havel's literary universe: it is not Vanek who, from the heights of his moral purity as a fighter for human rights, accuses the corrupt society of indifference; it is his society that accuses Vanek of the same—yes, of indifference. In the eyes of a citizen whose main concerns are promotion at his workplace, getting his daughter into a university, and building himself a dacha in the country, Vanek looks like a dangerous instigator and rabblerouser. What the Brewmaster in *Audience* says to his face would be echoed with equal sincerity by other characters in other plays, had their tongues been similarly loosened by the heavy intake of beer: "Principles! Principles! Damn right you gonna fight for your damn principles—but what about me? I only get my ass busted for having principles!" Vanek's original sin, all of them seem to think, is his indifference to other people, an attitude that he demonstrates merely by living among them and irritating them with his inflated conscience. He can afford to stick his neck out; we can't.

In specific plays, this reverberating "He can, we can't" is wrapped in different words, depending on the accuser's social status, intellectual acumen, and degree of cowardice. The Brewmaster's argument runs along the lines of social division: you can, but I can't, because I'm a simple worker whom nobody will care to defend and whose protest will go unheard anyway. In *Unveiling,* a married couple of friends who invited Vanek for the "unveiling" of their newly decorated apartment resort to an argument that reflects their philosophy of life: you can,

but we can't, because we need to live our lives to the full, while the pleasures of life apparently do not matter much to you. In *Protest,* a well-to-do screenwriter wriggles out of a moral obligation to sign a petition in defense of an imprisoned artist by invoking sophisticated arguments related to political tactics (he ends up endorsing "the more beneficial effect which the protest would have without my signature"), which essentially come down to the following: you can, but I can't, because your career has gone to the dogs anyway, while mine is still something I have to take care of.

These are all voices of human normalcy. Havel the pluralist has no choice but to register them, and even partly to agree with them. But Havel the moralist counters with a more powerful argument of his own: that in a totalitarian society it is precisely the "abnormal" troublemakers who have preserved the last vestiges of normalcy. Theirs is the ordinary human striving for freedom and dignity, the kind that ultimately matters more than the misleading normalcy of a full stomach. And Havel the self-ironist acknowledges, and brings into dramatic relief, the intrinsic irony of the dissidents' position: they may well be the only normal human beings around, but since they constitute a ridiculously powerless minority, their cause, noble though it is, will always be doomed to defeat.

In Havel's plays, Vanek serves as the central point around which these three lines of argument interlock, forming a triangular trap with no way out. He has no choice but to admit that people have basic rights to food on their tables and to a TV show after dinner. He realizes that his actions make people uneasy or put them at a risk. At the same time, he has no choice; he must stick to his own basic right to follow the voice of his conscience. That is not because of moral haughtiness, but for the simple reason that he is unable to force himself to do things or utter words that he considers wrong or false. In a sense, he lives among his compatriots like a foreigner in Paris: he is aware that all the French eat escargots, and he is even able to grasp abstractly their reasons for doing so, but he is physically incapable of forcing the slimy invertebrates down his throat. Finally Vanek has no choice but to realize his own comical awkwardness. In a society like his, he will always be the odd man out, a laughable exception to the prevailing rule.

The combination of these three necessities makes Vanek a highly complex dramatic character. This is clear even in the Vanek trilogy, in which Havel's protagonist is, in terms of sheer stage presence, the least exposed among all the characters. He might seem like little more than a taciturn straight man opposite his rambling and dramatically more developed counterparts. Yet his psychological profile would fill volumes. He is, oddly yet convincingly, heroic and anti-heroic, a centerpiece of tragedy as well as farce. He is never so blindly self-righteous as to forget that, after all, he shares with people their trivial needs, that therefore he is one of them. If his moral backbone is a little more erect than most people's, it is also a backbone that aches.

Vanek, in sum, is not comfortable with his nagging conscience, and he is not terribly proud of it, either. He realizes how little separates him from the less heroic human mass. In Audience, Vanek, apparently blacklisted, barred from any white-collar job, and forced to take up physical labor in a provincial brewery, does not wish at all to be a martyr; and it is this reluctance that motivates the entire plot. He would gladly swallow the bait of the less exhausting clerical position that the Brewmaster dangles in front of him, even at the cost of the fellow worker whom he would replace. The only reason that he rejects the offer is that the torture of toiling in the brewery's cold cellar is ultimately more bearable than the torture of the nonsensical informing on himself, which the Brewmaster requires as part of the deal.

In *Largo Desolato,* Havel's tendency to endow his dissident hero with anti-heroic features reaches an even greater extreme. Leopold Nettles is a dissident malgre lui, one who is not only aware of his weaknesses, like Vanek, but also doubtful about whether he is up to the task at all. He did not really become a dissident; he was made one. Some of his philosophical writings were denounced by the regime as ideologically harmful, and his quiet life of an introspective bookworm was irrevocably changed. We see him at the point of total exhaustion, on the verge of a nervous breakdown.

Ironically, his new status as a dissident has deprived him of his previous independence. Now everyone, his supporters and persecutors alike, expects something from him. His apartment is visited by an unending stream of friends who worry about his doing nothing, friends who worry about his not doing enough, friends who worry about his doing too much, friends who worry about his worrying. While expecting a secret police search and arrest any minute, he has to entertain his far-from-satisfied lover and at the same time handle a visit from

a pair of suspiciously enthusiastic working-class supporters who bear the unmistakable signs of agents provocateurs.

When the police finally turn up, their only demand is that Nettles renounce the authorship of his paper. When he refuses, the final blow falls: the police declare that his case has been adjourned "indefinitely for the time being," since it has become clear that his denial of his own identity "would be superfluous." Nettles cries, "Are you trying to say that I am no longer me?" The words aptly sum up what has happened to him. His self has been transformed into (to use the word Havel has applied elsewhere to his own life) a role. A role, in this case, definitely "assigned to him by destiny" rather than "invented by himself," but a role that he has been unable to "play well."

To what extent does Nettles personify the playwright's own doubts? Just as Havel the president is not a man of marble, Havel the dissident was not a man of iron. He has had his crises, his failures, his moments of despair. *Largo Desolato* was written in four days in July 1984, precisely at the low point of a bout of acute "postprison despair." Yet in *Disturbing the Peace* Havel plays down the autobiographical import of his play: "It is not about me, or only about me as such. The play has ambitions to be a human parable, and in that sense it's about man in general."

For Havel, though, writing about "man in general" means distilling some abstract concept of humanity out of concrete and individual experience. On the contrary, it means portraying man in his concrete surroundings, in the web of his innumerable entanglements, from the metaphysical to the trivial. (*Temptation,* with its Mephistopheles suffering from smelly feet, and its Faust immersed in the vulgarity of power games and sycophancy of his colleagues, is a particularly apt illustration of that range of vision.) Central among those entanglements is the individual's relationship to society and its institutions. In Havel, who is a matchless literary expert on the ironies of totalitarianism, this relationship takes on, as a rule, the shape of the most ironic of oppressions: the constant oppression of the individual by the institutions that he helped create.

Seen from this point of view, Havel's entire dramatic output may not seem to have progressed much beyond, say, Ionesco's *The Rhinoceros* or *The Bald Singer.* The similarities extend even to characteristic techniques in construing dialogue and dramatic situations. Not unlike Ionesco, Havel's favorite device is mechanical repetition. His plays are organized masterfully, almost like musical pieces, around recurring, intercrossing, and clashing refrains, usually utterances from a small-talk phrase book; the more frequently repeated, the more meaningless they are. The Brewmaster's "Them's the paradoxes of life, right?" and similar verbal refrains find their counterparts in repetitive elements of stage action (for example, the way certain characters conspicuously hold hands in *Temptation*). The despotic oppression of language, custom, stereotype, institution, any automatism with which man replaces the irregularity, spontaneity, and uniqueness of his self is a theme that runs through the Theater of the Absurd. Havel did not invent it, he merely transplanted the theme and its corresponding dramatic techniques onto the ground of the specific experience of the inhabitant of a Central European police state.

What he did invent was his counterbalance to the oppressive weight of that experience. That counterbalance is the weak, confused, laughable, and oddly heroic Vanek, in all his incarnations. Havel the moralist, Havel the pluralist, and Havel the ironist joined forces to produce a deeply human and exquisitely equivocal character. Precisely because Vanek is safe from the excesses of relativistic immoralism, he is able to help us put things in perspective. Precisely because he is safe from the excesses of dogmatic didacticism and self-righteous seriousness, he remains someone who teaches us something, who has to be taken seriously.

If he is an anti-heroic and comical version of Camus's Rebel, he is nonetheless a Rebel with a cause—and a Rebel with no streak of single-minded obsessiveness. A Rebel essentially powerless, true; but Vanek's obstinate defense of the core of his humanity expresses something more essential than the need for power: the need for values. In Central Europe in the mid-1970s, it was enough to realize the genuine presence of this need in the human world to begin to believe that "the power of the powerless," prophesied rather than described by Havel in his epoch-making essay of 1978, may one day manifest itself in real life. Last year it did. People very much like Havel's protagonist have woken up the rest of their society and won their seemingly lost cause. The symbolic credit for today's Czechoslovakia is owed not to Svejk, the bumbling soldier and relativistic philosopher of compromise. It is owed to Vanek.

Source: Stanislaw Baranczak, "The Memorandum: A Play," (review). *The New Republic,* Vol, 203, No. 4, July 23, 1990, p. 27.

Phyllis Carey

In the following excerpt, Carey places Havel's drama in three major phases: "The early absurdist comedies; the Vanek morality plays; and the psychological-prison plays."

If the language games of *The Garden Party* relativize the human out of the equation, the use of a synthetic language—*Ptydepe*—enables Havel in *The Memorandum* (1965), winner of the Obie Award (1967–68) for best foreign play, to focus on the process by which humans abdicate their humanity to linguistic and/or political systems.

Josef Gross, the Managing Director of an anonymous bureaucracy, receives a memorandum in *Ptydepe,* an artificial language designed to make human communication scientifically precise by making words as dissimilar as possible. In his attempts to get the memo translated, Gross experiences the paradoxes of bureaucracy: he can obtain the documents he needs to authorize the translation only by having the memorandum already translated. While he struggles with the irrationality of the system, he falls victim to a subordinate's power play, is demoted, but eventually convinces Maria, a secretary, to translate his memo; the message, ironically, confirms in *Ptydepe* the inadequacy of the new language, urging its liquidation. The play ends with Gross back in charge and with the prospect of a new synthetic language—*Chorukor*—which will operate on linguistic principles of similarity.

In *The Memorandum* Havel explores the scientific effort to transform language into a technological tool. Here, the drive for scientific precision contends with the apparently human need for unpredictability. The language instructor's lesson on saying "boo" in *Ptydepe* illustrates how analysis increasingly deadens spontaneity: The decision as to which *Ptydepe* expression to use for "boo" depends on the rank of the person speaking and whether the "boo" is anticipated, a surprise, a joke, or a test, as in "Yxap tseror najx." Another hilarious example of a simple expression made as complex as possible is the word "Hurrah!," which in *Ptydepe* becomes "frnygko jefr dabux altep dy savarub goz texeres."

The precision exercised on analyzing the trivial contrasts with the imprecision in expressing what

Several characters look on as Ferdinand Pillar, played by Steve Willingham, gives his lone speech in The Memorandum.

may be humanly significant. The ambiguous term ''whatever,'' deemed the most used human expression, is rendered by the shortest *Ptydepe* word, ''gh.'' Ironically, beneath all of the scientific pretensions, body language communicates and carries much of the action.

The preoccupation with using an artificial language in *The Memorandum* draws attention to the technological propensity to focus on means instead of ends. Enormous efforts to communicate precisely are undercut by the banality of what is expressed. Knowing the system, however, enables one to participate in the illusion of power and control. Like the specialized jargon of most professionals, *Ptydepe* represents an elitist code that paradoxically limits human communication both to a small group of *cognoscenti* and to those issues that can be analyzed and labeled.

Gross is caught between the need to fit into the system and his own humanistic platitudes. When Maria, fired because she translated the message without authorization, asks for his help, Gross excuses himself on the grounds that he cannot compromise his position as the ''last remains of Man's humanity'' within the system. He moves Hamlet's dilemma into Camus' theory of the absurd, and as so

often in a scientific age, the descriptive becomes the normative:

> Like Sisyphus, we roll the boulder of our life up the hill of its illusory meaning, only for it to roll down again into the valley of its own absurdity. . . . Manipulated, absurdity . . . automatized, made into a fetish, Man loses the experience of his own totality; horrified, he stares as a stranger at himself, unable not to be what he is not, nor to be what he is.

Gross, the would-be existentialist who is always wishing he could start his life over, cannot translate his own language into responsible action. If Pudnik is entangled in language games devoid of human integrity, Gross demonstrates that when language becomes an end in itself, even the most accurate or the most eloquent expressions become impotent.

In the tradition of Kafka, Camus, and Beckett, probably his most significant mentors, Havel explores in *The Garden Party* and *The Memorandum* the paradox of human rationality pushed to its absurd logical extreme. As in Kafka, anonymous authority figures loom behind the absurd context; as in Beckett, the habits and rituals of daily existence frequently deaden people from the horror of their predicament; as in Camus, there is occasional recognition of the absurdity. But Havel's characters, unlike those of Camus, do not rebel; rather they adapt and use the absurdity as an excuse for their own inhumanity.

Source: Phyllis Carey, ''Living in Lies: Vaclev Havel's Drama,'' in *Cross Currents,* Vol. 42, No. 2, Summer, 1990, pp. 200–11.

SOURCES

Barnes, Clive, ''Season's Last Show is a Czechoslovak Satire,'' in *New York Times,* May 6, 1968, p. 55.

Billington, Michael, review of *The Memorandum,* in *The Guardian,* March 30, 1995.

Hatch, Robert, review of *The Memorandum,* in *The Nation,* May 27, 1968, p. 709.

Havel, Vaclav, and Vera Blackwell, trans. *The Memorandum,* Farber & Farber, 1992, pp. 53-129.

Hemming, Sarah, Review of *The Memorandum,* in *Financial Times,* March 30, 1995, p. 17.

Hughes-Hallet, Lucy, Review of *The Memorandum,* in *Plays & Players,* April, 1995, pp. 32-33.

Kingston, Jeremy, Review of *The Memorandum,* in *The Times,* March 29, 1995, p. 28.

Meche, Jude R., ''Female Victims and the Male Protagonist in Vaclav Havel's Drama,'' *Modern Drama,* Winter, 1997, p. 468.

Oliver, Edith, ''Hayf Dy Doretob!,'' in *New Yorker,* May 18, 1968, pp. 73-74.

Review of *The Memorandum,* in *Time,* May 10, 1968, p. 74.

Skloot, Robert, ''Vaclav Havel: The Once and Future Playwright,'' in *Kenyon Review,* Spring, 1993, p. 223.

FURTHER READING

Carey, Phyllis, ''Living in Lies: Vaclav Havel's Drama,'' in *Cross Currents,* Summer, 1990, pp. 200-11.
   This essay gives an overview of Havel's work as a playwright, including a brief discussion of *The Memorandum.*

Goetz-Stankiewicz, Marketa, and Phyllis Carey, eds., *Critical Essays on Vaclav Havel,* G. K. Hall & Company, 1999.
   This collection of essays covers all of Havel's writings as well as his political life. Several discussions of *The Memorandum* are included.

Hvizdala, Karel, and Vaclav Havel, *Disturbing the Peace: A Conversation with Karel Hvizdala,* translated by Paul Wilson, Alfred A. Knopf, 1990.
   This book is composed of conversations between the authors in 1986, and includes Havel's own descriptions of his life and work.

Korbel, Josef, *Twentieth Century Czechoslovakia: The Meanings of Its History,* Columbia University Press, 1977.
   This book gives background on the history of Czechoslovakia from its inception to 1968, with one chapter focusing on the era *The Memorandum* is set in.

Kriseova, Eda, *Vaclav Havel: The Authorized Biography,* translated by Caleb Crain, St. Martin's Press, 1993.
   This biography covers the whole of Havel's life, including both his political and literary accomplishments.

Once in a Lifetime

GEORGE S. KAUFMAN
MOSS HART

1930

Moss Hart and George S. Kaufman's *Once in a Lifetime* was one of the pair's best collaborations, the first of eight they wrote together in the 1930s. Inspired by the rise of the talkies—movies with sound—and the excess of Hollywood, the play is a wisecracking satire, though not particularly mean or bitter. Hart had originally written the play in 1929. Kaufman, a more established comic playwright, collaborated with Hart on several rewrites in late 1929 and early 1930. After several problematic out-of-town tryouts, *Once in a Lifetime* opened on September 24, 1930, at the Music Box in New York City. It ran for 406 performances and won the Roi Cooper Megrue Prize for comedy in 1930. The play was very popular with both critics and audiences, giving them something to think about other than the growing economic depression. Since its original production, *Once in a Lifetime* was revived regularly through years, both on and off Broadway, as well as regionally and in Europe. Subsequent critics saw the play as a product of its time, but many believed its humor stood up well. The excesses of Hollywood were still contemporary, though some of the plays' references were dated. As the *New York Times*' Howard Taubman wrote in a 1962 review "*Once in a Lifetime* is still pertinent and funny. The film industry has been through more upheavals than an old-time banana republic, but the more it changes the more some of its foibles remain the same."

AUTHOR BIOGRAPHY

Hart was born on October 24, 1904, in Bronx, New York. He was the son of Barnett Hart, who was born in Great Britain and worked as a cigar maker, and Lillian (nee Solomon) Hart. Hart grew up in poverty after the advent of the cigar rolling machine made his father's profession outdated. When Hart left school in his mid-teens, he was already a confirmed fan of the theater. He got a job as a clerk to a theater producer, Augustus Pitou, Jr., and wrote a script for him, submitted under a pseudonym. The previews of *The Hold-Up Man or The Beloved Bandit* were awful, and Hart was fired.

While spending several years directing small theater groups and working as a social director at resorts during the summer, Hart continued to write plays, turning out one per year, none of which were produced until he got a break in the late 1930s. In 1929, Hart wrote *Once in a Lifetime,* based on what was happening with the advent of movies with sound. The only way Sam H. Harris would produce it, however, was if Hart rewrote it with a more experienced playwright, George S. Kaufman.

Kaufman was born on November 16, 1889, in Pittsburgh, Pennsylvania, the son of Joseph S. and Nettie (nee Schamberg) Myers Kaufman. He moved to Paterson, New Jersey with his parents while a teenager. After studying law for three months, before taking on a series of low-level jobs, Kaufman soon turned to the written word. After contributing occasionally to a column in the *Evening Mail,* Kaufman wrote his own column in the *Washington Times* in 1912. He wrote a column for several different papers before becoming a drama critic for the *New York Herald Tribune* and *New York Times* through 1930.

Kaufman began writing plays in the late 1910s. His first play, *Going Up* ''was not made, but led to more work.'' In 1921, he wrote his first play with Marc Connelly called *Dulcy.* The play was a big hit, and led to long-term success in the theater. While Kaufman had some successful collaborations with Connelly, including *Merton of the Movies* (1922), not all the plays they wrote together were successful.

Beginning in the mid-1920s, Kaufman wrote on his own again. He had several solo successes, including *The Coconuts* (1925) and *Animal Crackers* (1928) for the Marx Brothers. But Kaufman worked better with a co-writer, because, while he was good at developing interesting characters, plots were not his forte. Still, it was hard to find a good collaborator; and he worked with many over the course of his career.

In late 1929 and 1930, Hart and Kaufman rewrote *Once in a Lifetime* several times during out of town tryouts before it came to New York and was a box-office smash. At the time, Kaufman told audiences that most of the play was still Hart's. Hart and Kaufman wrote seven more plays together in the 1930s, including the Pulitzer Prize-winning *You Can't Take It With You* (1937). By 1940, the pair had gone their separate ways. Hart wanted to have an identity separate from Kaufman, who was still better known.

Hart both wrote his own material and collaborated with others in the 1930s, but spent the 1940s and 1950s writing primarily on his own. Beginning with *Lady in the Dark* (1943), Hart also directed many of his own plays, as well as plays of other playwrights until his death. Hart's writing was not limited to plays. Beginning in the early 1930s, he also wrote screenplays for major motion pictures. Hart wrote his last play in 1952, *The Climate of Eden.* Hart died December 20, 1961, survived by his actress wife, Kitty Carlisle, and their children, Christopher and Cathy.

Kaufman continued to write with and without collaborators throughout the 1930s and 1940s. He also directed many plays, including the 1941 hit *Mr. Big,* and later movies. In fact, many of his plays turned into movies. Kaufman both wrote and directed 1947's *The Senator Was Indiscreet.* He continued to work until his death. Kaufman was married twice. First to Beatrice Bakrow (with whom he adopted daughter Anne), who died in 1945, and later to Leuenn McGrath, an actress and playwright whom he divorced in 1957. Kaufman died of a heart attack on June 2, 1961, in New York.

PLOT SUMMARY

Act I, Scene 1

In a small furnished room in New York City, vaudeville partners George Lewis and May Daniels talk about their immediate future. Their third partner, Jerry Hyland, is supposed to be working on a booking for them. May worries because they have only $128 in their bank account. George is less concerned, sure that something will turn up.

When Jerry arrives, he announces that he has sold their act for $500. Jerry believes he has seen the future in the first sound movie, *The Jazz Singer*. Despite May's protests, Jerry insists that the three of them go to Los Angeles and get into the movies. Because films have been silent until this point, actors did not have to speak well. Jerry believes that stage-trained actors, who have voice training, will be in demand.

After agreeing with Jerry's decisions, May comes up with an idea about what they will do there. They will open a school of elocution (the art of public speaking) to teach film actors and actresses how to talk. They believe it will make lots of money, though none of them have actually taught it before.

Act I, Scene 2

On the train to Los Angeles, the three prepare to open their school. May discovers that Helen Hobart, the foremost film critic in the United States, is on the train. May knows Helen because they used to be in an acting troupe together. May convinces her to talk to them. They tell Helen that May taught elocution in England, Jerry is May's business manager, and George is a doctor and May's technical advisor. Helen becomes interested in their project, and agrees to introduce them to Herman Glogauer, the owner of Glogauer Studios.

Susan Walker, a young wannabe actress, finds Helen in the threesome's car. She is trying to get Helen to help start her acting career. George becomes interested in Susan, and escorts her back to her mother.

Act I, Scene 3

Inside the Gold Room of the Hotel Stilton in Los Angeles, actors, actresses, and wannabes work to see and be seen by others. Everyone, even the workers, has some connection to film. Susan and her mother, Mrs. Walker, come in. Susan is impressed by everyone in the room. George, May, and Jerry show up to meet Helen and Glogauer about their school. George sees Susan and promises to help her meet the studio owner. May and Jerry are not pleased that he has made this promise.

After Glogauer makes a sweeping entrance, Helen, May, Jerry and George meet with him. They convince him that their school would put him ahead of other movie moguls, playing on the fact that he passed on Vitaphone, the technology behind the talkies. George has Glogauer meet Susan, but her presence does not impress him.

George S. Kaufman (left) and Moss Hart

Act II, Scene 1

At the reception room of the Glogauer Studio, the secretary, Miss Leighton, manages the chaos of calls and visitors. A playwright, Lawrence Vail, waits for a meeting with Glogauer. Vail has been bounced between many people, and unhappy. His meeting is put off, and he is bounced around again.

May's school is in full swing. She is overworked, but Jerry and George are little help. Jerry is busy playing the Hollywood game, to the detriment of his relationship with May. George inquires about Susan's progress in her class, informing her that they will marry when she has a career. May tells him to talk to her before he does anything rash.

Their conversation is interrupted by the appearance of Mrs. Walker. She needs to take Susan to the hotel so they can take a long-distance call from Mr. Walker. George escorts the pair out. In the meantime, Vail is still waiting. Miss Leighton cannot remember who he is. He becomes angry that he cannot meet anyone and does not have enough work to do. Soon after he leaves, Helen comes looking for him. Miss Leighton does not know who he is when the movie critic asks.

May runs into Helen. Helen implies that the life of the school will be short. After she leaves, a man,

Flick, comes to take their names off the door of their office. This confirms the school's status. Jerry and George show up, and May tells them they have been fired.

George's first thought is of Susan and her career. Susan returns. Her father wants her to come home. George decides to look for Glogauer. He comes across Vail, who is shocked to learn that George has actually met Glogauer. Vail vents his frustrations on George, and Vail announces that he is quitting.

Glogauer appears, arguing with German director Rudolph Kammerling. Kammerling is angry about the casting of an actress who is totally wrong for the role. George steps in and suggests Susan would be more appropriate. When Glogauer tells him that they must have a name actress, George tells him off, using many of the same words that Vail used to describe the movie industry.

Glogauer is impressed by George's ideas. After casting Susan in the role and arranging for the publicity machine to go to work on her, Glogauer appoints George as the supervisor of the studio. George immediately hires May and Jerry, over the objections of Glogauer.

Act III, Scene 1

On the set of Kammerling's movie, *Gingham and Orchids,* all is chaos on the last day of shooting. As Kammerling starts to explain to everyone how the scene on the church steps will be shot, Susan claims she does not know this scene. May reminds Susan that they rehearsed it just five minutes ago, though it was called another name.

May's sarcastic attitude catches the attention of Jerry. While Jerry is enthusiastic about the movie and its future, May points out every fault. George appears and, the set temporarily focuses all its attention on him. Just as Kammerling and company return to work, Glogauer shows up. He is impressed that the movie is exactly on schedule. As a token of his appreciation, he gives George a solid gold dinner set.

Finally, the scene is shot. After it is over, Glogauer realizes that George had Kammerling do the wrong movie script. Glogauer suspends production and takes back his present to George. Jerry chides May for being sarcastic to Glogauer, while May points out that Jerry just kissed up to him. Susan refuses to speak to George. Glogauer fires everyone.

Act III, Scene 2

May is on the train back to New York. Vail comes aboard at a stop near a sanitarium. May has Vail read the reviews for *Gingham and Orchids.* To her surprise, they are very positive. Everything that was a mistake is praised. A telegram is given to her. It is from George who wants her and Jerry to come back. May decides she will return, if only to promote her agenda.

Act III, Scene 3

At Glogauer's studio, George is back in charge. Many demands are made on his time. Susan visits him, telling him about a premiere. George tells her that he has bought a number of aeroplanes. Glogauer appears and demands to know why he has bought 2,000 planes. He is extremely angry.

May enters, and George immediately wants to know where Jerry is. George tells her that Jerry went to find her when she left. While May wants to know more about that situation, George is more concerned about what to do with the aeroplane situation. Jerry appears and reassures her about their relationship. George is still worried about the aeroplanes. Glogauer interrupts, calling George a genius. Because he has bought all the planes, they are in demand by other studios. Glogauer is extremely happy with George's work. George is seen as even smarter as he allows the studio to be torn down so that a bigger one can be built.

CHARACTERS

May Daniels

May is one of the three vaudevillians who form the core of the play. Of the three, May is the worrier. From the beginning, she is well aware of how little money they have, and how much they need to work. She cannot believe that Jerry sold their act without her input. Yet May is also a survivor. She immediately forms the plan for what they can do in Los Angeles: open an elocution school. It is she who has the contact (Helen Hobart) that gets them the studio school. At the studio, she does most of the work at the school.

May sees through the falseness of Hollywood and takes no guff. When Jerry begins ignoring her, she calls him on how he has changed. May takes a similar attitude towards George when he screws up, as well as Herman Glogauer and others. May leaves

Los Angeles alone when she knows the move is right. Though May believes that *Gingham and Orchids* is garbage, she takes advantage of situations when they present themselves. The movie is a hit, and May returns to Hollywood to work for George and reunite with Jerry.

Mr. Flick

Mr. Flick is a door painter who works at the movie studios. He changes the names on the doors, using temporary paints because of the constant turnover.

Phyllis Fontaine

Phyliss Fontaine is a somewhat famous silent film actress. The switch to sound movies puts her at a disadvantage because of her accent. She attends May's elocution school at the studio so that she can work in talkies.

Herman Glogauer

Herman Glogauer is the owner of Glogauer Studios. He is a powerful mogul in Hollywood, who is vulnerable when Helen, May, Jerry, and George bring their elocution school idea to him. Glogauer turned down the Vitaphone technology that created the talkies, and does not want to miss out on the next big thing. Glogauer takes on the elocution school for a short time before getting rid of it. Glogauer is an impulsive man, trying to stay ahead of the game in Hollywood. He is also not used to being challenged, so when George tells him off, Glogauer immediately hires him as the studio head. Glogauer sees George's mistakes as genius, as long as they can benefit him in the end. Glogauer's only concern is the bottom line.

Helen Hobart

Helen Hobart is the foremost movie critic in the United States. She is also an acquaintance of May Daniels. They previously worked as actresses in the same troupe. May uses this relationship to get their elocution school idea heard in Los Angeles. It is Helen who arranges the meeting with Herman Glogauer, the owner of Glogauer Studios. Through this contact, the school gets started, though Helen gets half of the profits. When the school is about to be closed, Helen is not at all friendly to May. Helen is only interested maintaining relationships that are beneficial to her. She plays the Hollywood game

MEDIA ADAPTATIONS

- *Once in a Lifetime* was adapted as a film in 1932. Directed by Russell Mack, this version starred Jack Oakie as George, Aline MacMahon as May, and Russell Hopton as Jerry.

- A made-for-television version was aired in 1988, as an episode of *Great Performances* on PBS. Directed by Robin Midgley and produced by Shaun Sutton, it starred Zoe Wanamaker as May.

well, so well that the studios have bought her a house and kennel full of dogs.

Jerry Hyland

Jerry is one of the three vaudevillians who form the core of the play. Of the three, he is the doer. After seeing *The Jazz Singer*—the first sound movie with spoken dialogue—Jerry sees that the future is in the movies and that with their skills, the three could be a success in Hollywood. Without consulting his partners, Jerry sells their vaudeville act for $500 and decides that they are moving to Los Angeles. This does not sit well with May, with whom there is some romantic tension.

Once the three arrive in Los Angeles, Jerry does everything he can to be successful in the movie industry, though May does most of the work. May feels ignored in favor of Jerry's fast Hollywood life. It is only when she leaves after George is fired as studio supervisor that Jerry seems to realize what she means to him and what is important. Jerry goes after her, and when he catches up to her, declares his feelings. They are together at the end of the play.

Rudloph Kammerling

Rudolph Kammerling is a German movie director working in Hollywood. He is extremely frustrated that Dorothy Dodd has been cast in the lead role of the film he is directing. When he meets Susan through George Lewis's intervention, he sees that she is perfect for the role. Kammerling gets to direct *Gingham and Orchids* with her in the lead. After Herman Glogauer shuts down the production because George has given Kammerling the wrong script, Kammerling considers returning to Germany.

Florabel Leigh

Florabel Leigh is a somewhat famous silent film actress. The switch to sound movies puts her at a disadvantage because of her accent. She attends May's elocution school at the studio so that she can work in talkies.

Miss Leighton

Miss Leighton is the harried receptionist at Glogauer Studios. She does her best to keep everything she is juggling—numerous phone calls, people, and their needs—straight, but she forgets Lawrence Vail entirely. It her treatment of him that contributes to his quitting.

George Lewis

George is one of the three vaudevillians who form the core of the play's story. He is an actor, rather young, and single, and is somewhat carefree and oblivious. George follows the lead of May and Jerry at the beginning of the play. When Jerry announces that he has sold the act and they are moving to Los Angeles, George goes along. When May decides that they will open an elocution school, George goes along. He just wants to get along. One of his only decisive actions is to notice and fall for Susan Walker. He uses his good fortune to help her.

It is when George tries to further Susan's career that he lucks into his biggest break. George, May, and Jerry's school has been closed and they have all been fired. George hears that Rudolph Kammerling needs a new lead actress for his movie, and suggests Susan. After George stands up to Glogauer, Susan gets the part and George is appointed supervisor of the studio's production. Despite two setbacks, George manages to hang on to the job, keep his friends together, and get the girl. George is lucky, and he knows it.

Lawrence Vail

Lawrence Vail is a well-known playwright who is employed at the studio as a scenario writer. Vail is extremely frustrated. He cannot get a meeting with the studio head and is shuffled from person to person. Even the secretary, Miss Leighton, continually forgets who he is. Vail believes he is underemployed and does not like his job. He left behind a happy life in New York City to come to Hollywood, and while he draws a salary at the studio, he has not received one assignment. Vail finally quits and checks into a sanatorium that only takes such playwrights as patients. He meets May on the train back to New York City. Though she changes her mind and decides to go back to Los Angeles, he continues on to New York.

Mrs. Walker

Mrs. Walker is Susan Walker's mother. She does not know much about Hollywood, but supports her daughter's ambitions. Mrs. Walker does what she can for her before and after Susan has been case in *Gingham and Orchids*.

Susan Walker

Susan Walker is a nineteen-year-old wannabe actress from Columbus, Ohio. She is traveling to Los Angeles with her mother to pursue her career when she meets George Lewis. Susan is not particularly talented, but because George is enamored with her, she ends up starring in a movie. Susan has agreed to marry him after her acting career has started, and they are a couple at the end of the play.

THEMES

Friendship and Loyalty

At the center of the *Once in a Lifetime* is the loyal friendship of May, George, and Jerry. From the beginning, they stick together—they even have one bank account. The three had a vaudeville act, which Jerry sold when he thought there was better chance for them in Los Angeles. Though May, and to some degree George, did not like the fact that Jerry did not consult with them before making such a big decision, they go along with it. May comes up with their elocution school plan, uses her contract to get it going, and does most of the work when it is open.

Though their friendship is challenged by life in Hollywood, it does survive. May becomes somewhat resentful that she has to do much of the work and that Jerry, her love interest, has become wrapped up in life in the fast land. George does not like always feeling like the other two do not respect his intelligence or abilities. Jerry is temporarily oblivious of his responsibilities towards the other two. But when the chips are down, they rally around each other. After George is appointed head of the studio and insists that May and Jerry are hired as well, the pair comes through for George when he really needs their support. By the end of the play, their friendship is as strong as ever. *Once in a Lifetime* shows the importance of such relationships in an unstable world.

Hope and Optimism

Throughout *Once in a Lifetime,* there is an undercurrent of hope and optimism. No matter what life throws at May, Jerry, and George, or most of the other characters, they always have some positive feelings for the future. Jerry believes he, May, and George will improve their lot in Los Angeles. George believes that Susan will be a successful actress. Their optimism pays off in both situations: both of their hopes come true. Even the wannabe film-types, the actors, actress, and scenario writers who work in the hotel, do not have any doubts about their futures. They believe they will work in the movie industry.

The only person seemingly without hope is Lawrence Vail, the underused playwright and film scenario writer who is shuffled from person to person in an attempt to meet with someone about his work at the studio. Vail is frustrated because, while he draws a paycheck, he also has had no writing assignments. Though Vail is frustrated by the runaround he is getting, he knows that a better life is out there. Vail was happy in New York City as a playwright, and in Act III, he returns home, after a brief stay in a sanitarium just for playwrights such as him. *Once in a Lifetime* offered unbridled optimism in stark contrast to the economic situation in the United States at the time. It harkens back to the attitude of the Jazz Age of the 1920s, before the start of the Great Depression.

Success and Failure

Related to the idea of optimism, the theme of success and failure is also important to Once in a Lifetime. Nearly everyone is successful in some way in the play. There are no true failures depicted, save perhaps for Lawrence Vail, but even Vail fails only to get a meeting. He is still paid, though he does no work. May, Jerry, and George's elocution school at the studio fails and they are fired, but this is only a temporary setback. By standing up to the studio owner, Herman Glogauer, George is hired as studio supervisor, and insists that his two friends be hired as well. Though George gets himself in some sticky situations as studio head—he is fired when studio owner Glogauer realizes that George has ordered

TOPICS FOR FURTHER STUDY

- Research the history of the American entertainment industry in the late 1920s and early 1930s. What affect did the advent of sound movies have on vaudeville, theater, and radio, and those who worked in those mediums?

- Compare and contrast May in *Once in a Lifetime* with Karen in David Mamet's *Speed the Plow* (1988). How do both work to achieve success in Hollywood? How does the status of women in the United States affect their depictions?

- Use psychology to explain why George, Jerry, and May stick together throughout *Once in a Lifetime*.

- Research the changes in the United States economy from the late 1920s to the early 1930s. How did the faltering economy affect the common people, like George, Jerry, and May?

the wrong script to be shot and when he buys 2,000 aeroplanes for the studio—he retains his position and solidifies his status as resident genius in Glogauer's eyes. Success is depicted as easy in Hollywood, though sometimes short-lived.

STYLE

Setting

Once in a Lifetime is comedy/satire that is set in New York City and Los Angeles in the late 1920s, when sound movies were coming into their own. The action of the play takes place in several locations. Act I, scene i occurs in a small, shabby furnished room in New York City where George and Jerry live. This setting emphasizes the desperate straits the vaudevillians have found themselves in. Act II, scene ii and Act III, scene ii both take place on the train between New York City and Los Angeles. In the former, May, Jerry, and George formulate the plan for their future. In the latter, May and Lawrence Vail, the frustrated playwright, share their disillusionment about the movie industry. The rest of the scenes take place in Los Angeles, at the Gold Room of the Hotel Stilton, the Glogauer movie studio, its reception area, and on the set of *Gingham and Orchids*. In all of these scenes, the absurdity of Hollywood is front and center. As a whole, the setting of *Once in a Lifetime* provides the context for the comedy of the play.

Costumes and Props

In Hollywood, image is everything. Hart and Kaufman use this fact in the costumes called for in the directions of *Once in a Lifetime*. To add some visual comedy to the play, Miss Leighton, the receptionist at Glogauer, is supposed to wear a black evening gown and pearls, even though her scenes take place in the morning. Helen Hobart, the famous movie critic, dresses in similar fashion. Hart and Kaufman write ''Her ensemble is the Hollywood idea of next year's style a la Metro-Goldwyn.'' Glamorous is what is expected from Hollywood, even among its receptionists and film critics.

A similar excess is portrayed in the props of the studio reception. Everything there is bigger than life, especially the furniture and fixtures. This is in stark contrast to the furnishings of the room where some of the vaudevillians lived in New York City. The fleeting nature of Hollywood success is emphasized by another prop inside the reception room. One of the doors leads to the office of May, Jerry, and George, and their elocution school. May confirms that they have been fired when Mr. Flick comes to remove their names from the door. Such visual elements emphasize the humor in *Once in a Lifetime*.

Playwright as Actor Playing a Playwright

In the original production of *Once in a Lifetime*, Kaufman took on the role of Lawrence Vail for about eight months. Hart took over the role in the following year, still in the initial run. These casting choices added an element of realism and contributed to the comedy and irony of these productions. Both Hart and Kaufman had only written plays, and were not really actors. Neither of them had worked in Hollywood or the movies when they wrote the play, though they knew others who had. The frustrations they imagined for Vail were very real to them, and easy for them to portray. It was also a new gimmick that brought people into the theater, ensuring more would see the play.

HISTORICAL CONTEXT

Life in the United States changed dramatically on October 29, 1929. On that day, the stock market crashed. This marked the end of the Jazz Age and the beginning of the Great Depression. The 1920s had been an unprecedented age of prosperity in the United States. The stock market had captured the interest of the general public for the first time in the 1920s. People from all walks of life played the stock market.

In the summer of 1929, this interest turned into a craze. Warning signs of an impending crash were ignored: people traded more, creating an endless backlog of paperwork. After October 29 (called Black Tuesday), 1929, the American economy quickly slipped into a depression. President Herbert Hoover was not reelected in 1932 because of his perceived mishandling of the crisis. Life quickly grew grim in the United States. Unemployment increased exponentially. Banks failed (13,000 in 1930 alone), taking the savings of their depositors with them. Many people lost their homes. Hoover's federal government did not do much to relieve these conditions. Uncertainty ruled many people's lives.

Life for women in the United States changed greatly in this time period. Women had just gotten the right to vote in 1920. In the 1920s, more women went to work. Their numbers in white-collar office jobs especially increased. By 1930, 24.3 percent (11 million) of all women were in the workforce. But women were paid significantly less than men for the same work, especially in manufacturing jobs. Even educated women were restricted to so-called women's work, such as teaching or nursing. Before the Depression, 29 percent of married women worked. As it took hold, many single women called for married women to quit so that those without other means of support could find work. The rates of marriage, divorce, and childbirth changed during the Depression. It cost too much to get a divorce, so the procedure was put off. It became more common for women not to marry or have long engagements because their potential mates could not find employment. This also affected the birth rate in 1930. Fewer children were born because of the cost of rearing them.

One industry thrived during the 1930s. The movie industry came into its own, and made lots of money. The industry had been turned on its head when the first movie with spoken dialogue was made in 1927. Until that point, movies had been

COMPARE
&
CONTRAST

- **1930:** The American economy is in a downward spiral after October 29, 1929 stock market collapse. By the end of the year, more than 4.5 million will be out of work and the Great Depression would take hold.

  Today: The American economy is experiencing an unprecedented economic growth, seemingly without end. With a carefully regulated stock market, unemployment is very low.

- **1930:** Sound movies are still a novelty, with the full impact yet to be seen. Theaters are the only places to see movies. While early prototypes of televisions have been made, radio is the primary form of home entertainment.

  Today: Movies can be seen in a variety of places, not just movie theaters. Video, DVD, and other technology can be used to view movies in the home and on the go. There is uncertainty about how interactive games and computers will affect the film industry.

- **1930:** Most people travel the country by train; and commercial passenger air travel is only in its infancy.

  Today: Air travel is the preferred way of traveling the country. The appeal of train travel is limited, and Amtrak, the national passenger service, is subsidized by the government.

- **1930:** Only 27 percent of all women are in the workforce in the United States. Most are confined to "women's work," and paid less than the men for the same work. During the Depression, women are paid even less than men.

  Today: While some of these conditions have remained the same (women still make less than men for the same work) and a glass ceiling (an unofficial but real barrier) exists, there are many more women in the workplace, working in nearly every occupation, and some hold positions of power.

silent, with live music played at local music theaters. In 1926, the first movie with a synchronized music soundtrack was released, *Don Juan,* but the technology was not great and it was not particularly successful. *The Jazz Singer* (1927) was the first film with spoken dialogue and singing. It was made with Vitaphone technology. *The Jazz Singer* was a blockbuster smash.

The popularity of *The Jazz Singer* and sound movies changed the face of the movie industry. It affected how scripts were written, and how actors acted. Movie cameras had to be made differently, and theaters had to be rewired for sound. The question of how to deal with foreign-language markets had to be answered. By the end of the 1920s, as technology caught up, the number of talkies increased and silent films were generally no longer made. Musicals were especially popular. The popularity of the talkies killed off vaudeville, and provided serious competition for live theater. The 1930s

proved to be the golden era of cinema, an escape from the upheaval going on outside of the movie palace.

CRITICAL OVERVIEW

From its first run at New York City's Music Box in 1930, *Once in a Lifetime* has been popular with both audiences and critics alike. Of its opening night performance, J. Brooks Atkinson of the *New York Times* wrote "It is all swift shrieking and lethal. It is merciless and fairly comprehensive. If the fun lags a little during the middle sketches, it is only because the first act is so hilariously compact and because the best scenes all the way through are so outrageously fantastico."

Many critics of this first run had similarly minor problems with the play, couched always in

Jack Oakie, as George Lewis, and Aline MacMahon, as May Daniels, in a scene from the 1932 film adaptation of Once in a Lifetime.

the most positive terms. The unnamed critic in *Commonweal* took issue with the pacing of Hart and Kaufman's play, but ultimately found the production humorous. ''The movies are delicious satirical meat, which the authors have served up most humorously—even if the meal drags a bit at the end. Broadway now has its happy chance to even up an old score with its ancient enemy, the cinema, and to prod it nicely. In *Once in a Lifetime* the laugh is on the movies.''

Hart and Kaufman's satirical take on the movie business was quite popular with drama critics. Another review by the *New York Times*' Atkinson later in 1930 claimed that ''The dialogue is a St. Vitus dance of wit . . . Satire likes nothing quite so much as stupidity. Since Hollywood manufactures that commodity on the basis of large-scale production, the authors of *Once in a Lifetime* have an abundance of general material.

Once in a Lifetime was revived regularly over the years, to nearly universal praise. Though many critics noted that the play was somewhat dated in its references, they believed that most of the humor held up well. Most only took issue with the actual productions and the choices made by directors. For example, an unnamed *New York Times* critic did not

like (soon to be famous Hollywood) director Peter Bogdanovich's 1964 stage revival. The critic writes ''Nearly everything has changed since 1930, including Hollywood . . . But enough of the fun is left in *Once in a Lifetime* to warrant a revival if the director were thoughtful enough not to get in the way.'' Bogdanovich and other directors often added material to the play that diminished it in the eyes of critics.

The 1975 production at New York City's ETC Theater, directed by Frank Bongiorno, was similarly described by Mel Gussow of *New York Times*. The critic writes that ''Frank Bongirno's production mistakenly presents the comedy as a play within a television play. . . . The concept may have been motivated by a desire to comment on the play, to use television as a contemporary stand-in for the movies. If so, the result is no comment. It is merely a time-wasting intrusion that vitiates the satire.''

The 1978 revival at the Circle in the Square Theater in New York City was arguably the most successful since its initial staging. Richard Eder of the *New York Times* wrote that ''[S]ome bones have fallen from the meat of the 1930 comedy; its insane logic has lost some of its logic, but there is plenty of insanity left.'' T. E. Kalem of *Time* thought it light, though still enjoyable. Kalem argued that "[T]his show is a roller coaster of merriment, with hairpin turns of plot, zany swoops of emotion and a breakneck tempo. But for fanciers of substance in entertainment, soap bubbles would be solider." John Simon of *New York* had the most negative reaction, writing that "the entire play is about the purblind leading the blind by the nose, a spectacle as unfunny as it is intellectually unsatisfying."

Yet twenty years later, when *Once in a Lifetime* was revived at the Atlantic Theater in New York City, Simon had tempered his criticism at bit. Simon, still writing for *New York,* did not like this production any better, labeling the play "strained but occasionally funny satire about a Hollywood the authors had not set foot in." Later in the same review he claims "It is the sort of play that, in a perfect production . . . is worth seeing once in your lifetime." Robert L. Daniels of *Variety* saw the play's merits despite its age: "while some situations and characters have become cliches, the satirical romp remains an innocent nod to a bygone era."

CRITICISM

Annette Petruso

Annette Petruso is a freelance author and screenwriter in Austin, TX. In the following essay, Petruso discusses the depiction of female characters in Once in a Lifetime *and compares this with the reality of women's lives in the late 1920s and early 1930s.*

One interesting aspect of Moss Hart and George S. Kaufman's play *Once in a Lifetime* (1930) is its depiction of women. In this time period, the perception and status of women in the United States had recently undergone a fundamental change, and the play reflects the inherent contradictions. Some female characters have some complexity to them. This essay looks at the status of women in America in this time period, then the female characters in *Once in a Lifetime.*

By the late 1920s, many women in the United States had more power and much different social values than even a decade early. In 1920, women were finally given the right to vote, a fight that had been going on for many years. During the so-called Jazz Age of the 1920s, young women rejected the values of their mothers and grandmothers, wearing shorter skirts and bobbed hair as well as intensifying

their social contact with young men. According to *American Decades: 1920–29,* 11 million women were working by 1930, about 27 percent of the total workforce. Women worked in all areas of the economy—office jobs, factories, servants, farming, and professional—but those in manufacturing jobs, at least, made less than their male counterparts for the same work. Most professional women did what was termed "women's work," including teaching and nursing.

According to Sara M. Evans in *Born for Liberty: A History of Women in America,* the workplace, especially offices, were seen as places were one could meet a husband. Despite the fact that many women worked, marriage was still the ideal for them. They were expected to marry and lead domestic lives. While this expectation changed a little as the Great Depression deepened, and while marriage was seen as economically unfeasible for many, wife and mother were still the primary accepted social roles for women.

Yet in *Once in a Lifetime,* only Mrs. Walker clearly is married, and she is functioning away from her home and husband. Nearly every woman depicted in the play is single and has or wants a career. While show business was a semi-acceptable place for women at this time, the number of independent, sometimes powerful, women in the play is still extraordinary. Characters like May Daniels, who was part of a vaudeville act with two men and at the age of twenty-five still unmarried, and Helen Hobart, described as the foremost movie critic in the United States, are strong and in charge.

Most minor female characters do what were considered women's jobs. In Act I, scene iii, the cigarette girl and the coat check girl are both young women in the service industry. While they have aspirations to become more successful actresses—they take roles as they are available—for now they work in the hotel and search for their next part. Neither is married, and neither seems to be looking for a husband. A similar statement can be made about the maids to the famous actresses depicted in the scene, Phyllis Fontaine and Florabel Leigh. While they do domestic labor, they also look for acting work as well.

The receptionist at Glogauer Studio, Miss Leighton, does clerical work, another common job for women at this time Like the characters mentioned above, she is not obviously in pursuit of a husband. Though she is forgetful of the frustrated playwright for Lawrence Vail, Miss Leighton jug-

WHAT DO I READ NEXT?

- *Merton of the Movies*, a play written by Kaufman and Marc Connelly in 1922, also concerns the absurdities of life in Hollywood. It was one of the inspirations for *Once in a Lifetime*.

- *Speed the Plow*, a play written by David Mamet in 1988, also concerns the inner-workings of Hollywood. The story focuses on two film industry insiders, and the maneuverings of a woman to break in.

- *Which Lie Did I Tell?*, a memoir by William

Goldman published in 2000. The book recounts Goldman's life as a Hollywood screenwriter at the end of the twentieth century.

- *Merrily We Roll Along*, a play written by Hart and Kaufman in 1934, focuses on the pitfalls of success.

- *The Last Tycoon*, an unfinished novel by F. Scott Fitzgerald published posthumously in 1941. The novel is based on Fitzgerald's frustrating experiences as a Hollywood screenwriter.

---

gles phones, people, and information with calm ease, emphasized perhaps by her choice of an evening gown for daytime office attire.

Two women with more nontraditional career choices are Fontaine and Leigh, the successful actresses. Stars of silent film, Fontaine and Leigh do not seem particularly concerned with the advent of talkies, that is movies with a prerecorded, synchronized soundtrack. Like the other female, neither seems to be married or particularly concerned about it. Though Hart and Kaufman do not depict them as particularly bright—in Act II, scene i, May tells them that ''I won't be happy till you get the rigor mortis,'' a quip the actresses take as a compliment—they are prosperous single women with careers.

Similarly career driven is Susan Walker, the teenage wannabe actress who is on the train to Hollywood in Act I, scene ii. Escorted by her mother, Susan wants to become a famous actress, though she does not exactly know what that means. When she sees Helen Hobart, the famous movie critic, on the train, she tries to enlist her help. Susan later tries to get noticed at the Hotel Stilton. It is only through her relationship with George, and his connections, that she achieves her goal. She succeeds despite the fact that she is a horrible actress, as dumb as Leigh and Fontaine. Yet Susan has one very interesting characteristic: she will not marry

George until she has become a successful actress. Her career is more important than love and marriage.

The woman enjoying the most abundance is Hobart, described as ''America's foremost film critic'' by May. Again, she seems husband-free. Her occupation is somewhat unusual for a woman at this time, and her power as a film critic most certainly is. She is syndicated in 203 papers in the United States, and respected by men in lofty positions. Indeed, Hobart brags to May, George, and Jerry in Act I, scene ii that the studios shower her with gifts, including a twenty-two-room home in Beverly Hills. Hobart calls it Parwarmet, named after the first syllable in each of the major studios names: Paramount, Warner Bros., and Metro-Goldwyn. Fox Studios gave her a dog kennel, and she named each of the animals after an a studio executive.

May, Jerry Hyland, and George Lewis, appreciate her position. In that scene, they realize that her support could get their elocution school off the ground in Hollywood, and they get her on their side by lying about their background. Hobart arranges their meeting with Herman Glogauer of Glogauer Studios, and the school does open. However, Hobart gets a significant percentage of the profits. She is also a savvy businesswoman who knows how to get what she wants. Though in many way Hobart is a cog in the public relations machine that is the movie industry, she has milked it for all it is worth. She is the epitome of powerful woman in this play.

May Daniels, though, is the primary female character, just as powerful in her own way. She is one of the three vaudevillians who are looking to better their life in Hollywood. Of the three, May is the only woman and, in many ways, the center and leader of the group. George is malleable and goes along for the ride, while Jerry takes chances and arranges for their trip to Los Angeles. But it is May who comes up with the idea for the elocution school, and it is May who uses her connection to Hobart to get them jump-started in Hollywood. May takes the lead, and the others follow.

Yet when the three arrive in Los Angeles, and the school is opened, May does most of the related work. She teaches all the classes while Jerry leads a life in the fast land and George swoons over Susan. Thus while May is a leader among the three, she also fulfils a typical role for women of her day, that of teacher. After the school fails, May plays more of a supporting role to the men. Through a number of satirical twists, it is hapless George that ends up becoming a production supervisor at the studio. He needs May's expertise, as well as Jerry's help, for him to succeed and he knows it. George insists that she is hired, and though he and Jerry test her limits, May is there for them. She becomes something of a mother hen, all-knowing but supportive.

Unlike most of the female characters in *Once in a Lifetime,* May has a love interest, Jerry. This relationship, however, is subtle, if not underdeveloped, over the course of the play. In Act II, scene i, May chides Jerry for not spending any time with her. He broke a date with her to be with some Hollywood-types. Later, in Act III scene i, she becomes angry with Jerry for nearly selling her and George out after George has his director shoot the wrong script. She breaks up with him, telling him ''as far as I'm concerned, that's that.'' May leaves Hollywood in the next scene, intending to return to New York. She changes her mind after reading the reviews of *Gingham and Orchids* and returns in the next scene. It is only then that she learns that Jerry has left to look for her. When he comes back, they make up and it is implied that they are back together again. Thus May's future as a wife and mother seem assured.

Countering these strong, if not sometimes contradictory, images of women in *Once in a Lifetime* are the more conventional characters and characterizations of women. Mrs. Walker is retiring. She

> ❝ YET SUSAN HAS ONE VERY INTERESTING CHARACTERISTIC: SHE WILL NOT MARRY GEORGE UNTIL SHE HAS BECOME A SUCCESSFUL ACTRESS. HER CAREER IS MORE IMPORTANT THAN LOVE AND MARRIAGE.❞

supports her daughter's ambitions because she wants the best for her, yet when her husband calls them from Ohio, she wants to please him as well. It is only through George's intervention that Susan does get a role that allows them to stay, but Mrs. Walker would have gone home if her husband had demanded it. Also, on the film set, men and women play their traditional roles. The only women working on the film are May, Susan's coach, and the script girl. All the scenario writers are men, as is the director, the studio head, cameraman, electricians, and pages. These are minor details, however. In the big picture, *Once in a Lifetime* was ahead of its time in its portrayal of women.

Source: Annette Petruso, in an essay for *Drama for Students,* Gale, 2001.

Liz Brent

Brent has a Ph.D. in American Culture, specializing in film studies, from the University of Michigan. She is a freelance writer and teaches courses in the history of American cinema. In the following essay, Brent discusses the historical context of this play.

The play *Once in a Lifetime,* by Kaufman and Hart, takes place during a very particular phase in the history of the Hollywood film industry: the transition from silent film to sound film, or ''talkies.'' In order to fully appreciate the play itself, it is helpful to have a grasp of the specific elements of this era of Hollywood history which are referred to in the play.

This play was originally performed in 1930, and takes place in 1927, during the period of transition from silent film to ''talkies,'' or movies with

> IN THE PLAY BY KAUFMAN
> AND HART, WHEN SOMEONE REFERS
> IN PASSING TO THE CIVIL WAR,
> ANOTHER CHARACTER RESPONDS,
> 'THE CIVIL WAR? DIDN'T D. W.
> GRIFFITH MAKE THAT?'"

synchronized sound. The initial incident of the play occurs when Jerry returns from attending the film *The Jazz Singer,* which was the first feature-length sound film to be released by Hollywood, by Warner Brothers in 1927. Al Jolson (1886–1950) plays a Jewish boy who runs away from home to become a jazz singer and minstrel performer on the stage. *The Jazz Singer* featured four singing numbers in synchronized sound, while the rest of the film used standard silent film titles for dialogue. Between 1927 and 1930, all of the studios converted to sound film production, and by 1930 Hollywood was producing only "talkies."

In the play, Jerry explains to May and George that the "talking picture" he has just seen was made possible by the newly developed technology under the brand name Vitaphone. Vitaphone was developed and marketed as a subsidiary of Warner Brothers in partnership with General Electric in 1926. Vitaphone technology, however, had various problems and was replaced by more advanced sound film technology in 1931. In the play by Kaufman and Hart, George makes a big impression on the studio head, Mr. Glogauer, by pointing out that he had made a huge mistake in "passing up Vitaphone." In other words, this fictional head of a fictional studio within the story had passed up the opportunity to be at the forefront of the transition to synchronized sound. Mr. Glogauer at one point laments that the pioneering of sound film by the "Schlepkin Brothers" has forced the other studios to make this costly and complex transition; the fictional "Schlepkin Brothers" are clearly meant to represent the real life Warner Brothers who did, in fact, pioneer the production of "talkies."

This play refers to most of the major Hollywood studios and studio heads of this period in the history of the film industry. In order to appreciate

the significance of these references, it is helpful to understand the structure of the film industry at this time. From the beginning of the sound era until 1948, the Hollywood film industry was dominated by five major studios, known as "The Big 5," which included: Warner Brothers, Paramount, Twentieth-Century Fox, Radio-Keith-Orpheum Corp. (RKO), and Metro-Goldwyn-Mayer (MGM). All of the major studios are mentioned at various points throughout the play. For instance, the stage directions describing the character of Helen Hobart, the film critic, state that the outfit she is wearing "is the Hollywood idea of next year's style a la Metro-Goldwyn." Metro-Goldwyn, which later merged to become MGM, was known for the elaborate and sumptuous sets and costuming in their films. Later, Helen Hobart explains that she has named her home Parwarmet, after the three studios Paramount, Warner Brothers, and Metro-Goldwyn. She explains that she also has a kennel of dogs, all named after studio executives at Fox (which in 1935 merged with Twentieth Century studios to become Twentieth Century-Fox). Mr. Glogauer in the play also makes reference to the tendency during this era of Hollywood history for studios, such as MGM and Twentieth Century-Fox, to "merge"; he complains that the Schlepkin Brothers are "always wanting to merge, merge, merge."

The major Hollywood studios during this era were also known for their famous executive producers, referred to as "movie moguls," and included: Jack Warner at Warner Brothers, Louis B. Mayer at MGM, Y. Frank Freedman at Paramount, and Darryl F. Zanuck at Twentieth Century-Fox. The fictional character of Mr. Glogauer in this play is meant to represent a caricature of the famous movie moguls, known for their extraordinary power at all levels of the film industry.

The play also makes specific reference to such famous early movie moguls as the Laskys, the de Milles, and others. Jesse L. Lasky (1880–1958), in partnership with Samuel Goldwyn and Cecil B. De Mille (1991–1959), formed the Jesse L. Lasky Feature Play Company in 1913. In 1916, they merged with the Famous Players company to become the Famous Players-Lasky Corporation. This company later became Paramount, one of the major Hollywood production studios. De Mille's reputation as a successful producer is indicated in a line of the play by George. While they are on the film set, someone questions whether the pigeons that are supposed to be released during a wedding scene will know what to do; George replies, "Those pigeons know what to do. They were with Cecile De Mille for two years.''

This play also makes reference to D. W. Griffith (1875–1948) and the Biograph production company. D. W. Griffith is known as *the* master director of the silent film era. Many of his films were released through Biograph studios. D. W. Griffith is also controversial, however, for what some consider a masterpiece of American cinema, *The Birth of a Nation* (1915). While in many ways a brilliant work of cinematic art, *The Birth of a Nation* is an extremely racist depiction of the South during and after the Civil War. In the play by Kaufman and Hart, when someone refers in passing to the Civil War, another character responds, ''The Civil War? Didn't D. W. Griffith make that?'' The joke is in part that, while the first character was talking about the actual historical Civil War, the second character can only conceive of this historical event as a cinematic production. The play later refers to Biograph as a more significant element of the story. It is discovered after George directs his fist movie that he has directed from the wrong script. He has accidentally used a script for a movie made in 1910 by Biograph.

This play also refers to the development of early color film technology. Technicolor was originally a trademark name for a color film process; the first time a feature length movie was produced in Technicolor was 1917. In 1922, Technicolor incorporated to become the Technicolor Corporation. In the late 1920s, several feature films were produced in Technicolor. But, because the process was expensive, most films that used Technicolor had only one color sequence. By the early 1930s, with the Depression forcing the studios to cut costs, almost no color features were produced. In 1932, however, developments in the processing technology lead to a rise in the production of color films, and from 1932 to 1957 all color films were made using the Technicolor process. In this play, Mrs. Walker, the mother of the wannabe starlet Helen Walker, mentions that May had said Helen might do better on film in Technicolor. This comment is merely a joke at Helen's expense, implying that only extravagant film technology could counteract her poor acting abilities.

Sergei Eisenstein (1898–1948) is perhaps the most famous Russian film director and pioneer in the field of film theory. He is famous for his epic productions of events from Russian history, such as *Strike* (1925) and *October* (1928), about the Rus-

sian Revolution, as well as masterpieces such as *Battleship Potempkin* (1925). Eisenstein is best known in film theory for his theory of film ''montage,'' by which films are edited in such a way as to juxtapose images to create a symbolic set of meanings with the greatest impact upon the viewer. In the play by Kaufman and Hart, the fictional foreign director Kammerling makes reference to Eisenstein when he is fed up with the American film industry, and cries out, ''What a country! Oh, to be in Russia with Eisenstein!''

Will Hays was an important figure head of the film industry beginning in 1922, when he was appointed head of the Motion Picture Producers and Distributors of America (MPPDA), an association of Hollywood studios founded for the purpose of addressing public relations issues. The Hollywood industry had met with various forms of protest over the years in regards to the moral value of film content. Various sets of written guidelines for what was and wasn't considered acceptable film content were produced throughout the 1920s, but it was not until 1930 that the MPPDA adopted the Motion Picture Production Code, which became the standard basis of industry censorship until 1968.

In this play, reference is made to Will Hays when the receptionist at the film studio mentions that there had been a drunken man in the office. Helen responds that, ''they'll soon be weeded out. Will Hays is working on that as fast as he can.'' One of the concerns of the Production Code administration was that Hollywood movies not depict excessive consumption of alcohol. The joke is about Will Hays, suggesting that his crackdown on Hollywood morality threatens to extend to control of the behavior of those within the industry, as well as that of characters on the screen.

While all of the characters who actually appear in the play are fictional, reference is made to some of the most famous and successful film actors of the time, including: Gloria Swanson, Gary Cooper, Greta Garbo, Mae West, John Barrymore, Elsie Barrymore, and Janet Gaynor.

Source: Liz Brent, in an essay for *Drama for Students,* Gale, 2001

Robert L. Daniels

In the following review, Daniels provides an overview of the satire in ''Once in a Lifetime.''

George S. Kaufman and Moss Hart's 1930 satire on the dawn of talking pictures, *Once in a Lifetime,* still produces a goodly sampling of verbal and sight gags, and director David Pittu has whipped a cast of 21 actors (in more than 40 roles) into a briskly paced send-up. Pittu trusts his authors, and while some situations and characters have become cliches, the satirical romp remains an innocent nod to a bygone era.

Attempting to cash in on the Hollywood gold rush, three second-rate vaudevillians sell their tired act and head west to open an elocution school. Gaining the favor of a movie mogul, the trio gain a certain amount of influence in the industry before bringing near-ruin to the studio.

Peppered with extravagant performances and delightfully silly cartoon characters, the show never seems crowded on the Atlantic's small stage. Bell-hops, porters, chauffeurs and leggy starlets flit about trains, soundstages and hotel lobbies with giddy abandon. The break-neck tempo is vital and the antics suffer from any stalls along the way.

John Ellison Coulee is grand as a doltish vaudevillian who blunders into success by repeating simple words of theatrical wisdom he has read (most often in Variety). Johanna Day captures the flavor of the era as his aggressively flippant partner. When Larry Bryggman, as the hot-tempered, bumbling studio chief, points a dictatorial finger, it becomes a peninsula.

Cynthia Darlow is a gushing syndicated columnist from the Hedda Hopper mold, Kate Blumberg a winsome ingenue, and Peter Jacobson raps his riding crop with frequent frustration as the German film director.

Kaufman not only co-wrote the play, he also staged it and appeared as the neglected playwright in the original 1930 production; in homage to him, Pittu appears in that role of Lawrence Vail. (But he misses the manic desperation Max Wright summoned for the 1978 Circle in the Square revival.)

The period costumes are dapper and colorful, and the compact set changes, wrapped in a golden-edged proscenium. arch, boast a Technicolor gloss.

Adolph Green and Betty Comden May have refined the familiar elements of spoofing early talkies with their classic screenplay for *Singin' in the Rain,* but Kaufman and Hart got there first. Sixty-eight years years later, their first collaboration remains an amiable antic treat.

For the record, *Once in a Lifetime* opened at the Music Box on Sept. 24, 1930, and ran for 406 performances. Peter Bogdanovich directed a York Playhouse revival in 1964, and Adam Arkin appeared in an ETC Theatre Co. production in 1975. The 1978 Broadway revival at Circle in the Square featured John Lithgow, Treat Williams, Jayne Meadows Allen and George S. Irving.

Source: Robert L. Daniels, ''Once in a Lifetime,'' in *Variety,* Vol. 371, No. 5, June 8, 1998, p. 81.

Richard Eder

In the following excerpt, Eder details the comical absurdities that take place within ''Once in a Lifetime.''

When *Once in a Lifetime,* the first play that Moss Hart and George S. Kaufman wrote together, was revived here a number of years ago it ran for exactly one performance.

The Circle in the Square's leisurely but delightful version, which opened here last night, should do a great deal better. Some of the bones have fallen from the meat of this 1930 comedy; its insance logic has lost some of its logic, but there is plenty of insanity left.

And with John Lithgow sagging gently into a very large comic performance as George, the Heaven-favored fool who out-imbeciles Hollywood, and George Irving as athundering film tycoon constructed entirely of tiny gas-filled balloons, the Circle production surmounts the play's weakesses and its own blank spots to give New York something pretty close to ideal summer theater.

At its most alive, *Lifetime* has the wacky, mounting, improbable comic climaxes that distinguish the humor of the 1930s. The Marx Brothers had it, and at their best it was in a rhythm that raced and slowed but never dropped.

Quite a bit of *Lifetimes* drops. There is a lot of carpentry showing by now in this tale of the three out-of-work actors who set up an elocution school in Hollywood. It was the time when the talkies came in, and the stars who were the plumed swans of that particular puddle turned out to be as inaudible as swans.

There are grand chains of lunacy to the scenes in a Hollywood studio. A small but deadly not of bitter satire—Kaufman and Hart were New Yorkers, and Hollywood, which ate playwrights alive, was a joke that was no joke—gives the play some real bite. There is, as well, a good deal of stilted dialogue, particularly in the occasional scenes of sentiment. Caricatures wound better than they kiss.

But a lot of the limitlessness of the comedy of that time, the feeling that a joke could end up almost anywhere, remains. Sometimes it made for silliness and contrivance; sometimes for a beautifully irresponsible inspiration. Take the play's final joke.

Mr. Lithgow's George, whose mistakes that turn out lucky keep getting him alternately fired and promoted by the irascible Glogauer, makes one final mistake. He buys 2,000 airplanes. Now, at 50 years distance, this is something of a bald and heavy joke, especially for the climax of a long play.

But then somebody remarks hopefully that there must be some way you can use 2,000 airplanes. ''Sure,'' says May, the acid, good hearted heroine. ''Make applesauce.'' That afterthought, pure comic madness, is worth a ton of machinery and all the humor in a year's worth of *Saturday Night Live*.

The Circle production, directed by Tom Moore on a bare stage upon which furniture is toted in and out, does very well by the best moments, and nurses the longer worn spots with reasonable cheerfulness.

Mr. Moore is particularly good at some of the visual absurdities. The first entrance of Mr. Irving as Glogauer is a dignified retreat from the portable mob of sycophants he carries with him. He is pursued by a pair of emoting bellboys who, like everyone else in this hectic Hollywood of the imagination, are always auditioning. Even two electricians, having lunch, begin to improvise a song—it is ''Pretty Baby'' but they get it wrong—and wash off, presumably to see their agents.

Mr. Lithgow, as the bumbling George, is tall as Jacques Tati is tall. Like a mountain, his peak disappears into a cloudy of tentativeness. He looks like a cartoon of the 1930s, hips thrust forward, rocking back on his heels, and with one slow tugboat pulling bargeloads of silliness across his face. He moves in jecks, as if he were a sideshow.

In a scene with Max Wright, a playwright demented by underwork—he has been kept in an empty room for months and nobody has asked him for anything—Mr. Lithgow shows his art. Mr. Wright's performance, all hisses and jerks and twitches, embroiders its own embroideries. There is skill there but it is a sideshow and stops things dead.

> PEPPERED WITH EXTRAVAGANT PERFORMANCES AND DELIGHTFULLY SILLY CARTOON CHARACTERS, THE SHOW NEVER SEEMS CROWDED ON THE ATLANTIC'S SMALL STAGE. BELLHOPS, PORTERS, CHAUFFEURS AND LEGGY STARLETS FLIT ABOUT TRAINS, SOUNDSTAGES AND HOTEL LOBBIES WITH GIDDY ABANDON. THE BREAK-NECK TEMPO IS VITAL AND THE ANTICS SUFFER FROM ANY STALLS ALONG THE WAY.''

Mr. Lithgow, drooping, simply listens. He follows Mr. Wright's gyrations as a sunflower turns with the sun. He does nothing, in effect; he just stands there, and it is quite the best thing to do.

Mr. Irving is a comic roarer, a source of energy and noise but of considerable subtlety as well. His chin is an offshore continent, a kind of Iceland that precedes, the rest of his face and is full of glaciers an dvolcanic activity.

May, the heroine, is a fairly straight part, and difficult to do. Deborah May translates her gestures and expressions back into the 1930s; she is pert, tart and radiant.

Treat Williams is agreeable as Jerry Hyland, the ambitious but ultimately decent boyfriend of Miss May's. Julia Duffy makes a fine, brassy-haired and brassy-voiced young girl who possesses ambitions for stardom and the total doglike devotion of Mr. Lithgow.

MacIntyre Dixon, Jayne Meadows Allen, Beverly May and Bella Jarrett are all amusing in smaller parts. Jack Straw makes a fine screen bishop, who bets on horses between takes, and the rest of the cast is mostly good, too.

Source: Richard Eder, ''Stage: 'Once in a Lifetime,''' in *New York Times*, June 16, 1978, p. 237.

> " SOME OF THE BONES HAVE FALLEN FROM THE MEAT OF THIS 1930 COMEDY; ITS INSANCE LOGIC HAS LOST SOME OF ITS LOGIC, BUT THERE IS PLENTY OF INSANITY LEFT."

Richard Mason

In the following excerpt, Mason shows the collaboration between Moss Hart and George Kaufman and the styles that each employed to the making of "Once in a Lifetime."

Undoubtedly, Hart was fortunate in that his "formula" had a parallel in the work of George S. Kaufman, with whom he entered into a most fruitful collaboration after the success of *Once in a Lifetime*. In between, however, he had tested this formula as it buttresses many a musical book or revue sketch. Later, he was less fortunate in seeing fit to extend this formula into some serious works which reflect an ambition for his craft as do his comedies for his career.

Throughout this study distinctions between drama (content) and theatre (drama on stage) are continually made and must be continually understood. Such a distinction is inevitable in considering comedy—which gains so much from performance.

Further, comedy is accepted as [what Robert Lewis Shayon identified as] "a form of rational discourse, questioning and exposing absurdities and vices." Although the comic form may range from slapstick to verbal gymnastics, Louis Kronenberger, a connoisseur of comedy, identified a consistent characteristic when he writes [in *The Thread of Laughter*] that it is "a trenchant way of regarding life."

The nature and the effect of the comic have intrigued the poet and the philosopher from Aristotle to Sigmund Freud. Indeed, the theatre's comic mask has as many expressions and evokes as many varying responses as there are mirrors of distortion in an amusement park, but in pinning labels on them all, one runs the risk of echoing Polonius' category of plays.

Moss Hart took to the stage as a writer of comedy at the end of one of its most productive periods, and was highly active during its bleaker period when laughter was a precious commodity and cultural introspection unavoidable. We propose to gauge how Moss Hart met the challenge of his time, his theatre, and the venerable tradition of comedy. Hart's autobiography ended with the successful premiere of *Once in a Lifetime*. This study begins with it.

There is little doubt or mystery that Hart's involvement with Kaufman made a deep effect on his work. An investigation of Hart's plays can neither neglect *Once in a Lifetime* nor observe it cursorily. Fortunately, two versions exist: Hart's original, submitted to Kaufman, and the final, collaborative result. A comparison not only reveals the development of a play from its rough beginnings to a craftily polished stage piece, but it also indicates the authors' disposition toward the nature of comedy, their audiences, and the demands of their theatre as well. Importantly, a comparative study reveals characteristics repeated in the body of Hart's subsequent work, whether it be the product of collaboration or of solitary labor. These plays, *Once in a Lifetime* included, must be viewed partially in light of Hart's own recorded sentiment concerning an important aspect of his dramatic material:

> An audience is not interested in how hard an author has worked at his research, or how much material he has unearthed, and they do not take kindly to his parading in front of the footlights his hard-earned knowledge. They are quite right. They have not come to a school room; they have come to a theatre.

This was the theatre for which he desired to write, an inspiration notably described and detailed in his famous autobiography. Even its title, *Act One*, becomes particularly interesting in the context of Hart's lifelong preoccupation with the theatre world. It offers a somewhat tantalizing self-view of the author as a man of the theatre whose life runs like a play, and entices one to investigate the playwright on a psychological level. His plays, coupled with the available library of his personal papers, offer ample evidence that the work was an exceedingly personal extension of the man. . . .

Although Kaufman wrote in a fairly late letter to Hart "of those twin targets at which I have aimed so many times, business and politics. . . ." He too, had an affinity for the theatrical theme which must have contributed to the bond that was established between them with *Once in a Lifetime*. . . .

Admittedly, it is Kaufman rather than Hart upon whom the spotlight is mainly turned whenever their collaboration is under focus. In his eulogy to Kaufman, Hart admitted his "debt to George is incalculable." The beginnings of indebtedness would seem to have been established some time before Kaufman ever saw the young Hart's script, for there is much evidence of the strong influence of Kaufman's comedies in *Once in a Lifetime.* This initial influence stimulated Hart into (1) treating a theatrical milieu in (2) a farce frame.

Once in a Lifetime, a Comedy with Sound and Fury by Moss Hart, reads the title page of the script. It bears no copyright date but was written in either September or October of 1929. The garish film industry and its newly found "sound" are the subjects of Hart's play. This original version of *Once in a Lifetime* is obviously an apprentice work, but a highly promising one when it is considered that Hart was just past twenty years old, had never visited Hollywood, nor even written a comedy. [The critic adds in a footnote: "Hart tells us he had already written six serious plays."] What it lacks in structure and character development, it compensates for in energy and extravagance, and a sense of parody and satire. It is certainly "native" in its lack of cerebral subtleties, in the popularity of its aggressive farce form, and in its theme of the innocent (a Kaufman analogue) who stumbles his way to success, winning a beautiful bride along the way.

The script is so topical in its theme that the passage of time and the passing of a particular Hollywood era have robbed it of much of its original pertinence. Yet, Hart's script can claim an abundance of amusing moments and comic invention of situation and character. Although unsatisfactorily episodic in its dramaturgy, it is in its Hollywood caricatures that Hart's original is the most theatrically telling: Dahlberg, the man who rejected sound, who will not make a film without a "name" no matter how miscast the "name" may be, and to whom everything, regardless of subject, is "just too colossal," is in performance actually more humorously drawn than a description might indicate. It is the same with the narcissism of the mass-manufactured starlets; the ire of the foreign film director; and the ubiquity of the Hollywood hopeful, auditioning by way of vigorous, kaleidoscopic facial expression whenever important studio personnel appear.

It is of particular interest to note the grandly intense and "tragic" demeanor of the studio receptionist, a pose which anticipates the "bravura"

"UNDOUBTEDLY, HART WAS FORTUNATE IN THAT HIS 'FORMULA' HAD A PARALLEL IN THE WORK OF GEORGE S. KAUFMAN, WITH WHOM HE ENTERED INTO A MOST FRUITFUL COLLABORATION AFTER THE SUCCESS OF *ONCE IN A LIFETIME.*"

manner of the theatrical and royal folk of the later comedies.

But for all the theatrical heightening and comic absurdity, one repeatedly concludes that the reach exceeds the grasp as one fertile idea after another fails realization in a dramatically sustained way, or is so overdrawn as to blunt the edge of laughter. Repeated promise of genuine satire is lost or weakened amid the general and increasing extravagance.

The impression emerges, at least from a reading of *Once in a Lifetime,* that the play is a series of comic vignettes held together by a loose narrative rather than a dramatic plot. A lack of development in character treatment accounts for much of this. There is little conflict or story development, since Hart sacrifices narrative for burlesque sequences.

This native facility for "extravagance" can be traced throughout Hart's work. It contributes not only to the unique character of the comedies, but also to the later theatrical ingenuity of *Lady in the Dark* and the dramatic weaknesses of *Christopher Blake.*

Although the intent and spirit of the collaborative version sustains intact those of the original, it may be called an entirely new play in light of its more deliberate comic air and direction. The quality of burlesque remains the same as often does the incident of the original, but the accumulative effect is overwhelmingly superior to Hart's. This is mainly achieved through the infusion of an obvious theatrical skill and sureness of effect, a more sophisticated narrative, more dimensionalized characters, and smoother dialogue. A filling out of the drama's connective tissues has been added to Hart's skeletal schemes. An impression is gained that where Hart worked through intuition and an imitative sense, producing but the healthy embryo of an idea, Kaufman's theatrical disciplines helped ''humanize'' it.

Should one, however, find it failing to achieve on a satirical level what it has the potential to achieve, one could predicate of it the following view [expressed by James Agee in *Films in Review*]:

> Farce, like melodrama, offers very special chances for accurate observation, but here accuracy is avoided ten times to one in favor of the easy burlesque or the easier idealization which drops the bottom out of farce. Every good moment frazzles or drowns.

Even this collaborative version of *Once in a Lifetime* is, essentially, a parody less of Hollywood life and film-making than it is a parody of a typical genre film story, film decor, and the people involved in their production. Although possessed of moments of satire and satirical allusion, it is essentially a sympathetic lampoon.

On the other hand, as a carefully constructed farce containing timely and irreverent allusion, the collaborative version of *Once in a Lifetime* certainly possesses the merit to be included in the comedies which reflect the American scene as described by Alan Downer [in *Revolution in the American Drama*]:

> Here, in the mockery of the serious, the classic, the formal, and the eventual victory of the much-beaten underdog, is the theatrical equivalent of the tall talk and the comic folk story which reflect so accurately the American temper. Here, waiting for a playwright to put them to use, or give them form or purpose, were the elements of American comedy.

Twenty-four years later, Hart looked over his original script. He recorded his reaction in his journal:

> It was quite well constructed, the lines extremely funny, and I think perhaps, if a manuscript like this were submitted to me today, I would have to admit that the author had real talent for the theatre.

In 1954, Moss Hart entered the following observation in his journal:

> Again, I was struck by the fact that the three biggest hits of the season—*Teahouse Of The August Moon, Tea and Sympathy, and The Caine Mutiny Court Martial*—violate almost every theatre rule. It is a lesson that there are no rules whatever about the theatre, but one which is very hard to remember.

Yet, guided by principles of the theatre which had made their *Once in a Lifetime* a notable success, Hart and Kaufman apparently established a set of rules for themselves which they applied to their joint comedies and to which Hart returned with his *Light Up the Sky.*

A certain pattern emerges from the merest reading or viewing of these plays, and certain broad judgments are unavoidable. *You Can't Take It with You* is the most imaginative and exudes the most warmth and sentiment. Tonally, *The Man Who Came to Dinner* is reminiscent of the earlier Kaufman satires. It is of superior construction and, by way of Sheridan Whiteside, its caustic and principal role, proves a particularly effective sounding board for Kaufmanesque dialogue. Neither a reading nor viewing can disguise the fact that *George Washington Slept Here* is the weakest of the group, and strong in evidence that the collaboration was wearing thin or losing fire. Their joint authorship terminated with this play, but the influence of Kaufman thoroughly permeates the writing of *Light Up the Sky.* Although varying in degrees of accomplishment, the comedies suggest, by their very similarities, that the authors were writing for a theatre they knew and that they knew what that theatre wanted.

Once in a Lifetime proved to be the prime example of a formula constructed earlier by Kaufman and his various collaborators: the successful rise in a jungle world of the helpless innocent almost despite himself. Although such a theme has been replaced in the comedies written with Hart which are under scrutiny here, the formula persists in the theatrical frame and theatrical devices which are common to both.

Source: Richard Mason, ''The Comic Theatre of Moss Hart: Persistence of a Formula,'' in *The Theatre Annual,* Vol. 23, 1967, p. 60.

SOURCES

Atkinson, J. Brooks, review of *Once in a Lifetime,* in *New York Times,* September 25, 1930, p. 22.

———, review of *Once in a Lifetime,* in *New York Times,* December 7, 1930, section 9, p. 1.

Baughman, Judith S, ed., *American Decades: 1920–1929,* Gale, 1995, pp. 280-81.

Daniels, Robert L., review of *Once in a Lifetime,* in *Variety,* June 8, 1998, p. 81.

Eder, Richard, Review of *Once in a Lifetime,* in *New York Times,* June 16, 1978, p. C3.

Evans, Sara M., *Born for Liberty: A History of Women in America,* The Free Press, 1989, pp. 182-83.

Gussow, Mel, review of *Once in a Lifetime,* in *New York Times,* April 4, 1975, p. 22.

Hart, Moss, and George S. Kaufman, *Once in a Lifetime,* Samuel French, Inc., 1930.

Kalem, T. E., "Tower of Babble," in *Time,* July 17, 1978, p. 83.

Review of *Once in a Lifetime,* in *Commonweal,* October 8, 1930, p. 584.

Simon, John, "Forced Farce Cryer's Outcry," in *New York,* July 3, 1978, p. 74.

———, "No Man's Romance," in *New York Times,* June 22, 1998, p. 61.

Taubman, Howard, review of *Once in a Lifetime,* in *New York Times,* January 29, p. 20.

———, "Troupe in Capital Gives *Once in a Lifetime,*" in *New York Times,* October 30, 1962, p. 30.

FURTHER READING

Flexner, Eleanor, *American Playwrights: 1918–1938,* Simon & Schuster, 1938, pp. 216-20.
> This book considers the careers of the most important playwrights on the American stage, including Hart and Kaufman. Flexner considers and compares *Once in a Lifetime* and other plays.

Hart, Moss, *Act One: An Autobiography,* Random House, 1959.
> This memoir covers the whole of Hart's professional life, including details surrounding the conception and production of *Once in a Lifetime.*

Pollack, Rhoda-Gale, *George S. Kaufman,* Twayne Publishers, 1988.
> This critical biography on Kaufman's professional life includes a chapter on his collaborations with Hart.

Teichmann, Howard, *George S. Kaufman: An Intimate Portrait,* Atheneum, 1972.
> This biography includes Kaufman's personal and professional life, including his work on and in *Once in a Lifetime.*

Ring Around the Moon

JEAN ANOUILH

1947

Jean Anouilh's *Ring Around the Moon* first appeared in France in 1947 as *L'Invitation au Chateau.* Especially important in Anouilh's career, the play is the earliest of his *pièces brillantes,* a rather mixed group of four works moving from two lighter to two darker pieces. *Brilliantes* has been employed to describe the polished and sophisticated gemlike quality of this group, most prominently displayed in *Ring Around the Moon*'s complex plotting, ceaseless obstacles, and still—after all—the reconciliation of almost all of its characters to both love and wealth.

Perhaps because of its parody of upper-class vanity *Ring Around the Moon* is Anouilh's most produced play in the United States, where there is a tradition of holding the aristocracy in contempt. The play's numerous characters—engaged in ceaseless exiting and entrancing—enhance the quick-paced wit and tangy satire of upper-class pretension and lower-class ambition. Yet *Ring Around the Moon* is unexpectedly coupled to a fairy tale ending where nearly everything comes out better. For this reason, *Ring Around the Moon,* like some of Shakespeare's comedies, succeeds on the level of both entertainment and art—just one reason Anouilh is Europe's most popular post-World War II playwright.

AUTHOR BIOGRAPHY

Jean Anouilh was born in Bordeaux in the southwest of France in 1910. His father was a tailor known for his meticulousness, and his mother, a pianist, played in the orchestra of a casino in a seaside resort outside Bordeaux. At the resort, the young Anouilh was able to watch frequent operettas, which nurtured his interest in theater. At nine, Anouilh moved with his family to the Monmartre district of Paris, and by age twelve began writing verse plays acted for friends and relatives. At nineteen, he collaborated with Jean Aurenche on two plays, *Humulus le muet* and *Mandarine.* After briefly studying law at the Sorbonne, Anouilh became a gag writer from 1929–1931 for the cinema, and a copywriter at an advertising agency. In 1931, Anouilh married the actress Monelle Valentin and became secretary to one of the most important producer/directors in the French theater, Louis Jouvet, who was known for his elaborate and elegant productions. Jouvet produced a few of Anouilh's early plays, which were well received. When, in 1935, Anouilh sold the rights to MGM for *Y'Avait un Prisonnier,* he gained the financial independence to devote himself to writing. Two years later, Anouilh took his work to Georges and Ludmilla Pitöff whom Jouvet referred to as *les pitoyables* (the pitiful) for their spare productions. The Pitöffs produced two of Anouilh's plays and had a major impact on Anouilh's philosophy of theater: staging made subservient to ideas.

Anouilh first developed his chronic, and often comic, misanthropy when he attempted, unsuccessfully, to collect signatures from fellow artists to protest the death sentence given to novelist and dramatist, Robert Brasillach, who was accused of collaborating with the Germans. In 1944, Anouilh gained a wide audience with *Antigone,* a version of Sophocles' classical drama. *Antigone* was a thinly disguised attack on the Nazis and the collaborationist French government headquartered in the southern half of France, in the town of Vichy, during Nazi occupation of the north. After the war Anouilh was the most successful playwright in Europe. In the United States his "costumed" plays in the 1950s fared best. These include *L'alouette* (*The Lark,* 1953), about Joan of Arc, and *Becket* (1959), which won a Tony Award (1955) and was filmed with Peter O'Toole and Richard Burton. By the end of the 1950s Anouilh's works began to lose critical favor with the emergence of a new wave of "absurdist drama," which Anouilh welcomed, by Jean Genet,

Eugene Ionesco, and Samuel Beckett. In 1987, Anouilh died in Switzerland, survived by his second wife, the actress Nicole Lançon, and his four children. Anouilh was the recipient of the Grand Prize of French Cinema (1949), the New York Drama Critics Award (1957), the Cino del Duca Prize (1970); the French Drama Critics Award (1970), and the Paris Critics Prize (1971).

PLOT SUMMARY

Act I

Ring Around the Moon opens with the aristocratic *bon vivant,* Hugo, talking with Joshua, his butler, both discussing Hugo's brother, Frederic. Frederic has been sleeping outside his fiancée's bedroom window while she is a guest at the family's estate. Frederic and Hugo are identical twins, but Hugo is good with women and Frederic inept. Hugo and Joshua are unhappy with Frederic's fawning over Diana Messerschmann, his fiancée. Hugo hints he will do something about it. Hugo leaves and Frederic enters (they are played by the same actor). Frederic and Joshua now discuss Frederic's sleeping habits. Frederic assures Joshua that slumbering amidst rhododendrons is nothing serious. As one might expect from Frederic's behavior, Frederic's love for Diana is indeed insecure. Enter Patrice Bombelles (Messerschmann's male secretary) and Lady India (Messerschmann's mistress and Hugo and Frederic's cousin), who reveal their affair behind the back of the industrialist, Messerschmann. Patrice is especially worried because wealthy Messerschmann pays Patrice's salary and "keeps" Lady India. Lady India is less concerned with getting caught, is in fact fascinated by it. These two are replaced by Madame Desmermortes and her nephew, Hugo, he notifying her of Lady India's (her niece and his cousin) affair with Messerschmann. Hugo also informs Madame of Frederic's impending marriage to Diana. Madame is unhappy with Messerschmann's and Lady India's affair because Messerschmann is a mere businessman, not an aristocrat. Madame is displeased with the Diana-Frederic match because Madame believes the rich and confident Diana will overpower the subservient Frederic. Hugo again hints that marriage bells may not ring. Madame is now replaced by Romainville. Hugo informs Romainville he has seen Romainville doting on a young girl (Isabelle) and further, knows Romainville has brought her to the country to be with him. Hugo threatens to expose the meeting to

Jean Anouilh

Madame as a lecherous affair unless Romainville acquiesces to inviting Isabelle to the Desmermortes estate and pose as Romainville's niece. Isabelle and her mother soon arrive, the latter dazzled by the estate and the increased prospect of marrying Isabelle to a rich man. Isabelle thinks she has come just to dance. When Hugo greets them, Isabelle is preoccupied by his handsomeness. All exit and Madame and Joshua enter, planning the ball to be held that evening. In the next set of frequent entrances and exits, action is focused on an extended conversation between Hugo and Isabelle. Romainville's infatuation with Isabelle is revealed, as is Hugo's plan to parade the beautiful Isabelle at the evening ball so Frederic will fall in love with her, and out of love with Diana. Romainville rushes in to alert Hugo about a rumple in the plan: Isabelle's mother has recognized Madame's companion, Capulat, as her long lost friend. Romainville is worried Isabelle's mother will betray the plan to Capulat who will in turn tell Madame, giving away Romainville's apparently lecherous connection to Isabelle and ruining his relationship with the Desmermortes. Romainville's suspicions are confirmed after talking with the mother who has apparently already told Capulat too much. Hugo decides to tell Capulat to keep quiet, but before he can, Madame corners Romainville and intently questions him about his

family connection to the enchanting "niece," a grilling through which Romainville barely fakes his way. The final exchange of Act I has Capulat promising Isabelle's mother to help her win Hugo for Isabelle.

Act II

Act II opens at the ball with Capulat slyly giving up misguided bits of Hugo's plot to get Madame to connect Hugo and Isabelle. Madame is mystified as to Capulat's meaning and pulls her offstage to get the full story. Patrice enters with Lady India discussing Patrice's terrible fear that Messerschmann will discover Patrice and Lady India's affair. This excites India who romanticizes being poor. When Messerschmann enters, Patrice and Lady India leave, wondering if Messerschmann has seen them and guessed their affair. The next set of exchanges involve quick and uncomfortable meetings between Isabelle and Frederic. Isabelle finally tells Frederic—immediately after Hugo has kissed her to arouse Frederic's jealousy—that she is not, as it appears, in love with Hugo, but with Frederic. Hugo then tells Isabelle of his plan to inflame Frederic's love still further with another fictional lover pretending to challenge Hugo to a duel if Hugo does not cease his attentions toward Isabelle. Shots will then ring out and Isabelle, acting as if she thinks Frederic dead, will fake drowning. Hugo will then "rescue" her and carry her to Frederic. So happy will Isabelle act to see Frederic still alive, and so flattered will Frederic be that Isabelle attempted to drown herself on his account, Frederic will fall in love with her. After hearing Hugo's elaborate plan, Isabelle becomes so frustrated in her still-unstated love for Hugo, and so disgusted with Hugo's incredible stratagems, she runs off. Diana enters having seen Hugo and Isabelle together and is aroused to jealousy. Diana tries getting Hugo to say he loves her (Diana) but he refuses and leaves. Enter Messerschmann. Diana complains to him that she is being upstaged by Isabelle, that Isabelle is stealing the attentions of the men at the ball. Messerschmann promises his daughter he will take care of everything. Now Hugo enters threatening Patrice to expose his affair with Lady India if Patrice will not be the one to play the jealous lover and duelist in Hugo's crazy scheme. Patrice complies. Now Capulat enters with Isabelle's mother, richly dressed as "Countess Funela" a character Madame has given the mother to keep her occupied while Hugo and Madame manipulate the matches according to their own specifications. Romainville enters and tells Hugo he is distraught because Messerschmann has threatened to ruin Romainville financially unless Romainville gets Isabelle out of the Desmermortes house. Patrice now enters to play the jealous lover, insult Hugo, and challenge him to a duel. But Patrice is ignorant that by this time Hugo has forgotten the plan, preoccupied as he is with Romainville's hysteria and the ''Countess Funela.''

Act III

When Act III opens, Hugo, his plans in disarray, desperately discusses a new and fantastic plan— no longer to match Isabelle with Frederic by having her fake her drowning—but to embarrass the rich guests by exposing Isabelle as a humble girl, not an upper-class debutante as he led them to believe. Isabelle, again disgusted with Hugo, will have none of it. Hugo exits and Diana enters and complains to Isabelle about the misfortune of wealth. Isabelle, poor as she is, is incensed and ends up fighting with Diana. When Frederic discovers them, Isabelle mistakes him for Hugo, telling him off and confessing her love. Frederic admits he is not Hugo. Diana dislikes the attention Frederic and Isabelle pay each other and says she is leaving, demanding Frederic leave with her. Isabelle, now alone and distraught, is discovered by her mother. Isabelle tells her mother the charade is finished and that they are leaving. Messerschmann enters and tries to bribe Isabelle to leave the house. She tells him she is already planning to leave and refuses his money. He cannot believe it and continues raising his offers as fast as she rejects them. Suddenly, Messerschmann becomes disillusioned about the power of money and he and Isabelle begin tearing up stacks of bills. But both are still unhappy and Messerschmann hints at destroying himself. Isabelle then attempts to drown herself for real, but Hugo rescues her. Madame now begins to bring about a happy end. She persuades Isabelle to forget Hugo and has Frederic console her in order to match them. She then attempts to convince Hugo of his love for Diana. (Meanwhile Patrice, completely clueless to the new developments, again rushes in to play the jealous lover). Lady India now walks on to announce Messerschmann is financially ruining himself by selling off his assets. Diana enters and declares that since her father is poor and her marriage with Frederic finished, she will learn to be poor. Hugo, feeling sorry for her, advises reconciliation with Frederic. Romainville enters and announces he will propose to Isabelle, but learns Isabelle is now with Frederic. In a note from Hugo brought in by Joshua, Hugo confesses his love for Diana because he thinks her poor. Messerschmann then confirms the news of

his financial ruin. Lady India is moved and entranced by the adventure of being poor. The play ends with Messerschmann reading a telegram saying that his attempts at financial ruin were perceived as maneuvering, and have made him richer than ever. Messerschmann celebrates with his standard bowl of noodles, this time with a little salt.

CHARACTERS

Patrice Bombelles

Patrice Bombelles is male secretary to the wealthy industrialist, Messerschmann, and also the object of Messerschmann's mistress's (Lady India) attentions, which Bombelles has reciprocated for two years. Unsurprisingly, Bombelles does not want Messerschmann to find out about the secretive affair, since Bombelles believes it would mean his firing. So preoccupied is Bombelles to keep the affair with Lady India a total secret, he is constantly agitated, often forgetting or missing the subject of conversation and the latest change in the main character's (Hugo) ever-evolving plans.

Geraldine Capulat

Capulat is, as Anouilh describes her, Madame Desmermortes's ''faded'' servant/companion. She has a minor role until she is recognized by Isabelle's mother as a long-lost friend with whom she once played piano duets. Capulat is both a hopeless romantic and a loyal friend and so cannot help but satisfy Isabelle's mother in the attempt to get Madame to unite Hugo and Isabelle.

Madame Desmermortes

Desmermortes is the elderly, overly family- and class-conscious aunt of Hugo, Frederic, and Lady India. She is interested in her nephews and niece getting married to the right companions. By helping Hugo with his plans, by acting according to her own lights, and partly through sheer luck, Madame is successful. With a sometimes cruel, sometimes sober realism, Madame parries the hopeless romanticism of her servant/companion, Capulat. Madame's somewhat hardened view of life is at least partially due to her age and confinement in a wheelchair.

Frederic

Frederic is the identical twin brother of Hugo and played by the same actor. He is also the nephew of Mme. Desmermortes, and the zealous pursuer of Diana Messerschmann. He lacks confidence, and is self-deprecating, He constantly fawns over Diana from whom he cannot bear to be separated for a moment. Perhaps for this reason, Diana is not in love with Frederic, but Frederic's confident twin, Hugo. However inept Frederic is with women, Hugo thinks Frederic ''good, sensible, kind, and intelligent.'' Frederic eventually becomes disillusioned with Diana's domination of him and falls for Isabelle.

Hugo

Hugo is the identical twin of Frederic, but unlike Frederic, Hugo is a confident ladies' man and according to his own assessment, a kind of evil twin to Frederic. Hugo is the play's main character because the major action of the play revolves around his scheme to lure Frederic away from Diana, who does not love Frederic, but the more confident Hugo. While Hugo knows Diana loves him, he is convinced he doesn't love her because, he says, she is rich and ''badly spoilt.'' Hugo views himself as the enemy of upper-class vanity, and for this reason, some of the characters remark that he seems ''capable of absolutely anything.'' The observation is not without merit since Hugo blackmails Romainville, attempts to bamboozle Frederic away from Diana, pays Isabelle to act interested in Frederic, and finally, blackmails Patrice Bombelles to fake jealous love for Isabelle in order to stir up Frederic's desire. In the end, Hugo finally confesses his love for Diana after learning she is poor.

Lady Dorothy India

Lady India is the niece of Madame Desmermortes, cousin to the twins, Hugo and Frederic, and the mistress of both Messerschmann and Patrice Bombelles. She thinks she is in love with danger, and fantasizes about getting caught by Messerschmann in the arms of Patrice. Part of Lady India's attraction to danger is an unreal desire to be poor. She is at least partially sincere: at play's end, her love for Messerschmann is rekindled after learning he has just become penniless.

Isabelle

Isabelle, a young and attractive ballet dancer, has a somewhat uncertain relationship with the character of Romainville: it appears he furnishes her with money in the guise of ''patron of the arts.'' Whatever her motives, she accepts his attentions. At root, Isabelle is honest and considerate, but

she becomes swept up in playing the part of Romainville's niece because, like so many women, she is irresistibly drawn to Hugo. Along with Hugo, Isabelle shares a certain contempt for money, which she shows when refusing Messerschmann's offers to pay her off, and when joining him in tearing up his stacks of bills. Through the aid of Mme. Desmermortes's matchmaking, Isabelle realizes she loves Frederic, not Hugo.

Isabelle's Mother

Isabelle's mother is the only character in the play fully romanticizing money and culture, partly because she once had both. She pushes Isabelle to play the part in Hugo's charade so that Isabelle might have a chance to marry him, or at least marry *someone* with money. Isabelle's mother also turns out to be an old friend of Capulat. Fool that the mother is, she stands to give away Hugo's scheme through Capulat. To prevent her from subverting Hugo's plot, Mme. Desmermortes gives Isabelle's mother the character of ''Countess Funela'' to play at the ball. This fulfills the mother's fantasies of wealth and status. In the final distribution of partners, the mother gets her wish when Isabelle wins Frederic.

Joshua

Joshua has been the respectful butler at the Desmermortes family estate for thirty years. He makes sure Hugo's plans to separate Frederic and Diana is well executed. Joshua adds comic relief not only for his dignified language befitting the stock character of the butler, but also because he often loses his composure in the face of the unexpected. As Anouilh says, Joshua is ''crumbling.''

Messerschmann

A wealthy industrialist, Messerschmann is also an insomniac and eats only one thing: noodles without butter and salt. He has four primary roles in life: Diana's father, paramour of Lady India, Patrice Bombelles's boss, and owner of the pig-iron company managed by Romainville. Messerschmann represents money and the rich man's belief that every person has his or her price. When he finds Diana is jealous of Isabelle, he attempts to blackmail Romainville and bribe Isabelle to get her to leave the house. When his efforts fail with Isabelle, Messerschmann's rage and sudden disenchantment with money lead him to attempt to ruin himself financially, which, unexpectedly, makes him more attractive to Lady India.

Diana Messerschmann

Diana is the attractive daughter of the wealthy industrial magnate, Messerschmann; the aloof love object of Frederic; and the thwarted pursuer of Hugo. She settles for Frederic because Hugo does not love her. Diana becomes jealous of Isabelle for stealing the glances of the men at the ball and complains to her father. It is only when Messerschmann is reported to have lost his fortune that Hugo confesses his love for the now seemingly impoverished Diana.

Romainville

Romainville is an older man who studies butterflies, probably intent on making Isabelle his next specimen. He also heads a pig-iron company owned by Messerschmann. To guard against a possible smudge on his reputation, Romainville tries to keep his pursuit of young Isabelle a secret, and so is blackmailed by Hugo into getting Isabelle to pose as Romainville's niece, out to steal Frederic from Diana. But when Messerschmann finds that Isabelle is provoking his daughter's jealousy, Messerschmann threatens Romainville with financial ruin unless Romainville removes Isabelle from the house. In the last moments of the play, Romainville decides to confess his love and propose to Isabelle. He is, however, too late. Isabelle and Frederic have already become paired.

TOPICS FOR FURTHER STUDY

- Beginning a decade or so before the French Revolution (1789), research the history of industrialism in France, focusing on the friction between the old-money aristocracy and the new-money bourgeoisie. Then write an essay detailing some of the consequences of such friction.

- After researching the history and form of *commedia dell'arte* write an essay discussing how stock characters in that form resemble those in *Ring Around the Moon*.

- Study Anouilh's directions for music in *Ring Around the Moon*. Select (or compose) music to fit those scenes. Justify your reasons.

- Research the history of marriage in late eighteenth-century Europe, then write an essay describing what economic and social functions it served. Do any of these functions exist in today's United States? Which ones and in what segments of society?

THEMES

Wealth Versus Poverty

Two sets of class conflicts occur in *Ring Around the Moon:* that of older, aristocratic wealth versus newer, capitalist wealth, and both of these versus poverty. Old money is represented by Madame Desmermortes, her niece, and nephews; new money by Messerschmann, his daughter, and Romainville, head of Messerschmann's pig-iron company. When Madame makes her first entrance with Hugo, discussing Messerschmann's keeping of Lady India, Madame calls it ''monstrous'' and ''humiliating,'' because old money kept by new money indicates aristocratic demise, dependence, loss of status. In

Act III, Scene 2, Madame Desmermortes proceeds to make sure her two charges are married happily. This is a somewhat complex matter: Frederic must not marry Diana because she will be in complete control of him because she doesn't need his money and because he is servile. This is humiliating in terms of Frederic's wealth and status, and his gender. At least if the confident Hugo marries Diana, the emotional balance will tip in Hugo's favor. Further, if Diana is poor, then a marriage between Hugo and Diana will be even less objectionable, as she will be totally dependent upon Hugo. And Madame does not object to Lady India's swooning over Messerschmann's financial ruin because he will be unable to disgrace the Desmermortes family by keeping her. This is partially why Messerschmann wants his doubled wealth kept secret. At play's end, everyone is able to retain or increase his or her wealth. Even Romainville and Patrice keep their positions in Messerschmann's even stronger financial empire.

The other conflict in *Ring Around the Moon* is wealth versus poverty, the latter represented by Isabelle and her mother. But while Isabelle's mother has a generous dose of class envy—either new or old money being very acceptable—Isabelle is not only *not* envious but, at least as a result of Hugo's and Messerschmann's attempt to buy her, rather contemptuous of wealth. She therefore plays the heroine. Not only does Isabelle display enough strength of character to refuse Messerschmann's and Hugo's money, but after she and Messerschmann finish destroying the money, she realizes it might have been used to help the poor. Neither she nor Messerschmann feel as if destroying the money has been of any lasting value. Anouilh, then, while criticizing certain aspects of wealth (vanity, egregious power, pettiness) and poverty (envy and awe of the upper classes), denounces neither wealth nor poverty in themselves, nor class inequality. Instead, he spins out an ending unusual in the real world: both rich and poor get richer.

Appearance versus Reality

The most obvious example of the theme of appearance versus reality in *Ring Around the Moon* is the use of identical, indistinguishable twins played by the same actor. But readers have an "advantage" over audience members: while readers know who is speaking, audience members cannot always tell. This robs readers of an intended confusion accessible to only those seeing a performance. That is, unless a director dresses Hugo and Frederic differently, or alters their appearance.

The only characters confused about who is Hugo and who Frederic, are Diana and Isabelle. Diana's confusion is, however, far less total: while she mistakes their appearance on occasion—*or pretends to*—she is able to distinguish their personalities. Isabelle, on the other hand, hardly knows one from the other. If Isabelle had met Frederic before Hugo, she might even have been as infatuated with Frederic as with Hugo. Why does Anouilh wants to confuse not only the audience, but Diana and Isabelle? A partial answer is that he wants to preclude simplistic assessments like "The rich are all alike," since even identical, indistinguishable twins are not alike; are, in fact, opposites.

Two other violators of reality through physical appearance are Isabelle and her mother. Isabelle, a ballet dancer, is brought to the estate to play Romainville's niece and seduce Frederic. Isabelle's mother plays the part of Countess Funela. Both are meant to appear as though upper class. Though both

poor and of the same family and gender, Isabelle and her mother are also not alike: Isabelle dislikes deceit while her mother frolics in it. But whatever the case, the poor are paid by the rich to imitate the rich in order to fool the merely wealthy into thinking the poor are really rich. Less confusingly, Hugo and Madame (old money) attempt to bamboozle the new money guests at the party, such as Romainville, and those running companies that Messerschmann (also new money) ultimately controls.

There are other examples of appearance versus reality, but these have less to do with *being* a part than *acting* a part. While the twins, as well as Isabelle and her mother are pretending to be other characters, the violations of reality by Patrice and Lady India involve *acting* the part of not having an affair. Lady India is, in fact, attempting, though sometimes halfheartedly, to appear as if she is not having *two* affairs. In addition, Romainville must act as uncle to Isabelle, and Diana acts as though in love with Frederic. Finally, at the end of the play Messerschmann wants everyone to think him poor, though he is richer than ever. Why the charade? Because it not only provokes laughs, but points to the falsity of human behavior, and simultaneously, the facility of making fools of people, including—in the case of an identical actor playing Hugo and Frederic—the audience.

STYLE

Setting

Ring Around the Moon takes place at a French country estate in spring. Why spring? Probably because it is when romance is thought to "bloom." The additional setting of a glassed-in rococo winter garden looking out on a "wide expanse of park" contributes to this fertile atmosphere. The home belongs to Madame Desmermortes and is occupied by her nephews, Hugo and Frederic, and her niece, Lady India, all of them attended by the butler, Joshua. All other characters are guests at the chateau.

Dialogue

The dialogue in *Ring Around the Moon* is entirely social: it contains no soliloquies. Dialogue, as the word indicates, is always directed at someone, most often taking the form of persuasion, coercion, or attack. Recall the dialogue about money between Messerschmann and Isabelle, Hugo's numerous coercions of Romainville, Patrice, and Isabelle, and Diane's toying with Frederic. This is dialogue as manipulation.

Music

Music occurs primarily in Act II at the evening ball, where it may reinforce the idea that precise and numerous entrances and exits of a multitude of characters are a kind of comedic dance. When Hugo blackmails Patrice into acting as Isabelle's jealous lover, a kind of battle of wits results, and so Anouilh calls for a "heroic, warlike tune."

Movement

The movement of *Ring Around the Moon* consists of a multitude of precisely timed entrances and exits, especially of the identical twins, Hugo and Frederic, played by the same actor. In the final act of the play, Hugo must send in—"for reasons which you all know"—a note from offstage in which Hugo confesses his love for Diana Messerschmann. The reason? Frederic is already onstage. In Act I, Scene 1, just before Diana and Frederic exit, Diana states that Hugo is "capable of absolutely anything." Patrice and Lady India immediately walk on, Patrice speaking these same words, producing a neat transition between different situations and characters with Hugo's interference in common. Finally, it is fitting that in this play full of movement, the heroine, Isabelle, is a dancer.

HISTORICAL CONTEXT

During the course of World War II (1939–1945) the Germans invaded Paris and occupied the northern and western parts of France from 1940–44. The rest of the country was under the authority of the puppet government of Vichy led by Marshal Pétain and supported by much of the traditional French right. Simultaneously, General Charles de Gaulle was organizing the resistance movement of the Free French from London. Soon after the American, British, and Canadian military invasion on the Normandy beaches on June 6, 1944, de Gaulle entered Paris to head the new government.

France's defeat by the Germans unexpectedly prodded modernization forward after the end of Nazi occupation and the Vichy regime. The resistance movement that emerged, though existing in frictional coexistence, contained most of France's forward-looking elements. With the right discredited and the resistance elements committed to sig-

nificant change, the two-year life of the post-WWII liberation coalition after November, 1944 allowed a wide range of reforms. Extensive nationalization of industry endowed the central government with new power over the direction of France's economy and France's welfare state greatly expanded. Modernizing technocrats, represented by Jean Monnet and his planning commission, were eager to use the new state levers for rejuvenated control. Strong state influence pushed France's postwar development in a different direction from many other European countries whose industries were not nationalized.

Post-Liberation French governments did not fare so well at building new political institutions. Disputes between General Charles de Gaulle and the left over the role of the head of state led to de Gaulle's angry resignation and denunciation of the emerging "regime of the parties." In the Fourth Republic Constitution (1946–1958)—barely approved by the electorate—the National Assembly became the seat of all power. Its majority coalitions, made volatile with a new system of proportional representation, became even more unpredictable when the Cold War began in 1947. France's political alignment on the side of the United States forced the Communists, who represented twenty-five percent of the electorate, into quasi-permanent sectarian isolation. Governments thenceforth were constructed from among center-left and center-right groups that rarely agreed. The Fourth Republic drifted to the right and progressively fell under the sway of forces determined to preserve colonialism. Thus from 1946 to 1958 there was costly and divisive warfare, first in Indochina (1946–1954) and then in Algeria (1954–1962). The postwar years deeply changed French society: consumerism was born, the service sector rapidly expanded, and high-tech national projects were successfully launched. Modernization of the economy led to continuing attrition of aristocratic elements—represented in *Ring Around the Moon* by Madame Desmermortes—and their gradual replacement by the newer and more influential money of industrialists like Messerschmann.

CRITICAL OVERVIEW

Jean Anouilh's *Ring Around the Moon* first appeared in France in 1947 where it was and still is entitled, *L'Invitation au Chateau*. The play is especially important because it marked a transition

COMPARE
&
CONTRAST

- **1947:** Extensive nationalization of French industry becomes well established.

  Today: The French government retains considerable influence over key segments of each economic sector, with majority ownership of railway, electricity, aircraft, and telecommunication firms, but since the early 1990s has been gradually relaxing its control over these sectors.

- **1947:** With the Truman Doctrine of March 12, a policy of world communist containment by the United States is formally announced, an early landmark of the Cold War.

  Today: The Cold War is officially ended but is threatened again with the conflict in Yugoslavia—Russia aligned with Serbia, Europe and the United States aligned with elements against

Serbia. The Cold War is heated up further when U.S. bombs hit the Chinese embassy in Belgrade.

- **1947:** The American Marshall Plan, named for secretary of state, George C. Marshall, channels huge quantities of money into rebuilding Europe and strengthening anticommunist European governments.

  Today: A united, noncommunist Europe launches its first common currency, the Euro.

- **1947:** France greatly expands its welfare state.

  Today: France continues to refrain from cutting social welfare benefits and the state bureaucracy, preferring to trim defense spending and raise taxes to keep its deficit down.

---

between Anouilh's *pièces roses,* plays in which characters escape dark conditions through fantasy, illusion, and change of personality, to Anouilh's *pièces brillantes,* a more mixed group of four plays with *brillantes* referring to polished and sophisticated gemlike pieces. The first two plays of the *pièces brillantes,* which include *Ring Around the Moon,* were lighter plays closer to their "pink" precursors. The latter two plays were more ponderous, weighed down by gritty reality.

In *Jean Anouilh,* Alba della Fazia called *Ring Around the Moon* a "pleasantly jumbled fairy tale" and selects Isabelle as the play's heroine, primarily for her rejection of money and her understanding of when to end her part in the charade. In Jean Anouilh, Marguerite Archer echoes della Fazia's description of the play as a fairy tale: "Here, the ending is a happy one, achieved by Anouilh when he combines the themes previously exploited in the *pièces noires* [earlier, darker pieces in Anouilh's career], so that money and love can exist side by side in harmony." Lewis Falb in his *Jean Anouilh,* sees a darker center to Ring Around the Moon: "Though the action resembles a lighthearted charade, beneath the sur-

face there are disturbing undercurrents." Falb's comment is developed at length in Leonard Pronko's *The World Of Jean Anouilh.* Pronko says that Hugo is without feelings because, since he plans to pay Isabelle to act her part, and does not think she deserves consideration. Pronko goes on to say that in Anouilh's work, "men are so selfish that they seldom take their fellows into consideration. The primary social unit—the family—has broken down, and acts not as a group but as a heterogeneous mixture of individuals. With little regard for conventional morality, each goes his own way." For Pronko, then, Falb's "disturbing undercurrents" in *Ring Around the Moon* revolve primarily around selfishness issuing from monetary concern. Anouilh thereby becomes a critic of the intersection where society meets money. A more recent analysis of *Ring Around the Moon* reconciles the play's lighter and darker elements. H. G. McIntyre in *The Theatre of Jean Anouilh* sees this reconciliation in the marriage of form with content: "The vision of life may be bleak but an antidote to it lies in the comic form of the play ... Implicit in all this is an ethic of endurance not of rejection and self-sacrifice ..."

Margaret Rutherford, as Madame Desmermortes, talking to Paul Schofield, as Hugo, in a 1950 production of Ring around the Moon.

McIntyre goes further: not only does comedy help us endure, but so does the practice of theater.

CRITICISM

Chris Semansky

A playwright and poet, Chris Semansky teaches literature and writing at Portland Community College. In the following essay he discusses the role of class conflict in Anouilh's Ring Around the Moon.

Behind the thinner, lighter veil of Jean Anouilh's charade, *Ring Around the Moon,* lies two sorts of class conflict. First, is the friction between the older aristocracy ("old money") and the emerging and usurping industrialist bourgeoisie ("new money"). The second is the tension between both of these wealthy groups and the working class. The characters belonging to each camp are as follows: in the aristocracy, the Desmermortes side composed of Hugo, Frederic, Lady India, and Madame. In the wealthy bourgeoisie, the Messerschmanns: Messerschmann, Diana, and though not part of the family, Romainville, because he runs

Messerchmann's pig-iron company. Also in this class are many of the unnamed and unspoken guests at Madame's ball who, Diana states, work for Messerchmann. The last group, the working class or poor, includes Isabelle and her mother. All other characters fall somewhere between these camps since they are attached to the upper classes: Joshua and Capulat to the aristocracy, Patrice to the industrialist bourgeoisie.

The core conflict between old and new money erupts in the imminent marriage between Frederic (old) and Diana (new). Frederic, the "good" twin, cares little for class. But he is betrothed to the wealthy Diana. This is probably no mere coincidence since, usually, the moneyed classes are as segregated as the poor, self-segregation ensuring preservation of wealth and a sense of superiority. It is not clear what Diana is after by settling for Frederic when she really wants Hugo, but Diana's motivation might be her desire to marry into wealth, even if it means losing her happiness. But whether Diana marries old or new money seems of little concern to her. Nor does it concern Messerschmann since, after all, he has taken Lady India (old money) as a mistress. But it might be that the two Messerschmanns' do care, and con-

WHAT DO I READ NEXT?

- *Much Ado About Nothing*, is a comedy by William Shakespeare, written about 1598–1599. Like *Ring Around the Moon*, this is another play of mistaken identities and happy couplings at play's end.

- *As You Like It* is a comedy by William Shakespeare and first printed in 1623. This is yet another of Shakespeare's plays involving mistaken identities and an ending with a happy double marriage.

- *The Marx-Engels Reader* is an anthology of the writings of Karl Marx and Friedrich Engels, published in 1978. Of special importance to the issue of class warfare is "Manifesto of the Communist Party" (1848).

- *The Wealth of Nations* by Adam Smith was originally published in 1776. It is arguably the most important work in support of capitalist theory ever published. Smith's work is still quoted.

- *Pride and Prejudice* is a novel by Jane Austen first published in 1813. While there are no mistaken identities in Austen's work, the place of marriage in class relations is of central importance. One important difference between Anouilh's play and Austen's novel is the latter's emphasis on gender, specifically how women are forced by society to seek marriage in order to escape poverty or secure economic well-being.

---

sciously or unconsciously, pursue the old-moneyed Desmermortes to gain sophistication through association with "class," "breeding," and education. Through linkage with the Desmermortes the Messerschmanns might be able to have their wealth and eat it too.

The aristocratic Desmermortes, on the other hand, want little to do with the bourgeois Messerschmanns. Madame Desmermortes is humiliated by news that Messerschmann is "keeping" (paying for) her niece, Lady India. Madame exclaims: "She is a Fitzhenry! And through me, a Desmermortes. If only your uncle Antony were alive it would kill him." Desmermortes money has been transmitted by inheritance from generation to generation and is therefore "purified" by being kept within the family. Messerschmann's money, however, is recently gained through business, himself having been a member of the lower classes only "yesterday." Madame's humiliation over these matters is of less concern to Hugo with his narrower criteria for upper-class superiority. Hugo is less concerned with family than with breeding. For Hugo, money is not to be pursued or displayed as "mere" wealth, but instead, used for the sake of racheting up

one's civility, culture, and refinement. Hugo's complaint about mixing blood and money with the Messerschmanns apparently has less to do with them having it (after all, Hugo is rich), than with the way they deploy it. Although not fleshed out, Hugo's "healthy" contempt of money likely comes from the fact that he takes it for granted. Contempt for wealth (but not for breeding) Hugo likely thinks, is beyond the understanding of the bourgeoisie who continue to worship money like the lower classes, whom these Messerschmanns still are in disguise. And so, Hugo thinks, how dare Frederic stoop to Diana; how dare Lady India allow herself to be *had* by that mere businessman, Messerschmann.

And who does Hugo blackmail? Romainville, that second-tier wealthy bourgeois connected to Messerschmann, and Patrice, Messerschmann's secretary engaged in an affair with Hugo's aristocratic cousin, Lady India. Hugo's blackmailings are not mere means to break up the ill-fated Diana-Frederic love match, but ends, battles fought against those economic upstarts, the Messerschmanns, and their lackeys, Romainville, and Patrice. It is no coincidence Anouilh calls for battle music during the scene in which Hugo blackmails Patrice.

Finally, in the war between the upper echelons, there is Lady India, the peacemaker. Like Hugo, she takes wealth for granted. But unlike Hugo, Lady India does not manifest contempt for the bourgeoisie. After all, she is Messerschmann's mistress. But she is attracted to danger, specifically to "slumming," associating with the lower classes. This is at least part of her attraction to a mere secretary (Patrice). At the "further reaches" of danger, Lady India is not just attracted to the poorer classes, but to poverty itself. She believes so strongly that she would like to be poor, that she falls hard for Messerschmann when it looks like he is financially ruined. Lady India, unlike the play's other major characters, is in conflict with no one. She is the bridge not only between the upper classes, but also between upper and lower classes. While this might cast Lady India as the play's heroine—great bridger of all gulfs—Anouilh portrays her as a fool, in love with the state of poverty only because she has never visited. Thus, her poor sense of economic and social geography.

The battle between upper and lower classes involves both major and minor characters. For example, Joshua, Capulat, and Patrice partially escape inclusion in the working or poorer classes because they are attached to the upper classes, not just by working for them, but by living with them. Just as house slaves had more status than field slaves, so do Joshua, Capulat, and Patrice as "house slaves" have status over Isabelle and her mother, the "field slaves." There is, however, one last division among the lower classes. As Anouilh divided the upper classes into old and new money, he divides the poorer, working class into the envious (Isabelle's mother) and the complacent-if-not-contemptuous (Isabelle). Isabelle's mother shares features with both branches of the upper classes. With the aristocracy, she shares a love of breeding, as evidenced by having studied piano at a conservatory. Further, she has enabled Isabelle to study ballet, both of these, piano and ballet, being aristocratic pleasures. She also once belonged to the bourgeoisie: "Always remember, Isabelle, your grandfather was the biggest wallpaper dealer in the town. We've even had two servants at the same time." Isabelle's mother aspires to both branches of the upper class, if not for herself, then for her daughter. Isabelle's mother does not call her objects of aspiration old or new money, aristocracy or bourgeoisie, but sums them up with "beauty" (more often referring to old money rather than new) and "luxury" (more often referring to new money rather than old). Isabelle's

> AND SO, HUGO THINKS, HOW DARE FREDERIC STOOP TO DIANA; HOW DARE LADY INDIA ALLOW HERSELF TO BE *HAD* BY THAT MERE BUSINESSMAN, MESSERSCHMANN."

mother is not particular. She would be happy with either Romainville or Hugo as an upwardly mobile catch for Isabelle.

Isabelle, unlike her mother, aspires to love more than money. She does whatever chore needs doing, and doesn't dream of being rich so that, someday, servants will do it for her. Her mother's unabashed upper-class aspirations embarrass Isabelle who is not attracted to Hugo because of his wealth, but because he is handsome and confident. Money is nowhere apparent in her aspirations. Even Isabelle's ballet dancing seems a product more of her mother's aspirations than her own desires. Isabelle's disinterest in money turns to hostility in the memorable scene where Isabelle refuses offers of money from Messerschmann and from Hugo, and where she and Messerschmann tear up his stacks of bills. While Messerschmann tears up the currency because he resents money's loss of power, its death if you will, Isabelle tears it up to render it powerless, kill it. But neither Messerschmann nor Isabelle are made happy by such destruction. Isabelle remains unhappy because tearing up money does not help the poor. Moreover, Hugo does not care for her, and has only used her in his botched charade against upper class vanity, showing his contempt, as well, for the lower classes and those recently escaped, namely Messerschmann. And so through the insensitive and repellent actions of both old and new money (Messerschmann, Hugo, and Diana all display open class contempt), Isabelle finally ceases an outlook of quiet humility and satisfaction, becoming contemptuous of the rich. Revenge, however, is not open to one such as Isabelle, who can only separate herself from what is everywhere repellent by attempting suicide. When rescued, Isabelle becomes Anouilh's official hero by rewarding her more than any other character: only Isabelle moves up a few notches on the economic and social scale. But the other characters make out pretty well too: no matter what kind of folly absorbs them, Anouilh forgives them by letting them keep their money and status. He is forgiving ... unlike the world he assaults.

Source: Chris Semansky, in an essay for *Drama for Students*, Gale, 2001.

Liz Brent

Brent has a Ph.D. in American Culture, specializing in film studies, from the University of Michigan. She is a freelance writer and teaches courses in the history of American cinema. In the following essay, Brent discusses literary, biblical and mythological references in Anouilh's play.

Biblical, Mythological and Folkloric References in Ring Around the Moon

The dialogue of Anouilh's play *Ring Around the Moon* includes several references to folk, biblical, mythological, and English literature. A greater understanding of the sources of these references helps to illuminate the thematic concerns which run throughout the play.

Calliope. In Act I, Scene 1, Hugo discusses his twin brother Frederick with Joshua, the elderly butler. Joshua is informing Hugo that Frederick, who is in love with Diana, has spent the past five nights sleeping in the rhododendron bush outside of her bedroom window. Joshua explains to Hugo that he has slept in the rhododendron bush "beside that statue they call Calliope, a classical character, sir." In Greek mythology, Calliope is the primary of the nine Muses. The Muses are a group of goddesses, all sisters, daughters of Zeus, who were originally considered to be the patron goddesses of poets and musicians. They later each became associated with different branches of the arts and sciences, and statues of the various muses were popularly sculpted holding various objects indicating these associations. The name of Calliope means "she of the beautiful voice." Calliope is considered the muse of heroic or epic poetry, and sculptures often depict her with a writing tablet in her hand. She is considered to be the mother of Orpheus, the musician who played the lyre.

Croesus. Later in Act I, Scene 1, Hugo, in talking to Mademoiselle Desmortes, describes Mr. Messerschmann as being "as rich as Croesus." Croesus was a king of ancient Lydia, who reigned from 560 B.C. to 546 B.C., and was known for his great wealth. Main events during his reign include the conquest of the Greeks on mainland Ionia, and

subsequent defeat by the Persians. The name of Croesus continues to be associated with extensive wealth, and he was known for bestowing lavish gifts upon the oracle at Delphi, which appears in many Greek myths. While Croesus was a historically real person, his reputation and fate have taken on mythical status in the writings of ancient Greek historians. Some say that upon defeat by the Persians he tried to burn himself alive, but was saved from death by his captors; some say he was condemned to death by fire, but was saved by the god Apollo; and some say he was made a government official for the defeating nation. One of the prominent myths about Croesus, according to the ancient Greek historian Herodotus, is that he met with Solon, an Athenian law-maker, who lectured him on the virtues of good fortune, rather than wealth, as a source of happiness.

Reference to Croesus is significant because it indicates a central theme of Anouilh's play: wealth and poverty. Except for Isabelle, her mother, and the various servants, the central characters of the play are wealthy beyond all measure. The arrival of Isabelle and her mother into this world of rich socialites initiates a tension between rich and poor, and incites debates among characters over wealth and poverty. Messerchsmann is compared early on to Croesus, and this comparison is echoed toward the end when he realizes that wealth is not a source of happiness. Isabelle's role in this realization is comparable to the role of Solon, in that she provides Messerchsmann with a similar insight.

Helen of Troy. In Act I, Scene 2, Hugo tells Isabelle that the dress she has been given to wear "makes you look like Helen of Troy." Helen of Troy, in ancient Greek mythology, was a daughter of Zeus, and was the most beautiful woman in Greece. According to legend, she was the impetus behind the Trojan War, which explains references to her as "the face that launched a thousand ships." Isabelle's enchanting beauty is central to her role in Anouilh's play. It is agreed by all that she is the most beautiful presence at the ball, and her arrival is the catalyst which effects a change in the dynamics of the wealthy socialite world into which she has been thrust.

Cinderella In Act I, Scene 2, there is an exchange between Isabelle's mother and Hugo, in which the Mother refers to herself as "poor little Cinders." She is of course referring to the fairy tale Cinderella, in which the abused and neglected stepdaughter is visited by a fairy godmother who grants her the opportunity to dress in finery for a ball, at which she dances all night with the Prince himself. According to the *Encyclopaedia Britannica,* this folktale dates back as far as the 9th Century AD, and has appeared in over 500 different renditions. In Anouilh's play, Hugo asks Isabelle's mother if she would like supper brought to her in her room, to which she replies, "Just a crust, a crust and a glass of water for poor little Cinders." Isabelle's mother is an impoverished woman continually attempting to push her daughter on any rich man who comes her way. She is a selfish woman who embarrasses Isabelle, and continually laments her own poverty and lost youth and beauty. In comparing herself to Cinderella, the abused and neglected stepdaughter, the mother expresses a self-serving self-pity. Meanwhile, it is Isabelle who shares the role of Cinderella in Anouilh's play. She is a poor, beautiful, yet humble, girl who needs only to be dressed up in the finery of the rich to become, like Cinderella, the belle of the ball. And, by the end of the play, she does, in fact, find her prince charming in the form of the wealthy Frederick, the twin brother of Hugo (although she at first believes herself to be in love with Hugo).

English literature

Robinson Crusoe. In Act I, Scene 2, the wheelchair-bound elderly woman Mme. Desmortes makes reference to the classic English novel *Robinson Crusoe* (1722), by Daniel Defoe (1660–1731). *Robinson Crusoe* is the story of a castaway on a deserted island who must make do with limited resources in order to survive harsh and solitary conditions. In Anouilh's play, the excessively wealthy and privileged Mme. Desmortes compares herself to Robinson Crusoe when she is momentarily stranded in her wheelchair without a servant to escort her, and without a nearby "bell-rope" she could use to summon a servant.

> Mme. Desmortes: "Really, how marooned one is away from a bell-rope. I might be Robinson Crusoe, and without any of his initiative. If only one's governess, when one was a girl, had taught one something practical like running up a flag or firing a gun."

When a butler, Joshua, appears, she continues the comparison of being lost at sea, remarking, "Thank Heaven I'm on some sort of navigation route." She commands Joshua to "Put into land for a moment, my dear man, and rescue me. I was washed up here fifteen minutes ago, and I haven't seen a living creature since."

Mme. Desmorte's extended comparison of herself to Robinson Crusoe not only establishes her

> "THE ARRIVAL OF ISABELLE AND HER MOTHER INTO THIS WORLD OF RICH SOCIALITES INITIATES A TENSION BETWEEN RICH AND POOR, AND INCITES DEBATES AMONG CHARACTERS OVER WEALTH AND POVERTY."

character as extremely witty, with a keen, ironic sense of humor, but also demonstrates her ability not to take herself too seriously, as expressed by her tendency to jokingly exaggerate her circumstances. This reference also continues a theme of water imagery which runs through the play.

Byronic Poetry. In Scene 1, Act III, Hugo launches into an extended discourse in conversation with Isabelle, who listens attentively. Hugo has been using Isabelle in a scheme to distract his brother from his unrequited love of Diana. He explains that he is going to invent a lofty and romantic past for Isabelle, which he will use to deceive the guests at the ball as to her origins. Hugo muses that he will tell everyone that "you're the wonderfully wealthy side-issue of a Portuguese princess and an Admiral, an Admiral who wrote Byronic poetry and was drowned at sea." The idea of the Admiral drowned at sea picks up on the water imagery which runs throughout the play, such as in reference to the fictional character Robinson Crusoe. Hugo's mention of "Byronic poetry" refers to a style of Romantic poetry by the infamous English poet, Lord Byron (1788–1824). Byron is best known for his extended poem *Don Juan* (1819–1825), which is a satiric recounting of the adventures and exploits of a young man. In one segment of the poem, Don Juan becomes a castaway on a Greek island after surviving a shipwreck. The reference to Byron thus indirectly echoes Anouilh's theme of water imagery in the play.

Biblical stories

Samson. In Act III, Scene 1, the rich man Messerschmann has a conversation with the old butler, Joshua, in which Messerschmann mentions the Biblical myth of Samson. Samson is a figure from the Old Testament whom some scholars consider to be purely mythical, but whom others consider to be a historically real figure. The story of Samson is that his parents were told before his birth that he was to be a Nazarite, a person chosen by God to abstain from liquor, avoid contact with dead bodies, and never shave or cut his hair. Samson was known for his incredible physical strength, but his downfall was always his passion for Philistine women. The most famous story about Samson is that he was seduced by the Philistine Delilah, who tricked him into revealing the secret of his incredible strength: his long hair. As he slept Delilah cut his hair, depriving him of his strength so that he could be captured by the Philistines, blinded and forced into slavery. Samson's final act, although blinded and enslaved, was to use his strength to tear down the Philistine temple, where the worship of false gods was carried out, destroying both the Philistines and himself in the process. This act is seen as his final return to the service of the Jewish god Yahweh for which his life was originally intended.

In conversation with Joshua, Messerschmann recounts the tale of Samson, comparing himself to this mythical figure.

> M: ''You must have read your Bible when you were a little boy? J: Here and there, sir, like everybody else. M: Did you ever come across Samson? J: The gentleman who had his hair cut, sir? M: ''Yes; and he was very unhappy. Jeered at, my friend, always jeered at by everybody. They had put his eyes out. They thought he was blind, but I'm sure he could see. J: Quite possible, sir. M: And then, one fine day, unable to stand it any more, he got them to lead him between the pillars of the temple. He was very strong, terribly strong, you understand? He twined his arms round the pillars'' (he puts his arms around Joshua) like this.

Messerschmann continues, ''And then he shook them with all his might.'' He was so strong the entire temple crashed down on to the two thousand Philistines who were there praying to their false Gods and thinking Samson no better than a fool.'' Joshua points out that, ''it fell on him, too, sir,'' to which Messerschmann replies, ''But that wasn't of any kind of importance.'' Messerschmann then explains to Joshua that he will be ''putting through an overseas telephone call'' that night. Messerschmann tells Joshua that he will be doing this, ''Like Samson. With my eyes tight shut.''

This conversation between Messerschmann and Joshua occurs late in the play, just after an extended exchange between Messerschmann and Isabelle, the impoverished young dancer whom he has in-

vited to his home with the intention of making her his mistress. Messerschmann is like Samson in that his lust for women has been the cause of his moral depravity. Through his conversation with Isabelle, he comes to realize that his wealth is no source of happiness, and he rashly decides to make a financial decision that will undoubtedly impoverish him. Messerschmann's intention is to alter his financial situation with a single phone call. Like Samson tearing down the temple, Messerschmann plans to perform a final act of moral good by symbolically tearing down the temple of wealth in which he and his fellow socialites worship the false gods of money and luxury. Messerschmann performs this act ''blindly,'' like Samson, meaning that he does not stop to consider the consequences of such as brash act as turning himself from a rich man into a poor man. And, like Samson, he may bring on his own ruin in the process of performing an act for the cause of a greater good.

Source: Liz Brent, in an essay for *Drama for Students*, Gale, 2001.

Charles Isherwood

In the following review, Isherwood presents negatively the revival of ''Ring Around the Moon'' through its actors.

Lincoln Center Theater's revival of Jean Anouilh's *Ring Round the Moon* is a real heartbreaker—but for all the wrong reasons. Christopher Fry's adaptation of Anouilh's comedy has not often been staged since its original London and Broadway productions in 1950, and it's easy to see why: The play is uncommonly delicate, a poetic mixture of farce, romance and comedy of manners that must also accommodate a whiff or two of mortal thoughts (it was written in the shadow of World War II). Fry subtitled his sparkling adaptation *A Charade With Music,* and indeed it has the sweeping rhythms of a dance—not for nothing is the play's heroine a ballerina. Unfortunately, what's onstage at the Belasco Theater more often than not has two left feet. Gerald Gutierrez's largely miscast production betrays the play's gossamer sensibility; what should taste like a spun-sugar confection goes down more like chewy taffy.

The disenchantments begin even as the curtain rises on John Lee Beatty's set, a rather literal-minded reworking of Oliver Messel's famed London original. Beatty's garden gazebo manages the signal feat of seeming both flimsy and oppressive. The airiness that is the soul of the play is lost—the characters cavort in this chamber like trapped moths. (The play cries out for the liberating imagination of a Bob Crowley.) The young British actor Toby Stephens plays the central roles of the twins Hugo and Frederic, and here, too, delicacy is lacking. Stephens comes from sturdy theatrical stock—he's the son of Maggie Smith and Robert Stephens—and he's definitely an actor in the grand English tradition. As such, he does not have a natural, light touch, as anyone who saw him in the Almeida Theater Co.'s recent Racine plays at BAM could attest (and surely the producers did).

Stephens does have an authentic upper-crust charm, and is amusingly snippy as the heartless Hugo, whose scheme to wean his twin brother from his love for Diana Messerschmann (Haviland Morris)—who in turn loves Hugo—sets the carousel of the plot in motion. But as the lovesick Frederic, he's really just Hugo sulking—there's no soul in his Frederic, no romance. His performance is professional but artificial, and more artifice is the last thing this sweet piece of whimsy needs.

The play is set in 1912 France, at the chateau of the twins' aunt Madame Desmermortes (Marian Seldes), an imperious woman whose reliance on a wheelchair hasn't kept her from ruling her little fiefdom with an iron fist.

Guests at the chateau include Diana's father, Messerschmann (Fritz Weaver), a Jewish business magnate who controls the destinies of his fellow visitors; Lady India (Candy Buckley), Messerschmann's mistress and Desmermortes' niece; and his secretary Patrice Bombelles (Derek Smith), who also happens to be India's lover.

Hugo has invited to the chateau a beautiful ballerina from Paris, Isabelle (Gretchen Egolf), in the hopes that by turning her into the belle of the ball he can turn Frederic's head, curing him of his hopeless love for Diana. But the sensitive Isabelle, as fate would have it, falls instantly for Hugo himself, and it takes some sorting out before she is united in bliss with the equally sensitive Frederic.

With everyone either in love, trying to get out of it or observing it with variously cynical, practical or sentimental attitudes, the play is a comic poem on the vagaries of romance. It also contains wry reflections on the elusive nature of happiness: Diana's riches can't win her the love of Hugo and her father's constitution is so poisoned by the excesses delivered by his wealth that he has been relegated to a diet of unsalted, unbuttered noodles.

"UNFORTUNATELY, WHAT'S ONSTAGE AT THE BELASCO THEATER MORE OFTEN THAN NOT HAS TWO LEFT FEET. GERALD GUTIERREZ'S LARGELY MISCAST PRODUCTION BETRAYS THE PLAY'S GOSSAMER SENSIBILITY; WHAT SHOULD TASTE LIKE A SPUN-SUGAR CONFECTION GOES DOWN MORE LIKE CHEWY TAFFY."

But the subtle strains of melancholy and the affectionate tone that suffuse the comedy mostly are muted here. Emblematic of the production's clumsiness is the bull-in-a-china-shop performance of Joyce Van Patten as Isabelle's mother. Her character is supposed to be silly and pretentious, but Anouilh observes even her with a measure of sympathy. You'd never guess it from this production, which turns her into a crass buffoon with an American accent.

Indeed all the characters in *Ring Round the Moon* are dusted with poetry, even the most fiercely pragmatic or comically cynical. And yet virtually none of the performers in this production give lyrical or graceful performances. The fault is the director's; Gutierrez plays the comedy too heavily and lets the tender essence of the play evaporate.

Morris' Diana is a flat, shallow interpretation of a character whose haunted depths are revealed in a striking monologue in the second act, when she recalls a traumatic childhood experience of anti-Semitism; this feeling should infuse the rest of the performance, but it doesn't. The pathos of Messerschmann himself is only hinted at by the gruff Weaver. Buckley's India, replete with tongue-in-cheek English accent, isn't even convincing as a small-L lady, and her business with Smith's Patrice is overcooked.

The beautiful Egolf has a graceful, willowy presence and comes very close to capturing the ethereal spirit of Isabelle. But the role requires an actress who can suggest infinite feeling with the subtlest of inflections, and Egolf ultimately cannot (merely to look at a photo of Claire Bloom in the original production is to be enchanted).

The estimable Seldes is gloriously entertaining as she dishes out Desmermortes' eloquently phrased, Lady Bracknellesque put-downs, but she is not entirely right for the role. Her astringent delivery of the part's waspish witticisms ultimately obscures the essential goodness of the character. (Irene Worth was to have played it, with Seldes gallantly doing one performance a week, but Worth had to withdraw because of a stroke.)

While Simon Jones strikes just the right, straightforward note in his small role, it's really only Frances Conroy, as Desmermortes' companion, who manages to walk the fine line between tender feeling and high comedy that runs through the play. Her overwhelmed effusions about the young lovers' fates are both brilliantly funny and tinged with a real pathos. She isn't onstage for long, but Conroy makes the most of her time.

Sadly, the same can't be said for the production itself. This revival of a lovely play about romantic opportunities seized is a theatrical opportunity lost.

Source: Charles Isherwood, ''Ring Around the Moon,'' (review) in *Variety,* Vol. 374, Issue 11, May 3, 1999, p. 94.

SOURCES

Anouilh, Jean, *Ring Around the Moon,* translated by Christopher Fry, Oxford University Press, 1950.

Archer, Marguerite, *Jean Anouilh,* Columbia University Press, 1971.

Della Fazia, Alba, *Jean Anouilh,* Twayne, 1969.

Falb, Lewis W., *Jean Anouilh,* Frederick Ungar, 1977.

McIntyre, H. G., *The Theatre of Jean Anouilh,* Barnes and Noble, 1981.

Pronko, Leonard Cabell, *The World of Jean Anouilh,* University of California Press, 1961.

FURTHER READING

Chiari, Joseph, *The Contemporary French Theatre: The Flight from Naturalism,* Macmillan, 1959.
    Chiari's text charts the course of French theater from Naturalism to Realism to Theater of the Absurd.

Curtis, Anthony, *New Developments in the French Theatre,* Curtain Press, 1948.
    Curtis's subject, like Chiari's, charts varied approaches toward achieving realistic theater.

Grossvogel, David I., *The Self-Conscious Stage in Modern French Drama,* Columbia University Press, 1958.
    Grossvogel concentrates on psychological aspects of late nineteenth and early twentieth century French theater.

Kuritz, Paul, *The Making of Theatre History,* Prentice Hall, 1988.
    Kuritz's ambitious study encompasses Asian and Occidental theater. The book is organized according to time period beginning with ancient Greek Theater and proceeding to the present.

Seven Against Thebes

AESCHYLUS
467 B.C.

Seven Against Thebes was first staged in 467 B.C., as part of a tetralogy that includes *Lauis, Oedipus* and the satyr play, *Sphinx*. The first two plays in the trilogy have been lost, as has the satyr play. *Seven Against Thebes,* the story of the conflict between Eteocles and Polyneices, the sons of Oedipus, won Aeschylus a first prize at its initial performance. Aeschylus could count on his audience knowing the story depicted in the tragedy without his having to fill in a lot of details. Epic poems told the story of the Oedipus tragedy and the battle for Thebes, and Greek audiences would know these stories very well. The challenge was not in the details of the story but in the poetic depiction. Aeschylus is celebrated for the poetic beauty of Chorus, and indeed, in the Chorus has a major role, with more lines than any other character. The sounds of battle, which are often heard in the background, and the weeping of the Chorus, and later of the sisters, emphasize the tragedy that is unfolding, but these same elements also illustrate the strengths of Aeschylus's tragedy. The conflict between fate and justice is important for the Greek audience, for whom battle and honor are important characteristics of Athens's strength. Aeschylus was a deeply relig-ious man who was concerned with ethics, hubris, and with justice. The Oedipus tragedy is very con-cerned with these issues and thus it provides a natural choice for Aeschylus's trilogy. Many early Greek poets saw themselves as the purveyors of moral and ethical wisdom. It is clear that with *Seven*

Against Thebes, Aeschylus is fulfilling this role for his fifth-century B.C. audiences.

AUTHOR BIOGRAPHY

Aeschylus was born in 525 B.C., probably in Eleusis, just outside Athens. Few details are known of his childhood, but Aeschylus entered his first dramatic competition, the Dionysia, in 500–501 B.C. He enjoyed his first real success as a playwright in 484 B.C., but Aeschylus was more than a dramatist; he was also a soldier, having fought in several of the battles that marked the wars between Athens and Persia. The relative peace that followed these battles allowed Aeschylus time to focus on his plays.

The first of his tragedies appears to have been performed around 500 B.C. Aeschylus presented his tragedies as trilogies, each grouping having a common theme. The drama trilogy was then followed by a satyr drama, a comedy involving a mythological hero. Aeschylus is credited with introducing the second actor into Greek drama and with reducing the size of the chorus. These innovations allowed for a greater complexity of plot and dialogue. Aeschylus also made use of more frightening masks and costumes than had previously been used. He also introduced limited scenery. Aeschylus is said to have written between 80–90 plays; however, only seven are known to have survived. His plays won many awards at drama competitions, including several first prizes. Most dramatists were also actors, and so Aeschylus probably acted in his own plays.

Because of his own experience in battle, Aeschylus's battle scenes are particularly vivid, easily evoking the terror and sounds of death. Aeschylus died in 456 B.C., having lived through the greatest period of Greek theatre. He set a formidable example for other dramatists, such as Sophocles and Euripedes. After his death, Aeschylus received many honors, and is now known as the Father of Greek Tragedy. The seven plays that survive today are *The Persians* (472 B.C.); *Seven Against Thebes* (467 B.C.); *The Suppliant Women* (c. 463 B.C.); the three parts of the *Orestia* trilogy, *Agamemnon, The Libation-Bearers,* and *Eumenides* (458 B.C.); and *Prometheus Bound* (undated).

PLOT SUMMARY

Seven Against Thebes opens with Eteocles calling forth every man in the city, whether child or aged, to the fight and the threat, which is at hand. Everyone must be ready to defend the city in battle. At that moment, the Scout enters with news that the enemy is just outside the walls and is preparing for battle. There are seven commanders ready to attack the seven gates of Thebes. After delivering the news, the Scout departs, and Eteocles prays to Zeus for his favor in the battle to come. The Chorus, which has entered as the Scout has related his news, begins a lament as they hear the approach of the armies. They beg their gods to protect them and their city. Eteocles hears the Chorus' fearful pleadings as he enters and chastises them for their fear, which he says will not help their beloved Thebes. Instead, Eteocles promises that the Chorus will be stoned to death for their mindless fear, as their fear will incite the city's residents into an instinctive fear of their own, which will disable and defeat the city. But the Chorus is not appeased, and they continue with their warnings as Eteocles warns them of the risk they create with their wailing. Eteocles again warns the Chorus to remain inside and to hold back their panic. At their continued warnings and fearful exclamations, Eteocles responds with attacks on the nature of women, their weaknesses, and their fears. Finally the Chorus promises to restrain their fear and remain silent, and Eteocles again prays to the gods, with promises of sacrifices and trophies if Thebes is successfully defended. After Eteocles leaves the stage, the Chorus continues to voice their worry at the coming battle and the risk they face if they are taken and become slaves.

When the Scout enters, he brings news of who will lead the attack at each of the city's gates. At the news of each opponent's assignment, Eteocles assigns one of his men to defend that particular gate. When Eteocles is told that his brother, Polyneices, will lead the attack on the seventh gate, Eteocles decides that he will defend that gate. At this news, the Chorus warns Eteocles that he should not shed his brother's blood, but Eteocles is beyond listening to warnings. He acknowledges the curse of his father, Oedipus, but Eteocles says that fate will determine the outcome, and if the gods are determined that he shall be destroyed, then this will happen. The chorus is dismayed at Eteocles departure and cry out that if each bother slays the other, there will be no family to see to a proper burial. The Chorus then begins to remind the audience of the story of Oedipus and the curse that followed his father, himself, and now his sons. At that moment, the Scout again enters with the news that Thebes has crushed her enemy, and the city is victorious. Six of the seven gates have withstood the onslaught of the enemy's armies, but the battle at the seventh gate has ended in tragedy. Both Eteocles and Polyneices are dead, each at the others hand. The Scout reminds the Chorus that the city must mourn the death but also celebrate the end of the curse. The Chorus asks is they should mourn these deaths or celebrate the triumph of Thebes' victory. With the arrival of the brother's bodies, the Chorus acknowledges the tragedy that has unfolded. The bodies are followed closely by Ismene and Antigone, who have come to bury their brothers. The Chorus addresses the sisters, with grief and with sadness at the resolution of the curse. The two sisters respond to the Chorus with their own grief, as they lament the curse that damned both brothers. As Antigone wonders where they will bury the brothers, a Herald enters with an announcement that the council has met. The council has determined that Eteocles is a hero and will be accorded an honorable burial. However, Polyneices would have laid waste to Thebes, and thus, his corpse is to lie unburied, to be picked apart by the birds of prey. Antigone promises that she will bury her brother, as she will not be bound by the Theban council's ruling. A brief argument with the Herald ensues, but Antigone will not be threatened, and finally, the Herald leaves to report to the council. The play ends with the Chorus divided. Half will accompany Eteocles to his grave; half will accompany Polyneices to his burial.

Aeschylus

CHARACTERS

Antigone

Antigone is a sister to Eteocles and Polyneices. She appears briefly at the end of the play to mourn the deaths of her brothers. When she learns that Polyneices is to be denied a proper burial, she vows to oppose the state and follow her own conscience. She is brave enough to argue with the Herald and to promise defiance of the council's edict. Antigone exits at the play's conclusion with Polyneices' body, intent on burying him.

Chorus

The chorus of Theban maidens sings sections of the play. Their purpose is to explain events or actions that occurred previously and to provide commentary on the events that are occurring. As the play opens, the Chorus learns of the impending battle and attempt to seize the city. The Chorus is afraid that Eteocles will lose the battle and the city will be captured. Because they fear they will be made slaves, the Chorus is very loud in their lamentations. But finally, Eteocles manages to quiet them, but not without considerable effort and threats. When the Chorus learns of Eteocles' plan to defend the seventh gate against his brother Polyneices, they warn Eteocles that brothers should not shed one another's blood. They also worry that the brothers will have no family to attend to their burials. The Chorus functions to tell or remind the audience about the curse of Oedipus. They also serve to share in the sister's grief at the brothers' deaths.

Eteocles

Eteolcles, ruler of Thebes, is one of the surviving sons of Oedipus. As the play opens, he is preparing for battle. Eteocles is angered at the worries and fears displayed by the Chorus. He responds with threats to have them all killed if they cannot control their fear. When Eteocles learns that his brother will lead the attack at the seventh gate, Eteocles decides to lead the battle at that gate, himself. Eteocles ignores the warnings of the Chorus, pointing out that fate will determine his success.

MEDIA ADAPTATIONS

- There are no specific film productions of *Seven Against Thebes*. However, *Seven Against Thebes* does have a central role in an Italian film from 1998, *Rehearsal For War*, directed by Mario Martone. In this film, which depicts the war in Yugoslavia, theater rehearsals of Aeschylus's tragedy serve to illustrate the tragedy that is unfolding in the streets outside the theater.

- *The Oresteia*, is a film production of Aeschylus's trilogy, consisting of three videocassettes (230 minutes). It was directed by Peter Hall for the National theater of Great Britain and was a production of Channel 4 (1990, 1983).

Eteocles is stubborn and unwilling to listen to the concerns of the Chorus. He dismisses their worries as the hysteria of women, who have little worth. When Eteocles is killed, the council rewards his bravery with an honorable burial.

Herald

The Herald appears at the play's conclusion to bring word of the council's decision regarding the funerals of Polyneices and Eteocles. When Antigone announces that she will bury her brother in violation of the council's decree, the Herold argues with her. He leaves to tell the council of Antigone's plans after it becomes apparent that she will defy their edict.

Ismene

Ismene is another sister to Eteocles and Polyneices. She appears at the end of the play to mourn her brothers' passing. She is not as strong at Antigone, nor as willing to defy the council's edict.

Polyneices

Polyneices is the second of Oedipus' sons. His body is seen at the end of the play, and he has no lines to speak, but his presence in leading the attack

on the seventh gate is a significant cause of the deaths that follow.

Scout

The Scout (also called the Spy) has infiltrated the enemy camp, and it is he who brings news to Eteocles of the impending battle. The Scout's return with news that Polyneices will lead the attack on the seventh gate leads to Eteocles' decision to defend that gate. Without such precise information, Eteocles might have assigned another warrior to defend the seventh gate.

Spy

See The Scout

THEMES

Anger and Hatred

Anger and hatred are emotions that can control the protagonist and blind him to his obligations and choices. Eteocles is a victim of his own anger. When told by the Scout of the planned attacks on the city gates, Eteocles quite rationally assigns one of his warriors to each gate, each matched to the skills of the attacker. But when the Scout relates that Polyneices is to attack the seventh gate, Eteocles assigned himself to defend that gate. The rational decisions, which provided the best possible defenses for the city, are forgotten in the hatred that he feels for his brother. Because Eteocles is blinded by his hatred, he and his brother die, and only the seventh gate is not successfully defended.

Choice and Fate

Eteocles recognizes that the gods are in control of his destiny. When the Chorus begs Eteocles not to meet his brother, Polyneices, in battle, Eteocles says that fate has already determined his future: ''Why kneel to Fate when sentenced to death already?'' This surrendering to fate allows Eteocles a way to escape responsibility for his actions. He may make bad choices, as he does when he decides to fight his brother, but he is not responsible, since the he is only fulfilling his destiny. This approach to fate relegates the gods to little more than puppet masters, who simply pull man's strings, and it means that man need not reason, need not be responsible, and need not search for a greater purpose in life. It is all decided by the gods anyway.

Death

Death has a significant role in Aeschylus's play because death is the fulfillment of the curse that doomed Laius, Oedipus, Eteocles, and Polyneices. But death does not result in the end of the tragedy. *Seven Against Thebes* ends with the decree that Eteocles is to receive a hero's funeral, but Polyneices, his brother, is to remain unburied, a target for the vultures to pick apart. His sister, Antigone will not allow the council's edict to stand unchallenged, and follows her brother's body offstage, where the audience knows she will attend to his burial. Antigone's defiance of what she will call man's law (to distinguish it from god's law), will result in her death and the deaths of many more people. The deaths of Eteocles and Polyneices do not end the curse, as it should, but instead leads to more deaths and a continuation of the tragedy.

Human Laws versus Divine Laws

In the Judeo-Christian tradition, God is a powerful, though forgiving and beneficent creator. Man views his relationship with God in a cause and effect manner, in which good deeds and faith are rewarded with God's grace. But early Greek men had a different relationship with their gods. There were many gods, and man's relationship with these gods was marked by the arbitrary nature of each god. Whether or not a man was good, honest, or brave had no bearing on how the gods treated him. Instead, man's treatment depended on how the gods were feeling at any given time. If the gods were warring amongst themselves, they would quite likely inflict some revenge upon men, rather than on the offending deity. This very arbitrary nature of the gods meant that men could not determine their own fates, nor could they even assume responsibility for their own behavior. The relationship with the gods was without rules and dependent solely on whim. This created a very unstable and precarious world in which to live. The effects are clearly seen in this play when the two sons of Oedipus are doomed, even though the initial curse that governs their lives was promised to their grandfather, Laius.

Honor

In Greek life honor is the virtue that governs man's actions. As in the opening, Eteocles is calling upon all men, regardless of age, to join him in defending Thebes from the invaders. That all men would do so, unquestionably, is a function of honor. For Eteocles, honor is the one strength he thinks he possesses. He knows that the gods control his fate,

TOPICS FOR FURTHER STUDY

- The story of Oedipus' tragedy is an very old one and one that was the subject of several tragedies. Try to research this story and determine its origin and source. How old is the Oedipus tragedy? Under what circumstances did it originate?

- Spend some time looking for Greek art that represents the Oedipus tragedy. What kind of things are depicted in art of 5th-century B.C. Greece?

- Research the role of early Greek drama in Greek life. What lessons might 5th-century Greek men learn from this play?

- Research 5th-century B.C. Greek society. What is the role of women in this society? Is Eteocles' reaction to the Chorus typical of the way men address the concerns of women?

- Eteocles ignores the Chorus's warning, citing fate as the controlling factor in his destiny. What is the role of fate in the Classical Greek belief system?

and that the familial curse controls his destiny, but Eteocles finds his strength in honor, the only thing he can control. Eteocles's reply to the Chorus' pleadings against fighting Polyneices, is a statement that, "when misfortune and dishonor join as one, no worth fame results." There is no dishonor, he says, when evil intervenes, but there is dishonor in not succeeding. Eteocles is willing to die for his honor, as were many other Greek heroes.

STYLE

Audience

Audience is the people for whom a drama is performed. Authors usually write with an audience in mind. Aeschylus writes for an audience interested in drama as entertainment, but this is also an audience that would expect the playwright to include important lessons about life. Aeschylus also views this moral lesson as an important role for the dramatist and so he emphasizes important lessons in his plays. In there are lessons about the role of honor and of destiny, as well as lessons about hatred and facing death.

Character

A character is a person in a dramatic work. The actions of each character are what constitute the story. Character can also include the idea of a particular individual's morality. Characters can range from simple stereotypical figures to more complex multifaceted ones. Characters may also be defined by personality traits, such as the rogue or the damsel in distress. ''Characterization'' is the process of creating a lifelike person from an author's imagination. To accomplish this the author provides the character with personality traits that help define who he will be and how he will behave in a given situation. In the characters have names that depict their characters. For instance, Polyneices means ''full of strife,'' a name that reveals his role in the play.

Chorus

In ancient Greek drama, a chorus consisted of a group of actors who interpreted and commented on the play's action and themes, most often singing or chanting their lines. Initially the chorus had an important role in drama, as it does in *Seven Against Thebes* , but over time its purpose was diminished, and as a result, the chorus became little more than commentary between acts. Modern theater rarely uses a chorus.

Drama

A drama is often defined as any work designed to be presented on the stage. It consists of a story, of actors portraying characters, and of action. But historically, drama can also consist of tragedy, comedy, religious pageant, and spectacle. In modern usage, drama explores serious topics and themes but does not achieve the same level as tragedy. *Seven Against Thebes* is a traditional Greek drama, and as such, provides important lessons for men about their relationship with the gods.

Genre

Genre is a French term that means ''kind'' or ''type.'' Genre can refer to both the category of literature such as tragedy, comedy, epic, poetry, or pastoral. It can also include modern forms of literature such as drama novels, or short stories. This term can also refer to types of literature such as mystery, science fiction, comedy or romance. *Seven Against Thebes* is a Greek tragedy.

Plot

This term refers to the pattern of events. Generally plots have a beginning, a middle, and a conclusion, but they may also sometimes be a series of episodes connected together. The plot provides the author with the means to explore primary themes. Students are often confused between the two terms; but themes explore ideas, and plots simply relate what happens in a very obvious manner. Thus the plot of is the battle for Thebes, which results in the deaths of two brothers. But the theme is how fate and destiny and the will of the gods must be fulfilled.

Setting

The time, place, and culture in which the action of the play takes place is called the setting. The elements of setting may include geographic location, physical or mental environments, prevailing cultural attitudes, or the historical time in which the action takes place. The primary location for is the battle for Thebes. The action occurs within the city as Eteocles prepares his city for the impending attack.

HISTORICAL CONTEXT

Theater was an important part of Greek life, since it illustrated for the audience important lessons about morality and the function of the gods. The time during which Aeschylus was writing was known as the High Classical Period. During this period, the Greek city-states flourished, although war was a constant factor of Greek life. The Persian Wars, which occurred in 490 B.C. (First Persian War) and 480 B.C. (Second Persian War), were a contemporary event in Aeschylus's life, who had fought during the wars himself. The victory of Athens over the invading Persians was an important one, since the Persian force was significantly larger. The Athenian naval victory over the Persians provided the basis of Aeschylus's play, But most theater was based on the ancient myths and the conflicts between man and gods. The theater was considered an important enough feature of Athenian life that the state paid the actor's salaries. Wealthy patrons paid

COMPARE & CONTRAST

- **c. 467 B.C.:** The Greeks triumph over the Persians and defeat the invasion of their country. The Persian force was significantly larger than the Athenian forces, and this victory infuses the Greeks with pride.

  Today: Greece, which has been dominated by military coups and turmoil with neighboring Turkey since the end of World War II, is no longer considered a dominant military force.

- **c. 467 B.C.:** The Greek poet Pindar moves to Thebes, where he composes lyric odes to celebrate triumphs at the Olympic games.

  Today: Today's athletes are also celebrated for their victories, but the celebrations often focus on advertising contracts and endorsement contracts that make the athletes very wealthy. Few have poems written about them.

- **c. 467 B.C.:** Alfalfa is grown by the Greeks, who were introduced to this grain by the Persians, and use this grain to feed their livestock.

  Today: Grain is still useful as a by-product of war. Although the United States spent many years seeking military and economic victory over the Russians, when victory was assured, the United States began shipping wheat to the Russians to supplement their meager harvests.

- **c. 467 B.C.:** The dramatist Sophocles becomes a major competitor of Aeschylus for the annual drama prizes at the Dionysus competition. The prizes are sought after, and for several years both dramatists will continue to challenge the other for the greatest plays.

  Today: Drama competition continues with prizes for film and theater eagerly sought each spring. Winners of the Best Film at the Academy Awards or the Best Play at the Critic Circle Awards are assured of accolades and monetary rewards that will ease the production of subsequent work.

for the other expenses, staging the production and feeding everyone associated with the play. There were government officials to maintain order, but the audience attended because it was a serious civic obligation to attend. Of course, the plays were very entertaining, as was the competition between playwrights, which was also important.

Theater had its beginnings in Athens at religious festivals, which later began to include public competitions in drama. The drama contests were held outside in huge amphitheaters, with the Dionysus competition being held in a theater that seated 17,000 people. In this competition, considered to be the largest and most prestigious, three playwrights were chosen to present a total of twelve plays. The playwrights, actors, and choruses all competed for prizes. Women were involved only as spectators, boys played women's roles and men wrote the plays. Originally, theater began with just choruses that sang hymns or narrative lyrics. Over time, the first actor appeared. He was masked and entered into a dialogue with the chorus. Aeschylus introduced a second actor to the play, and this enabled him to create a more complex plot. The chorus, which consisted of six to twelve young men, wearing long, flowing robes and identical masks, also joined the actors. The two actors wore different masks, and oftentimes, elaborate costumes. They also wore platform shoes that made them taller and more imposing. Costumes were decorated and sometimes revealed the social status or position of the character. The sources for plays were past and sometimes more recent wars, but might also include familiar Homeric epics and stories of how gods treated mankind. Oftentimes, there was an emphasis on the power of gods, as well as their ability to use trickery. Other topics included man's response to fate or the hopelessness of man's dreams in the face of gods' desires. The story of Oedipus and his sons tells of how one mistake with a god can lead to disaster for all subsequent generations.

Plagues and famines were frequent problems for people of the ancient eastern Mediterranean world. These disasters were usually blamed on the gods, since people had no real understanding of how weather patterns functioned or of the earth's geological movement. Early Greeks believed that the gods were responsible for weather disasters, outbreaks of disease, or the occasional volcano erupting, and they believed these events signaled a punishment from the gods. The Greeks believed in an orderly world, one in which the gods determined their well-being or success. When a significant disaster occurred, these early Greeks looked toward the one thing they could control, their behavior, for answers. In the Oedipus myth, Laius defied the gods. It was appropriate that he was punished, and it was not unusual for this punishment to be extended to all his offspring. Their acceptance of the punishment is seen in Eteocles's acceptance of his forthcoming death. It is determined by the gods as a fit punishment. It does not matter that Eteocles was not even born when his grandfather received the god's curse. The injustice of his death is not even a factor for the audience. This is the way Greek life functioned. Everyone in the audience would be aware of this story cycle, and they would be acutely aware that their own survival depended on pleasing the gods. Eteocles is fulfilling his duty and fulfilling a destiny determined long before his birth.

CRITICAL OVERVIEW

Seven Against Thebes depicts the third story in the Oedipus trilogy. The first story in the trilogy tells of the curse that is visited upon Laius, which threatened Thebes if Laius had any offspring. In the second tragedy, Oedipus cannot escape his father's curse, and fulfills it with the murder of his father and marriage to his mother. When Oedipus discovers that he has fulfilled the prophecy, he blinds himself and promises that his sons will have to do battle over his property, thus setting up the actions of the third part of the trilogy, the fight between Eteocles and Polyneices. The story of Antigone and of her insistence on following her conscience, which she places before the laws of the state, is also the subject of a tragedy, Sophocles's *Antigone*.

We do not know how Aeschylus's audience reacted to *Seven Against Thebes,* but we can assume

that the reaction was favorable, since he received a first prize for the trilogy, of which it is a part. It is important to remember that Greek drama was not nightly entertainment, but was a part of festivals, which were staged only a few times during the year. Plays were not intended to hold up a mirror to life, but the playwright did hope that his play would touch the audience, forcing them to consider the implications of the behavior depicted on stage. Audiences listened very intently to the actors and the Chorus, even reacting with fear to an actor's persona, costuming, or mask. Tragedy was intended to teach a lesson, reveal a moral truth, or create an emotional response in the audience, such as pity or fear. In a particularly effective tragedy, the play would produce a catharsis of these emotions in the audience. The audience would learn that sometimes these emotions are destructive, and therefore, they would attempt to avoid them in their own lives. In *Seven Against Thebes,* Eteocles teaches the audience that hatred is destructive in its blindness. Eteocles and Polyneices should have united in strength; instead they opposed one another and so both died.

Aeshcylus's plays are not often produced, since many directors find his works difficult to stage before a modern audience. However, there is still an occasional production, as one would expect, in Greece, such as a recent presentation of *Seven Against Thebes* in Athens in August 1995. Occasionally, productions are attempted elsewhere, as in a 1994 staging at the Macunaima Drama School in Sao Paulo, Brazil. There was also a 1996 staging at the Stagecraft theater in New Zealand. Of the latter production, a review by John Davidson mentions the difficulty in staging Aeschylus. In this performance, the director included a lecture on the mythical background and a staged conversation between Oedipus and Antigone, in which the two discussed their family history. These devices preceded the performance, but Davidson argues that "a straightforward delivery of the essential features of the story would probably have been more useful." Davidson also noted that the Chorus was unequal to the role, lacking emotional force. In spite of the problems of the performance, Davidson credits the actors playing Eteocles and the messenger as particularly effective. One addition that pleased the reviewer was a pageant of Theban champions, whose shields matched the descriptions delivered by the messenger. A too-small theater and uneven acting, according to Davidson, could not diminish the glimpses of the "raw power of Aeschylus." We cannot compare modern productions and the audience's response to how a Greek audience might have responded to this tragedy. By the time the ancient Greek audience witnessed *Seven Against Thebes,* they had been following this familial tragedy through productions of the first two parts of the tetralogy. Since the first two plays have not survived, a modern audience will never experience these plays in their entirety. Nor is a modern audience as familiar with the myths that lie behind the trilogy. Aeschylus's audience was informed and attentive, with the events on stage having a meaning for the audience that is lacking in a modern audience. Davidson noted in his review that this production of was followed by a staging of *The Persians* with a production of *Agamemnon* planned the following year. Occasionally an audience is lucky enough to experience Aeschylus's work, and for a few moments, they are transported back to ancient Greece.

CRITICISM

Sheri E. Metzger

Metzger has a Ph.D., and specializes in literature and drama at The University of New Mexico, where she is a Lecturer in the English Department and an Adjunct Professor in the University Honors Program. In the following essay, she discusses Aeschylus's depiction of women, as observed in the interactions between Eteocles and the Chorus in Seven Against Thebes.

A modern audience is at a distinct disadvantage in studying Aeschylus's *Seven Against Thebes.* This tragedy is the third play in the tetralogy; thus to see or read only the third play is a bit like walking into a film as it nears its completion. The audience is in time for the denouement, the resolution of the plot, but the important information, the reason these events occur, is missing. The first two plays of Aeschylus's series relate the events of Laius' curse, the birth and abandonment of Oedipus, his discovery of his destiny, and his attempts to avoid his fate. Aeschylus's *Laius* and *Oedipus* provide the background for the third play, the reasons behind Eteocles' decision to fight his brother, and they help establish why Polyneices would consider attacking his brother, who was also his twin. That missing information may also help illuminate Eteocles' harsh treatment of the Chorus in *Seven Against Thebes.* In truth, the cold, merciless manner in which Eteocles addresses

the Chorus is more a function of his personal family tragedy, than a reflection of the way women were treated in Aeschylus's fifth-century B.C. Athens.

> The female Chorus, with their loud laments and cries of fear, represent all women, and women have failed Eteocles. His relationship with his mother, who is also his sister, is enveloped in shame and destruction. Eteocles identifies all women with the woman who betrayed him.

The brief fragments of the first two plays in this trilogy offer little information as to the specifics of their content. The Oedipus narrative, his father, Laius' story, and the tale of the destruction of Eteocles and Polyneices were familiar legends to Aeschylus and to other Greek playwrights. Sophocles also used these legends as source material in his play, but we cannot know exactly what aspects of the legends Aeschylus chose as a focus. There are many different renditions, with slight changes, including different reasons why Oedipus cursed his own sons. It is sometimes reported that the curse resulted from the sons offering their father an inferior cut of meat. This might appear to be an insignificant cause to a twentieth century reader, but hospitality was a serious issue to ancient Greeks, since a traveler's life might depend on the level of hospitality received. Indeed, the initial curse on Laius and his offspring resulted from a violation of the laws regarding hospitality. The curse warned Laius that he should remain childless so that he might save the city of Thebes. But should he have a child, the gods prophesied that the son would murder his father and marry the mother. The son, Oedipus, did, in fact, murder his father, though unknowingly, and he did wed his mother, again unknowingly. As a result of his union with his mother, Jocasta, Oedipus fathers two sons who are destined to destroy one another: Eteocles and Polyneices. This is the story told in the first two plays of Aeschylus's trilogy. As a result of these events, the relationship with his mother/sister, Jocasta, may lie behind Eteocles' animosity toward the female Chorus.

When *Seven Against Thebes* opens, his past and the family curse are recent events for Eteocles. The play opens with the sounds of battle, and as J. D. Conacher observes in his study of Aeschylus's early plays, *Aeschylus: The Earlier Plays and Related Studies,* these are the sounds of "one of the great 'battle plays'" in Western literature." All the battles occur offstage, and yet, their presence is so intrusive that the sounds of the fierce battle fill the stage and theatre with tension. The Chorus is frightened, nearly reduced to hysteria as they imagine the battle

WHAT DO I READ NEXT?

- *Prometheus Bound*, by Aeschylus (undated), is the story of how Prometheus is punished for disobeying the god Zeus.

- *The Persians*, by Aeschylus (472 B.C.), is a history play that recounts an event from the Greek and Persian Wars.

- *Oedipus Rex*, by Sophocles (c. 430–426 B.C.), is the story of one man's attempts to escape his fate. This play tells the story of the events that precede *Seven Against Thebes*.

- *Antigone*, by Sophocles (c. 441 B.C.), is a literary and mythical sequel to *Seven Against Thebes*. This tragedy also deals with the problems of excessive pride and stubbornness. It also delves into the responsibility that all men have to bury the dead.

- *Bacchae*, by Euripides (c. 405 B.C.), is often regarded as a condemnation of religious excess.

drawing closer, the threat more immediate. The cries of the Chorus, the images they create with their pleas to the gods, are intermingled with images of battle. Together, these noises pull the audience into the scene, involving them through sounds almost as realistic as the actual presence of war. Conacher points out that this use of sound and image creates for the audience, "something of the terror of the off-stage battle preparations." These sounds of the approaching army, according to Conacher, are what most frighten the Chorus. Aeschylus establishes through sound the noise and confusion of battle, and by transporting the audience into the sounds of battle, he passes that fear and tension to the listening spectators. Thus, when Eteocles enters to confront the Chorus, his attack appears even harsher. Eteocles addresses the Chorus as "you stupid creatures," and expresses the hope that "Whether it's hard times or good old happy days, / don't put me in with the women." It is the Chorus that Eteocles addresses as "bossy" and "mindless," and who he accuses of bringing aid to the enemy with their fear. This hysteria is what Eteocles says happens when "a man lives with a woman." He continues with a reminder that war and battles and sacrifices to the gods are the dominion of men, and women ought not to tell men what to do. Conacher mentions that this scene provides great theatre, with the contrast between "the strength and masculinity of the protagonist and the terror of the female Chorus." This

is what Conacher labels a "piteous spectacle," which depicts the terror that awaits women in the face of war. The female Chorus has sound reasons for their fright, but Eteocles is unmoved by these images of feminine doom. In fact, Eteocles reacts with particularly fierce brutality to the Chorus' fear.

Of interest in this exchange between Eteocles and the Chorus is the threat of death that he adds to his chastisement to be silent. Anyone who fails to support him will be stoned to death, and Eteocles interprets the Chorus's fear as lack of support or belief in him. In her essay, "Language, Structure, and the Son of Oedipus," Froma L. Zeitlin suggests that Eteocles' ambivalence toward the Chorus is a manifestation of his relationship with his parents, particularly with his mother, Jocasta. Zeitlin first reminds her readers that "the women in the parodos [the ode] speak both for the city and for the family, sanctioning the norm by their appeals to the gods of both genders who hold sway in Thebes." Thus, the Chorus is fulfilling what females in this society are expected to do: voice their concerns for the well-being of the city and pray to their Greek gods for protection. And yet, their fulfillment of this duty compels Eteocles to threaten the Chorus with death. Zeitlin acknowledges that in chastising the Chorus, Eteocles may only be fulfilling his role as king of Thebes, maintaining order and protecting the best interests the population. But Zeitlin also suggests that Eteocles' "misogynistic tirade against *all* women for *all* time demonstrates precisely the status of Eteocles as a child of an incestuous union.'' As the child of such a union, Eteocles has fclt the abhorrence his parent's marriage has produced. The Chorus, too, is aware of the deviation from norms, since their pleas in the play's opening are for protection from the pillaging, and thus the rape and abduction that is too often the fate of women during war. As Zeitlin notes, ''war and incest both interrupt the normal exchange of women, one in excessive exogamy, one in excessive endogamy.'' Consequently, women are deprived of the normal marital relationship they might reasonably expect, and instead, are forced to either mate with their captors or unite within their immediate family or tribe. The Chorus is aware of this risk to their chastity, and since their response to the implied threats of the battle is appropriate, it is worth considering why Eteocles' response to the Chorus' fear, including the threat of death, is so extreme.

During the fifth century B.C., women in Greece enjoyed extraordinary freedoms. According to Thomas R. Martin's study, *Ancient Greece: From Prehistoric to Hellenistic times,* Athenian women contributed to almost all aspects of Greek society, except in the political forum. Women contributed to their society in several ways, including the bearing of legitimate children, whose parentage was especially important. Greek women earned significant freedoms once they had supplied the desired, legitimate heirs. Women earned respect, Martin says, by obeying society's norms. There was significant pressure on both men and women to ensure that a woman's reputation remained chaste and pure. The events that surrounded Eteocles' birth, when revealed, resulted in a complete breakdown of the accepted social norms. Oedipus, having blinded himself, fled in exile from the city, and Jocasta killed herself. The shame of these events was significant, and not surprisingly, Eteocles reacts in a crisis situation with a condemnation of all women.

The modern audience can never know what Aeschylus had in mind when he provided Eteocles with such a cruel condemnation of all women. Since Greek society valued women and encouraged their role as significant contributing members of society, Eteocles' attack would be out of character for most Greek men. But Eteocles is not any ordinary citizen. He is a victim of his father's curse, his parent's incest, and his mother's shame. The female Chorus, with their loud laments and cries of fear, represent all women, and women have failed Eteocles. His

> THUS, THE CHORUS IS FULFILLING WHAT FEMALES IN THIS SOCIETY ARE EXPECTED TO DO: VOICE THEIR CONCERNS FOR THE WELL-BEING OF THE CITY AND PRAY TO THEIR GREEK GODS FOR PROTECTION.''

relationship with his mother, who is also his sister, is enveloped in shame and destruction. Eteocles identifies all women with the woman who betrayed him. He will shortly fulfill the prophecy and his destiny; he will die, as will his brother. A rational response to the Chorus' hysteria is, perhaps, not to be expected.

Source: Sheri E. Metzger, in an essay for *Drama For Students,* Gale, 2001.

David H. Porter

In the following essay, David H. Porter examines the parallelism of the play, believing that the main movement of the play ''finds imitation at virtually every level.''

There are many unresolved questions about Aeschylus' *Seven Against Thebes.* Does the play fall into two imperfectly linked sections, the first dealing with the conflict between Thebes and the Argive invaders, the second with the effects of Oedipus' curse on his sons? Does Eteocles act with freedom of choice, or is he merely the unwitting agent of the curse? Does he make his selection of defenders as the play actually unfolds, or has he already made this selection before he appears for the great central scene? What is the precise nature of the curse which Oedipus has cast upon his sons? Is Eteocles' death to be seen as a sacrifice willingly undertaken in order to save the city? Are we to accept as genuine those portions which at the end of the play introduce Antigone and Ismene and the subject of Polyneices' burial? What was the relationship between the *Seven,* originally the final play of a trilogy, and the two plays which preceded it, the *Laius* and the *Oedipus?*

> THE MOVEMENT OF THE PLAY IS THUS A MOVEMENT FROM THE WAR TO THE CURSE, FROM THE COLLECTIVE TO THE INDIVIDUAL, FROM THE EXTERNAL TO THE INTERNAL, THE FOREIGN TO THE NATIVE, THE PUBLIC TO THE PRIVATE, THE *POLIS* TO THE *GENOS*."

On one matter, however, most critics agree—the basic movement of the play. The emphasis in the first half is clearly on the invasion that threatens Thebes—a public danger posed by the enemy outside the walls; the emphasis in later scenes is just as clearly on the curse that threatens two individuals—a private, family danger, one that grows, as it were, straight out of the soil of Thebes. The movement of the play is thus a movement from the war to the curse, from the collective to the individual, from the external to the internal, the foreign to the native, the public to the private, the *polis* to the *genos*. In the early scenes the chorus' lengthy odes express their hysterical fear over the threat of invasion, sacking, and rape at the hands of the foreign invaders, while in the equally long later odes their fears are for the fate of Eteocles and his family. Their concern at first is over the possibility that they themselves may become victims of war, at the end that Eteocles and his brother may become victims of the curse. One verbal motif, to which I shall return later, aptly sums up this dominant movement of the play as a whole. At the start we hear a great deal about the foreigners who are attacking the city; later, the foreigner repeatedly mentioned is the Chalybian stranger, that mysterious and haunting embodiment of the curse of Oedipus; thus we move from numerous foreigners threatening a whole city to a single Theban-rooted *xenos* who threatens the royal family.

There *are* other basic movements in the play, of course, and to one of these we shall return later in this chapter. But the most obvious and deeply ingrained is the progression just identified, a movement which finds imitation at virtually every level of the play—within larger and smaller inner components, in the relationships between balancing sec-

tions, in imagery and verbal motifs. This ubiquitous parallelism of movement serves many functions in the *Seven*, as we shall see in the remainder of this chapter, among them, of course, that of contributing to the coherence of a play some have judged lacking in unity.

In what follows I shall analyze the play section by section, first showing how each section as a whole reflects the play's basic movement and then commenting on other reflections within those sections. I divide the play into five major parts [with line numbers referring to the original Greek text]: 1–77 (Eteocles' opening speech and his exchange with the messenger); 78–286 (the *parodos* and Eteocles' dialogue with the chorus); 287–791 (the great central scene, including the balancing odes which enclose the selection scene); 792–821 (the short dialogue between the messenger and the chorus); 822–1004 (the lamentation over the death of the two brothers).

The first major section of the play, 1–77, contains both a clear reflection of the basic movement in the scene as a whole and also several smaller, more subtle imitations within. The focus at the beginning and through most of the scene is on the collective enemy outside the city: note the emphasis on the size of the invading force, on the collective nature of the defense, and on the public nature of the threat (it is the city and the land which are threatened) From this stress on the war, its public nature, and the numerous individuals who will be involved, Aeschylus moves at the end to clear, if not yet emphatic, suggestions of the narrowing of focus that is to come—to Eteocles' explicit (and somewhat surprising) mention of his father's curse; to the herald's emphasis on the degree to which Eteocles himself must now take charge. . .; and to Eteocles' personal acceptance of the responsibility placed upon him.

In passing we should note that in the two early sections (1–77, 78–286) the focus on the public, external menace of war dominates while the theme of the curse and Eteocles' personal involvement sounds only distantly and at the very end of the scenes, whereas in the last sections (792–821, 822–1004) the public issue of the city's safety appears at the start of scenes only to be swiftly overwhelmed by the now-dominant theme of the curse and its impact on Eteocles and Polyneices; in the great central panel (287–791) the two contrasting themes receive equal stress. This gradual shift of emphasis from scene to scene is, of course, yet one more reflection of the overall movement of the play.

As I have mentioned, even within the first section there are hints, albeit slight, of this same larger movement. Eteocles' address to the assembled Cadmeians and his generalizing *hostis* move rapidly, as will the play, to a focus on his own involvement; his description of the external threat to the city and his commands to the citizens as a group lead to his statement of his own, individual role; the messenger's speech itself moves from description of the invader to injunctions aimed primarily at Eteocles himself; and the messenger's focus on the foreign enemy is answered by Eteocles' emphasis on the native gods and land of Thebes, a movement that foreshadows the play's overall shift of focus from a foreign danger to an indigenous, earth-rooted curse.

The next section, 78–286, similarly contains parallel motion on several levels at once. Again it begins with the public, external threat of a large army. In the *parodos* the women as a group express their collective concern for the land as a whole, stressing the multitude and the foreignness of the invaders (multitude; foreignness) and repeatedly emphasizing the gods' obligation to protect the state. From this emphasis in the *parodos* on the many, the foreign, and the state, the last lines of the scene move to Eteocles, the Theban individual who by his own actions will bring the curse upon himself:

> I will take six men, myself to make a seventh and go to post them at the city's gates, opponents of the enemy, in gallant style, before quick messengers are on us and their words of haste burn us with urgency.

The scene thus ends, appropriately, with a far more ominous sounding of the ''Eteocles theme'' than that heard at the conclusion of the first section.

Several features within this elaborate section help foreshadow these final lines with their emphasis on Eteocles. For one thing, with the king's arrival at 181 attention shifts from an external to an internal danger. For just as the play as a whole moves from the threat of foreign war to the threat of the native curse, so this section moves from the danger posed by the foreign invader (in the *parodos*) to the danger posed by the Theban women. . . . Furthermore, whereas the women feared for the city, Eteocles perceives the women's hysteria as a threat not only to the city but also to himself, a fact emphasized by the very confrontation here between the many women and the one man. In the scene as a whole the opening section thus focuses on the

external danger, the final section on Eteocles' own participation; and the intervening discussion effects a gradual and skillful transition from the many to the one, the foreign to the Theban, the public to the private.

There are again inner parallels as well. The *parodos* creates the illusion of an army that is coming ever closer, an illusion obviously related to the way in which, in the play, the focal danger moves from outside Thebes to within Thebes; and the chorus' cries contain another distant variation on the same theme in the repeated movement from description of foreign invaders to invocation of native divinities. With the central section of the scene we move from the domination of the many (i.e., the women) to the domination of the one (i.e., Eteocles), a shift underscored by the almost precise numerical balance of 181–202 (22 lines), which stress the collective danger posed by the many, with 264–286 (23 lines), which express Eteocles' reestablished dominance. Still smaller components also reflect the same pattern: Eteocles' speech at 181–202 moves from description of the collective threat posed by the women to emphasis on his own necessary dominance, the *stichomythia* at 245–263 from the women listening to the sound of the enemy to them listening to Eteocles, and Eteocles' final speech from his statement of what the *women* must do to his statement of what *he* will do.

As we might expect, the play's great central scene contains the climax not only of the play's action but also, both qualitatively and quantitatively, of its parallelism. Virtually every aspect of this vast scene displays clear reflections of the play's larger movement. On the most obvious level, one so obvious that little need be said about it, there is the movement from the chorus which opens the section to the chorus which closes it, with the former focusing almost exclusively on the collective danger of foreign war, the latter almost exclusively on the threat of the Theban curse to Eteocles and Polyneices (cf., for example, the fear of the army at the start of the first ode, with the fear of the curse at the end of the second)

We may note also that these two contrasting odes exemplify almost perfectly the principles which were our theme in the Introduction: the centrifugal thrust of balanced opposites on the one hand, the centripetal pull of motivic links and parallel structure on the other. For although the two odes point to the two contrasting themes of the play, they are bound together by numerous verbal motifs and by a clear parallelism of structure. . . .

The climax of the relationship between the two odes comes in their final sections . . . . Both the events and the language in this section of the earlier ode carry strong connotations of Oedipus. Thus *domaton stugeran hodon* is reminiscent of the journey on which Oedipus met and killed Laius, a journey which we know was explicitly mentioned in the previous plays . . . , and the references to murder similarly recall the parricide; the description of new-born babes crying as they are torn from breasts reminds us of Oedipus' exposure, an event not explicitly mentioned in the ode at 720 f. but one certainly suggested by *ekbolan,* a word used in Euripides of an exposed child and a word which in the *Seven* corresponds metrically to *Oidipoun* in the antistrophe; the comparison of rapine in the city to the pouring of fruit on the ground not only parallels Oedipus' spewing of his curse on his sons but also reminds us of the frequent fertility language associated with Oedipus and his family. . .; the ''bitter eye'' of the stewards . . . Oedipus' recalls destruction of his own eyes. . .; the wretched *eunan* of the captive maids recalls the wretched marriage of Oedipus (*athlion gamon;* and the final description of the fate of women captured in war is phrased so ambiguously as to suggest the marriages of both Oedipus and Laius:

> *elpis esti nukteron telos molein pagklautōn algeōn epirrothon.*

Finally, the lines which begin this whole section of the first ode suggest Oedipus in a remarkable way:

> Man stands against man with the spear and is killed.
> Young mothers, blood-boltered, cry bitterly for the babes at their breast.

While the overtones of Oedipus and his family in the ode at 287 f. are fresh in mind, we should note that this ode itself contains yet one more inner reflection of the overall movement of the play. Just as the play moves from the war to the curse, from the danger to Thebes to the danger to the children of Oedipus, so this ode begins with the women's response to the war but moves to a conclusion filled with rich reminiscences of the curse and its effect on Oedipus and his family. Furthermore, the ode's progression from the women's generalized concern for the city to their more specific concern for themselves reflects in microcosm the play's movement from public concerns to private.

The principal function of the ode at 720 f. is to conclude as emphatically as possible the great movement from war (287 f.) to curse (653 f.) which shapes the central scene of the play. If, however, this ode as a whole contains only subtle hints of the play's dominant rhythm, its brief passages about Laius and Oedipus contain clear imitations in that both first focus on the safety of the city, then turn their attention to the family curse.

In the central episode itself, that involving the matching of the seven pairs of antagonists, the overall parallelism to the play's basic movement is again so apparent as to require little comment. Just as the play as a whole moves from a focus on Thebes' foreign enemies to a focus on a Theban curse, so in the earlier parts of this episode the war and the danger to the state are uppermost in Eteocles' mind, but from 653 on the curse clearly dominates his thinking. . . . This shift of focus is not unprepared: in different ways Parthenopaeus and Amphiaraus, the last two champions before Polyneices and Eteocles themselves, begin to shift the emphasis from the collective to the individual, from the war to the curse, from a foreign threat to a native one, and from the state as a whole to Eteocles in particular.

Parthenopaeus, unlike the previous Argive champions, carries on his shield a distinctively Theban emblem, the Sphinx, an emblem which, moreover, has a special relevance to the curse-laden royal house of Thebes. He is also described in the language of fertility that is usually reserved for the Theban *Spartoi* and their kings. . . . In addition, Parthenopaeus is more fully individualized than are the four previous champions. With him, and with Amphiaraus, we begin to focus less on a collective invasion and more on certain individuals, a movement which will reach its climax in the close-up focus on Eteocles and Polyneices at the end of the scene.

Amphiaraus brings us still closer. Again there is the distinctively Theban agricultural imagery, this time in greater profusion. Furthermore, Eteocles recognizes in Amphiaraus a kindred spirit, and the king's words about him bear an ominous, if hidden, relevance to himself:

> In all man does, evil relationships are the worst evil. . .
> (tr. Dawson)

Finally, to underline the relationship, Amphiaraus, like Eteocles, is a man fighting a losing battle against a Theban-born curse.

Thus as we move from the threat of foreign invasion to that of the native curse, the foreign invaders begin to take on Theban characteristics, a movement that reaches its destination in the seventh Argive champion, Polyneices, who is not only himself a Theban but also, like Eteocles, the specific target of the curse. At the same time, Eteocles is becoming increasingly involved on a personal as against a merely strategic level, a movement that effectively begins at 282, that accelerates in the responses to Parthenopaeus and Amphiaraus, and that leads ultimately to the impassioned outburst at 653 f. At the end of the central scene, as at the end of the second section of the play, Eteocles is at center stage in dispute with the chorus, the one against the many, his mind focused on a danger that is Theban rather than foreign. This danger now, however, is not the collective danger of the Theban women's hysteria but the personal danger of the Theban curse.

I have already spoken of several of the smaller parallels within parallels that this great central scene contains. Suffice it to add that in the descriptions of the various pairs of opponents at the gates there are still more parallels: the movement within each pair, as within the play as a whole, is from foreign to Theban; and just as Eteocles' public generalship and even his words diabolically recoil upon himself in personal disaster, so, through Eteocles' verbal manipulations, the public mission and the emblems and words associated with it recoil upon each Argive champion in turn.

For two reasons I shall deal but briefly with the concluding sections of the play. First, the text of these last portions is corrupt and in dispute at so many points that at best one can do no more than suggest their general movement. Second, while these scenes do contain clear reflections of the play's basic rhythm, these reflections do not possess the many-layered complexity found in the earlier sections.

As already mentioned, the dominant theme in these last scenes is that of the curse, just as the dominant theme in early scenes was that of the war. At the beginning of each section there is, however, a clear, if short-lived, recurrence of the war theme. Thus the fourth section (792–821) begins with the messenger's explicit reference to the city's victory in war (792 f.), a theme that soon gives way to his and the chorus' preoccupation with the curse-determined death of the brothers; and the long choral passage beginning at 822 similarly opens its lamen-

tations over the brothers and the curse with a clear glance at the new-found safety of the city (825 f.)

Source: David H. Porter, ''The Magnetism of Destruction: Aeschylus' *Seven*,'' in *Only Connect: Three Studies in Greek Tragedy,* University Press of America, 1987, pp. 1–44.

Froma I. Zeitlin

In this essay, Zeitlin discusses autochthony in relation to Eteokles, as well as the structure and identity of his role in the play.

III. Mythos—Polis/Genos: Autochthony/Incest

The climax of the drama, after the seventh shield, when the two codes, that of the city and that of the family, diverge, does not constitute a sudden reversal, as many have suggested, a substitution of one set of terms for another, but is rather the culmination of a process which has governed the logic of the text from the beginning. The relations of oppositions and homologies which underlie the text are strained to their limits by the inherent but unnatural contradiction of *genos* and *polis* exemplified in the person of Eteokles who is always *both* the ruler of Thebes *and* the son of Oedipus. Thus the text resonates throughout in both registers, each voice dominant now in one part and recessive now in another. At times these voices reply to each other antiphonally; at times, they join in unison. This tension between the two codes is demonstrated on the structural level of plot in the complex relationship between the two major episodes, that with the *women* of Thebes *inside* the city and that involving the shields of the *men outside*. These two scenes are both opposites and doublets of each other. As a confrontation between two opposing attitudes, the first scene is, in fact, a rehearsal of the other; it is also its dynamic mover, since the conflict provokes from Eteokles his promise to include himself as the seventh combatant in the approaching battle.

Limitations of space do not permit the analysis of the role of the women of the chorus who carry the largest burden of the text, with whom and through whom Eteokles activates the doom which awaits him. Here I would point only to the operation of the sexual code, which, through its various inversions, establishes the proper norm for the city. That norm insists upon a dual allegiance—to the general collective of the group as exemplified in the unifying myth of autochthony (origin from one, the mother earth) and to the individual family in its exogamous union of male and female (origin from two). The women in the parodos speak both for the city and for

"IN AESCHYLEAN DRAMA,
NOTHING CAN COME INTO
EXISTENCE BEFORE ITS NAME HAS
BEEN UTTERED. CONCEPT IS FULLY
EMBEDDED IN IMAGE, AND FIGURE
IS INSEPARABLE FROM IDEA."

the family, sanctioning the norm by the nature of their appeals to the gods of both genders who hold sway in Thebes.

Eteokles, however, invokes only the myth of the autochthonous origin of Thebes. He appeals to this myth on the one hand, as a good general might, to serve the interests of patriotic ideology. For the resort to the myth of birth from the mother earth serves as a reminder of the absolute duty of her hoplite sons to defend their city. On the other hand, autochthony is a dangerously seductive model for Eteokles: first, he is not truly a Spartos, but the son of Jocasta and Oedipus, and hence he is not fully an insider in the city. His identification with the Spartoi therefore implies a potential misrecognition of himself and his own origins. Second, and conversely, since autochthony, like incest, posits a single undifferentiating origin, Eteokles all too easily transposes the pattern from one domain to the other and runs the risk of contaminating the city's myth of solidarity with the negative import of his own story.

For the city, single autochthonous origin is only a point of origin, one which precedes the next stage when different families are founded in Thebes. Ares, as the chorus indicates in the parodos, is the deity who makes this transition possible. For he faces in both directions, first, as the founder of Thebes through his connection with the Sown Men; second, as the consort of Aphrodite with whom he united to engender Harmonia who, in turn, was given to Kadmos. For the chorus, on the other hand, the city has two primordial mothers: Gaia (earth) and Aphrodite *promator*.

Return to the notion of a single origin excludes the circulation of females as signs of exchange who guarantee continuing differentiation within the system. Eteokles, when he attempts to silence the unruly women at the altars and insists upon the rigid

antithesis between the sexes, is perhaps performing his proper military role in the interests of group morale and demanding from the women only what the social conventions expected from them. But the addition of his misogynistic tirade against *all* women for *all* time demonstrates precisely the status of Eteokles as child of an incestuous union, who knows only how to repress the "speaking signs" that are essential to the city for its genealogical diversity in favor of a homogeneous commonality ruled by a single principle.

The import of this repression is emphasized when the chorus in the first stasimon evokes the polar opposite of incest/autochthony, namely, the vision of the forcible rape and abduction of the city's women by the alien attackers. This is exogamy in its most negative form as unlawful appropriation of women which accompanies and is homologous with the pillaging of the goods of the city and its homes. When the violence of strife has entered the city, both extremes, that of excessive distance and that of excessive closeness, are correlated in the hidden mantic message of the choral ode. For war and incest both interrupt the normal exchange of women, one in excessive exogamy, one in excessive endogamy.

ENDOGAMY
within the city
autochthony/incest
single origin: same
unlawful appropriation
ENDOGAMY/EXOGAMY
within the city/without the city
orderly exchange
same/other
lawful marriage
EXOGAMY
without the city
rape/abduction
other
unlawful appropriation.

Eteokles' flight from woman, a refusal both of genealogy and generation, substitutes asexual autochthony for hypersexual incest, and replaces the biological mother with the symbolic mother of the collective city. But his antithesis of either/or cannot stand. Polarity is also analogy, for in the language of the Greek city, the woman imitates the earth and the earth imitates the woman. Each term lends to the other the appropriate metaphorical quality by which literal and symbolic stabilize one another in an integrative system of values. An attack upon one is, in truth, equivalent to an attack upon the other. Eteokles' dissociation of the two is paradoxically only the sign of their inherent relationship, since incest is the hidden paradigm of autochthony. The denial of this analogical connection between mother and earth can only encourage a false claim to autonomy; it will therefore establish a system in which reciprocal relations must take the form of antithetical violence, whether with the women inside or the warriors outside.

That analogy is already at work, for the curse of Oedipus was precipitated by the sons' neglect of *trophe,* the nurture they owed in return for their *trophe,* the same *trophe* owed in the language of autochthony to the mother earth as her Dike. The terms of the father's curse, when fulfilled, will perfect the paradigm, for the sons, as citizens of Thebes, will repeat the violation of *trophe,* this time against the mother earth, by Polyneikes' attack against it and by Eteokles' willingness to pollute the earth with fratricidal blood.

Eteokles' single adherence to *polis* in his appeal to the myth of the city's single origin can and does confirm a positive political ideology *for* the group. But when construed also as a defense *against genos,* Eteokles' appeal also reconnects *genos* to *polis* by invoking now the *negative* paradigmatic force implied by the terms of the origin myth. For when the brothers reenact the crimes of the father against one another for possession now of their father's goods and of his city, they are, at the same time, reenacting the regressive aspect of the city's founding myth, which first led to destruction before it culminated in solidarity. The fratricide of the sons of Oedipus follows the model of the Sown Men, who, springing up in autochthonous birth from the dragon's teeth in the soil of Thebes, slew one another in mutual combat, with the exception of five who survived to establish families in Thebes and to profit from the prestige of their indigenous origins. The city is saved, not for the first time, but for the second, when Laios proves to have died without issue. And the second time proves a repetition of the first time, when Eteokles is enrolled at last among the Spartoi only after his death. Autochthony, in its ambiguities in the political and mythic codes, is therefore the sign that Eteokles will function as the bridge between a defective model of city and a defective model of family; he will serve as a negative mediator between the two. His is a monocular gaze whose partial vision will betray him in the reading of the signs on the warriors' shields.

IV. Hero: Structure, Sign, and Identity

If we can speak of the power of the family over its offspring as a "genealogical imperative," in the

case of the family of Laios we can speak of a negative "genealogical imperative," which now decrees not life but death to its progeny and which regulates the text from its beginning to its end. From this perspective, Eteokles' defensive strategy, one might say, is dedicated both to preserving the integrity of the walls that protect the besieged city of Thebes and to preserving his unique singular identity. The encroachment of "no difference" heralds the fall into plurality with his brother and hence back into genealogy as the son of Oedipus.

On the one hand, Eteokles, who characterizes himself as "one" (*heis*), at the beginning of the play, only to juxtapose the term with *polus* ("many"), prophesies more truly than he knows that he alone, as the son of Oedipus, will be separated out from the many, those citizens of Cadmos' city whom he addresses. On the other hand, once the distinction between the two brothers fails, so does the line between singular and plural. Thus Eteokles will quite literally be absorbed into the pluralizing name of *Poly*-neikes. In other words, he will prove to be singular with regard to his fellow citizens and plural with regard to his brother when the two identities merge.

The potential loss of Eteokles' name carries a double jeopardy. In general terms, a name is the guarantee of identity and of existence, of difference from others in the world at large and at home. Surrendering one's name is a dangerous act, even in the interests of survival, as Odysseus well knows when he reasserts his name at his peril after he names/unnames himself as Outis, "No One," in the cave of the Cyclops. The name also attests to the legitimacy of the father's prerogative to name his progeny and to inscribe the bearer of that name together with his patronymic in the continuing line of the family.

In specific terms, maintaining a stable relation between signifier and signified in the name, Eteokles (truly famed, full of *kleos*), offers another hope in the face of the shadow of negation that broods over the family. For the alternative to generation as the guarantee of immortality through the continuance of *genos* is the winning of individual *kleos,* of singular heroic renown in battle so as to survive through the memory of tradition on the lips of men. In the economy of praise and blame which structured archaic Greek society, Eteokles (*kleos* × fame × praise) and Polyneikes (*neikos* × strife × blame) are lexical signs of the opposition itself. This dichotomy opposes positive (presence of praise) to negative (absence of praise), memory to oblivion, clarity to obscurity, the brightness of fame (to be named) to the darkness of ill repute (anonymity); in short, opposes immortality to extinction. But the fulfillment of the curse through fratricidal combat must inevitably defeat Eteokles' claim to moral and personal identity which his name represents and which he had hoped his virtuous allegiance to the city would protect. Instead, the deflection of heroism to fratricidal combat fulfills the hidden, sinister significance of his name, i.e., ''truly bewept,'' or ''true cause of weeping'' [*klaio* = weep, lament]. Thus, as Bacon persuasively argues, Eteokles' own name, like that of his father, functions as a riddle and prophecy of his fate, namely a death without *kleos* that will be truly bewept. The last stage of the drama will efface his name when both brothers are jointly characterized as Polynei*keis,* the plural form of the singular, *Poly* neikes. The name, *Poly*neikes, already contains within itself the notion of plurality (''much,'' ''many''), and the grammatical plural redoubles, as it were, the annulment of Eteokles' name and identity.

Thus, in broadest terms, Eteokles' best defense against the curse of his father and on behalf of his own name is attention to language and control of the discourse. The best defense against the collapse into ''no difference'' is attention to the maintenance of the binary opposition. And, in thematic terms, as we have seen, the best defense against *genos* is exclusive adherence to *polis.*

No other play is as generous and as repetitive in establishing the competing codes and values at work in the system according to the fundamental dichotomies which regulate Greek thought: male/female, enemy/friend, Greek/barbarian, inside/outside, self/other, man/god; and there is none that specifically elevates the task of making and unmaking binary oppositions to the level of a crucial and explicit action of the drama.

Binary opposition informs both the structure and content of the two major episodes in the play, the first when Eteokles encounters the unruly Theban women of the chorus, and the second, the centerpiece of the drama, the shield scene. There, through seven paired speeches between himself and the scout, Eteokles seven times pairs enemy with defender until the ''barrier of the antithesis'' that guarantees the opposition begins to break down when brother faces brother at the seventh gate. Polarized difference then yields to doubling homology, as the double progeny of a doubly seeded womb meet in a duel and collapse their single selves into the grammatical category of the dual. The enemy brothers thus act out on the synchronic level of fraternity (i.e., of the same generation) their status as offspring of the diachronic collapse of generational distinction that the two original acts of the father represented, i.e., parricide and incest. The erotic vocabulary of passion (*eros*) and desire (*himeros*) used to characterize Eteokles' eagerness to confront his brother in mortal combat, suggests the merger of Eros and Thanatos—the conflation of the two transgressions that engendered the two brothers.

The shield scene, located strategically at the midpoint of the drama, acts as a model system that condenses, climaxes, and hypostasizes the problems of structure and language that inform the play from the beginning when war establishes the legitimacy of the polar opposition, and Eteokles, as the ruler of Thebes, determines to speak the proper words (*legein ta kairia*). Throughout, the privileged field of combat is the semantic field. The speech act is truly performative.

Semiotics, the study of the system of signs and how they communicate, can provide a hermeneutical tool for analyzing the synergetic system of relations that comprises Aeschylus' distinctive world view. In Aeschylean drama, nothing can come into existence before its name has been uttered. Concept is fully embedded in image, and figure is inseparable from idea. Conflict in the *Seven* is literally war, while the antithesis is a pairing of opponents with antithetical names. Homology is the identity of kin (*homoios/homaimon*), the oxymoron is the enemy brother. *Moira* as fate is literally *moira* as portion, since the destiny of the brothers is the apportioning of the father's patrimony, and the equal *moira* of death will prove to be the equal *moira* of land for their interment. Above all, the shield devices, *semata,* are signs, iconic emblems, that speak and move within a system that is not only tactical (military), but syntactical (linguistic). Language is therefore action and action is language through which the ''genealogical imperative'' of the accursed family at last asserts itself. Eteokles will create a text which claims linguistic competence in the ''langue,'' i.e., the public language of civic values, which will insure the victory of Thebes over Argos, but through which his own ''parole'' will ''speak itself,'' the language upon which his personal identity rests, and which once discovered in wits signification, will constitute the language of curse and oracle.

Here then in the shield scene is a coded demonstration of the science of signs and how they operate within the social system in regard to the special status of tragic language in its necessary and intrinsic ambiguity. This demonstration, in turn, raises the more general question of language as a means of communication and as a guarantee of identity and truth. Literature has been defined as ''a language, but a language around which we have drawn a frame'' by which we ''indicate a decision to regard with a particular self-consciousness the resources language has always possessed.'' From this formalist point of view, the language of the shield scene is doubly marked: first, by the artful frame of formal design which characterizes the scene within the larger structure of the literary text of the play, and second, by reason of its explicit oracular activity.

Oracles, by their nature and the mode of their operation, inevitably direct attention to the problematics of language and reality and point to the potential slippage in the sign between signifier and signified. Once personal identity becomes equivalent to the proper name and once oracle and riddle, as forms of speech, translate the problems of personal identity into those of the linguistic sign, the decipherment of language claims first priority as the hermeneutic way into those fundamental human issues which the dilemma of Oedipus (or his progeny) best represents. In a semiotic perspective, the case of Eteokles to an even greater extent than that of Oedipus, exemplifies the ''power of the signifier to be both instrument of power and through the deception inherent in it, a cause of misfortune'' and destruction. What then are the rules of the semiotic game? How and why do they function as they do?

Source: Froma I. Zeitlin, ''Language, Structure, and the Son of Oedipus,'' in *Under the Sign of the Shield: Semiotics and Aeschylus' ''Seven against Thebes,''* Edizioni dell'Ateneo, 1982, pp. 13–52.

William G. Thalmann

Thalman looks at several facets of the city in Seven Against Thebes *and regards the brothers' relationship as a microcosm of the city.*

The Theme of Blood

One other persistent theme of the play ought to be mentioned here: the theme of blood. It is closely related to that of the family, though it is more relevant to the brothers themselves than to the city. Most of the occurrences of this theme have been noted in the preceding pages, but its development should be sketched. At first, blood is a feature of the

war generally. The Argive Seven plunge their hands into a bull's blood and vow either to sack the city or to spill their own blood. Blood is prominent in the destruction of the city contemplated by the chorus in the first stasimon. During the shield scene the chorus fear that they will see the ''bloody fates'' of their [*philoi/friends or allies*]. They have, of course, general slaughter in mind, but that is just what they will see in the case of Eteocles and Polynices. The transition of this theme from the city to the brothers comes when the chorus urge Eteocles not to go to the seventh gate: This is a mark of how the scope of the war has shrunk; Thebes' involvement in the conflict is no longer the central concern, even though Polynices prays as a Theban. The incongruity of his invocation of the city's gods when he is the aggressor only draws attention to the fact that the actual issue is between the two brothers.

> [But it is enough for Argives that Cadmeian men come to blows, for that blood is cleansing.]

Whatever the exact meaning of the last phrase, there is a clear contrast between the [*haima/blood*] of 680 and the blood shed in fratricide, for the chorus continue:

> [But the death of two men of the same blood in this way is by their own hand, there no old age for this pollution.]

This kind of bloodshed is unlawful. There follow, later on, the references to the ''bloody root'' which grew from Oedipus's sowing and to the brothers' blood spilled and mingled on the ground. Blood is common to the members of a family: they are *homaimoi/of the same blood.* But in the blood of this family runs a curse. If the *Laius* contained a description of Oedipus tasting his father's blood, then this theme may have run through the whole trilogy.

The Gods

The city's ties with the land are important, but its relations with its gods are basic to its existence. In this case too, Aeschylus presents a picture of a normal pattern of life, from which the ruling family is excluded and which it threatens to overturn. Eteocles invokes this relationship in urging the citizens to defend the altars of their gods. . . .

The gods are ''native''; the implication is that Thebes has a special claim on their protection. The chorus therefore beg them for help in the parodos and first stasimon. One of the pairs of gods to whom the chorus appeal in lines 109–50 [in the Greek text] is especially ''native,'' Ares and Aphrodite, parents of Harmonia and so the divine ancestors of the

Theban race. Thus the chorus summons up the whole mythical past of the city as a basis for their prayers.

What binds the gods to the city and the city to the gods is a systematic interchange between them. This is clearly expressed by Eteocles at the end of his prayer in the prologue:

> [But be our strength. I expect that I speak about the common good. For a city that fares well honors its divinities.]

This has sometimes been understood as a mark of Eteocles' cynicism in religious matters. But such a view ignores the fact that the chorus end their own pleas in the parodos by reminding the gods of sacrifices received from the city. Similarly, in the first stasimon, they claim that the gods could not depart to a better land than Thebes and promise them future honors in return for their aid. Sacrifices matter to the gods; the idea is at least as old as Homer. In the *Iliad,* Zeus grants Troy's destruction to Hera only reluctantly. The Trojans are dear to him, he says, for they have never failed to honor him by sacrifice. In the *Seven* this relation, systematized by ritual, is yet another sign of the "norm" which the war threatens to disrupt. The gory sacrifices performed by the Argives express a distorted version of this norm. Their gods are Eres, nyo, and Phobos. Moreover, Parthenopaeus reveres his spear more than a god; and, of course, the Argives' boasts, detailed in the shield scene, are hybristic.

Is Eteocles in any way impious? Golden, for example, considers his religious outlook "highly pragmatic. . . . He is able to manipulate all of the doctrines of the conventional religion to suit his purposes and will." Certainly his relations with the gods are uneasy, but the case does not appear that simple. His words early in the play seem to indicate that passive trust in the gods is not enough to meet the present situation; military steps are also necessary. At the same time, Eteocles recognizes the limits of human endeavors, conceding that the final outcome will be decided by the gods. Yet the first episode, in its total effect, does tend to isolate Eteocles from the usual relationship between men and gods. As in the case of the earth, he apparently understands its value, but something prevents him from engaging in it fully. That can only be the curse. Rather than insist on a characterization of Eteocles, however, we ought perhaps to consider themes in the play which are associated with the gods.

The ambiguity of Eteocles' position is clearly brought out in the repetition of the word [*telein/to*

complete or accomplish]. Like [*krainein*], it is a favorite word with Aeschylus and is always significant when he employs it in reference to the gods, particularly to Zeus. In the *Seven,* it is first used in the prologue, when Eteocles encourages the Thebans. From there, it can be traced through the chorus's fearful doubts, prompted by the war, in the parodos to a similar outburst of fright in the second stasimon; but here they fear that the Erinys will "accomplish" the curses of Oedipus. Finally, after news of the battle, the chorus lament the completion of the curse. In this respect as in others, the play moves from the general to the specific, as the conclusion to be feared becomes no longer that of the war (for the gods do protect the city) but that of the curse which ruins the house.

A more direct statement of Eteocles' situation with regard to the gods is given in his prayer in lines 69 ff. There he appeals not only to Zeus, Earth, and the gods of the city, but also to the curse and his father's Erinys. This is in accord with his double role as political leader and accursed individual, and at this point in the play both aspects seem fused. But then he asks, "do not uproot the city at least. . . ." Is a distinction being made here between Eteocles and the city? Perhaps, instead, a distinction is being blurred, which only later becomes prominent. The curse at this point is threatening the whole city; private and civic are identified, and that may be why the curse is asked, along with the other gods, not to destroy the city. In the last pair of speeches in the shield scene, when it is becoming evident that the real conflict is the personal quarrel, a prayer of Polynices is reported, which forms an important contrast to Eteocles' earlier one. . . .

Polynices calls upon the native gods of Thebes, much as Eteocles does. That is probably intended as a mark of piety; but the phrase [*theous genethlious . . . patroias ges*] inevitably evokes the curse and the Erinys, the family's own divinities. Thus Polynices implicitly juxtaposes civic and individual gods as Eteocles did explicitly; but he does so to plead his case against his brother, not (like Eteocles) in the city's behalf. This is a mark of how the scope of the war has shrunk; Thebes' involvement in the conflict is no longer the central concern, even though Polynices prays as a Theban. The incongruity of his invocation of the city's gods when he is the aggressor only draws attention to the fact that the actual issue is between the two brothers. Thus Polynices' prayer seems to balance and shed light on the earlier one of Eteocles.

It is right at the break in the play, when Eteocles has learned who his opponent at the seventh gate will be, that the family's alienation from the gods becomes explicit, and the reason is the curse. . . .

In the scene which follows, the chorus suggest to Eteocles that the curse can be appeased with sacrifice. Wilamowitz dismisses this idea as "die Gesinnung des Ablasskramers." But sacrifice is the expression of the city's relations with the gods, and on it they have based their prayers for safety. Eteocles rejects this course, however; the entire family is so deeply enmeshed in the curse that there is no way out. The gods, he has said, leave a captured city. Though they will not depart from Thebes, they have abandoned his family:

> [We have already been abandoned by the gods some-
> how, and the boon from us perishing is admired, why
> then would we still fawn upon a destructive destiny.]

This is the rhetoric of desperation; the only favor the gods will accept from the family is its obliteration. The contrast with the city is sharply drawn.

If the city has its particular gods, so does the family. Apart from the Erinys, there are two gods with whom the family has a special relationship, and it is a vexed one. First there is Apollo. In line 691, the race of Laius is said to be "hated by Phoebus." As argued above, this is not because of Apollo's spite against Laius. In this line, [*stygethen/ hated thing*] recalls [*mega stygos/great hatred or abomination*] of line 653. The cursed family is hateful to all the gods, and to Apollo in particular; the nature of its fate is alien to his worship. In addition, he watches over the fulfillment of his oracle. His prophecies will bear fruit, not only in the case of Amphiaraus, but in regard to this family as well. The fatal battle takes place at the seventh gate under Apollo's supervision, and the number is appropriate, as line 800 indicates, for it is specially associated with the god. The Medicean scholiast explains that Apollo was born on the seventh day of the month. In fact, by Aeschylus's time consultations at Delphi took place regularly on the seventh of each month of the oracle's operation, to commemorate that event.

The other god whose position in the *Seven* is ambiguous is, of course, Ares. In terms of the war itself he has a double aspect. On the one hand he is the terrifying spirit of battle, throwing everything into confusion, the embodiment of imbalance and the particular deity of the Argives. They swear their oath by him. His blast drives the wave of Argives against Thebes. Hippomedon, like a Bacchant, is [*entheos Arei/possessed by Ares*]. And when a city is sacked, it is Ares who "pollutes reverence." On the other hand, he is the ancestor of the Thebans, [*palaichthon/ancient inhabitant*] who once loved the city well and to whom the chorus particularly appeal. It is symptomatic that these two facets of the god appear side by side in the parodos. To the Argives' Ares the city opposes its own special deity.

But Ares also appears in a third guise. In regard to the family, he is neither external threat nor beneficent ancestor, but the personification of internal division—literal division, for he is the arbiter of the brothers' dispute. The *Seven,* then, is a "drama full of Ares" in several senses, and Benardete only slightly exaggerates when he says that "*the* question" of the play is "[*Ti estin Ares?/what is Ares?*]"

The importance of Ares furnishes an example of how the various themes in the *Seven* are related to each other. In this case, the theme of the gods and the nautical imagery overlap. Early in the play, Ares is the source of the wind which hurls the wave of the enemy upon the city. Later, the wind which sweeps away the vessel of the family is its daimon or Oedipus's imprecations. Thus nautical language is applied to the family just as its true relations with the gods are made explicit. Ares himself disappears as the cause of the wind (that is, as the deity of warfare in general), but later reappears in a more specific capacity as the arbiter between the brothers. A third image, that of the lot, is thus brought into alignment with the other two.

Language of Debt and Commerce

The reciprocal relationship with its gods is one facet of the city's balanced life. It has a similar relationship with the earth. The latter is expressed at the beginning of the *Seven* in terms of a debt. The earth, says Eteocles, brought up the Thebans: [*pisto th' hopos genoisthe pros chreos tode/And that you be faithful in regard to this debt*]. Here commercial language is an expression of the city's way of life; but it comes to have a more specific application to the fate of the brothers.

It is used in the shield scene in connection with the war. The Theban champions are called "guarantors of a debt" ([*pherenguoi*]) who "stand before" the city to protect it. They are faithful to the obligation expressed in the prologue. Parthenopaeus, by contrast, is repaying his own debt of nurture to Argos and is no petty retailer of war.

Eteocles turns the boasts of Tydeus and Capaneus to advantage: [*Kai Twide Kerdei Kerdos allo Tik Tetal/and another profit is born to the profit for this man*]. This line evidently means that in Capaneus's case ([*Kai Twide*]) new profit ([*Kerdos allo*]—Capaneus's arrogance, which will anger Zeus) is being added; with interest to the profit already in hand ([*kerdei*]—Tydeus's boasts, which will be self-destructive). Eteocles is triumphant. The situation is different when he follows his exclamations over the fate of his family with the words:

> [But it is fitting neither to weep nor to wail, lest a lamentation more difficult to bear be born.]

There is no longer any question of profit, but of interest accruing in the form of a still more serious cause for lamentation—as in fact happens with his own and Polynices' deaths. In the subsequent exchange with the chorus, however, Eteocles does mention gain, and his language stands the whole notion of profit on its head. The curse sits near him: [*legousa kerdos proteron hysterou merou/saying profit [is] earlier than later doom*]. Winnington-Ingram plausibly suggests that [*Kerdos*] here should be connected with the same word in line 684 ([*monon gar Kerdos en tethnekosi/for there is only profit among the dead*], and that both refer to killing Polynices. "Kill him and then die"—it is a ghastly reciprocity.

The only gain the brothers can expect, then, is each other's murder, for as members of Laius's family they have been under an obligation to the curse. The development of commercial language culminates when, after the death of the brothers, the chorus observe that Oedipus's curse has exacted payment of the debt owed it, and the influence of Laius's transgression is felt in the background:

> [The votive speech from his father has exacted vengeance and has not failed; the disobedient plans of Laius have endured.]

The curse is the creditor, to whom the brothers' destruction has been due. It has shaped events, and any hope for gain on their part has been illusory.

But what of the city? Its guarantors have discharged their function faithfully, and it has not been ruined. When he announces Thebes' victory, the messenger's repetition of the commercial language associated with the champions contrasts sharply with the application of such language to the brothers' fate:

> [And the tower protects, and we have fortified the gates with champions, giving their pledge and fighting in single hand-to-hand combat.]

Themes Associated with the War

The themes used to characterize the war can be treated more summarily. As the scope of the war narrows, they gradually focus on the brothers and on the final result of the play. But at first they are associated with the Argive army and with the reaction its attack provokes in the city.

From start to finish, the *Seven* is pervaded by discordant and terrible noise. There is, first, the sound of the Argives as they advance—the clatter of their weapons, for example ([*ktypos*], or the neighing of their horses. Eteoclus shouts ([*boai*]) his boast, silently but unmistakably, in the letters on his shield (line 468). Between the two extremes that these examples represent lie many other harsh noises which issue from the Argives and create an impression of terrifying force. There is a corresponding confusion within the city, and the sounds of the maidens' panic answer those made by the enemy. Their first word in the parodos is [*threumai/I cry aloud*], and the dochmiacs there provide a fitting and impressive medium for their cries of terror. These shrieks are, without question, dangerous to the city. But it is interesting too that the sounds both outside and within the city combine to give a total picture of the confusion wrought by war. Then, when the conflict narrows to the fight between the brothers, the sounds of war give way to those of lamentation.

Perhaps the following pair of passages illustrates this best. The city, threatened by the enemy, groans from its roots in the earth. . . . But after the brothers' mutual murder, the city, the towers, and the plain groan again—now not in confusion or terror, but in sorrow. . . .

Similarly, the chorus's [*oxugooi litai/shrill-wailing prayers*] to the gods are replaced by the [*gooi/wailings*] of grief at the end.

In this play, Aeschylus often represents the sounds in terms of music. Haldane describes well his general use of this imagery:

> Thus Aeschylus found in the various types of music and song practised in his day a convenient set of symbols, the significance of which would be immediately apparent to his audience. Around each clustered associations of occasion, atmosphere, and emotion which could be counted upon to awaken a definite, predetermined response. With skillful manipulation such images could be used to focus a climax, to highlight a moment of conflict or irony or, linked together from scene to scene, to underline the pattern of a drama.

This is certainly what he does in the *Seven*. The Argives have on their horses and chariots noise-making devices which produce a grotesque distortion of music and which are themselves described as musical instruments. The chorus's songs are anything but harmonious. . . . Eteocles tries to induce them to sing the paean instead, the auspicious song chanted by Greek custom before a battle. But just as his own well-omened words in the shield scene issue in the fulfillment of the curse, so in the end music is again distorted. The chorus sing a lament over the brothers, and the curse raises its own shrill song of victory.

Related to the music is a strain of Dionysiac language in the play. The chorus depict their dirge in lines 835–39 as a Dionysiac song; it is actually an inversion of that cheerful music. Earlier in the play there are also traces of the Dionysiac. Hippomedon revels like a Bacchant, but he is inspired with Ares. Similarly, the chorus describe the noise of the Argives in words that are appropriate to Dionysus. [*Bremein/to roar*] and [*bromos/roaring*] occur several times. One of the titles of Dionysus was *Bromios*. They speak of the [*o tobos/din*] of the Argive chariots; the word is not inappropriate to the music of a flute. There is also a suggestion in line 214 that the chorus are like maenads . . .; what goads them, however, is not ecstasy but terror.

This language is part of the more comprehensive theme of madness. The latter is used in the play to link all the stages of the family curse. It has been remarked already that Laius's error was due to atê resulting from the curse. Oedipus in turn was in a rage when he cursed Eteocles and Polynices; he was [*blapsiphron/deranged*], and he uttered the curse [*mainomenai kradiai/with maddened heart*]. In the third generation the curse has brought on the war; the Argives boast [*mainomenai phreni/with maddened mind*]. And in the ending of the quarrel, the brothers kill one another [*eridi mainomenai/in maddened strife*]. Eteocles refers to the letters on Polynices' shield with scornful alliteration . . .: And he describes his brother as a [*phos pantolmos phrenas/ a man all-daring in his wits*]. The chorus term his own determination to fight Polynices an irrational desire, a product of hate. It is, therefore, no accident that the iron which is to be the arbiter between the brothers is called [*homophron/savage-minded*]. The madness of war is but an external sign of a mental imbalance within this family which has infected the whole city. Finally, in the parodos the "spear-shaken *aether*" rages with the violence of war . . . , but at the end of the play the chorus's hearts rave

with grief. . . . This contrast marks the shift from general warfare to the curse's particular result.

Divination and Prophecy

The outcome of the war cannot be foreseen. But from the beginning of the play there is what seems to be an effort either to predict or to shape its course. Various forms of divination, for example, are mentioned. In the prologue there is the seer with his ornithomancy, who has informed Eteocles that the Argives are planning an attack. There is a sort of retrospective oneiromancy, as Eteocles realizes, in the light of his new situation, the truth of some dreams he has had. The mention of Ares' dice may be a reference to cleromancy; as will be argued in the next chapter, the lot plays an important role in the *Seven*.

Finally, cledonomancy, the gathering of omens from chance utterances, is prominent, especially in the shield scene. Words in the play are effective, as Cameron says, "in the need for silence at solemn moments so as to avoid ill-omened chance utterance, in the manipulation of chance utterances to the advantage of the one who accepts them, in cursing, and in the invocation or acceptance of the omen implicit in a name." Names are particularly important. There is a consistent feeling that a name ought to reveal something about its bearer. This is a common Greek belief. But against this background there is special point when Amphiaraus emphasizes the component parts of the name Polynices, or when the chorus play on the names of both brothers. . . .

Divination and attention to words are not, however, the only means in the play of straining toward the future. At several points, alternatives are posed which give what seem in each case the likely results of the action. These shift somewhat and become more specific as possibilities are gradually eliminated and the play moves toward *the* final outcome. Eteocles utters the first pair of choices in the prologue. Both of these possibilities come true in the end, though neither is an accurate forecast in itself. The outcome is really a third possibility not contemplated at the beginning of the play. Thebes *does* fare well, and at the same time Eteocles *is* "hymned"—in mourning.

The Argives are more accurate when they vow either to sack the city or to spill their blood. The latter is what happens. Similarly, the second term of Eteocles' prediction in lines 477–79 is fulfilled in the event. Both of these examples refer to the war, and Thebes' survival can be in no serious doubt after the fourth pair of speeches in the shield scene. But as the play moves to its climax and the focus shifts to the brothers, Polynices utters his own oath:

> [[He asks in prayer] to be brought together with you and in slaying you to die nearby, or if you live (you who drive one from his home and are in this way a dishonorer), to pay you back in the same manner with banishment.]

This is devastating accuracy. The natural alternatives would be "to drive you out or die in the attempt." Polynices, it seems, has slipped into a way of speaking which will turn out to have been prophetic.

The concern throughout the play with divining the future culminates in line 808, where the chorus, anticipating the news they are about to hear, exclaim, [*mantis eimi ton kakon/I am a prophet of evil things*]. Thus prophecy has focused on the specific horror of the result. Similarly, the Erinys of Oedipus has a particular kind of foresight, for a little earlier she was called [*kakomantis/prophesying evil*]. Like Apollo's oracle, the Erinys possesses her own logic, which is unimpeachable, though most easily followed in hindsight. Her inexorable procedure according to this logic is reflected in the imagery of allotment, which will be examined next.

Source: William G. Thalmann, "Imagery I: The City," in *Dramatic Art in Aeschylus's "Seven against Thebes,"* Yale University Press, 1978, pp. 31–61.

Helen H. Bacon

Hecht and Bacon provide a brief history and summary of the play and the characters in this essay.

I

With some important exceptions, scholars and translators, from the nineteenth century onwards, have been virtually at one in their indifference to *Seven Against Thebes;* an indifference which has been deflected from time to time only into overt hostility and contempt. The play has been accused of being static, undramatic, ritualistic, guilty of an interpolated and debased text, archaic, and, in a word, boring. The present translators find themselves in profound disagreement with such assessments, and cherish a slight hope that the translation offered here—which is also an interpretation, as any translation must be—will help restore to the play some of the dramatic and literary interest it deserves to have even for those with no knowledge of Greek.

This translation has aimed at literal accuracy insofar as that was possible within the limitations of our own imaginations and understanding; our English text departs from the original mainly through that sort of extrapolation we have thought useful to a modern audience not likely to be acquainted with all the minor Greek deities, for example, or with their ritual attributes. Thus, where Phobos alone will do in the original, here he is identified as the god of fear. This kind of expansion, as well as complete independence from the Greek of the English lineation, has made our text some three hundred lines longer than the original. But we are confident—as confident as our scruples and a certain fitting modesty will allow us to be—that in this we have not violated the tone or dramatic intention of the play. A scholarly defense of such liberties as we may be thought to have taken will appear, as it ought to, elsewhere.

Still, it must be admitted that even to the most sympathetic of readers *Seven Against Thebes* suffers under a special handicap. It is the last play of a trilogy of which the first two plays have been lost. It is, of course, impossible accurately to reconstruct the enormous dramatic and linguistic forces that must have been contrived and set in motion to culminate in this play; but one may perhaps guess at the magnitude of the loss if one were to think of the *Oresteia* as surviving only in the text of the *Eumenides.* We do know the names of the first two plays of this trilogy: *Laios* and *Oedipus.* And what we know of the ancient legends and sagas of the Curse of the house of Laios, of the traditional lore concerning the founding of Thebes by Kadmos, and of the subsequent history of the city, may provide us with some of the background with which Aeschylus approached this final drama in the series.

II

Like the "history" of the Trojan War, Theban "history" was preserved in epic poems, now lost, but almost as familiar to fifth-century Athenians as the *Iliad* and *Odyssey.* Aeschylus could count on his audience knowing not only his specific shaping of the stories of Laios and Oedipus in the two earlier plays, but also the broad outlines of the whole story of Thebes as preserved in the poetic tradition. It is a story of violence and wrath from beginning to end.

Kadmos, the founder of the city and the royal house, came from Tyre seeking his sister Europa. He killed a dragon that guarded a spring at what would become the site of Thebes and, at Athena's direction, sowed the dragon's teeth in earth. The teeth sprouted as a crop of armed men who, when Kadmos pelted them with stones, began to murder each other. The five survivors of this fratricidal battle, the so-called "sown men" (Spartoi), were the ancestors of the people of Thebes. The lost epics went on to tell the stories of Laios and his descendants, but did not end, as the trilogy does, with the defeat of the Argive army, the death in battle of the army's leaders, and the fratricide of the sons of Oedipus. They pursued a narrative that took up the story again ten years later when, just before the Trojan War, the sons of the leaders of the Argives returned for their revenge at the head of another Argive army, and completely destroyed Thebes. This sack of Thebes by the Epigonoi, as the sons of the seven Argive captains were called, was one of the most firmly fixed elements of the tradition: among the famous cities of Greece, only Thebes is missing from the catalogue of the ships in the *Iliad.* Aeschylus' audience could not fail to associate the many hints of future disaster for Thebes appearing throughout this play with the total destruction of that city by the sons of the "Seven."

The principal mythological figures of *Seven Against Thebes,* Ares, the Fury, the Curse (also referred to in the plural as Curses, perhaps suggesting the separate words of the imprecation), Dike, and Apollo, interact in a context taken for granted by Aeschylus' audience, but which for us perhaps requires some explanation. Ares, the Fury, and the personified Curse of the house of Laios (the Curse of which Laios and Oedipus were the victims and which in turn Oedipus laid upon his two sons) represent the forces which are let loose when Dike, the personification of the fundamental principle of right and order, is violated. The trilogy dramatized a chain of outrages (outlined in this play in the third choral song, . . . the Fury chorus) starting with Laios' defiance of Apollo's word—which said that if Laios refrained from begetting offspring the city would be safe. The traditional reason for this prohibition was that Laios had kidnaped, violated, and murdered the little son of his host and friend, Pelops. For this violation of the sacred tie of hospitality, childlessness was a fitting punishment. Like the banquet of Thyestes in *Agamemnon,* this, or a similar outrage, was probably the crime behind the crimes in *Laios.* To these acts of violence, Laios added the attempt to destroy his own son, Oedipus, the child of forbidden intercourse. And violence begets violence. Oedipus killed his father and married his mother; his sons, by an act of outrage against him (we do not know which of several versions of their crime Aeschylus used in *Oedipus*), provoked their father's Curse, and they then attempted to take possession of their mother city by

> AESCHYLUS TAKES THE RICHEST POSSIBLE ADVANTAGE OF THESE AMBIGUITIES IN *SEVEN AGAINST THEBES;* AND BEHIND THE AMBIGUITIES, OF COURSE, LIE THE UNRESOLVED PROBLEMS OF FREE WILL AND JUSTICE. THAT IS TO SAY, DOES A MAN CHOOSE HIS LOT, OR IS IT CHOSEN FOR HIM? DOES HE GET WHAT HE DESERVES, AND BY WHAT OR WHOSE STANDARDS? WHILE THESE PROBLEMS ARE WOVEN INTO THE BACKGROUND OF ALMOST EVERY TRAGEDY, IN THIS DRAMA WE ARE MADE TO TAKE PARTICULAR NOTICE OF THEM."

violence (Aeschylus in the lament makes plain that Eteokles too has used force on Thebes) and ended by murdering each other. Dike represents the sanctity of the basic relationships between god and man, host and guest, parent and child, brother and brother, relationships which Laios and his descendants defied. When these are violated Dike is violated.

The Fury, wrath (her Greek name Erinys is derived from *eris,* wrath or strife), and Ares, violence and hostility, are the instruments with which Zeus comes to the defense of Dike, but they are in turn the cause of new outrages in an apparently endless sequence. The Curse is another expression of the same psychological fact. It is the prayer of a victim, which is implemented by Ares and the Fury in their capacity as enforcers of Dike. Where this complex of forces occurs Delphic Apollo will always be found as well, in his role as restorer of harmony and health, the purifier from all kinds of contagion. Only when the miasma of violated Dike has been cleansed away does the Fury cease raging and become the gentle cherisher that she is at the end of the *Oresteia.* Though in *Seven Against Thebes* she appears only as a destroyer, it should not be forgotten that she destroys in defense of the helpless and in order that life and the social order that sustains life shall be cherished. Her contradictoriness is the contradictoriness of woman—the tender mother ready to kill in defense of those she cherishes. Several images and figures in this play express this enigmatic quality of the female—the moon, Hekate, Artemis, the land of Thebes, the Sphinx. . . .

An Athenian audience would also have recognized the parallels in *Seven Against Thebes* with their own recent history, and responded to them with a special set of feelings and values. The return of an exiled ruler to claim his rights with the support of a foreign army, a not infrequent occurrence in Greece, was regarded with the same kind of religious horror as was felt toward attacks on parents. *Seven Against Thebes* was produced in 467 B.C. Twenty-three years earlier, in 490 B.C., Hippias, the exiled son of the tyrant, Peisistratos, and himself a former tyrant, landed at Marathon with the Persian army, prepared to be reinstated as ruler of the Athenians. According to Herodotos, whose account is later than our play and could even have been influenced by it, the night before the landing Hippias dreamed that he slept with his mother. At first he interpreted this hopefully, as a sign that he would pass his old age peacefully in Athens. However, when he landed there was another portent. He was seized with a fit of sneezing and coughing, and, being an old man, coughed out one of his teeth, which fell upon his native soil and could not be found again. He then said, ''This land is not ours and we will not be able to conquer it. My tooth has my whole share of it.'' Herodotos adds that this statement was Hippias' interpretation of the dream. In this story, as in *Seven Against Thebes*, the attack on the parent land is equated with incest, and its consequence is that the attacker receives only a token share of his native soil. Hippias received as much Attic earth as his tooth possessed, Eteokles and Polyneices each as much Theban earth as it takes to bury a man. Whether this story of Hippias is older than Aeschylus' play, or came into being as a result of it, its existence suggests that the Athenians would have understood the play in the light of their own great national crisis. It also suggests that parallels between the crimes of Oedipus and those of his sons would have been more immediately obvious to the Athenians than they are to a modern audience.

III

The action of *Seven Against Thebes* we conceive to be profoundly unified and profoundly dramatic. It unfolds in four stages, of which the Fury is the organizing principle. In the first stage the Fury is set in motion when Eteokles calls on her in conjunction with his father's Curse, to defend the city which is being attacked by one of her own children. In his prayer Eteokles seems clearly to assume that if any violation against Dike has been or is being committed it is by his brother, Polyneices; he seems to have forgotten or blocked out of his mind the earlier crimes performed jointly with his brother that brought down on both their heads their father's Curse; and seems as well to have forgotten that his exiled brother has as much right as he to be king in Thebes. In the second stage the Fury comes to the defense of Dike by implementing the Curse. She rages unchecked as Eteokles decides to meet his brother in single combat. In the third stage, Dike is temporarily re-established and the Fury seems to subside. The inheritance is justly divided when the brothers, in death, are apportioned their equal shares of Theban earth. The plays ends with a new outbreak of the Fury as the magistrates of Thebes reopen the conflict by refusing burial to Polyneices—refusing him, that is, his just share of the inheritance—and in so doing once more implicate the city in the fate of the house of Laios, edging Thebes and her entire population one step nearer to their ultimate destruction at the hands of the Epigonoi.

Modern scholars, with a few notable exceptions, regard this last scene, which dramatizes the final stage, as a fourth-century interpolation whose purpose is to bring the play into line with the popular Sophoclean version of the aftermath of the brothers' deaths. They see no justification for introducing a new speaking role in the person of Antigone, who raises what they consider to be a problem new to this play and wholly outside the dramatic unity of its action: the problem of the burial of Polyneices, after the conflict of the brothers has been resolved. Yet the scene is integrated with the entire design of the play; and to an audience familiar with the Theban epics, the second song of the Chorus, which visualizes the sack of the city, is not an unfulfilled fear but a prophecy of her ultimate fate. And that prophecy is brought nearer to its consummation in this final scene when the city brings upon herself the promise of total annihilation by repeating Eteokles' repudiation of Dike. The scale of the tragedy is enlarged, pity and fear intensified by this fresh outbreak of the Fury. It is not a new problem but a new stage and development of the old problem: how to allay the wrath let loose in Thebes by the chain of outrages stemming from

Laios' original violation of Dike. It is a wrath that spreads from the individual members of the house of Laios until it includes, first, the magistrates of Thebes rising up to deny Polyneices his inheritance, and ultimately all the inhabitants of the city that is to be brought to destruction; a wrath that promises a countering wrath, a continued struggle to an exhausted and demolishing end.

IV

The language of *Seven Against Thebes* is markedly concerned with noise, and with two kinds of noise in particular: the noise of battle and the noise of lamentation, that is, of strife and of weeping. At the start of the play, the noise of battle is outside the walls of Thebes, and the noise of lamentation (in the form of the first choral song) within. By the time the drama is over, these two noises will come to be identified with the two contending brothers, Eteokles and Polyneices; and not merely because one has been inside and the other outside the walls, but because of their names and their fates, as will appear. Eteokles is more than merely ''justifiably angered'' by the fears and lamentations of the Chorus: he is enraged and unhinged by them, and proceeds to some quite extraordinary calumnies upon womankind in general. His nominal grounds for wrath are that the Chorus, by their womanly weakness, are undermining manly courage and endangering military morale inside the city. There is a certain plausibility to this, to which, after all, the Chorus acquiesce. But Eteokles' rage seems so extravagant that we might at first suppose that he is himself afraid of losing his nerve. Since, in the event, this does not prove to be the case, there must be some other reason for it. And, indeed, as the drama unfolds, we come to see that this play is not merely the culmination but the terrible re-enactment of the tragedies of Laios and Oedipus, of disobedience, parricide, and incest. And Eteokles' misogyny might be not only an unconscious sense of his inheritance, but a fear that he is doomed to repeat it. He is determined not to. Nevertheless, he does.

As in the case of his father, he is called upon to protect Thebes from what appears to be an outward danger. And, as in his father's case, he seems to undertake this in a manly way. The city of Thebes and its outlying pastures and folds are consistently spoken of in maternal terms, in metaphors of a mother who nurtured, cherished, and brought up her sons, and who must therefore not be violated. The violent desire for exclusive possession of the mother is a tragedy Oedipus unconsciously acted out, be-

coming blind that he might see what he could not see with his eyes. The violent desire for the exclusive possession of the mother land, the unwillingness of either to be content with a lesser or equal share, drives Oedipus' two sons, who are also his brothers, to murder each other, each one blindly believing justice to be on his side. And each, by murdering his brother, sheds his father's blood. As in the case of Oedipus, a problem is posed, a riddle must be untangled, in order that the city may be saved. For Eteokles this is, in fact, not one riddle but seven. These are the devices on the shields of the seven champions who attack the city.

It may be worth attending to this scene in some detail, for it has often been singled out as one of the most tedious blemishes of the play, and it constitutes about a third of the whole. In hearing the report of the Scout and undertaking to construe in terms of magic and numinous power the nature of each of seven successive threats to Thebes, and in proposing a counter-magic for the defense of the city, Eteokles is taking upon himself the role of seer, as once his father did. Yet even before these seven opportunities for divination occur, Eteokles has several times been warned; what he is at pains to conceal from himself is precisely who he is, the nature of his inheritance, and the possibility that he cannot see everything clearly and for what it is. And while the Scout punctiliously addresses him as ''most fittingly king of the Kadmeians,'' the Chorus, with more intimacy and greater point, address him as ''son of Oedipus.'' Moreover, in their high-strung emotional debate with him, they defend their devotion to and utter reliance on the gods by observing that not only are the gods more powerful than men, but that the gods alone can assist humankind when its vision and understanding are obscured. These are implicit warnings against blindness and impiety, and they are augmented by the off-stage but telling presences of two genuine seers and diviners, who are also priests: Teiresias and Amphiaraos. Nevertheless, as commander of the defending troops, Eteokles does not hesitate to assume the role of seer.

There are seven contending champions, and therefore, seven riddles (though there is in addition one great and central riddle, concerning Eteokles' name, which lies at the very heart of the play, and which we will come to later). In general, it may be said that Eteokles conceives these riddles as applying purely to the fate of the contending champions and, by extension, to the fate of Thebes; never does he seem to suppose that the riddles might have any bearing upon his own fate. It may be added that with most of the defending champions he nominates, Eteokles takes pains to advertise the distinction of their genealogies as well as their military prowess and excellence of character. This is, of course, quite in accordance with heroic tradition. But in emphasizing the nativity—the legitimacy, as it were—of these local sons of the mother land, their title by birthright to be her defenders, he appears never to consider that this is a right he must, by the same token, share equally with his own brother. And the fact that two of the defending champions, Hyperbios and Aktor, are themselves brothers, does nothing to remind him of this.

1. The first of the attacking champions is Tydeus. We learn that he abuses and insults a priest of Apollo, Amphiaraos. Yet, while Eteokles does not hesitate to accuse Tydeus of impiety (as indeed he does in the case of every attacker but one—and that one worth noting), neither does he scruple himself to abuse and insult Amphiaraos when later the priest, the true seer, presents himself as the sixth of the champions outside the walls. It is true that Eteokles cannot quite bring himself to accuse so unblemished a man as Amphiaraos of impiety; but the priest is charged with blindness and bad judgment, which Eteokles might do well to consider with respect to himself. And in abusing Amphiaraos, he is imitating the impious enemy, Tydeus. In addition to the dark night (ignorance, inability to see) which is Tydeus' device, the moon, associated with Hekate, goddess of the three ways, might serve to remind Eteokles of the beginning of his father's catastrophe, the curse of the house of Laios, the penalty for blindness. Tydeus' helmet is triple-crested, a part of the riddle to which we will return in due course. Most importantly, Eteokles proclaims that his defending champion, Melanippos, is a blood-relative of Dike, "goddess of all orders, of justice human and divine," and that she will favor him. If Dike is to side with the defending forces, she cannot at the same time side with the attackers, as from the claims of Polyneices it appears she does, unless she is to play some impartial role, and deal with the claims of both sides as being equal.

2. The second of the attackers, Kapaneus, the giant, is an enlargement, a grotesque exaggeration, of the impiety of Tydeus; he defies all the gods, and Zeus in particular. As opposed to Tydeus, whose emblem was darkness, Kapaneus' device is a naked man armed with a flaming torch (which is light and knowledge, the ability to see, to construe the truth), but this light has been perverted into a destructive weapon, intended to reduce the city to ashes (just as the Chorus has feared and prophesied). It might therefore be a warning to Eteokles in his self-assumed office of seer.

3. The third is Eteoklos, whose name is so close to the protagonist's as surely to invite a moment's thought. He is clearly "Eteokles Beyond the Walls," the attacking double of the defender; Eteokles, by this extension, is both outside and inside the city, and therefore it is folly to fear, to observe, to take precautions chiefly against the danger of what is outside. Here is a representation of Eteokles as his own worst enemy, and, pointedly, he has nothing whatever to say about the character of this attacker. Whereas in every other case he is quick to bring accusations of blasphemy, impiety, and folly, here he moves swiftly to name his chosen defender, and makes unusually brisk work of the matter, turning instantly to the next contender.

4. This is Hippomedon, who bears Typhon, the earth god, on his shield. Now, from the very first speech of Eteokles, the earth has been seen as a nourishing parent, child-bearer, kindly provider. But just as the Fury has what seems to be a double nature, or at least two aspects of a single nature, so here is the earth transformed, represented by a monstrous offspring, "breathing fire, black smoke, sister of glittering fire, pouring from his mouth," the universal tomb. This is not unlike the earlier vision of the Chorus.

5. Parthenopaios, "savage-minded" but with a boyish beauty, himself suggests the two aspects of the Fury. And his device, the Sphinx, not only recalls the whole Theban and family saga, but specifically points it toward the problem of knowing who you are. It is declared of Parthenopaios that he reverses his blade "above god and his own eyes," which is to say that he puts violence, military glory, and ambition above piety and knowledge; and it recalls the theme of blindness.

6. The case of Amphiaraos is rich and complicated. He is, first, a priest of Apollo, the god who is foreteller, knower of what awaits, who long ago warned Laios of what would happen if he begot a child, and who warned the youthful Oedipus of his parricidal and incestuous fate. These facts are all clearly known to the Chorus, and therefore may be supposed to be known to Eteokles as well. As the god's priest, Amphiaraos is not merely a holy man, one who wishes not to seem but in fact to be the best, undeceived by appearances and undeceiving; he also has special access to the wisdom of the god. He

clearly denounces the impiety, violence, and violation that Tydeus and Polyneices are about to offer the city, and in the most condemnatory terms; he speaks of this in the highly charged language and metaphor of rape and incest. Eteokles' answer to this riddle is noticeably weak and evasive. Perhaps that is because there is no device for him to perform magic with. But possibly the true piety and self-knowledge of this man has come home to him. In any case, he makes Amphiaraos guilty by association, and, while not doubting the priest's piety—which, incidentally, consists in part in his refusal to attack the city—all but calls him foolish and blind for getting mixed up with wicked men against his better judgment, that is to say, ignorantly. Yet if, as Eteokles himself says, Apollo does not lie, then all the prophecies of disaster which have been accumulating throughout the drama, and which Eteokles has now been given six chances to fathom and to attempt to avert, are obviously pointing to something he does not see, yet knows to be inexorable.

7. At last, the brother, mighty Polyneices. His claim is plain, violent and sexual.

> He declares he will scale and bestride the walls,
> proclaimed lord and subjugator of the land.

He makes explicit his equality with Eteokles (which Eteokles has never acknowledged):

> he will fight you hand to hand;
> and either, in killing you, lie dead beside you,
> or else drive you into dishonored exile
> just as you forced such banishment on him.

The insistence on ''equality'' in Polyneices' boast should be noticed. He does not propose, as he might, to kill his brother and take upon himself the kingship; rather he says that either they shall both die, or they shall change places with each other. And just as Eteokles has done, he calls upon the gods of the race of his own land, entreating their support. This exclusive claim to the motherland as a sexual possession is stated at its clearest in Polyneices' device.

> A stately woman guides forward a warrior
> in full armor who is hammered out in gold.
> She says she is Dike—goddess of all orders,
> human and divine—
> and inscribed there are these words:
> ''I shall bring this man to his harbor,
> and he shall enjoy his father's city,
> shall tumble and make free with his house.''

The great blow, and the final irony, for Eteokles, is not that his brother should be revealed as a champion, for it was generally known that his brother was among the attacking troops, and no doubt the entire siege has been undertaken at his behest and with an eye to his restoration to the kingship. Clearly, then, he could have been expected to play a major role in the attack. What unhinges Eteokles is in part the claim that Dike is aligned with the forces outside the walls, and with his brother in particular, since he has already assumed that she has allied herself with the defenders. Her impartiality in this, as well perhaps as the discovery that Eteokles is not only inside but outside the walls in the person of Eteoklos, reveal to us at last the true equality of the two brothers in their inheritance, their fate, their shared guilt of origin and of ambition.

But this sense of equality Eteokles is determined to resist to the end, and while he feels he has been mocked and manipulated by fate, he goes to meet his brother in a frenzy of blindness, a man fully armed, turned into iron, himself a weapon. And the Chorus, perhaps recalling the warning that appeared with the very first of the attackers, the triple-crested helmet of Tydeus, proceeds, in the next ode, to recall the first of all the warnings to this blind family:

> Three times the Lord Apollo
> in the midmost Pythian navel,
> the prophetic center, spoke:
> If Laios were to live
> childless, without issue,
> then the city would be safe.

And they echo the present storm outside the walls:

> Like a plunging and storm-agitated sea, disaster
> drives the wave;
> first one wave falls, a second rises up,
> a third, three-crested, crashes at the stern
> of the city in angry foam.
> Between our perilous home
> and total jeopardy,
> our hull is the mere width of the city walls.

While it is clear enough that, in the first instance, these waves represent the hordes of attacking troops, they have also by this time come to refer to the three destructive and self-destructive generations of the house of Laios, each of which in turn put Thebes in peril, and were themselves the whole cause of her troubles, and, in effect, her attackers.

V

Like Oedipus, whose name means both ''knowing foot'' and ''swollen foot,'' the sons of Oedipus have names which express their fates. The applicability of Polyneices' name, ''full of strife,'' to his actions as the leader of a foreign army attacking his native city is reasonably clear. Amphiaraos, Eteokles, and finally the Chorus, all brood over it in the section of the play that leads up to Eteokles' climactic decision to meet his brother in single combat. The etymologically correct meaning of Eteokles is "justly famed" (from *eteos,* just, true, and *kleos,* fame), and in the argument with the Chorus about whether or not he will go to the seventh gate, Eteokles dwells on fame and honor as though, in deciding to confront his brother, he hoped to implement this meaning of his name. However, another possible meaning of Eteokles, "truly bewept" or "true cause of weeping" (combining *eteos* with *klaio,* weep), is fearfully suggested in Eteokles' opening speech, and alluded to with increasing dread throughout the play. It suggests to him a fate which he tries with all his powers to evade; hence his prohibition of weeping to the Chorus, and his own refusal to weep when he feels that fate has pointed him toward fratricide at the seventh gate. And just as the measures Oedipus took to avoid the fate spelled out for him at Delphi nevertheless brought about its complete fulfillment, so Eteokles' attempt to avoid the fulfillment of this second, more ominous meaning of his name results in its implementation; as even he himself perhaps begins to recognize when he says,

> let the generations of Laios go down to
>   the last man,
> blown wind-wracked along the weeping river
>   of Hades.

In the act of killing his brother he finds the answer to the riddle of his own identity and fate, a riddle posed by the double meaning of his name. The second, or buried meaning, "true cause of weeping," "truly bewept," is literally acted out as the Chorus of Theban women, joined by Antigone and Ismene, perform their lament over the bodies of the brothers who have murdered each other. At this point it is clear that the names and fates of the brothers are interchangeable. Reconciliation and total equality are achieved together. Polyneices is just as "truly bewept" in this scene as Eteokles. In the preceding scene the Chorus warns Eteokles,

> do not take on the violence of your brother
> of evil name and fame . . .

But by the end of the scene Eteokles has done just that. In deciding to meet his brother at the seventh gate he becomes the counterpart of Ares, the emblem of strife in the house of Laios.

Both in imagery and action the play is an elucidation and dramatic unfolding of these two names. The storm of strife, presided over by Ares and the Fury, is realized in the Argive army outside the walls, and in the Chorus's fearful visualization of the final destruction of Thebes in their second song. The storm of weeping is realized in the Chorus's entrance song as well as in the final lament.

VI

There are many texts, both ancient and modern, that maintain, with elegiac eloquence, that it is the lot of mankind to be born, to suffer, and to die. However sagely we may assent to this universal condition of existence, no particular man likes to think that this is the governing limit of his own life; and when he speaks of his lot, though he may acknowledge it as a limited one, he is inclined at the same time to feel that it entails certain rights and prerogatives, that it is truly and only his, and not to be shared by anyone else. It is therefore associated most easily with what he comes to regard as his just due, his personal fortune, a wealth, either earned or inherited, though that wealth may be expressed in any number of ways, such as strength or courage or a gift for music or telling jokes.

Aeschylus takes the richest possible advantage of these ambiguities in *Seven Against Thebes;* and behind the ambiguities, of course, lie the unresolved problems of free will and justice. That is to say, does a man choose his lot, or is it chosen for him? Does he get what he deserves, and by what or whose standards? While these problems are woven into the background of almost every tragedy, in this drama we are made to take particular notice of them. The first speech of the Scout recounts the drawing of lots. It appears that both Eteokles and Polyneices, while realizing that a part of their inheritance must include their father's Curse, seem also to feel that it includes title to the kingship of Thebes. As for the Curse itself, Eteokles at least seems to feel, when at last he is brought to acknowledge that it cannot be evaded, that it is confined purely to the prophecy that the sons of Oedipus shall divide his wealth with a sword; that is to say, he thinks of the Curse as something laid upon his brother and himself by his father, not as something laid upon his grandfather, his father, and the two brothers in their turn, for the original and continuing violations and crimes of the house. The father's wealth, for which the brothers are prepared to fight to the death, is the city of Thebes, its land, its fecund, life-giving sustenance. What they actually win in their duel is just enough of that land to be buried in. Yet the land is truly a part of their wealth, and indeed of the wealth of all the inhabitants of Thebes; it is life itself. To the

Chorus, who are women, this appears to be much clearer than it is to the two ambitious brothers. The Chorus sing movingly about the richness and fertility of the land, and the horror of its despoliation; and their sympathy with the land might perhaps derive from their sharing with it a common gender. At the same time, and perhaps for the same reason, they conceive human life itself as being a form of wealth:

> Our city's wealth of men
> climbs to the battlements.

And, again, later

> The city's wealth,
> this heavy freight of men, this swollen horde
> must, from the stern, now be cast overboard.

That, as in the Book of Jonah, a forfeit must be paid, some wealth rendered up to protect and preserve the remainder, the mariners on the ship to Tarshish or the inhabitants of Thebes, appears to these women a natural if terrible part of the economy of justice; life must be paid out that life may be sustained. For the two brothers it means, with a disastrous, ultimate irony, that the wealth for which they fight is precisely what they must forfeit: their lives.

Source: Anthony Hecht and Helen H. Bacon, Introduction to *Seven against Thebes*, in *Seven against Thebes*, by Aeschylus, Oxford University Press, 1973, pp. 3–17.

T. G. Tucker

Tucker introduces the play by discussing its structure, as well as the history of the time.

Though we do not demand of a modern drama that it should convey a definite moral or political lesson, and though we should not be too exacting in this respect when we deal with the corresponding form of art in antiquity, it is nevertheless a notorious truth that the early Greek poet, and not least the dramatic poet, was commonly regarded—and regarded himself—as an exponent of religious, ethical, and political wisdom. In its primary purpose a tragedy was doubtless a composition of art, intended for the public entertainment on its more serious side; but it was meanwhile expected of the tragedian that he should 'improve the occasion' and play the part of teacher to the audience. The stage Euripides is not expressing simply his individual opinion, when he maintains in the *Frogs* of Aristophanes that poets can only claim admiration. . . .

The traditional [*sophia/wisdom*] of the poet is to show itself not merely in the varied lore for

> IF THE FUNCTION OF TRAGEDY IS TO EVOKE KEEN SENSATIONS OF [*ELEOS KAI PHOBOS/ PITY AND FEAR*], WE MUST ESTIMATE THE SUCCESS OF A PIECE, NOT BY THE STANDARD OF OUR OWN SOCIAL, MORAL AND RELIGIOUS CONCEPTIONS, BUT BY THAT OF THE ATHENIANS IN REGARD TO THE SAME MATTERS."

which he has to thank Mnemosyne, the mother of the Muses, but also in the [*gnomai/opinions* and *paraineseis/exhortations*] which are to be expected of his more profound thought and keener insight. His function is not only [*To poiein/make poetry*], but also [*To chresta didaskein/teaching good things*]. Most obviously valuable, and most readily appreciated, was wise admonition applied to contemporary circumstance. When Athens was in sore straits just before the end of the Peloponnesian war, Dionysus seeks to bring back a tragic poet from Hades. . . . And, when Aeschylus has been chosen and is departing to the upper world, the prayer is made that he may be the means of suggesting

> [. . .good plans of good and great things for the city.]

In writing the *Septem* Aeschylus duly performs this function of admonisher. But while the general and permanent moral lesson involved in the fate of the sons of Oedipus is obvious, there was also conveyed a special political lesson with a contemporary reference, a lesson so little obtruded that it has apparently escaped the notice of commentators. When Dionysus asks in the *Frogs*

> [and what did you do, Aeschylus, that you taught them to be so noble. Speak!]

the poet is made to reply

> [I made drama—full of Ares. . . .]

that drama being

> [. . .the Seven against Thebes, and when each and every man saw it, he would have loved to be destructive.]

And doubtless something might be caught of that *aura* of valour which so peculiarly pervaded the piece, and which suggested to Gorgias this apt description 'full of martial spirit.' Besides dramatically enforcing his invariable warning against [*hybris/pride*] and [*To agan/excess*] in any shape, Aeschylus does indeed stimulate Athenian manhood with the desire [*daioi einei/to be destructive*]. But he meanwhile 'improves the occasion' in behalf of a debated public policy, or one which at least required the spur. This was the policy initiated by Themistocles, continued by Cimon, and accomplished by Pericles; namely, the policy of fortifying Athens with such completeness that it might thenceforth be secure against assault, whether from barbarian or from hostile Greek. To suppose this purpose included in the 'wisdom' of the play is no idle fancy. The date of the *Septem* is B.C. 467. The date of the commencement of Cimon's wall of the Acropolis is B.C. 468. Themistocles had previously built the new (if hasty) [*peribolos/enclosure*] of Athens, had fortified the Peiraeus, and had probably devised a larger scheme, which was delayed, and doubtless in part discredited, by his fall and exile in B.C. 472. There were no doubt financial difficulties also. The spoils of the battle of Eurymedon supplied Cimon with the means to accomplish the work upon the Acropolis which is associated with his name. According to Plutarch he also commenced the building of the Long Walls, although the actual carrying out of that supremely important work was left for Pericles (B.C. 460–458).

It is manifest that for some time before and after the production of the *Septem* the question of the nature and extent of the fortifications of Athens was one of chief public prominence. Nor could it be otherwise. In B.C. 480 not even the Acropolis, much less the larger city, had been defensible against the Persians. The Athenians had been compelled to take refuge within their 'wooden walls.' In the following year Mardonius had completed the destruction of the city. No one knew when such an experience might be repeated. Nor was assurance against the Peloponnesians much greater than that against Persia. Far-sighted statesmen with the large conceptions of a Themistocles or a Cimon perceived what was necessary. But, as on similar occasions ancient and modern, the more far-sighted the conception, the more difficulty may be found in persuading the body politic to adopt it comprehensively. Especially is this the case when the execution involves heavy financial burdens. That the Athenians required no little pressure of persuasion is manifest, first, from the delay in carrying out the full scheme (whether it be due to Themistocles or to Cimon), second, from such indications as that afforded by Plato, who refers to a speech delivered by Pericles in favour of building the Long Walls. For the sake of brevity historians speak of Themistocles or Cimon or Pericles as doing this or that; yet these greater men were but agents of the will of the people, even though they may first have been the moulders of that will. It was but human nature that the eagerness displayed immediately after the Persian invasion should diminish as the younds of that invasion healed.

In the *Septem* Aeschylus is indubitably lending his aid to the formation of public opinion in support of the Cimonian policy of fortification. He is insisting upon the text 'Trust in the gods, but see to your walls.' Though the scene of the action is in Cadmea, the language is carefully adapted to Athens. If Athena Onca is implored to hold her protection over the Cadmea, it is easy to grasp the allusion to Pallas Athena of the Acropolis, ... If she is to guard her [*heptapylon hedos/seven-gated dwelling place*], the Athenian would at once think of the [*ennea pylon/nine-gated one*]. These are occasional reminders, but at frequent intervals throughout the play the importance of the defences is emphasised. The Cadmeans are bidden to man the [*purgomata/fenced walls*] . . . and there to take their stand. . . .

The Scout bids Eteocles

[And you, as a diligent rudder-turner of a ship, fortify the city, before the blasts of Ares rush down like a storm.]

To the Chorus the tutelary gods are [*gas tasde purgophylakes/tower-guards of this land*]; they are besought not to 'betray the bulwarks.' When the Chorus surrenders itself on the Acropolis to a helpless passion of supplication, Eteocles bids it offer a prayer more to the purpose. . . .

The Chorus itself in a [stasimon/*song of the chorus*] of some length describes vividly the fate of a captured city; how it is enslaved, befouled with smoke, and reduced to ashes. The allusion to the burning of Athens by the Persians is unmistakable. And this havoc, it is said, occurs when 'the defences fail' (332). The boasts and threats of the Achaean champions are addressed to the [*purgoi/towers*] of the besieged town, and, in answer, the Chorus prays that the enemy may never get within gate or wall, but may perish [*prosthe pylan, purgon ektosthen/in front of the gates, outside of the towers*]. After the failure of the assault the Scout reports

[And the city is both in calm weather and has not taken on any bilge-water from the many blows of the wave.]

It would have been impossible for the poet to communicate his lesson more plainly without violating (as Euripides is so apt to do) the canons of dramatic art.

The action of the play is simple, and requires no further analysis than that which is supplied in the commentary. Whereas Homer infused into his epic [*mimesis/imitation or representation*] a dramatic life, on the other hand the dramatic [*mimesis/imitation or representation*] of Aeschylus, especially in its earlier stages, is wont to retain much of the epic character. Apart from its choruses the *Septem* is in a large measure epic put upon the stage. There is much description, there would be considerable scenic effect, but there is little action in the modern sense. As a study of [*praxeis, pathe, and ethe/ actions, sufferings, and customs*] the play is apt to strike the reader as somewhat slender. Of the [*melopeiia*] we have no information, but it would necessarily count for much. In [*opsis/appearance*] it may be readily imagined that the play would not be lacking. We have the burghers in the opening scene, the distracted Chorus amid the images, the armed champions, the funeral procession and the dirge, besides the dancing and acting. When we have supplied these to the best of our ability, we are called upon to allow for sundry differences between the Greek point of view and our own in regard to a dramatic creation and its performance. Our own conception of 'action' is not the same as the Greek conception of [*praxis/action*]. A passage of [*elengchos/rebuke*], or a scene of argument in which a certain mental [*pathos/feeling*] is produced, removed, or changed, is sufficient in its 'action' for the Athenian, who loved these altercations, so long as the degree of [*dianoia/thought*] exhibited on either side was sufficiently keen or solid to maintain his intelligent admiration. Meanwhile he experienced a lively appreciation of the dexterity or beauty of the language employed. 'Action' also is the 'keening' over the bodies of the slain brothers. To the Greek, with his lively sympathies and his ready response to a call upon his emotions, this formed an interesting chapter in the [*mimesis biou/imitation of life*] of the stage. It was not merely that he took—as one modern sarcastically remarked of another—'a melancholy pleasure in the contemplation of a funeral.' It was that the attendant ceremonial of death and burial was to him a thing of real significance, for the simple reason that he entertained strong views of the vital importance of such duty to the dead.

If the function of tragedy is to evoke keen sensations of [*eleos kai phobos/pity and fear*], we must estimate the success of a piece, not by the standard of our own social, moral and religious conceptions, but by that of the Athenians in regard to the same matters. If it seems easy for us to realise the tremors which might pass through an audience when the Chorus depicts the miseries of slaughter, desolation, and enslavement in a captured city, we still can hardly experience them with the same liveliness as a people who recognized their literal truth and to whom they were more or less imminent possibilities. If we can understand a shudder of horror at the impending slaughter of brother by brother, we nevertheless cannot experience it with precisely the same acuteness as a people who regarded the tie of blood from a far more superstitious standpoint, and to whom the Erinyes were dreadful and ever-present realities. The curse of a father is to us a deplorable and shocking thing from the point of view of sentiment, but we cannot regard it, like the Athenians, as an embodied and operative power which can work madness in the brain and relentlessly and irresistibly achieve its dire object. To a people accustomed to the enigmas of oracles and prophecies, prone to look for their fulfilment with awe, and keen to feel the irony when the language was interpreted by the event, there were thrilling sensations of apprehension and premonition which are scarcely realisable by a sceptical modern reader, to whom such riddling rede is apt to present itself in a less venerable light. The refusal of burial to Polyneices is to us a cruel and disgusting action, possible only to a stage of civilisation from which we have emerged. To the Athenian such a prohibition came nearer home; it moreover amounted to perpetual damnation of the departed spirit, and the situation is therefore one of much more crushing grief to Antigone and her sympathisers than we can now realise without considerable effort. To us therefore, who have little regard for Erinyes or Curses or cryptic utterances, who have minimised the interest and importance of obsequies, and who have shifted to a different plane our conceptions of the claims of kinship, the *Septem* must lose much of its tragic force. The particular motives of pity and fear which it employs, though not without their effect upon ourselves, have lost not a little of their edge. They have at least lost the peculiar quality of poignancy which they would possess for a Greek of the early part of the fifth century B.C. Not only do we miss much that the piece actually contained, together with the acting, [the *orchesis/dancing,* the *melopoiia/ making of lyrical music,* and the *opsis/appearance*];

we have also been taught by the romantic drama to look for something at which classical tragedy does not aim, to wit, rapidity of action in a plot more 'complex,' and subtlety of characterisation probing to greater depths of 'philosophy,' than even the writer of the *Poetics* would have contemplated. One thing, however, which no competent reader can miss is the Aeschylean power of language, with its extraordinary specific gravity, its magnificent compression, and its brilliant figurativeness, by means of which the poet brings into the modest compass of a little over a thousand lines enough matter to have furnished forth as many more in many another writer.

The epic character of the play appears especially in the descriptions of the several Achaean champions with their accoutrements and their utterances. It is chiefly here that modern criticism, proceeding on *a priori* principles as to what is or is not dramatic, raises some question. Have these descriptions a legitimate place in drama? If so, are they seasonable in the mouth of the Scout? Is it, moreover, possible for the Messenger to have seen and heard all that he reports? It is not easy to act the [*lytikos/solver* to these *problemata/problems*], if we are to apply to ancient drama the strictest canons of modern realism. But though we are not called upon to undertake this impossible task, in view of the accepted conventions of the Greek stage, it may at least be answered that the criticism is largely misconceived. It is an entirely false notion that the Scout and the King are wasting time in talk while the enemy may be taking advantage of the situation. A point so obvious is not one which would escape so experienced a playwright as Aeschylus. At the very beginning of the Messenger's report we are told that the operations of the enemy are suspended

> [And the seer does not allow him to cross the Ismenus passage, for the sacrifices are not coming out good.]

It is characteristic of Aeschylus that he does not elaborate this excuse. He is too good a dramatist to add 'and therefore I may proceed to give my account at leisure.' We may, if we choose, regard the device itself as not particularly convincing. Yet Aeschylus believed it to be sufficiently so for his audience. Here, as elsewhere, he credited that audience with the quick intelligence which accepts few words in place of many. Doubtless he often took that intelligence too readily for granted. But whether the device be an entirely natural one or not—and there is at least nothing irrational in it—if it is once granted, criticism falls to the ground. For how long, after all, does it take the Messenger to make this report and for Eteocles to answer it with his disposi-

tions? The whole scene until Eteocles himself departs occupies 345 lines. Comprised in these there is no interval, and the time thus 'wasted' amounts to neither more nor less than it would take to deliver that number of lines upon the stage. It is not even the space of time which a modern critic spends in reading and pondering the lines, but the time which he might take, as a Greek of the date of Aeschylus, in uttering and acting them. This would be measured in minutes. To the spectators almost no time would appear to elapse. There are several single scenes in Shakespeare which are as long, and some which are longer. It can hardly be contended that the delay is rationally out of proportion to the justification offered for it.

Of two passages of Euripides which are supposed to be aimed at this scene in the *Septem,* one will be found on examination to have no such reference whatever. In the *Supplices* Theseus says to Adrastus.

> [And I will not ask you one thing, lest I bring laughter on myself, whom each of these is joined with in battle or has received the wound from a troop of enemy spearmen. For these words are empty, both those of the ones hearing and those of the one speaking, who, having gone in battle when a close-packed troop of spearmen is coming before his eyes, has reported clearly who is good.]

But what application has this passage to the Messenger's descriptions in our play? Euripides is simply ridiculing the man—probably too frequently in evidence at Athens—who pretends to know the full details of a fight in which he has been himself engaged. As every veteran acknowledges, the field of observation in a battle is limited to the soldier's own immediate neighbourhood, and sometimes he can render no very clear account even of his own experiences. But the Scout in the *Septem* has nothing to tell of any fight in which either he or anyone else has been concerned. It should be obvious that to force the lines into a criticism of his fellow-dramatist is to do an injustice to Euripides.

More relevant might seem the passage in the *Phoenissae,* where Eteocles says

> [And these things will be: having come to the seven-gated city, I will arrange troop commanders before the gates, as you say, setting equals opposite equal enemies, and it would be a great waste of time to say the name of each while the enemies are sitting under the very gates, but I go, in order that I may not leave my hand idle, and may it happen for me. . . .]

Though this particular [*rhesis/saying or speech*] is rightly suspected to contain a number of interpolations, and though it might be hoped, for the artistic credit of Euripides, that the dramatically unnatural—because obviously forced—passage [*onoma. . .chera*] is one such, we need not avail ourselves of that suspicion. It is enough to remember that the *Phoenissae* is of exceptional length, and that the poet has crowded into it (if it is all his) an unusual variety of matter. His lines here are no reflection whatever upon Aeschylus; they are a defence of himself. If anyone is criticised, it is the audience, which looked for such detail and description, but which Euripides does not this time propose to satisfy. The playwright is aware that he cannot spare room for this matter, and he accounts to the audience for the omission. The tone is not one of sarcasm, but of apology: 'I cannot name them now; it would take time, and the enemy are pressing us.'

It is sometimes further objected that the descriptions themselves are merely picturesque, and therefore undramatic. The same criticism would sweep away many a fine passage of Shakespeare. Aesthetic dogmatism is of little value unless founded on the facts of experience. That the Athenian audience was intensely interested in such descriptions pure and simple might doubtless be put down to that [*astheneia/weakness*] to which it was subject. The keen interest itself is beyond doubt. The same taste is met by Euripides. And if the strangeness to the modern reader lies not so much in the descriptions of the warriors as in the details of their shields and blazons, it is precisely here that the Greek appreciation was especially lively. How deeply ingrained in the Greek constitution was the love of skilful workmanship and of the contemplation of masterpieces in any kind, can scarcely be more conclusively shown than in the prominence given to verbal pictures of such things from epic times downwards. The shield of Achilles in the *Iliad* and in the *Electra* of Euripides; the shield of Heracles in the *Scutum* of the pseudo-Hesiod; the sculptures of Delphi in the *Ion;* the breastplate of Agamemnon in Homer, the bowls in Theocritus, the [basket] of Europa in Moschus, the [*diplax/double-fold*] of Jason in Apollonius Rhodius, the chest of Cypselus in Pausanias, are a few of the instances in point. It was part of epic convention that a shield of more or less miraculous workmanship should be described, with a combination of sheer joy in decorative art and naive wonder at the marvel of craftsmanship. The earliest Hellenic invaders of Greece could never sufficiently admire the technical productions of their 'Aegean' predecessors or of oriental workmen. As warriors they would be especially concerned with such work upon shields, breastplates,

and daggers. They would be eager to possess, and, if they possessed, they would hugely prize, accoutrements so distinguished. Their bards would magnify the possibilities of skill and dream dreams of wonderful inlaying and colour-toning. They would vie with each other in equipping their heroes with a shield of which, as of Nestor's, [*kleos ouranon hikei/fame reaches heaven*]. Of the shield of Achilles in the eighteenth book of the *Iliad,* Leaf remarks that 'though of course beyond the power of early Greek, as of any human art, to execute, it yet requires to explain it only such works of art and technique as we know to have been accessible to the Greeks, at least in foreign imports, in pre-Homeric times.' He illustrates by the dagger-blades found by Schliemann at Mycenae.

Exquisite inlaying was realised in fact, and so far there is nothing unreal in such instances as *Il.* 18.474, where Hephaestus blends bronze, gold, silver and tin. . . . Nor is the *tour de force* in *Scut.* 233, of the Gorgon's head in a net, beyond execution. Greater marvels, such as of moving reliefs, belong to the fancy of a later age.

Above all it was the shield which lent most scope both for the execution and the display of such work, and hence no epic is complete without its highly-wrought 'shield.' Vergil cannot fail to supply his Aeneas with one of the type. It is practically certain therefore that both Aeschylus and Euripides are led to their descriptions primarily by the *Thebais.* Pindar had evidently found similar matter in the *Epigoni.* Nevertheless the artistic and technically wonderful emblazoning of shields was no mere convention of epic. Later times knew and admired such accoutrements among contemporaries, although miracle had been compelled to give place to more sober possibilities. We should take the sense literally when Mamercus writes.

> [And we captured these shields, painted purple and overlaid with gold, ivory and amber by means of these worthless little shields.]

The contemporaries of Aeschylus were connoisseurs in work of the kind glanced at by Pindar. . . . If therefore Aeschylus takes the hint for describing the shields from the epic *Thebais,* he is by no means to be charged with introducing matter into his play for no better reason than that it happened to exist in the epic. Rather he introduces it for the same reason which led the epic writer to employ it first, namely, because to the audience of the drama, as to the audience of the epic, it caused a whole-hearted delight.

Doubtless the question of dramatic fitness is not settled by this consideration. Though the descriptions may please the audience, are they sufficiently in place when addressed by the Scout to Eteocles? In other words, would a messenger in ancient Greece conceivably render a report in such manner and kind? We may venture to hold that Aeschylus is incapable of a gross irrelevance. It is not merely that the Scout is himself carried away by the characteristic Greek gusto for the technical wonders which he has seen (although no Greek would be surprised at such behaviour on his part); it is also that his descriptions of the blazonry are part of his descriptions of the men. They mark the special temper and character, the insolence or self-assertion, which Eteocles is to confront. In effect the Messenger says in each case 'Such is the man; such are his boasts in word or blazon; it is for you to choose his antagonist.' In each case the king proceeds to select the opposing champion, and he either chooses him with some special reference to the blazon or draws some augury of victory from the temper which it betrays.

In one point we are apparently asked to accept a physical impossibility. It is difficult to convince ourselves that any scout could possibly see and hear all that the [*angelos/messenger*] reports. There are seven champions at seven different gates, and the Scout has observed them all at close quarters, heard their words, and even noted their expressions. He would presumably do this in making a circuit of the walls. In the *Phoenissae* Euripides employs the rather crude device of making his [*angelos/messenger*] the bearer of the [*xunthema/signal or agreement*] to the various [*lochoi/bands of armed troops*] concerned with the several gates. To name such a procedure is however, only to bring out its difficulties. Aeschylus, with more tact, glides over the exact proceedings of the [*kataskopos/scout or spy*]. We may be sure that, during the time of the performance, scarcely anyone among the audience would raise the question. It is one which only occurs after consideration or to the critical student. For the practical playwright this acceptance for the time being was sufficient. But while admitting that there is some violation of strict probabilities, we must again remember that pause in the assault which affords the Messenger time for observation. We must also remember the comparative smallness of the epic city. Nor are we, of course, to regard all the reported actions and utterances of the champions as synchronous. The Scout began his observations with the first approach of the Argives, and they would not all reach their gates at the same moment. These considerations do not indeed achieve an entire rationalising of the situation, but they go no little distance towards removing any very gross or palpable irrationality. As to the mere hearing and seeing of the besiegers by the besieged there is no difficulty whatever. When Sulla was besieging Athens taunts were hurled upon him from the walls. The same thing occurred to Maximinus before Aquileia. A proximity possible at such dates and in the siege of such cities was still more possible at the siege of a smaller town in epic days.

Source: T. G. Tucker, Introduction to *The Seven against Thebes of Aeschylus:* The Play of Aeschylus, in *The Seven against Thebes of Aeschylus:* by Aeschylus, Cambridge University Press, 1908, pp. xlii–lv.

SOURCES

Conacher, D. J., *Aeschylus: The Earlier Plays and Related Studies,* University of Toronto Press, 1996.

Davidson, John, review of ''Aeschylus's *Septem,*'' in *Didaskalia* Vol. 4, No. 1, Spring, 1997.

Martin, Tomas R., *Ancient Greece: From Prehistoric to Hellenistic Times,* Yale University Press, 1996.

Slavitt, David R., and Palmer Bovie, *Aeschylus, 2,* University of Pennsylvania Press, 1999.

Zeitlin, Froma L., ''Language, Structure, and the Son of Oedipus,'' in *Under the Sign of the Shield: Semiotics and Aeschylus's ''Seven Against Thebes,''* Edizioni dell'Atenceo, 1982, pp. 13-52.

FURTHER READING

Ashby, Clifford, *Classical Greek theater: New Views of an Old Subject,* University of Iowa Press, 1999.
    This text is an examination of Greek theater, based on architectural evidence. The author has traveled extensively and examined many of the remaining theater sites in Greece, Southern Italy, and the Balkans.

Bovie, Palmer, and Frederick Raphael, eds., *Sophocles, 1: ''Ajax,'' ''Women of Trachis,'' ''Electra,'' ''Philoctetes,''* University of Pennsylvania Press, 1998.
    This book provides original and fresh translations of several of Sophocles' tragedies. The Penn Greek Drama Series intends that their new translations should make reading Greek drama accessible to any reader.

Gressler, Thomas H., *Greek Theater in the 1980s,* McFarland & Company, 1989.

This is a study of theater in modern Greece. The author focuses on the social and cultural influences on theater, discusses the history of theater, and provides a look at productions and the restoration of theaters.

Griffith, R. Drew, *The Theater of Apollo: Divine Justice and Sophocles's ''Oedipus the King,''* McGill Queens University Press, 1996.

This is a reinterpretation of Sophocles' *Oedipus Rex* that focuses on Apollo's role in bringing about this tragedy. This book also attempts to recreate the play's original staging.

Rehm, Rush, *Greek Tragic Theater,* Routledge, 1994.

This book is helpful to readers who want to understand how Greek tragedy works. This author looks at performances of several plays and encourages readers to consider the context in which the plays were performed.

Walton, J. Michael, *Living Greek Theater,* Greenwood, 1987.

This text focuses on the staging and performance of Greek theater. The author attempts to integrate classical theater and modern theater, while providing a great deal of information about a number of the most important plays from this period.

Wise, Jennifer, *Dionynsus Writes: The Invention of Theater in Ancient Greece,* Cornell University Press, 1998.

This author discusses the relationship between literature and theater by examining the influences of a newly emerging literary world on drama. This text also provides some interesting ideas about the role of the oral tradition on theater.

Zelenak, Michael X., *Gender and Politics in Greek Tragedy,* Peter Lang, 1998.

This book offers some insight into the status of women in Greek culture and theater and provides interesting analysis of many women characters from Greek drama.

Sizwe Bansi is Dead

ATHOL FUGARD

1972

Sizwe Bansi Is Dead was written in collaboration with two African actors, John Kani and Winston Ntshona, both of whom appeared in the original production. It made its debut on October 8, 1972, in Cape Town, South Africa. The play made its British debut a year or so later and won The London Theatre Critics award for the best play of 1974.

The genesis of *Sizwe Bansi Is Dead* can be traced to Fugard's experiences as a law clerk at the Native Commissioner's Court in Johannesburg. At that time it was required that every black and colored citizen over the age of sixteen carried an identity book that restricted employment and travel within in the country. In court, Fugard saw the repercussions of this law: blacks were sent to jail at an alarming rate. Although these restrictions are specifically South African, critics have noted that the play's greater theme of identity is universal. Critics and scholars have also observed that *Sizwe Bansi Is Dead* contains elements of absurdism, especially its sparse setting and surreal subject matter.

AUTHOR BIOGRAPHY

Fugard was born in Middleburg, Cape Province, South Africa, on June 11, 1932. When Fugard was three years old his family moved to the diverse city of Port Elizabeth. Growing up, Fugard was keenly aware of the racial divisions in the city and their economic and social consequences. Fugard attended the University of Cape Town on a scholarship, where he studied philosophy and social anthropology. In the middle of his senior year, he dropped out of college and became a sailor. Fugard was the only white crew member on the ship for two years, an experience that eliminated his racial prejudice.

When he returned to South Africa in 1956, he met and married Sheila Meiring, an actress. Fugard wanted to be a novelist—indeed he finished a manuscript—but watching his wife audition for plays, Fugard became interested in the theater too. They formed the Circle Players in Johannesburg.

In 1958 he took a job as a clerk with a local court to support his family. There, Fugard saw racial injustice firsthand. He also became friends with black people and saw their living conditions. This experience inspired his first play, *No-Good Friday,* which was performed privately for white audiences. In 1959 he and his wife went to London to gain more theatrical experience. Within a year, they returned to South Africa and he wrote the first of his so-called ''Port Elizabeth plays,'' *The Blood Knot.*

In 1962 five Xhosa tribesmen approached Fugard wanting to start a theater company. After some initial reluctance, Fugard formed the Serpent Company, which became the first successful nonwhite theater company in South Africa. On account of this success, several members of the company were arrested. In 1967 Fugard's passport was withdrawn by the South African government (it was returned in 1971), yet he continued to write plays exploring the implications of apartheid in South Africa.

During this time period, Fugard wrote his most successful play, *Boesman and Lena* (1960). Performed both Off-Broadway and in London, the play garnered international praise. In the early 1970s Fugard experimented with developing scripts in improvisational theater format. The best-known result was *Siswe Bansi is Dead* (1972).

In the early 1980s Fugard became associated with the Yale School of Drama, which hosted the first production of *Master Harold and the Boys.* Widely acclaimed, this play was representative of Fugard's autobiographical period, which continued into the 1990s. In 1999, Fugard wrote *The Captain's Tiger,* which explores some of his early writing experiences. Today, he splits his time between the United States and South Africa.

PLOT SUMMARY

Sizwe Bansi Is Dead opens in the photography studio of a man named Styles. The studio is located in New Brighton, Port Elizabeth, South Africa. After reading a newspaper article on an automobile plant, Styles tells a humorous story to the audience about an incident that occurred when he worked at Ford Motor Company.

Styles continues to read the paper and talks about his photography studio. His musings are interrupted when a customer, Sizwe Bansi, arrives. Sizwe asks to have his picture taken, but when Styles asks him for his deposit and name, Sizwe hesitates. Sizwe says his name is Robert Zwelinzima. Styles asks Sizwe what he will do with the photo, and Sizwe tells him he will send it to his wife. When the picture is taken, the moment is frozen into what the photograph will look like. It comes to life and Sizwe dictates the letter to his wife that will accompany the photo.

In the letter, Sizwe tells his wife that Sizwe Bansi is dead. He writes that when he arrived in Port Elizabeth from their home in King William's Town, he stayed with a friend named Zola who tried to help Sizwe find a job. His employment search was unsuccessful; as a result, he was told by the authorities that he must leave in three days. Sizwe went to stay with Zola's friend, Buntu.

Sizwe Bansi is Dead returns to present time. Staying at Buntu's house, Sizwe tells Buntu about his problems—unless a miracle happens, he will have to leave town in three days. Buntu is sympathetic to the problem and suggests he work in the mines in King William's Town. Sizwe rejects the idea as too dangerous. Buntu decides to take Sizwe out for a treat at Sky's place, a local bar.

The focus switches back to Sizwe as he continues to compose the letter to his wife. He describes his experiences at Sky's Shebeen, where he was served alcohol by a woman in a respectful manner.

Sizwe Bansi Is Dead shifts to the outside of Sky's after Sizwe and Buntu have been drinking. Buntu decides that he needs to get home to go to work tomorrow. He goes into an alley to relieve himself and finds a dead man there. Sizwe wants to report the body to the police. Buntu nixes the idea, but he retrieves the dead man's identity book to find his address. Buntu finds that the man, named Robert Zwelinzima, has a work-seeker's permit—the very thing that Sizwe needs to stay in town. They take the

Athol Fugard

book. At Buntu's house, Buntu switches the photographs in the books. He proposes that they burn Sizwe's book—effectively making him dead—and have Sizwe adopt the dead man's identity so he can stay in Port Elizabeth. Sizwe is unsure about the plan; in particular, he worries about his wife and children. Buntu contends that they can remarry. After much discussion, Sizwe agrees to the switch.

Sizwe finishes dictating the letter to his wife. In it, he tells her that Buntu is helping him get a lodger's permit. The scene shifts back to Styles' photography studio; Sizwe is getting his picture taken.

CHARACTERS

Sizwe Bansi

The protagonist of the play, Sizwe (also known as Robert Zwelinzima and The Man) is a young African man with a wife and four children. He has come to Port Elizabeth from his home in King William's Town to look for work and a better life. Unfortunately, he is refused an official permit and is told to leave town in three days.

When he finds the body—and identification papers—of the dead man, Sizwe assumes the man's

identity in order to stay in Port Elizabeth. It is not an easy decision for him: he worries about the loss of his identity and what it means. When he goes into Styles's studio to get his picture taken and announces his name is Robert Zwelinzima, it reflects his acceptance of his new identity.

Buntu

Buntu is the friend who convinces Sizwe to assume the dead man's identity. He is a good man and generous friend: he lets Sizwe sleep on his couch; takes him out drinking; and helps him find a way to stay in town. After Sizwe assumes the dead man's identity, Buntu helps Sizwe find a decent job.

The Man

See Sizwe Bansi, Robert Zwelinzima

Styles

Styles is the owner of a photography studio in New Brighton, Port Elizabeth, South Africa. He is courageous enough to quit a steady job and start his own business, which was difficult for a black man at that time. He enjoys his work because it gives people a personal history and record of their lives. Styles takes pictures of all kinds of people from families to individuals.

Robert Zwelinzima
    See Sizwe Bansi, The Man

THEMES

Identity

The primary theme of *Sizwe Bansi Is Dead* is identity. The quest for or changing of identity deeply affects each of the major characters.

For Styles, identity means several things. First, Styles was able to forge a new identity as a photographer; previously, he had worked on the line at the Ford Motor Company, which was not a satisfying identity for him. Second, through his work, Styles is able to record the identity of his patrons. By taking photographs of common people, they are not lost to history—their descendants will remember them.

Sizwe Bansi's identity issues are more problematic. His passbook—essentially his identity—has disappointed him; he does not have the proper documentation to stay in Port Elizabeth and look for a job to support his family. The stamp in his passbook says that he must report to a bureau in his home of King William's Town.

Sizwe stays with Buntu, a friend of a friend. After a night of drinking, they come across a dead man and take his identity book. It is Buntu's idea that Sizwe Bansi take on the identity of the dead man, who has the proper documentation to work.

This potential change of identity troubles Sizwe Bansi: his children have his name; he is unsure what would happen to his wife; and he could get into serious trouble with the authorities if the switch is discovered. Yet to ensure his family's survival, Sizwe Bansi reluctantly becomes Robert Zwelinzima.

In *Sizwe Bansi is Dead,* one's true identity is knowing who you are—not what your name is.

Family

The importance of family is another theme of *Sizwe Bansi Is Dead.* Styles believes that the photographs he takes will link families through generations; moreover, they allow descendants to see what their ancestors looked like. He says that his best business comes from family groups because their sheer numbers guarantee lots of copies sold.

Sizwe Bansi has come to Port Elizabeth to find work to support his wife and four children. He goes as far as to take on a dead man's identity to make

MEDIA ADAPTATIONS

- *Sizwe Bansi Is Dead* was filmed for television by the BBC and British Open University in 1978. The production was produced and directed by Andrew Martin. It features Jose Ferrar as a presenter, and Ossie Davis and Ruby Dee. The tape also includes discussion of stylization, avant-gardism, realism, and Black Theater. It was released on videotape in the United States by Insight Media in 1992.

sure he can stay in the city and find a decent job. He has his photograph taken at Styles' studio to show his wife that he is still the same man.

Buntu's family situation—his wife is a domestic who only spends weekends at home, and his child lives with his or her grandmother—allows him to take in Sizwe and help him with his problems. Buntu treats him like family.

Limitations and Opportunities

Though both Sizwe Bansi and Styles (as well as Buntu) are limited by circumstances—such as racism—they are able to seize opportunities for positive change.

For example, Styles felt stifled and overworked at the auto plant. During the Christmas shutdown, he finds out about a room near a funeral parlor and gets permission to use it as a photography studio. Now, unlike many of his peers, Styles owns his own business. He is independent.

With Buntu's help, Sizwe also takes advantage of opportunities. He cannot stay in Port Elizabeth to find work because his identity book has restricted his movements. When he finds a dead man in an alley, Buntu picks up the dead man's identity book.

After reviewing Sizwe's options, Buntu suggests that he take on this man's identity so Sizwe can stay and find a job in Port Elizabeth. Though Sizwe's options have been limited by apartheid, taking on the dead man's identity gives him the

TOPICS FOR FURTHER STUDY

- Research the policies of apartheid as practiced by the South African government in the 1970s. How do these policies affect each of the characters in *Sizwe Bansi Is Dead*?

- Compare and contrast *Sizwe Bansi Is Dead* with *The Island*, another play written by Fugard and his collaborators during this time period. The two plays are often performed together. What does each play express about apartheid?

- Research the psychological aspects of identity. How will Sizwe's choice affect his psychological makeup? Write a short story about Sizwe a year later. How has he changed?

- Some critics believe that *Sizwe Bansi Is Dead* has elements of existentialist and absurdist theater. Research the history and philosophy of these two kinds of plays. Do you agree with these critics?

opportunity to make a decent living and support his family.

STYLE

Setting

Sizwe Bansi Is Dead is set in New Brighton (an African township) in Port Elizabeth, South Africa, in 1972. The action of the play takes place in three locations. The first is Styles's photography studio located near a funeral parlor, where Sizwe Bansi (as Robert Zwelinzima) gets his picture taken.

The second is Buntu's house, where Sizwe stays when he has nowhere else to go in Port Elizabeth. The last setting is the streets of New Brighton outside of the local bar. This is where Buntu discovers the dead body of Robert Zwelinzima.

Each of these settings emphasize the fact that these characters inhabit a certain part of South

African society that places limits on the movements of its African citizens.

Monologue/Stream of Consciousness/ Improvisation/Transitions

Large parts of the one-act *Sizwe Bansi Is Dead* consist of stylized monologues.

In the original production, the actor who played Styles, John Kani, was allowed to improvise his opening stream-of-consciousness monologue. As the script calls for Styles to read from and comment on a newspaper, actors who play the role sometimes update it to reflect topical concerns of his location at the moment. These touches allow *Sizwe Bansi Is Dead* to stay relevant.

Styles's long monologue also introduces the themes of the play. In revealing some of his life story (how he came to own the photographic studio) and his opinions (how the photographs he takes allow the common person to leave something of themselves behind), Styles reflects on the results of apartheid.

Sizwe Bansi and Buntu's monologues have different forms and purposes. Sizwe's monologue is in the form of a letter to his wife, who lives in King William's Town. Fugard uses the letter to give background to the story.

For example, in the beginning of the letter, Sizwe tells his wife that ''SizweBansi, in a manner of speaking, is dead!'' He chronicles the raid at his friend Zola's and how he came to stay with Buntu.

The action shifts to Buntu's house and Sizwe's arrival there. Sizwe Bansi's letter gives *Sizwe Bansi Is Dead* structure and organization. Each segment after the beginning of the letter is set up by such a Sizwe monologue.

Buntu's monologues are more traditional. Most of them occur at his house, when Sizwe is analyzing his problem and proposing feeble solutions. Buntu counters every one of Sizwe's ideas and chronicles long stories about recent events in his own life that are relevant.

HISTORICAL CONTEXT

In 1972, South Africa had a system of repressive apartheid; segregation occurred socially, economically, politically, and culturally. For years, black Africans and ''coloureds'' (the South African term

COMPARE
&
CONTRAST

- **1962:** The head of the African National Congress, Nelson Mandela, is sentenced to five years in prison for leaving the country illegally. Two years later he is sentenced to life in prison for treason and violent conspiracy. In the following years he becomes an international symbol of resistance to apartheid.

  Today: Finally released from prison in 1990, Nelson Mandela was elected President of South Africa in 1994. He has announced his retirement from public life.

- **1969:** In South Africa people of color are segregated into certain areas. They are prohibited from living in white areas.

  Today: In South Africa, laws are enacted to redistribute land among citizens of color.

- **1972:** The South African economy is strong, but there is extremely high unemployment among the black population. The salary gap between white and black is about five to one.

  Today: The South African economy is struggling. There is an extremely high unemployment rate and a rising crime rate.

---

for those of mixed race) had been the overwhelming majority, yet their rights and opportunities were severely restricted by the white minority.

From the beginning of the twentieth century, the white minority in power restricted ownership of land, education, employment, and movement within South Africa. Races were not allowed to intermarry. Many blacks lived in crowded areas and could not live in the same areas as whites. Blacks and coloureds were paid less than their white counterparts. The white-controlled government tried to restrict all dissent by whites and blacks.

Yet there seemed to be some positive progress in 1972. Three black homelands—Bophuthatswan, Ciskei, and Lebowa—were given self-governing territory status within South Africa. This move was supposed to promote self-government, which meant that each territory could have their own cabinet, legislative assembly, official language, flag, and national anthem.

The South African government was trying to geographically consolidate black homelands. Yet such events were seen as empty, politically suspect gestures by much of the world.

In 1973 new forms of black resistance, including the burgeoning Black Consciousness Movement, became prominent in South Africa. Black trade unions staged a number of strikes. They demanded higher wages (the disparity in wages between whites and blacks was about five to one) and better working conditions. The strikes publicized the situation in South Africa worldwide, starting a backlash against the brutality and inhumanity of apartheid. The United Nations General Assembly declared the system of apartheid a "crime against humanity."

CRITICAL OVERVIEW

The initial audiences of *Sizwe Bansi is Dead* were the black audiences who saw the production at the Space in Cape Town, South Africa. Although the play was popular, many audience members left during the opening monologue when they discovered the subject matter—they feared the police would raid the theater.

When *Sizwe Bansi* made its American debut on Broadway in 1974, critics generally praised the play and its exploration of controversial topics. For example, Jack Kroll of *Newsweek* contended: "What Fugard, 42, and his astonishing collaborators have created is theater of unique dramatic impact and

Actors Winston Ntshona and John Kani, shown here, appeared in the original production of Sizwe Banzi Is Dead.

crucial significance in its relationship to reality—the Kafkaesque reality of South Africa.''

On Broadway, the play was performed with another Fugard one-act piece, *The Island.* Many reviewers compared the two plays. Harold Clurman of *The Nation* maintained that ''Athol Fugard's two one-act plays *Sizwe Bansi Is Dead* and *The Island* are important—not simply because they provide an insight into the life of blacks in South Africa but because in the writing and in acting they are examples of original theatre.''

Brendan Gill of *The New Yorker* provided another perspective on the play. He asserted: ''*Sizwe Bansi* is, in formal terms, scarcely a play at all; rather, it is an explanation and an indictment. It renders with impassioned eloquence the feelings engendered by the social injustice practiced under law in South Africa.''

Other critics agreed that the unconventional aspects and profound political statements were quite powerful. Gerald Weales of *Commonweal* maintained, ''These two plays are the most exciting things that I have seen in any theater for a long time.'' Weales contended that the play's ''triumph lies not in any social or political message, but in the fact that they have imposed life on the stage at the Edison. It is not plot, nor situation, nor even character in the conventional sense that is communicated by these plays, but a quality of being.''

Another critic, Catharine Hughes, concurred: ''I doubt very much that most people would consider *Sizwe Bansi* and *The Island* 'good plays.' They are not. But they are powerful, moving, compassionate theatrical experiences.''

Many of the critics who liked the play commented on the power of the lengthy opening monologue. Clurman praised the stream-of-consciousness technique: ''It conveys a vivid impression of what it means for a black man to be working in such a place as a South African factory.''

Kroll of *Newsweek* saw something more. He stated: ''It opens with an amazing monologue by John Kani in which he becomes all by himself the protean black man of South Africa, the most omnipresent invisible man in the world, the 15-million-faced disinherited man who has been debriefed of his humanity by a total bureaucracy that shrinks him down to a rogues-gallery head in a passbook.''

There were some dissenters among American critics. Stanley Kauffmann of *The New Republic* believed that was potential in the production, but that it ultimately failed: ''Both plays are drawn from the innermost feelings of three gifted and committed men. So it's something more than sad to report that, for me, both plays are disappointing.'' Regarding the play's premise, Kauffmann asserted: ''Now this might make a good ironic short play of 30 minutes or so. But it begins with a very long monologue, about two-fifths of the play. Buried in this ramble are a few glints of relevance, but mostly it seems a consciously theatrical attempt by addressing the audience and bringing members of it up on the stage briefly—devices by now so familiar that their triteness works against the freshness that it's aimed at.''

Russell Vandenbroucke in his book on Fugard, *Truths the Hand Can Touch,* concurred that *Sizwe Bansi* was problematic. He maintained: ''Despite this process of refinement, the major inadequacy of the text remains its repetitiveness. Consequently, a fairly short play 'feels' rather bulky. The drunk scene and Bansi's disorientation last too long . . . [S]o much factual information is imparted that the text becomes overburdened and briefly threatens to become a general survey of living conditions for blacks in South Africa.''

CRITICISM

Annette Petruso

Annette Petruso is a freelance author and screenwriter in Austin, TX. In the following essay, Petrusso discusses the role of photography in Sizwe Bansi Is Dead.

Athol Fugard has maintained that the genesis of *Sizwe Bansi Is Dead* lies in an unforgettable photograph he saw hanging in a studio window. It was of a South African black man wearing his best suit and an angelic smile. He carried a pipe, a walking stick, and a newspaper.

> Styles is selling Bansi dreams of more than what is currently available to him under apartheid. Styles's photograph is made up of several lies about Bansi, though the man's face can never hide the truth of his life.

Something about this photography spoke deeply to Fugard, and his collaborators on the play, actors Winston Ntshona and John Kani. They speculated

on the man's life as they wrote the play. Thus, *Sizwe Bansi is Dead* is built on a picture, a concrete illusion of reality. The story is driven by issues of control—or the lack thereof—over one's life and one's photograph. This essay explores how these ideas are expressed in *Sizwe Bansi Is Dead.*

The man who seeks some measure of control over his life is Sizwe Bansi. He has come to Port Elizabeth to get a better job to support his family. In Bansi's hometown of King William's Town, there are few opportunities other than the mines. Bansi equates such a job with death. When the place he is staying at is raided, the authorities discover his passbook is not in order. He does not have the proper paperwork to be looking for a job in Port Elizabeth. Bansi has three days to report to a government office in King William's Town.

With the help of a friend of a friend named Buntu, Bansi tries to find a way to avoid deportation. After an evening of drinking, the two men stumble across a dead man whose passbook is in order. Buntu gets the idea to solve Bansi's problem by having Bansi take over the identity of the dead man, Robert Zwelinzima. Bansi resists, but ultimately sees the benefits of the plan. He takes over Zwelinzima's identity with a mere photograph. Buntu switches the men's identity by pasting Bansi's photograph in Zwelinzima's passbook. If Bansi gets into any trouble, the authorities could discover the deception when fingerprints are compared. It is a risky solution to Bansi's problem. Yet the photograph is all the identity Bansi needs to find work.

This identity switch gives him a new lease on life. To explain what has happened to his wife, Bansi goes to a photographic studio run by Styles to have his picture taken and sent to her. By this time, the switch has paid off. Bansi has found a job working for a company called Feltex and has a new suit. Yet the photograph Styles takes reveals that the control Bansi has over his life is just an illusion in many ways. As a photographer, Styles has several contradictory aspects. Throughout his opening monologue, Styles talks about the power of photographs, or ''cards,'' as he calls them. At one point, he says, ''You must understand one thing. We own nothing except ourselves. This world and its laws allow us nothing, except ourselves. There is nothing we can leave behind when we die, except the memory of ourselves.''

Yet Styles insists on placing Bansi/Zwelinzima in a false pose for the photograph. He makes him put

WHAT DO I READ NEXT?

- *Waiting for Godot* is a play written by Samuel Beckett. Published in 1965, it is an existentialist play featuring humorous and disaffected characters.

- *South Africa: A Visual History, 1972* (1973), is a pictorial history of South Africa in 1972. The book is published by the Republic of South Africa, and is comprised of the government's version of the events of 1972.

- Fugard's *Boesman and Lena* (1969) is a play that focuses on two characters barely surviving under the repressive regime of apartheid in South Africa.

- Arthur Miller's play, *Incident at Vichy*, was published in 1965. The play focuses on human responsibility.

on his new hat and hold his new pipe, but pushes the issue when he gives Bansi a lit cigarette to hold in the other hand. Styles flatters Bansi by telling him that he will soon be chief messenger at Feltex. To emphasize the matter, he pulls down a backdrop that is a map of the world—a world that illiterate Bansi does not know much about. Excited by his work, Styles convinces Bansi to pose for a second picture. The backdrop is the city of the future, and Styles tells Bansi he could be the head of Feltex in this city. Styles poses Bansi with a walking stick and a newspaper (though Bansi insists he cannot read) as he poses him walking in this city of the future.

These poses could be interpreted several ways. Styles wants to sell photographs, so boosting Bansi's ego makes for a larger sale. Yet there is more going on here: Styles is selling Bansi dreams of more than what is currently available to him under apartheid. Styles's photograph is made up of several lies about Bansi, though the man's face can never hide the truth of his life. Styles can relate to Bansi's situation. Like Bansi, Styles once held a low-paying job, but better than most; in fact, he worked in a Ford factory before opening his studio. During his monologue, he tells a story about an experience he had there. Henry Ford II, one of the executives at Ford Motor Company, was scheduled to visit the plant. The workers had to prepare for the visit: safety measures were put in place; lines and words were painted on the floor to mark dangerous areas; and each of the workers were forced to take showers and

were given new uniforms. For Mr. Ford's benefit, the line would be slowed down and the men were instructed to sing. Yet when Mr. Ford finally made his appearance, it took all of a few seconds. He took three strides out of his car and three strides back to it. All this preparation is parallel to the process of posing Bansi for his picture. The effect is a superficial change, yet Bansi's picture lasts forever. The photographer appreciates his power—he has learned the importance of image well.

Because Styles is an independent businessman, he knows he has more control over his life than most men of his race do in South Africa. To gain control, he had decided to become a photographer and looked for a place to set up shop. After getting permission to take over the space, Styles had to solve some problems. The place was a mess and infested with cockroaches. He had to control the cockroaches with some help of a cat, after a product called "Doom" failed him. These concerns were superficial in many ways, but shop had to look presentable to customers so that Styles could sell dreams to people who wanted them.

Styles makes money off the very things that oppress his customers. The stage directions call for his sign to read "Styles Photographic Studio. Reference Books; Passports; Weddings; Engagements; Birthday Parties and Parties. Prop.—Styles." The first thing on this list is reference books, another name for the passbooks that cause Bansi's problems in the first place. Styles is a businessman in a difficult environment. Yet the fact that he contributes to his people's oppression this way is ironic, though necessary. Of these pictures, Styles says "I sit them down, set up the camera—'No expression, please.'—click-click—'Come back tomorrow, please.'" There is no posing, no playing with the truth in these pictures. Styles knows that his clientele have to get these photographs somewhere. He never says another word on the subject because he is more interested in making a record of people who will not be remembered any other way.

Throughout the text of *Sizwe Bansi Is Dead,* death is a recurring theme. Bansi gets a chance to stay in Port Elizabeth because of a dead man. Bansi worries about losing his identity as Sizwe Bansi, implying that part of him might die. Indeed, in the letter to his wife that will accompany Styles' photograph of him, Bansi writes "Sizwe Bansi, in a manner of speaking, is dead!" Yet a photograph pasted in the dead man's passbook gives Bansi a new life. Styles often talks about photographs as the only way common people will be remembered by their descendants after death. He describes one photograph he took of a family comprised of twenty-seven members. The experience of taking the picture was frustrating to him. When the eldest son returned for the photographs a week later, he told Styles that his father had died two days after the sitting. This had a big impact on Styles.

While death cannot be controlled, a person's image in a photograph can be—even if it is not completely honest. Styles points to a picture of his father dressed in a uniform from his days fighting in World War II. Styles reflects, "That's all I have of him." What his father wears in the picture and how he is posed does not matter: it is the photograph itself that counts.

Source: Annette Petruso, in an essay for *Drama for Students,* Gale, 2001.

Andre Brink

In the following essay, Brink explores the difficulties encountered by a playwright addressing social, political, and ideological problems in an artistic, moral, and existential arena.

In the play *Sizwe Bansi Is Dead,* which was "devised by" Athol Fugard, John Kani, and Winston Ntshona, Sizwe Bansi is stranded without a work

> *... THE PHOTOGRAPH STYLES TAKES REVEALS THAT THE CONTROL BANSI HAS OVER HIS LIFE IS JUST AN ILLUSION IN MANY WAYS."*

permit in Port Elizabeth. The only solution to his dilemma is summarized in Kafkaesque terms by his benefactor Buntu:

> You talk to the white man, you see, and ask him to write a letter saying he's got a job for you. You take that letter from the white man and go back to King William's Town, where you show it to the Native Commissioner there. The Native Commissioner in King William's Town reads that letter from the white man in Port Elizabeth who is ready to give you the job. He then writes a letter back to the Native Commissioner in Port Elizabeth. So you come back here with the two letters. Then the Native Commissioner in Port Elizabeth reads the letter from the Native Commissioner in King William's Town together with the first letter from the white man who is prepared to give you a job, and he says when he reads the letters: Ah yes, this man Sizwe Bansi can get a job. So the Native Commissioner in Port Elizabeth then writes a letter which you take with the letters from the Native Commissioner in King William's Town and the white man in Port Elizabeth, to the Senior Officer at the Labour Bureau, who reads all the letters. Then he will put the right stamp in your book and give you another letter from himself which together with the letters from the white man and the two Native Affairs Commissioners, you take to the Administrative Office here in New Brighton and make an application for a Residence Permit, so that you don't fall victim of raids again. Simple.

The problem is that Sizwe Bansi knows no white man to start with. In the circumstances, Buntu's evaluation of the situation is straightforward: "There's no way out, Sizwe. You're not the first one who has tried to find it. Take my advice and catch that train back to King William's Town."

However profound the personal implications for Sizwe Bansi may be, the problem as formulated by Buntu appears to be a purely social one. Within moments, however, another dimension grows from it. When Buntu suggests, as the only other "way out," a job on the mines, Sizwe refuses point-blank. "You can die there." Whereupon Buntu, prompted *"into taking possibly his first real look at Sizwe,"*

A scene from Sizwe Banzi Is Dead.

remarks, "You don't want to die." And Sizwe affirms, "I don't want to die."

The statement is echoed in Antigone's acknowledgment in *The Island* that "I know I must die," and in the resignation to "a susceptibility to death" in *Statements after an Arrest under the Immorality Act.* This is Unamuno territory: "The man of flesh and bone; the man who is born, suffers, and dies—above all, who dies." The man who dies and who does not want to die. It is also Camus territory, as we know from Fugard's illuminating *Notebooks,* and from Dickey and many other commentators. It is not irrelevant to note that, according

to Walder, one of the Serpent Players' major productions, only months before *Sizwe Bansi,* had been Camus' *Les Justes.*

Much of the impact of this moment in *Sizwe Bansi* derives from the way in which it represents an interface between the play's two key dimensions: the sociopolitical and the existential. *Sizwe Bansi* has long been recognized not only as "an indictment of the depravity and inhumanity of apartheid," but also as a "watershed" of a "new theatre" in South Africa. Stanley Kauffmann even dismissed the play as "superficial" because it was, he believed, "only about the troubles of South

African blacks.'' On the other hand, it is well known that Fugard himself has always aimed at transcending the ''merely'' sociopolitical. Significantly, in the seven-page introduction that precedes the three *Statements* plays, he concerns himself with some of the dramaturgical and philosophical problems he confronted in them, *without a single reference to their ideological or sociopolitical context.* ''Facts,'' writes Fugard in a characteristic pronouncement, ''are flat and lacking in the density and ambiguity of truly dramatic images.'' In a corroborating passage John Kani provides a cameo of Fugard as director, trying to outwit the censors: ''Find a simpler statement. *Disguise this statement. That is politics. Try and find the artistic value of the piece.*''

In the present post-apartheid era it is perhaps time to take a more dispassionate look at some problems illuminated by *Sizwe Bansi Is Dead:* not only the interaction between sociopolitics and theatre within a given text, but the dilemma of the writer as a person with both artistic integrity and a social conscience. Or, in terms of Fugard's own explanation of his improvisational technique in his preface to the play. ''The basic device has been that of Challenge and Response'': the problem of reacting to an *ideological* and/or *political* challenge (apartheid and the struggle for liberation) with a response on a different level altogether—theatrical, existential, and moral.

In several interesting respects N. Chabani Manganyi provides an early articulation of the terms of the problem:

> Sisyphus is the absurd hero. Pushing the rock uphill is the price I pay . . . for what? I am not Camus, nor am I the West. I the black Sisyphus am social—not metaphysical. It is the social which constitutes the horizon of my futile labour. Going downhill I come face to face with the social—my tormentors. I make the only logical jump I know, i.e. ignoring suicide in favour of something so painfully pragmatic—murder. . . . I did not participate in the rebellion of the West. Yet I carry the burden of the questions they raised.

With reference to Arthur Miller's *Incident at Vichy,* Manganyi highlights ''the interface between personal troubles and public issues,'' concluding that ''It is the personal troubles, the individual destinies, that add a dimension to the problem of the historically extreme situation.'' In this context the artist occupies a special position through his preoccupation with ''images'' rather than ''action.'' As Manganyi notes, the artist's ''first solution for the problem of subordination and its consequent violent and rebellious impulse is symbolic rather than actual. He responds at a more primitive level by

''. . . THE QUESTION REMAINS WHETHER THE DISGUISE OF THE POLITICAL STATEMENT THROUGH PLAY-ACTING MAY NOT BE SEEN AS A WITHDRAWAL INTO THE COMPARATIVE SAFETY OF AESTHETICS.''

placing his whole weight behind ritualisation on a symbolic level in the place of a real murder as a social act.''

Sizwe Bansi opens with a now-famous improvisation by the character Styles (a photographer) on themes provided by whatever news is topical on the day and in the locality of the performance. We know that this improvisation, which in the printed version of the play covers about fifteen pages and in the filmed version about thirty minutes, sometimes stretched to as much as an hour and a half once John Kani was in his stride. Whatever the importance of this variable introduction of political satire and reference in any given performance, its dramatic significance lies in its contribution to the definition of the character Styles and his history. And the *mise en scene* assumes a peculiar circular form which is of decisive importance for the reading of the play I am attempting to offer here. The play opens in the here and now of Styles's photographic studio, where he finds himself, facing his audience, waiting for a customer to turn up. From this point Styles returns to his beginnings, his first job as a worker in the Ford Factory in Port Elizabeth, and traces the vicissitudes of his life along the route which will bring him back to this studio, as T. S. Eliot puts it in *Four Quartets,* to ''know the place for the first time.'' There is indeed, in Styles's seemingly lighthearted excursus, an acknowledgment of Eliot's proposal that ''every moment is a new and shocking / Valuation of all we have been.'' This interaction of ''time past'' and ''time present,'' in many respects the lifeblood of drama as a literary mode, establishes a base and a model for the further evolution of the play.

Undoubtedly the Styles story contains a strong and explicit political text: the lack of choices available to him as a black worker in a white-owned factory; the dreary realities of job reservation, of group areas, of the whole complex of laws that define apartheid as a system; the futile pleasure derived from a momentary reversal of white and black roles (when Styles makes a fool of ''Baas'' Bradley by saying in Xhosa what cannot be said in English, by standing erect while the foreman is ''kneeling there on the floor,'' by ''wearing a mask of smiles,'' by changing the customary order of *perception* as a key to the racial power play at work in the scene—''We were watching them. Nobody was watching us''); the process of transformation into a self-made man with his own studio.

Below this explicit text there are signs of a more problematic ideological subtext. Two such signs are the economic choice implied in Styles's evolution (which appropriates precisely some of the practices of apartheid that have proved most successful in establishing a society of haves and have-nots, exploiters and exploited), and the choice of language in the play.

The choice of private enterprise as a response to the dehumanization of the apartheid system is in itself significant. Consider a similar response by Sizwe Bansi when he thinks of ''start[ing] a little business'' as a ''way out'' of the vicious circle described by Buntu. The choice of private enterprise certainly goes against the ideological grain of black South African playwrights who define ''the system'' not only in terms of racial oppression, but most particularly in terms of *economic* exploitation. For example, Zakes Mda's ex-soldier Janabari, in *We Shall Sing for the Fatherland,* says: ''Serge, I have been trying to tell you that our wars were not merely to replace a white face with a black one, but to change a system which exploits us, to replace it with one which gives us a share in the wealth of this country.''

Language offers an even more subtle disturbance. Unlike Mda, Mbongemi Ngema, and other black playwrights, who readily incorporate African languages like Xhosa in their texts, *Sizwe Bansi* is written/performed almost exclusively in English—even, and particularly, in the factory scene, where ''Baas'' Bradley's unilingualism in an environment where his workers poke fun at him in Xhosa is the source both of fun and of political power play. This is imperative, of course, if the play is performed for a white and/or foreign audience, otherwise the whole point of the scene will be missed. But in contextual terms it means that the play, at least in its published form, is aimed primarily, if not exclusively, at

audiences from the dominant white culture. This would appear to place it outside the current of protest or struggle theatre. The implications are fascinating, especially in the light of Fugard's often stated passionate concern for ''a much more immediate and direct relationship with our audience.'' Viewed in this light, the play becomes a doubly mediated *interpretation* of the ''black situation,'' through the collaboration of black and white writers and actors, to a primarily white audience. If this explains the ''weighting'' of the existentialist load of the text, may it not also result (I am perhaps playing the devil's advocate here) in a concomitant compromise of the ideological text?

If so, it would explain something about the curious confusion of metaphors which arises from Styles's account of his life's journey. Upon first acquiring his studio he faces a problem of infestation by cockroaches, and the first remedy he reaches for is an insecticide, ''The Mass Murderer! Doom!'' Clearly, in this scene the cockroaches become a metaphor for the black masses infesting the white capitalist's ''condemned'' premises. This becomes most evident in the *failure* of the attempt to ''doom'' the ''pests.'' But for the metaphor to work, Styles himself becomes, at least temporarily, allied to the forces of white repression. An even more convoluted situation arises when the failure of the first attempt to evict or kill the cockroaches is followed by a much more efficient method: a cat called Blackie does the job. Even if one resists the temptation to tread much further through this particular labyrinth of metaphors, Styles's appropriation of the strong-arm tactics that traditionally characterized the apartheid regime sends some unexpected signals.

What marks the Styles circle above all else is his resort to role-playing, which is, interestingly enough, a strategy in any number of resistance plays by black writers in South Africa. Much more than a mere device to resolve the problem of tedium presented by straight narrative, role-playing operates within several systems of signification.

In the first place, role-playing extends the scope of the character's involvement in the narrative. Instead of being merely *this* individual implicated in *this* situation (a photographer and ex-factory worker in his township studio), Styles becomes a crowd, reaching beyond the twenty-seven members of an extended family who turn up to have their photograph taken to a whole community (the township), a whole society (the blacks in South Africa). ''The most powerful moments in the *Statements* plays, their most memorable images, take us beyond the private pain in which [Fugard's] own concerns are rooted,'' says Walder, ''to suggest the shape of suffering and hope for an entire community.'' In this process the plurality already hinted at in Styles's very name is actualized. This is the strategy through which Styles legitimizes his concern, not with himself as an individual or with other individuals, but with ''the simple people, who you never find mentioned in the history books.'' In short, his concern is identical with that of Brecht in *Questions of a Reading Laborer:*

> Who built the seven-towered Thebes?
> In the books we find the names of kings.
> Did the kings lug the quarried rocks to the place?
> And the often destroyed Babylon—
> Who rebuilt it so many times? In which houses
> In the gold-shimmering Lima did the build-
>   ers live? . . .
> Every ten years a great man.
> Who paid for the food?
> So many reports.
> So many questions.

Inhabiting the stage with a multitude of invisible yet highly significant people—a startlingly effective demonstration of Derridean presence of absence and absence of presence—Styles not only highlights the Camusian tenet *Je suis, donc nous sommes,* but also proposes its converse: We are, therefore I am.

In the second place, role-playing makes it possible to represent the all-encompassing yet invisible System on the stage. The representation of the objects and victims of the System is inevitable and inescapable—that is what the play is ''about.'' But for the full effect of both their suffering and their possibilities of resistance to be communicated to the audience, the *subjects* of the System must also be represented. That is why Styles's impersonation of ''Baas'' Bradley carries such peculiar weight. It demonstrates not only the existence and omnipresence of the System's *subject,* but also the possibility of subverting him by appropriating him in a totemizing function. However, if this has a positive side, namely the discovery that ''Baas'' Bradley can be manipulated and dominated in this representation, it can also be read negatively. Even when he is not physically present he continues to inhabit the minds of his victims—who can only, through play-acting, acquire a temporary ascendancy, because he is and remains *there.* After all, what does not threaten does not need to be exorcised. Through play-acting, and only through play-acting, can the actor, in the primary sense of ''actant,'' enter into a full understanding of the System, which helps to subvert it from the inside—even as it confirms it.

Representation of the System also bestows a function of relative power on the representer. Both as photographer and as narrator/producer, Styles captures, like a writer, ''in my way, on paper the dreams and hopes of my people so that even their children's children will remember a man''—a statement (and this *is,* one is constantly reminded, one of a triptych entitled *Statements*) which is confirmed by the camera's flash at the very end of the play. But the statement, as we know from Fugard's injunction quoted earlier, is offered in (distorted by?) *disguise;* and this is yet another function of play-acting in the text. This raises once again the question of the play's potential for involvement in ideological discourse through acting as a response to a very specific sociopolitical challenge. Of course, disguise need not imply denial, rejection, or even repression. It may be an acknowledgment of a variegated or stratified reality. This would involve the primary façade adopted by black people in the face of apartheid, which Lewis Nkosi refers to as ''the fantastic ambiguity, the deliberate self-deception, the ever-present irony beneath the mocking humility and moderation of speech.'' It would also involve the demonstration of what Vandenbroucke calls ''the facade as facade,'' and thereby blur the boundaries between the political and the existential. Even so the question remains whether the disguise of the political statement through play-acting may not be seen as a withdrawal into the comparative safety of aesthetics. This problem will have to be returned to later, once the text has been scrutinized in greater depth.

Another fascinating ambiguity highlighted by the processes of role-playing involves the identification of apartheid (the ideology of oppression) with death (the existential experience of the *neant*), and of political survival with life. Many commentators have noted the play's context of omnipresent death: the proximity of Styles's studio to a funeral parlor, the extermination of the cockroaches, the death of the old man two days after posing for his photograph, the funeral of Outa Jacob, who accepts ''the terms of his contract with God'', the death of Robert Zwelinzima, who literally provides Sizwe with a ''Book of Life,'' etc. The commentators have also noted the play's concomitant insistence on, and even celebration of, the forces of Life. In the process of role-playing, the past itself is identified with death, and the theatrical act with (re-)incarnation—

which affirms the present as life, and opens the possibility of a future.

This, more than anything else, elucidates the importance of the Styles improvisation which introduces the play. For it is only in the process of drawing, with all its meanderings and ambiguities, the first circle of the play, the Styles circle, that the audience is conditioned to evaluate the second, which gives the play its title. Styles does not merely establish a prologue to the play, but rehearses the conditions for its interaction with the audience. He does not simply precede the narrative, but surrounds it and contextualizes it. Approached in this way, each of the two parts becomes a "dangerous supplement" to the other.

A second circle opens as Sizwe, significantly indicated in the text or theatre program as an anonymous "Man," makes his appearance at the very moment when Styles appears to close his own. But as a result of what the spectator has already witnessed, the Sizwe circle is differently loaded. The strategy of the Styles circle had been to draw a cyclic life story, starting at the end (i.e., the narrative or theatrical present), then going to the most distant past, and proceeding back to the starting point. The Sizwe circle is not a simple repetition of this strategy, but is just as much the product of Sizwe's narration as of Styles's creative intervention. From the moment Styles greets Sizwe as "a Dream," he at the very least co-invents and co-imagines Sizwe's life. It is Styles's evocation of a possible future for Sizwe, his conversion of Sizwe from a static image, a mere "card," into a life, a "movie," which makes the reinvention of the past possible. Interestingly enough, this also involves a transformation from straight narrative (Sizwe's account of his life to Styles) via a transitional stage of slightly more highly charged dramatized narrative (the encounter with Buntu is acted out in front of the spectators, but still involves the *telling* of his story), to full-blown role-playing (the re-enactment of the scene where the dead body of Robert Zwelinzima is discovered, urinated upon, then robbed of its identity document).

The real point of the play's discourse, and its interaction with both its sociopolitical and its philosophical context, is confronted in the final debate about the significance of adopting the dead man's identity. If Styles demonstrates that survival as a "man" is possible only on the condition that the self-respect and the dignity of the individual is guaranteed, the argument presented by Buntu (who

in the second circle represents a "role" played by the same actor who was Styles in the first) is that Sizwe's only hope of survival lies in his renunciation of that dignity and self-respect embodied in his name. "Survival," writes Fugard in his *Notebooks,* "can involve betrayal of everything—beliefs, values, ideals—except Life itself."

It becomes, inevitably, a debate—the immemorial debate—about "having" and "being." The nameless "Man" who "is" both the old Sizwe and the new Robert, appears to affirm the notion of an identity divorced from all processes of naming. And as Sizwe (who announces his own death almost as soon as he appears on the stage: because, in fact, his appearance is conditional upon that death) assumes more and more the role and the identity of Robert, a process as theatrically impressive as the transformation of Arturo Ui, the distinction between a "man" and a "ghost" becomes more and more pertinent. If a black man is dehumanized in the perception of whites to the point of becoming a mere number and a ghost, argues Buntu, then "All I'm saying is be a real ghost, if that is what they want." Or, in other words, "What I'm saying is shit on our pride if we only bluff ourselves that we are men."

If the spectator's moral sympathies reside inevitably with Sizwe, who is reluctant to shed his notion of identity as the *essence* of a name, the Styles circle, which has established the processes of play-acting as the *raison d'etre* of the play itself, predetermines the outcome. Names, that first circle has demonstrated, *are* indeterminate and random: in fact, only by playing the game of the relative, which manifests itself as an endless series of versions and possibilities, is survival, and life itself, conceivable. But what, then, becomes of authenticity? And what becomes of the possibilities of authentic revolution or of any radical change in any given system? This is where a crucial problem of the play becomes obvious. Can one ever act oneself out of a given situation, or only ever more and more deeply and fatally into it?

The problem becomes even more complicated as one approaches the end of the second circle: Sizwe's transformation into Robert Zwelinzima is complete, his letter to his wife is rounded off, his excursion into the past restored to the present. Simultaneously, he returns to the pose struck for the photograph Styles has set up. (Would it be over-indulgent to wonder whether this double unfolding of a life in a single moment—first Styles's, now Sizwe's—is a demonstration of the old belief that this is what happens at the moment of *death*?) As Sizwe's smile, which is an affirmation of *life,* is petrified into a photographic image, both circles of the play are rounded off—and closure means death. Surely it would not be far-fetched to see in this circular action a theatrical manifestation—and affirmation—of the closed circle of sociopolitics within which the action has been located and from which no exit is possible. The System, in the devastating formula proposed by *Statements . . . ,* has "no vestige of a beginning, no prospect of an end." In this vicious circle the ancient hero as the man who conquers is reduced, at best, in the familiar Camusian terms, to the one who simply manages to endure.

All three *Statements* plays offer this image of closure. In *Sizwe Bansi* it resides in the circularity of the action, the confinement of Styles's studio, the inescapable present to which all flights of recollection or the imagination return. In *The Island* it is encapsulated in the image of the island itself, from which none can escape. Even if John, whose sentence has been remitted, is to return to the outside world in three months' time, the society he returns to embodies the deadly system that has created the island as prison. As in *The Tempest,* mainland and island are supplementary to each other, and life is inevitably rounded with a sleep. Ultimately, even if the play does hold out the hope of release for John in the future, the final *action* of the play is a repetition of the beginning: an endless running in a circle. In *Statements . . .* all the vicissitudes and open possibilities of life are forever frozen in half a dozen photographic images, in an implacable series of "statements": "And then at the end as at the beginning, they will find you again."

Moreover, through their presentation as a triptych with a common title, the plays interpenetrate one another: the photographs of *Statements . . . ,* images of death, inform the images of life taken by Styles; the finality of the island image also rounds off *Sizwe Bansi* and *Statements . . .*; the ancient play performed in *The Island* becomes a silent accompaniment to the action in all three, illuminating the ultimate acceptance of the fact that "Because life lives, life must die."

The only way the System can be beaten, it would seem, lies in a denial of identity, in playing the game, in remaining fully within closure. If Sizwe confronts the world as a "new" man and challenges it on its own terms, he offers no hope, and no example, to anyone else. His confrontation cannot but remain a purely personal motion. If John leaves the island, his departure neither brings nor affirms freedom for anyone else—in fact, he is as much an exception to the rule as Sizwe, his "freedom stinks." The condition of man is reduced to being "nothing." Even when Buntu provides the means of survival it can never be more than temporary. Sizwe embraces it in the full knowledge that a black man cannot *stay* out of trouble: "Our skin is trouble." The System is all-powerful and all-embracing; if Denmark's a prison, then is the world one.

Yet the end of the play is not defeatist; the rounding of the circles appears to challenge the finality of absolute closure. Buntu's last words to Sizwe are "See you tomorrow," and in the final paragraph of his letter to his wife Sizwe undertakes "to send some more [money] each week." Vandenbroucke even asserts that "Inasmuch as individual action can make a difference, *Sizwe Bansi* is far more hopeful and optimistic than the plays written solely by Fugard." If there is justification for this it would have to be located in strategies to break the either/or deadlock of traditional approaches to ideology and existentialism, to politics and theatre. Most particularly, it would have to be located in strategies to escape from the aesthetic insularity of the rounded play, to break out of the deadly circularities of structure, to transcend the fate of the individual—those solitary males whose plight dominates the action of *Sizwe Bansi,* of *The Island,* and to a large extent even of *Statements. . . .*

The most obvious device, already broached in the discussion of role-playing, involves the peopling of the theatrical space of the play with a wide variety of representatives from the society which surrounds the action and the actors. In *Statements . . .* the policeman represents not only the System, the forces of law and order, but—notably through the statement of Mrs. Buys—the outside world which invades the lovers' haven. In both the other plays the two central actors themselves re-present the absent multitude—all the more persuasive because in their invisibility they come to inhabit, to possess, the actors. In Styles and Sizwe, in John and Winston, as I have indicated above, an abstract System finds its local habitation and its name. The characters conjured up through the role-playing inhabit an intermediate space between actors and audience, moving in both directions, and thereby *involving* both. By the same token they go a long way toward fusing the "purely" political and the "merely" aesthetic.

One particularly pertinent strategy in the attempt to break out of the circle involves an appeal to the absent woman. This is illuminated by a crucial observation in *Notebooks:* "A sudden and clear realisation . . . of how, almost exclusively, 'woman'—a woman—has been the vehicle for what I have tried to say about survival and defiance."

In *Statements. . .,* of course, the woman is physically present as "the other person on the floor." Yet from the beginning, even before the intervention of the Immorality Act, the relationship between the play's protagonists is in the process of breaking down ("Is there nothing any more we can do except hurt each other?") If she represents an attempt toward human wholeness ("And he . . . And I . . . And we . . ."), it is the failure of this wholeness, through a progressive exclusion and denial of the woman by the man toward the end, that results in the irremediable bleakness of the outcome, a near-total darkness quite uncharacteristic of Fugard.

In *The Island* an accumulation of denigratory references to woman and the "place" of a woman ("You got no wife here. Look for the rag yourself"; "I'm a man, not a bloody woman") runs parallel to expressions of lack and deprivation caused by her absence (consider especially the imaginary telephone conversation which concludes Scene One)— to be resolved in the crucial play-within-the-play which figures Antigone in the central role. If in *Statements . . .* it is the very presence of the physical woman that confirms the absence of femininity, the absence of woman becomes an overwhelming presence in *The Island.* The ultimate degradations are possible *because* the figure of woman is absent from prison.

This also happens, in different ways, in *Sizwe Bansi.* The Styles circle already anticipates it. Woman may appear to figure only as the provider of food ("Get the lunch, dear"), but she is also the guarantor of family cohesion and management: "Go to your mother. . . . Look after the children, please, sweetheart." "Family" is a key word throughout the play. In the Styles circle the important role of woman is understated; but as soon as Sizwe enters she becomes the pivotal figure of the action. His experiences come to make sense, and to acquire an aim and a purpose, only by virtue of their all being interpreted in the letter to his wife Nowetu, which occupies the whole second circle of the play. Addressing himself to her in the distant King William's Town, 120 miles from where he has ended up in his

attempts to provide for her and the family, Sizwe literally reaches out from the confinement of Port Elizabeth. In perhaps the most poignant scene in the play, Sizwe strips off all his clothes to reduce himself to the barest existence of a poor fork'd creature—in which, like Shylock, he most acutely represents the whole of humanity. This is how he then defines himself: "Look at me! I am a man. I've got legs. I can run with a wheelbarrow full of cement! I'm strong! I'm a man. Look! I've got a wife. I've got four children." Being a man *means* having a wife, means acknowledging femininity as part of the self. It is his very absence from home, the family, his wife, that has resulted in all his present troubles. Eventual restoration and return to the absent Nowetu is the only resolution, and it is symbolically prefigured in the act of writing to her.

The importance of the subtext on male/female relations cannot be emphasized too much, most especially as it forms part of the interface that connects the existential and the political. Nowetu may represent the "female principle" as part of the existential experience, even possibly as part of a metaphysics of being—but she is *also* a black woman in a township suffering the degradations and deprivations imposed by apartheid. In the terms of Fugard's *Notebooks,* Nowetu is both "woman" and "a woman." In this respect, as in many others, the play does *not* represent an act of withdrawal from (sociopolitical) reality into the island of aesthetics, but rather the opposite: a demonstration of a new aesthetics as a plunge into Heideggerian "facticity" and an assumption of moral responsibility. Far from being "something out there," Nowetu is very much, and very urgently, someone *in here.*

We have seen how role-playing in *Sizwe Bansi* can be read either as part of a mere statement (registering the past) or—worse—as an escape into the imagination. But play-acting transcends the mere recapitulation or remembering of the past: it is also a reshaping, a reinvention, of that past. Because "Who controls the past . . . controls the future: who controls the present controls the past." Which is why at the very least role-playing represents the artist's victory over whatever menaces him.

It is more than a pyrrhic or private victory. It represents, in fact, the most basic function of the writer in a closed society where "normal" artistic creation is inhibited and everything is politicized: the need to *record,* the need to bear witness. It is the primary reaction, which precedes all resistance. "To mark the paper," insisted Winston Smith, "was the decisive act." This kind of "writing" implies a correction of "the conspiracy of silence" in South African history, in history generally. Unless one recognizes in this action, not a renunciation of sociopolitical action in favor of an aesthetic and/or existential response, but a highly charged *confluence* of the two, the often superficial debate about the efficacy of *Sizwe Bansi* will never proceed beyond the obvious.

Thanks to this strategy, Styles's photography—like the creative collaboration of Fugard, Ntshone, and Kani that resulted in this text—transcends the level of mere recording or witnessing toward an act of the imagination which *also* has sociopolitical implications and repercussions. Because, through role-playing, not only the past is reinvented but the present ("reality" itself) is approached *as* invented, that is, as a version of the possible or the imaginable. What Styles does involves the recording of images: but it involves also the active stimulation, in fact the creation, of dreams. His studio becomes, in that much-quoted phrase, a "strong-room of dreams." When Sizwe erupts into this space he is announced, not as a "customer," but as "a Dream."

This does not posit a simplistic binarity of "dream" versus "reality": if dream is the *mask* of reality, or reality the acting-out of the dream, each is informed by the other. And if reality itself is acknowledged—as happened *consciously* in the theatre ever since Calderon's *La Vida Es Sueno*—as imagination and fabrication (i.e., as *version,* or in postmodern parlance as *text*), it is, as Brecht would have it, not a fate to be endured but a fact which can be changed. Far from being a trap which ensnares its victim, the circle of the play is presented as a challenge to be responded to. In this lies much of the explosive revolutionary potential of the interaction between the existential and the ideological. Aesthetics here *becomes* an act of ideological choice—not of withdrawal but of immersion.

This reading of Fugard's dramaturgy in *Sizwe Bansi* returns us to what he himself, at a time when he was a particularly enthusiastic exponent of Jerzy Grotowski's Poor Theatre, regarded as basic to the theatrical experience: an "immediate and direct relationship with our audience." It means that for a more comprehensive evaluation of the interaction between aesthetics and politics we should look at the text as *performance,* i.e., as part of an experience that has no "outside" to it. In such a reading the audience assumes a vital importance. The narrative in the play may indeed present images of closed circles in which Buntu's words reverberate ad infinitum: "There's no way out, Sizwe." But the act of confronting an audience with such images cannot but stimulate a response, and this in itself is already a breaking of the circle. In the narrowest sense of the word, the play can be read as the response by a group of artists to the challenge of a sociopolitical situation. In performance it is the play that acts as challenge to elicit a response from the audience. *"Freedom is the freedom to say that two plus two make four. If that is granted, all else follows,"* said Orwell.

In conclusion I note that, in one way or another, all South African writers under apartheid faced the same dilemma; but there were, inevitably, a wide variety of responses. In Zakes Mda's play *The Hill* there is unmitigated gloom in the portrayal of the system of migrant labor as ultimately omnivorous. In *The Road* Mda presents violence as the only "way out" of the impasse of the System: the Laborer, driven beyond endurance, kills the Farmer. A more subtle end is that of *We Shall Sing for the Fatherland:* after their death from exposure, two veterans of the wars of liberation, forced into a futile life of deprivation in the margin of the "new" society, return as ghosts to haunt not only the park in which they died but the conscience of the audience. In this manner an all but direct appeal is launched to do something about the injustices that have survived racism to be perpetuated in capitalism.

One of the most forceful and exuberant plays from the Struggle is *Woza Albert!* by Mtwa, Ngema, and Simon. Going far beyond the statement of suffering under apartheid, it succeeds in combining political action with religious revivalism in appealing to the heroes of the past to replace the white man's Christ and redeem their people.

Fiction, too, demonstrates the challenge of ideology to the artistic mind. As may be expected, apocalyptic writing by white writers has found the reconciling of political and moral conscience with Western aesthetics to be problematic. In many ways John Conyngham's *The Arrowing of the Cane* is an archetype of the liberal dilemma: faced by the end of his familiar world, the spoiled scion of an English settler family, renouncing all hope of procreation, withdraws into his cellar and commits suicide after secreting the narrative of his end in a fissure which resembles a vagina. Here writing turns upon itself. A crack in a wall is hardly a cure for impotence. Wholly unlike *Sizwe Bansi,* Conyngham's creative act celebrates its own white futility.

Nadine Gordimer's response in *July's People* is fascinating. With great skill she establishes both her white and black characters as acting on behalf of larger social groupings. The white Smales family, seeking refuge in the remote community of their erstwhile trusted servant as Armageddon is unleashed on the country, represent "their kind." Their servant, July, represents "his kind." The hut in which they all are sheltered becomes archetypal, the mother of all huts, the womb. However, when in the brilliantly ambiguous final scene Maureen runs out toward a helicopter, "whether it holds saviours or murderers," it is presented as an utterly individual act—"like a solitary animal at the season when animals neither seek a mate nor take care of their young, existing only for their lone survival." What is ultimately important here, however, is not the privacy or the immediacy of her choice, but the *fact* of it: that is, the discovery that the interregnum between the convulsions of the old world and the emergent new can only be transcended through an act of *conscious and individual choice* which opens the way to the future irrespective of what that future may be. The remarkable coincidence of private decision and public responsibility, of individual integrity and social commitment, resembles in many respects the same fusion of opposites in *Sizwe Bansi*.

J. M. Coetzee's *Life and Times of Michael K* also explores the Final War, and also focuses on individual choice in an endorsement, complicated with irony, of Voltaire's *Cultivons notre jardin.* But once again, however private and imaginary the final action, it transcends the purely personal—in this case because Michael K's resolution implies the survival, not just of an individual, but of a set of values. These values are articulated only after Michael's identification with all the poor naked wretches who bide the pelting of a pitiless and universal storm. Which once again endorses the subtler meanings of *Sizwe Bansi Is Dead* and re-establishes it as, in so many ways, a key text from the apartheid experience.

Source: Andre Brink, "'No Way Out': *Sizwe Bansi Is Dead* and the Dilemma of Political Drama in South Africa," in *Twentieth Century Literature,* Winter, 1993, Vol. 39, no. 4, pp. 438–54.

Hilary Seymour

In the following essay, Seymour argues that Sizwe Bansi is Dead *is the least political and most palatable to a mass popular audience of any of the three plays that make up Fugard's trilogy.*

In the current corpus of Athol Fugard's work, the trilogy *Statements,* can be described as the political trilogy following the family one. Of the former, *Sizwe Bansi is Dead* has been the most popular component, with enthusiastic receptions in Lagos, London, Accra, Ibadan, Toronto, etc. It is the nature of its popularity that I wish to explore, for in many ways *The Island* and *Statements after an arrest under the Immorality Act* confront and explore their political themes with greater depth and penetration, particularly the latter, which as a theatrical experience must be harrowing in its impact on the spectators, whereas, *Sizwe Bansi is Dead* can be experienced at a more superficial level, with an emphasis on entertainment—that is, it can be experienced and responded to in the typical way western urban audiences consume commercial entertainment.

It is always relevant to consider the nature of the audience in relation to their responses: "Life is not determined by consciousness, but consciousness by life." Audiences, like critics and playwrights, confront plays and performances with their world-view, which is a product of the dynamic interaction between actual social relations and private sensibility, the one influencing and influenced by the other. The social characteristics of an audience are useful factors in analysing its responses to the play. In this instance, the audiences whose responses have been recorded in newspaper reviews and in literary journals are: (a) bourgeois liberals within South Africa and outside, e.g. in Britain and North America, and (b) student (i.e. sub-elite) and elite audiences in West Africa.

Apartheid laws and machinery marred and obstructed performances of the play in South Africa. The problematic nature of drama as a functioning art form in a racist police state is highlighted in an interview with Athol Fugard, where he describes how performances of the play to white audiences were stopped by the police, who also interfered with the performance of the play to a coloured audience, because of the participation of two black actors, the performance being threatened with prosecution. It is interesting to note that after these experiences, Athol Fugard registered surprise at the permission given by the South African authorities to take the play to Britain: "I cannot understand why we were finally given passports, because the work we were doing was intended only for South Africa: and *we were trying to be as courageous as possible in that context, in indicting a social system.*" Perhaps that "indictment," for all the furore it briefly provoked in South Africa in 1972 and 1973, was less damaging to apartheid officialdom than he assumed. Indeed, statements on racism which ignore its class basis are not in essence radical. The notion that the ruling Nationalist Party of South Africa should move away from discrimination based on race and colour has its advocates within the party itself, hence the divisions between the so-called *"verligtes"* (''enlightened'' liberals) and *"verkramptes"* (hardliners). Consequently, when we read comments such as the following, the limited perspective they express needs amplifying and explaining:

> That such highly political plays have been performed in South Africa surprised a British audience which was, at a guess, unanimous in its opposition to the South African government.

This critic, and the British audiences referred to, appear to be, not surprisingly, parochially ignorant of such divisions. Surely, the Oppenheimers, Anton Ruperts and Pik Bothas are representative of a section of white South African ''liberal'' opinion; and would they not be sympathetic to the reformist message of the play? It is this section of South African opinion to which Athol Fugard and his co-devisers give artistic expression.

The play, we are told, contains ''indictment.'' It is the nature of this indictment and its limitations that I shall attempt to explore, taking as my starting point the final quotation in the preface. It is, too, the nature of the indictment and its limitations, which partly explains the play's international popularity.

1 The Pass Laws are shown to be inhuman and absurd; but they are also shown to be entrenched and man it appears can do little or nothing to change social structures that rob him of his humanity and ''manhood.''

2 The most vigorous character in the play, the photographer Styles, succeeds in moving from working-class to petty-bourgeois status. Consequently, what he comes to represent is acceptable within the class framework advocated four years after the first performance of the play by M. P. Botha in 1976, and by Harry Oppenheimer and associates in 1977.

3 The message of liberal humanitarianism evades and ''ignores'' what Joe Slovo refers to as ''the class basis of racism.'' Herein lies the answer to Athol Fugard's puzzlement at the granting of permission to perform *Sizwe Bansi is Dead* to audiences outside South Africa, by the authorities of that country.

> AUDIENCES ARE 'INVOLVED' TO THE EXTENT THAT THEY ARE ASKED TO 'FEEL' FOR THE PLIGHT OF SIZWE AND PARTICIPATE IN AN EMOTIONAL AND ABSTRACT RITUAL OF IDEALISED LIBERAL BROTHERHOOD.''

The strengths and achievements of the play have been widely acclaimed by liberal critics:

> The degree of political acuity won by Fugard's use of a dramatic form unconstrained by narrative demands, in which he can write 'into space and silence' without being diverted by the linear, temporal exigencies of episode, is exemplified in *Sizwe Bansi is Dead* (1972).

In his introduction to the 1974 edition of *Statements,* Athol Fugard discusses the function of *silence,* and it becomes, with the South African context in mind, a technique of ''indictment.'' Several critics and writers, notably Nadine Gordimer and Oswald Mbuyiseni Mtshali, have noted that after the post-Sharpeville silence of the 1960s, the 1970s have seen a ''resurrection of black writing'' within South Africa, mainly in poetry—a poetry which operates through understatement and irony and what has been aptly termed ''the cryptic mode.'' ''Silence'' may be thought-provoking, intellectually and emotionally stimulating, or it may signify a failure to make connections, in which case it will serve a negative function. Behind Styles's statement that he wants to be his own ''baas'' (quoted in the preface), weighs a heavy silence. As I perceive it, his articulation of his ambition is in no way ironic.

Athol Fugard's choice of a small number of characters and emphasis on actors 'staking' their ''personal truths,'' derives in part from the influence of Jerzy Grotowski's ''theatre laboratory.'' In both cases, the method is one whereby the characters reveal themselves to the audience. *Sizwe Bansi is Dead* is a play based on the elaboration of personal biography. A small number of case histories, situated in appropriate social contexts, serve as social commentary. The focus on a small number of isolated individuals is appropriate to the liberal conceptual framework. In evaluating this method and its application it is pertinent to ask the following questions:

(i) What aspects of South African life do the characters in the play represent and how effectively?

(ii) What are the ideological implications of their responses to society?

(iii) How do these reveal the playwright's perspective on the issues of class and colour in South Africa?

The preliminary stage directions indicate something of Styles's role in the society. He is a member of the black petty bourgeoisie, a small-scale entrepreneur who owns his business. In the list of services he offers, pride of place is given to "Reference books," followed by "Passports" and then "Weddings; engagements, birthday parties and parties." "Reference books" is a euphemistic term designating the notorious documents all African workers are required to carry under the Pass Laws. These booklets must contain a photograph of the bearer. Therefore, Styles in his New Brighton studio is in a position to capitalise on this aspect of apartheid.

Styles has made an adaptation to the system, which also represents his dependence on it, although this aspect of "personal" and public "truth" is not probed. Silence weighs heavy. The first performance of the play was on 8 October 1972, in Cape Town, more than a decade after the campaign of passive resistance which culminated in the Sharpeville killings and the declaration of a state of emergency in 1960, and four years before the Soweto uprising. Indeed, from this particular aspect—Styles's fundamental passivity and pragmatism—the play belongs conceptually more to the 1960s than to the 1970s. The Treason Trials of 1958–61 and the Sharpeville Shootings of 1960 belong to a period when organised opposition to apartheid policies was being systematically smashed and the failure of the tactics of passive resistance had weakened morale. The 1960s was also a decade of ruthless censorship systematically imposed, a period when many South African writers were driven to despair and exile. Styles's response makes sense as a passive and pragmatic individual response to the social circumstances he finds himself in. Exploration does not go beyond this point, however. The play satirises the absurdities of the Pass Laws, yet one of the three characters, whose individualistic entrepreneurial initiative is portrayed in a positive light, paradoxically contributes to the functioning of those very laws. On this issue the playwright is significantly if

understandably silent. Styles has learnt to survive as an individual—indeed, individual survival is the play's major theme—but his success story is the exception and not the rule. His studio is *a strong-room of dreams,* his function much of the time to encourage the illusions and self-delusions of the black working class, to provide them with temporary catharsis, emotional escapism and a fantasy world of unrealisable aspirations, all of which serve to maintain a system of economic and racial exploitation:

> *Styles:* That's my man! Look at this, Robert. (*Styles reverses the map hanging behind the table to reveal a gaudy painting of a futuristic city.*) City of the Future! Look at it. Mr Robert Zwelinzima, man about town, future head of Feltex, walking through the City of the Future!

In certain respects, Styles's studio, his "strong-room of dreams" is analogous in its function to the church in Oswald Mtshali's poem "An old man in church." But where Mtshali recognises the pacifying function of religious ritual in relation to the social services it performs, Fugard's presentation of Styles as a guardian of illusions misses out on the political implications of that role. The poem is a brilliant piece of sustained, sharp and controlled irony:

> I know an old man,
> who during the week is a machine working at
>   full throttle:
> productivity would stall,
> spoil the master's high profit estimate,
> if on Sunday he did not go to church
> to recharge his spiritual batteries.

Similarly, Styles's photographic services "recharge" the "spiritual batteries" of the black urban poor, so that after a brief respite in his retreat, they may return passive and docile to factory, mine and urban slum, their capacity for patient endurance and acceptance renewed by escapist indulgence in fantasy worlds. The playwright's perspective on his subject is limited, because descriptive rather than interpretative, with the areas of description themselves being highly selective. Interest in individual character and personal truth overrides other concerns, such as the need to relate the individual to his class and to understand the nature of his social relations in historical and political perspective.

Styles's responses to apartheid capitalism differ according to his role as wage labourer and petty businessman. As a wage labourer, his relationship with fellow workers is characterised by an intimate camaraderie, whereas the nature of the dialogue, reported and actual, between entrepreneur and client is manipulative and patronising.

In his role as translator of the general foreman's instructions to the car plant workers, Styles conveys not only the necessary instructions and prescriptions, but demonstrates the contradictions in labour relations and conditions for the automobile factory. Through irony, paradox and carefully-chosen descriptions, which highlight the absurdities characteristic of working conditions in the factory, he achieves a skilful and indirect verbal indictment of industrial relations. He begins to articulate the general conditions of wage-labour exploitation, conditions which highlight the international exploitative nature of the multinationals as they seek to maximise profits by investing in those countries offering a plentiful supply of cheap and readily-available labour. In the play, management is shown to be loyally eager to impress the visiting American Ford boss on his inspection tour of the South African subsidiary, that this labour force is more manageable, more malleable than its Afro-American counterpart, or that, in other words, American investment is secure and will continue to yield high profits.

Styles, in his role as intermediary, comes to the point where he is capable of triggering off potential dissent among his listeners. His role allows him to play a curious verbal power game.

> "Styles, tell the boys that when Mr. Henry Ford comes into the plant I want them all to look happy. We will slow down the speed of the line so that they can sing and *smile* while they are working."

> Gentlemen, he says that when the door opens and his grandmother walks in *you must see to it that you are wearing a mask of smiles.* Hide your true feelings, brothers. You must sing. The joyous songs of the days of old before we had fools like this one next to me to worry about!. . ."(Emphasis added.)

Here, he is not just passively relaying messages, he is using language creatively to provoke his receptive listeners into perceiving the contradictions of their situation (and his). The humour is caustic, sharp, double-edged and to the point. By contrast, his use of language in his role as photographer is flat, dull, cliché-ridden, vague and sentimental.

However, Styles's response to his heightened awareness of the exploitative nature of the multinationals remains fundamentally individual and individualised. Thus the devisers of the play do not explore the potential of the material they have only sketched into space and silence. There remains an evasion of underlying and fundamental issues. Styles does not develop his skills as potential spokesman and intermediary between local white management and black employees. On the contrary, he

chooses to withdraw from the situation and to assert his "manhood." He chooses personal assertion, not public commitment, in the interests of maintaining the family of which he is the head and chief bread-winner. To succeed in his business, he is forced to change and modify his voice and the nature of his communication with his exploited brothers and sisters. He no longer shares the same aspects of a common economic and social reality with them. Instead of highlighting the contradictions and absurdities of industrial apartheid, he becomes a skilful manipulator of individual sensibilities, a public relations officer retailing acceptance of the status quo. Same talent, different objectives and different effects! Styles encourages in individual clients the expression of sentimentality at the expense of reason and thus he performs a socially mystifying and intellectually soporific function. Styles's "upward social mobility," new economic status as entrepreneur and sense of personal achievement are marked by a change in his social relations. The implications of these changed social relations are neither recognised nor explored. Styles the photographer still likes to think of himself as some sort of spokesman for "his people," providing them with a valuable service.

As a character, Styles is static, at times almost grotesque in his antics, like the "monkeys" he so scathingly refers to in his long monologue at the beginning of the play. There can be no character growth, because Styles the entrepreneur has defined the limits and nature of his social relations and has found himself a niche, albeit not a very cosy one, in the established order. Styles's clients are told to hide their pain, to suppress and submerge their true feelings, to conform to the norms and expectations of society, even when these are directly inimical to their interests.

Contrast this image with the one which emerges from the poems of Sipho Sepamla, published four years later. These are in the main, angry, assertive disclosures of pain. The anger is both private and public, rooted in the historical reality of the Soweto uprisings of 1976. The future is not seen as a closed door but as a door that has to be forced open. Look at the following extracts from "At the dawn of another day":

> it was on that day children
> excused the past
> deploring the present
> their fists clenched full of the future
> and:
> at the height of the day
> youth spilled all over the place

unleashing its own energy
confounding the moment
exploding the lie
take away
your teachings
take away
your promises
take away
your hope
take away
your language
give
me
this
day
myself
i shall learn myself anew
i shall read myself from the trees
i shall glean myself from all others
i shall wean myself of you . . .

In a subsequent poem in the same collection, Sepamla, unlike Fugard and his co-dramatists, assesses clearly the shifting political sands of the petty traders and entrepreneurs of Soweto. During periods of social crisis, they cannot be relied upon:

but sis'rosie
the one with the biggest business
she declares
in the presence of her customers
i'm not mad
i must live
i must pay the rent
i must pay school-fees
i have no husband
i swear
i won't sell on tick
only take-away

Sis' Rosie, the Soweto she been queen, is another version of Styles. She too is a petty entrepreneur, who is anxious not to lose her precarious foothold in the system. The difference in presentation is that Sipho Sepamla's poem "Queens/Kings," places Sis Rosie's individual response with all its understandable limitations within a broader and a more specific social and political reality. Here *silence,* that is the lack of poetic commentary, functions as indictment.

Sipho Sepamla's pain cannot be suppressed. Indeed, his experiences and responses, trigger off the need to articulate pain:

I want to remember these things
because I had never known such hate before
I remember the click of my tongue
my muscles tightening round my chest
I looked at his covered face
feeling the crush of pain as he was being felled
by that bullet

There is here an insistence on the need to recall images of pain; the poet wrestles with words (to paraphrase T.S. Eliot) to discover, to make coherent and to hold on to the reality of his identity.

On the contrary, Styles the photographer/salesman encourages his pliant customers to dream unattainable dreams and "smile" at the world. And yet we know Styles has been critical of an economic system that makes the factory worker a slave to a machine. The cost of Styles's economic success is a stifling of his nascent political awareness and an attempt to stifle that of others. The 48-year-old municipality worker, holding his Standard Six Certificate, Third Class and dreaming in front of Styles's camera of becoming a "graduate, self-made," is typical of Styles's customers, in orientation and aspiration. The image of the self-made man pulling himself up by his boot straps is a key concept in the mythology and ideological superstructure of industrial capitalist societies.

The difference between the devious sentimentality of the entrepreneur and the realistic appraisal of the factory worker exposing the hypocrisy of management and foreman can be demonstrated in the use Styles makes of the key word SMILE in these two contrasting situations.

(a) Styles's role as interpreter/translator affords him, as I have already argued, the opportunity of exposing the foreman and management to ridicule and this ridicule fulfils two functions. First, it serves to sharpen the self-awareness of Styles and his brothers—an awareness, which in its apprehension of socio-economic realities is demystifying. And secondly, exposing the white foreman to ridicule punctures the official mythology propping up the concept of white superiority. That which is officially sacred is made to look absurd, grotesque. Baas Bradley's linguistic limitations render him temporarily dependent on the man he is used to ordering about. Styles's translations and adaptation of Bradley's instructions implicitly and skilfully make the point that if the workers "smile" for the American managing director of the multinational corporation, they are conniving in their own alienation, they are playing the role of "monkeys," puppets, clowns, formally allotted them. When Styles conveys the message "you must see to it that you are wearing a *mask of smiles,"* he underlines the point that they are performing in false consciousness, a role that is in diametric opposition to the expression of authentic feelings and responses. Like the machines they operate, they are groomed and programmed for inspection. Nor are they rewarded for "smiling"—they are required to make up for lost time and lost profits, after the rapid departure of the visiting American boss, by the same management which gave the instruction for the productive process to be slowed down. The word *mask* signals the fundamental opposition between appearance and reality. Styles is conscious of this dichotomy and exploits his role of interpreter to mediate powerfully and arouse in his brothers a consciousness of their true position. His efforts are so effective that he is taken aback by the assertive and vigorous responses he provokes. But uncertain of his intentions and lacking any clear political direction or objective, he puts a brake on his verbal provocations, which ultimately become only temporary and spontaneous diversions from the normal, work routine. Styles's monologue evokes something of the mounting tensions and potentially explosive nature of tightly controlled and rigid industrial relations. It is significant that on the threshold of political initiative, he draws back, afraid of the forces he is beginning to unleash:

> "Gentlemen, he says we must remember, when Mr. Ford walks in, that we are South African monkeys, not American monkeys. South African monkeys are much better trained. . ."
>
> Before I could finish, a voice was shouting out of the crowd: "He's talking shit!" I had to be careful!. . .

He withdraws into caution and individual self-interest and leaves factory floor for photographic studio. In the final analysis, the games he plays at the expense of the credibility of the managers of industry have more entertainment than politicising value and, due to his restraint and self-imposed limitations, serve only as a safety valve allowing frustrated workers to let off steam, to release tensions partially and temporarily. Indeed, after the fleeting appearance of the big white boss from the USA, "It ended up with us working harder that bloody day than ever before."

In reviewing his situation, Styles determines to seek a more permanent escape from the conditions he has described so well. Chance and lucky coincidence enable him to succeed. But, from a broader perspective, his individual success has to be balanced against the unmentioned failures, against the many who do not succeed in finding a way to escape from the conditions of wage labourers on the factory floor, from conditions that make men feel they have lost their "manhood."

(b) Styles the photographer is continuously asking his customers to smile, and not just at the camera but at the world. "Smile" is the last word of the play and his parting advice to Robert/Sizwe. The function of Styles's verbal skills has changed. He no longer uses them to distinguish "mask" from reality. Reality and fantasy are fused in the dream worlds he sells to his customers. As it is demonstrated to us, Styles's commercial success depends on the gullibility, sentimentality and good-natured naivety of his customers. They are all stamped with the same quality of amiable simplicity and exhibit a certain dull docility. Indeed, they belong to a stereotype that has links and affinities with the standard presentation of "good," i.e. passive black characters in South African fiction of the liberal, Christian humanist tradition. Such characters are humble, passive and stoic. Simplicity and docility can be associated with Sizwe Bansi and his willing and pathetic participation in the fantasy world populated by self-made men and propagated by proprietor Styles. Like Styles, Sizwe directs his energy towards the immediate goal of individual survival, with his responsibilities to wife and children uppermost in his mind. His one angry outburst is made while drunk and is directed against the shallow hypocrisy of the establishment of so-called "independent homelands."

> *MAN (To the audience)* I must tell you, friend . . . when a car passes or the wind blows up the dust, Ciskeian Independence makes you cough.
>
> I'm telling you, friend . . . put a man in a pondok and call that Independence? My good friend, let me tell you . . . Ciskeian Independence is shit!

Sizwe's comment is a spontaneous response which offsets and undermines official pronouncements on the subject. But it is an atypical and isolated outburst. Our main impression of Sizwe is of a man who is simple, humble, intellectually limited and politically unaware, a man unaccustomed to asking questions, a man who readily complies with Styles's repeated injunctions to smile at the world. These injunctions and what they conceal, signal Styles's new status and economic position. His social mobility is an example of how capitalism contains and absorbs potential voices of dissent. It is the failure to probe the empty clichés of the photographer Styles, and their political implications, that leaves an uneasy sense of dissatisfaction in the minds of those who seek more from theatre than entertainment or descriptive narrative that reminds guilty liberal consciences, especially outside South Africa, that the Pass Law system is inhuman, unworkable and absurd.

There emerge two contradictory messages in the play: a cry of outraged human dignity stemming from the indignities of the urban situation confronting Sizwe Bansi (a cry echoed in Styles's earlier commentary on his work routine at the factory) and a plea for patient endurance on the part of Styles the photographer, a plea which at moments does not escape the charge of complacency. The nature of these contradictions is inevitable, for they are embedded in the liberal position itself. The cries of outrage against the alienating conditions of the South African wage-labour system have to be balanced against the more persistent voices of accommodation. Contradictions also occur *within* the fragmented consciousness of individual characters such as Sizwe and Styles, who contain within themselves different and opposing voices.

Sizwe, in contrast to his customary tone of patient perplexity, does make one direct appeal to the audience for sympathetic understanding of his simple, indeed simplistic, plea: the right to urban employment and identity.

> What's happening in this world, good people? Who cares for who in this world? Who wants who?
>
> Who wants me, friend? What's wrong with me? I'm a man. I've got eyes to see. I've got ears to listen when people talk.
>
> I've got a head to think good things. What's wrong with me? (*Starts to tear off his clothes.*) Look at me! I'm a man. I've got legs. I can run with a wheelbarrow full of cement! I'm strong! I'm a man. Look I've got a wife, I've got four children. How many has he made, lady? (*The man sitting next to her.*) Is he a man? What has he got that I haven't . . .?

The questions he puts to the audience are purely emotional appeals to "man's better nature," a key concept in liberal philosophy, which at this point in the play manifests itself as an undefined existential assumption to be shared by actor and audience. Audiences are "involved" to the extent that they are asked to "feel" for the plight of Sizwe and participate in an emotional and abstract ritual of idealised liberal brotherhood.

At this point Sizwe shows himself to be a victim of acute alienation. Underlying the apparent simplicity of the Man's plea can be detected deep psychological malaise. First, Sizwe's or the Man's initial assertion is negative, self-deprecating, almost apologetic. The contrast in tone with Sipho Sepamla's "At the dawn of another day" again springs to mind. Secondly, he sees himself through the eyes of others. Where the "i" of Sepamla's poem is self-defining, the "I" of Sizwe's appeal is defined for

him by others. He is implicitly trapped in labels and categories that bear little relation to his experiences and perceptions of the world around him. It is only when he is drunk that a more authentic response surfaces, as I have already noted. There is a rupture between individual sensibility and its expression on the one hand, and societal norms and expectations on the other, where the former represent class interests fundamentally at odds with the latter. Liberal rhetoric and ritual appeals to universal brotherhood can only "dodge" this issue. Thirdly, not only does Sizwe lament his degraded status in the eyes of the ruling white bourgeoisie, he also laments, though he does not understand, the state of alienation that reduces black urban workers to fragmented islands of defensive and exclusive material self-interest. The lesson of self-interest, as the best strategy for survival in a ruthless and reified world, is the one that Buntu attempts to teach his unwilling pupil; it is the same lesson that Leah preaches to Xuma in Peter Abrahams' *Mine Boy,* and it receives the same instinctively hostile reception.

Behind Sizwe's appeals and the dialogue that follows, we find a thinly-veiled indictment of the Pass System. But there is more at stake: Sizwe and Buntu are less than "man," not simply because of their colour but because of their class. The problem of alienation is not simply a problem of colour. Replacing Baas Bradley and other "bigger bosses" by black counterparts would not change the real face of capitalism.

In the closing lines of the play, Robert/Sizwe is asked to smile. Styles is in his position behind the camera, but the audience is left feeling uneasy about Robert Zwelinzima's precarious urban future and the long-term outcome of the false identity game Buntu persuades him to play. Styles's final message to Robert carried more than a literal meaning; for here "smile" involves the adoption of a mask and identification with it. It also means accepting a split personality, torn between a public image and a suppressed private reality with which it is inevitably at odds. The devisers of the play have themselves exercised caution in the focus they give to the situations and characters they have chosen to sketch on to the silence of the stage. However, this may paradoxically explain the acclaim with which middle-class audiences in the West, and indeed elsewhere, have received the play. At times, the laughter is a little too light, the smiles a little too thin; for ultimately neither laughter nor smiles are adequate even if ambivalent responses to the painful realities of a strife-torn land.

The play belongs to a liberal tradition which is both international and national.

By way of conclusion, I wish to focus on certain ideological affinities *Sizwe Bansi is Dead* shares with two earlier South African novels, namely Alan Paton's *Cry the Beloved Country* and Peter Abraham's *Mine Boy*. The perspective of these writers is that of the liberal visionary. (In this respect it is misleading to argue that *Mine Boy* is a proletarian novel whose plot displays a marxist perspective on life, just as it is misleading to discuss *Sizwe Bansi is Dead* as though it carried a politically radical message.)

1 The humanitarian impulse is uppermost in the characters presented sympathetically to audience or reader. Characters like the Reverend Stephen Kumalo, Xuma, and Sizwe Bansi constantly appeal to the better side of human nature—an existential assumption never defined or contextually specified.

2 The message of the liberal visionary writer is reformist, often at odds with the reality described. It is a message which papers over cracks which in reality threaten the whole edifice. The vision of society, in this kind of literature, is static and pessimistic with regard to material conditions and progress. Appeals are made to the emotions at the expense of reason. Such appeals gloss over hard social realities by a dubious process of sublimation and idealisation. Pessimism with regard to material progress is offset by directing readers' and audiences' attention to spiritual or material fantasy worlds, in which problems miraculously disappear.

3 To carry the reformist message, everyman figures and ostensibly universal types are frequently used. Thus, Sizwe Bansi is referred to as "the Man" and Xuma as "the man" who comes "from the north." The Reverend Stephen Kumalo is, par excellence, the suffering Christian pilgrim and a direct descendant of John Bunyan's allegorical hero. The novel, however, is not allegorical but borrows from the later traditions of social realism. Social contexts, periods and places are all to a limited extent particularised and specified, though they lack the vivid situational immediacy that characterises the work of such writers as Alex La Guma. The reformist message produces a tension of modes and methods in the three works cited for comparison.

4 Great emphasis is attached to the importance of individual morality. Characters held up for our approval are usually those who accommodate them-

selves, in one way or another, to a status quo inherently inimical to their material interests.

Thus we meet the paradox of the cult of the individual given literary expression in contexts clearly inimical to individual self-fulfilment. Ndotsheni (Natal), Claremont (Johannesburg), Malay Camp (Johannesburg) and New Brighton (Port Elizabeth) are shown to be environments, in which the practice of a privatised or minority code of liberal ethics becomes problematic to say the least. The treatment of Ndotsheni in Alan Paton's *Cry the Beloved Country* is an interesting example of the failure of the liberal position to connect the superstructure to the social and economic bases of society. Stephen Kumalo's moral code, romantic pastoral attachment to the land and the "tribe" and his repeated lament over the rural exodus to the towns are typical of the ahistorical notion that individual moral precept can change social conditions and that morals make men, rather than men morals. Kumalo's, and by extension the author's moral vision, ignore: (a) the historical background of the area. In Natal "the use by the settlers of state power to force the African peasantry to become workers," by depriving them of their land and liberty, had led to the Bambata Rebellion of 1906, in which "some 4,000 Africans and 25 whites were killed in the fighting." (b) that the commercial success of John Jarvis and his kind depends on the continuing exploitation and expropriation of rural black labour, deprived of their ancestral farm lands and forced into either a rural or an urban wage labour system. Thus, Stephen Kumalo's moral injunctions have no historical or practical validity, except perhaps in heaven.

Kumalo, Xuma and Sizwe Bansi are models for the moral message their creators use them to convey. They are long-suffering, passive and accommodating by nature. At the same time, they often exhibit feelings of helpless moral anguish and intense loneliness. The authors' literary pursuit of the cult of the individual tends to isolate characters from group experience. We see little of Xuma in his work situation, more attention being given to the romantic love theme. Sizwe and Xuma do assert the right to urban identity and residence, a position Alan Paton would appear to shy away from in *Cry the Beloved Country*. Nevertheless, Xuma offers himself as a sacrificial lamb to the legal and penal machinery of a system he has labelled unjust. Motivated by personal loyalty to his white liberal brother, he contemplates an act of futile heroism that can serve no social function. Ironically, considerations of colour override those of class. True sacrifice, argues Kihika, the freedom fighter in Ngugi's *A Grain of Wheat,* should have a practical objective and impact.

It is interesting to note that Athol Fugard has linked his political and artistic position and his responses to that position with those of Alan Paton, who, par excellence, represents South African liberalism:

> I think I can go on producing plays under segregation (mixed audiences are not allowed) even admitting some non-whites to private readings. But eventually I may have to take a stand like Paton's (i.e., a certain degree of political commitment). We are in a corner. And all we can do is dodge here and push there. And under it all there's a backwash of guilt.

No matter how well or effectively it is presented, the liberal position tends to be negative in its impact. It is a position caught in the web of its own contradictions. As a response to the South African situation it remains inadequate, characterised by "dodges" and evasions. Kumalo performs a salvage operation for members of his family lost in urban iniquity and tries to hold family and "tribe" together in a Christian, pastoral vision, which is blind to past and present realities. Xuma, like some latterday Don Quixote, dedicates his life to a personal crusade waged in the name of universal brotherly love. Sizwe/Robert smiles at a world that robs him of his "manhood," and Styles asserts his manhood at the price of serving a system whose inhumanity he once deplored.

Source: Hilary Seymour, "*Sizwe Bansi Is Dead:* A Study of Artistic Ambivalence," in *Race and Class,* 1980, Vol. 21, pp. 273–89.

SOURCES

Clurman, Harold, review of *Sizwe Bansi Is Dead,* in *The Nation,* December 12, 1974, pp. 637-38.

Gill, Brendan, "The Great Ratiocinator," in *The New Yorker,* November 25, 1974, p. 131.

Hughes, Catharine, "Two from South Africa," in *America,* December 21, 1974, p. 415.

Kauffmann, Stanley, review of *Sizwe Bansi Is Dead* and *The Island,* in *The New Republic,* December 21, 1974, pp. 16, 26.

Kroll, Jack, "The Beloved Country," in *Newsweek,* December 2, 1974, p. 98.

Vandenbroucke, Russell, *Truths the Hand Can Touch: The Theatre of Athol Fugard,* Ad. Donker, 1986, p. 167.

Weales, Gerald, review of *Sizwe Bansi is Dead,* in *Commonweal,* January 17, 1975, pp. 330-31.

FURTHER READING

Brink, Andre, "'No Way Out': *Sizwe Bansi is Dead* and the Dilemma of Political Drama in South Africa," in *Twentieth Century Literature,* Winter, 1993, pp. 438-55.
  This article focuses on the play's cyclic nature and treatment of apartheid.

Donahue, Francis, "Apartheid's Dramatic Legacy: Athol Fugard," in *The Midwest Quarterly,* Spring, 1995, pp. 323-31.
  This interview provides an overview of Fugard's career, including *Sizwe Bansi Is Dead.*

Lester, Eleanor, "I Am in Despair about South Africa," in *New York Times,* December 1, 1974, Section 2, p. 5.
  This article features an interview with Fugard and discusses the genesis of *Sizwe Bansi Is Dead.*

Peck, Richard, "Condemned to Chose, But What? Existentialism in Selected Works by Fugard, Brink, and Gordimer," in *Research in African Literatures,* Fall, 1992, pp. 67-83.
  This article explores the existential aspects of Fugard's plays.

Walder, Dennis, "Crossing Boundaries: The Genesis of the Township Plays," in *Twentieth Century Literature,* Winter, 1993, pp. 409-23.
  This article surveys Fugard's "township plays."

The Three Sisters

ANTON CHEKHOV
1901

Chekhov referred to *The Three Sisters* as a "drama," preferring to avoid the more confining labels of either "comedy" or "tragedy," although later critics have argued for both of those labels. It is one of the four major plays that he wrote at the end of his life. Chekhov was an accomplished fiction writer, one of the one of the most influential short story writers of all time. At the time that his plays were being produced there was some criticism that his dramas too closely resembled the style of fiction. Traditionalists found the action too cramped and the characters too inexpressive, noting that there were too many people on the stage at any one time, doing nothing, for audiences to be able to register the significance of it all. Contrary to expectations, though, Chekhov's plays were very popular in Moscow, where they were staged by the famous Moscow Art Theatre under the direction of Constantin Stanislavsky.

The Three Sisters was the first play that Chekhov wrote specifically for the Moscow Art Theatre, having experienced commercial success in his previous collaborations with the company, *The Seagull* and *Uncle Vanya*. Like many of Chekhov's works, it is about the decay of the privileged class in Russia and the search for meaning in the modern world. In the play, Olga, Masha, and Irina are refined and cultured young women in their twenties who were raised in urban Moscow but have been living in a small, colorless provincial town for eleven years. With their father dead, their anticipated return to

Moscow comes to represent their hopes for living a good life, while the ordinariness of day-to-day living tightens its hold. First performed in 1901, *The Three Sisters* is a perennial favorite of actors and audiences.

AUTHOR BIOGRAPHY

Although Anton Pavlovich Chekhov was trained as a physician and practiced as one, he came to dominate not just one field of literature, but two: plays and short stories. He was born in 1860 in Taganrog, a provincial town in the Ukraine area of Russia that was similar to the one described in *The Three Sisters*. His family had a small grocery business that went bankrupt, forcing them to move to Moscow in 1876, although Chekhov stayed behind in Taganrog to finish his education. With a scholarship to Moscow University, he studied to be a doctor of medicine, going into practice in 1884. At that time he started publishing short humorous sketches in the Moscow newspapers, though he had no serious artistic aspirations. His writing career became earnest when he moved to St. Petersburg in 1885 and befriended the editor of a literary journal, who recognized his talent and encouraged him. He did write plays, and some of these were produced, but his most memorable work from that period were his short stories, and by late 1880s, he was one of the world's great masters of short story writing.

It was in the late 1890s, when Chekhov became associated with the Moscow Art Theatre, that he reached full maturity as a playwright. The theater, under director Constantin Stanislavsky (whose theories about acting method are standard texts for theater students today), produced *The Seagull* in 1896, followed by *Uncle Vanya* (1899), *The Three Sisters* (1901) and *The Cherry Orchard* (1904). Chekhov was very involved in the Moscow Art Theatre's productions of his plays, offering suggestions for the actors and constantly rewriting passages. He courted an actress from the company, Olga Knipper, who played Masha in the original production of *The Three Sisters* (he wrote the part with her in mind); they were married in 1901, just four months after the play opened. During much of their marriage, they were apart, because Chekhov, suffering from tuberculosis since 1884, often went to country retreats for medical treatment. He died of tuberculosis in Yalta in 1904, when he was forty-four years old.

PLOT SUMMARY

Act I

Act I takes place on May 5th of an unspecified year, in an unspecified provincial town in Russia. It is the twentieth birthday of Irina, the youngest of the sisters mentioned in the play's title. It is also the one year anniversary of the death of their father, Colonel Prozorov, who moved his family there from Moscow eleven years earlier. Irina and her older sisters, Olga and Masha, receive visitors, members of the military battery that is assigned to the town. The sisters discuss how bored they are with the town, how they long to move back to Moscow, and their brother Andrei, who will probably become a university professor. Olga, who is twenty-eight and the oldest sister, expresses interest in the new lieutenant colonel who has been assigned to the town, Vershinin, but is told that he is married, with two children. Chebutykin, the drunken old doctor who had been in love with the girls mother, gives Irina a silver samovar for her birthday, which is considered an inappropriate gift.

Vershinin arrives, explaining that he knew the sisters' father back in Moscow, and that he remembers them from when they were girls. When he talks philosophically about how time makes all their lives insignificant, Solyony, a rough staff captain, mocks him by spouting gibberish. The sisters explain that they have been teasing their brother Andrei for being in love with a local girl, Natasha, who is married to the chairman of the county board, Protopopov. Masha's husband, Kulygin, arrives to take Masha to a school function, but she angrily refuses to go. Tuzenbach, an army lieutenant, expresses his love for Natasha, but she expresses her disinterest in him. When Natasha enters, Olga feels sorry for her poor fashion sense and suggests that her belt does not match the rest of her clothes. When everyone else leaves for the dining room for the celebration, Andrei tells Natasha of his love for her and asks her to marry him.

Act II

Almost a year later, in mid-February, Andrei and Natasha are married and living in the family house. The sisters have invited their friends and some performers from the carnival that is in town over to the house, but Natasha tells Andrei that she objects to letting them in because she is worried about the health of their baby, Bobik. Ferapont, an old servant, enters with paperwork for Andrei, who is the secretary of the county board. When they leave the room, Masha and Vershinin enter and discuss their love for each other. Irina and Tuzenbach enter; he still is in love with her, and she is still uninterested. They discuss the great gambling losses that Andrei has incurred. Vershinin is called away by a letter from his daughter, saying that his wife has attempted suicide once again. Solyony arrives, is rude to Natasha, and is threatening to Tuzenbach, the reason for which becomes clear later in the scene, when he expresses his love for Irina and vows to kill any rivals. Natasha has the carnival performers sent away when they show up at the door, and, while Irina is upset about Solyony's threatening words, asks her to move out of her bedroom and into Olga's so that the baby can have her room. She goes to the door when she hears a sleigh bell and comes back acting surprised that it is Protopopov, come to take her for a ride, explaining that she feels that she has to accept. Kulygin and Vershinin enter the scene again—the former's meeting is over and the latter's wife is all right—to find that everyone has gone. The scene ends with Olga complaining of her terrible headaches and Irina repeating her wish to return to Moscow.

Act III

Act III takes place nearly four years after the opening of the play; Irina, who was twenty then, tells Olga that she is "almost twenty-four" while explaining how washed up she feels. This act takes place in the bedroom Olga and Irina share, while a fire is spreading across the neighborhood outside. Olga is choosing clothes from her closet to give to the fire victims, who have lost all of their belongings. She has invited people who have been made homeless by the fire, particularly Vershinin and his family, to spend the night there, but when she enters Natasha objects, saying that she doesn't want her son and new daughter to be exposed to the flu. Natasha discussing firing Anfisa, the old nurse who, as Olga explains, has been with the family for thirty years. Kulygin enters, again unable to find Masha, and brings the news that the doctor, Chebutykin, is drunk. When he enters, feeling guilty about a patient that has died, Chebutykin picks up a clock that once belonged to the girls' mother and breaks it: in his embarrassment, while everyone is staring at him disapprovingly, he blurts out that Natasha and Protopopov are having an affair. When Masha arrives, she and Vershinin communicate to each other in code, with musical notes. Kulygin tells Masha how much he loves her, how important she is to him, but she asks him to leave her alone to rest for a short while. When everyone is gone, the sisters talk about

Anton Chekhov

how difficult their lives are and about how difficult Natasha has made Andrei's life. Olga's advice to Irina, who hates her job, is to marry Tuzenbach, whether she loves him or not. After Natasha passes through the room with a candle, Masha confesses to her sisters that she is in love with Vershinin. Andrei enters and tells them that he has mortgaged the house to pay his gambling debts and given control of his money to Natasha. Irina announces that she will marry Tuzenbach.

Act IV

About a year after the previous act, in the garden outside of the house. The soldiers have been assigned to a new post and are stopping by throughout this scene to say goodbye. There is gossip about a fight that took place the previous day outside of the theater, during which Solyony challenged Tuzenbach to a duel. Olga is living at the school where she teaches, and Irina is planning on leaving with Tuzenbach later that day for Moscow. Chebutykin leaves to be a witness to the duel, and Andrei enters, pestered by his assistant to sign more and more paperwork for the county board. As Masha cries over being left by Vershinin, her husband, Kulygin, tries to comfort her, not admitting that he knows what she is upset about. Natasha already has plans for the rooms of the house being vacated: she is moving Andrei down to Irina's room, ever further from her own, so that her baby Irina can have his room. Word comes that Tuzenbach has been killed in the duel, and at the play's end Irina, Olga, and Masha think about the future, hoping that they may one day understand the meaning of it all.

CHARACTERS

Anfisa

The old governess who has been with the Prozorov family for thirty years, Anfisa is worried that she will be turned out on her own in her old age. Her concerns are justified—while the Prozorov sisters care enough about tradition and sentiment to laugh at the idea of abandoning Anfisa, Natasha is adamant that the old woman is a drain on the household funds, and it is Natasha who is taking over the running the house. In the end, when everyone is going their separate ways, it is only Anfisa who seems happy about the future—she is to live in a government apartment with one of her girls, Olga, and she asks nothing more of life.

Ivan Romanovich Chebutykin

An old friend of the sisters, a military doctor, a failure, an alcoholic who laments the patients of his who have died. He lives in the basement of the house. In the first scene, he brings a silver samovar to Irina's birthday party: the silver samovar is traditionally a wedding present, indicating that Chebutykin is either confused or trying to send a signal. His most important scene occurs when he drops he clock in Act III, smashing it. The sisters are horrified because the clock had belonged to their mother, the woman Chebutykin loved, but he tries to cover up his mistake by turning philosophical, discussing whether the clock actually existed or not, and when that doesn't work he blurts out the commonly-known secret of Natasha's affair with Protopopov before storming out of the room. In the last scene, as he is preparing to leave, Chebutykin gives Andrei some friendly advice about his marriage to Natasha: leave, go far away, "keep going, don't ever look back."

Alexei Petrovich Fedotik

A second lieutenant in the army, Fedotik is seldom on stage. When he does show up, he usually has something to give to somebody—a musical top

for Irina, or a toy for the baby. He also takes photographs of people whenever he is on stage.

Ferapont

Ferapont is an old man who works for the county board. He is sometimes confused and sometimes has trouble hearing, but in general he is level-headed, taking care of required business. While the sisters and Andrei dream of Moscow as a place where life will finally be good, Ferapont associates Moscow with bizarre stories that he thinks he has heard, about a man eating forty or fifty pancakes and dying, or of a rope stretched across the city. In the middle of the play, Andrei, feeling the pressure of life with Natasha, takes his trouble out on Ferapont, insisting that the old man address him as "your honor," while in the last act, when Natasha has taken over the house, the two of them are left together on fairly equal footing as her servants.

Fyodor Ilich Kulygin

Kulygin is Masha's husband, a disappointment to her. Recalling when she was married, Masha explains, "He seemed terribly learned to me then, intelligent, and important. It's different now, unfortunately." He is an assistant principal, and is willing to play the role of the underling, shaving off his moustache because the principal shaved his off and struggling to convince himself that he does not mind having his actions thus controlled: "Nobody likes it, but it doesn't make any difference to me. I am satisfied. With a moustache or without a moustache, I am satisfied." At the end of the play, when his wife is upset because her lover is leaving, Kulygin tries to cheer her up, echoing the loss of his facial hair by pulling out a false beard and moustache that he has confiscated from a student and putting them on. During that scene, he is aware of why Masha is grieving, and he offers her support while struggling to avoid the subject of her grief. "You're my wife, and I'm happy, no matter what happens . . . I don't complain. I don't reproach you for a single thing." It is an attitude is not based on sharing her suffering, but on weakness and a wish to avoid unpleasantness.

Natalya

See Natasha Ivanovna Prozorov

Irina Prozorov

Irina is the youngest sister, not just in age but in her vibrant personality. Act I starts with Irina's twentieth birthday, with her feeling girlish and happy with the world. Having been raised in an aristocratic family, she idealizes work as the solution to all of life's problems, knowing that work can solve the great problem faced by characters in this play, that of living life with meaning. When Tuzenbach proposes to her in Act I, Irina changes the subject to work. A year later, in the Act II, Irina is exhausted from her work at the telegraph office, which is ruining her personality: she recalls an incident when she was impatient with a woman who was upset her son's death. Solyony professes his love to her, and threatens that no one else will have her, but she does not take him seriously. Like Olga, Irina longs to live in Moscow, but she is too young to remember what life was like there: instead, she dreams of it as an enchanted, magical place. Irina accepts Tuzenbach's proposal of marriage out of a sense of duty to her family. In the final act, she says a touching farewell to him, knowing that he will not survive the duel (''I knew, I knew . . .'' is her response later when the doctor brings news that he is dead). She still plans to go to Moscow, alone, and still dreams that work will set all of her troubles straight.

Masha Prozorov

Masha's marriage to Kulygin was not a joyful one from the beginning—''They married me when I was eighteen, and I was afraid of my husband because he was a teacher and I was barely out of school,'' she later explains. Masha is a talented pianist, but she does not play any more because she is bored and disappointed with her life. That changes when she meets Vershinin and begins an affair with him. As she later explains it to her sisters, ''At first he seemed strange to me, then I felt sorry for him . . . then I fell in love with him.'' Masha is happy during her affair with Vershinin, laughing openly and frequently, even though she is frightened when he expresses his love. She is the most forthright and honest of the sisters, sometimes harshly so, lashing out angrily at others—the stage directions *(angrily)* and *(sternly)* appear often with Masha's lines. Her most moving speech comes in the third act when, having watched Natasha walk past with a candle and noted to her sisters ''She walks like the one that started the fire,'' she quietly confesses her affair to Olga and Irina, as if, having seen Natasha take on the role of anger and suppression that she used to play, Masha wishes to talk about her new life and remind herself about being in love. In the end, when Vershinin leaves, Masha has a hard time, crying

MEDIA ADAPTATIONS

- Members of New York's Actor's Studio, including Shelley Winters, Sandy Dennis, and Geraldine Page, are in a video edition of the play, filmed in 1965. Directed by Paul Bogart. Released by Hen's Tooth Video in 1998.

until she is able to raise her anger, refusing to go into the family house, which Natasha has taken over and spoiled.

Natasha Ivanovna Prozorov

During the first act, the sisters look down on Natasha's (also known as Natalya) way of dress and her coarse manners. By the time the second act begins Natasha is married to Andrei, and they have one son, Bobik, whom she dotes on, repeating every little thing that he says or does with complete fascination. She leaves the house at the end of Act II to go for a ride with Andrei's superior, Protopokov, in his sleigh, pretending that it is a chore that she must put up with. By Act III, her affair with Protopokov is openly known. As time passes, Natasha comes to increasingly dominate the household. She hates eighty-year-old Anfisa, who was the Prozorov sisters' maid when they were children, planning to dismiss her, with no concern for the sentiment that her husband's family might feel for the old woman. She arranges to move Irina into Olga's room, claiming that the baby's health is at risk. Her maneuvers for control are undertaken with the pretense of acting for the well-being of her children. Andrei is aware of this and tells Chebutykin confidentially, ''She's honest, sincere—well, kind, but at the same time there's something in her that makes her a kind of blind, petty, hairy animal.'' At the end the play she has Protopokov inside the house with her and her husband outside—''Protopokov's going to sit with Baby Sophie, and Andrei Sergeevich can take Bobik for a ride''—indicating to some reviewers that she has taken over the Prozorov family's house with Protopokov, and that the younger child, Sophie, is actually Protopokov's.

Olga Prozorov

Olga is the oldest sister and the voice of rationality among the three of them. She is struggling to live up to the code of nobility that the family has traditionally followed and, therefore, struggling with life's changes. As a result, she is constantly weary. Unlike her sisters' sense of anticipation, Olga's dream of Moscow is nostalgic, looking back to when they lived there, not forward with anticipation. She thinks of their coming trip to Moscow, which the family left eleven years ago, as "going home." As the trip is delayed by uncertainty, Olga finds herself steeped in a sense of purposelessness. Throughout much of Act II she is offstage, in bed with headaches that appear closely related to her inability to cope with her life. In Act III, when resentments and desires are being discussed, Olga's dialog is marked by her efforts to avoid thinking. "How terrible it all is!" she says about the fire, "And how sick of it I am!" Her greatest emotion shows when Natasha is rude to Anfisa, the family's old servant: Natasha tries to win her favor by assuring her that she will one day be the school's headmistress, but Olga, says that she would not accept such a position: "I'm not strong enough. . . .You were so rude to nurse just now. Forgive me, I just haven't the strength to bear it . . . It's all getting black before my eyes. . ." By the end of the play, though, Olga has gathered her strength. She expresses hope in the play's last speech: "Oh, dear sisters, our life isn't over yet. We shall live! The music is playing so gaily, so joyfully, and it seems as though a little more and we shall know why we live, why we suffer . . . If only we knew, if only we knew."

Andrei Sergeevich Prozorov

The sisters' brother is a teacher who aspires to be a great scholar in Moscow. Two problems arise to thwart Andrei's plans. The first is Natasha. Andrei proposes marriage to Natasha at the end of the first act. By the time of the second act, a year later, he is a henpecked husband, annoyed that Natasha is overly worried about the health of their baby, Bobik. He is somewhat resistant to Natasha's schemes, such as canceling the carnival dancers or moving Irina into Olga's room, but he retreats before an argument starts, letting her have her way. He attends business meetings because he is bored at home, and he regrets that the opportunity to become a great scholar has slipped away. Although he has an active home life, he also is, as he explains to

Ferapont, lonely. He seems aware that Natasha is having an affair with his supervisor, but he cannot do anything about it because he cannot afford to be fired. Andrei's second problem is that he loses money gambling. This forces him to mortgage the house, which leaves his sisters and him at the mercy of Natasha. In the final act, Andrei is pushing a baby carriage around. He has a speech about how the town is full of ignorant, slow-witted people—"the divine spark within them dies, and they become the same pitiful, absolutely identical corpses that their mothers and fathers were before them." He recognizes that this is the fate that has come to him too, but he also has hopes for freedom for himself and his children in the future.

Vladimir Karlovich Rode

Rode always appears with Fedotik, but he is more loud and boisterous. He teaches a gym class at the high school.

Vasili Vasilevich Solony

Solony is a hard, angry character who mocks the social conventions of polite society with his seemingly nonsensical statements. He is aware of his own crudeness, though, and regrets it, as evinced by the fact that he is constantly sprinkling perfume over his fingers because they "smell like a corpse." He has fought and presumably won two duels already. He models his life after Lermontov, the nineteenth-century Russian poet who killed a rival in a duel, and believes himself to be so in love with Irina that he is willing to kill any other man that she would choose over him.

Nikolai Lvovich Tuzenbach

Tuzenbach is a Baron of German descent, although, as he is emphatic about pointing out, he is not German. He is somewhat disgusted with himself for the easy life he has lived, noting that he has never worked a day in his life but anticipating a time in the near future when everyone will work. His belief in the redemptive powers of work resembles that of Irina, with whom he is in love. In the fourth act, Tuzenbach is happy and excited about the life to come—"Tomorrow I'll take you away," he tells Irina, "we'll work, we'll be rich, my dreams will come true." His excitement extends to an appreciation of the little town he is leaving, in all that surrounds him, even though he knows that he might die in the duel with Solyony. "See that tree, it's dried up, but the wind moves it with the others just the same,'' he explains before going off to the duel. ''So it seems to me that if I die in some way or other I'll have a share in life.''

Alexander Ignatyevich Vershinin

When Vershinin is first discussed early in the play, the sisters are uninterested in him, until they hear that he is from Moscow. He was in the same brigade as their father eleven years ago, and when he arrives he is able to recognize them all. Vershinin has two daughters and a wife who is mentally ill, trying to commit suicide often—at one point he receives a note that she has tried suicide again and he leaves, annoyed, only to return later with the news that it was a false alarm. His attitude toward life in a provincial town is the opposite of Andrei's: while Andrei is lonely and longs for the cultural life of Moscow, Vershinin recalls being lonely in Moscow and appreciates the things the small town has to offer. His affair with Masha offers them both a chance for excitement in their deadening marriages.

THEMES

Alienation and Loneliness

Despite the fact that they have been there for over ten years and that their house is full of visitors, the Prozorov sisters feel lonely in the town where they live. For one thing, they are better educated than the people around them, which isolates them intellectually. Even though Vershinin tells them that he doubts there could even be a town ''so boring and so dismal that it doesn't need intelligent, cultivated people,'' it is clear that they do not share his optimistic viewpoint and his ability to look to the future. Their friends in town are, for the most part, from the military, who are posted there temporarily and are inevitably going to move on, as they actually do in the end. Andrei shuts himself in his room with his violin and Olga removes herself from company, complaining that she has headaches. Even the engagement between Irina and Tuzenbach, which she enters into with reluctance because she feels the need to be more involved, ends with abrupt violence, ruining her chance to break through the wall of alienation that has surrounded her family since their father's death. Their hope that life in Moscow would make much difference by putting them among their own type of people is cast into doubt by

Vershinin, who has just come from Moscow and recalls being lonely there.

Love and Passion

This play is a net of interwoven romances, all of them presenting differing degrees of sincerity and passion. Each character gives readers a different view of love. Andrei's love is that of the hopelessly exploited, while Natasha acts as the exploiter to him and as a martyr to her children. Masha and Vershinin are sincerely happy with each other, escaping confining marriages, while Kulygin, though unimaginative, displays a pure and selfless love by comforting his wife when she is upset over losing her lover. He confides also to Olga that he should have married her, not Masha, indicating that he is bound to Masha by devotion. Irina has an open and jocular relationship with Chebutykin, who dotes on her, even though a relationship between them is out of the question because of their age difference; Chebutykin also keeps alive his memory of their mother. Tuzenbach is content with his own love for Irina, even though he knows that she does not love him, while Solyony, who is perhaps incapable of love, patterns his life on the romantic figure of a poet. None of these relationships ends up happily, although there is an admirable nobility to the way that all of these characters hop on to their elusive passions.

Meaning of Life

There is a lack of meaning in their lives at the core of the misery felt by these three sisters. And the other characters in this play reflect the various attitudes that the sisters attach to the meaning of life. Olga spends her time trying to recapture the past through memory, especially by recalling her mother and father in detail—it is not surprising that she ends up as a teacher, dealing in established ideas and living in an apartment with Anfisa, who functions as a living relic of her childhood. Masha, who once was artistic, has fallen into despair and claims to have forgotten her piano skills. As she explains it, there is no point to being cultured in a provincial town: ''We know a lot that isn't any use.'' Her affair with Vershinin reawakens her talent, though, and she uses music to communicate nonverbally with him in public. Irina is full of hope for the future, but her conception of the future—of what exactly it is that she is looking forward to—is vague, so she can hardly do anything to make it become real. She is willing to marry Tuzenbach if that will enable her to

TOPICS FOR FURTHER STUDY

- In his letters, Chekhov said that he had the city of Perm in mind as a model for the type of provincial city where this drama takes place. Research what life would have been like in a provincial Russian town at the turn of the century, and compare it to what Moscow would have been like.

- Research the role that servants would have played in a Russian household at the turn of the century, between the emancipation of the serfs in 1858 and the Russian Revolution in 1917, and explain what the social customs tell about the roles of Ferapont and Aneisa in *The Three Sisters*.

- Read some of the poetry of Russian writer Mikhail Yurievich Lermontov, as well as some biographical information about him. Use this to explain the significance of Solyony's observations that "I have a disposition like Lermontov's . . . I even look a little like Lermontov . . . so I'm told."

- What would these characters do if the play were set in modern America? Since the army is not quartered with civilians here, the characters in the army would have to be given different occupations. Would Protopopov still be the chairman of the county board? Where would Irina work? Try to give them occupations that you are familiar with in daily life.

- Explain how you think each of these characters would have fared under communism in the Soviet Union after the Russian Revolution, and why.

- Read one of Chekhov's short stories, such as "The Gooseberries" or "The Lady With the Pet Dog," and show the similarities between the story and this play, focusing on characterization and themes.

---

go to Moscow, where she hopes to find true love. The contradiction in her plan is apparent, but she is unable to come up with anything less self-defeating. She ends up dedicating herself to the equally vague idea that work will bring meaning to her life, although she does not know exactly how.

The people who come to the Prozorov house toss around ideas about what gives life meaning, discussing the mysteries of existence as of they were involved in a game, as when Vershinin says, "Well, if they won't give us any tea, at least let's philosophize," and Tuzenbach responds, "Yes, let's." Vershinin supports the idea that work gives life meaning, even of no results are visible. Solyony represents an absurdist view that discussion is just meaningless chatter, which he mocks with the purposely meaningless comments he utters. Chebutykin echoes this idea of meaninglessness when he drops the clock that belonged to the woman he loved and argues that what seems to be reality might not be. Tuzenbach learns to appreciate the world around him only when he is faced with death in a dual.

STYLE

Setting

The setting of this play is given as "a provincial city." Describing it this way, Chekhov takes the middle ground between those stories that are unrelated to the towns where they occur and those that could only occur in particular locations. It is important, of course, that *The Three Sisters* takes place in a province, because the emotion that occurs on stage is centered around what the main characters think of where they live. Olga, Masha, Irina, and Andrei all feel that their lives would be much better if they were living in Moscow; Vershinin arrives from Moscow, and extols the charm of life in a small country town; Natasha is able to consolidate her power through her allegiance with a local politician, making her the proverbial big fish in a small pond.

More specifically, all of the action takes place at the Prozorovs' house, which is a sort of meeting place for an assortment of local characters. The soldiers assigned to the town are comfortable there because of their affiliation with the sisters' father, Colonel Prozorov. Aside from the connection to the military, though, the house is presented as a sort of center of culture for the town—certainly, its inhabitants are more refined in their manners and better educated than most of their fellow citizens. It is a grand house, likely the finest structure in the neighborhood, as indicated by the fact that it is not even evacuated when the wooden houses surrounding it are burning down.

Conflict

All dramas rely upon conflict between opposing forces, in order to keep readers interested in seeing which side will overcome. In *The Three Sisters,* the conflict in implied, not stated, and this accounts for the feeling that some audiences get that "nothing happens." From the very beginning, the sisters focus their concern on getting out of this small town and returning to Moscow, and the play follows a series of events that place obstacles in the path to that goal. There is no clear-cut conflict with any one obvious force interfering with their plans, but everything that happens in the play, from the fire to the feud to Natasha's dominance of the household, all serve to raise questions about whether Olga, Masha, and Irina will be able to find their happiness by returning to Moscow. The play's ending provides no clear-cut conclusion to this conflict. Only one of the sisters is going to Moscow, and none of them has been able to hold onto happiness, but they have hope that the future will be better and that they might be able to understand the significance of their lives sometime, so all is not lost.

Realism

At the end of the nineteenth century Realism became a major movement in the arts. The best way to understand Realism is to see it in terms of what it is not. It does not require its audience to know artistic traditions in order to understand what is being presented to them. It does not use educated language or complex plot structures that play well on the stage but that do not reflect the ways that people in life actually speak and act. Chekhov is often associated with Realism, especially in his short stories. Early audiences found this degree of reality to be confusing, because it meant that the characters in his plays seemed to just stand around and talk about whatever came to mind. The structure and language of his work is less obviously

"artistic" than it is in traditional drama, providing audiences with fewer clues but leaving a stronger impression on those who figure out the play's meaning for themselves.

Antagonist

The issues that the sisters are concerned with in this play are not clear-cut but abstract philosophical issues that affect every moment of life equally. In order to define these issues more clearly for readers and audiences, Chekhov has provided an antagonist for the Prozorov family. An antagonist is a force in a play that acts in opposition to the protagonist, or main character, in this case three main characters (or four if you count Andrei). In addition to the many moral issues that the Prozorovs struggle with, their lives are also met with direct opposition from Natasha. She represents what they are not: she is ill-mannered, with no fashion sense, and sentimental and greedy and aggressive and manipulative. The fact that she is able to move Irina out of her own room in the second act and then move her husband out of his room in the end can be read as Chekhov's commentary that rudeness triumphs over refinement, although critics have pointed out that she is victorious in areas that the three sisters had already rejected—she becomes a powerful figure in a town that they had already rejected and she takes over a house that they had hoped to leave from the very start.

HISTORICAL CONTEXT

Social Order

Traditionally, Russia had been a society with a rigid class system. From the seventeenth century through the middle of the nineteenth, this included a system under which most of the people were serfs, which meant that they were practically slaves of the people who owned the land on which they lived, and were at their mercy. Growing pressure throughout the first half of the 1800s, brought on by the international movement toward freedom that had already caused the American Revolution and the French Revolution, led to government reform, giving the serfs their freedom in 1861, soon before slavery was abolished in America. Not much changed when the serfs were freed. The arrangement was for them to inherit control of the land they worked, but they had to pay back the aristocrats that they received it from, and so they ended up working the same jobs under the same bosses. As the twentieth Century began, 81.6 percent of Russian citizens

COMPARE
&
CONTRAST

- **1901:** The first trans-Atlantic telegraph message was sent from England to Newfoundland, where Guglielmo Marconi received it. It was the letter ''s,'' sent in telegraph code across radio waves.

  1917: The idea of the American Marconi Company's system of broadcasting sounds through the airwaves was adapted to music and entertainment broadcasts.

  Today: Wireless technology broadcasts millions of voices across the world at any given moment, more and more radio broadcasts are being taken off of the airwaves and transmitted across cable wires for better clarity, and it is possible to experience fine art and music just about anywhere.

- **1901:** The oppressive policies of Russia's Czar Nicholas II pushed the country toward the revolution after the First World War that left the country as the cornerstone of the communist superpower, the Union of Soviet Socialists Republic.

  Today: After the USSR disbanded in 1991, many of its former constituent countries, including Russia, have struggled with establishing political democracies with capitalist economies.

- **1901:** Tuberculosis, from which Chekhov suffered for twenty years and which eventually killed him, was untreatable, and killed approximately 188 people per 100,000 in America.

  Today: Vaccines have reduced the danger of tuberculosis to less than one in 100,000, although outbreaks still arise in impoverished nations that cannot afford vaccine programs.

were classified as peasants, although this name covered a broad category, from poor people in the cities to wealthy farm owners; 9.3 percent were merchants and what we might today consider the middle class; 6.1 percent were in the military; 0.9 percent were clergy; and 1.3 percent were the gentry, or the ruling class. Most of these class distinctions were inherited, so that the children of former serf-owners still lived luxurious lives, as the Prozorovs do in this play. As Tuzenbach explains it, he was ''born into a family that never knew what work or worry meant,'' although he expects that in his lifetime, everybody will work. Only the military was not a hereditary class, so that many young men became soldiers in order to improve their status in the world. The Russian social order was not equipped to accommodate people who did not follow their inherited place—for instance, a son of merchants who did not become a merchant was categorized on his passport as ''raznochintsy,'' which meant ''of no particular class.'' There was nonetheless much social change, especially in the huge government bureaucracy. Even in the late 1800s, before the rise of communism, Russian society was run by a huge, centralized bureaucracy that approved all local changes, all construction of government projects, from the center of government in St. Petersburg. In a country of over six and a half million square miles (twice that of the United States) before modern means of communications, including telephones, it was impossible to really control all local decisions from the capital. This left the opportunity for local government officials, like the play's chairman of the county board, Protopopov, to wield control. The Russian bureaucracy had fourteen ranks that an individual could rise through with careful political manipulation, which is a central reason why Andrei does not want to raise trouble with the superior who is having an affair with his wife.

The Revolution

At the turn of the century, Russia was ruled by Tsar Nicholas II, the last of the Romanovs that had ruled Russia since 1613. Russian society was falling apart, mainly because of a failing economy that could not even provide enough food for its citizens, and as a result the public sentiment was against the royal family. The huge centralized bureaucracy made it difficult to change production practices, and the ruling family did not show any indication of caring about the suffering of the people. In 1904 the Tsar committed the country to war against Japan. The Russo-Japan War was one that the country was unprepared for, and the cost of fighting the war further strained the economy and food resources. After Russia lost the war in 1905, general strikes broke out in St. Petersburg, and soldiers fired into the crowd, killing striking peasants. The 1905 revolution was suppressed, and the Tsar and his wife withdrew even further from the concerns of the citizens. They began relying on advice from Rasputin, a mystic, and eventually let him make decisions about who should be appointed to government positions. Most of his appointees turned out to be incompetent. When World War I broke out in 1914, Russia was involved, but performed badly: Nicholas took personal control of the military, and the country's defeats were blamed on him. In 1917, after the war, the Russian Revolution changed history by establishing a communist government based on principles that Karl Marx and Friedrich Engels had proposed in *The Communist Manifesto* in 1847. Nicholas and all of his family were executed.

CRITICAL OVERVIEW

The Three Sisters was written late in Chekhov's life, staged just three years before he died. At the time, he had a solid reputation for his short fiction, and his previous play, *Uncle Vanya,* had been a critical and popular success for the Moscow Arts Theatre. Chekhov's fame as a playwright during his lifetime was neither widespread nor universally positive. Today he is considered a primary figure in the Realist movement that swept Russian drama in the beginning of the century, and, like a forerunner in any movement, his work was sometimes misunderstood. One of the most painful criticisms must have been the rejection of Russian literary giant Leo Tolstoy, author of *War and Peace* and "The Death of Ivan Ilych." Early in his career, Chekhov idolized Tolstoy's writing, but when he went to see him in the winter that *The Three Sisters* was first performed Tolstoy kissed him but then whispered in his ear, "But I still can't stand your plays. Shakespeare's are terrible, but yours are even worse!" (qtd. in Kirk, pg. 145).

According to his biographer Henri Troyat, early audiences for *The Three Sisters* misunderstood the play, criticizing it as "slow and colorless" because they were unfamiliar with his style. To some early audiences and especially to critics, Chekhov's stage work seem casual, rambling, as if he had no design but just wrote off the top of his head. Modern audiences are familiar with dramas using ordinary people behaving as they would in real life, but audiences expected more artifice on the stage a century ago. As Soviet critic A. Shaftymov pointed out more than a half century later, "theater critics reproved Chekhov most of all for introducing into his plays superfluous details from everyday life, and thus violating the laws of stage action. The presence of such details was put down to his ineptitude, to the habits of the writer of tales and short stories, and to his inability or unwillingness to master the requirements of the dramatic genre." Audiences began to appreciate Chekhov's modern style before critics: while critical discussions continued about whether *The Three Sisters* violated tradition out of defiance or ignorance of the rules, audiences grew larger and larger throughout the play's run.

Outside of Russia, the world was slow to appreciate Chekhov as a playwright. His plays were performed occasionally in Munich and Berlin and London, but with no great lasting effect. After World War I ended in 1918, the Moscow Art Theatre toured the world, with stops in Germany, France, and the United States, which helped bring Chekhov's plays to the world. The turning point came in the mid-1920s, when the London theater world embraced Chekhov. Martin Esslin, one of the foremost theater critics of the twentieth century, considered the acceptance of Chekhov's plays in London to be a natural pairing. England was a great empire that was near its end, just as Russia had been at the turn of the century, so that the themes that Chekhov dealt with, especially the downturn of fortune that had the social elite losing their traditional privileges, would have been familiar. Another important aspect was that London in the 1920s had a wealth of young, talented actors who were eager to put on shows that challenged traditional ideas about art. According to Esslin, such actors as John Gielguld, Peggy Ashcroft, Laurence Olivier, Alec Guinness and Michael Redgrave "made Chekhov their own, and . . . he has remained one of the most performed standard authors for over fifty years."

In Russia, the vast political changes that redefined the country helped to elevate Chekhov's reputation. After the Russian Revolution, the Moscow Art Theatre was designated the official model for

A scene from the 1970 film adaptation of The Three Sisters.

"proper" Soviet theater, and Chekhov, because of those same "realistic" elements that earned him the resentment of his early critics, was presented as the model dramatist. Most of the highly propagandistic plays that came out of the Soviet Union, with its tight political controls on all aspects of life and art, showed little resemblance to Chekhov in any matters other than portraying ordinary citizens in their unglamorous lives. Still, the state's official approval helped to make the author known by school children across the land. Today, Chekhov is one of the most-performed playwrights in English, and *The Three Sisters* is considered one of his four great plays (along with *The Seagull, Uncle Vanya,* and *The Cherry Orchard*).

CRITICISM

David Kelly

Kelly is a teacher of Drama and Creative Writing at Oakton Community College in Illinois and the author of a full-length drama. In the following essay he examines whether Soyony really loves Irina, as he claims, and the significance of this to the play overall.

The characters in Anton Chekhov's drama *The Three Sisters* present various emotional conflicts, but one generalization that can be made about all of them is that they all hope that love will provide release. The sisters of the title feel themselves being dragged down by boredom, and two of them turn to love affairs to do for them what circumstances haven't. It might at first seem that "boredom" is the wrong word, because we tend to think of boredom as slight, as an inconvenience that will pass, but it is clear that Olga, Masha, and Irina are suffering acutely from a lack of intellectual stimulation, that the small town cannot keep up with their trained minds. What is not so clear is whether Chekhov wants us to believe that love really is itself a value that can stop lives from going to waste, or if it is just an illusion that these characters fool themselves with to make their situations bearable.

Masha loves Vershinin, even though they have opposite interests—she dreams of the city and he, bored with the city, values the country. Nor does the fact that he has nothing in common with her stop Andrei from falling in love with Natasha. Chebutykin promises at the end to return to Irina, the daughter of the woman he once loved, as "a sober, G- G- God-fearing, respectable man." Irina is not in love with Tuzenbach, but she does believe that there is some-

WHAT DO I READ NEXT?

- Chekhov's thoughts as he was writing this play, and the considerations that came up while it was in production, are discussed in his letters. Long out of print, there is a new edition of *Anton Chekhov's Life and Thought: Selected Letters and Commentary* available from Northwestern University Press. There is also much about *The Three Sisters* in *Dear Writer, Dear Actress: The Love Letters of Anton Chekhov and Olga Knipper*, translated by Jean Benedetti.

- The actors who presented this play during Chekhov's time for the Moscow Art Theatre were under the direction of the legendary director Constantin Stanislavsky. Readers can find out more about the acting method these performers followed in Stanislavsky's three books, *An Actor Prepares*, *Building a Character* and *Creating a Role*. All three are available in reprint editions from Theatre Arts Books.

- In addition to his fame as a playwright, Chekhov is considered one of the greatest writers of short stories ever. His stories are collected in *Anton Chekhov's Short Stories*, published by W. W. Norton Company.

- One of Chekhov's closest friends and confidants was the Russian writer Maxim Gorky, who was more popular than Chekhov at the turn of the century. His best-known play is *The Lower Depths*, first performed in 1902 and available in a Yale University Press collection *The Lower Depths and Other Plays*.

- *The Three Sisters* was Chekhov's second-to-last play, and, according to some critics, was surpassed only by his last play, *The Cherry Orchard*.

- Comparisons have been made between this play and *Hedda Gabler*, by Norwegian author Henrik Ibsen. Ibsen's play, first produced in 1890, concerns a strong-willed newlywed aristocrat who takes her frustrations and disappointments out on those around her.

- "Errend," a short story by American author Raymond Carver, captures the feel of Chekhov's writing while presenting a fictionalized version of the playwright's last hours before death. It is available in Carver's collection *Where I'm Calling From*, published in 1988.

---

one in Moscow who is destined to be her true lover. All of these attempts at romance, from halfheartedly to perpetual, seem motivated by the characters' attempt to inject some reality back into their otherwise controlled, colorless lives. It makes perfect sense that people finding themselves confined should look to love for escape. Whether what they are feeling is "true" love is a broad philosophical question that Chekhov just does not provide enough information to answer.

Strangely, the one character whose motives for love are most clearly presented is Solyony, the boorish, angry staff captain. By all indications, Solyony should be incapable of love. He is a cretin, a braggart, and a bully, an insecure man who mocks intelligent conversation when he is unable to under-

stand it and who kills men he feels threatened by. Soon before the end of Act II, this obnoxious man declares his deep love for Irina, using vocabulary that is strange for him. For one thing, his speech is more straightforward than it has ever been, not hidden behind a joke or a snarl as it is everywhere else in the play. For another, it is here that he uses graceful, colorful language, such as adjectives ("exalted," "pure," "marvelous," "glorious," "incredible") and similes for comparison. He seems earnest about his emotions and about his wish to express them.

It would be easy to make light of Solyony's declaration of love as a weak attempt to take advantage of Irina, which would fit with his cynical personality. It is also tempting to see his clumsy attempt to romance her as his bid to take place in the carnival of romance that is going on around him. It's most unlikely that Solyony might really be in love, but that is a possibility that has to be considered also.

To me, it seems that Solyony is sincere in his claim to love Irina, but that his sincerity is not, as he seems to hope, enough to free him from his dark personality. Considered this way, Solyony can be seen as more than merely a plot device to sprinkle comic or tragic relief onto an otherwise uneventful, talky play. Taking him seriously as a lover proves him to be a key player near the intellectual and emotional center of *The Three Sisters.*

Solyony's function throughout much of the play is to disrupt the flow of the conversations going on around him. Conversations in polite society, even those concerned with meaning, tend to fall into patterns and lose their sense of urgency without someone like Solyony to challenge the speakers. When his method works as he presumably intends, he ends up, like the fool in Shakespeare's *King Lear,* exposing the shallowness of the culture that surrounds him. For instance, in the first act, with Masha turning nearly hysterical over the prospect of having to go and send a boring evening with her husband's boss, Solyony cuts into a serious conversation with, ''Here, chicky, chicky, chicky!'' It is somewhat cruel to mock Masha for following along like a mindless animal, pointing out the dreariness in her life that she is already fretting over, but it is a welcome change from the polite supporters who surround her and give her encouragement.

Clearly, Solyony sees his apparent senselessness as the brave stance of one man willing to cut through the pretense of polite society, brave enough

to show polite company the nonsense at its core. Often, though, his non sequiturs fail to unmask hypocrisy, and instead they just leave listeners shaking their heads, as when he explains that the train station is far away ''[b]ecause if the station was here it wouldn't be way off there; and if it's way off there, then of course it can't be there.'' Solyony draws attention to himself before this pronouncement, obviously expecting it to either pass for intelligence or to parody conventional logic, but it's met with embarrassed, awkward silence.

Thinking of himself as the one honest person in the middle of hypocritical society, Solyony cannot tell when his peers are embarrassed because he has shown them the truth, from when they are embarrassed on his behalf, when they feel he has acted like a fool. His goal is often to shock and cause discomfort. When someone asks what the liquor they are drinking is made of, he responds, ''Cockroaches,'' which might have a deep meaning about the evils of liquor but is more likely meant to make someone say, ''How disgusting,'' which Irina does. Solyony cannot grasp the difference between an unusual statement that provokes thought and one that is just odd, or one that gets a reaction more like annoyance than enlightenment. He is too comfortable with being an outsider, which he equates with being a romantic figure, because romantic figures are usually outside of the mainstream.

Accustomed to being considered odd, but certain of his offbeat moral superiority, Solyony has an inverted sense of social status. For him, it is social success when people cringe, whereas smiles and laughter are signs that one is playing society's game, acting as its pawn. With this sense of values, it is hardly likely that he could be romantically successful. There are slim odds that he can find a woman who thinks of romance in the same way that he does, especially not in a small provincial town. If he found one, it would be unlikely that he could make his desires known to her. And yet, he knows that his sort of life has been romantically successful before. The poet and novelist Mikhail Lermontov (1814–1841) was a romantic figure who told the truth, who looked at life from his own unique angle and who stood up to the drones of society, and he earned the country's respect for it.

It is not surprising as it might seem at first to find a tough, offensive character like Solyony modeling himself after a poet, not if the poet is an outlaw who died young and his admirer is uncomfortable with himself for accepting the confines of society, following army regulations, and eating cake at birthday parties in the homes of the socially prominent. Surrounded by the mainstream culture, Solyony would naturally need an alternative culture to call his own. It is his belief that he is following different rules that no one but he and Lermontov would understand that makes him want to be dangerous, but also to be loved for it.

His role in the play is bracketed between the threat to someday put a bullet through Baron Tuzenbach's head and his murder of the Baron at the end. He has already killed two people in duels. Some critics define him as a killer, as if he just happened into the Prozorov sisters' social circle by chance or their bad luck, but that view of him comes from looking at him with his own eyes, taking him for what he wants to think he is. But he is not an out-and-out murderer, he is a dueler. In dueling there is an element of risk and courage, but there is also a strict social code that is missing from ruthless killing. For all of his mockery of it, Solyony wants social acceptance. This much is clear from the fact that he tries to cover up the scent of past killings at his hands, a smell that no one else would detect, with perfume.

The question about the love that he declares for Irina hinges on whether it is, as Solyony himself seems to believe, the great secret tenderness that his gruff exterior is defending, or whether, like the perfume on his fingertips and chest, it is an attempt to rise above his crudeness and fit in with cultivated society. Unlike the other characters, who seem ready to fall in love at the earliest opportunity, Solyony seems to be dragged into love against his will. But the fact that he believes that he does not want love is no proof that love has taken control of him. There is no evidence that Solyony really has a soft, romantic self hidden deep within his hardened shell, and plenty of reason to doubt that he does.

In Act II, he tells Tuzenbach that he is really shy and depressed when other people are around, talking nonsense in his discomfort: "But just the same, I'm more honest and sincere than lots of people—lots and lots of people." This confession is touching, until it is put into the context of his threat to kill Tuzenbach in the beginning of the play and the actual killing at the end. Solyony may be so insecure that he could only let down his thorny facade to someone who he knows will die, but it is just as likely that the sensitive Solyony is just an act, a nervous defense against Tuzenbach's direct question about why they do not get along better.

It is only a few minutes later that Solyony declares his love for Irina, calling her "the only one there is that can understand me." Why Irina? She is a sad young woman, but she does not seem any sadder than either of her sisters—Olga, by comparison, seems flat-out miserable, if neediness is what he identifies with, while Masha seems more in his league in terms of bitterness. Solyony's passion for Irina seems to last for just a few lines, racing quickly through her purity and incredible eyes before he settles on more familiar ground, male aggression, and decides to concern himself with how to deal with rival suitors rather than with her.

Does he believe he loves her? Of course. Does he actually love her? If he were more honest about his antisocial tendencies, if he really were a truth-teller and not just truthful by chance sometimes in his senseless babbling, then it would be easier to believe that he actually understands himself. As it is, too much of Solyony's self-concept is tied up in his image of himself as a troublemaker, a voice of truth in the social wilderness, and especially his identification with Lermontov. Lermontov dueled with his friend Lensky over Lensky's fiancée, and Lermontov won. He only stayed with the fiancée for a few weeks, though, before her abandoned her. In the same way, Solyony seems to honestly want to be in love, but it is hardly likely that he would know what to do with it if he got it.

Source: David Kelly, in an essay for *Drama for Students,* Gale, 2001.

The Economist

The following review discusses the new possibilities that director Yefremon provides to Chekhov's "Three Sisters."

Sad evenings by the samovar, birch trees, an inexplicably breaking string and three young women moaning about their provincial lives. Few things are duller than bad Chekhov. The boredom can be as painful for theatregoers as the stifled hopes and unrealised dreams are for his characters.

If moroseness is one way to kill Chekhov, another method, favoured outside Russia, is to turn his plays into stiff drawing-room comedies. In his homeland, Anton Chekhov (1860–1904) has tended, by contrast, to have the life revered out of him as Russia's "national playwright." This was especially true in Soviet times. Apart from a courageous burst of experiment in the 1960s, Chekhov on stage was reduced in the Stalin period and after to a

> FEW THINGS ARE DULLER THAN BAD CHEKHOV. THE BOREDOM CAN BE AS PAINFUL FOR THEATREGOERS AS THE STIFLED HOPES AND UNREALISED DREAMS ARE FOR HIS CHARACTERS."

thumping message about the decay of the past and the promise of the future.

Things, happily, have changed, and Moscow's autumn theatre season is full of productions which put the life back into Chekhov. The revival is most striking at the Moscow Arts Theatre, where his plays all had their premieres at the turn of the century, but where the weight of tradition has hung since like an old curtain. Oleg Yefremov's production of *Three Sisters* is only the third at the theatre this century and it took him a year and a half of rehearsals to cut loose from the past.

The Moscow Arts Theatre's 1940 production of the play had a set designed by Vladimir Dmitriyev in which a line of birch trees stretched into the far distance. The vista symbolised the Soviet interpretation of the play: when the visiting colonel, Vershinin, dreams of a future that is "unimaginably beautiful, astonishing," he is predicting the achievements of communism. So strong was this orthodoxy that a more adventurous staging of *Three Sisters* in 1967, directed by Anatoly Efros, in which Vershinin spoke ironically, had to be closed down. Several actors from the Moscow Arts Theatre wrote an open letter to the press, complaining that the production had travestied Chekhov.

Mr. Yefremov frees *Three Sisters*. His set is a long portico of the Prozorovs' house surrounded by a grove of tall birch trees in which the changing light of the seasons is reflected. At the end, when the sisters deliver their final speech the house disappears and they are hemmed in by trees, searching for a way out, lost. The birch alley has become a forest.

The delicacy of the acting reinforces the sense of hopelessness. Viktor Gvozditsky, who plays the luckless lover Tuzenbakh, speaks for many when he says he was bored in childhood with "school-

primer Chekhov," and could never see the point of all those pauses and repetitions. Working with Mr Yefremov, he discovered the emotional power of the playwright. His Tuzenbakh is a poignantly vulnerable character, nervously optimistic but fatally passive as he agrees to a pointless duel.

Mr. Yefremov works up perhaps too powerful a mood of gloom. Even in the first two acts, when they should radiate some illusory optimism, the three Prozorov sisters seem almost paralysed as their nouvelle riche sister-in-law Natasha slowly takes over their house and their lives.

Judging by the keen response to the new production, Chekhov is striking a chord with audiences. One reason perhaps is that contemporary Moscow society has a little more time for reflection. The pace of change has slackened and Russians are preoccupied less with the threat of civil war than with bewildering economic transformation, much like their bourgeois great-grandparents in the 1890s. "The main mood in Chekhov is one of longing and apprehension. People look around them and wonder about their lives. When everything is falling apart it's more difficult to stage him," says Anatoly Smelyansky, associate artistic director of the Moscow Arts Theatre. During the short burst of artistic experiment before and after the Russian revolution, he points out, Chekhov was more or less ignored.

The novelist Andrei Bitov goes one step further, musing that Russian audiences are only now starting to appreciate Chekhov. His characters come from a property-owning class whose identity is bound up with a conception of money and ownership that for most modern Russians is still distant. "Why is Chekhov so popular in the West?" Mr Bitov asks. "Because western people still know about what it is to own property and go bankrupt, these problems are close to them."

It is appropriate that the most popular play of the moment is Chekhov's last, *The Cherry Orchard*. In a new production at the Sovremmenik Theatre, directed by Galina Volchek, an appreciatory murmur goes through the smart audience as the debt-plagued landowner Ranevskaya and the serf-turned-millionaire Lopakhin argue over the future of the orchard, which Lopakhin wants to chop down and turn into dacha plots. But that is so vulgar, complains Ranevskaya, expressing the distaste of the old intelligentsia for the brash new business class.

Ms. Volchek's production crackles with sexual comedy and class conflict as the household falls apart and finally disperses. It is full of that Russian social interaction that is always close to anarchy and veering madly between laughter and tears. At the heart of the play is a grand performance by Marina Neyolova, playing the mistress of the house Ranevskaya as a wayward prima donna. Like Ranevskaya, Ms. Neyolova lives most of the time in Paris, which adds an edge to her depiction of a character torn between the Russian provinces and France.

The production, which has just set off to the United States on tour, restores the social contours to the play, the only one in which Chekhov gives the servants a say and lets them openly mock their masters. The upstart Yasha is played a touch too overtly as a "new Russian" wearing a yellow suit and lime waistcoat, while Lopakhin, hard-working and dressed in black, is more inclined to win people's sympathy. At the curtain call the four non-aristocrats take their bow separately.

Both these productions stay within the naturalist tradition started by Chekhov and pursued by his first director, Konstantin Stanislavsky. The playwright himself left very precise instructions on how his characters should look and be played. He gave them exact ages and left instructions that Uncle Vanya, for example, should have smart, but crumpled clothes. These new stagings suggest that faithfulness to this tradition does pay off. The plays are made up of a thousand nuances and abrupt changes of mood that give them their coherence and their emotional strength. They also show that it takes top-class acting to restore the immediacy to Chekhov. For many the lines are so familiar that even Mr Yefremov sometimes drowns them out with music in a way a western director would never do, as though assuming his audience knows them anyway.

Another production directed by Yury Pogrebnichko, a pared down *Cherry Orchard* at a little over two hours, is witty and discursive-Chekhov for those who already know him by heart. There is no decoration, just a white brick wall with a single railway line running in front of it. It is not only the railway mentioned in the play, but symbolises its themes of industrialisation and the coming new life. In the final act the servant Firs undoes his shoelaces as he lumbers on stage as though he has arrived in a prison camp. The servants, who are dressed in orange smocks-Soviet railway workers or Buddhist monks-scatter white cherry petals over the departing characters. This ritual promising rebirth nicely captures the ambiguity of the play's ending.

Mr Pogrebnichko's production is more a brilliant raid on Chekhov and his themes, than a full staging of *The Cherry Orchard,* but it shows that Chekhov in 1997 is open to new possibilities. By the centenary of the playwright's death in 2004, Russia may even have caught up with him.

Source: "Three Sisters," (review) in *The Economist,* Vol. 344, no. 8041, November 1, 1997, p. 89.

Celia Wren

In the following review, Wren summarizes "Three Sisters" through the character's unique personalities.

The Prozorov sisters' much desired and eternally thwarted journey to Moscow gleams through Anton Chekhov's *Three Sisters* like Zeno's arrow in reverse: as time goes by, the distance between the sisters and their dream city increases, though in Act 1 they appear to be on the verge of arriving, and though they would arrive if it were possible to dose a gap with pure longing.

Even if they did get to Moscow, though, chances are that Olga, Masha, and Irina would still be thinking too much. Thinking too much causes much unhappiness in this play, which Chekhov wrote in 1901. In a moment of inspiration, early in Act 1, Irina's suitor, Baron Tuzenbach, rebukes the sisters' bad habit of asking what it all means: "What does it mean?.... It's snowing outside—what does that mean?" By the end of the play, though, he is as bad as all the rest. Everyone is thinking—about the purpose of life, about ambitions and careers, about society's future, about why birds fly south—and because they think, they feel perpetually unsatisfied.

Thought may also be getting in the way of the Roundabout Theater's production of *Three Sisters,* which despite several winning performances and numerous comic moments seems a little un-rooted, as if everyone had thought a great deal about the nuances of Chekhov without ever feeling at ease with his characters. Using an unobtrusive translation by the gifted playwright Lanford Wilson, director Scott Elliott has adopted a straightforward, naturalistic approach that takes advantage of the script's comic potential. Overall, his distinguished actors execute their roles with grace, but the energy level never feels terribly high—something of a problem in a play that is three-and-a-half-hours long.

Though the directorial touches are more subtle here than in director Elliott's other current Broadway production, *Present Laughter,* there are some

A scene from John Gielgud's production of The Three Sisters, *performed at London's Queen's Theatre.*

discreetly inspired moments, such as when the bizarre, ill-tempered Captain Solyony (Billy Crudup), seated at the back of the stage, rudely polishes his silverware on his dinner napkin while his hostess looks on. And if the comings and goings of the characters, the confessions and the non sequiturs, have a hint of staginess, that is certainly a problem that could seem almost inherent to Chekhov.

A handsome but not extravagant set designed by Derek McLane succeeds in emphasizing the scenes and personalities that Chekhov keeps off the stage. For example, the row of French windows in the Prozorovs' dining room, in Acts I and II, gives a nice symmetry to the production's beginning and end. In Act II a frosty moonlight slants through the panes, and when Irina stands looking out at the carnival revelers who have been turned away from the house, she really does seem separated from the gaiety of life.

By contrast, Act IV is set in the garden just outside these same windows. We can see through them to the dining room where Andrei Prozorov's shrewish wife Natalya (Calista Flockhart) is crowing over her children. The windows' transparency makes it all the more noticeable at this point that we do not see Natalya's visiting lover Protopopov, whom Chekhov chose to make an invisible, though sinister, presence throughout the play.

More practically, McLane's set gives the characters room to pace about as they ponder the meaning of existence. After all, this production's greatest claim to fame is its cast of eminent actors, including several refugees from Hollywood. Unfortunately, some of the performances are a little disappointing. Amy Irving creates a measured and dignified portrait of Olga, her acceptance of suffering seeming to improve her immaculate posture. Jeanne Tripplehorn has seductive moments as the flaky Masha. But Lili Taylor is nothing short of disastrous as the youngest sister, Irina: Taylor delivers all her lines in the same breathy tone, leaning forward from the waist in a way that makes her delivery even more strained and unbelievable.

Among the supporting characters, Jerry Stiller is hilariously deadpan as the decaying doctor Chebutykin. Eric Stoltz and David Marshall Grant give amusing but curiously superficial depictions of the Baron and of Masha's pompous schoolmaster husband Kulygin.

Two of the best performances extend the play's atmosphere of sadness and disillusionment beyond the eponymous sisters. Paul Giamatti's excellent comic timing in the role of Andrei complements the character's more reflective moments, such as when he sits in his darkened living room passing his finger through a candle flame.

And David Strathairn is truly moving as the disappointed dreamer Vershinin, the Battery Commander whose love for Masha cannot tarnish his gallant behavior toward his family. Strathairn has perfect stage presence, and his smallest movements—his cautious, restless glances, his soldierly carriage, his slightly uneasy workings of the hands—suggest great passion and pain held in check by impeccable manners.

In a way, Vershinin becomes the play's saddest figure because he is such an idealist, and has such naive faith in an idea of mystical progress. As he says in Act 4 (according to an older translation than Wilson's): "Life is hard. It seems to many of us blank and hopeless; but yet we must admit that it goes on getting clearer and easier, and it looks as though the time were not far off when it will be full of happiness."

It was probably this kind of philosophical strain, running through the play, that gave another New

York director, Richard Schechner, the idea for a recent experimental version that situated each act at a different point in Russian history, with matching performance style (Act I set in 1901 a la Stanislavsky, Act II in the first years of the Communist state with the mannerisms of biomechanics, Act III as a political critique set in a 1950s labor camp, and Act IV as a postmodern meditation on the end of the Soviet Union). As this intriguing concept suggests, visions of a perfect society and a better future haunt *Three Sisters,* a little as the specter of Moscow does.

Fortunately, Chekhov never reduces his characters to spokespersons for ideas. Olga, Masha, Irina, and friends are more than the sum of their circumstances. That is why if, one day, the Act IV curtain rose on a domicile miraculously transferred to Moscow, the members of the Prozorov household would still be themselves. And they would still be thinking.

Source: Celia Wren, ''Three Sisters,'' (review) in *Commonweal,* Vol. 124, no. 5, March 14, 1997, p. 15.

Karl D. Kramer

In the following essay, Kramer argues that the three sisters are symbolic of faith by examining the meaning behind the play.

For all the talk about *Three Sisters,* it is still extraordinarily difficult to determine exactly what the play is about. One prominent school places the emphasis on the sisters as inevitably ruined creatures. Beverly Hahn, for instance, speaks of the ''inbuilt momentum towards destruction'' in the sisters' world. Another commentator claims that we cannot avoid contrasting the success of Natasha and Protopopov with the failures of the sisters. We might do well to examine just what the first two do achieve: a house, an affair, and a businesslike manipulation of the professional positions of the others. It would, of course, be absurd to suggest that the sisters have in some way failed because they do not aspire to such heights of crass avarice as Natasha and Protopopov. But there is still the claim that the sisters continually yearn for a quality of life that they do not possess, and yet do very little, if anything, to make their dreams come true. Chekhov invited this response by initiating the to Moscow line. That goal remains unattained, while the desires of Natasha and Protopopov are richly fulfilled. This seems to present an opposition between those who get what they want and those who don't, as if the goals were equivalent, but abilities not. Natasha wants the big house on the hill and a union with the man who runs

> FORTUNATELY, CHEKHOV NEVER REDUCES HIS CHARACTERS TO SPOKESPERSONS FOR IDEAS. OLGA, MASHA, IRINA, AND FRIENDS ARE MORE THAN THE SUM OF THEIR CIRCUMSTANCES.''

things in town—the boss. These may be attainable prizes, and certainly Natasha does wrestle their house away from the sisters, but the sisters never really enter into combat with her over such issues. If they did, they would themselves be transformed into first-class Natashas, an extremely dubious achievement at best. Natasha sees living in the big house at the top of the hill as an end in itself. The sisters' aspirations go considerably beyond this. Moscow as destination is equally illusory. Natasha, incidentally, isn't even up to that aspiration on the fanciful scale; she's quite content with a good view in a city much like Perm. The questions the sisters seek answers to are considerably more basic: how to seize and properly evaluate one's own experience, how to cope with experience, and when all one's delusions have been cast aside how to go on somehow from there. The particular area of experience around which the majority of the action in the play revolves is the question of love. The stance of nearly every character is determined by his ability to establish a close relationship with another. Love gone awry is in most instances the pattern. Olga seems to have the least chance of finding a mate—a situation to which she has become largely reconciled, though in Act I she chides Masha for failing to value the man she does have. Kulygin himself—aware of the failure of his own marriage—pathetically suggests to Olga in the third act that if he hadn't married Masha, he would have married her. Irina ultimately admits that her desire to reach Moscow is directly connected with her desire to find her true love. Masha is the only one of the sisters who does at least temporarily find real love, and in this sense her experience is the standard against which the experience of nearly all the other characters is to be measured. Chebutykin once loved their mother but has long since lost that love, and with it his involvement in actual experience. Soleny, on the other hand, capitalizes on his inability to inspire love by deliberately creating hostile relationships. But to determine the structure of the play as a whole and the way in which the experience depicted adds up to a statement about human capabilities, we must look in considerably more detail at the variety of responses to love among the main characters.

It is Andrei's fate to make the most ghastly miscalculation of them all in believing he loves Natasha. How could he, an educated man, brought up in the same environment as his sisters, believe he has fallen in love with her? Masha in the first act discounts the possibility that he could be serious about her. The answer seems to lie in a recognition that he has been constantly living under pressures he can't bear. ''Father . . . oppressed us with education. . . . I grew fat in one year after he died, as if my body were liberated from his oppression,'' he tells Vershinin. He has been preparing for a university career, bowing to his father's wishes—a course he abandons immediately after his marriage. Since the father's death, Andrei has been under constant pressure from his sisters to deliver them from this provincial town. His love for Natasha is simply a means of escaping these various responsibilities, which have been thrust upon him. But a relationship based on such motivation becomes a trap from which Andrei desperately wishes to escape. In some dialogue that Chekhov eventually deleted from the play, Andrei dreams of losing all his money, being deserted by his wife, running back to his sisters, crying, ''I'm saved! I'm saved!'' In the finished play, Andrei and Chebutykin argue about the efficacy of marriage, Andrei maintaining it is to be avoided, Chebutykin asserting loneliness is worse. But by the end of the play, even Chebutykin admits that the best course for Andrei is to leave, ''leave and keep going, don't ever look back''. This is, indeed, the course Chebutykin himself adopts at the end of the play. Andrei's escape from responsibility through love thus seems to lead only to an entrapment from which he would be only too happy to flee by the end of the play. His predicament stems not so much from Natasha's nature as from his own desire to avoid experience by hiding behind a very illusory kind of love.

Chebutykin's problems turn equally on love. He had at one time known a real love for the sisters' mother. That has long been in the past, but the only vaguely positive way he can deal with immediate experience is by the illusion that this love can be sustained through his relationship with the sisters, particularly Irina. His other protective screen is his growing insistence that nothing and nobody really exists and that therefore nothing matters. In his first appearance at stage center, he is talking sheer nonsense about a remedy for baldness and duly noting down this trivia. Shortly thereafter in Act 1 he displays his tender—almost sentimental—affection for Irina by presenting her with a silver samovar on her name day. The fact that the silver samovar is the traditional gift on the twenty-fifth wedding anniversary surely suggests that he is honoring the memory of the woman he loved and is exploiting the occasion of Irina's name day for this purpose. During the first two acts he alternates between these two poles—the attempt to sustain a lost love and an abiding interest in trivia. The chief sign of the latter is his constant reading of old newspapers, a device for distracting himself from the actuality of the present moment.

In Act III his failure to handle his experience reaches a crisis when, drunk, realizing he is responsible for the death of a woman who was under his care, he retreats into a pretense that nothing and nobody exists. It may be a measure of his feeling that he so retreats, but I would suggest that he associates this recent death with that death in the past of the woman he loved. Death has denied him his love, and the recent event vividly reminds him of his own earlier loss. Within moments of this breakdown he smashes the clock which had belonged to the sisters' mother. This may of course suggest that he is trying to destroy time itself, which separates him from his love, but he is also deliberately destroying a material object that belonged to her; it may also be a gesture of denial—a denial that his love ever existed. He tries to cover this by suggesting that perhaps there was no clock to break, and he accuses the others of refusing to see that Natasha and Protopopov are having an affair. The assumption is that if others don't see what's right before their eyes, why shouldn't Chebutykin refuse to recognize anything in the world that may hurt him? In any case, what comes out of this episode is our discovery that Chebutykin cannot deal with a death that takes away his love. His final stance in the play—''The baron is a fine fellow, but one baron more or less, what difference does it make?''—is a pathetic indication of the lengths he is driven to in trying to cope with a love long since lost.

Soleny is the only character in the play who turns away from love—turns away so completely that he commits himself to murder instead. He has an uncanny knack for turning a situation that is initially friendly into one of enmity. In Act II

Tuzenbakh attempts to bury the hatchet with Soleny, who immediately denies that there is any animus between them, thus provoking an argument and indirectly testifying to the correctness of Tuzenbakh's view of their relationship. Their discussion ends with Soleny's "Do not be angry, Alexei," which distorts Tuzenbakh's friendly overtures into a rivalry, presumably over Irina. Dissatisfied in his exchange with Tuzenbakh, Soleny seizes upon the first opportunity for further quarrel. Chebutykin enters, regaling Irina with an account of a dinner given in his honor. He is particularly pleased with the *chekhartma* (lamb). Soleny insists that *cheremsha* (an onion) is totally disagreeable. This pointless argument ends with a victory on Chebutykin's side when he says: "You've never been to the Caucasus and have never eaten *chekhartma.*" Chebutykin is the clear victor here, because Soleny prides himself on being a reincarnation of Lermontov, the nineteenth-century Russian romantic poet whose setting is regularly the Caucasus Mountains. To suggest that Soleny has never been there totally undercuts his stance as a hero in the Lermontov mold. Having lost the argument with Chebutykin, Soleny immediately proceeds to avenge himself in the best Lermontov tradition by picking a quarrel with Andrei over the number of universities in Moscow.

It is true that he declares his love for Irina toward the close of Act II, but one senses that he had expected a cool reception from her. In any case, the scene ends with what seems to be Soleny's real message—that he will brook no rivals. To put it another way, Soleny employs his declaration of love to establish a hostile relation with Tuzenbakh. We might also view the episode as a parody of the opening scene in Act II, where Vershinin declares his very real love to Masha. The initial exchange between Masha and Soleny in the first act suggests that we are to view them as polar extremes in some sense. Soleny's first speech implies a $1 + 1 = 3$ equation: "With one hand I can lift only fifty-five pounds, but with two hands I can lift a hundred and eighty—two hundred, even. From that I deduce that two men aren't twice as strong, they're three times as strong as one man . . . or even stronger . . .". Masha's opening speech implies a retort to Soleny: "In the old days, when Father was alive, there'd be thirty or forty officers here on our name days, there was lots of noise, but today there's a man and a half . . .". In view of the fact that the only officers present are Soleny, Tuzenbakh, and Chebutykin, Masha's equation is apparently $3 = 1.5$. Soleny immediately picks up on this banter, if that's what it

"THE FINAL INTERCHANGE BETWEEN CHEBUTYKIN AND THE SISTERS MAY SUGGEST NOT AN EITHER/OR RESPONSE TO LIFE, BUT A MEASURE OF THEIR CAPACITY FOR ENDURANCE. AFTER ALL, LOVE IS LARGELY A MATTER OF FAITH."

is, and compares one man philosophizing with two women trying to philosophize, the latter being equal to sucking one's thumb. Masha thereupon cuts him off: "And what is that supposed to mean, you terribly dreadful man?." This exchange between Masha and Soleny in the opening moments of *Three Sisters* is a vitally important one because, on the question of love, they represent polar extremes within the play: Masha is willing to take a chance on love; Soleny can only capitalize on love as a pretense for a duel.

The wooing scenes between Vershinin and Masha are masterpieces in Chekhov's whimsical art. The process is initiated in the first act as Olga and Irina laugh together over recollections of Moscow. It is Masha who suddenly pins down a real moment of connection in their lives when she recalls that they used to tease Vershinin as the lovesick major. In the first of his rather protracted philosophical speeches, Vershinin offers a justification for existence in response to Masha's statement that the sisters' lives will go unnoticed. She immediately responds to his attention by announcing she'll stay to lunch after all. This exchange initiates that special relationship between them. Shortly after this, Vershinin offers Masha another view with which she must be wholly in sympathy: ". . . if I were to begin life over again, I wouldn't get married. . . . No! No!." This is the precise moment Chekhov chooses for Kulygin's entrance.

In Act II, Vershinin's speech on what life will be like in two or three hundred years is clearly directed toward Masha; indeed, his philosophical ramblings are primarily a way of wooing her. She understands this and laughs softly during his speech. Tuzenbakh is clearly not privy to this particular form of lovemaking. He believes he is engaged in a serious discussion with Vershinin and cannot understand why Masha is laughing. Vershinin, of course, has no reason to ask. It is interesting to note, incidentally, that in his musings about the future Vershinin almost never responds to Tuzenbakh's attempts to join in the discussion. Indeed, Chekhov revised the text of *Three Sisters* at a number of points to eliminate Vershinin's responses to Tuzenbakh's remarks. In the first act Tuzenbakh announces Vershinin's arrival to the assembled company; Vershinin ignores the introduction and proceeds to identify himself by name. In his first monologue on the future, Vershinin dismisses Tuzenbakh's attempt to enter the discussion with a curt ''Yes, yes, of course.'' In the musings about life in two or three hundred years in Act II, Vershinin suggests the theme and Tuzenbakh offers his opinion about the future. Vershinin is apparently ruminating on his own views as Tuzenbakh speaks—the stage direction reads: ''*After a moment's thought.*'' His subsequent remarks bear no relation to Tuzenbakh's; we get the distinct impression that Vershinin has not the slightest interest in a debate, thus emphasizing the real motive for his musings, to converse indirectly with Masha. The ostensible discussion continues with Masha's observations on the necessity for meaning in life:

> It seems to me a man must believe, or search for some belief, or else his life is empty, empty. . . . To live and not know why the cranes fly, why children are born, why there are stars in the sky. . . . Either you know what you're living for, or else it's all nonsense, hocus-pocus. . . .

In effect, her words confirm her need for the kind of reassurance Vershinin has been offering her, that what man is presently doing is creating the possibility for future happiness and understanding. Vershinin's next line—''Still it's a pity our youth has passed''—is almost a reproach to Masha: since youth has passed and each of them is set in his respective relationship, their mutual happiness is impossible for any protracted period of time. Masha greets his reproval with the famous line from Gogol: ''It's dull in this world, gentlemen.'' Tuzenbakh, not comprehending the private dialogue, answers with a paraphrase of Masha's reference to Gogol, expressing his frustration over a conversation he was never meant to follow. Chebutykin does apparently follow at least the drift of the conversation— love—as he notes that Balzac was married in Berdichev. Irina, either consciously or unconsciously, picks up on this drift as she repeats Chebutykin's observation. Tuzenbakh, now attentive to one strand

in the discussion—what can we do with our lives?— announces he's leaving the service. Having argued that life will always be pretty much the same, he now asserts that he will change the direction of his own. This is an important aspect of that contradiction of position so characteristic of Tuzenbakh and Vershinin. It is highly ironic that Vershinin consistently denies there is any happiness for us now, while achieving at least a momentary happiness with Masha. Tuzenbakh, on the other hand, argues that he is happy right now, in his love for Irina, while he is denied any return of that love. Masha, characteristically, disapproves of his determination to change, feeling herself denied any such opportunity.

In the third act, Vershinin's musings on life in the future are a direct response to Masha's arrival on the scene. After Chebutykin's rather shocking references to Natasha having an affair, perhaps partly to distract everyone's attention from the assumption that he and Masha are, too, Vershinin launches into a peroration on what his daughters have yet to go through in their lives. When Masha enters, he almost immediately shifts theme from daughters to life in the future, as though the topic has already become a secret code between them. His musings are intermixed with his laughter and expressions of happiness. Everybody has fallen asleep except Masha and Vershinin, making clear that his philosophizing *is* a way of talking about love. The episode ends with their strange love duet from Chaykovskiy's *Yevgeniy Onegin.*

Near the end of the third act Masha has her frank talk with her sisters. Olga refuses to listen; Irina listens most attentively, as she presumably longs for a love of her own. Despite Olga's disclaimers, Masha's confession of love brings the sisters closer together than they have been at any point in the play thus far and prepares the way for their final scene of coming together in the finale.

In the fourth act Masha speaks to Chebutykin of her love, implicitly comparing her own position with his at an earlier time:

MASHA: . . . Did you love my mother?

CHEBUTYKIN: Very much.

MASHA: Did she love you?

CHEBUTYKIN *after a pause:* That I don't remember anymore.

MASHA: Is mine here? That's the way our cook Marfa used to speak of her policeman: mine. Is mine here?

CHEBUTYKIN: Not yet.

MASHA: When you take happiness in snatches, in little pieces, and then lose it as I am, little by little you get coarse, you become furious. . . .

The ambiguity in Chebutykin's reply to Masha's question about her mother is remarkable. Is he trying to protect the honor of the woman he loved? Did she perhaps not return his love? Or is his reply part of his attempt to deny the past experience itself? We have no way of knowing. Masha's use of "mine" must refer to Vershinin, and Chebutykin so understands it. If he thought she were speaking of her husband, he could not reply "Not yet," for he has just seen Kulygin go in the house. Masha's remarks on happiness contain little joy, and yet she is admitting she has now known love, and the indications are that it will not turn her away from experience as it has Chebutykin. We shall see more of this in the finale.

As far as love is concerned, Irina would seem to be in the best position of the three sisters. She is unattached; two suitors pursue her; and yet she is unhappy because there is an imaginary third lover, whom she associates with Moscow. It is the dream of going to Moscow that animates her in the first act, and, although it is not clear why Moscow is so important to her at this point, it does become clear by the end of Act III. Still, there are hints, even in the opening scene, that it is love Irina seeks. When Tuzenbakh reports the arrival of the new battery commander, it is Irina who pricks up her ears, inquiring, "Is he old? . . . Is he interesting?." Her desire to work looks like a second choice, and Tuzenbakh is at his most pathetic as he tries to ingratiate himself with her by sharing her desire for work: "That longing for work, Oh Lord, how well I understand it!". Tuzenbakh seems to use the work theme to promote his standing with Irina in very much the way Vershinin talks of the future to woo Masha. Irina's cry at the end of Act II—"To Moscow! To Moscow! To Moscow!"—suggests that it is an appeal to love, if we look at the context out of which it arises. Soleny has just made his rather ridiculous and thoroughly repulsive declaration of love to her; Vershinin has just returned bearing the news that his wife didn't poison herself after all; Kulygin is unable to find his wife; Natasha has just left with Protopopov; Olga makes her first appearance in the act, complaining of professional responsibilities and of Andrei's gambling losses. Each situation suggests an abortive love relationship, including the absence of a love for Olga. If all this is what provokes Irina's cry, it may well mean she is looking to Moscow for the kind of love that is simply unavailable to her here.

Her association of Moscow with love becomes explicit in the third act when she says: "I always expected we would move to Moscow, and there I would meet my real one, I've dreamed of him, I've loved him. . . . But it seems it was all nonsense, all nonsense . . . ." In the final lines of Act III she agrees to marry the baron, but still wants to go to Moscow: ". . . only let's go to Moscow! I beg you, let's go! There's nothing on earth better than Moscow! Let's go, Olga! Let's go!." These words come after Masha's declaration that she loves Vershinin and would seem to suggest that though Irina has agreed to marry Tuzenbakh, she looks forward to finding her real love elsewhere, as Masha has.

Olga has had the least opportunity to find happiness through love, and yet Olga seems to cope with her situation better than the other two. She has very nearly reconciled herself to a single life even at the opening of the play, and during the course of it she expresses her love in an entirely different fashion. We see her love in her readiness to help with both clothing and lodging for those who have been left homeless by the fire; we see it in her comforting Irina in the third act and in the way she silently acquiesces to Masha's love for Vershinin, as she steps aside to allow them their last moment alone together.

Finally, we must compare the situations at the opening of the play and at its end to gather some measure of just what the intervening experience has meant for the sisters, how it has altered their conceptions of human possibility. Harvey Pitcher has observed that the fourth act is very nearly an "inversion" of the first. He lists any number of actions and situations that occur in Act I and again in altered form in the fourth. He makes a convincing argument for seeing the finale as a negation of most of the positive elements that appeared in the opening, but I think that in addition to such negations, we see a number of positive elements in the finale that invert the hopeless and desperate attitudes of the opening. In one sense, the play moves from both naïve faith and despair to a heightened awareness of possibilities in life and a more solidly rooted ability to endure. At the opening, the sisters are both physically and temporally separated; Olga is primarily oriented to the past as she recollects the death of their father a year ago and comments on how the last four years at the high school have aged her. Irina disclaims any interest in this past, as she remarks to

Olga: "Why talk about it?." She also shares some of Irina's naïve faith in a future in Moscow, but even Moscow is in part a past orientation; certainly for Olga it must be, since she is the eldest and would have the clearest memory of what their life had been like there. Irina's Moscow, on the other hand, is the land of the future; she can look only forward to Moscow and to going to work. Masha restricts her observations to an occasional whistle, is not particularly interested in either Olga's sense of the past or Irina's hopes for the future; she is, as she sees it, buried in a present without hope. When Olga suggests that Masha can come up to Moscow every summer to visit them, Masha's only comment is to whistle, as if, knowing her own present, she recognizes Olga's wishful thinking as a mere whistling in the wind. Perhaps Masha's only departure from a present orientation is her remark about her mother: "Just imagine, I've already begun to forget her face. Just as they won't remember us. They'll forget." But even here she seems to exploit both past and future to affirm the worthlessness of present existence. Thus, at the opening the sisters are totally at odds, as they contemplate three different perceptions of reality. Perhaps the only common strain here is their shared dissatisfaction with the present. Spatially, there is some sense of their occupying a restricted area, particularly with Olga, who either sits at her desk correcting papers or walks to and fro about the room. Even Masha seems initially restricted to her couch. Temperamentally, they are also separated from one another here, each involved in her own activity—Olga correcting, Masha reading, Irina lost in thought, their dresses dark blue, black, and white.

Olga's opening speech is full of strands connecting past, present, and future:

> Father died exactly a year ago on this very day, the fifth of May, your name day, Irina. It was very cold then, snow was falling. I thought I couldn't bear it, you lay in a dead faint. But a year has passed and we remember it easily; you're wearing a white dress now, your face is radiant. *The clock strikes twelve.* And the clock was striking then. *Pause.* I remember, when they were carrying Father, there was music playing and they fired a volley at the cemetery.

The play opens with the recollection of a death, just as it will end with the news of a death at the present moment. At the same time, Olga's recollection of death is associated with birth; it is also Irina's name day. Olga's reflections next focus on the difficulty of facing the loss of a father whom both Olga and Irina presumably loved, but, as if in anticipation of their stance at the end of the play,

Olga notes that they did survive the calamity. In short, Olga's speech is a kind of summary of their reactions to calamitous experience: it is both unendurable and endurable, and calamity itself is mixed with elements of joy. The contrast between the weather a year ago and the weather today ("sunny and bright") underscores a recurrent cycle of anguish and joy. The funeral music of the military band of a year ago will be transformed at the end of the play into music that is played "so gaily, so eagerly, and one so wants to live".....

The process of redressing natural relationships which were at the very least strained in Act I gets under way near the end of Act III. First, there is Masha, who refused to join in the sisters' conversation at the opening. In Act III she draws the sisters together, although against Olga's better judgment, in her frank discussion of her love for Vershinin. This is followed shortly by Andrei's confession to at least two of his sisters that he is desperately unhappy, which constitutes a considerably more honest response to the family than his rapid departure from the scene as early as possible in Act I. The setting in Act IV is the garden attached to the house. On the one hand, it is true that Natasha dominates the house, but at the same time, if we recall that sense of the sisters' confinement in the living room of Act I, there is a compensatory feeling of openness in Act IV. The garden is unquestionably preferable to the living room now, and one is uncertain whether the sisters have been evicted or liberated—perhaps a combination of the two. The final tableau certainly contrasts the separation the sisters felt in the opening scene with their physical closeness at the end— *"The three sisters stand nestled up to one another."* But the physical closeness reflects a far more basic sense of unity. Harvey Pitcher has quite justly commented on this scene: "The sisters feel perhaps closer to one another now than they have ever done before." In the departure of the regiment and the death of Tuzenbakh, they give themselves to one another as they have not done earlier. They give themselves to their love for one another and discover a strength in this to endure.

Masha has the first of the sisters' final speeches, and I would like to look at her words, not as they are printed in texts today, but as they appear in Chekhov's original version of the speech, which, unfortunately in my view, has never been restored to the play. The speech was cut at the request of Olga Knipper, who found the lines difficult to speak. It would appear that Chekhov silently acquiesced. I've indicated the deleted lines by brackets:

Oh, how the music is playing! They are leaving us, one has really gone, really and forever; and we'll stay here alone to begin our lives anew. I shall live, sisters! We must live. . . . [*Looks upward.* There are migratory birds above us; they have flown every spring and autumn for thousands of years now, and they don't know why, but they fly and will fly for a long, long time yet, for many thousands of years—until at last God reveals to them his mystery. . . .]

The reference to migratory birds connects a series of images that run through the play and that have two reference points for their meaning. The first is the rather familiar metaphor of birds' flight as man's passage through life. Irina is the first to use the image in Act I: "It's as if I were sailing with the wide blue sky over me and great white birds floating along." Chebutykin picks up on this metaphor in Act IV when he tells Irina: "You have gone on far ahead, I'll never catch up with you. I'm left behind like a migratory bird which has grown old and can't fly. Fly on, my dears, fly on and God be with you". Chebutykin makes the metaphorical meaning clear here: he may be too old a bird to continue the flight himself, but Irina must of necessity be engaged in her passage through life. Shortly after this Masha refers to the birds, apparently with reference to Vershinin: "When Vershinin comes, let me know. . . . *Walks away.* Migratory birds are leaving already. . . . *Looks upward.* Swans, or geese. . . . My dear ones, my happy ones . . .". Like Chebutykin, Masha here refers to others whose lives go on, but in her final speech her "we must live" is connected with the bird imagery so that it becomes a positive image for her as well; her life—the life of all the sisters—will go on.

There is a second reference point for her speech, however, and that occurs in Act II when Tuzenbakh, as well, invokes the image. It comes in the midst of that scene in which Vershinin muses about the future, as a way of wooing Masha—a scene in which Tuzenbakh is largely left out of the proceedings. He says: "Migratory birds, cranes, for instance, fly and fly and whatever great thoughts or small may wander through their heads, they'll go on flying, knowing neither where nor why. They fly and will fly whatever philosophers may appear among them; and let them philosophize as much as they like, so long as they go on flying . . . ." Masha's last speech is equally a tribute to Tuzenbakh. In paraphrasing his lines she both acknowledges his conception of experience and reconciles it with her own point of view, that eventually we must have some understanding of why we do what we do. Irina's betrothed—whatever the degree of affection

she may have had for him—has just died. Masha has just parted with the man she loves, but she transforms their shared sorrow into a virtual panegyric to Tuzenbakh and finds in it a reason why the sisters must go on living. In any case, the sisters have clearly come a long way from that point a year before the play began when death seemed unendurable.

In Olga's final speech she answers that remark of Masha's in Act I—"they'll forget us too"—when she says: ". . . They'll forget us, forget our faces, our voices, and how many of us there were, but our sufferings will be transformed into joy for those who live after us, happiness and peace will reign on the earth and they will remember with a kind word and bless those who are living now." Essentially, she is reiterating Masha's appeal that we must go on living because the experience is worth the effort, and reaffirming that the purpose will be revealed in the future. But whether it is or not, the continuation of living is essential.

The sisters' final speeches are interspersed with Chebutykin's nihilistic observations on the total indifference of the universe to anything that happens. The interchange may be read as an ultimately ambivalent attitude toward the nature of experience, or it may be read as a final tribute to the sisters' faith. They have not retreated to Chebutykin's fatalism, though their experience of love has been no more encouraging. The final interchange between Chebutykin and the sisters may suggest not an either/or response to life, but a measure of their capacity for endurance. After all, love is largely a matter of faith.

Source: Karl D. Kramer, "Three Sisters, or Taking a Chance on Love," in *Chekhov's Great Plays,* edited by Jean-Pierre Barricelli, New York University Press, 1981, p. 61.

Eugene K. Bristow

In the following essay, Bristow illustrates the theory of how the number three is a key factor within Chekhov's play.

Even a casual reading of *The Three Sisters* reveals that the concept of three is somehow intertwined in the fabric of the play. And so it is. No matter what is seen or what is heard, the answer is usually three—or its multiple. Let's begin with, say, the number of characters. Fourteen characters are named in the dramatis personae; there is, however, a fifteenth character—Protopopov, the chairman of the District Council—who never sets foot onstage, but his presence offstage touches or ensnares all members of the Prozorov family, including the three sisters, their brother Andrei, and his wife (after the first act) Natasha. Five of the fifteen are female; the remaining two thirds, male. If Protopopov, his old watchman Ferapont, and the old Prozorov nurse Anfisa are set aside momentarily, the remaining twelve characters divide evenly into soldiers and civilians.

The concept of three shows up in the ages of the characters. For example, at the beginning, Irina, the youngest of the three sisters, is in her twenty-first year. Baron Tuzenbakh is almost thirty; Vershinin is forty-two; Chebutykin is almost sixty; Anfisa is seventy-eight and has been with the family twenty-seven years. All are multiples of three. The calendar time—from the beginning to the end—is three and a half years. The second act takes place twenty-one months after the first; the third, eighteen months later; the last, three months later. The time of day follows a similar pattern. At the beginning, the clock strikes twelve—it is noon. During the second act, the hour of nine in the evening rolls by; during the third, three in the morning; and the last act takes place at twelve noon. Not only is the time of each act three or its multiple, but also the diurnal/nocturnal time span could conceivably total twenty-four hours—again, a multiple of three. Moreover, even though four acts divide the play, only three settings define the locale: drawing room/ballroom; bedroom; garden.

The basic architecture of the play is apparently constructed in terms of three; that is, three characters, three parts of a triangle, three time orientations (past, present, future), and so on. As the first act begins, so does the last act end. At the beginning, for example, three female characters are downstage, and three male characters are upstage. At the close of the play, three female characters are downstage, and three male characters are upstage. The close of the play is arranged like the beginning, not only to illustrate the circular effect, but also to emphasize the precise balance, or parity, of a six-part conclusion on the meaning of existence. Both concepts of the circle and parity are closely associated with the concept of three in the play.

The effect of Chekhov's opening and closing in *The Three Sisters* is similar to that of the chorus in ancient Greek tragedy; that is, two groups, separated in space, sing and dance their choral odes; the first is called a strophe; the second, antistrophe. At the beginning, the answering group upstage consists of three military officers, Tuzenbakh, Soleny, and

Chebutykin, who are talking together. What is heard by the audience, however, is an ironic comment on what the downstage group (the sisters Olga, Masha, and Irina) is doing and saying. That Chekhov deliberately arranged this opening in terms of the Greek chorus is verified by a comparison of the Yalta manuscript (an early version) with the Moscow manuscript (a late version). The three verbal combinations of the upstage group have been added, including Tuzenbakh's apparent comment to Soleny (in reality, a summary conclusion on the optimistic dreams of the sisters): "You're talking so much nonsense I'm sick of listening to you." It should be noted that not one character in either group is aware of the chorus device. The aspirations expressed in the downstage odes are consistently denied by the negative comments in the upstage odes. The result is an appropriate stalemate in which the downstage three sisters are perfectly balanced by the upstage three military officers.

The grouping of characters in threes occurs throughout; moreover, membership in one group does not exclude membership in another, since both members and groups are constantly in flux. The Prozorov family is a good example.

> Olga
> Irina Masha
> Andrei

The family quartet is viewed as a foursome only for a few moments in the first act, when Andrei is called in to meet Vershinin, and for a single moment in the third act, just before Masha leaves to meet Vershinin. Combinations of these four Prozorovs into threesomes, however, take place on six or perhaps seven occasions. For example, in addition to the opening and close, the sisters share important scenes with Vershinin in Act I and Natasha in Act IV and develop one of their own in Act III. Andrei, Masha, and Irina are together for the party in Act II, and Olga and Irina behind their screens apparently listen to Andrei's confession near the end of Act III. It might be argued that this last scene—the seventh—is not really a threesome, since Andrei is the only visible character onstage, and neither sister acknowledges his presence or his words once they have escaped behind the screens.

The concept of three pervades the stories, particularly the love stories, in the play. Love triangles, with varying combinations, complicate the action, adding interest and suspense. Three triangles are apparently the most important. Baron Tuzenbakh loves Irina, as does Soleny who tells Irina his feelings in Act II. . . .

Irina, however, does not love either one, but is persuaded by Olga in Act III to become the fiancée of Tuzenbakh. In the first act, Kulygin loves his wife Masha, who, in turn, is falling in love with Lieutenant Colonel Vershinin. Vershinin declares his love in Act II, and in the following act, Masha tells her sisters that she has fallen in love with Vershinin. Masha does not love her husband, nor does Vershinin love his wife. At the end of Act I, Andrei declares his love to Natasha, and between Acts I and II they marry and Natasha births a son, whom she calls Bobik. Her affair with Protopopov is discussed later in this essay. Andrei, who is very much aware of Natasha's adultery, inexplicably still loves her, as he tells the doctor in Act IV.

Three subsidiary love triangles exist; one seems more important than the others; and, in terms of parenting, the result is probably conjecture, perhaps even surmise. For example, the old doctor Chebutykin could easily be seen as the surrogate father to the Prozorov children, and perhaps in his special relationship with Irina as her biological father. Both the mother and her husband the general are dead by the time the play begins, and thus their relationship depends solely on Chebutykin's memory. Chebutykin professes his love for their mother on three separate occasions. As to evidence pertaining to biological parenting, however, whatever conclusion is reached can only be the result of guesswork. In the last act, when Masha asks Chebutykin if their mother loved him, he confesses, after a pause, "That I don't remember anymore." The other two love triangles are Tuzenbakh-Irina-the man of her dreams and Vershinin-Masha-Vershinin's wife. In terms of the six love triangles, if the Chebutykin-Mother-General triangle of the past is excluded, three characters participate in adulterous affairs (Natasha, Masha, Vershinin), and, if Irina's dream man and Vershinin's wife are included, a total of seven characters experience unrequited love (Irina, Tuzenbakh, Soleny, Andrei, Kulygin are the five seen onstage).

Trios abound throughout, and in keeping with Chekhov's striking a balance, parity is consistently observed. In the first act, for example, Vershinin waxes eloquently on the loss of personal identity, the mutability of human mores, and the essence of culture and education. The three sisters are enchanted, but three other characters are not. Soleny snarls insults at Tuzenbakh for joining in the philosophical discussion; Chebutykin tries to turn it all into a joke; and Andrei wanders off to his room to play the violin.

THE BASIC ARCHITECTURE OF THE PLAY IS APPARENTLY CONSTRUCTED IN TERMS OF THREE; THAT IS, THREE CHARACTERS, THREE PARTS OF A TRIANGLE, THREE TIME ORIENTATIONS (PAST, PRESENT, FUTURE), AND SO ON. AS THE FIRST ACT BEGINS, SO DOES THE LAST ACT END."

Linking characters in groups of three is a common technique in *The Three Sisters*. For example, three characters thoroughly enjoy mulling over metaphysical matters, as is evidenced in Act II, when Vershinin, Masha, and Tuzenbakh perform a musical trio on the meaning of life. Olga, Kulygin, and Irina are linked by their occupation of teachers and potential teacher. Natasha, Soleny, together with Protopopov, form another group of three who have been characterized as "the forces of darkness," in opposition to "the forces of life and culture," such as the sisters, Andrei, Tuzenbakh, and Vershinin. Although three characters play the paino, only Tuzenbakh and Natasha are heard. In Act III, Tuzenbakh claims that Masha is an exceptional pianist, which is denied by Irina's assertion that Masha has forgotten how to play, since she "hasn't played in three years . . . or four." To illustrate the superiority of Tuzenbakh over Natasha in terms of talent and training, their playing (in performance) reveals a significant contrast between Tuzenbakh's better-than-average rendition of his waltz and Natasha's inept thwacking of "A Maiden's Prayer."

In the language itself, Chekhov constructed sets of three. That is, three subjects, verbs, predicates, attributes, and so on, have been carefully threaded into a multitude of words, phrases, clauses, sentences. Indeed, the opening line of dialogue illustrates the basic ternary formula:

Father died exactly one year ago,
on this very day,
the fifth of May,
on your saint's day,
Irina.

The three adverbial modifiers stress in rhythm (accent marks) and sounds (assonance italicized) the ternary construction. What Chekhov begins at the very opening is consistently practiced, with variations, throughout. At times, a word is simply repeated, and a new word added to conclude the threesome.

Vprochem, byl *dozhd'* togda. Sil'nyy *dozhad' i sneg.. . . .*

Or perhaps two verbs have been chosen, and one of the two is repeated to make three.

Segodnya utrom *prosnulas', uvidela* massu sveta, *uvidela* vesnu. . . .

Sometimes a word or phrase is said and then twice repeated by a character, as in the following famous exchange in Act III.

KULYGIN: Ya dovólen, ya dovólen, ya dovólen!

MASHA: Nadoyélo, nadoyélo, nadoyélo. . . .

Kulygin's ''I am satisfied'' is musically matched by his wife's ''[I am] bored.'' The sense in the exchange (Kulygin's contentment versus Masha's ennui) vies with rhythm (anapests) and sound (Kulygin's *yada* rhymes with Masha's *nada*) to gain control, and the result is a perfect balance at this moment between husband and wife.

Recurring phrases between two characters occur here and there. For example, in the opening moments Olga begins a thought, Irina continues it, and Olga finally concludes it.

Olga: I tol'ko rastet i krepnet odna mechta . . .

IRINA: Uyekhat' *v Moskvu.* Prodat' dom, pokonchit' vse zdes' i *v Moskvu* . . .

Olga: Da! Skoreye *v Moskvu.* . . .

It is also apparent that, besides the three instances of *v Moskvu,* Irina's second sentence incorporates three action verbs (the last is missing but is understood as the first word in her speech). As the example illustrates, the unity of the three sisters as a family group is explained in part by Chekhov's subtle use of ternary construction in the dialogue.

Chekhov's preoccupation with trinominal combination in language was not restricted to *The Three Sisters.* In examining the syntax of his stories, both Derman and Yefimov verify the ternary formula and note that it occurs regularly enough in prose written early as well as late in his career to pass muster as a consistent feature of Chekhov's writing style. Moreover, it seems that Chekhov frequently chose this device, according to Derman, ''especially in dramatic, lyric, and generally 'touching' places'' in the stories. A great share of the lyric and compassionate moments assigned to *The Three Sisters* by critic after critic may be attributed to the trinominal combinations in the dialogue.

Tuzenbakh's farewell scene with Irina in the last act is a good example. In the space of less than a page and a half of printed text, almost a dozen separate sets of trinominal combinations develop contrapuntally elaborations (in rhythms and sounds) on the theme of unrequited love. The scene begins appropriately with Tuzenbakh and Irina commenting on Kulygin, who crosses the stage calling for his wife Masha. Both understand that Kulygin is happy at seeing the soldiers leave, since his wife's lover, Vershinin, is marching away, too.

Tuzenbakh, like Kulygin, is experiencing unrequited love. Tuzenbakh's chief rival in his love triangle, however, is not Soleny, who is waiting across the river for their forthcoming duel; instead, his chief rival is the unknown man in Irina's dreams. Although Irina and Tuzenbakh plan marriage the next day, she does not love him and tells him so, explaining that her soul ''is like a beautiful piano that has been locked up and the key is lost''. This is the second time in the play that a key is mentioned; the first ''lost'' key apparently prompts Andrei at the end of the third act to seek out Olga and ask for a replacement. . . .

It is apparent that Irina, like Tuzenbakh, is experiencing unrequited love, in that she has not yet met in actuality the man of her dreams. What Tuzenbakh desperately seeks is ''only that lost key'' (the third and last time a ''lost'' key is mentioned) that torments his soul and gives him no sleep. He continues:

TUZENBAKH: Tell me something. *Pause.* Tell me something . . .

IRINA: What? What (can I) say? What?

TUZENBAKH: Something.

IRINA: Enough! Enough! *Pause.*

Occurring as it does in the central moments of their final duo, the sextet of *chtos*—evenly divided between the pair—aptly illustrates their inability to assuage the other's pain. Tuzenbakh's threefold request for ''something,'' or ''anything,'' is crisply denied by Irina's impersonal ''what.'' Even their choice of rhythms is appropriate. Tuzenbakh's dactylic *chtónibud'* is countered by Irina's trochaic *chtó skăzát'* and, subsequently, *Pólno! Pólno!*

In Tuzenbakh's long speech following this exchange, he at first tries to explain the events and attitudes leading to the duel. Irina apparently does not understand what he is saying, since he couches his remarks in Aesopian language. Tuzenbakh then turns to the here and now. And to the ternary formula, as well. ''As if [it's] the first time in [my] life I [actually] see these *firs, maples, birches,* and everything is *looking* at me, *questioning,* and *waiting.*'' His plea that a beautiful life should go hand in hand with the beautiful trees is punctuated by Skvortsov's shout, ''Au! Gop-gop!''—a signal reminding Tuzenbakh of the impending duel. Before he goes, however, he sees the dried-up (dead) tree swaying in the wind with the live trees and concludes that he, if he should die, will participate in life (like the dead tree), ''in one way or another''. Kissing Irina's hand, he speaks in threes once more.

> Your papers,
> that you gave me,
> are lying on my table,
> under a calendar.

Their scene breaks off abruptly when Tuzenbakh ''quickly leaves.'' His departure follows his piddling request that coffee be prepared since, ''not knowing what to say,'' he lamely explains that he had not ''drunk coffee today.'' Tuzenbakh knows, as does the reader, that he will probably die in the duel. It is, after all, Soleny's ''third duel'', and Soleny himself predicted three years earlier that Tuzenbakh ''will die of a stroke,'' or Soleny would lose his temper ''and plant a bullet'' in his forehead ''in about two or three years.'' Irina's inability to respond to Tuzenbakh's request that coffee be prepared perhaps only clarifies their understanding that the *coffee* is simply a substitute for her *declaration of love.* In short, the two end their final scene in the same way that Tuzenbakh begins his long speech in it—with Aesopian dialogue.

As the example of the final duo scene between Irina and Tuzenbakh illustrates, the trinominal combinations in the language itself contribute to an understanding of structure, character, and thought. In fact, the duo scenes of Irina and Tuzenbakh in the remainder of the play reveal that the uses of three are subtle, consistent, and—above all—numerous.

Irina and Tuzenbakh have three duo scenes where the two are alone; their duo scene in Act III is monitored by Masha, although Tuzenbakh—in the beginning—believes that he and Irina are alone and thus speaks to Irina ''tenderly.'' Their duo scene in Act II is confined to Irina's complaint of being tired and to Tuzenbakh's ternary statements about his three surnames, the dominance of his Russian qualities over the German, and his persistent attention to Irina's welfare. Their next-to-the-longest duo scene alone, lasting about a half page of printed text, takes place near the end of Act I, when the other characters are upstage in the ballroom. Their conversation is limited to three topics: Soleny, love/life, and work. Their duo scene in Act III, although Masha keeps telling Tuzenbakh to leave the bedroom, is also focused on three topics: work, love/life, and erosion by time. . . .

Not only are trinominal combinations interlaced in the Russian language, but they are also apparent in the other two languages, Latin and French. In keeping with Chekhov's addiction to the concept of three, *The Three Sisters* is indeed trilingual. Latin is spoken by Kulygin who teaches that language in the school; French, by Natasha who is apparently trying to ''better'' herself. How ironic that the Prozorov family admit their knowledge of three languages and in reality know twice that number but speak only Russian, whereas Natasha whose origins are socially inferior to the Prozorovs, coming as she does out of the *mesh-chane* (an estate next to the peasantry in Old Russia), persists in speaking French. She speaks it badly, of course, enough so that Tuzenbakh must suppress his laughter, but she speaks it only two times—once in the second act, and once in the fourth act. French is, however, spoken a third time in the play—by Chebutykin in the second act when he asks Irina to come into the ballroom.

Kulygin's Latin phrases and sentences (two in every act except the second when only one is spoken) can be viewed as annotations, injunctions, or even Chekhovian signatures as to action and character. Two examples may suffice to illustrate the device. In the first act, Kulygin presents Irina with a copy of his book on the history of the school and concludes his presentation speech with a Latin injunction, which reads (in translation): ''Do what you can, let those who are able to do it better''. Apparently, he is referring to the result (his book) of his own efforts as historian. When Irina points out that she had already received a copy from Kulygin last Easter, Kulygin then makes a gift of the book to Vershinin—an ironic action, since the book still carries with it the Latin injunction. In a short while, Vershinin and Masha fall in love, and it is apparent that Masha considers Vershinin far superior to Kulygin. Moreover, the Latin injunction pervades other stories in the play, as well as the Kulygin-Masha-Vershinin love triangle. For example, Natasha apparently believes her lover Protopopov abler than her husband Andrei. Irina picks the man of her dreams over both Tuzenbakh and Soleny. Vershinin prefers Masha to his own wife. And so on throughout the play. In terms of control of the house, for example, both Natasha and Protopopov are superior to the Prozorov family by the end of the play. So is Soleny topmost when it comes down to dueling.

A second example of Kulygin's Latin takes place in the third act. Chebutykin is drunk and, in a touching speech, excoriates himself and others for their hypocrisy, ignorance, and philistinism. Shortly thereafter, Kulygin slaps Chebutykin on the shoulder, thereby appointing to the doctor Cassandra's gift for prophetic truths as he announces, *"In vino veritas,"* or "In wine there is truth." Whatever the doctor says and does in this third act may be considered the truth, or close to the truth, and like Cassandra, the doctor is scarcely listened to. For example, he drops mama's clock, smashing it to pieces—an appropriate action that depicts time itself as going to pieces, or the Prozorov family's dream of Moscow as falling apart, or the very house in which they live as no longer belonging to them. The doctor repeats his nihilistic avowal of nonexistence. And he reports that Natasha is having an affair with Protopopov. Since the rules of linear time no longer apply (mama's clock is smashed to pieces), the doctor's statement about the affair is not only current, but travels back into the past and forward into the future, as well. In fact, Natasha's sexual affair with Protopopov ostensibly begins with their sleigh ride at the end of Act II, since Natasha's new child, Sofochka, announced at the beginning of Act III, is probably Protopopov's. It is possible, of course, that the affair began much earlier; for example, Masha—at the beginning of the play—reports the rumor of their forthcoming "marriage." Thus, the "truthful" messages—blessed with Kulygin's Latin—that Chebutykin drunkenly brings into the third act reveal incontinence, putridity, even manslaughter.

In addition to the trilingual explorations in sound and sense, three instances of nonsense sounds have been selected, since they permeate certain characters and their actions: Soleny's barnyard irritant; the love duet between Masha and Vershinin; and the doctor's nihilistic song. Soleny comes up with the nonsense sound *tsip* three times on each occasion, and since there are five occasions (four in Act I, one in Act III), the sound is heard fifteen times—a multiple of Chekhov's three. It is an irritating sound—high pitched, piercing, grating—and designed by Soleny to needle his rival Tuzenbakh. Not until act III, when Soleny quotes from Krylov's "The Geese," is the sound clarified, its origin

discovered, and the threat to Tuzenbakh's welfare intensified.

The famous love duet in nonsense sounds occurs in three separate instances in the third act. The first comes after Vershinin sings a line or two from Pushkin's *Yevgeniy Onegin* (the music is probably Chaykovskiy's).

MASHA: Tram-tam-tam . . .

VERSHININ: Tam-tam . . .

MASHA: Tra-ra-ra?

VERSHININ: Tra-ta-ta. *Laughs.*

The three-syllable exchange of vows is undoubtedly their mutual declaration of love, and Masha's agreement to a consummation of their affair probably takes place in their second interaction a few moments later as Vershinin prepares to leave.

VERSHININ: Tram-tam-tam.

MASHA: Tram-tam. . . .

And their final exchange is heard near the close of Act III.

VOICE OF VERSHININ *offstage:* Tram-tam-tam!

MASHA *Rises, loudly:* Tra-ta-ta!

This last three-syllable interaction is an appropriate culmination of the previous scene between Masha and her two sisters, during which Masha describes her profound, abiding, inexplicable love for Vershinin. When he finally calls her from offstage, she answers boldly and then leaves, knowing full well that she is replacing her reputable marriage state with the life of an adulteress. Her farewell moments with her sisters and brother are impeccable Chekhovian signatures as to the end of one role and the beginning of the next.

The doctor's nihilistic song occurs only in the last act (twice in the early part, twice at the end). It consists of twelve syllables (a multiple of Chekhov's three); the first six are nonsense sounds; the last six essentially mean "Sitting on a curbstone am I." The entire line, composed in almost perfect dactyls and aptly punctuated with Chekhov's trinary series of three dots, runs: *Tarara . . . bumiya . . . sizhu na tumbe ya . . .* Its apparent purpose is chiefly to help balance the six part ending of the play.

Another word that seems to be a nonsense sound is the interjection *gop* that appears only in the last act. In Chekhov's day, the sound was used to spur animals into jumping or leaping, and its choice is effective. It is first used at the beginning by Rode.

Takes in the garden at a glance. Farewell, trees! *Shouts.* Gop-gop! *Pause.* Farewell, echo!...

As produced at the Moscow Art Theater, there is a third *gop,* that is, the echo itself that is heard in place of the *pause,* and thus Rode's youthful, lyric, compassionate moment of farewell is carefully constructed in threes. A few moments later, Rode repeats his farewell *gop-gop* upstage and in production the third *gop* is heard. The same interjection, combined with another sound for attracting attention—"Au! Gop, gop!"—occurs three times in the act. In place of the touching effect witnessed with Rode, this phrase is designed to sound a note of impending doom. When it is first heard, for example, Irina "shudders," explaining that "Everything somehow frightens me today." When it is repeated, it follows Chebutykin's comment on the baron's chances in the duel: "The Baron is a fine person, but one Baron more, one Baron less—what does it matter, anyway! Let them! It doesn't matter!" After the sounds are heard, Chebutykin explains, "That's Skvortsov shouting, he's the second. He's sitting in a boat." And the last time the phrase occurs, it signals Tuzenbakh to the duel.

Musical instruments and their sounds apparently go in threes, too. In Act I, three instruments are heard: onstage piano (Tuzenbakh); offstage violin (twice played by Andrei); onstage humming top (Fedotik's gift to Irina). In Act II, three instruments: offstage accordion (heard at the beginning and end of the act); onstage guitar(s) played by Fedotik and/or Rode; onstage piano (waltz by Tuzenbakh). In Act III, the only "musical" instrument is the fire alarm bell that is struck three times (beginning, middle, end). In Act IV, however, a piano and two groups of instruments are heard: offstage piano (Natasha playing "The Maiden's Prayer"); offstage and onstage violin and harp; offstage military band.

Embedded firmly in the play are numerous threads of folksong, poems, folklore, literary allusions and names, and rituals that stitch point to patterns of meaning that are easily understood or felt only by audiences familiar with the Russian language and environment. A partial listing includes writers such as Dobrolyubov, Gogol', Griboyedov, Lermontov; poems such as Krylov's "The Geese" or Pushkin's "Gypsies"; literary concepts like superfluous (*lishniy*), freeloader (*prizhival*), or the universal concept of *poshlost'*. The daily rituals of eating, drinking, and interacting combine with the larger rituals associated with individual rites of passage: celebration of a saint's day in Act I; births (Bobik and Sofochka); and death (Tuzenbakh in Act IV). Group rituals occur throughout, including a rite of intensification in Act II (Carnival Week), as well as that of fighting the town fire in Act III, and the arrival (Act I) and departure (Act IV) of the soldiers. In most of these instances, the concepts of the circle, triads, and parity clarify the patterns and complicate the action of the play. Two examples should illustrate Chekhov's technique.

Early in Act I, the first words spoken by Masha are the opening lines of the prologue to *Ruslan and Lyudmila* (1820) by Aleksandr Pushkin.

> By the curved seashore stands an oak tree green;
> A golden chain to that oak is bound....

Masha then repeats the second line. These lines are appropriate in all aspects: structure, character; thought; diction; music; spectacle. They introduce a long fairy tale that, in turn, is based on seventeenth-century popular narrative, and thus in *The Three Sisters* clarify the beginning of the Vershinin-Masha-Kulygin triangle in terms of awe, mystery, ecstasy of new love. Having introduced Pushkin's poetic image, Masha returns to that image twice. At the end of Act I, these same two lines are repeated by Masha, who then adds, "Now, why on earth do I keep saying this? Those lines have been bothering me since early morning...." What is not said, but is well known to all educated Russians, are the third and fourth lines.

> And linked to the chain with a scholarly mien
> A tomcat is seen going round and round and....

The poetic image of the tomcat chained to, and circling round, the oak tree underscores both the repetition (Act I) and the final effect (Act IV) of Masha's two loves: first, for her husband Kulygin (about four years before the play begins); second, for Vershinin during the course of the play. The cyclical effect of Masha's love is stressed at the end of the first act when Fedotik gives a spinning (and humming) top to Irina, and thus the images of the cat circling the tree, as well as that of Masha and the love cycle, are reinforced both visually and aurally. At this point in Russian productions, all the actors onstage (except Masha) usually "freeze" into a tableau, and only the humming sound of the top and Pushkin's lines, reinforced by the sight of the spinning top and the slight movement of Masha, are heard and seen. Masha's third and last reference to Pushkin's poem occurs immediately following the farewell scene with Vershinin in Act IV. There, of course, she is so distraught, she scrambles the poem and refers to "A tomcat green ...." At no point in the play is Masha ever consciously aware of the subtle connections between Pushkin's poem and the complex of emotions, meanings, and action.

A second example of Chekhov's craftsmanship occurs shortly after the introduction of the Pushkin poem in Act I, and like the earlier image, the second is twice repeated; unlike the first, however, the second image exemplifies the action of several characters. Soleny overhears the sisters in conversation, makes a stupid remark, and is quickly ripped apart by Masha. ''What is it you wanted to say, you loathsome, terrible person?'' Masha asks, and Soleny replies, ''Nothing at all.'' He then adds two lines.

> Before he had time to let out a yell,
> The bear was squeezing him to hell.

The lines are from *The Peasant and the Workman* (1815), a well-known fable by Ivan Krylov. By quoting these lines, Soleny refers to the suddenness of Masha's attack; the *he* in the fable is Soleny himself; and the bear is Masha. In the last act, Soleny arrives to take Chebutykin to the duel and repeats the Krylov lines. Then Chebutykin repeats the same lines, and it is clear that Chekhov has linked Soleny and his action to the action of the bear. The *he* in the fable is associated with Tuzenbakh. Both the fable and the Pushkin poem meld in the last act. At the very moment Kulygin forgives Masha for her love affair with Vershinin, the gunshot that kills Tuzenbakh is heard.

> KULYGIN: She's stopped crying . . . she is a good woman . . .
>
> There is heard a faint shot, far off.
>
> MASHA: By the curved seashore stands an oak tree green; A golden chain to that oak is bound . . . A tomcat green . . . an oak tree green . . .
>
> I'm getting it all mixed up. . . .

Not only does Chekhov link the fable and its bear to Soleny and his action, but he also links it to Protopopov and his. In Act I, immediately after Soleny quotes from Krylov, the nurse Anfisa and Ferapont enter with a cake—a gift to Irina on her saint's day. Anfisa says, ''From the District Council, from Protopopov, Mikhail Ivanych . . . A cake. It is tempting to associate Protopopov with the two lines in the fable, particularly with the bear in the fable. The common nicknames of Mikhail (Protopopov's first name) are *Misha* and *Mishka,* which are also common nicknames for the Russian bear ('*medved*'). The action of Protopopov from beginning to end, as David Magarshack points out, resembles the swift action of the bear in the fable. The *he,* in this instance, is associated with the three sisters, who have been forced out of their home by

Act IV, whereas Protopopov is comfortably seated inside—a guest of his paramour Natasha. The last verbal reference to the image of the bear occurs in French, when Natasha at the window shouts at Andrei: ''It's you, Andryusha? You'll wake up Sofochka. *Il ne faut pas faire dú bruit, la Sophie est dormée déjà. Vous êtes un ours''.* In translation, ''Don't make a noise, Sophie is already asleep. You are a bear.'' The baby Sofochka at this moment is in the carriage Andrei has been wheeling outdoors. Natasha then orders Ferapont to take the carriage from Andrei. Natasha's accusation and decision are—unwittingly for her—ironic comments on the condition of Andrei. He, too, resembles the bear in Krylov's fable. His marriage to Natasha is the beginning of a downward glide that ends in cuckoldry and alienation from his sisters. On the way he mortgages the house to pay his gambling debts, and Natasha holds the money. Andrei is as much the bear as is his rival Protopopov. Moreover, when Natasha shouts, ''You are a bear,'' the *you* can refer not only to Andrei outside but also—unwittingly for Natasha—to Protopopov sitting next to her inside. It may be that the removal of Sofochka from Andrei is perhaps a symbolic gesture of emasculation—as much as it is symbolic of Natasha's drive for order. That is, at the end of the play, Andrei is outside, wheeling his son Bobik, while Protopopov is inside, holding his daughter Sofochka—an effective ironic conclusion, in keeping with Natasha's manipulation of persons. To each child, her or his own father. Both actions are the result of Natasha's own decision. . . .

All these moments grow—not only linearly but also geometrically—into clusters of ideas, feelings, and images that recur, multiply, and strike consistent balances. *The Three Sisters,* perhaps more than any other Chekhovian play, is centrally concerned with the meaning of existence. What goes into the making of happiness? How should we live out our lives? Why do people suffer? ''Nothing happens,'' Olga concludes in Act IV, ''the way we want it to''. . . .

Chekhov's questions that he raises throughout the play come together at the very end. Just as the seasons change (each of the four acts takes place during one of the four seasons), the life cycle starts over again at the end. And the ending resembles the beginning. Only a strophe and a half, separated by an antistrophe, conclude the play. It begins with the three sisters downstage, ''pressing next to one another,'' and each sings and dances her own song. Masha begins, and borrowing from Tuzenbakh's ideas, she stresses the necessity of simply to keep on living. Repeating Vershinin's faith in the future, Irina returns to her own beliefs (first expressed in Act I) that personal salvation can be realized only through work. Olga, cribbing too from Vershinin's ideas pertaining to the loss of personal identity and optimism in the future, searches for the raison d'être: "The band plays so joyfully, so happily, and it seems that in a little while we shall know the reason we live, the reason we suffer . . .". And then Olga adds her famous dactyl plea, "*Yesli by znat'*," which is repeated. The statement, usually translated "If only we knew," is a hypothetical conditional statement, so constructed without a stated subject but with an infinitive. Any subject could be added— *I, you, he, she, one, they,* in place of *we,* or, more to the point—all subjects could be added, thus encompassing everyone in listening range. And so ends the first ode, a three-part harmony on existence.

The antistrophe, consisting of two mute male characters (Kulygin and Andrey) and the speaking doctor, is a three-part answer to the sisters' ode. Kulygin, carrying Masha's hat and cape, is "happy, smiling," apparently convinced that everything will return to the way it was before Masha's affair with Vershinin. The Latin teacher had previously expressed his belief that life is very real, by no means an illusion, and like the Romans, a person's life style must be ordered, following its routine, regimen, rules. Andrey, emasculated by his wife and neglected by his sisters, wheels the carriage, in which Bobik is sitting, a consistent reminder of his vanished dreams. Earlier in the act, he condemns the town (audience) for their indifference, deceit, and philistinism, charges that could perhaps be leveled at the speaker himself. The third member of the upstage chorus, Chebutykin, sits on a bench and denies the optimism expressed by the sisters. He *"sings quietly."*

> "Tara . . . ra . . . boom-di-yah . . . sitting on a curb today . . ." *Reads newspaper.* It doesn't matter! It doesn't matter!

The antistrophe ends, and Olga begins the second strophe: "If only we knew, if only we knew! . . . ."

And the curtain falls on two choruses. In each chorus are embodied three characters, each singing and dancing her and his viewpoint on the nature of existence. The play has come full circle, in keeping with the persistent cyclical patterns. Moreover, it has consistently followed the ternary construction from beginning to close. And the characters, usually cast in groups of threes, together with their ideas,

emotions, and images, have been carefully balanced to reveal an equivalence rarely seen in the drama since the Renaissance.

Source: Eugene K. Bristow, "Circles, Triads, and Parity in The Three Sisters," in *Chekhov's Great Plays,* edited by Jean-Pierre Baricelli, New York University Press, 1981, p. 76.

SOURCES

Bruford, W. H., *Chekhov and His Russia: A Sociological Study,* Archon Books, 1971.

Esslin, Martin, "Chekhov and the Modern Drama," in *Anton Chekhov,* edited by Harold Bloom, Chelsea House Publishers, 1999, pp. 139-50.

Kirk, Irina, *Anton Chekhov,* Twayne Publishers, 1981. pp. 144-45.

Shaftymov, A., "Principles of Structure in Chekhov's Plays," in *Chekhov: A Collection of Critical Essays,* edited by Robert Louis Jackson, Prentice-Hall, Inc., 1967. p. 72.

Troyat, Henri, *Chekhov,* E. P. Dutton, 1984.

FURTHER READING

Hahn, Beverly, "Three Sisters," in her *Chekhov: A Study of the Major Stories and Plays,* Cambridge University Press, 1977, pp. 284-309.
    Hahn's study, often cited by other critics, examines the interplay between sadness and hope in the play.

Gerhardie, William, *Anton Chekhov: A Critical Study,* St. Martin's Press, 1974.
    This book is a reprint of the 1923 edition, one of the first critical studies of Chekhov before his genius was widely recognized throughout the world. It is considered the one book that any serious student of Chekhov *must* read.

Karlinsky, Simon, "Chekhov: The Gentle Subversive," introduction to *The Letters of Anton Chekhov,* Harper & Row, 1973, pp. 1-32.
    A political analysis of Chekhov, who is usually treated by critics as an artist who was removed from politics. Russia at the turn of the century had a delicate political balance, and Karlinsky examines how Chekhov reflected that balance and toyed with it.

Peace, Richard, "The Three Sisters," in his *Chekhov: A Study of the Four Major Plays,* Yale University Press, 1983, pp. 74-116.
    This short analysis of the play is mostly useful for its wealth of background information clarifying references that the play mentions quickly without explanation.

Pritchett, V. S., *Chekhov: A Spirit Set Free,* Random House, 1988.

> Pritchett, one of the great novelists and short story writers of the twentieth century, produced this wise critical biography when he was in his eighties, and the feeling of one master story teller's appreciation of another helps readers understand why Chekhov is so universally admired.

Stroeva, M. N., "*The Three Sisters* in the Production of the Moscow Art Theater," translated by Robert Lewis Jackson, in Jackson's *Chekhov: A Collection of Critical Essays,* Prentice Hall, 1967.

> Stroeva's essay, originally printed in Moscow in 1955, is a meticulously researched piece giving a theatrical background to the act of bringing this play to life.

Szondi, Peter, "The Drama in Crisis: Chekhov," in his *Theory of the Modern Drama,* University of Minnesota, 1987.

> This essay emphasizes the dramatic device of the monologue, and Chekhov's unique deployment of that device.

Tiny Alice

EDWARD ALBEE
1964

Tiny Alice first opened to audiences in New York in 1964. Almost immediately, the play spurred intense controversy and sparked a debate that was played out almost daily in newspapers and magazines. What did the play mean? demanded critics and viewers alike. Albee claimed in a press conference, and in his Author's Note when the text was published in 1965, that the play was quite clear, even simple, and thus did not need his explication. Despite Albee's assertions, people continued to have a hard time deciphering the play, in which characters are symbols, words and actions have multiple dimensions, and religious expression mixes with sexual fantasy.

Fortunately, a large body of work helps the current reader understand many important parts of the play, including symbolism, imagery, and underlying assumptions about religion. Critics have also been interested in how *Tiny Alice* fits in with the body of Albee's work. They have examined such specific aspects of the play as language, theme, and genre. Many scholars, however, maintain that *Tiny Alice* remains one of Albee's most difficult—but ultimately satisfying—plays.

AUTHOR BIOGRAPHY

Edward Albee was born in 1928 somewhere in Virginia. Two weeks after his birth, Reed and

Frances Albee, who lived in Larchmont, New York, adopted him. The Albees were wealthy, and Reed Albee was part owner of a chain of theaters his father started. Albee grew up in the lap of luxury, and as a child, often attended matinees in New York City. Many show business personalities also visited the Albee home. Albee began writing poetry as a young child.

When Albee was eleven years old, he was sent to the first of a series of boarding schools. His academic record was poor. His teachers at Choate, however, encouraged his writing, and he worked in every genre—poetry, short stories, plays, and even the novel. One of his poems appeared in a literary magazine in Texas.

In 1946, Albee attended Trinity College in Connecticut. He left school a year and a half year later, returning home, where he worked as a writer for a radio station. In 1950, with the financial assistance of a trust fund left to him by his grandmother, Albee moved to Greenwich Village. He supplemented his income by working in various jobs. He also spent six months in Italy, where he wrote a novel.

Albee came into contact with literary luminaries such as W. H. Auden and Thornton Wilder, who gave him advice on his writing. At this point, Albee mainly worked on his poetry. Immediately following his thirtieth birthday, however, Albee started work on a play, *The Zoo Story,* which he completed in three weeks. *The Zoo Story* premiered in September 1959 in Berlin. Four months later, Albee's play shared a double bill with one of Samuel Beckett's at the Provincetown Playhouse in Greenwich Village. It was generally received as the creation of a formidable talent. The following year, Albee won the Vernon Rice Memorial Award for the work.

Albee continued to achieve critical and popular acclaim for his one-act dramas, and his work was compared to that of Tennessee Williams—whose work Albee greatly admired—and French writer Eugene Ionesco. In 1959, he published *The American Dreams* and *The Sandbox,* both of which, along with *The Zoo Story,* established Albee as an astute critic of American values and of human interaction.

The production of *Who's Afraid of Virginia Woolf?* in 1962, however, catapulted Albee from avant-garde attention to public notoriety. Many critics still continue to find this play his most important work, and it was made into a film four

years later. Albee followed up this success with a number of full-length works, including *Tiny Alice* (1964). Three of Albee's plays have won the Pulitzer Prize: *A Delicate Balance* (1966), *Seascape* (1975), and *Three Tall Women* (1991).

Since his emergence in the theatrical world, Albee has continually produced plays that have been staged both in the United States and abroad. He also established the Edward Albee Foundation, which maintains an artists' colony on Long Island. Albee has also taught at the University of Houston, and worked at the Alley Theater, where he directed one play a year.

PLOT SUMMARY

Act I, Scene 1

The play opens in a garden. Lawyer is talking nonsense to a pair of cardinals in a cage as Cardinal, a cardinal in the Catholic Church, enters. Conversation reveals that the two men went to school together and maintain a lasting dislike for each other. The two men throw around insults. Cardinal says it is fitting that Lawyer, who always was a cheater and a liar, has chosen the legal profession, and Lawyer counters that it is fitting that Cardinal, an arrogant, pompous whore, is in the Church. Eventually, the men turn their attention to the business at hand: Lawyer's employer, Miss Alice, wants to give two billion to the Church. The Cardinal is very excited at the prospect of so much money (though the currency is never named). At Lawyer's request, he agrees to send his secretary, Julian, a lay brother to Miss Alice's house to take care of the "necessary odds and ends."

Act I, Scene 2

In Scene Two, Julian has just entered the library of Miss Alice's mansion. The room's most prominent feature is a huge doll house model of the mansion itself. Butler, Miss Alice's butler, comes into the library. He sees Julian looking at the house and points out that it is an exact replica of the mansion. Butler asks if anyone is in the replica, which startles Julian, who ascertains that the model is empty. Lawyer enters the library. He reveals that he knows Julian's history, with the exception of a six-year blank period, which Julian refuses to talk about. Then Lawyer proceeds to slander Cardinal, which causes Julian to protest. Lawyer eventually leaves to get Miss Alice. Once he is gone, Julian tells Butler about those six years. He lost his faith in God, suffered a nervous breakdown, and put himself into a mental institution. His loss of faith stemmed from his inability to reconcile himself with the difference between God and human's representation of God. Julian tells Butler that his faith is his sanity. A chime sounds, indicating that Miss Alice will now see Julian.

Act I, Scene 3

When Julian enters the sitting room, he sees an old lady. He is surprised, for Cardinal had said Miss Alice was young. Lawyer leaves the two alone, and Julian is forced to yell in an effort to be heard, but then Miss Alice takes off a wig and her old lady mask, revealing her own, much younger face. She says she was just playing a game to lighten the mood. Alice asks what Julian thought of Butler and Lawyer. Miss Alice says that Butler was once her lover and that she is the mistress of Lawyer, but that he is a pig. Then she asks Julian about his missing six years, and Julian gives much the same explanation he gave Butler. Alice asks if Julian has slept with many women, but he does not know. Although celibate, as a lay brother must be, while in the asylum, Julian had a hallucination that he had sex with another patient who believed she was the Virgin Mary. However, he does not know if this really took place. Miss Alice changes the tone of the conversation back to business. She suggests that Julian move into the castle so he will be on hand to take care of the business, and he assents.

Act II, Scene 1

Lawyer chases Miss Alice into the library, while she is yelling at him to stay away. Lawyer is angry that Julian is at the house all the time. He tells Miss Alice that she should ''get it done with.'' He thinks that she is sleeping with Julian. Miss Alice talks of her loathing for Lawyer but at the same time, lets him fondle her. Butler and Julian return from their tour around the mansion. Julian notices that the model is on fire. Butler looks out the windows and he sees that the chapel is burning. The men run off to put out the fire, and Miss Alice stays in the library. Alternating between a ''prayer'' voice and a natural voice, she asks that the fire be put out and the mansion be saved. Julian returns with news that the fire is out. He wants to know why

Edward Albee

the real chapel and the model chapel were both in flames, but Miss Alice says she doesn't know why.

Act II, Scene 2

Butler and Lawyer are in the library. Butler says the fire in the chapel helped bring Miss Alice and Julian together. Lawyer expresses his distaste of them sleeping together, but Butler reminds him that the situation will not last long. Lawyer has to go see Cardinal again, so they decide to play act; Butler takes the role of Lawyer and Lawyer plays Cardinal. Butler, as Lawyer, tells Cardinal that Julian will be taken from the Church in return for the 2 billion. The men slip in and out of their roles, discussing what Lawyer will say. Butler suggests that Cardinal marry Miss Alice and Julian. Then Butler takes the role of Julian, while Lawyer stays in the role of Cardinal. The men discuss what God is. Butler/ Julian contends that God is an abstract ideal, but Lawyer/Cardinal asserts that while there is an abstract God, that God cannot be understood or worshipped. Lawyer says that Alice can be understood, however.

Act II, Scene 3

Julian and Miss Alice are in the sitting room. Miss Alice speaks of sex, asking Julian about his body hair. Miss Alice continues to tease him. Julian makes a slip of the tongue and says that she is tempting him. He speaks of his desire, when he was younger, to serve humanity, but Miss Alice tells him that he has done great service to the Church through his interactions with her. He speaks of his dreams of sacrifice and martyrdom. Alice asks him to marry her and to sacrifice himself to her. She engulfs him within the winglike arms of her dressing gown.

Act III

Julian and Miss Alice have just married. Julian enters the library where Butler is covering all the furniture with sheets. Julian wonders where everyone, including Miss Alice, has disappeared. Julian wonders why Miss Alice did not invite friends to the ceremony, but Butler says that she does not have friends. Then Miss Alice comes in the room, but when she sees Julian, she immediately leaves again. Then Cardinal comes in the room, and Butler leaves. Julian speaks to Cardinal excitedly about doing service for God through his marriage to Miss Alice. Cardinal advises Julian to accept what may happen in the future as part of his service and part of God's will. After Lawyer comes into the room, Julian exits to look for Alice. Cardinal looks at the model, asking obliquely if it is really true. Lawyer says it is. He opens a drawer and takes out a loaded pistol. When Cardinal questions this, Lawyers say they may have to shot Julian. Soon enough, everyone is gathered in the library. Butler opens the champagne and Lawyer starts a toast to the "ceremony of Alice." As Lawyer toasts Alice and Julian and their house, lights begin to flicker on in the model. Julian makes his own toast to his love for Miss Alice. As soon as he is done, Lawyer announces it is time to go. Julian realizes that something is going on that he does not understand. Lawyer tells Julian that they are going, while he will stay behind with Alice. Miss Alice tells Julian that she has done her best to imitate her, meaning Alice in the model, but Julian, who has fought his entire life against "the symbol," does not want to stay behind with Alice. He believes that he has married Miss Alice, but she informs him that he has married Alice through Miss Alice. Julian charges that "there is no one there," meaning in the model, but everyone else tells him to accept that Alice is there. Julian resists, declaring that he is "done with hallucination," but Miss Alice proclaims that she, not Alice, is the illusion. Julian refuses to do as they ask and declares his intention of going back to the asylum, so Lawyer shoots him. Julian sinks to the floor in front of the model. Miss Alice holds him while he bleeds. Cardinal leaves,

after agreeing to send his new secretary to pick up the money. Miss Alice asks Lawyer how long they must do this, implying that they have acted out this drama before and will continue to do so again and again. Julian is in great pain, and Miss Alice talks to Alice in the model, asking her to take him in. Then the three say goodbye to Julian and leave him alone.

Julian begins his final soliloquy. He talks about his abandonment by Miss Alice. He finds it hard to believe that he is dying. He remembers a boyhood accident that parallels his current situation. He also addresses Alice in the model, asking if she has forsaken him like all the others. He looks in the model at "his chapel," but starts with fear when the light suddenly goes out. He begins to speak to the phrenological head that wears Miss Alice's wig, asking if she is his bride. he wonders if this is his priesthood and demands that his bride—Alice, God—show herself. He begins to hear the sounds of heartbeats and breathing, growing louder and louder. A great shadow fills the room, darkening the stage. His final words are that he accepts God's, Alice's will. Julian dies with his arms spread wide like the crucifixion.

CHARACTERS

Miss Alice

Miss Alice is a young, beautiful, wealthy woman. She manifests several contradictions, for instance, vacillating between being flirtatious and being businesslike, or despising Lawyer but being his lover. She intends to donate billions to different charitable institutions such as Jewish organizations, hospitals, universities, and the Catholic Church. It is this gift that brings her in contact with Cardinal, and thus, Julian, his secretary. Though she seems to sincerely like Julian, she, along with the other members of her household, are plotting against him. She seduces and marries Julian in order to sacrifice him to Tiny Alice. Despite the affection she shows for him, she matter of factly leaves him when the time comes.

Butler

Butler is Miss Alice's butler and her former lover. He claims to derive his name from his job, which gives him the function of serving the others. Butler demonstrates some empathy and liking for

Julian. The two men seem to forge an immediate bond, and it is only with Butler that Julian shares the more complete story of why he went into the asylum.

Cardinal

Cardinal is a cardinal in the Catholic Church. Lawyer approaches him with Miss Alice's gift, but the two men already are acquainted—and heartily dislike each other—through their boyhood school. As Lawyer asserts, Cardinal is pompous and full of self-importance. He is also a hypocrite, "selling" his personal secretary—a man of faith—to Alice's agents for a vast sum of money. He is complicit in the plan against Julian, as indicated in Act III. He even knows that this action might end in Julian's death—because Lawyer tells him so—but he does not protest.

Julian

Julian (also known as Brother Julian) is the middle-aged secretary of Cardinal. He is a lay person, but he never became a priest because he experienced a crisis of faith years ago. He came to believe that people were worshipping the image of God they created, not God himself; they were worshipping the symbol of God. When this happened, he checked himself into a mental asylum for six years. While in the asylum, he had difficulties telling the difference between hallucination and reality, as demonstrated by his lack of knowledge of whether he had sex with another patient or simply imagined it. Throughout his life, however, his fantasies of martyrdom—all of which are heavily tinged with sexuality—are so vivid as to become almost real to him. At the time that the play takes place, Julian allows himself to be drawn to Miss Alice. He succumbs to her seduction and agrees to marry her. After the wedding, however, Miss Alice leaves him to die of a gunshot wound. Through his final soliloquy and death, he comes to accept what either is a hallucination or a personification of an abstract force, both of which go against his belief system.

Brother Julian

See Julian

Lawyer

Lawyer is the lawyer who handles the transfer of Miss Alice's money to the church. He is also Miss Alice's lover, but he disgusts her. He is a cruel, crude, and thoughtless man. He dislikes Cardinal, calling him the son of a whore and profiteer, and he is jealous of Miss Alice's affections for Julian. He kills Julian at the end of the play, though Miss Alice believes that such an action was not necessary. He remains completely unaffected by Julian's impending death as he leaves the mansion.

THEMES

Illusion and Reality

Julian is torn between conflicting desires for truth and illusion. He claims to respect only that which is real, but at the same time, he is drawn to the world of his imagination. He wants to worship God in the abstract form and he rails against those people who create God in their own image for their own purpose. This incompatibility of illusion and reality caused him to lose his faith, and thus his sanity, forcing him into the asylum. While in the asylum, he experienced even greater confusion about what was real and what was illusion. To the present day, he is never sure whether or not the sexual experience that he remembers did happen. When he tells Miss Alice about this, she wonders, "Is the memory of something having happened the same as it having happened?" vocally illustrating the sometimes unavoidable merging of illusion and reality. Julian's leave-taking of the asylum also illustrates this principle: he was persuaded that hallucination was inevitable and even desirable.

By the end of the play, however, Julian has been thrown into such a state of confusion that he questions whether he was actually sane during the time he spent in the asylum. He cannot accept Miss Alice's assertion that she, not Alice, is the illusion. He realizes that he has "given up everything . . . For hallucination." He declares his intention to return to the asylum, his "refuge . . . in the world, from all the demons waking," at which point Lawyer shoots him. In his dying soliloquy, Julian becomes enmeshed in his debate between truth and reality. Earlier, while looking at the model he had shouted, "THERE IS NOTHING THERE!," but now, even while continuing to deny the physical representation of the abstract, he calls for Alice-God to come to him, and he begins to hear heartbeats and breathing that grows increasingly louder. These sounds continue after his death. Albee has said that he

TOPICS FOR FURTHER STUDY

- Imagine that you are a theater critic who has just attended a performance of *Tiny Alice*. Write the review to run in your local paper. Consider the essential message of the play in your article.

- Find out more about the Theater of the Absurd. Read plays from this school, such as Eugene Ionesco's *The Bald Soprano* or Samuel Beckett's *Waiting for Godot*. Based on your research and your readings, do you think *Tiny Alice* is Absurdist drama. Why or why not?

- Read another of Albee's plays. Compare the play to *Tiny Alice*. Consider themes, characterization, symbolism, and philosophical underpinnings.

- Conduct research to find out about some major controversies that have existed in the belief system within the Church. What are different ways in which people have regarded God and faith over the years?

- The Catholic Church and its rituals are filled with many symbols. Find out what some of these symbols are. How many religious symbols do you find in the play?

- The 1960s were a time of great change in the way Americans regarded religion. To many people, religion had lost its influence. How has religion been regarded in the 1990s? Has there been many changes in the way people have used religion and religious thoughts and ideals?

- Find out more about Albee's works. How would you categorize his body of work? What issues were of greatest concern to him? How do his early plays differ from his later plays?

---

intended the audience to think of these sounds as either Julian's hallucination or as the personification of an abstract force. Either way, Julian is submitting to an illusion instead of the reality—the pure abstraction of God—that he claimed he wanted.

The mutable nature of illusion and reality is underscored by many other elements in the play. Miss Alice convincingly appears as an old woman—it takes only a face mask and a wig to turn a young beauty into a crone. Cardinal also demonstrates that how something or someone appears is not fixed. He speaks in the royal "we," but excited about the amount of money Miss Alice is going to give to the Church, he slips into the more informal "I." The model, which has the power to signify what happens in the mansion, is another example of the overlap between illusion and reality. What happens in the model happens in the mansion, such as the fire in the chapel. "It is exact," says Butler, but that is not true, for in the model Alice resides and in the mansion Miss Alice, Butler, and Lawyer reside. Further, he and Julian question whether the model is an accurate model of the mansion—does it have a

model within the model? Trying to answer this question would prove the impossibility of discerning with utter certainty the distinction between illusion and reality, for if the model is an accurate replica of the mansion, the smaller models within would extend into infinity.

God and Faith

Julian's primary struggle has centered on the limits of his faith. He is a lay person, thus, in Butler's words, Julian is "*of* the cloth but [he has] . . . not taken it." This position indicates Julian's indecision and his inability to accept the human-made institution of religion. Alone with Butler again, he clarifies his position: he fled to the asylum because he had lost his faith in God. He could not accept that humans made God into a "false God in their own image." Julian's rejection of this representation shows his distaste for making God into a symbol for worship; instead, he thinks, people should merely worship God. Julian says of the asylum, "I did not go there to *look* for my faith, but because *it* had left me." His faith and his sanity, "they are one and the same.'' The implication is that without his faith, he is insane, so in leaving the asylum, he was affirming his faith. However, one significant change took place during the asylum: he came to accept that hallucinations were inevitable and *not* the mark of insanity.

The idea of faith arises again at the end of the play. Faced with Lawyer, Butler, Miss Alice, and Cardinal, all of whom want him to stay with Alice—all of whom want him to accept the representation of God—Julian says he is unable to do so. Lawyer tells him to accept this "act of faith." Cardinal seconds Lawyer's suggestion, declaring it to be "God's will." Julian visibly recoils at this suggestion. Having fought so hard to regain his faith, he knows that acknowledging Alice as the personification of God will leave him empty.

Sexuality

Tiny Alice ripples with both heterosexual and homosexual energy. The opening scene of the play, acted out between Cardinal and Lawyer, is filled with hostility, yet it makes numerous references to sexual tensions that have existed over the years between the men. Lawyer speaks of the "obeisance" that he used to demand from Cardinal, who in turn reminds his enemy that Lawyer's nickname, Hyena, derived from the animal's habit of eating its prey through the anus. Lawyer counters by implying in a manner that is "too offhand" that Cardinal may have sexual relations with other cardinals. Lawyer muses on the "vaunted celibacy" of priests. When he was young, he and Cardinal attended a Catholic boys' school where "everyone diddled everyone else," and they naturally assumed that the priests did the same. The homosexual tension extends beyond these men. Lawyer calls Butler "Darling" and "Dearest." Butler, too, when he kisses Julian goodbye on the forehead gives him "not a quick kiss." Julian describes his attraction to a Welsh stableman with hairy hands.

Despite his vow of celibacy, Julian has numerous and intense sexual fantasies for both men and women. His description of his hallucination of his sexual encounter with the fellow patient is vivid, mimicking orgasm, but it is not as sexually evocative as his homosexual fantasies. In his dreams of martyrdom, the entrance of the gladiator's fork is simultaneous with his sexual mounting by the lion. He relishes the "bathing" of his groin with his own blood and the press of the lion's belly, which changes into the gladiator's belly, against him. While retelling this fantasy, Julian works himself

into a trancelike state which ends in him giving himself to Miss Alice, who opens her gown wide so he can enter within "the great wings." Thus, he has transforms his homosexual fantasies into heterosexual carnal desire.

STYLE

Symbolism

Of the five characters, three bear the title of their profession. Lawyer, Miss Alice's lawyer, represents civil law, and Cardinal, a cardinal in the Catholic Church, represents divine law. Instead of standing for justice and God's love, respectively, each man symbolizes the perversion of power and hypocrisy. Cardinal acts as Julian's pimp, willingly selling his secretary to Miss Alice and her cohorts. The papers transferring the money are signed on the day of the wedding. "[T]he grant is accomplished;" Cardinal tells Julian, "through your marriage . . . your service." Lawyer arranges for this transaction, obtaining a human under the guise of making a donation. As Cardinal points out, though, Lawyer was a "cheat in your examinations, a liar in all things of any matter." Further, the two men are made increasingly powerful through Miss Alice's money, a symbol here of corruption. Butler, whose actual name signifies his position, is frequently seen serving wine, which is the Christian metaphor for blood. Julian has a symbolic profession. He is a lay brother—of the cloth but not fully a priest. In his relationship with Miss Alice, Julian escapes this celibacy without priesthood and unknowingly replaces it with priesthood without celibacy—a position denied by the Church.

The model house is the most important symbol in the play. The house in which Tiny Alice lives—where Julian will join her—is sealed tightly. In this respect, it is like the "glass dome" that "descended" on Julian before he entered the asylum. The sealed world of the model also represents the unrealistic world Julian has tried to create for himself since then. He had sought safety in the Church but that institution turns out to be his greatest enemy. The model, which captivates Julian, ends in symbolizing his death.

Imagery

Religious imagery abounds in the play. After Lawyer has shot Julian, Miss Alice takes him in her arms so that "they create something of a Pieta." Julian dies with his arms wide spread, forming himself into a figure suggests that suggests Jesus on the cross. Cardinal's cardinals cause him and Lawyer to reference Saint Francis and also draw improbable likenesses between these men and the saint. Both Cardinal and Lawyer also engage in nonsense talk to the birds, demonstrating a more tender side but one that never reveals itself to humanity.

This vulnerability is echoed in other images of birds throughout the play. Miss Alice's gown has arms that resemble great wings to enfold Julian. Alternately, Julian is described as Lawyer and Miss Alice as a "bird of prey," "a drab fledgling," and a "little bird, pecking away." Like a bird, he is trapped in a cage, ready to be destroyed by Alice. For her part, Alice has been first compared to a mouse in Lawyer's effort to demean God, and then she has been likened to a hungry cat, one ready to dally with and destroy her prey.

Allegory

Many readers have perceived *Tiny Alice* as an allegory. An allegory is a narrative technique in which characters representing objects or abstract ideas are used to convey a message, which is most often moral, religious, or ethical. Julian represents pureness in the world; that pureness is murdered by the impurities in the world, which are represented by the other characters. On a more complex level, Butler, Cardinal, and Lawyer have been seen as forming an "unholy trinity" who pervert traditional religious faith. In the final scene, each man becomes his function. Cardinal serves the greed of the Church, not the souls it is supposed to care for. Lawyer efficiently finishes negotiations of the unholy barter in front of Julian's dying eyes, attempting to give the 2 billion to Cardinal. Butler completes his last task of service for Julian, fetching a cushion to place behind his back. And Julian, the layperson, the nonpriest who still practices celibacy, becomes a priest wed to Alice—he becomes a son of God despite the shaking of his faith.

Setting

The setting is significant in its very indistinctness. Time and place are not specified in the play. The sums of money talked about are in the millions and billions but no currency is named. The only references to the outside world come as inconsequential details: the temperature in Cardinal's gar-den is 96 degrees; the port that Julian drinks was bottled in 1806; Miss Alice's mansion was brought over stone by stone from England. The generality of these facts gives the play a universal quality, reinforcing the idea that what happens in the play could happen anywhere and to anyone. At the end of the play, as well, Miss Alice makes specific yet vague references to future plans. She, Lawyer, and Butler will move to "the city" before they embark on "the train trip south." They will have a "house on the ocean" and a Rolls Royce that takes them "twice weekly into the shopping strip." Clearly, the three agents of Alice have enacted this drama before and will do so again. They will use the same props to lure their prey: wealth, beauty, and mystery.

Theater of the Absurd

The Theater of the Absurd was a post-World War II dramatic trend characterized by radical theatrical innovations. In these works, nontraditional characterizations, plots, and stage sets reveal a meaningless universe in which human values are irrelevant. Absurdist drama features a vision of bewildered and anxious humanity struggling to find a purpose. Traditional aspects of support, such as religion and society, have often collapsed. By the mid-1960s, many absurdist innovations had been absorbed into mainstream theater.

Some critics find *Tiny Alice* an absurdist drama. Albee first was categorized with the major absurdist playwrights—Eugene Ionesco, Samuel Beckett, Jean Genet, and Harold Pinter—after the staging of his first play, *Zoo Story*. Like these European absurdists, Albee has also tried to dramatize the reality of humanity's condition. Albee differs from them in that he focuses on the illusions that screen humans from reality instead of on life's alogical absurdity. Julian, for example, uses his belief in God to shield him from the hypocrisy of religion and his own repressed sexuality.

HISTORICAL CONTEXT

The Sixties

The 1960s was a decade that ushered in great change in the United States. The decade began with voters electing John F. Kennedy as president. At that time, he was the youngest man ever to hold the office, and he brought a spirit of youth and hope to the nation. After his assassination, Kennedy was

COMPARE
&
CONTRAST

- **1960s:** In 1965, advanced degrees in theology are awarded to 1,739 Americans, out of a total U.S. population of close to 194 million.

  1990s: In 1996, advanced degrees in theology are awarded to 8,479 Americans, out of a total U.S. population of close to 266 million.

- **1960s:** By the end of the decade, there are 145 institutions conferring degrees in legal studies. In 1970, 14,916 L.L.B. or J.D. degrees are awarded to students.

  1990s: By the middle of the decade, there are 183 institutions conferring degrees in legal studies. In 1996, 39,828 L.L.B. or J.D. degrees are awarded to students.

- **1960s:** In 1965, a bit over $12 million (in 1965 dollars) is donated to charities. Individuals donate about $9.3 million of this sum. Close to $6 million is given to religious interests.

  1990s: In 1997, almost $144 billion (in 1997 dollars) is donated to charities. Individuals donate just over $109 billion. In 1995, 31.5 percent of American households give some money to charity. Just over 15 percent donate more than $1,000. Forty-eight percent of people give money to religious interests, and the average donation is $868.

- **1960s:** In 1965, 24.9 percent of American households have an income of $10,000 or higher.

  1990s: In 1997, 18.4 percent of American households have and income of $75,000 or higher.

- **1960s:** In 1965, there are just over 46 million American members of the Roman Catholic Church, which is about 24 percent of the U.S. population.

  1990s: In 1998, 27 percent of the American population are Roman Catholic. Forty percent of all Americans attend church or synagogue each week.

---

succeeded by Lyndon Johnson, whose administration effected great change in tax cuts, civil rights, and the war on poverty. By the middle of the decade, the Civil Rights Act and the Voting Rights Act had been passed, which barred discrimination and led to a mass registration of African American voters in the South, respectively.

Many young people rebelled against mainstream America. These members of the counterculture questioned conformity and societal institutions, such as churches. The enrollment in college courses in religion grew dramatically as students searched for alternative answers. The women's movement also experienced a widespread revival, which forced the government to reconsider women's rights.

Changes in Religious Expression
In 1962, Pope John XXIII attended the Second Vatican Council to discuss what would become historical changes to Church practices. The pope and the other delegates decided that mass should be performed in local languages instead of in Latin. Laypeople also began to acquire a larger role in determining Church affairs.

The U.S. Supreme Court also handed down a historic decision in response to *Engel v. Vitale.* The Court's decision brought an end to religious worship in public schools. In 1962, twenty-four states either permitted or required school prayer, but the Supreme Court stated that special time designated for prayer violated citizens' First Amendment right to freedom of religion. This decision sparked widespread controversy. In the ensuing years, there were 144 proposed constitutional amendments to allow prayer and Bible reading in school; none of them passed. However, the Court's decision seemed to reflect the growing consensus of the American population that religion was losing its influence on American life; a poll conducted in 1969 showed that

70 percent of the respondents agreed with such a statement.

The Art World

Drama and dramatists have moved to the forefront of the arts. Tennessee Williams, Archibald McLeish, Frank Gilroy, and Edward Albee were among the most respected playwrights of the period. Plays by these writers and others were performed regularly on college campuses and by amateur theater groups throughout the country. Unconventional theater also grew in popularity. Plays such as "Hair," about members of the counterculture living under the cloud of the Vietnam War generally opened off-Broadway, but many became enormous hits.

In literature, novels that had previously been censored were becoming hits in the bookstores. D. H. Lawrence's *Lady Chatterly's Lover* and Henry Miller's *Tropic of Cancer* were published in inexpensive paperback editions. College students studied novels that had previously been considered too risqué, such as James Baldwin's *Another Country,* which featured a homosexual character. Other authors portrayed their heroes as victims of an inhumane, insane, and authoritarian society. Joseph Heller's *Catch 22,* which takes places against a mad backdrop of war, and Ken Kesey's *One Flew Over the Cuckoo's Nest,* whose protagonist was an inmate in an insane asylum, were popular novels that were made into movies.

CRITICAL OVERVIEW

Tiny Alice first opened in New York in 1964 and soon appeared, with the inclusion of material that had been deleted for the stage, in book form. Albee's publisher asked him to provide a preface to the published play. Albee instead wrote an Author's Note in which he explained that many had hoped that he would clarify "obscure points in the play— explaining my intention, in other words. I have decided against creating such a guide because I find—after reading the play over—that I share the view of even more people: that the play is quite clear." Despite Albee's affirmative words, many contemporary audiences and critics were unsure what to make of *Tiny Alice* or what the play, in fact,

meant. Within a month after its opening, the play had already garnered a mass of reviews, many enthusiastic, that awarded kudos to Albee for his literary technique, language, and audacity. The controversy over *Tiny Alice,* however, which continues to the present day, had begun. Contradictory statements—often in the same review—were rampant. Theater critics ran the gamut of calling Albee's work "a masterpiece" that "established Albee as the most distinguished American playwright to date" to "pretentious" and "willfully obscure" to "a set trap that has no bait." The reviewer for *Newsweek,* for example, while admitting that *Tiny Alice* was a "thoroughly confused play," also found that it contained unique "scenes that break down the walls of reticence and safety ... [of] the commercial theater."

One element that many reviews had in common was a noticeable refusal to attempt to explicate the drama they had witnessed. Henry Hewes, writing for the *Saturday Review,* was a notable exception. Hewes openly interpreted action and character in the play and even boldly stated what he believed to be misinterpretations on the part of other reviewers. In the same issue of *Saturday Review* was a psychiatrist's "look" at *Tiny Alice* by Abraham N. Franzblau. Franzblau asserted that the reason viewers were so "disturbed," "puzzled," and "fascinated" by the play, simultaneously, was that "Albee penetrates the superficial layers of our conscious personality and, using the mysterious escalators of the unconscious, reaches the citadels of our private certainties and shoots them full of questions marks."

Reviewers certainly understood that Albee raised issues of the nature of faith and evil, but they immediately engaged in controversial debates over the play's meaning. Some reviewers contended that it was an allegory. Others advised to look for deeply embedded clues, such oblique references to homosexuality as Julian the Apostate and even *Alice's Adventures in Wonderland.* Albee biographer and scholar Richard E. Amacher wrote in his study of the author, *Edward Albee,* that the play was "subjected to a confusion of interpretation by the critics" because they "refused to accept it on its own surrealistic terms."

Certainly, the body of Albee's work up to the production of *Tiny Alice* included works that challenged the audience with authorial messages about social relationships, the connection between love and aggression, loss and isolation, illusion and

Actors David Warner and Irene Worth in a production of Tiny Alice.

reality, and the concept of God. In the words of Leonard Casper, writing in 1983—almost twenty years after the play was first staged—''*Tiny Alice* has continued to be considered exceptionally difficult.''

Scholars have often looked at the play as an allegory. Harold Clurman was one of the earliest critics to make a definitive statement about *Tiny Alice;* he was cited in Caspar's ''*Tiny Alice:* The Expense of Joy in the Persistence of Mystery,'' as calling it an allegory in which ''the pure person in our world is betrayed by all parties,'' who are themselves corrupt. ''Isolated and bereft of every hope, he must die—murdered.'' Later, Anne Paolucci, again cited in Caspar, worked out a more intricate allegory in which Butler, Cardinal, and lawyer compose an unholy trinity who act out a parodic ritual of faith. Michael Rutenberg (cited in Caspar) saw the play as an allegory of diabolic forces eager to trade a billion ordinary souls for one soul who is particularly sensitive—and thus worth corrupting.

Other critics have focused on specific aspects of the play. Leonard Casper denied the play was an allegory at all, contending that *Tiny Alice* resists such treatment ''because its meaning lies in the persistence, rather than the resolution, of mystery.''

Ruby Cohn called it a ''modern mystery play'' in which the mystery is twofold: the mystery of what is happening on stage, and the mystery of what happens in the ''realm of ultimate reality.'' Julian N. Wasserman focused on Albee's use of language in *Tiny Alice* and how this illustrates the confusion of illusion and reality. For instance, Wasserman equated Julian's descent into madness with his loss of the ability to hear and comprehend language. Katharine Worth asserted that the play ''trumpets its symbolism from the start and indeed could hardly be interpreted on any but a symbolic level'' and that the players in the drama are play-acting in order to achieve a significant ''psychic change.'' Other critics have even proposed that the whole play takes place in Julian's mind.

More recently Foster Hirsch proposed an interpretation of *Tiny Alice* as a ''multi-focus drama, which is at once a busy religious allegory about one man's loss and recovery of faith; a satire on the worldliness, the corruption, and greed of the Church; a parable about appearance and reality, the symbol and the substance, the abstract and the concrete; a morality play about man's inevitable defeat in reaching for the Platonic Ideal.'' Hirsch's reading of the play is perhaps most in keeping with Casper's assertions that the prevailing body of criticism about the play "ignored the possibility that any definitive reading is too narrow for Albee."

CRITICISM

Rena Korb

Korb has a master's degree in English literature and creative writing and has written for a wide variety of educational publishers. In the following essay, she discusses why Julian was chosen as the sacrifice and how it changes his views on God.

When *Tiny Alice* opened in New York in December 1964, the theatergoing world was immediately abuzz. At once complex and simple, graphic and understated, abstract and concrete, the play challenged viewers to find a true meaning, but for the most part, they were unsuccessful at this task. In defense of his play, in March 1965, Albee addressed the press to share his thoughts and ideas.

> A lay brother, a man who would have become a priest except that he could not reconcile his idea of God with the God which men create in their own image, is sent by his superior to tie up loose ends of a business matter between the church and a wealthy woman. The lay brother becomes enmeshed in an environment which . . . contains all the elements which have confused and bothered him throughout his life: the relationship between sexual hysteria and religious ecstasy; the conflict between selflessness of service and the conspicuous splendor of martyrdom. The lay brother is brought to the point . . . of having to accept what he had insisted he wanted: union with the abstraction, rather than [a] man-made image of it, its substitution. He is left with pure abstraction . . . and in the end . . . one of two things happens: either the abstraction personifies itself, is proved real, or the dying man, in the last necessary effort of self-delusion[,] creates and believes in what he knows does not exist.

Albee asserted that his play was "perfectly straightforward," adding "it is the very simplicity of the play, I think, that has confused so many," but he also noted that in order for the play to be "not at all unclear," the audience needs to "approach it on its own terms."

Indeed, the plot sequence progresses carefully along a preordained script. The agents of Alice—Miss Alice, Butler, and Lawyer—clearly have played their parts before and will do so again. Everything has been planned, especially the selection of Julian as their sacrifice. That they have investigated him and actually chosen him is apparent in Lawyer's reference to the report that they have on Julian. On one level, Julian has been chosen because he occupies an intermediate space—he is neither secular citizen nor religious body—yet he has excelled in the church hierarchy, becoming "the only lay brother in the history of Christendom" to serve as a cardinal's secretary. Julian's role as a layperson—one who takes on the priest's vow of celibacy without being a priest—indicates his extraordinary faith; and his position within the church further shows the Church's recognition of him. It is for these reasons that Lawyer picks Julian as the sacrifice. He wants to strike out at Cardinal, an enemy from childhood. When Lawyer reminds Julian of his duty to the Church and to Miss Alice's household, he points out, that Julian has "this present job be*cause* I cannot stand your Cardinal."

But Lawyer also wants to strike out at the "august and revered" Church. Though Lawyer early in the play insists that he has learned "never to confuse the representative of a . . . thing with the thing itself," he still finds Cardinal's acceptance of money in exchange for Julian's soul to exemplify the hypocrisy of the Church. Lawyer calls the Church "wily" and mocks its "inscrutable wisdom" in appointing "that wreckage [Cardinal] as its representative." He holds no respect for institutionalized religion and enjoys holding power—via Miss Alice's money—over it.

Not only does Lawyer succeed in gaining control of his childhood foe (and the Church), he also perverts him by making him become an agent of Alice, for Cardinal is complicit in the sacrifice of Julian. Although Cardinal understands right away that something important is at stake when Lawyer asks that Julian be given the assignment, the first certain indication of his knowledge comes in Act III when he points at the model and asks Lawyer, "Then it is . . . really true? About. . . *this?*" Lawyer knows exactly what is the "this" to which Cardinal refers, and he responds in the affirmative. A few moments later, Lawyer tells Cardinal, "You know we may have to shoot him; you know that may be necessary." Although the Cardinal reacts with sadness to this news, he makes no attempt to put a halt to the plot. He initially tries to delay the inevitable, but once Lawyer announces that Julian will stay behind to his "special priesthood," Cardinal goes along with everyone else. Because of all people, he knows Julian best, he is even able to remind the secretary that "it has been your desire always to serve; your sense of mission." He further draws on his knowledge of Julian's past when he tells Julian to "be glad, yes, be glad . . . our ecstasy," thus

WHAT DO I READ NEXT?

- Jean Genet's *The Balcony* (1956), influenced by the Theater of Cruelty (the theater philosophy of Antonin Artaud) takes place in a contemporary European city in the midst of a revolution. The protagonists of the play recreate a world of illusion, which they convince the revolutionaries is better than reality.

- Eugene Ionesco's *The Bald Soprano* (1950), called an ''antiplay,'' by the author, is an important example of the Theater of the Absurd. It consists mainly of a series of meaningless conversation between two couples.

- Albee's *Who's Afraid of Virginia Woolf?*, also made into a popular movie, remains the author's most well-known work. It centers on two married couples who reveal their secrets in one, long evening. By the end of the play, the middle-aged couple decides to face realities and stop living in their fantasy world.

- *Suddenly Last Summer* (1958) is a two-act play by Tennessee Williams. The play circles around disturbing and violent themes: insanity, lobotomy, pederasty, and cannibalism. It was also made into a movie.

---

referencing Julian's ecstatic sexual fantasies of martyrdom. It is also Cardinal who initiates the chorus of voices telling Julian to ''accept'' Alice. Perhaps without Cardinal's involvement, Julian may have escaped the plot against him. Lawyer never unearths the truth about those missing six years of Julian's life, which indicates that he is neither infallible nor omnipotent. This secret further demonstrates that Julian has exercised choice—with whom he will share his story—even though by the end of the play his right to freely choose has been taken from him.

Miss Alice and the rest do more than take away Julian's free choice: they take away his very belief system. Julian chose not to become a priest because he was ''not wholly reconciled'' to the use people make of God. As he tells Miss Alice, ''Man's God and mine are not . . . close friends.'' He rebels against people's personification of God in their own image, making a God ''created by man'' instead of allowing God to be the creator. Lawyer and Butler role-play a conversation Lawyer would like to have with Julian. Butler/Julian declares that there is ''a *true* God.''

> Lawyer: ''There is an abstraction, Julian, but it cannot be understood. You cannot worship it. Butler: There is more. Lawyer: There is Alice, Julian. That can be understood. Only the mouse in the model. Just that. Butler: There must be more. Lawyer: The mouse. Believe it. Don't personify the abstraction. Julian, limit it, demean it. Only the mouse, the toy. And that does not exist . . . but is all that can be worshipped.

Lawyer is essentially describing a world without God. God is an abstraction, but since you cannot worship an abstraction, you cannot worship God. Unlike others, Lawyer does not ''personify'' God into his own image, but instead makes of God something insignificant and worthless, and even a pest: he makes God a mouse. At the end of the scene, however, Lawyer transforms God/Tiny Alice/Mouse into a cat. ''Rest easy;'' he says to the model, ''you'll have him . . . Hum; purr; breathe; rest. You will have your Julian. Wait for him. He will be yours.'' With the transformation of the mouse into a cat, Lawyer intimates that God/Tiny Alice/Cat is hungrily awaiting the feast of Julian.

This transformation further recalls Julian's dreams of martyrdom in which a gladiator's trident enters him at the same time that a lion climbs on top of him and sinks in its teeth. This fantasy is so powerful that when Julian recalls it for Miss Alice, he falls into a trance, but his fantasy inevitably merges into the sexual hallucination he had when he was in the asylum. This lapse of Julian's conscious-

> JULIAN'S FAILURE IS ONLY MADE GREATER WHEN HE CAN'T HELP BUT GIVE HIMSELF TO MISS ALICE AND EVEN DECIDES TO LEAVE THE LAITY IN ORDER TO MARRY HER."

ness demonstrates how closely linked are his religious urges and his sexual urges. Having this knowledge makes it easy to understand why Julian's hallucinations ''were saddening to him.'' Although he says that they were ''provoked, brought on by the departure of my faith,'' thus intimating that his sadness stemmed from his lack of faith, on a more suppressed level, they also represent his inability to subdue his sexuality despite his religious calling. As such, they indicate a personal failure. Julian's failure is only made greater when he can't help but give himself to Miss Alice and even decide to leave the laity in order to marry her.

The betrayal on Miss Alice's part—and her ability to make Julian change his mind about something so important to him—foreshadows the end of the play. Left alone and dying, Julian is forced to confront and question his most basic religious tenet: that humans should not personify God in their own image. Who was real, he wonders, Miss Alice with ''warm flesh'' or Tiny Alice ''THE ABSTRACT.'' He understands that if Tiny Alice is real and Miss Alice is the illusion, as she claimed, he has betrayed himself. He looks at the phrenological head that wears Miss Alice's wig, but since it is not real, it represents Tiny Alice and not Miss Alice. He speaks to the head as if it were Alice. ''Is thy stare the true look? . . . And her eyes . . . warm, accepting, were they . . . not real? Art thou my bride?'' He realizes that he has brought this lonely situation upon himself: ''It is what I have wanted, have insisted on. Have nagged . . . for.'' He at last understands the human need to create something solid and graspable out of something that is wholly abstract.

Julian makes his final demand: ''IS THIS MY PRIESTHOOD, THEN? THIS WORLD? THEN COME AND SHOW THYSELF! BRIDE? GOD?'' The heartbeats and breathing become louder. The light in the bedroom of the model goes out and begins to move across the upper story, indicating that someone or something is moving across the upper story of the mansion at that very time. Julian becomes fearful. ''You . . . thou . . . art . . . coming to me? . . . ABSTRACTION? ABSTRACTION!'' Julian is ''sad'' and ''defeated,'' for he now actively seeks the personification of God to save him from his solitude. ''How long wilt thou hide thy face from me? . . . Consider and hear me, O Lord, my God,'' he cries, desperate for a God who can share this moment. Right before Julian's death, a momentous occurrence happens: he sees ''a great presence filling the room.'' It is either the personified God or Julian's hallucination of a personified God. Either way, Julian's ending shows his rejection of his earlier contentions. What could be seen as defeat, however, has a positive twist, for in losing his former faith, Julian has gained a new, more sustaining faith.

Source: Rena Korb, in an essay for *Drama for Students*, Gale, 2001.

Steven Drukman

In the following essay, Krukman describes Albee's career by taking a look into a variety of his productions.

The much-besieged playwright defies conventional critical wisdom with a dazzling new play and a Broadway revival

This oblique aphorism, about obliquity, was first uttered on a Berlin stage in 1959. One year later, when *The Zoo Story* came home to inaugurate the new Off-Broadway, the New York Post trumpeted Edward Albee as the ''next Eugene O'Neill.'' For decades afterward, critics scorned him for trying to live up to the title. Jerry's insight proved to be an uncanny forecast of Albee's career in the American theatre. Albee has gone a long distance out of the way from that two-character one-act over the past four decades; his short-distance, four-year ''comeback'' seems, at age 70, correctly on track. Albee's 1994 *Three Tall Women* earned him his third Pulitzer; a fine-tuned revival of *A Delicate Balance* won three Tony awards in 1996; and now, after his 1964 *Tiny Alice* was widely praised last year at Connecticut's Hartford Stage Company (and is currently gearing up for a Broadway stint this spring), it seems that, in typically indirect fashion, Albee is asserting himself as one of the greatest living American playwrights. Suddenly, it seems, everyone's asking: ''Where has he been for so long?''

Of course, Albee's been here the whole time, but Americans had gotten used to treating him like the unwelcome guests that populate so many of his plays. After a long career that began with a burst of breathless praise, followed by denunciations and even downright excoriation, we may now be ready to sit up, take notice and, as Albee once implored in an interview with the Dramatists Guild Quarterly, bypass our "conscious barriers" and let the plays seep into our unconscious minds, uncensored.

I, too recently traveled a long distance—to London—to see the world premiere of *The Play About the Baby,* Albee's newest, consistently funniest and, to my mind, best play yet. Without giving too much away, the plot concerns—as Albee explained it to me—"a baby who ceases to exist." Even more than in *Who's Afraid of Virginia Woolf?,* the baby (to be more accurate we might call this absent presence "the baby") is endowed with a powerful symbolic valence. In fact, George and Martha's illusory baby from Virginia Woolf almost seems to haunt the new play's opening moments: The character named the Girl announces to the Boy, "I'm going to have the baby now," and we hear an otherworldly Lamaze class of heavy breathing, then water breaking. The "baby" is born, and the frisky young couple goes on to tickle, taunt and play (note the pun) with their bundled-up offspring. *The Play About the Baby* is a pared down, more perfect Virginia Woolf as well as its onstage deconstruction: Two intruders, named the Man and the Woman, arrive to take away both the baby and the younger couple's rose-hued view of the future.

As he did with *Zoo Story,* Albee has taken the showbiz tradition of opening out of town to trans-Atlantic extremes. No matter: He is busy making plans to produce his short, sharp shock of a play stateside. When that happens, *The Play About the Baby* should go a long distance to erase any doubt that Albee has always been one of this country's greatest playwrights.

Last summer Albee and I discussed the European dramatists who are often cited as his influences. I asked him to name his favorites. He rarely hesitates when asked a question (there's none of Jerry's obliquity in his conversational manner), and the answered directly: "Beckett, Genet, Ionesco. In that order."

Those three words—"in that order"—intrigued me more than the three names, which any barely attentive undergrad could have guessed. Following the success of his early one-acts, Albee was often

IT OCCURRED TO ME THAT THIS WAS WHEN THE TROUBLE ALL BEGAN FOR EDWARD ALBEE IN AMERICA—A COUNTRY THAT LIKES ITS FOURTH WALL LEFT INTACT."

called the "American Ionesco." He explained: "I intentionally made *The American Dream* an homage to Ionesco. And anybody who's bright enough could realize what I was doing. But critics were saying, 'Oh, he's just imitating Ionesco.' Idiots!"

It occurred to me that this was when the trouble all began for Edward Albee in America—a country that likes its fourth wall left intact. The label of absurdist stuck too soon and too well. If this fresh-from Europe arriviste was not going to write realism, most Americans felt, he should stick to doing Ionesco: Keep us laughing with nonsensical language, with incontinent old people and babbling bourgeois couples, a la Bald Soprano. Martin Esslin's embrace of Albee in the 1968 second edition of his landmark book *The Theatre of the Absurd*—tying Albee's assault on the "foundations of American optimism" to Ionesco's lampooning of the French middle class—only exacerbated the problem.

Critics took their brickbats to *Tiny Alice* for not providing the easy earmarks of Ionesco-styled Absurdism. But it wasn't meant to be clear-cut Absurdism. Nor was the 1966 *A Delicate Balance* (which Albee calls "naturalism")—Gerald Gutierrez's realistically nuanced production, winner of the 1996 Tony for best revival, proved that the play is in fact a "delicate balance" of the real and the symbolic. When Agnes and Tobias are visited by their frightened longtime friends, Harry and Edna, they are met by terror that is not only metaphysical but also mundane, the existential anguish of life's prosaic moments—like when we are shooing out guests, not when we are reading Cainus. Clearly, Albee was moving in new directions.

Or trying to. For many, Albee's move up that three-tiered ladder of playwrights he mentioned had him breathing air too rarefied. Early on, when critics noticed that *Who's Afraid of Virginia Woolf?* may actually have been the beginning of something else—when they detected French whiffs of (gulp) Jean Genet's game-like rituals—a handful of them begrudgingly allowed him this dalliance. It soon became clear, though, that Americans simply do not do Genet on Broadway; perverted rituals were fine as Greenwich Village fare, but they were not serious mainstream theatre. Virginia Woolf became famous for, among other things, not winning the Pulitzer prize in 1962, when committee member W. D. Maxwell deemed it "filthy," causing a flurry of protests and resignations.

And what of Beckett, the first name on Albee's list? Beckett was usually mentioned as a writer he should not emulate, lest he embarrass himself. (One noteworthy exception was Clive Barnes's review of *Seascape,* a rare instance of a favorable comparison between Albee and Beckett in the popular press.) Even Esslin's lapidary study, generous enough to mention Genet vis-a-vis Virginia Woolf, resisted calling Albee and Beckett theatrical bedfellows (despite noting that *The Zoo Story* and Krapp's *Last Tape* shared a bill at Provincetown Playhouse in 1959).

So what has Albee been up to all these years, and how do Americans usually make a narrative out of his remarkable career? Until his sudden reappearance in 1994 with *Three Tall Women,* the story often went like this: After *The Zoo Story* and his absurdist one-acts (*The American Dream, The Sandbox*), Albee dipped into social protest with *The Death of Bessie Smith.* Then, despite a blip (albeit a revolutionary blip for American theatre) called *Who's Afraid of Virginia Woolf?,* it was a steady slope downward. There were occasional successes—*Tiny Alice* and *A Delicate Balance* were generally perceived as last gasps—but mostly a mess of half-baked adaptations of other authors' work. He got a lot of bad reviews for his 1975 *Seascape,* yet, despite the critical carping, managed to put Frank Langella in a lizard suit and walk away with his second Pulitzer. The '70s were the beginning of the end, mostly: plays like *Counting the Ways, All Over* and *Listening* are all but forgotten. And the '80s? Well, John Simon called *The Lady from Dubuque* "one of the worst plays about anything, ever." Albee was either experimenting too wildly or repeating himself too cravenly. His last desperate experiments—*The Man Who Had Three Arms* (1983), for example—only proved that he was a charlatan from the start, and that he had merely capitalized on a wave of Sartre-struck sentiment in this country in the early '60s. If he exists at all, he's a mere shadow of his former Woolf.

To anyone doing the math, however, this account would never add up. After all, Albee is mentioned, without hesitation, by American playwrights Terrence McNally, Christopher Durang and Tina Howe as a primary influence, and several up-and-comers of the next generation—Nicky Silver and David Ives jump immediately to mind—have also sung his praises. The roster of dramatists Albee has assisted financially includes Adrienne Kennedy, Sam Shepard and John Guare. And his years of teaching at the University of Houston, where he was named distinguished professor of drama in 1988, have turned out a profusion of Albee-mentored one-acts and full-length plays. Still, even though his presence in American drama is redoubtable, the trajectory of his career has been narrated as a gradual diminution, Beckettian only in its slouching toward absence.

Some might say that Albee has been Protean to a fault, refashioning his style so much that his imprint keeps disappearing. The problem has been that critics have not kept up with him. While other major American playwrights have been allowed room to grow, granted laissez passer to mix genres within plays or jump from genre to genre as they develop, Albee was issued a moving violation. Suspicious of his every move, critics kept up a weary and wary vigilance throughout the years, responding to Albee's dramaturgical gauntlets as if they were deceptive gambits.

In language typical of so many reviews, Robert Brustein lamented of *Virginia Woolf,* "Albee is a highly accomplished stage magician, but he fails to convince us that there's nothing up his sleeve." Albee, it seems, was only out to dupe us.

One explanation for critics seeing chicanery instead of innovation may rest on Albee's own explication—or lack thereof—of his own work. As one of three regnant living American playwrights—Miller and Mamet being the only others with similar stature and longevity—Albee is the member of this troika who resists theorizing about himself. He has written cogently about art, including an excellent 1980 article on Louise Nevelson in *Art News,* and, not content to merely adapt their works for the stage, penned critical essays on Carson McCullers and James Purdy; his early poetry relied as much on philosophy as it did on musicality. But there has never been Albee's version of Miller's *Tragedy and the Common Man* or even Mamet's *Uses of the Knife* or *True and False.* (Even O'Neill, never a great theoretical mind, hashed out his own confused aesthetic project in *Memorandum on Masks.*) While these authors have written their separate works to (even if only on the strategic level) justify the plays they like to write, Albee has rarely been more programmatic than to ask us—with his typically acerbic wit—not to think about where we parked the car upon leaving the theatre.

A rare defense came after *Tiny Alice,* when, at a press conference, he was just beginning to fight charges of obfuscation that would dog him for decades. "*Tiny Alice* is a fairly simple play, and not at all unclear, once you approach it on its own terms," he said, following with a step-by-step plot development, no more, no less. Albee didn't quote Kierkegaard or offer any apologia for his new type of drama. He didn't dub Julian the existential Loman—though he certainly could have. Instead, he concluded: "It is, you see, a perfectly straightforward story. It is the very simplicity of the play, I think, that has confused so many." Albee was in effect telling the audience to stay awake and pay attention.

The question audiences seemed to throw back was: Pay attention how? Without the clues and confines of a single genre, we don't know whether we're watching a doomed love story about a defrocked priest and an heiress, or a Pirandellian puzzle about Platonic forms. The characters seem to be real—well, most of the time. Still, they're named Butler, Lawyer, Cardinal—earthly symbols for the abstract forces they represent, right?

But *Tiny Alice* had already been the last straw in many critics' long-suffering wait for Albee to come clean. Now he was not only playing tricks with an audience's enjoyment, he was offending their psychosexual values. Deviously, he was floating gay content past unsuspecting men and women. Philip Roth's outraged review of *Tiny Alice* ended by asking: "How long before a play is produced on Broadway in which the homosexual hero is presented as homosexual, and not disguised as an angst-ridden priest, or an angry Negro, or an aging actress, or worst of all, Everyman?"

Of course, Albee had heard a lot of that before, especially around *Who's Afraid of Virginia Woolf?,* the play where he first supposedly bamboozled Broadway houses by smuggling in a covert homosexual relationship. As Stanley Kauffmann complained in a 1966 *New York Times* Arts and Leisure article that became notorious, Albee's first play about "the baby" reeked of "disguised homosexual influence." Albee—who is never directly named by Kauffmann but is called one of those "reputed homosexuals [whose] plays often treat of women and marriage"—was "streaked with vindictiveness toward the society that constricts and, theatrically, discriminates against them." In that article, the unnamed Albee was compared to Genet, but unfavorably, as Genet "is a homosexual who has never had to disguise his nature." (Albee told me with a rueful laugh that he was never in the closet and, since boarding school, has always been very happy being gay—a point that evaded Kauffmann's analysis.) Not only the journalists but the academics were lifting the veil: In *The Drama Review,* Richard Schechner inveighed against *Virginia Woolf's* "morbidity and sexual perversity, which are there only to titillate an impotent and homosexual theatre and audience." Already, a mere three years into this wunderkind's career, Schechner was "tired of Albee."

And Georges-Michel Sarotte, in the book *Like a Brother, Like a Lover,* wrote that *Virginia Woolf* "is a homosexual play from every point of view, in all its situations and symbols. It is a heterosexual play only in outward appearance, since in 1962 it had to reach the mass public, and also because Albee does not want to write a homosexual work.".

This attack on Albee did some damage. Coupled with his infuriating genre-bending, people began to think he was now pulling one over on us because he was sick and couldn't admit it. It has taken 25 years to see the irony in the fact that it was disguised homophobia that accused Albee of disguising homosexuality.

Autobiography is the last refuge of a baffled critic. In 1978, Foster Hirsch wrote a book-length study of the "evasions" of Edward Albee's personal life (titled *Who's Afraid of Edward Albee?*), which the author believed to be the question to pursue now "at this diminished moment in the career of an enormously gifted writer." Albee couldn't pull the wool over Hirsch's eyes: "The answer, in the evidence of his progressively claustrophobic and indirect plays, from which his biography is carefully omitted, is—Albee himself."

After all these critical jabs—with kidney punches outnumbering the fair hits—it's small wonder that Albee seemed down for the count through the '80s. In one respect, he was on the mat for a while, spending a lot of time directing—including a Los Angeles revival of *Virginia Woolf* with Glenda Jackson and John Lithgow in 1989 and plays by Shepard, Mamet and Lanford Wilson at the English

Theatre in Vienna in 1985. But his career was resuscitated. He premiered two of his own new plays, again way out of town, in Vienna: *The Marriage Play* in 1987 and an intriguing play in 1991 that was frankly autobiographical—*Three Tall Women*. When it made its U.S. premiere in 1994, *Three Tall Women* won not only the Pulitzer but a spate of other awards. Even Albee was surprised. He told me that *Three Tall Women* was, after 35 years of writing plays, his first ever to receive unanimous critical praise, adding, "Just wait. I'll be out of fashion again soon enough."

But I'm not so sure. In 1994, he was the featured playwright at New York's Signature Theatre and won an Obie award for sustained achievement, and in 1996 he received Kennedy Center honors for his lifetime contribution to the nation's culture.

Albee recently showed me a notebook that included his new play, *The Goat* (he claims to never use a computer because he delivers plays nearly complete in longhand, direct, it seems, from the unconscious—storing fragments on a hard drive would defeat this method). Albee calls the play the most "politically involved" he's ever written, and he may finish another he's "threatened to unleash for several years now, about Attila the Hun." So, in fashion or not, Albee has more to write.

> "Define your terms. Honestly, the imprecision!"
> Leslie in *Seascape*

What many have perceived as Albee's long disappearance from the stage, a vanishing act akin to, well, that darned "baby" in the play, may be a signal to critics that he will not follow their directions. But *The Play About the Baby* may finally force us to acknowledge Albee's presence, even adopt him as our own. By evoking what must be by now his invisible theatrical signature—the nonexistent baby—Albee answers back to the charges of subterfuge that have followed him since *Virginia Woolf.* At the end of the new play, the Man, who has threatened to take "the baby" away, performs a bit of legerdemain: He unrolls the blanket to reveal—presto!—there's no baby there. The moment is terrifying, an absurd coup de theatre and, at the same time, Albee's showing of his hand to the critics. You see, Albee might be saying, you believed in the illusory baby, despite the fact that I told you it doesn't exist. The trick, in other words, is no trick at all. There was never anything up my sleeve.

More than hocus-pocus, though, Albee has written a harrowing and hilarious four-character

play, pristine in structure, pure in intent, even Beckettian maybe his Godot. *The Play About the Baby* combines playful self-reflexive commentary with wicked humor while tapping the existential terror of lost youth and passion's inevitable demise. Imagine the demons of *Rosemary's Baby* enacting their rituals in the manner of Vladimir and Estragon, and you begin to get a sense of the vaudevillian theatre of cruelty that surrounds the play's action.

At one point in *The Play About the Baby,* the Man asks the audience if we've ever noticed that, when we take a trip, the journey back always seems much shorter than the time spent headed to our destination. The moment, of course, echoes Jerry's insight in *Zoo Story,* but it's classic Albee for other reasons, too: a question about home and belonging, delivered across the footlights to an uneasy-because-they're-implicated audience, fusing mundane speculation with metaphysical possibility. It's that possibility that Albee has teased us with for decades now - the possibility suggested by the first playwright on his favorites list, Beckett, when *Endgame*'s Hamm speculates, "We're not beginning to . . . to . . . mean something?"

As this 70-year-old comeback kid keeps writing, will American audiences finally believe that Albee means something, and isn't just up to something? Even if they don't, let's hope the pedants and pundits have him to kick around for many more years. The "next Eugene O'Neill" doesn't show up every day.

Source: Steven Drukman, "Won't you come home, Edward Albee?," in *American Theatre,* Vol. 15, Issue 10, Dec, 1998, p. 16.

Markland Taylor

In the following review, Taylor depicts that the success of the production lies within its "coruscating dialogue."

Hartford Stage continues to carry the flame for Edward Albee's rarely produced 1964 enigma *Tiny Alice,* its current revisitation being the play's first major revival since Hartford Stage mounted it in 1972. It was well worth a second visit, for no matter how much of a puzzlement the play may be, there's no denying that it contains some of Albee's most gleamingly coruscating dialogue. Has Albee ever written anything more brilliantly, bitingly vicious than this play's opening scene between a lawyer and a cardinal who have utterly loathed each other since they were at school together?

And since one of the greatest pleasures of theatergoing is hearing and seeing accomplished actors exploring and reveling in splendid dialogue, this production is undoubtedly one of the highlights of the New England theater season, not the least because of its excellent cast, direction and setting.

If the play's third act (to which the playwright has restored some cut material) doesn't truly deliver on the promises of its two preceding acts, *Tiny Alice* is still one of Albee's most endlessly fascinating creations, not the least because it is such a tantalizing puzzle.

As the play's central character, a lay brother who has survived a major loss of faith, Richard Thomas gives one of his most admirable performances. Robed and bespectacled, he performs with tremendous technical skill in the service of a portrayal of potent simplicity and humility. He's superb.

But so is the rest of the cast, beginning with Gerry Bamman and Tom Lacy as the opening scene's antagonists. They are glorious sparring partners, Bamman a viciously cruel lawyer, Lacy a plumply pompous prelate. And in what is in a sense the play's comic-relief role (except for the fact that the whole play is shot through with comedy), John Michael Higgins is deliciously sly and wry as the butler named Butler whose casual insolence is so playful.

In the difficult title role of Miss Alice, apparently a multibillionairess offering a gift of multibillions to the Catholic Church—who may or may not be a stand-in for God—Sharon Scruggs performs with considerable panache and does not let the production's high acting standards down. She is not, however, helped by Constance Hoffman's costumes, and she may not be ideally cast, lacking the cool, ladylike elegance Irene Worth gave the role in its original Broadway production.

Thomas, on the other hand, may be better cast than John Gielgud was originally as Brother Julian. In any case, Scruggs and Thomas work wonderfully together, especially in the second act's still-shocking seduction finale.

Mark Lamos, in a return to the theater of which he was artistic director for so many years, has directed at the top of his form. And set designer John Arnone has given the play's various locales a chilly minimalist grandeur that suits Albee down to the ground. The model of the elaborate castle in which Miss Alice lives (shipped stone by stone from

> HAS ALBEE EVER WRITTEN ANYTHING MORE BRILLIANTLY, BITINGLY VICIOUS THAN THIS PLAY'S OPENING SCENE BETWEEN A LAWYER AND A CARDINAL WHO HAVE UTTERLY LOATHED EACH OTHER SINCE THEY WERE AT SCHOOL TOGETHER?"

England by her father) dominates the stage as it should, and there very well might be a *Tiny Alice* living in it. Or is it a mouse?

Much of the play could well be said to be a comedy of manners, its dialogue quite up to the quality of Shaw and Wilde. There are also suggestions of theater of the absurd, notably Beckett, of T. S. Eliot and even of Tennessee Williams in his lush *Suddenly Last Summer* mode as it explores "the relationship between sexual hysteria and religious ecstasy," to quote Albee.

But at the same time, *Tiny Alice* is pure Albee, and at the Hartford Stage it's receiving a production that really should be seen beyond Hartford in order for the play to be seen and reassessed more widely.

Source: Markland Taylor, "Tiny Alice," (review) in *Variety,* Vol. 371, no. 4, June 1, 1998, p. 52.

Mardi Valgemae

In the following essay, Valgemac provides a parallel between The Great God Brown *and* Tiny Alice.

Critics who have grappled with Edward Albee's *Tiny Alice* have conjectured about its possible sources. These range from *Alice's Adventures in Wonderland* to the plays of Noel Coward, T. S. Eliot, Jean Genet, and several other European playwrights. Surprisingly, no one has mentioned Eugene O'Neill. Albee himself has repeatedly admitted being "an enormous admirer" of "late O'Neill." "By late O'Neill, do you mean *Long Day's Journey Into Night?*" asked an interviewer. "Yes," replied Albee, "and *The Iceman Cometh* and those of that period when he started writing good plays." The interviewer: "Do you mean after he got over his gimmicky period?" Albee: "Yes." Yet it is precisely the O'Neill of the "gimmicky period" who seems to have influenced the Albee of *Tiny Alice.*

Tiny Alice, said Albee at a press conference, was "something of a metaphysical dream play which must be entered into and experienced without predetermination of how a play is supposed to go." Since Albee was not so much explicating his play as lecturing the New York critics, his warning about "predetermination" in all probability referred to thinking conditioned by the conventions of theatrical realism. For by calling *Tiny Alice* "a metaphysical dream play," Albee placed his own play in the tradition of dramatic expressionism that goes back to Strindberg's dream plays and eventually became naturalized, as it were, with the experiments of O'Neill. Thus we are justified, I think, in approaching *Tiny Alice* as an expressionistic objectification of Brother Julian's nightmare or hallucination. Further external evidence to support this contention is found in Albee's statement that "Brother Julian is in the same position as the audience. He's the innocent. If you see things through his eyes, you won't have any trouble at all."

"Things" are seen through the eyes of the protagonist also in O'Neill's expressionistic plays, where the action on the stage is distorted in order to capture a character's subjective view of the world. In *The Great God Brown,* the most complex and imaginative of O'Neill's experimental plays, the most salient expressionistic device is the mask. Masks are worn by all the major characters, thus objectifying the duality between their outer and inner selves, between illusion and reality. Most of the characters in *Tiny Alice* from time to time don metaphoric masks, Butler refers to the Cardinal as having to "wear a face," and when Julian first meets Miss Alice, she appears in a matted wig as well as the mask of an old hag. By removing both mask and wig, Miss Alice is suddenly transformed into an attractive woman. Yet this is not her real identity, either. For as we discover later in the play, she is the symbol of the abstraction Tiny Alice. The transformation of Miss Alice from an old crone into an attractive woman—an action that has puzzled critics—suggests that all is not as it appears to be on the surface and foreshadows the stripping away of illusions that Julian must undergo in order to confront the abstraction, or Alice, which derives from the Greek word for truth.

Miss Alice's seemingly surreal transformation brings to mind Strindberg's "expressionist manifesto"—his preface to *A Dream Play*—in which he proclaims that in a play governed solely by dream logic, "Characters divide, double, redouble, evaporate, condense, float out of each other, converge." Albee's debt to Strindberg has been investigated by Marion A. Taylor and Robert Brustein, in his *New Republic* review of *Tiny Alice,* has suggested parallels between that play and Strindberg's *A Dream Play.* Yet Miss Alice's unmasking is also reminiscent of the action in scene ten of O'Neill's *The Fountain,* where an old woman appears to Juan. *"In a flash,"* read the stage directions, *"her mask of age disappears"* and the beautiful Beatriz stands before the hero. More indirectly, Miss Alice, masked and unmasked, brings to mind the objectification of the split personality of John and the masked Loving in O'Neill's *Days Without End.* And like Billy Brown in *The Great God Brown,* who at times wears the mask of Dion Anthony, Butler and the Lawyer in *Tiny Alice* assume for a while the personae of Julian and the Cardinal.

Related to the mask as an expressionistic device in *Tiny Alice* is the castle, which contains an infinite number of proportionately smaller models of itself. The castle can easily be related to the more traditional House of God, thus forming yet another link with *The Great God Brown.* In *Tiny Alice* the Lawyer suggests that the very foundation of the castle is "a wreck". As Butler phrases it, "Something *should* be done about the wine cellar. I've noticed it—as a passerby would—but Brother Julian pointed out the extent of it to me: bottles have burst, are bursting, corks rotting . . . something to do with the temperature or the dampness. It's a shame, you know". The connection between the house of mouse-god Alice and a more conventional if similarly metaphorical House of God is established by the Lawyer, who says: "When Christ told Peter—so legends tell—that he would found his church upon that rock. He must have had in mind an island in a sea of wine. How firm a foundation in the vintage years." The parallels between the rock of Peter in a sea of wine and Dion's cathedral, into which he has concealed a blasphemous, wine-loving Silenus, are equally apparent.

Dion's cathedral, argues Doris Falk in her study of O'Neill's plays, "is a metaphor of the neurotic process . . . which O'Neill seems to have understood thoroughly throughout the play. Man's normal need to transcend himself, to build spires toward the infinite, is blasphemed and travestied when its energies are all diverted inward to the struggle with masks of self.'' Professor Falk's observation suggests an interesting point of comparison between the two plays, especially in the light of Brother Julian's erotic hallucinations. For the castle, like the cathedral in *The Great God Brown,* has certain affinities with the neurotic process occurring within Julian's mind. Hence the fire in the chapel serves as an objectification of Julian's physical passion for Miss Alice, which threatens to destroy the tenuous order he has established for himself as a lay brother. The scene opens with Miss Alice running away from the Lawyer, telling him to ''KEEP OFF ME!'' To the Lawyer's ''Don't be hysterical, now,'' she replies, ''I'll *show* you hysteria. I'll give you *fireworks!,''* thus linking *fire* and the Greek *hysteria* for *womb.* When the actual fire breaks out in the chapel, it guts the altar area, just as Brother Julian's sexual fantasies destroy his attempts to come to grips with religious experience. For Brother Julian's road to religious ecstasy is paved with sexual hysteria (to use Albee's own terminology), and before he can embrace his God in a not so metaphoric marriage, Julian must be seduced. As Butler remarks at the beginning of the next scene, referring to Julian and Miss Alice, ''the fire in the chapel . . . brought them closer,'' after which the lovers go picnicking and partake of an almost O'Neillian ''Montrachet under an elm.'' (Also decidedly O'Neillian is a conversation between Brother Julian and Butler. The former states that he dislikes being left alone. ''Like a little boy?'' questions Butler, ''When the closet door swings shut after him? Locking him in the dark?'' In *The Great God Brown* Dion Anthony speaks similar words about his mother: ''I remember a sweet, strange girl, with affectionate, bewildered eyes as if God had locked her in a dark closet. . . .'')

The union of Brother Julian and Miss Alice is consummated in the flesh, but the fusion of their bodies is merely a further concretization of abstract states. For as in *The Great God Brown,* the characters in *Tiny Alice* are not merely individuals but rather expressionistic types: the Cardinal, the Lawyer, and Butler, the butler. The parallels between the protagonists of both plays are fairly obvious. In Dion Anthony, as his name implies, struggle ''the creative pagan acceptance of life'' and ''the masochistic life-denying spirit of Christianity.'' Brother Julian, who narrates at length his erotic experiences, has a Christian martyr complex: he has ''dreamed of sacrifice''. O'Neill's protagonist experiences a fourway tug of war between the Christian, pagan, aes-

> O'NEILL WOULD CERTAINLY HAVE AGREED WITH ALBEE'S DISCARDING THE OLD IMPLEMENTS OF DRAMATIC REALISM IN HIS ATTEMPT TO DIG AT THE ROOTS OF THE SICKNESS OF TODAY.''

thetic, and materialistic forces within him (and within society). So Julian's soul is at the mercy of the Cardinal, the Lawyer, Butler, and Miss Alice. Julian, like ''Dion Brown'' (as Cybel calls the composite of the Dion Anthony-Billy Brown multiple personality in *The Great God Brown*), who is shot by a police officer, is killed by a representative of law and order, in his case, the Lawyer. Similarly, O'Neill's statement to the press about Brown: ''in the end out of this anguish his soul is born, a tortured Christian soul such as the dying Dion's, begging for belief, and at the last finding it on the lips of Cybele'' could almost describe Julian's death scene. He, too, is a ''tortured Christian soul'' begging for affirmation of his belief.

Miss Alice, in turn, displays similarities not only to Cybel but also to Margaret, both of whom represent aspects of the *Ewig-Weibliche* in the O'Neill play. In the fire scene in *Tiny Alice,* where she speaks in her *''little-girl tone'',* Miss Alice approaches O'Neill's ''girl-woman'' Margaret. When Julian is dying, Miss Alice cradles him in her arms, the two forming ''something of a Pietà'', which is one way of describing Cybel's and Brown's relationship at the end of *The Great God Brown.* And just as Brown gratefully snuggles against Cybel as he dies, saying, ''The earth is warm,'' so the dying Julian finds comfort in Miss Alice: ''Closer . . . please. Warmth. . . .''

The constant putting on and removing of masks in *The Great God Brown* not only objectifies the characters' inner states but also creates a ritualistic pattern. In *Tiny Alice* the ''ceremony of Alice'' concretizes Julian's distorted view of the Eucharist and combines it with a sinister *rite de passage* that portends Julian's death and links him to Alice. Against a background of carefully positioned characters and considerable patterned movement, Butler, whose name derives from the Old French *cupbearer,* serves Julian his symbolic Last Supper. But since the God of Wrath has become literally mousy, the more substantial traditional red wine has now been diluted into a quickly staling, though deceptively bubbly, champagne.

In this scene Albee throws a little more light on the basic allegory in *Tiny Alice.* While Miss Alice is trying to tell Julian that she is merely an agent of the mouse that lives in the model of the castle, Butler links the mouse to God: "Do you understand, Julian?" asks Miss Alice. "Of course not!" replies Julian. Miss Alice: "Julian, I have tried to be . . . *her.* No; I have tried to be . . . what I thought she might, what might make you happy, what you might use, as a . . . what?" "*Play* God," says Butler. Miss Alice continues: "We must . . . represent, draw pictures, reduce or enlarge to . . . to what we can understand." Julian's next speech returns us to his basic metaphysical dilemma: "But I have fought against it . . . all my life. When they said, 'Bring the wonders down to me, closer; I cannot see them, touch; nor can I believe.' I have fought against it . . . all my life . . . All my life. In and out of . . . confinement, fought against the symbol" . . . .

In *The Great God Brown* Dion Anthony dies unmasked at the feet of his alter ego, the crass, materialist Billy Brown. With his last breath, Dion speaks the first two words of the Lord's Prayer. Julian also dies at the mercy of materialistic forces. He, too, struggles to accept the god in the model while the Lawyer and the Cardinal banter over the two billion in the briefcase. And here, in the final scene of *Tiny Alice,* we once more encounter the mask. Dying, Julian asks of God, "How long wilt thou hide thy face from me?" A few moments later the Lawyer enters with Miss Alice's wig and places it on a phrenological head. (In William Ball's highly acclaimed American Conservatory Theatre production of *Tiny Alice* the mask was used more extensively than the published text warrants, and it remained attached to the wig throughout the play.) Phrenology is supposed to tell us something about the mind inside the skull, but here is an empty mannequin. To the accompaniment of the gradual crescendo of the audible heartbeat, an effective borrowing from O'Neill's *The Emperor Jones,* Julian notices the wig on the phrenological head, crawls toward it, and half kneels in front of it. He is alone with this inscrutable dummy, and he addresses it as if it were the mouse-god Alice:

> Thou art my bride? Thou? For thee have I done my life? Grown to love, entered in, bent. . . accepted? For

thee? is that the. . . awful humor? Art thou the true arms, when the warm flesh I touched. . . rested against, was. . . nothing? And *she* . . . was not real? Is thy stare the true look? Unblinking, outward, through, to some horizon? And her eyes. . . warm, accepting, were they. . . not real? Art thou my bride?. . .

It is ironic that Julian, who has "fought against the symbol" all his life, should now turn to the mask, as does Margaret in the final moments of O'Neill's "gimmicky" *Great God Brown:* having never really understood Dion, she worships his mask even in death.

Both Albee and O'Neill, like most modern writers, grapple with the meaning of life and religion in a materialistic world. Albee has said that *Tiny Alice* "is essentially an attack on modern institutions, modern materialism, and the illusory nature of modern life, indicating much of the evil caused by the misuse and misunderstanding of the institutions." Albee's statement brings to mind O'Neill's widely quoted remark to George Jean Nathan about the playwright's having to "dig at the roots of the sickness of today as he feels it—the death of the old God and the failure of science and materialism to give any satisfying new one for the surviving primitive religious instinct to find a meaning for life in, and to comfort its fears of death with." These fears are comforted in both plays. Dion Brown dies, "*exultantly*" repeating the words of Cybel: "Our Father—?. . . Who art!" Julian accepts Tiny Alice. Albee has said that "Once Julian accepts the existence of what does not exist, his concept (his faith) exists for him. Or, if one does not accept God, then, there is nothing. Since Julian accepts Tiny Alice, his God becomes real." O'Neill would probably have agreed.

O'Neill would certainly have agreed with Albee's discarding the old implements of dramatic realism in his attempt to dig at the roots of the sickness of today. For most serious playwrights have by now grasped the more imaginative tools of expressionistic dramaturgy in order to hack through "the banality of surfaces," as O'Neill put it, and penetrate into "the characteristic spiritual conflicts which constitute the drama—the blood—of our lives today." The parallels between *Tiny Alice* and *The Great God Brown* suggest that in breaking away from the realistic mode, Albee has been influenced not only by Strindberg and recent European playwrights but also by Eugene O'Neill.

Source: Mardi Valgemae, "Albee's Great God Alice," in *Critical Essays on Edward Albee,* ed. Philip C. Kolin and J. Madison Davis, G. K. Hall & Co., 1986, p. 101.

John Stark

In the following essay, Stark claims that Tiny Alice *should be "considered an experiment" due to its considerable amount of obscurities.*

. . . The best way to begin clarifying *Tiny Alice* is to consider the one point about which the critics agree: that it is obscure. This condition, rather than ending analysis of the play, should begin it. After all, readers have come to accept the creation of obscurity as a literary technique, especially in poetry. One should not be bothered, for instance, by the deliberate ambiguity of the stage directions, which are like those in the Theater of the Absurd. (At one point Albee describes one setting and then another that is "an alternative—and perhaps more practical," and later he says that "maybe" some noise should be made. After one accepts this kind of obscurity he can concentrate on Albee's reasons for creating it.)

Some explanation for this obscurity can be found in Sontag's work. Although she has not written about *Tiny Alice,* her two major essays, "Against Interpretation" and "Notes on 'Camp'," appeared in 1964, just before *Tiny Alice* was first produced. Albee had read Sontag; when an interviewer mentioned that a critic's ideas about *Tiny Alice* seemed similar to some of Sontag's ideas, Albee replied, "this critic . . . what he has done is to misinterpret my attitudes, Miss Sontag's attitudes." So, there is a possibility of influence. But even if there were no influence, the similarity between Sontag's and Albee's ideas is worth exploring because it sheds light on the play.

Three of Miss Sontag's essays are relevant to this play. One is her definitive description of Camp in "Against Interpretation." Robert Brustein has noticed Camp's influence on Albee's play (and undoubtedly is the critic about whom Albee and his interviewer were talking); "*Tiny Alice* is a much more ambitious work than the usual variety of 'Camp,' but it shares the same ambiguity of motive." Brustein, however, does not pursue his insight. It is necessary to go to Sontag's essay and look for ideas that will clarify *Tiny Alice.* She writes that Camp was originally created by homosexuals, and homosexuality—at least in mock form—is evident in *Tiny Alice.* The Lawyer, in the rough and tumble conversation that opens the play, imputes homosexuality to the Cardinal and to Catholic clergymen in general. He refers sarcastically to "their vaunted celibacy . . . among one another," and to the Cardinal's supposed desire for "some good-looking young novice, all freshly scrubbed, with big

> *TINY ALICE* SHOULD BE CONSIDERED AN EXPERIMENT. AS MANY EXAMPLES DEMONSTRATE, ART ABOUT ART CAN BE GREAT BUT UNFORTUNATELY THE OBSCURITIES AND COMPLEXITIES INHERENT IN CAMP ART-ABOUT-ART SEEM TO MAKE COMPLETE SUCCESS IMPOSSIBLE."

working-class hands." He also jokingly exchanges a "dearest" and "darling" with Butler. . . .

According to Sontag, Camp joking eventually became self-conscious and began mocking modern culture. Much of *Tiny Alice's* obscurity results from the jocular attitude Albee takes toward some of his most important themes, like sex and religion. The sexual theme provides the play's most spectacular moment, the second act curtain, when Miss Alice opens her cloak, reveals her body to Julian and then enfolds him in the cloak. But sex is also sometimes treated comically—in a Camp manner—in, for example, the erotic puns. Brustein mentions the pun about the unused organ; other puns concern Julian's status as a lay brother and the Lawyer's British title of Solicitor. In her essay "On Style," Sontag explains the attitude of writers who recognize the potential seriousness of certain themes yet treat them comically. This ambivalent point of view will almost inevitably cause obscurity: "'Stylization in a work of art, as distinct from style, reflects an ambivalence (affection contradicted by irony) toward the subject-matter. This ambivalence is handled by maintaining, through the rhetorical overlay that is stylization, a special distance from the subject."

Albee also treats religion in the ambivalent and obfuscating manner Sontag describes. An example is his failure to clarify the source of Julian's name. It is not clear which of two very different religious persons he is named after: Julian the Apostate, an emperor who abandoned Christianity and later persecuted its followers, or Julian of Norwich, a female medieval mystic and author of *Revelations.* Religion is also important in the play's ending, when

Julian assumes a crucifixion pose, but even this is burlesqued. He asks for "the sacramental wine" but also for his "cookie," not a wafer. The frequent comic reference to wine, especially to the exploding bottles in the cellar, make this image far from serious in the play. The most ironic part of the religious theme is a macabre joke about a woman at the insane asylum who believed her womb contained Christ when it really contained cancer. Finally, inside the model and purporting to be a kind of god is Tiny Alice: a mouse, a comic kind of god indeed.

Another essay of Sontag's that is relevant to *Tiny Alice* is "Against Interpretation." In it she argues that art should not be mimetic and that interpretation is therefore an improper response to art: "the modern style of interpretation excavates, as it excavates, destroys; it digs 'behind' the text, to find a sub-text which is the true one." She argues against interpretation because "in a culture whose already classical dilemma is the hypertrophy of the intellect at the expense of energy and sensual capability, interpretation is the revenge of the intellect upon art. Even more, it is the revenge of the intellect upon the world." These ideas help explain the play's most baffling feature, the model. It is a Chinese box, representing the house, and inside it is a model of the model and so on *ad infinitum*. Art, according to Plato, is just such an indirect representation of reality: "the tragic poet, too, is an artist who represents things; . . . he and all other artists are, as it were, third in succession from the throne of truth." Thus, according to Plato, works of art are part of a Chinese box system. But Sontag and probably Albee disagree with Plato because his theory states that art is mimetic. Albee seems to mock mimetic theories of art by using a schematization of them (the model) as part of his scenery and by placing inside it, as its ultimate representation of reality, a mouse.

In *Tiny Alice* Albee's complaint with the mimetic theories of art is that it argues that art is related to the world, rather than holding that art is self-contained and cut off from external reality. Albee makes his point by presenting a change in Julian's conception of the relation between art and reality. Before the main action of the play Julian had experiences—hallucinations—that should have warned him to be skeptical about believing in a simple relation between reality and representations of it, with the latter mirroring the former. These hallucinations should have suggested to him that it is not always easy to determine precisely what is

reality and what is something else, but Julian remains secure in his orthodox conceptions about reality; in fact, he holds to these conceptions throughout most of the play. Near the end he affirms the Lawyer's statement that he, Julian, is dedicated to reality, not to appearance. It is the Lawyer who has occasionally been insinuating into Julian's mind another possibility: that non-real things purporting merely to copy reality are not related to everyday reality at all but are themselves an ultimate—perhaps the only—reality. For example, early in the play the Lawyer says: "I have learned . . . Brother Julian . . . never to confuse the representative of a . . . thing with the thing itself." "Representative" is of course a pun on "representation." By the end of the play the Lawyer, with help from other influences, prevails, and Julian decides to forsake other realities for the reality of the model, the representation.

Rather than merely copying part of the everyday world, this play itself, like the model, is in some important respects "about" itself. To be specific, it is a play that examines the validity of representing reality by means of plays. The first thing Miss Alice does is assume the role of an old crone. This role-playing, according to Sontag, is characteristic of Camp: "to perceive Camp in objects and persons is to understand Being-as-Playing-a-Role." Another involution is the play within the play, in which the Lawyer and Butler act out new identities. In fact, Julian—along with the more perceptive members of the audience—senses that he is the victim of a troupe of highly skilled actors. Thus the actors in *Tiny Alice* play characters who are actors playing roles. The result is indeed a Chinese box system, with the play moving inward toward a core of dramatic "reality" rather than toward a copy of reality.

Tiny Alice also has the effect of being self-enclosed and separate from external reality because it stresses that to a large extent reality is linguistic. In this it resembles the story of another Alice: *Alice in Wonderland*. In Carroll's book Alice leaves the world of external reality and goes to a world that seems to be linguistically composed (i.e., figures of speech, such as "mad as a hatter," are made manifest). Albee's Alice is reminiscent of Carroll's, particularly late in the play, when her actions become very childish and Albee says that her reaction to Julian is "*surprisingly little-girl fright.*" The many puns in the play also emphasize language's role in forming conceptions of reality. Butler indirectly suggests to Julian that this is so when he claims that it was a semantic problem that caused Julian's mental illness. Julian's final acceptance of Alice is, among other things, an acceptance of the power of language; he is convinced more by assertion than by evidence. His acceptance is also his validation of drama as not only a representation of reality but *as* reality.

In short, both Albee and Miss Sontag are interested in Camp sensibility and the nature of art. Another way to demonstrate Albee's interest in these matters is to set *Tiny Alice* into its chronological place in his work. The relevant works are *Who's Afraid of Virginia Woolf?* (1962), *Tiny Alice* (1964), and *Malcolm* (1965). *Ballad of the Sad Cafe* (1963), a dramatization of a novella by Carson MacCullers, deals with other themes.) The first of these plays develops the themes of reality, representation and the creation of fictitional alternatives to reality, particularly in its treatment of the fiction about George and Martha's "child." Albee himself mentioned this aspect of *Virginia Woolf* to an interviewer: "and of course, who's afraid of the big *bad* wolf ... who's afraid of living life without false illusions." *Malcolm* is an adaptation of James Purdy's novel, which is a classic of Camp literature, a peculiar *Bildungsroman* that describes a boy becoming a Camp object, and it is full of Camp characters, rooms, clothes and other trappings. Its Camp theme is recapitulated in the motto of Malcolm's first wife. "Texture is all, substance nothing," which recalls Susan Sontag's statement that "Camp art is often decorative art, emphasizing texture, sensuous surface, and style at the expense of content." Albee's decision to adapt Purdy's novel immediately upon finishing *Tiny Alice* shows his continuing interest in Camp.

One can speculate about Albee's reasons for creating art about art and for treating his in a Camp manner. A probable cause is the large number of critics who turn their attention on the work of contemporary writers. The most striking feature of the interview with Albee in *Paris Review* is his knowledge of the criticism written about him. At one point he says, "about four years ago I made a list, for my own amusement, of the playwrights, the contemporary playwrights, by whom critics said I'd been influenced. I listed twenty-five." Note, too, the strained and uneasy irony of "for my own amusement." His response is certainly understandable, because too much criticism can make any writer uneasy about his work and can even encourage him to fashion what Brustein called a "huge joke on the American culture industry." Once again

Sontag has a relevant comment: "a great deal of today's art may be understood as motivated by a flight from interpretation. To avoid interpretation, art becomes parody. Or it becomes abstract. Or it may become ('merely') decorative. Or it may become non-art."

Tiny Alice exemplifies some of the alternatives for art that Sontag proposes. Albee's treatment of the themes of sex and religion is parodic rather than profound, and his development of the theme of art is not immediately clear. The ending, especially in the longer printed version, is ludicrous, probably deliberately so. Julian takes longer to die than a villain in a bad western movie, and his final speech is extremely over-blown. Nigel Dennis' complaint about some other playwrights at first seems to apply also to Albee: "when [Beckett, Ionesco and Genet] got into difficulties ... they filled up the void with make-believe of meaningless words and stage 'business.' This now has become the approved way, with the difference that as the tradition grows more and more decadent, the firmness of grasp becomes feebler and feebler, and the accumulation of meaninglessness greater and greater." Dennis' complaint is over-stated, but he does sound a useful warning. This criticism should not be applied to Albee, however, since he has artistic reasons for the apparent flaws in *Tiny Alice*.

Tiny Alice should be considered an experiment. As many examples demonstrate, art about art can be great but unfortunately the obscurities and complexities inherent in Camp art-about-art seem to make complete success impossible. Even more unfortunate, this experiment seems to have tainted Albee, for never again has he risen to the heights of his early one-act plays and *Who's Afraid of Virginia Woolf?* But the fad of the Camp sensibility has waned since *Tiny Alice,* which leaves hope that Albee (and the other writers who were affected by it) will return to his previous level of accomplishment.

Source: John Stark, "Camping Out: Tiny Alice and Susan Sontag," in *Critical Essays on Edward Albee,* ed. Philip C. Kolin and J. Madison Davis, G. K. Hall & Co., 1986, p. 162.

SOURCES

Albee, Edward, Author's Note, in *Tiny Alice,* Atheneum, 1965.

Amacher, Richard, *Edward Albee,* G. K. Hall & Co., 1999.

Casper, Leonard, "*Tiny Alice:* The Expense of Joy in the Persistence of Mystery," in *Edward Albee: An Interview and*

Essays, edited by Julian N. Wasserman, University of St. Thomas, 1983, pp. 83-92.

Cohn, Ruby, article, in *American Writers,* Vol. 1, Charles Scribner's Sons, 1974, pp. 71-96.

Franzblau, Abraham N., "A Psychiatrist Looks at *Tiny Alice,*" in *Saturday Review,* January 30, 1965, p. 39.

Hewes, Henry, review and discussion of *Tiny Alice,* in *Saturday Review,* January 30, 1965, p. 38.

Review of *Tiny Alice,* in *Newsweek,* January, 1, 1965, p. 75.

Wasserman, Julian, "'The Pitfalls of Drama': The Idea of Language in the Plays of Edward Albee," in *Edward Albee: An Interview and Essays,* edited by Julian N. Wasserman, University of St. Thomas, 1983, pp. 29-53.

Worth, Katharine, "Edward Albee: Playwright of Evolution," in *Essays on Contemporary American Drama,* edited by Hedwig Bock and Albert Wertheim, Max Hueber Verlag, 1981, pp. 33–53.

FURTHER READING

Bloom, Harold, ed., *Edward Albee,* Chelsea House Publishers, 1987.
    This is a collection of critical essays on Albee's most significant plays.

Gussow, Mel, *Edward Albee: A Singular Journey: A Biography,* Simon & Schuster, 1999.

Volpone

BEN(JAMIN) JONSON
1605

Jonson was a serious classicist who modeled his plays on classic Roman and Greek tragedies. Jonson thought that the poet had a moral function to educate, and the purpose of *Volpone* is to teach lessons about greed. The topic is quite serious, although this is comedy, and there are many moments of humor in the play, especially when Volpone is feigning illness and lies disguised. This play is, in many ways, a play within a play. Volpone and Mosca are actors playing roles throughout, but they are also directors leading the three fortune hunters, Corvino, Voltore, and Corbaccio, through their performances. Jonson differed from other playwrights of the period in that he did not use old stories, fables, or histories as the sources for his plays. Instead, Jonson used a plot "type" as the source for most of his plays. In *Volpone,* the plot is the familiar one of a swindle. The action is set in Venice, which many Englishmen thought was a center of debauchery and sin. Jonson's characters are not well defined, nor do they have any depth. Instead, they are "types" familiar to the audience: the dishonest lawyer, the jealous old husband married to a beautiful young girl, and the miserly old man who cannot be satisfied until he can amass even more money.

Volpone was first performed in 1605. Since there were no reviews, the audience's exact reaction cannot be known. But we do know from letters and diaries that Jonson was not popular with audiences. His plays provided morals and tended to preach to the audience, something they resented. William

Shakespeare's plays were much more popular, since they set out to entertain, and this fact was not lost on Jonson, who is credited with being privately annoyed at Shakespeare. *Volpone* is considered Jonson's most popular work, since it is the one most frequently staged.

AUTHOR BIOGRAPHY

Jonson was born in about 1572. The date is uncertain since Elizabethans were very casual about the recording of exact dates. He was a scholar, a poet, and a dramatist. Jonson was born near London shortly after the death of his father. He was educated at Westminster School and for a short period worked as a bricklayer for his stepfather. Jonson was briefly in the military, where he killed an enemy in single combat. In his next career, as an actor, Jonson also wrote dialogue in some of the works in which he acted. After killing another actor in a duel, Jonson was arrested but released after claiming benefit of clergy, which meant that he was an educated man. Jonson converted to Roman Catholicism during this period, and although he escaped hanging, he was still labeled a felon after his release. Jonson's first play, *Every Man in His Humour,* was written this same year, 1598, with William Shakespeare playing one of the roles on stage. Jonson continued with a new play every year for the next few years: *Every Man out of His Humour* (1599), *Cynthia's Revels* (1600), and *Poetaster* (1601). Perhaps best known for his court masques, Jonson wrote the first of many, *The Masque of Blackness,* in 1605.

Although Jonson became well established as a playwright with works such as *Volpone* (1606), *Epicene, or the Silent Woman* (1610), *The Alchemist* (1610), *Bartholomew Fair* (1614), and *The Devil was an Ass* (1616), he is also well known as a poet. Jonson was not formally appointed England's poet laureate, but he was awarded a pension in 1616 by King James I, thus acknowledging that Jonson was essentially performing that function. That same year, Jonson became the first poet or dramatist to publish a folio edition of his *Works.* Since not even Shakespeare had published a compilation of his work, Jonson received some criticism for this action. However, he was awarded with an honorary M.A. from Cambridge University in 1616. Among Jonson's patrons was the Sidney family, for whom he wrote one of his most famous poems, *To Penshurst,* one of the best known poems to cele-

brate an estate and family. The beauty of this poem and the skill with which Jonson composed it is evident to visitors who abandon the road to approach Penshurst from the back of the estate.

Jonson was not always popular with audiences, who while attending his plays were often critical of the writer. During the height of his creativity, Jonson was as popular a writer as Shakespeare, who was also Jonson's friend. But he saw much of his popularity diminish later in his life while Shakespeare's continued to grow. Although Jonson was largely responsible for the publication of the first folio of Shakespeare's work in 1623, for which he wrote a poem, he was less generous with his praise in private. Still, there is no doubt that Jonson both liked and admired Shakespeare. While Jonson was a talented writer, his misfortune was to be writing plays during the same period as a talent as enormous as Shakespeare. Jonson spent the last nine years of his life bedridden after suffering a stroke. He died in 1637 and was buried in Westminster Abbey

PLOT SUMMARY

Act I

When the play opens, Volpone and Mosca are discussing the great wealth that Volpone has amassed and that he enjoys seeing and touching. Volpone has no family and no heirs, and he enjoys the game of acquiring riches far more then he does the actual wealth he amasses. Volpone is in excellent health, but when his first visitor is announced, the lawyer Voltore, Volpone quickly feigns grave illness for his visitor, who has brought Volpone an expensive gift. Mosca suggests that Volpone is due to die at any moment and that if Voltore visits often, each time with an expensive gift, Voltore will inherit all Volpone's wealth. After Voltore departs, Volpone and Mosca repeat their performance for the next visitor, the miser Corbaccio. After Corbaccio leaves, Corvino enters, and the routine is repeated, with Corvino convinced that he will inherit, just as the two previous visitors were also convinced. Volpone celebrates his new gifts and the successful deceit of his visitors.

Act II

Peregrine and Sir Politic Would-be are attempting to impress each other with their relative importance in the world. While this conversation is going on, Volpone enters disguised as a Mountebank (a quack doctor). He sets up a stand and begins to promote his medicines. After listening to a disguised Volpone promote his medicines and cures, the two Englishmen begin arguing with Volpone over prices. Attracted by the commotion, Celia leans out her window and is noticed by Volpone, who is immediately smitten. Volpone decides he must have this woman and instructs Mosca to make it possible. When Corvino emerges and sees his wife at the window, he begins to beat on Volpone and chastises his wife to remain cloistered inside.

Mosca goes to Corvino and tells him that Volpone is very ill, and that the doctors have said he might be better if only he has a beautiful young woman to sleep beside him. Corvino suggests that Mosca hire a prostitute, but Mosca warns that such women are dishonest and might attempt through trickery to take Volpone's wealth. After Corvino is convinced that Volpone is too ill to make use of a woman, and that his wife would be safe, Corvino offers his own wife to sleep by Volpone. This act ends with Corvino telling Celia to get ready; they will be going to visit Volpone.

Act III

Mosca, who has been augmenting Volpone's plots with some of his own, meets Bonario on the street. He tells the young man that his father, Corbaccio, is going to disinherit his son in favor of Volpone. To prove his accusation to the disbelieving Bonario, Mosca invites him to Volpone's house to overhear Corbaccio's meeting with Volpone. While waiting for Mosca to return, Volpone's three freaks entertain him until a guest arrives. Lady Politic Would-be enters, but her constant chatter about meaningless things almost overwhelms Volpone, who begins to think that her chatter might actually kill him. At this moment Mosca returns. To rid Volpone of this annoying woman, Mosca tells her that he saw her husband with one of the most beautiful courtesans of Venice.

Mosca, who has brought Bonario to witness his father's meeting with Volpone, now hides the young man in Volpone's gallery, as Corvino arrives with Celia. Celia is taken into Volpone's presence, who is feigning grave illness at her approach. As Mosca takes Corvino away, Volpone jumps up and attempts to attack Celia. Bonario comes to her rescue and the two young people exit the room. Volpone recognizes that he is in danger and his plots may soon be revealed if he is turned over to the police. Mosca takes advantage of Corbaccio's sudden appearance to tell him that his son reacted violently to

Ben Jonson

his accidental discovery that he was to be disinherited. In response, Corbaccio does, indeed, disinherit his son. Voltore, who has also arrived and who has heard much of the plotting, is convinced by Mosca that he has misunderstood. Voltore is told that Bonario has convinced Celia to lie about Volpone so that Corbaccio will not change his will. Voltore agrees to help Volpone and the three go to the senate to seek legal action against Bonario.

Act IV

Sir Politic Would-be is telling Peregrine about his plots and secret plans for several inventions and ways to get rich. When Lady Politic Would-be enters, she thinks that Peregrine is a woman in disguise, but apologizes when she realizes that Peregrine is, indeed, a man. The result of the Lady's actions is that Peregrine becomes convinced that Sir Politic Would-be is a man without honor. At that moment, Mosca enters and tells the Lady that the courtesan, who was earlier with her husband, has been arrested. Meanwhile, at the senate, the conflicting stories confuse the magistrates, but Voltore provides a masterful defense of Volpone and an attack on Celia and Bonario. The magistrates are convinced of Celia's lewdness after Lady Politic Would-be testifies that she saw the lady with Sir Politic Would-be; at the same time, Bonario is portrayed as Celia's lover. While all this is going on around him, Volpone lies on a stretcher and points out that he is too ill to have performed the attack of which he is accused. The magistrates are convinced, and Volpone emerges victorious.

Act V

Volpone's success makes him even more confident of his superior intellect, and he hatches a new plan. His servants are dispatched to announce that Volpone has died and a new will leaves everything to Mosca. Mosca is dressed in Volpone's dressing gown and is told to count his riches as Voltore, Corvino, Corbaccio, and Lady Politic Would-be enter. Volpone hides and listens, but none of these disenfranchised heirs dares to speak out. While the deception with Volpone continues, Peregrine disguises himself and seeks revenge on Sir Politic Would-be, who has no idea why any of these events are occurring. The action then moves back to Volpone, who is enjoying his deception so much that he instructs Mosca to go out into the streets and gloat at his victory. However, Volpone has underestimated his victims, and overstated his reliance upon Mosca, who has plans to seize the wealth and leave. When Voltore recants his testimony at Volpone's trial, the magistrates send for Mosca. The entire plot is revealed, and Volpone admits his role when Mosca's own plans are foiled. As a man of lower ranking, Mosca is first whipped and then sent to the galleys as a prisoner. Volpone is sent to prison and his goods seized and donated to a hospital. Voltore is disbarred and banished, while Corbaccio must retire to a monastery and turn his estate over to his son. Corvino faces public humiliation and must return his wife to her father, with her dowry tripled in value.

CHARACTERS

Androgyno

Androgyno is a hermaphrodite and a member of Volpone's household, whose sole purpose seems to be the entertainment and flattery of Volpone. Androgyno, Castrone, and Nano's appearance in Act I is devised by Mosca as a way to further ingratiate himself into Volpone's good favor. The trio reappear during the play, as Volpone needs additional distraction or entertainment.

Avocatori

Avocatori are the four judges, who hear the trial of Volpone. In the first trial, they are deceived by Voltore's accusations against Celia and Bonario and the witnesses who have been called to testify. After Voltore is disinherited, he goes to these magistrates and admits his crime. The four judges, who are confused, discover the truth after Volpone admits his plot. These four magistrates pass sentence on all the conspirators and find justice for Bonario and Celia.

Bonario

Bonario is Corbaccio's son. Mosca tells Bonario that his father is about to disinherit him and leave his estate to Volpone. And although he does not want to believe ill of his father, Mosca's tears convince Bonario of the servant's honesty, and Bonario agrees to listen to Volpone and Corbaccio's conversation. Bonario is an honest and good man, who saves Celia from Volpone's advances. However, because of Lady Politic Would-be's testimony, Bonario and Celia are accused and tried as schemers against Corvino. After the plots are discovered, Bonario is given his father's estate and his honor is returned.

Castrone

Castrone is a eunuch, one of the freaks that Volpone maintains in his household. With Androgyno and Nano, Castrone's role is simply to entertain Volpone when he is bored or needs distracting.

Celia

Celia is Corvino's wife. She is honest and pure, the opposite of almost every other character in the play. As Corvino's wife, she is subject to his misuse, even when her gives her to Volpone in hopes of being made heir. Celia is told that Volpone is in such poor health that she will be safe sleeping by his side, but she is still unwilling to obey Corvino's wishes. When Volpone tries to attack her, Celia is saved by Bonario. Celia faces her trials with nobility, even when found guilty at the first trial. Celia illustrates the problems of women in this period. She is just some man's property, an object to be disposed of or sold.

Corbaccio

Corbaccio (also called The Raven) is an old miser who also wants Volpone's estate. Corbaccio is feeble, deaf, and greedy. Volpone convinces Corbaccio to disinherit his own son, Bonario, and to replace him with Volpone, who will then leave his estate to Bonario. Corbaccio is completely taken in by this plan and even plots to hasten Volpone's death through poison. Corbaccio is so corrupted by Mosca's plots and desire for Volpone's money, that he even testifies against his own son at the trial. In the final act, Corbaccio is punished, when the magistrates send him to a monastery and instruct him to turn his estate over to Bonario.

Corvino

Corvino (also called The Crow) is a rich merchant who seeks Volpone's estate. He is mean-spirited, cowardly, and jealous of his wife, Celia. But he is also greedy, and when he finds out that Volpone wants Celia, Corvino is willing to sacrifice his wife's virtue for money. Corvino leaves her in Volpone's hands as a ploy to get his inheritance, after Mosca tells Corvino that Volpone's doctors have said that a beautiful young woman should sleep by his side. To assure himself of Volpone's gratitude, Corvino volunteers his own wife, although he has been assured that Volpone is too feeble to take advantage of her. Corvino's punishment is the loss of his wife, who must be returned to her father with her dowry tripled.

The Crow
See Corvino

The Fox
See Volpone

The Gadfly
See Mosca

Lady Politic Would-be

Lady Politic Would-be is the wife of the English tourist. She affects strange airs and talks constantly. She is very shallow and not very intelligent. Her constant empty chatter is so offensive to Volpone that he would rather lose money than have to listen to her one more moment. She is unreasonably jealous and acts the fool when told her husband is having an affair with Celia. Lady Politic Would-be gives false testimony at the first trial, and thus, she helps save Volpone. She tries to hide her mental defects behind cosmetics and dress.

Mosca

Mosca (also called The Gadfly) is Volpone's flatterer, who plots against everyone else. He is

MEDIA ADAPTATIONS

- Industrial Cinematográfica produced a Spanish version of *Volpone*, entitled *Tiburón*, in 1933. The film is distributed through Empressa (USA).

- Île de France Films produced a version of *Volpone* in 1940. The film has been distributed through A. Z. Distribution in France.

- United Artists produced a version of *Volpone*, entitled *The Honey Pot*, in 1967.

---

malicious but also very witty. It is Mosca's job to convince each gift-giver that he or she will be the honored recipient of Volpone's will. Mosca carries out Volpone's plans, but he also conceives of pranks that take his master's plots just one step further. Mosca teases his master with descriptions of Celia, playing upon Volpone's desire for the woman, and ultimately leading to the collapse of the plots. Mosca is in love with himself, and like many men who are wrapped up in their own ego, Mosca underestimates his master. Whereas, Volpone loses with dignity, Mosca whines and curses as he is dragged away at the play's end. As a commoner, his punishment is more severe then Volpone's, and thus, Mosca pays a greater price for his greater plotting.

Nano

Nano is a dwarf, one of the freaks that Volpone keeps in his household for amusement, whose sole purpose seems to be the entertainment and flattery of Volpone. Nano, Castrone, and Androgyno's appearance in Act I is devised by Mosca as a way to further integrate himself into Volpone's good favor. The trio reappear later in the play when Volpone needs distracting.

Peregrine

Peregrine is a wise and sophisticated traveler, the very opposite of Sir Politic Would-be. When Lady Politic Would-be mistakes Peregrine for a courtesan, with whom she thinks her husband has been dallying, Peregrine thinks Sir Politic Would-be is without honor, and so devises of a plot to seek revenge and to diminish the English knight's ego and power.

The Raven

See Corbaccio

Sir Politic Would-be

Sir Politic Would-be is an English knight, who represents the English tourist traveling through Venice. He has many projects to advance, but he is also naïve and gullible, seeing a spy around every corner. Sir Politic Would-be is eager to be thought an insider of politic doings. He also admires Volpone, does not understand that Volpone ridicules him, and in fact, wants to imitate Volpone. Since Volpone is never what he pretends, Sir Politic Would-be's imitation is an imitation of an imitation. Sir Politic Would-be is made a greater fool by Mosca, although it is unwittingly and unknown to the knight. As a result, Peregrine is also moved to make the knight the butt of his joke.

Volpone

Volpone (also known as The Fox) is an old ''magnifico,'' who is more interested in the game of acquiring money than he is in the real property of money. He leaves no family to inherit his estate, and finds that pretending to leave his estate to his followers has created quite an interesting game. Thus, Volpone pretends to be ill in order to manipulate several men, who think they will become his heirs, and from whom he has acquired many expensive gifts. It can be argued that Volpone has some integrity, since he is not interested in tricking widows and children out of their money, although in truth, Volpone simply considers widows and children too gullible for his interests. Instead, he picks victims who present a challenge. Volpone enjoys the performances he devises and the disguises that he assumes. However, he has three weaknesses that make his plots susceptible to failure. The first weakness is Volpone's total trust in Mosca. The second weakness is Volpone's desire for Celia, at any cost. And the third weakness is Volpone's overconfidence in his own intelligence and his lack of appreciation of his opponent's intelligence. When his plots are discovered, Volpone is accepting of his punishment, even showing humor and resignation at the outcome.

Voltore

Voltore (also known as The Vulture) is a lawyer who presents Volpone with elaborate gifts. Voltore is not alone in competing for Volpone's estate, since there are two others who are also showering Volpone with gifts. Voltore is a scavenger who seeks the spoils of the dead and who preys on the dying. He helps Volpone in his first trial, securing his acquittal, even suborning witnesses. But Voltore is dangerous, and when Mosca pretends that Volpone is dead and has left Voltore nothing, he engineers the collapse of all Volpone's plotting. Voltore is disbarred and banished when the truth is finally revealed.

The Vulture

See Voltore

THEMES

Appearances and Reality

What Volpone and Mosca's victims perceive as reality is not the truth of the play. Each one thinks that he will be made heir to Volpone's fortune. Voltore attempts to deceive the court and is punished when the deception is revealed. Corvino is willing to seduce Volpone with Celia's body, although Corvino is also deceived into thinking Volpone too ill to make use of the young woman. Corbaccio is deceived into sacrificing his son's inheritance in a ploy to make even more money. The reality is that each will be left with less wealth. However, Mosca, whom Volpone trusts without question, is also deceiving Volpone. Mosca is the only participant who clearly understands the depth of the deception.

Class Conflict

On first reading, it is not readily apparent that *Volpone* is concerned with class, and this is probably because class was not Jonson's concern in writing the play. However, the inequities in punishment provided at the play's conclusion create some questions about the role of class in this play. The judges say that Mosca, ''being a fellow of no birth or blood,'' shall be whipped and then sent to a lifetime in the galleys. His punishment is much more severe than the that of the other participants because he has no social rank. Mosca is seized and dragged from the stage, as he cries out. In contrast, the other men involved accept their punishment,

TOPICS FOR FURTHER STUDY

- The setting for *Volpone* is Venice, which the English considered a center of sinful vices. Thus, Jonson felt very comfortable using this city as a setting for a story about greed. Shakespeare also used Venice as a setting for several of his plays, including *The Merchant of Venice* and *Othello*. What was Venice really like in the sixteenth and seventeenth centuries? Was it a center of sinful vices, as these playwrights depicted?

- Sir and Lady Politic Would-be represent the out-of-place English tourist, who are pretentious and too loud, much the way American tourists are regarded in the twentieth century. Research the role of the tourist during the seventeenth century. How accurate is Jonson's depiction of the English knight and his wife?

- Spying was an important element in early seventeenth century life. There was a lot of spying going on in the courts of both Elizabeth I and James I, and so, this was a common motif in plays of this period. Sir Politic Would-be represents this motif, as he is very concerned with spying, which allows Peregrine to finally best him. Investigate the spying that occurred in court and how it might have influenced other elements of English society.

- Eventually Jonson turned to writing masques, which were much more popular with audiences than his plays, especially at court. But masques were more expensive to produce than plays, and ultimately, the exorbitant cost indirectly led to the English Revolution and the beheading of Charles I. While Jonson did not cause the English Revolution, the king's constant taxing of his subjects to pay for masques, did play a huge role in Cromwell's victory. Research the history of the masque and its staging and the role the masque played in the beheading of Charles I in 1649.

---

which does not involve whipping, with dignity. Only Mosca, as someone without birth or blood, is subjected to physical punishment and the indignity of being dragged screaming from the court.

Deception

The plot of Jonson's play is based on deception. Each of the three victims attempts to use deception for financial gain. But the victims are each self-deceived. Their willingness to believe allows the game to succeed. Each of the victims attempts to deceive Volpone, as each pretends to be a caring petitioner. Mosca and Volpone deceive each victim with the promise of greater wealth as a return for exorbitant gifts. The deception is largely dependent on none of the victims uniting against Volpone. Thus, when Volpone fakes his death and the three are brought together to witness Mosca's triumph, their joint misery and recognition of their deception leads to Voltore recanting his defense of Volpone.

Greed

It is the victim's greed that permits Volpone's plot. Each victim seeks more wealth than he deserves. And each man attempts to bargain himself into a better position through more and more extravagant gifts. Volpone is also not immune, but his greed is not for more money but for more fun at his victim's expense. It is Volpone's greedy need to see his victims humiliated that ultimately leads to the plot's unraveling.

Morality

The play's resolution leads to the lesson, which is that greed will result in each man's downfall. Corvino loses his wife and her dowry, which he must repay at three times its worth. Corbaccio is banished to a monastery, and the estate he denied his son is turned over to the son, while the lawyer, Voltore, is disbarred and banished from Venice. Volpone is imprisoned and all his goods are dispersed to a hospital, a just punishment, since Volpone pretended to be ill. The worst punishment is provided to Mosca, who is of a lower class than the other men. Mosca is whipped and sent away to be a prisoner in the galleys for the rest of his life. Each man is justly punished for his greed and the morality of the play's resolution provides an important lesson for the audience.

Victim and Victimization

Volpone puts the definition of victim to the test. The initial victims of the Volpone's plot are victims because they are duped by Volpone into losing money and gifts, and they have enriched Volpone through their victimization. But are they are victimized by Volpone and Mosca or are they victimized by their own greed? They, perhaps, see themselves as victims of Volpone's cruel joke, but the audience would not have sympathized with them. The true victims are Bonario and Celia, who are unjustly accused and convicted of crimes they did not commit. And yet, as punishment is being dispensed in the final act, Celia pleads for the court's mercy for her husband, who would use her so basely.

STYLE

Act

A major division in a drama. In Greek plays the sections of the drama signified by the appearance of the chorus and were usually divided into five acts. This is the formula for most serious drama, from the Greeks to the Romans, and to Elizabethan playwrights like William Shakespeare. The five acts can sometimes denote the structure of dramatic action, which are exposition, complication, climax, falling action, and catastrophe. The five-act structure was followed until the nineteenth century when Henrik Ibsen combined some of the acts. *Volpone* is a five-act play. The exposition occurs in the first act when the audience learns of Volpone's deception and meets his victims. By the end of Act II, the complication, the audience has learned that Mosca is expanding on Volpone's plans and that Celia is to be catalyst for the climax, which occurs in the next act. The climax occurs in the third act when Celia arrives, is attacked by Volpone, and then is rescued by Bonario. The trial provides the falling action, and the catastrophe occurs in the last act when all the plotting begins to unravel and the punishment is dispensed.

Character

A person in a dramatic work. The actions of each character are what constitute the story. Character can also include the idea of a particular individual's morality. Characters can range from simple stereotypical figures to more complex multifaceted ones. Characters may also be defined by personality traits, such as the rogue or the damsel in distress. "Characterization" is the process of creating a lifelike person from an author's imagination. To accomplish this the author provides the character with personality traits that help define who he will be and how he will behave in a given situation. The characters in *Volpone* are stereotypes, since the characters are not well-defined and appear as little more than types. The audience does not really know or understand the character as an individual. For instance, Voltore is a dishonest lawyer, revealing all the stereotypes often associated with this career.

Genre

Genres are a way of categorizing literature. Genre is a French term that means "kind" or "type." Genre can refer to both the category of literature such as tragedy, comedy, epic, poetry, or pastoral. It can also include modern forms of literature such as drama novels or short stories. This term can also refer to types of literature such as mystery, science fiction, comedy or romance. *Volpone* is a comedy.

Setting

The time, place, and culture in which the action of the play takes place is called the setting. The elements of setting may include geographic location, physical or mental environments, prevailing cultural attitudes, or the historical time in which the action takes place. The location for Jonson's play is Venice, which is significant because it automatically signals the audience that this play will deal with a vice. Venice was considered the center of depravity, according to most English thought of the day. The action occurs during the course of a day.

HISTORICAL CONTEXT

The period from 1576 to 1642 is considered the Golden Age of English drama, although it was probably not golden for those who lived through it. For more than 100 years, farmers had been displaced by enclosure acts that fenced off agricultural

COMPARE & CONTRAST

- **1605:** The Gunpowder Plot is discovered. This is a plot to blow up the House of Parliament. The plot is attributed to Roman Catholics; and the English, who worry a great deal about the Catholic Pope's influence in their country, are reminded of the danger that Catholics and the Italian Pope present.

   Today: Terrorism is still a part of British life, with random bombings remaining a principle means of the Irish Republican Army's method of warfare.

- **1605:** Tobacco, a late sixteenth century export to England, was the recent subject of a pamphlet published by James I, in which the king referred to the habit as dirty and unhealthy. He will change his mind in 1612, when the Virginia tobacco trade adds significant wealth to his coffers. The desire for wealth easily eclipses honor and duty.

   Today: Tobacco continues to be a subject of much controversy. While the United States government pursues settlements with tobacco companies, the government collects huge revenues in taxes on tobacco, which it uses to subsidize tobacco growers.

- **1605:** The forests of England have been severely diminished for several years, and imports of wood continue to escalate in price, thus contributing to inflation and economic hardship and to peasant unrest.

   Today: The queen has been under increasing pressure to reduce her expenses and the cost of maintaining the royal presence. In response, she has agreed to pay taxes and to cover many of the expenses previously paid through taxation of the public.

- **1605:** The plague continues to kill many in England, although the death toll is not as severe as two years earlier. A significant contributor to the reoccurrence of plague is the crowding and poverty of London, caused in large part by the forcing of peasants from the country and into the city.

   Today: The plague still continues to threaten lives, but in smaller number. A more significant plague is to be found in HIV infections, which in spite of promising treatments, continues to infect many new victims each year.

- **1605:** The English continue their exploration of the Americas, with the voyage of explorer George Waymouth, who lands off the coast of North America, an area he will call Nanticut.

   Today: After nearly three hundred years of colonization, the English no longer seek to discover and colonize new lands, and are more focused on solving the social problems of their own country.

land for pastures. This created severe unemployment in the countryside with accompanying high inflation. Crop failures, the threat of war abroad, and brutal religious strife had shaken English society by the time Elizabeth I assumed the throne in 1558. The reign of Elizabeth produced relative stability, but her failure to name a successor brought discontent and the threat of civil war even before her death. The rule of James I was greeted initially with enthusiasm in 1603, but religious, class, and political divisions soon intensified. In spite of this turmoil, or perhaps because of it, the most important drama in Western history was produced during this period. Rural unemployment drove many people to London, making it the largest city in Europe. However, attempts at civil order led to widespread disorder and the establishment of a capitalistic economy in place of the feudal agrarian social order. The writers of this period grappled with new ideas about science and philosophy, religion and politics. In addition, there was also a new emphasis on individual thought, action, and responsibility.

Playwrights thought of themselves as poets, but were not regarded as serious artists, much as we regard screenwriters today. In fact, playwrights turned out a commercial product. Once sold, plays became the property of acting companies and when published, were more likely to bear the name of the acting company than the author's name. It was not until the seventeenth century, when Jonson published his plays (in 1616) and a folio of Shakespeare's works were published (in 1623), did the idea that plays have literary merit occur. But because plays weren't regarded as serious literature, playwrights had the opportunity to deal with any subject that interested them. In 1576, the first permanent theatre was built. This led to greater social status for theatre people. The location was out of town, due to religious problems. Puritans thought actors were sinful, with substandard morals, because the social milieu of the playhouse was loose, and often libertine. There was also the philosophical argument that acting was lying, role-playing. In spite of these problems, plays brought large numbers of people together and correspondingly increased crime and disease, so city officials often sided with Puritans in wanting theatres outside town. Theatres also enticed people from their jobs and so affected trade.

Every script had to be reviewed by the Master of Revels, who could force revisions and censure. Most concerns were with religion and politics, not with sexual content. In a very real sense, religious theology governed politics. Topics that might offend the queen, such as the abdication scene in William Shakespeare's *Richard II,* or incite treason were banned. Some plays might be closed, or might never open for such offenses. In spite of this official censorship, the court and queen, and later king, were huge fans of theatre. Since actors could be arrested as vagrants, they needed the protection of the court and its patronage. Because theatre reached the illiterate, its influence was widely felt. The audience was mostly upper class. Since there was no lighting, plays were presented in the afternoon, and thus, most working people were not able to attend. However, gentlemen attended, and for a penny (one pence), others could stand in front of the stage and watch. Respectable women could attend, if they were escorted by a male, but prostitutes also attended to increase trade. In spite of many obstacles, such as the open air and problems with English weather, stage presentation and performance over-

came the shortcomings of the audience and their lack of a classical education. Although education was growing, its presence was still very limited. Still, even with a limited education, the feeling and ideas of the play could still be grasped and enjoyed by the audience.

CRITICAL OVERVIEW

Volpone is Ben Jonson's most popular comedy. The con or swindle was a familiar theme, and one which Jonson found to be a natural topic for comedy, since he also used the swindle in *The Alchemist.* There is little information about how Ben Jonson's *Volpone* was received by the public, since plays were not reviewed during the period in which this play was composed. Instead, response to a play may be determined by examining how often it has been produced in the years since its creation. Yet another way to gauge a play's popularity is through anecdotal evidence: letters, diaries, and journal entries from the period. Most Jonson scholars acknowledge that Jonson's plays were not generally well received. The audience was often loudly critical, and several of Jonson's plays were hissed from the stage. This is not necessarily because the plays were not entertaining or topical, but rather, the play's reception reflected the audience's attitudes toward the author. Jonson is often described as arrogant and difficult. Unfortunately, in the case of *Volpone,* there is little evidence of letters or diaries that reveal the play's initial reception. There is also little information about how long any play remained in production and on the stage during the early part of the seventeenth century. Although all plays were licensed by a government official, the Master of Revels, his original records have not survived, although collected passages were published in 1917. The details of performance that are so readily available in the twentieth century, length and dates of performance and the theatre in which a production played, are not available for the period during which Ben Jonson wrote.

Although there were no critical reviews early in the seventeenth century, within a hundred years, reviews, via letters and other correspondence began to appear. When theatres reopened after the Restoration in 1660, *Volpone* was being staged regularly enough to be noted in correspondence of the late seventeenth century. Among the comments is one by Samuel Pepys, the diarist, who observed that a

1665 production of *Volpone* was a ''most excellent play; the best I ever saw, and well acted.'' However, there are few compliments for Jonson, since many of these writers were intent on dissecting the plot of Jonson's work, looking for inconsistencies and flaws. A 1696 production moved John Dennis to complain that the plot made no sense to him and that Mosca and Bonario's movements, which set up the action of Act III, ''seems to me, to be very unreasonable.'' Dennis's additional complaints deal with characterization and Volpone's actions, which Dennis argues, are inconsistent. In 1709, Richard Steele felt so strongly about Jonson's play that he wondered ''why the modern writers do not use their interest in the house to suppress such representations.'' Since many playwrights owned the theatres in which their plays were staged, Steele contends that they should simply ban some plays, rather than take a chance on boring and turning away the audience. Steele continues by saying that after seeing Jonson's comedy the audience will no longer have any interest in attending comedy, since the audience is required to constantly question the characters and plot, and thus these questions, ''will rob us of all our pleasure.'' These questions on characterization continued to plague *Volpone* throughout the eighteenth century. Peter Whalley noted in 1756 that the character of Sir Politic Would-be ''seems to be brought in merely to lengthen out the play,'' since his character appears to serve no purpose. However, Whalley differs from many other writers in that he does admire the characters of Volpone and Mosca and finds that their actions in the final act lend themselves to ''true comic humour.'' An anonymous theatre reviewer of 1771 also admired the plot, which he says ''is perfectly original, ''but the writer goes on to say that that play is best suited to ''afford pleasure in the Closet, than on the Stage,'' since *Volpone* fails to elicit the passion and genius that Shakespeare's plays offer the audience. Jonson was unable to escape Shakespeare's shadow while they both lived, and it appears that 150 years later, the comparisons continued. Certainly, if there had been no Shakespeare, Jonson might be remembered as a greater playwright. But the Elizabethan and Jacobean eras provided some of the greatest dramatic works the Western world has ever known. With competition, such as that offered by William Shakespeare, Christopher Marlowe, John Ford, John Webster, and Cyril Tourneur, Ben Jonson almost becomes lost in a plethora of great dramatists. Of this group, only Shakespeare has emerged with the timelessness of a great playwright. Today, Jonson is staged infrequently, as is the case for all these playwrights

An illustration by Aubrey Beardsley for Volpone.

except Shakespeare. Frequently, audiences must travel to England to see the great Renaissance plays on stage, while Shakespeare is readily available at theatres or on videos worldwide. Jonson would be even more envious than he was nearly four hundred years ago.

CRITICISM

Sheri E. Metzger

Metzger has a Ph.D., and specializes in literature and drama at The University of New Mexico, where she is a Visiting Lecturer in the English Department and an Adjunct Professor in the University Honors Program. In the following essay, she discusses the role of Venice in Ben Jonson's Volpone.

The setting for Ben Jonson's *Volpone,* is Venice. Many Renaissance playwrights, including William Shakespeare, used Venice as a setting for their plays, since this location represented, what many Englishmen considered to be the world's center of vice and debauchery. But, it can be argued that

WHAT DO I READ NEXT?

- Ben Jonson's *The Alchemist*, written in 1610, is another play that uses the farce or the con game as a plot device. In this case, a servant takes advantage of his master's absence to swindle a succession of people with the promise of turning base metals to gold.

- Geoffrey Chaucer's "The Miller's Tale" is another parable about greed. As he did elsewhere in his *Canterbury Tales*, written c. 1387, Chaucer uses an old man's greed and lust to reveal people's vulnerability.

- *Twelfth Night*, by William Shakespeare, was first presented in 1600. Although the plot is not about a swindle, it does involve the use of disguise and trickery to bring about order and resolution. Since Shakespeare was a contemporary of Jonson's, his comedies provide a useful contrast to Jonson's.

- *The Merchant of Venice*, also by Shakespeare, was first presented in 1596. This play likewise involves disguise and deceit, but it is interesting because the ending creates many questions about the definition of comedy. A complete moral resolution is missing, but in the case of this Shakespearean play, the plot raises many complicated questions about prejudice and honesty.

- *The Art of Renaissance Venice*, published in 1993, is a study of the art of Venice. Author Norbert Huse incorporates architecture, sculpture, and painting into one volume containing more than 300 illustrations.

- *Art and Life in Renaissance Venice*, is a 1997 text that attempts to recreate Venice during the Renaissance. In this text, Patricia Fortini Brown tries to answer reader's questions about how the people lived and why Venetian art differs from that of the rest of Italy.

Jonson used Venice better than any other playwright because he depicted it in greater detail. This detail was essential, since Jonson used several of the myths associated with Venice—its sexuality, its wealth, and its corruption. Ralph Cohen, in his essay, "The Setting of *Volpone*," points out that Venice is a setting that functions as symbol and theme, presenting a lurid atmosphere. It is this atmosphere that makes the machinations of Volpone and Mosca appear so believable, and which allows the audience to enjoy the plotting. If the setting had been moved to London, Volpone and Mosca's plots would lack any levity, appearing simply evil. But in Venice, the two easily fit into the city's reputation, where they are only performing as Venetian men are expected to perform. This setting is so essential to the performance of this play, that when Jonson published his *Works,* he left the setting of *Volpone* intact, although he changed the setting of *Every Man in His Humour*. Perhaps he realized that *Volpone* would not work in a London setting.

The audience is never allowed to forget that the setting of *Volpone* is Venice. Cohen points out that to remind the audience of the Venetian setting, Jonson creates two visiting Englishmen, who clearly are out of place in this Italian setting. Sir Politic Would-be and Peregrine represent the innocence of the Englishman abroad, and are juxtaposed with the duplicity of the Venetian men. This subplot is sometimes considered a distraction without purpose, as it was for some eighteenth-century critics. But as Cohen notes, the Englishmen's presence separates the Venetian setting from the London performance, and Sir Politic and Peregrine's meeting allows Jonson to "flavor his play with topical comedy without compromising his setting." London audiences can enjoy the antics and misunderstandings of the two innocent travelers and still imagine themselves as more sophisticated visitors should they visit Venice. The ending of the play, with its harsh punishments, can also serve to remind the audience of yet another of Venice's excesses, its reputation for severe punishment, as it makes the audience thankful, once again, to be Englishmen. Mosca, Volpone, and their three intended victims all receive harsh punishments, as the London audience would expect. This serves to contrast with Jonson's London setting for *The Alchemist,* in which the plotting servant is easily forgiven. Cohen states that London audiences would have known of Venice's harsh justice and would have anticipated a severe punishment. The justice dispensed in the last act, in keeping with reality, would have made the London audience grateful to be Englishmen and not citizens of Venice.

The English response to Venice as a place of great interest and excitement, balanced with a certain amount of trepidation, is based largely on the city's dual nature. Venice was both a city of great beauty, defined by its prominent reputation for art and wealth, and a city of sin, defined by an extensive population of courtesans and the lust associated with excessive sexual freedom. It is not as if there were no prostitutes in London; there were. But in Venice there was an openness, with women readily displayed in revealing gowns, that was missing from London society. Somehow, in the warmth of Venice, sexuality appeared more exciting than in the cold, drafty halls of the London court. Consequently, Venice drew many Englishmen to visit, so many, observed McPherson in *Shakespeare, Jonson, and the Myth of Venice,* that the Pope complained. This duel nature of Venice was also an attraction, since with any adventure, there is an allure in perceived danger. Jonathan Bate quotes a visiting Englishman, whom he says describes Italy as "'a paradise inhabited with devils.'" In his essay, "Elizabethans in Italy," Bate argues that "Italians are characterized by a combination of politeness and perfidy." And yet, there was certainly an attraction to both the politeness and the perfidy. Although many Englishmen were opposed to the Pope and viewed him as a significant threat to Protestant England, Italy remained a popular destination for English visitors. Bate mentions that "since Italy was not a unified country, different impressions were gained from different cities and principalities." Rome had a strong association with the Catholic Pope, but as Bate notes, Venice appeared independent from the Pope and Rome, and it "could be imaged as an anti-Romish island like England itself." Thus Venice could continue to draw tourists to visit, and drew audiences to the theatre. Venice provided the perfect setting—warm and sensual, dangerous and wicked, neither England nor Rome.

> VENICE PROVIDED THE PERFECT SETTING—WARM AND SENSUAL, DANGEROUS AND WICKED, NEITHER ENGLAND NOR ROME"

It provides one other attraction as a setting, according to Bate: "Venice is also a place of performances." Bate mentions that public performance was not limited to the theatre, where women were permitted to act on stage, but ordinary citizens preformed in the streets, with elaborate embraces, kissing, and displays of bare breasts. This street performance is obvious in *Volpone,* when Volpone disguises himself as a Mountebank, who engages in performance upon a small stage, which he erects in the street. The three victims of Volpone's plots are also engaged in performance, as they seek to fool Volpone with their generosity. Of course, Volpone is also directing their performances, all of which illustrate the ease with which Venetians engage in performance, an ease that Jonson adapts to the stage.

Much of the action in *Volpone* is focused on the myths attached to Venice. McPherson says that Venice was frequently described as "rich," and that the city's publicists boasted of the city as the richest city "under the heavens." This wealth is certainly an element in Jonson's play. Volpone is fixated on acquiring more wealth. That he is rich is evidenced in the counting of his riches that occurs in Act I. However, Volpone is not only interested in having more wealth, although it is important to him; instead, he is transfixed by the art of acquiring wealth. This art is also an element of Venice's reputation for political wisdom. McPherson cites the crafty nature of the Venetian, of whom travelers warn, and who should not be trusted. Volpone exemplifies this nature, but he is not alone. Every Venetian male in the play, except for Bonario, is engaged in deception. None of these men is as he appears, and this results in a severe punishment for each. As previously mentioned, Venice enjoyed a reputation for harsh justice. McPherson points out that this Venetian justice "was praised frequently for its severity," frequently by visiting Englishmen. At the conclusion of *Volpone,* Celia pleads for leniency, but is abruptly dismissed by the judges, who think her pleas do her a disservice. It would appear that there is no place in Venetian justice for easy dismissals; in this respect, Jonson is echoing reality, where harsh punishments, including the cutting off of hands, a tongue, or even the putting out of an eye, were expected and accepted.

Another important myth of Venice was its reputation for pleasure. McPherson calls Venice ''the pleasure capital of Europe,'' with many of the pleasures being legitimate. There was art and architecture to be admired, wonderful festivals to attend, and great food to be sampled. The Venetians encouraged tourism and it was a major source of revenue, with much effort placed on pleasing these visitors. But among the pleasures to be enjoyed were those associated with prostitution. According to McPherson, ''the favorite vice to attribute to the Venetians was sexual licentiousness,'' a characteristic was well known to the tourists. McPherson asserts that courtesans made up a significant portion of the population, with estimates running at high as 10 percent. This accounts for Lady Politic Would-be's easy acceptance of Mosca's lie that he saw her husband with a courtesan. Any English tourist would have been effortlessly convinced that, although only separated for a short period of time, one's husband might have been readily approached by and seduced by a prostitute. One by-product of the accessibility of courtesans was that their loose style of apparel was adapted by married women. As a result, married men, who frequented these courtesans, worried when their wife adopted the dress of prostitutes. Venetian men responded with jealousy to their wives' new dresses and to their implied threats. Although some women did stray, McPherson says it was difficult, since husbands guarded their wives so carefully. This jealousy is portrayed in *Volpone,* by Corvino's extreme jealousy of Celia.

It is easy to see why Jonson would not have changed the setting of *Volpone* to London. This play exemplifies many of the elements of Venetian society, which are essential to its success on the stage. A Volpone hatching his plots in the cold, wet atmosphere of London would have held no magic for the audience, with the tragic elements outweighing the comic. But transfer Volpone to the warmth of the wealthy, sensual atmosphere of Venice, and the play becomes a comedy, dependent on the illusion of debauchery to awaken its potential.

Source: Sheri E. Metzger, in an essay for *Drama for Students,* Gale, 2001.

Don Beecher

In the following essay, Beecher traces the legacy of the prankster leading up to Jonson's comedy Volpone.

It was from the *Satiricon* of Petronius and Lucian's *Dialogues of the Dead* that Jonson derived the idea of creating Volpone's Venice as a city of dissemblers divided between he who pretended to infirmity in order to attract gifts and those who feigned friendship and generosity in order to attract the legator's consideration. The patterns of the tale of Eumolpos are visible in the play: the shipwrecked wayfarer who gets rich in a foreign land by posing as a childless old man and by speaking only of his wealth and the rewriting of his testament between fits of coughing. But it was from the tale of the death-feigning fox of medieval legend that Jonson drew the mythological substructure of the play. A Latin bestiary from the twelfth century recounts a version of the tale of the hungry fox who besmears himself with red mud to resemble blood, and who then lies on his back holding his breath in order to attract carrion birds which, as soon as they alight, he grabs and devours. Jonson clearly recognized the analogy between this primordial trickster who maintained himself by audacious cunning and the Romans who fraudulently lured gifts from expectant *captores.* The Roman matter combined with the tradition of Reynard pointed the way towards a more vigorous strain of satiric comedy, such as Jonson had been seeking, one free from the taint of romance and sentimentalism, one which emerged by superimposing the microcosm of the fox upon a portrayal of greed in contemporary society.

Little remains to be said on the thematic and imagistic implications inherent in the allusions to beast fable in *Volpone,* but that the crafty fox serves as an appropriate analogy for the kind of trickster protagonist Jonson depicted is worth further notice. The fox is motivated by a cunning which is instinctual and amoral; he seeks to satisfy fundamental appetites rather than to serve, consciously, any moral or humanitarian ends. His craft is a life-style pervading his entire being and not merely adopted disguise. To the extent that he can be said to be aware of his own acts, the art of pulling a clever jest on the less wary is his supreme joy. His world is a narrow one in which knavery is carried out half as play, half in accordance with the logistics of survival. Such a prankster, with his sheer primitive drive, differs markedly from the festal trickster who assumes disguises in order to achieve precalculated

A scene from the National Theatre's 1977 production of Volpone.

ends, the literary intriguer of learned comedy who presides, by licence, over the creation of rites of passage, gentle ridicule and carnival. Fox is hero in his own world, not servant, and his tricks are the central transaction of the story. In keeping with his nature and the tradition of tales which fostered him, the fox is, typically, now the wily hunter, now the hunted one forced back upon his ruseful resources in order to save his own neck. The tale of the folk trickster contains, characteristically, the waxing hero exulting in his piracy and the waning hero who is made to endure mortification. In *Volpone,* not only is the trickster of folk lore fully accommodated to the English stage as hero, but his rising and falling destiny is redeployed in the context of an intrigue drawn from the conditions of contemporary society. In this lies the substance for a response to Partridge's comment that *Volpone* is ''a drama too complex in nature and unique in effect to be encompassed by the traditional categories.'' Volpone behaves neither as a romantic hero nor as a tragic one despite his magnificence, the apparent depths of his motivation and his so-called flaw and lamentable catastrophe. But there is a subgenre of comedy implicit in the figure of the trickster hero with its own themes and conventions. The rise of this class of comedy is one of the salient achievements of the English theatre in the Renaissance to which there

were notable contributions by several of Jonson's contempories. Yet they were never able to free themselves, as Jonson did, from the established conventions preventing Trickster from arriving at his full dramatic potential. By such a measure *Volpone* attains a special place in the development of intrigue comedy.

If Jonson's handling of the protagonist is an innovative one, it is set even more in relief by the fact that the dramatic tradition which he held in highest esteem, that of Plautus and Terence (and their followers in Renaissance Italy), offered no precedent for the trickster as hero. In Roman comedy he had reached his nadir, both socially and in terms of his ties with the primordial figure. Classical models dictated a highly conventionalized use of the slave whose wits were in the exclusive employ of his master, a commission which invariably entailed, in the cause of true love, the outwitting of a refractory parent or a threatening rival. Though the writers of the *commedia erudita* allowed him more novel disguises and a freer range in their well-honed, multifaceted intrigue plots, he remained a low-life character, monodimensional, subservient to his betters and ever restrained by the variables of plotting which led only to happy issue for the lovers accompanied usually by reconciliation and the prom-

> JONSON'S VISION WAS TO SEE THE DIVERSE MANIFESTATIONS OF SOCIAL TRAFFIC REGULATED BY A VARIETY OF TRICKSTER FIGURES WHO INCORPORATE SELF-INTEREST AND ACCIDENTAL BENEFACTION, WHO ARE MORAL LEGISLATORS AND BUFFOONS, AND WHO, AS MISCHIEVOUS MASTERS OF CEREMONY, PRODUCE NEW ORDER THROUGH THE COMIC JUSTICE IN THE PLAYS WHOSE INTRIGUES THEY UNWITTINGLY DESIGN."

ise of carnival. Jonson refers to the Italian character types in justifying his handling of Volpone's demise and he mentions the *"quick comedy, refined as best critics have designed* swerving *From no needful rule"* as the source of the plotting and general ambiance of the play. These were the conventional utterings of a classicist in action and no doubt Jonson believed he was writing a play directly in the learned tradition. *Volpone* is, indeed, classical in its sense of economy of plot, the following of the unities and its critical attitudes towards excess in the spirit of the Roman satirists. But there were no models among the ancients, or their Renaissance imitators, for the kind of captains of intrigue in which Jonson specialized.

There is a sense in which the rise of realist satiric comedy in England was synonymous with the emancipation and diversification of the intriguer figure as internal plotter and satiric persona. Marlowe, Chapman, and Marston all laboured towards that end. Each in his own way raised the station and intelligence of the trickster figure in order to broaden his social currency, which in turn accommodated him more naturally to the contemporary settings and, as a satirist, gave him access to folly in high places. Marston devised the duke in disguise whose high station and lofty moral purpose guided him infallibly through a maze of trials and obstacles.

Chapman created the urbane, witty Elizabethan gentleman as intriguer. Lemot (*An Humorous Day's Mirth*) is full of verve which he deploys in wooing the puritanical Florilla from her prayer garden to a lovers' rendezvous. But Chapman's calculated moral programming causes Lemot to teach her a lesson by humiliating and scorning her rather than by seducing her on the spot. The moral design of the trickster-intriguer's role is more veiled in Rinaldo (*All Fools*) and Lodovico (*May Day*) who evince greater sense of the primordial trickster's love of freedom, the outsider's pleasure in controlling the destinies of others, the drive for personal expression and the joy of sheer waggery. Yet, they remain subordinate in position to the lovers they serve, they are untainted by material ambitions of their own, and they serve plots which must make the metamorphosis from satire into the neutralized atmosphere of festival. The progress of both writers in relation to the dramatic tradition was marked and both achieved a form of literary trickster drama. But it was Jonson who turned the comic intriguer into a self-serving knave, driven by appetite and greed, who set him up as a rich magnifico and the central protagonist of the play. Volpone harbours no concern either for his victims or the good of his society. He is free from all the restraints of the intriguer compounded of conscious literary attitudes and functions. In his new freedom he becomes synonymous with the ancient prankster who had not died out entirely in the native story-telling tradition.

Volpone has no direct literary forebears in the native theatre, but there are a handful of plays which feature prankster rogues, in some cases even as heroes, from which Jonson no doubt drew certain fundamental lessons. Chapman's *Blind Beggar of Alexandria* comes to mind as *Volpone's* closest relative, since the hero is not only a prankster of the first order but styles himself as an oriental magnifico on his way to becoming King of Egypt. In this episodic multi-disguise plot the knave of the Interlude peeks through, without doubt as part of the burlesque of the Marlovian hero Tamburlaine, which Chapman surely intended. Irus sets up a confidence operation in which he poses as a sage clairvoyant who makes prophecies which he is able to fulfil through a series of adopted disguises. His gulls include a nobleman, three beautiful sisters and the Queen herself. His most outrageous achievement is to marry two of the sisters at once, giving the third to his parasite Pego, and then to cuckold himself twice by seducing each wife as the husband of the other. (Of course, by eliminating a disguise he could eliminate a wife, a rather neat trick in any age.) The play has none of Jonson's hard polish or satiric intensity, but it does prefigure the ambitious master trickster in love with power and sheer devilry. A detail of interest is that Pego, like Mosca, reminds his master at the end of the action of all he knows and could reveal about Irus' devious climb to power and so claim a greater share in the spoils. Chapman lets the matter fall because the parody would have collapsed with the mortification of the hero, but he was aware of the dramatic potential in the situation. That this play has so many correspondences with *Volpone* should be submitted with the caveat that it belonged, at the same time, to a class of multiple-disguise plots, which by 1600 had run its course with such plays as *Look About You* and *The Blind Beggar of Bednal Green* and had all but disappeared. More important, Irus is a mono-dimensional figure who lacks those qualities which pertain to the trickster of folklore.

The folk trickster, in his most fully realized state, possesses a double nature which makes him both the hunter and the hunted at once. He is an outsider who is both a marauder and a mocker who shames his victims into conformity. He maintains at once the ways of the prophet and apostate, the benefactor and the bandit. It is this inter-relationship of opposites which is the key to his character. Endemic to trickster is what Herford and Simpson called "the fatuities of the overweening." The more dangerous and thus exhilarating the exploit, the greater the risks in executing it, and thus the greater the risks of being cashiered. Self-confidence blinds and the greatest tricksters invariably precipitate themselves towards error or self-betrayal. This dual nature does not make the character complex in himself, but it provokes complex reactions in those who watch him pass through a society. In *Volpone* the benefactor's contribution, the satiric exposure of gulls, is a by-product of the trickster's own pursuit of wealth, pleasure, and, above all, the joys of artful intrigue.

> *I glory*
> More in the cunning purchase of my wealth,
> Then in the glad possession; since I gaine
> No common way (I.1.30–3),

declares Volpone. Even when all hope of gain is past, he takes to the streets in another disguise for the sheer delight of further plaguing his victims. The double dénouement of *Volpone* is in perfect keeping with the character of the pristine trickster; like Chaucer's Russell the fox in *The Nun's Priest's Tale,* who now enjoys the victory of his sophistry, now suffers humiliation for his folly, Volpone knows perfect success before he puts his head in the noose.

The Winnabago trickster cycle, which is one of the finest of the Amer-indian literary legacies, offers several examples of this dual nature of the trickster. In a rapid succession of tales the hero demonstrates his remarkable inventiveness and his naïve stupidty. In one adventure he seduces the chief's daughter across a lake with his infinitely extendible penis; in another he allows it to be whittled down to size by a sharp-toothed woodchuck while employing it to prod the beast out of a hollow log. In this way trickster forfeits his god-like phallus, yet redeems himself as a benefactor by planting the retrieved pieces which produce edible tubers of great value to his tribe. Trickster stories generically tell how the hero both deceives and is deceived in keeping with his nature; both tales are seen to be equally comic.

Trickster undertakes these adventures merely to express himself, amuse and furnish himself, which he cannot do unless he has a society to sport with, nor can he pass through that society without altering it for better or for worse. Jonson realized that the best story is not that in which the trickster is made to carry the author's moral burden as part of his own psychological outlook and the rationalizing voice behind his every deed, but that story in which he struggles to do his worst and nevertheless produces an unforseen good. Volpone was Jonson's ironic maker who created a well-turned comic artifact which both teaches and delights. As in the earliest trickster tales, Jonson sees how social benefit, cultural development and moral stability come about by accident through the civilizing force of trickster.

Comedy depends for its success on its capacity to regulate the degrees of distance between the action and the observer, between the artifice which feigns the real and the intellectually perceived values and judgements which the play raises. This has to do with the kind and degree of spectator involvement with the actions and characters. The fully realized trickster hero poses certain problems which Jonson renders particularly subtle by superimposing in the plot of *Volpone* the tales of the fox in the ascendant and the fox in decline. The fox in the ascendant invites a special attachment. Mosca boasts that he can "*Shoot through the aire, as nimbly as a starre,*" which we must admire, in spite of lingering moral reservations. In the combined performance of these two knaves there are brilliant deceptions, a compelling use of verbiage and sheer audacity. Their intrigues are carried out in an atmostphere of serious play. We support their strategies in a context from which we are eager to transfer the joys of the victors to ourselves, the fundamental goal of any spectator sport. Jonson has arranged for our involvement and carries us with them to the pinnacle of success. After extricating themselves from the court scene in Act IV, Mosca gloats and warns at once:

> *Here, we must rest; this is our master-peece;*
> We cannot thinke, to goe beyond this (V.2.13–14).

Irony abounds as we discover just how far beyond this they are determined to go. But for a moment we sense the full flush of victory, the satisfaction of having prevailed momentarily in a situation of pure knavery. In a related sense, we also abandon ourselves to the entire topsy-turvy world as to a carnival. L. A. Beaurline suggests in reaction to the overmoralized views of Jonson's comedy, that it should be viewed as having ''a more relaxed, playful air, tempting spectators to enjoy and perhaps give tacit assent to decadent but delightful release of inhibitions.'' Here is therapy through the release of aberrant impulses and through self-projection into the illusions of the comic theatre.

Jonson's own best trick as comedian is to let us align ourselves with the rogues until we too are exposed for our complicity. We are fascinated by the dizzying centrifugal force of the intrigue, the ever more daring ventures and the more spectacular saves. In the spirit of play we want the game to go on and we invite the heroes to greater dangers, seeking for ourselves, as does Volpone, one last ''*rare meale of laughter.*'' At the same time we are implicated in the moral ambiguities of their behavior. Through the introduction of a code of legal values into this world of criminal schemes, our involvement in the sport is brought up short. We are forced to detach ourselves through sober reflection. But it is not a reflection about the personal destiny of the hero. He is but the animator of a whirligig which carries us along until the scheme explodes from sheer internal pressure.

This brings us to the tale of the trickster in defeat. Trickster out-tricked is never tragic; his foolishness leads him to the absurd which is risible by definition. He never laments his fate and does not ask it of others. As Paul Radin explained, the aboriginal trickster can never be philosophically motivated, for the moment he becomes self-conscious, his powers to act capriciously and ruthlessly

are impeded by his own mind. Volpone never reflects upon his deeds; when he goes down he is merely deflated. As Quomodo, the intriguer in *Michaelmas Term,* says after he is caught out, ''*for craft, once known, / Does teach fools wit, leaves the deceiver none.* '' The trickster is a born overreacher, engaging in his successes, comic in his defeat. The Lord Admiral's Men kept a bevy of such plays in their repertory, perhaps best characterized by the title of the now lost play, *'Tis No Deceit to Deceive a Deceiver,* indicating both the degree of comic justice and the lack of culpability which pertained to the central transaction of the play. Volpone shares in common with such plays the tradition of the rogue repaid in kind.

Una Ellis-Fermor speaks more appropriately of Samson than of Volpone when she says that ''with one last terrific gesture, utterly unbefitting a comedy and all but precipitating it into tragedy, Volpone pulls down disaster upon himself and his enemy alike.'' She goes on to compare him with the Duchess of Malfi who stood so nobly alone in the final hour of her life. But such reflections hail from romantic sensibilities alien to Jonson's comedy. To be sure, with the proper degree of abstraction, a sense of the narrowing sphere of operations and the feigned sickness and death which prevent Volpone from returning to a state of normalcy may be nursed into intimations of tragedy. One may assume that Volpone's desperate rush for the rewards of the game, for wealth and sexual pleasure, reflect a degree of fear, longing, and a suspicion that all is a cheat. Something Faustian can be teased out of the patterns of mutability, the *carpe diem* images, the grandeur of Volpone's stature and the fact that he loved the sport more than the rewards. Such a Volpone must go down, unfulfilled, a victim to insensitive justice. But Marlowe, himself, saw the other side in Barabas the Jew of Malta, who plays his hand in a serious game with malicious verve and vitality. In the end he, too, is double-crossed and finds himself in a boiling cauldron destined for his enemies, where he continues to shout in a final burst of remorselessness. Like *Volpone,* this play defies easy categorization and for many of the same reasons, including its parody of tragedy. T. S. Eliot called it a ''serious farce.'' No gull is so comic as he who believes that everyone else is his gull. That irony excites laughter in the cases of Voltore, Corbaccio and Corvino. So it must when Volpone and Mosca follow suit. And where we must laugh at the knave we must also laugh at ourselves if we have been so tender as to take him to our bosom.

In *Volpone* Jonson achieved, willy-nilly, a resurrection of trickster comedy with his promotion of the comic intriguer to the level of a guileful voluptuory. He recaptured the fundamental antinomies of the trickster nature, the scourge and the buffoon, and he understood the alternating of tales of success and failure. There is one further innovation to Jonson's credit in this play, namely the mechanism required to reveal dramatically these two sides of trickster's nature. Jonson's technique was to develop the conventionally static relationship between master and and servant into a dynamic one in which the parasite uses his inside position to defraud his patron, thereby reversing the fortunes of the protagonists. The concept was available to Jonson in a number of seminal forms, any of which he could have relied upon for triggering his management of the dénouement in *Volpone*. The master-servant relationship in drama is at least as old as Aristophanes and no doubt was the substance of comic scenes in the mimes before that. Plautus' Palaestrio in the *Miles Gloriosus* is perhaps the most outstanding example from the Roman period of the slave whose wit enabled him to abuse his master relentlessly even while he was busy cozening him out of his mistress. So effective is the flattery that he is able to get away with money, the girl (who is restored to her former lover), and his own freedom. A different model, nearer to hand, is the Ithamore-Barabas entente in the *The Jew of Malta* in which Ithamore tries to blackmail his master and, failing that, manages to confess all of his nefarious deeds before Barabas' poisoned flower was able to silence him. Here is a sequence of double-dealing prefiguring the double betrayals in *Volpone*. Herford and Simpson argue cogently for an even nearer source in Jonson's own Roman history play *Sejanus* which deals essentially with "the league of two noble villains, master and servant, ending in a deadly struggle between them." It was through a development of this pattern that Jonson found the means to mortify his fox. Jonson's handling of the dénouement of *Volpone* is a variation on the plot of the servant who attempts to usurp his master's wealth and position. Both villains struggle in a contest for supremacy with an uncertain outcome. Such an employment of trickster bears little relation to the witty servant of romance comedy whose success is guaranteed by the sacredness of the cause he espouses. Master and servant, in turning upon one another in active combat, produce a wholly different model of action through which the satirist can indict the follies of greed and ambition.

In *Volpone* both the patron and the parasite ostensibly work together; both are tricksters wholly dependent upon one another for the advancement of their confidence game. Yet by degrees, the audience comes to appreciate Mosca's burgeoning sense of independence. The high-tide of their confederacy and the height of Mosca's sense of injured merit arrive simultaneously. When the gulling of the others was complete there was no other direction possible except an internecine struggle. The imperturbable Mosca took note of his master's nervous sweating during the court scene and counted it for a weakness. Where he had been wont to say "*Alas, sire, I but doe, as I am taught; / Follow your graue instructions*" he changed for, "*You are not taken with it, enough, me thinkes?*" Mosca has not only been in disguise to the gulls, but to Volpone as well, with his camouflage of flattery. Yet if Volpone underestimated his knave for cunning, the latter underestimated his master for pride and stubbornness. This was the final phase of the game by which they had lived and sportsman-like they carried it through to the victory or the defeat which every such context must hold in store. It is in precisely that spirit that Mosca declares his intentions:

> *To cosen him of all, were but a cheat*
> Well plac'd; no man would construe it a sinne:
> Let his sport pay for't, this is call'd the Foxe-trap.

Mosca had not calculated Volpone's one remaining trump, that one which was furnished by the conventions of comic art. Volpone opted to strip away his mask, preferring a double check-mate to an uncontested victory for his parasite. Justice was ready to serve sentence once the truth was out, but it was the last all-or-nothing toss which brought about that revelation. In this way the two cats of Kilkenny reduced themselves to none.

Trickster is the comic projection of one dimension of human nature, a greater-than-life embodiment of the appetites which he attempts to satisfy through his wits. Success and failure alike bring laughter to those who look on. Such a being delights in imposing his view of the world upon others, who often imagine themselves to be doing the same but who are merely victims of delusions and self-betrayal. This is why the trickster is so valuable to the comic plotter and to the satirist. The essence of the character is unchanging, but individual tricksters are always products of national mentalities and individual geniuses working on the materials of their own times and cultures. Jonas Barish claimed that "the most obvious trait of Jonson's style, its realism, thus brings to a climax a process toward which comedy had been moving for generations, perhaps since its origins.'' Jonson, in *Volpone*, was on his way home from his literary peregrinations in the classical world and on the verge of finding comedy in the streets and halls of London. His revival of old forms was partially an archeological enterprise, but he made his forms appear to spring *sui generis* from the unique circumstances generated in his plays. Jonson's vision was to see the diverse manifestations of social traffic regulated by a variety of trickster figures who incorporate self-interest and accidental benefaction, who are moral legislators and buffoons, and who, as mischievous masters of ceremony, produce new order through the comic justice in the plays whose intrigues they unwittingly design. In keeping with his picture of a society driven by greed and rapaciousness Jonson devised the confidence artist as hero. It was a master stroke, taking the trickster hero to his apogee in *Volpone* after a long period of development. Marlowe, Chapman, and Marston had already supplied trickster with new guises and contemporary habiliments, but Jonson freed him from conventional roles, from socio-moral subservience, rediscovering the dual nature of the primal folk hero. These alterations had such a powerful reorienting effect that the standard definitions of comedy must expand to accommodate them.

Source: Don Beecher, ''The Progress of Trickster in Ben Jonson's *Volpone*,'' in *Cahiers Elisabethains,* April, 1985, Vol. 27, pp. 43–51.

C. N. Manlove

In the following essay, Manlove argues that the ''instructive'' and the ''delightful'' elements of the play are ''increasingly opposed during the play.''

Current discussions of the ''instructive'' and ''delightful'' elements in *Volpone* (1604) tend, variously, to accept that both are united to give a single dramatic effect. The object of this article is to reargue the case that the two elements are increasingly opposed during the play.

In common with the comedy next written by Jonson—*The Alchemist* (1610)—the subject of *Volpone* is the gulling of dupes for profit by schemers; there are many incidental points of similarity in the plots and ''humours'' of both plays. Yet *Volpone* has a character very different from that of *The Alchemist*. Where Jonson's story of the magnifico is set in the luxurious and exotic world of Venice, *The Alchemist* takes place in London, in the house of the bourgeois Lovewit. In *Volpone* the bumbling Eng-

lish traveller, self-appointed man of the world and manipulator, Sir Politic Would-be, and his wife, whose assumptions of refinement only the more surely reveal her vulgarity, point up the gulf between the English temperament and that of the supersubtle Venetians, to the advantage of the latter. The world of *Volpone* is on a far grander scale than that of *The Alchemist* or *Bartholomew Fair* (1614). Volpone has enormous wealth and is surrounded by an array of dwarves, eunuchs and parasites who minister to him and execute his purposes. He demands far more of those he gulls than Subtle and Face do in *The Alchemist*. Not only does he demand large sums of money or valuable jewels and plate, but he even demands of the obsessively jealous Corvino, his own wife. The most in this respect which Subtle and Face ask in *The Alchemist* is his sister of Kastriland her name is Pliant. Moreover, the performance in court of one of Volpone's dupes, the lawyer Voltore, goes far beyond that required of any character in the later play: when, at Volpone's instigation, he for a second time retracts a false case made by him against previous defendants, he pretends to have been possessed and feigns a fit in which he vomits out ''evil spirits.'' The nearest we come to this performance in *The Alchemist* is Dapper's enforced sojourn in the jakes. In *The Alchemist* too the payments exacted by Face and Subtle of their clients—Mammon's andirons, the dollars of the Puritans, Drugger's tobacco or portague, Dapper's twenty nobles or his ''paper with a spur-ryal in't''—are trivia by comparison, typified by the final inventory of the ''confederacy'':

> *Face.* Mammon's ten proud; eight score before. The Brethren's money, this. Drugger's and Dapper's. What paper's that?
>
> *Dol.* The jewel of the waiting maid's, That stole it from her lady, to know certain—
>
> *Face.* If she should have precedence of her mistress?
>
> *Subt.* Yes.
>
> *Dol.* What box is that?
>
> *Subt.* The fishwives' rings I think, And th' alewives' single money. Is't not, Dol?
>
> *Dol.* Yes, and the whistle that the sailor's wife Brought you to know and her husband were with Ward.
>
> *Face.* We'll wet it tomorrow; and our silver beakers, And tavern cups. Where be the French petticoats, And girdles, and hangers?
>
> *Subt.* Here, i' the trunk, And the bolts of lawn.
>
> *Face.* Is Drugger's damask there? And the tobacco?
> (V. iv. 108–21)

With these vulgar commodities we can be more familiar, as indeed with the wishes of most of the gulls. But with the desire of the rich to be richer still, as we find it in *Volpone,* there is much less scope for this level of engagement.

The motives of the gullers are also different. Volpone loves wealth not because it gives material or social advancement, but because it gives power: he is in his way a megalomaniac. He is by no means a miser, for he keeps an extensive house and has luxurious tastes. He simply worships money because of its magnetic strength of attraction, its power to break all other links which stand in its way and draw in its victims. Wealth is seen as the focus of the universe:

> Hail the world's soul, and mine! More glad than is
> The teeming earth to see the longed-for sun
> Peep through the horns of the celestial Ram,
> Am I, to view thy splendor darkening his;
> That lying here, amongst my other hoards,
> Showst like a flame by night, or like the day
> Struck out of chaos, when all darkness fled
> Unto the center. O thou son of Sol,
> But brighter than thy father, let me kiss,
> With adoration, thee, and every relic
> Of sacred treasure in this blessed room.

Every other value is transcended, swallowed by wealth, until riches become God himself. Volpone sees the substance that is gold, like God, reducing all else to shadow by its sheer facticity:

> Thou being the best of things, and far transcending
> All style of joy in children, parents, friends,
> Or any other waking dream on earth.

What fascinates him is the image of the stasis of wealth that puts all other things in a state of flux, the sheer inertia of this mineral which engrosses to itself all states of existence or value that are above it in the scale of being:

> Dear saint,
> Riches, the dumb god that givst all men tongues,
> That canst do nought, and yet mak'st men do
>   all things;
> The price of souls; even hell, with thee to boot,
> Is made worth heaven! Thou art virtue, fame,
> Honor, and all things else. Who can get thee,
> He shall be noble, valiant, honest, wise—

In these lines Olympian detachment combines with complete commitment: Volpone speaks in apparently detached wonder at the power of gold and yet can testify to that power over himself. In the last three lines he is saying both, "You subsume all value," and "Look how benighted man is, that he will attribute to one who is wealthy all spiritual value." This double position of involvement and ironic distance is the key to Volpone's motivation in the play: it enables him to jest while he is in earnest, to laugh at the follies of the gulls who seek his

> " THE POINT IS THAT VOLPONE AND MOSCA ARE NOT TO BE STOPPED BY OUTSIDE FORCES . . . BUT STOPPED BY A PROCESS WHICH WILL MORE FULLY EDUCATE THE READER IN THE NATURE OF EVIL, A PROCESS INVOLVING SPONTANEOUS COMBUSTION."

money while he delights in the power of, and homage paid to, his wealth. The essence is to do nothing while others do everything: as his gold is "lying here," so too does Volpone for most of the play on his sick bed, attended by a constant succession of would-be heirs. The stress is on the enclosed nature of his world: he does not go out to get his wealth, for it comes to him without his stir; he does not have an impact upon the outside world, for that world is pleased to visit him:

> I gain
> No common way: I use no trade, no venture;
> I wound no earth with ploughshares; fat no beasts
> To feed the shambles; have no mills for iron,
> Oil, corn, or men, to grind' em into powder;
> I blow no subtle glass; expose no ships
> To threat'nings of the furrow-facèd sea;
> I turn no monies in the public bank,
> Nor usure private—(I. i. 32–40)

What begins as a picture of the sophisticated manner in which he makes his gold turns into a protestation of innocence—"I do not interfere with the world." But it is interesting that he conceives the hurting which he has avoided more as a hurting of things, not of people: the earth is not wounded except under the terms of the pathetic fallacy, or unless one considers the earth to be animate. Fatting beasts to feed the shambles is not generally considered cruelty. The upset of hierarchy behind Volpone's words is seen in the way he speaks of "iron, / Oil, corn, or men" as the same sort of commodity for mills and in his picture of the mills as causing suffering to inanimate substance the same way they cause suffering to men ("grind 'em into powder"). Thus when he speaks of ships rather than of men exposed "To threat'nings of the furrow-facèd sea," we are inclined to take the ships simply as vessels rather than as vessels containing men—an inclination reinforced by the animate status given to the sea. Aware, no doubt, that this protestation of innocence is somewhat misdirected, Mosca now turns it to more human contexts:

> No, sir, nor devour
> Soft prodigals. You shall ha' some will swallow
> A melting heir as glibly as your Dutch
> Will pills of butter, and ne'er purge for't;
> Tear forth the fathers of poor families
> Out of their beds, and coffin them, alive,
> In some kind, clasping prison, where their bones
> May be forthcoming, when the flesh is rotten.
> But, your sweet nature doth abhor these courses;
> You loathe the widow's or the orphan's tears
> Should wash your pavements, or their piteous cries
> Ring in your roofs, and beat the air for
>   vengeance—(I. i. 40–51)

He covers a range of impact from the soft prodigals, who might deserve their loss, to the innocent, who would not: again the portrayal of Volpone's guiltlessness is founded on his self-enclosure, not on any distinction he makes between those who deserve fleecing and those who do not. Moreover, in the very manner which Mosca paints the refusal of his master's "sweet nature" to seize on the undeserving and cause pain to their families, along with his equal refusal to "devour" prodigals and "melting heir[s]," we see that no such sweet motive really exists; we are nearer the truth in Volpone's objection to any invasion of his privacy by tears washing his pavements or by piteous cries ringing in his roofs (an objection portrayed in his reactions to Lady Would-be throughout the play).

What we have in Volpone is a man whose scale of values is entirely perverted by money, but who, at the same time, without applying the condition to himself, is able to see how wealth overthrows all values in other people. He is a man who has taken on an Olympian position, but who himself is one of those he mocks—a man who is in a fundamentally ironic position throughout the play. Hence, a part of his weakness is that he who manipulates others can himself be manipulated. Mosca is not plotting Volpone's ruin when he raises his interest in Corvino's wife Celia in terms of her likeness to gold; he is playing on his master's Pavlovian responses:

> Bright as your gold! and lovely as your gold!
>
> *Volp.* Why had not I known this before?
>
> *Mos.* Alas, sir, Myself but yesterday discovered it.
>
> *Volp.* How might I see her?

> *Mos.* O, not possible; She's kept as warily as is your gold, Never does come abroad, never takes air But at a window. (I. v. 114–20)

Celia, spiritually Volpone's opposite, is like him and his wealth in that she never goes out to the world (though in her case she is imprisoned). Yet, this portrait of her by Mosca draws Volpone to abandon his usual posture: he is forced to go out to someone rather than have them come to him. That inconsistency is in fact the beginning of his undoing.

Like his master, Mosca is at pains to disconnect himself from the world, even from himself:

> Success hath made me wanton.
> I could skip Out of my skin, now, like a
>   subtle snake,
> I am so limber. O! your parasite
> Is a most precious thing, dropped from above,
> Not bred' mongst clods and clodpolls, here on
>   earth. (III. i. 5–9)

He goes on to distinguish himself from inferior sorts of parasites whom he sees as tied to the earth and to pleasing the senses of their masters:

> I mean not those that have your bare town-art,
> To know who's fit to feed 'em; have no house,
> No family, no care, and therefore mold
> Tales for men's ears, to bait that sense; or get
> Kitchen-invention, and some stale receipts
> To please the belly, and the groin; nor those,
> With their court-dog-tricks, that can fawn
>   and fleer,
> Make their revènue out of legs and faces,
> Echo my lord, and lick away a moth.
>   (III. i. 14–22)

In some degree, by thus refusing the conventional image of the parasite, Mosca is denying that he is, finally, dependent on his master in the way that others are—a prognostic of his later truancy. The picture of his own class of parasite which follows continues the idea of separation from the earth in the vision of his movements in terms of an aerial being:

> But your fine, elegant rascal, that can rise
> And stoop, almost together, like an arrow;
> Shoot through the air as nimbly as a star;
> Turn short as doth a swallow; and be here,
> And there, and here, and yonder, all at once;
> Present to any humour, all occasion;
> And change a visor swifter than a thought.
>   (III. i. 22–29)

In the last two lines the notion of constant metamorphosis is so pitched as to suggest total loss of any inner and fixed identity. Indeed it is by constant movement, rather than the stasis of other parasites, that Mosca characterizes himself—an interesting contrast with Volpone's praise of his gold or with his own supine position for most of the play. Mosca further separates true parasites from the idea of earthliness or from any public dependency when he makes a Horatian distinction between those parasites who are born dependent and those who have to learn the craft:

> This is the creature had the art born with him;
> Toils not to learn it, but doth practice it
> Out of most excellent nature: and such sparks
> Are the true parasites, others but their zanies.
> (III. i. 30–33)

The true parasite is not dependent on anything outside himself for the knowledge of his craft; we are reminded of Volpone's severance from the world.

Both Volpone and Mosca have a form of creative delight in their schemes: the gulling of Corvino, Corbaccio and Voltore is engineered not so much for gain as for the pleasure that results from skillfully-managed deception and for the mirth that arises, whether from the success of the deceptions themselves or from the way that the gulls are only too ready to assist in their own duping. After Mosca has persuaded Corbaccio to disinherit his son and make Volpone his heir, expecting that out of gratitude for such generosity the dying Volpone will in turn make Corbaccio his heir, Volpone is almost beside himself with laughter:

> O, I shall burst!
> Let out my sides, let out my sides.
> *Mos.* Contain
> Your flux of laughter, sir. You know this hope
> Is such a bait it covers any hook.
> *Volp.* O, but thy working, and thy placing it!
> I cannot hold; good rascal, let me kiss thee.
> I never knew thee in so rare a humor. (I.
> iv. 132–38)

Typical of their relationship is the mobility with which Mosca engineers the fun for the static Volpone to enjoy, and typically, too, he cunningly disclaims responsibility and dupes his master:

> Alas, sir, I but do as I am taught;
> Follow your grave instructions; give 'em words;
> Pour oil into their ears, and send them hence.
> *Volp.* 'Tis true, 'tis true. (I. iv. 139–42)

This delight in creativity, however perverse, gives enormous zest and energy to the play. Such energy is missing from *The Alchemist,* where the gulling of people who believe in the powers of alchemy is carried on specifically as a business venture for gain by the league of Dol, Face and Subtle.

It is an energy which, however immoral by all the canons, themes or imagery of the play, threatens to upset the norms invoked. Here it is worth contrasting Volpone with the luxur of *The Alchemist,*

Sir Epicure Mammon. When Volpone is attempting to seduce the virtuous Celia, he tries to sway her with a picture of the sensuous delights they may both share:

> See, behold,
> [*Pointing to his treasure.*]
> What thou art queen of; not in expectation,
> As I feed others, but possessed and crowned.
> See, here, a rope of pearl, and each more orient
> Than that the brave Egyptian queen caroused;
> Dissolve and drink 'em. See, a carbuncle
> May put out both the eyes of our St. Mark;
> A diamond would have bought Lollia Paulina
> When she came in like star-light, hid with jewels
> That were the spoils of provinces; take these,
> And wear, and lose 'em: yet remains an earring
> To purchase them again, and this whole state.
> A gem but worth a private patrimony
> Is nothing; we will eat such at a meal.
> The heads of parrots, tongues of nightingales,
> The brains of peacocks, and of ostriches
> Shall be our food, and, could we get the phoenix,
> Though nature lost her kind, she were our dish.
> (III. vii. 188–205)

Unnatural, of course, but beautiful—and alive. The rhythm almost enacts Mosca's picture of the true parasite, rising, stopping, shooting and turning. The run-on lines make these pleasures mobile, not stagnant, as do the rising and dipping rhythms: "See, behold . . . / Dissolve and drink 'em''; "See, a carbuncle / . . . That were the spoils of provinces" (not quite a full close, followed by the dolphin-like rhythm of "take these, / And wear, and lose 'em: yet remains an earring / To purchase them again, and this whole state"). Compare this with Mammon:

> I will have all my beds blown up, not stuffed:
> Down is too hard. And then mine oval room
> Filled with such pictures as Tiberius took
> From Elephantis, and dull Aretine
> But coldly imitated. Then, my glasses
> Cut in more subtle angles, to disperse
> And multiply the figures as I walk
> Naked between my succubae. My mists
> I'll have of perfume, vapored 'bout the room,
> To loose our selves in; and my baths like pits
> To fall into; from whence we will come forth
> And roll us dry in gossamer and roses. (II.
> ii. 41–52)

The rhythm is no longer various, but stops and starts in short breaths, flopping inert at each cadence: "Down is too hard," "From Elephantis," "But coldly imitated," "To loose our selves in," "To fall into." Where in Volpone's lines the partial cadences come on significant injunctions, here we see them fall on mere desultory afterthoughts, "Down is too hard," "From Elephantis," "and dull Aretine / But coldly imitated." Each item is one in a list, and has a corresponding deadness: ''my beds,'' ''And then mine oval room,'' ''Then, my glasses,'' ''my succubae,'' ''My mists,'' ''my baths''; and his continual use of ''my'' limits his pleasure by possession, where Volpone's impersonal pleasures seem more independent and alive. It seems apt that the element of collapse—losing, falling and rollingshould become explicit in the last lines. Mammon's speech continually deflates itself rhythmically, pointing up not only his limited sensual capacity, but puncturing the absurdity of his pictures—''I will have all my beds blown up, not stuffed; / Down is too hard,'' ''multiply the figures as I walk / Naked between my succubae'' (suggesting sudden detumescence).

Other features in *Volpone* besides the energy and creative delight of both Volpone and Mosca make our—and Jonson's—attitude to them more complex than simple condemnation, although the imagery and their thematic placing by such standards as inversion of value or self-enclosure ask us to condemn them. For one thing, all the would-be heirs whom Volpone and Mosca gull are portrayed either as disgusting and depraved birds of prey (Corbaccio, Corvino and Voltore) or as vulgar fools (Lady Would-be), so that we can be led to feel that their manipulation gives Volpone and Mosca a certain moral credit, however much they share their standards of value. Secondly, the energy and wit of Volpone and Mosca, when compared to the stupid monomanias of their victims, make us admire the former for reasons which have little to do with morality, in precisely the way that we admire a fine performance.

What then of Jonson's view? In *The Alchemist* the schemer Face is forgiven at the end for his practices when the master of the house returns, and that master's name is Lovewit. Of course, neither the deeds nor the mind of Face are in any way as corrupt as those of Volpone, and there is less to forgive; however, the name, Lovewit, nonetheless reveals the draw on Jonson himself to admire a scheme well and wittily handled. We may also observe that his bringing in the virtuous innocents in *Volpone* may well have been the product of a sense that the play was getting up and walking away with the moral nail; conversely, from his dedicatory Epistle, we know how uneasy Jonson subsequently was at the way he hammered it down again. As we have said, the effect of surrounding Volpone and Mosca with evil and stupid characters is to make them the more admirable, however much their language and attitudes may reveal moral perversion: it may be that, aware of this, Jonson tried to make sure

of damning Volpone and Mosca by having them hurt innocence as well. The result, as has often been remarked, is unfortunate: Celia and Bonario, not belonging to the world of the action, come as a jolt, not least in their language:

> Forbear, foul ravisher! libidinous swine!
> *He leaps out from where* MOSCA *had placed him.*
> Free the forced lady, or thou diest, impostor.
> But that I am loth to snatch thy punishment
> Out of the hand of justice, thou shouldst yet
> Be made the timely sacrifice of vengeance,
> Before this altar, and this dross, thy idol.
> [*Points to the gold*.]
> Lady, let's quit the place, it is the den
> Of villainy; fear nought, you have a guard;
> And he ere long shall meet his just reward. (III. vii. 267–75)

This language recalls the stridency of the brothers of the Lady in Milton's *Comus;* it has even the smack of some of Jonson's Puritanical figures about it. That Jonson feels the need to insert such a direct judgment into the play suggests that he feels Volpone to be flying above moral censure.

What control Jonson has over Volpone and Mosca comes as we have seen through the imagery of perversion; it should also come through the plot. For at the end Jonson tells us through the First Advocate that the play has demonstrated a process whereby evil eventually always destroys itself: ''Mischiefs feed / Like beasts, till they be fat, and then they bleed'' (V. xii. 150–51). The point is that Volpone and Mosca are not to be stopped by outside forces (Bonario and Celia are easily outwitted and imprisoned thanks to the twisted testimony of Volpone's dupes in court), but stopped by a process which will more fully educate the reader in the nature of evil, a process involving spontaneous combustion. First Volpone, having heard of the beauties of Corvino's wife Celia, goes forth disguised to see her. Then Mosca eventually succeeds in persuading Corvino to bring her to his master at a fixed time. Meanwhile Mosca brings Corbaccio's son Bonario to overhear his father disinherit him before Volpone (and so perhaps be fired to slay his parent, leaving Volpone heir), but when he arrives at Volpone's house he finds that Corvino, anxious to make certain of his chances, has come with Celia before he was due. Mosca therefore places the now suspicious Bonario out of hearing in a book gallery, hoping to keep him there and to delay Corbaccio's approach while Volpone interviews Celia. Nevertheless, Bonario does overhear Volpone with Celia, and the first court case must then ensue if he is to be silenced.

We may at this stage ask whether Mosca might not have sent Corvino home again rather than compound his difficulties with a "Well, now there's no helping it, stay here"; and we may too ask why Mosca is wrong in his calculation that Bonario will not hear anything from the gallery (we are not told that he has come any nearer, but that "*he leaps out from where Mosca had placed him*" (III. vii. 268)).

In court Bonario and Celia are both discredited, not only through the machinations of Volpone's dupes, particularly the lawyer Voltore, but through the corrupt timeserving nature of the advocates; outside factors will not be able to destroy Volpone. When Volpone returns from court, he says,

> Well, I am here, and all this brunt is past.
> I ne'er was in dislike with my disguise
> Till this fled moment. Here, 'twas good, in private,
> But in your public—*Cave,* whilst I breathe.
> (V. i. 1–4)

But instead of resolving to lie quiet for a time and consolidate his success, he decides to proceed even further in his schemes. His reason is that if he did not he might fall ill of his fears:

> A many of these fears
> Would put me into some villainous disease
> Should they come thick upon me. I'll prevent 'em.
> Give me a bowl of lusty wine to fright
> This humor from my heart. Hum, hum, hum!
> *He drinks.*
> 'Tis almost gone already; I shall conquer.

Yet he does not stop there:

> Any device, now, of rare, ingenious knavery
> That would possess me with a violent laughter,
> Would make me up again, (V. i. 14–16)

This scheme, of course, eventually becomes one of making Mosca his heir. The motivation is clearly tenuous. That the cautious fox should so risk himself with another plot goes against the grain of what we expect; that he should attempt this scheme even when most of the unanticipated motive for so doing has been removed by the drink is even more hard to accept. Mosca, when now called for, puts the first point:

> We must here be fixed;
> Here we must rest. This is our masterpiece;
> We cannot think to go beyond this (V. ii. 12–14)

and Volpone later is astonished at how we could have been so foolish:

> To make a snare for mine own neck! And run
> My head into it wilfully, with laughter!
> When I had newly 'scaped, was free and clear!
> Out of mere wantonness! O, the dull devil
> Was in this brain of mine when I devised it.
> (V. xi 1–5)

Even then he does not know that his scheme has allowed Mosca to betray him. One wonders how Volpone proposed to undo the trick. One solution might have been for him to have servants take him to court on a stretcher and there to claim that Mosca had locked him up and forged a will in his favour (we are told that only the name has to be filled in (V. ii. 71–73)). Clearly Volpone had no such notion in mind: he seems to have been determined to blow up the gulls' hopes for good, without considering what they could do against him in reply ("I will begin e'en now to vex 'em all, / This very instant" (V. ii. 56–57)).

Again, Volpone could have used the way out just suggested when he discovers Mosca has betrayed him (and after he has just beaten his breast over his previous stupidity). Instead he goes to the court to bargain with Mosca and then, that failing, to bring down his parasite with himself by disclosing his own identity. If we are to take this behavior as typical of him, we must begin to find the name "Volpone" (the fox) a little inapposite. The more reasonable view here, however, is surely that the motivation is thin and that this thinness is unconsciously deliberate on Jonson's part. He is unwilling to show Volpone as self-destructive by any other than partly trumped-up motives.

Objections to the fifth act of the play as forced rather than natural were first expressed by Dryden in 1668 and expanded by the dramatist Richard Cumberland in 1788; Jonson himself also reveals doubts in his dedicatory Epistle. Yet modern criticism has so far attacked these views to the point where Jonas A. Barish can claim:

> The inquest opened by Dryden into the structural peculiarities of Act V would seem to be closed; few today would dispute Swinburne's and Herford's verdict, that Volpone's compulsive resumption of his hoaxing, far from being a desperate shift to galvanize a flagging plot, forms one of the master strokes of the action.

The word "compulsive" is the key to most current opinion of what drives Volpone forwards: it is said that he is incapable of rest and is driven on to his end by poisoned creative exuberance which has grown throughout the play. No one, however, seems to have considered that while this may partly be true, it would better be brought home to us if Volpone had not been portrayed as he is in Act V, scene i, where he expresses his fears at the degree to which he has already overreached himself. Nor has it been remarked that he could have saved himself even after going further and that, to this extent, the "dull devil" which he berates in himself continues long after its supposed dismissal-in-recognition. Moreover, there is disparity in the fact that V. ii, the first scene in the play which Volpone rather than Mosca arranges, reverses the earlier dichotomy of Volpone exerting power while static and Mosca while in motion.

Jonson could not, as we have seen, let Volpone get away with it in this play because he has, at least in the first scene, and in much of the imagery, subjected him to moral analysis. However, as he wrote he came to admire his own creation to the extent that he could not find it in him to give the creation fully adequate motives answering to the governing notion of evil being self-detonating.

Source: C. N. Manlove, "The Double View in *Volpone*," in *SEL: Studies in English Literature: 1500–1900,* 1979, Vol. 19, pp. 239–52.

Ralph A. Cohen

In this essay, Cohen discusses the significance and detail of the setting of Volpone.

Theseus' observation that poets give "to airy nothing a local habitation and a name" is nowhere more confirmed than in the works of Ben Jonson. To his great plays Jonson has given local habitation a hundred names and made the sense of locale in those plays almost tangible. His plays are filled with scenes that go beyond an attempt to suggest a place and try instead to re-create it in all specifics. Where Shakespeare would supply a setting with a few bold impressionistic strokes, Jonson etches in every detail with Hogarthian thoroughness. Jonson first toyed with a precisely imagined setting in *Every Man out of His Humour* in 1599, but he did not approach setting consistently until he wrote *Volpone* in 1606. From that time on, Jonson takes pains to locate his comedies in a strict geography. The deliberate setting of *Volpone* functions as symbol, as theme, and as a principle of unity and dramatic tension; it suggests the extent to which setting is structural, not ornamental, in Jonson's great plays.

Jonson's choice for *Volpone* of an Italian—specifically, a Venetian—setting contributes to what C. H. Herford describes as a "lurid atmosphere." In the eyes of Jonson's English audience, Italy "represented the very acme of beauty and culture, of licence and corruption." And of all Italian cities, Venice, as Herford points out, "stood in the front rank for this sinister repute," so that "to make the Fox a Venetian grandee was thus to give him and his

story the best chance of being at once piquant and plausible."

To the Englishman, Venice was the most fabulous of wealthy Italian cities; it was a place where houses were "worthily deserved to be called, Pallaces, some hundred of them being fit to receive Princes...." Venice was a city famed for its jealous husbands and closely kept wives on the one hand, and for its courtesans and brothels on the other. Thomas Coryat marvels that such "places of evacuation" were necessary "for the gentlemen do even coope up their wives always within the walles of their houses ... as much as if there were no Cortezans at all in the City." The reputation of Venice for licentiousness was matched by its reputation for harsh justice, and the *Catastrophe* of *Volpone* reflects not only Jonson's own strenuous morality but also the fame of a Venetian punishment "sufficiently severe and righteous to frustrate ... the villainy its society presumably tolerated."

This reputation of Venice for vice, opulence, jealousy, and cruelty made Jonson's choice of it as the setting for *Volpone* not simply a sound one, but the *sine qua non* of the action, the characters, and even the language of the play. Little wonder that when Jonson published his *Works* ten years later he used *Volpone* as it stood and did not transfer it to London as he did his other important play with an Italian setting, *Every Man in His Humour*. But Jonson was not the first English dramatist to appreciate the aptness of Venice as a setting for a play about greed and harsh judgment. What separates the Venice of Volpone from the Venice of Shylock is Jonson's detailed depiction of that setting.

Jonson clearly establishes the Venetian setting of *Volpone* and preserves that setting consistently throughout. Unlike the Florentine setting of the first *Every Man In* (Quarto), for example, the Venice of *Volpone* does not grow transparent and reveal, as the play progresses, a thinly disguised London beneath an Italian setting. Unlike the *Insula Fortunata* of *Every Man Out,* the Gargaphy of *Cynthia's Revels,* or the Rome of *Poetaster,* the Venice of *Volpone* is not meant as an allegorical London. Nor has Jonson created, as he did in *Poetaster,* a setting which, though true to the Italian model, is carefully drawn to resemble London. Venice is simply the best setting possible for the play, and throughout *Volpone* Jonson's steady execution of that setting shows he knew its value.

The care with which Jonson draws the Venetian setting of *Volpone* anticipates the accuracy and technique of his finest London comedies, and this despite the fact that Jonson never visited Venice. Jonson's diligence appears in the references to currency, in allusions to literature and politics, in the language, and in the imagined topography of the play. Twelve kinds of coin are named in *Volpone,* more than in any other of Jonson's plays, and his use of six denominations of Venetian currency testifies to his careful research. Nowhere does an errant reference to English money spoil the consistency of the setting.

Jonson shows the same care with respect to works of literature. In the Milan of *The Case Is Altered,* Jonson alludes at length to the English stage. In the Florence of *Every Man In* (Quarto), the fops steal poetry from Heywood and Marlowe and pay homage to Kyd's *Spanish Tragedy.* Despite their settings of Gargaphy and Rome, *Cynthia's Revels* and *Poetaster,* respectively, are extended references to the literary society of London and are designed as salvos in the *Poetomachia.* Only *Volpone* of all Jonson's non-English comedies is innocent of displaced allusions to English letters.

Even the allusions to public figures and history show Jonson's eagerness to give *Volpone* an accurate Italian setting. Volpone, as Scoto, searching for a simile to express his rejuvenated appetite, tells Celia he is "as fresh / As hot, as high . . ." as when he acted Antinous for "the great Valoys" (III. vii. 157–162). The reference is to a 1574 reception for Henry of Valois, the Duke of Anjou, given by the Doge and senators of Venice—a reference perfectly apt for a Venetian in 1606 who is recalling his youth.

The most obvious way in which Jonson has matched the language of *Volpone* with its Venetian setting is the occasional Italian term with which he has seasoned the speech of the play's characters. Italian vocabulary that finds its way into this English play includes: *sforzati,* "gallie-slaves"; *scartoccios,* "a coffin of paper for spice"; *canaglia,* "raskalitie, base people, the skum of the earth"; *gondole; saffi,* "a catchpole, or sergeant"; *clarissimo,* a grandee; *strappado,* a Venetian torture; and *Pomagnia,* a popular wine in Venice. Jonson's attention to these Italian touches as well as his care in such details as literary references and coinage contributes bit by bit to the exotic and foreign atmosphere of the play as a whole.

But the language of *Volpone* heeds the location of the play in a more important way: only the two tragedies avoid the tones and rhythms of everyday London speech more carefully than *Volpone.* From

the elegance and blasphemy of Volpone's hymn to his riches—"Good morning to the day, and next my gold"—Jonson maintains a heightened verse in keeping with the reputation of Venice for the perversely exotic. Nowhere in the play is there a trace of the lower-class colloquial English found in every Jonson comedy from *A Tale of a Tub* to *The Magnetic Lady.* Although the London travelers—Peregrine, Sir Politic and Lady Would-be—provide some relief from the sumptuousness of the play's language and emphasize its foreignness, even they do not speak in the English of the London streets.

Indeed the English subplot is itself a clever device for separating the Venetian setting from London. First, the very presence on the scene of two "affectate travellers" is a constant reminder that London is *not* the setting of the play. Second, the harmless English folly of the Sir Politic Would-bes acts as a foil to the vicious Italian knavery of the other characters and thus enhances the menacing Venetian atmosphere. And third, by channeling all topical English allusions into the Would-be scenes, Jonson can flavor his play with topical comedy without compromising his setting. Act Two, scene one, for example, in which Sir Politic enlightens Peregrine on the subject of international intrigue while Peregrine reports the news from home, is a veritable gazette of current London news and gossip, but in the context of two Englishmen meeting abroad the whole scene serves to emphasize the Venetian setting.

The most impressive aspect of London's thoroughness in creating his Venetian setting is his handling of place itself. There are forty-four topographical allusions to Venice in *Volpone.* Altogether, including Venice, thirteen different places are mentioned. Venice is referred to sixteen times, St. Mark's Cathedral eight times, the Piazza of St. Mark's five times, the *scrutineo* or court four times, the port twice, and eight other locations once each. By contrast, in *The Merchant of Venice,* though Shakespeare refers to Venice seventeen times, the only other place name he mentions is the Rialto. These numbers confirm the importance of setting to the playwright; since Jonson had never been in Venice, such allusions cannot be the echo of actual experience but are rather a conscious effort to provide an accurate and thorough background. This nearly documentary approach to dramaturgy appears to have been fundamental to Jonson's larger purpose—the making of a unified play.

The Prologue declares, ''The lawes of time, place, persons he observeth'' (1. 31), and, in fact, Jonson strictly enforces the unities of time and place. By setting all of *Volpone* in Venice, Jonson easily fits the action into a single day, a feat he had already managed in *Every Man In, Cynthia's Revels,* and *Poetaster. Volpone,* however, represents a significant development in Jonson's technique, not because the action of a day is limited to one city, but because the action is confined to a certain part of a city. In this play Jonson begins the technique he never abandons of focusing his comedies within the sharp outlines of a narrow and well-conceived section of a city. Jonson squeezes the action of *Volpone* into the Piazza of St. Mark's and its surrounding buildings.

The text specifically locates all the scenes except Sir Politic Would-be's quarters and Volpone's house itself. Ten of the play's scenes take place in the Piazza of St. Mark's, which Sir Politic calls ''this height of Venice.'' Three more—the three at Corvino's house—take place in ''an obscure nooke of the piazza'' for which it is likely that Jonson envisioned no movement at all, but intended that the scenes be played on the upper stage, while the main stage continues to represent the piazza. Nine scenes are set in the *scrutineo* or senate house that makes up one side of the Piazetta adjacent to the main piazza. Thus Jonson sets twenty-two of *Volpone*'s thirty-nine scenes in the most renowned section of Venice, the magnificent Piazza of St. Mark's and its adjoining Piazetta. Of the seventeen unlocated pieces in the puzzle, one is Sir Politic's house, for which there simply is no evidence, and sixteen are Volpone's house. Having so scrupulously conceived the other parts of the setting, Jonson would hardly have been

indifferent to the location of Volpone's house in his imaginary Venice. The care, moreover, with which Jonson has placed the majority of the scenes around the center of Venice strongly suggests that he envisioned all of the play within a narrow scope of the city, namely in close proximity to the piazza.

Such a conjecture finds support in Volpone's taunt to Voltore in V. ii:

> I meane to be a sutor to your worship,
> For the small tenement, out of reparations;
> That, at the end of your long row of houses,
> By the *piscaria:* it was, in Volpone's time,
> Your predecessor, ere he grew diseas'd,
> A handsome, pretty, custom'd bawdy-house,
> As any was in Venice (none disprais'd)
> But fell with him; his body, and that house
> Decay'd, together.
> (ll. 7–15)

The phrases, ''fell with him,'' and ''his body, and that house / Decay'd, together,'' suggest that Volpone is talking about his own lodging, a place corresponding in both moral and physical terms with the nature of its master—a decayed ''bawdy-house.'' The ''*piscaria*'' in Venice was on the wharf along the south side of the piazza. In light of the configuration of the other settings and in view of this reference to Volpone's ''long row of houses, / By the *piscaria,*'' Jonson apparently envisioned all of the action, including that at Volpone's house, in the area of St. Mark's Piazza.

The question is ''why?'' Later, Jonson's extraordinary care in limiting and locating the settings of his London comedies might have given his audience a good deal of fun, but the audiences who saw *Volpone* would not even realize, much less enjoy, Jonson's precision with the Venetian setting. I would like to suggest that the limited and detailed setting first used in *Volpone* and thereafter in *every* Jonson comedy worked as a principle of construction for the author. It provided him with a framework that resulted in the tensions, the atmosphere, and the unity that have come to be associated with Jonson's great work. Beyond whatever sense of ''being there'' his deliberateness gave the audience, the careful setting unifies and heightens the action, enhances the symbolism of the spatial relationships on and off the stage, and lends meaning to the play.

For the playwright, the cumulative effect of the many concretely imagined details of the piazza in *Volpone* is that of a container which unifies the action simply by keeping its different parts in the same place. Madeleine Doran has rightly pointed out that unity of place is not an end in itself but a way of insuring unity of action. Because the scope of the setting is limited, Sir Politic can break off his conversation with Peregrine to watch Volpone perform nearby as the mount-bank; Mosca, leaving Corvino's house, can meet accidentally with Bonario; Lady Would-be, leaving Volpone's house to apprehend her husband, can find him in the piazza with Peregrine; and so on. Thus the limited imaginary setting helps Jonson hold the various actions together. Working from this premise, Jonson can give the audience a sense of concentration that leads in turn to a heightened excitement, because the container, which confines Jonson's action so closely that the characters must frequently meet one another, raises the audience's expectation of collision.

By extending the principle of movement within an imaginary container to the action on the stage—the visible container—Jonson achieves the intense expectation of collision which is the essence of the excitement in *Volpone* and *The Alchemist*. In both plays, Jonson creates excitement by a theatrical application of Boyle's Law—he puts more and more characters into a chamber in quicker and quicker succession, and thereby increases the probability of collision and the exhilaration of each near miss. In *Volpone,* Mosca's deft shuffling of the dupes in and out of Volpone's house generates tension until they collide at the end of Act Three, while in *The Alchemist* the three rogues prolong and aggravate the tension until Act Five. The excitement in both the London play and the Venetian play is a function of Jonson's carefully concentrated setting—both on the stage and in the narrowly conceived section of the city beyond.

His precisely delineated setting helps Jonson establish the symbolic significance of the spatial relationships on stage. As simple a relationship as "high" and "low," for example, acquires a rich complexity. In the mountebank scene the stage is divided into three levels: the stage floor, the platform on which Volpone speaks, and Corvino's balcony. Sir Politic, Peregrine, and the "flock" stand on the first; Volpone as Scoto of Mantua, on the second; and Corvino's wife, Celia, on the third. Their positioning on stage is a visual comment on each. The mob, fooled by Volpone's disguise, represents the fox's victims and is, therefore, on the bottom; Volpone, a Venetian grandee who preys on the greedy but is unable to corrupt the virtuous, is situated above the crowd but below Celia, who, as befits her name, is placed nearest heaven and out of the reach of Volpone. Logically, Corvino, who is in the house, should be above to discover Celia at the window, and his extreme jealousy would erupt there on the spot. But since the appearance of such a despicable character on the highest level with the innocent Celia would destroy the careful symbolism of the spatial relationships, Jonson has preserved his high-low scheme by having the enraged Corvino appear on the stage floor level to chase Volpone/Scoto away.

Jonson also uses the "in" and "out" spatial relationship on stage for its symbolic impact. Volpone's house, particularly his room—the inner sanctum—is the goal of all the scoundrels and, therefore, the play's symbolic "in." When Mosca betrays Volpone in V. v, he expresses his triumph in terms of in and out: "My Foxe / Is out on his hole, and, ere he shall re-enter, / I'le make him languish, in his borrow'd case . . ." (ll. 6–8). Though being "in" the fox hole after the fox is gone is the ambition of all the dupes, the metaphor cuts the other way as well, for Volpone's room is, above all, a trap. Corvino, Voltore, Corbaccio, and Lady Would-be are all caught in that "Foxe-trap," but the scene that most vividly expresses the negative sense of "in" as entrapment is III. vii, where Celia, dragged into Volpone's room by her husband, is caught by the Fox and pleads, "If you have touch of holy saints, or heaven, / Do me the grace, to let me scape" (ll. 243–244).

Jonson establishes an over-all opposition of place within the play. Volpone leaves the safety of his lair to prey on the innocent Celia and his subsequent assault on her brings in the opposite moral pole—the *scrutineo*. Through Mosca's brilliant manipulation, he and his master escape the Venetian justices and return to Volpone's inner sanctum. Act Five finds Volpone secure and ready to bring his plans to fruition, but Volpone's desire to torment his victims makes him leave his house in Mosca's hands and the tricky servant springs the "foxe-trap." From this point on, the action is determined by the play's second magnetic field—the *scrutineo*—where all the scoundrels are punished and the play ends. Thus the fifth act repeats in miniature the movement of the play by restating the struggle between Volpone's house—pleasure, falsehood, and lawlessness—and the *scrutineo*—severity, truth, and law. At the opening of the act, Volpone and Mosca are in control of events in the fox's lair; then Volpone's arrogance moves the action to the piazza, away from the safety of his house; and finally the forces of law represented by the *avocatori* take control of the action, resolve the complications, and punish the evildoers.

The often-remarked severity of the play's conclusion voices Jonson's own response to the meaning of the play's setting. Venice was renowned in the English mind for its excesses—in wealth, in beauty, in corruption. That atmosphere of excess exaggerates familiar domestic faults: it transforms jealousy into the viciousness of Corvino; turns the misunderstanding between father and son into the bitter enmity of Corbaccio and Bonario; materializes the dreams of a voluptuary into Volpone's attempted rape of Celia; surpasses a charlatan's promises with Volpone's actual wealth; transmutes the folly of English "gulls" into the frightening avarice of the carrion birds—Corvino, Corbaccio, and Voltore; and inflates the pranks of clever servants and the con games of rogues into the crimes of Mosca and Volpone. These excesses were rooted in the English concept of Venice, and Jonson responded to them by using yet another reputation of Venice—its harsh justice—to punish its sins.

Volpone might fairly be viewed as a turning point in Jonson's work for the public stage. In *Volpone* he treats setting with a deliberateness which is surprising in view of his earlier comedies but which signals his approach to place in the masterpieces that follow—*Epicoene, The Alchemist,* the revised *Every Man In,* and *Bartholomew Fair.* The Venice of *Volpone* is much more than appropriate ornamentation for Jonson's play. Although, like Shakespeare, he chose Venice because his audience associated that city with wealth, corruption, viciousness, and judicial severity, Jonson drew Venice with an unparalleled accuracy and detail. His remarkable care in such matters as references to coins, history, and literature, and his obvious research into Venetian topography bespeak a purpose in his methodical madness. Through these efforts, he provides the imagined world of the play with a fixed and detailed setting and with a narrowly limited field of action. Jonson's best comedies share these two characteristics in their settings and reflect their benefits. Primarily, such a setting provides Jonson's plays wtih a sense of concentration. It can accelerate the movement of characters from place to place—an effect he exploits in *Epicoene.* It can increase the plausibility of a chance meeting and raise the expectation of collision, thus heightening the excitement of the play—a device most dramatically demonstrated in *The Alchemist.* Perhaps most important, the tightly drawn setting accounts for what T. S. Eliot calls Jonson's "unity of inspiration"—his ability to "do without a plot"—by holding the various actions so tightly together that

they appear intertwined—a technique fundamental to the coherence of *Bartholomew Fair.* Jonson's handling of setting in *Volpone* is a departure from his earlier work, a departure that corresponds with and in part explains the beginning of his greatest period.

Source: Ralph A. Cohen, "The Setting of *Volpone*," in *Renaissance Papers,* 1978, pp. 64–75.

Dorothy E. Litt

In this essay, Litt shows the relationship between the seemingly incongruous themes in the play, which many criticize "for its seemingly irrelevant subplot, fool interludes, and mount-bank scene, as well as for the near-tragic tone of its denouement."

Ben Jonson's *Volpone* has for centuries been acclaimed a masterpiece; yet it has been condemned for as long a time for its seemingly irrelevant subplot, fool interludes, and mountebank scene, as well as for the near-tragic tone of its denouement. With these charges against it, the play has nevertheless won such admiration and respect as to suggest that there is much in it to be appreciated which, though overlooked by the critics, must be implicit in its performance.

In 1953 Jonas A. Barish took the first step toward finding a connection between the main plot and the subplot by identifying their respective protagonists as Volpone and Sir Politique Would-bee, justifying their relationship through the theme of disorder. Although his interpretation opens up possibilities for greater appreciation of the play, the so-called discordant parts remain so for the most part, and the analogy between Volpone and the knight seems forced, since there is little parallel in the play's action to support the relationship.

A more meaningful analogy may be found by contrasting Would-be with Volpone's would-be heirs. Peregrine exploits the knight's desire to appear sophisticated and knowing in the subplot, just as Volpone exploits his clients' desire for his gold in the main plot; each is the "center attractive" of his own plot. In both cases it is their victims' blindness which makes their exploitation possible. In their victims' blindness we find the unifying theme for the play: self-deception. Through this theme the subplot may be seen to mirror the main plot; the would-be sophisticate operates in a world of folly, while the would-be heirs operate in a world of vice.

Jonson, by this theme, strikes at a universal human characteristic, as perverse as it is persistent, to believe what flatters our hopes at the expense of denying truth. It is a tendency as timeless and ubiquitous as Oedipus' refusal to believe Tiresias in ancient Thebes, or as Willy Loman's denial of his own truth in contemporary Brooklyn.

We are offered numerous variations on this theme, revealing how all men fall victim to self-deception when they are tempted sufficiently to hope for impossible goals. In every case in the play, except for Lady Would-be, the handmaiden of self-deception is flattery; thus the flattery of others, whether open or subtle, causes each to flatter himself into faith in false hopes. Not only simpletons like the Would-bes succumb, but crafty fortune hunters as well as brilliant manipulators like Volpone and Mosca yield to this deceptive self-flattery.

The knight and his lady are clearly self-deceived in their desire to appear worldly. Volpone's suitors, too, willfully blind themselves to the truth because they want so desperately to win his fortune, although they see clearly enough when they choose. Each has a moment of doubt which is instantly set aside at Mosca's equivocal reassurances. None seriously questions how Volpone could be dying for so long a time, or that Mosca is the exclusive "creature" of each to the exclusion of all the others.

Unlike the Would-bes, Volpone and Mosca are neither simple-minded nor merely crafty and blinded by false hope. Their great success lies in their self-knowledge; Volpone glories in being an old fox and Mosca takes pride in being a parasite. Neither is flattered by the professions of love and concern by Volpone's clients. Mosca is clearly never deceived by them; he, further, makes it his business to expose each suitor to his master (except for Lady Would-be, who, as a result, Volpone later reveals he believes loves him). Yet eventually Volpone and Mosca also deceive themselves, revealing the all-pervasive power of self-deception more emphatically; mocking the blindness of their victims these clever deceivers succumb to that same malady.

From the earliest moments in the play Volpone reveals a predilection for flattery, foreshadowing his ultimate capitulation to it. It is generally assumed that Volpone's downfall begins when he supposedly "overreaches" himself by feigning death, but it really begins in the first scene of the play, when we find him boasting that he earns his gold in "no common way." Mosca slyly converts his master's claim into a moral statement through flattery:

> But your sweet nature doth abhorre these courses;
> You lothe, the widdowes, or the orphans teares

> IF THE THEME OF SELF-DECEPTION IS ACTUALLY THE KEY TO THE PLAY, AS I HAVE SUGGESTED, IT SHOULD BE SUPPORTED IN THE PLAY'S DENOUEMENT, AND SO IT IS, BUT IN A PERVERSE WAY THAT IS PECULIARLY JONSON'S OWN. JONSON PUTS A 'SNAFFLE' IN THE MOUTHS OF HIS CRITICS, SHOWING WHY VICE *CANNOT* BE PUNISHED IN HIS 'INTERLUDES'—IT WOULD NOT TRULY 'INSTRUCT TO LIFE' AS HE IN THE 'OFFICE OF A COMIC POET' IS OBLIGED TO DO."

> Should wash your pauements; or their
>   pittious cryes
> Ring in your roofes; and beate the aire, for
>   vengeance.—(I.i.48–51)

The unsuspecting Volpone melts in agreement: "Right MOSCA, I doe lothe it." Shortly each of these claims will be violated: Celia's tears shall wash his floor, and Corvino's betrayal shall make her plight as pitiable as any widow's, while Bonario, financially orphaned by Mosca's plot, shall soon cry out for vengeance.

Mosca goes on to flatter his master's generosity, and Volpone, enchanted with Mosca's vision of him as a generous patron, reciprocates with a gift. In spite of being realistic about his clients Volpone is as malleable as they when he is flattered. It is significant that we see Mosca flatter Volpone *before* he flatters the fortune hunters. Jonson meant us to see the parallel, which differs only in timing; Volpone's descent into self-deception is gradual, while the clients' is an accomplished fact from their first moments on the stage.

Volpone begins to hope for the impossible once he decides to win Celia through Mosca's efforts. Helena Baum considers his passion "heroic," and few commentators have observed that it is mis-guided and doomed to failure. Yet Volpone's passion is precisely what Jonson derides in him; a successful old fox with clients who cooperate in deceiving themselves, Volpone is out of his depth as a lover. Celia, unlike the clients, is singularly unimpressed by his flattery and has no desire to join him in the sports of love. His refusal to recognize this, after their first few moments alone, makes his lyrical outpourings ridiculous and self-deceptive. And when Celia promises to ''report, and thinke'' him virtuous if he will only release her, he reveals a new, unrealistic interest in appearances that had not interfered with his dealings with his clients:

> Thinke me cold,
> Frosen, and impotent, and so report me?
> That I had NESTOR'S *hernia,* thou wouldst
>   thinke. (III.vii.260–62)

He has altered his motive: he now wants only to prove his manhood. His sudden degeneration from wooing in Catullus' vein to raping in Tarquin's becomes highly comic. Celia's terror, however, contrapuntally played against this changing mood from lover to rapist, makes the scene one of the high points of satire in the play, for it reveals self-deception in a more serious light. Indeed Volpone's short-lived career as a lover is singularly ill-starred; he is beaten by Corvino, shunned by Celia, and ignominiously discovered by Bonario. It is not accidental, surely, that Volpone dons the costume of a mountebank to play the lover.

Not only does Volpone fail to win Celia, but his seeming victory at court, won at the cost of his being publicly declared impotent, is Pyrrhic for a man who has begun to fancy himself a lover. We see him, indeed, in ''dislike'' with his disguise for the first time, and it is his dislike for the price he has to pay, I believe, that leads him to abort his lucrative venture by giving out that he is dead. He has been undone in appearances just as he has begun to believe in them.

Like his master, Mosca also falls victim to flattery, but he is somewhat more realistic. He flatters himself at his great success with Corvino, which leads him to boast that he is superior to all other parasites (III.i.13–22); yet each quality he scorns in ordinary parasites is evident in himself. Mosca also begins to deny reality, as he joins the ranks of the Would-bes. Taking pride in being able to assume any shape, he is later deceived into believing that he may don the costume of a grandee and thereby be one in reality. He forgets that he is only a parasite, dependent on his patron, forgets, too, that his most potent weapon with his master is

flattery. Once he becomes blunt, Volpone, no longer blinded, exposes their venture—to Mosca's surprise, whose cynical view of mankind has not taken into account the fact that men need not act like animals, although the would be's of the play do. Mosca thus deceives himself when he overestimates his own ability and underestimates his master's.

The play reveals exceptions, those who do not deceive themselves—because they are never tempted into unrealistic hopes. In the main plot these are Volpone's fools, who tell of their metamorphoses from Apollo in a steady downward process of degeneration but, ironically, never into self-deception. All the would-be's desire to be other than themselves, but the fools willingly remain fools. Their deformities are visible, hence undeniable; appearance and reality are united in their physical deformity, affording ironic contrast to the moral and spiritual deformity of the main characters.

The deformed trio of the main plot are fools by profession and entertain Volpone; in the subplot Peregrine pretends to be a fool with Sir Politic—to entertain himself. At first glance it would seem that Barish's thesis was supported by a certain correspondence here between Volpone and the knight, but in it lies another of the play's ironies. Those who act as fools are only such in appearance; those they serve are the true fools in their self-deception. Volpone in his would-beism is like Sir Politic, but in his disabused exploitation of his clients he remains the counterpart of Peregrine.

Long ago the exchange between Volpone and Mosca in V.ii.18–27 was pointed out, by William Gifford, as the best ''defence of the plot of the Drama.'' In it Volpone tries to understand his suitors' blindness, and Mosca, the shrewd psychologist, points out:

> True, they will not see't.
> Too much light blinds 'hem, I thinke.
>   Each of 'hem
> Is so possest, and stuft with his owne hopes,
> That any thing, vnto the contrary,
> Neuer so true, or neuer so apparent,
> Neuer so palpable, they will resist it—

Hope blinds each would-be to the truth. And something has prevented the critics who pause to comment on this passage from seeing its wider application, not simply to the fortune hunters, but to all the major characters of both plots, except Peregrine and the fools.

To recognize self-deception as the unifying theme can be to comprehend the importance of the mountebank scene in II.ii, which has often been criticized for its length, or indulgently tolerated for its color. It is a key scene in the play structurally as well as thematically. In it Volpone steps out of his role as fox to take on the role of lover, i.e. to become seriously involved in self-deception. The preceding scenes have been devoted mainly to exposition— introducing the world of gold-worship in I.i, the ironically ideal world of the fools in I.ii, Volpone's suitors in I.iii to I.v, the subplot, the world of folly, in II.i. The mountebank scene opens the action proper. Volpone is smitten by Celia's beauty; Mosca sets out to win her for him; from this scene forward Volpone resigns his role as chief manipulator to Mosca, reclaiming it partially when he decides to revenge himself on his clients by pretending to be dead, but not fully regaining it until his final confession.

Self-deception speaks in the imagery of the scene: Scoto's oil, a metaphor for flattery, makes it possible. The oil is dispensed by Mosca to gull the clients and his patron; by Peregrine to Sir Pol, in the oblique form of feigned innocence, which flatters the knight into a conviction of omnipotence; by Voltore to smooth his way with the Avocatori. In II.vi Mosca cynically tells Corvino that Scoto's oil has restored his dying master, which we may take as a way of saying that Volpone has flattered himself into believing that flattery (and gold) may win the love of Celia. As for the powder Scoto offers her, the magic powder of cosmetics is the means whereby women deceive themselves. Later in the play the flattery of the Aesopian raven by the fox is applied to the would-be heirs as Volpone taunts his suitors in his guise as commandadore.

The correspondence between the two plots develops in the play's ensuing action, which is propelled by accusations and counter-accusations which are similar in nature and outcome, although different in regard to veracity. Volpone is accused of attempted rape while Peregrine is accused of attempted seduction of Sir Politic. Both charges are dropped at the Lady's intervention under Mosca's direction, and apologies are thereupon made to those accused: the court apologizes to Volpone and the Lady apologizes to Peregrine. New charges are then made: Celia and Bonario are accused of being a team of prostitute and pander, and Peregrine makes the same charge against the English couple. The difference in seriousness of the charges is in keeping with the worlds of vice and folly which the plots reflect.

The two actions are linked, further, in Sir Politic's imagined plots, which find their counterpart in the real plots of the main action. Whereas he imagines plots exist everywhere, the would-be heirs ignore the real plots which flourish all about them; each is blind to the schemes of the others against him as well as to the Fox's plot against them all. The protagonists of both actions revenge themselves by mortifying their victims through their faith in false plots: Volpone uses the fortune-hunters' faith in his own plot, which is based on the belief that he is a dying man, to pretend that he is dead; Peregrine exploits the knight's faith in intrigues to pretend that he has been accused of intriguing against Venice. Volpone, in disguise as a court officer, humiliates his victims, while Peregrine, in disguise as a merchant, parallels Volpone by making the knight crawl literally. Finally, both protagonists show by example that deception need not lead to self-deception, for each strips himself of his own disguise.

Linking both actions is the role of Lady Would-be, who acts as a catalyst, but does not fully belong to either action. She is a would-be heir, like the other clients, and a would-be sophisticate like her husband, yet she is different from the others in that she affords no pleasure to Volpone or Peregrine, both of whom enjoy ''milking'' their other victims. Further, while everyone else is named for what he really is, her title indicates only what she *should* be, an English gentlewoman—the role in which everyone in the main action sees her. Her uninhibited freedom in a society which restricts its women shocks Volpone, Mosca, and even Nano, who sits in judgment on no one else in the play. (It is of course ironic that Volpone and Mosca should sanctimoniously deplore her behavior just as they are about to arrange for Celia's seduction.) Peregrine, however, is totally unimpressed by the Lady's title. She is different from all the others, moreover, in being the only character who is chastised in both actions, and the only one of the would-be heirs who is not punished in court. Jonson's purpose in setting her apart from the others would seem to be to make the point that even a fool may become vicious in a vicious environment.

Another of Jonson's purposes in using the Lady to span both actions may be found in examining Mosca's role, which also encompasses both actions, for his hand guides her; he is thus responsible for a tonal change in both through the Lady's intervention. In the main action he is responsible for the most bitingly satiric scenes: Corvino's offering Celia, Volpone's subsequent attempt at seducing her, and the first court scene. In the subplot, too, he is responsible for the farcical tone established by the Lady's accusation of Peregrine. Hence Mosca's intervention on Volpone's behalf from the mountebank scene when he takes the reins, with the Lady as his assistant, may be seen as a third line of action which sits astride and commands the worlds of vice and folly. He is thereby responsible for the sombre tone which has struck the notice of so many commentators.

Through the third line of action Mosca becomes the third protagonist and we find another variation on the theme of self-deception. A clever young Englishman manipulates a would-be sophisticate to entertain himself and the consequences are comic and benign; a Venetian voluptuary manipulates would-be fortune-hunters for gold and the consequences are still comic but less benign, yet not altogether to be condemned; a Machiavellian manipulates whomever he can out of contempt for mankind and the consequences may be deadly and tragic; such consequences are averted only because the Machiavellian is himself trapped in self-deception and thereby overreaches himself.

Another link between the worlds of vice and folly may be found in Sir Politic's schemes, which function on two levels; on the surface they are comic, and for this reason have been virtually ignored by commentators. Barish, however, notes that the onion scheme has ironic value as a reminder of the "moral plague prevailing in Venice," and all three schemes indeed serve to mock self-deceivers who are plagued by lies they cannot distinguish from truth. The knight plans to sell red herrings to Venice if his two "mayne" projects fail. From its use in the text the term "red herring" would seem to have meant for Jonson what it is commonly understood to mean today, that is, a false scent, an attempt to divert attention from the issue at hand. Sir Politic offers his schemes at a crucial point in the play, in the first scene of Act IV. Immediately thereafter we are deluged by red herrings in false accusations which carry equal weight with the truth. Thus, if Sir Politic's schemes fail, Venice will stand in need of red herrings, which he will furnish at a profit. The schemes aim at making deception visibly and olfactorily foul to warn those incapable of reason. The tinder box scheme attempts to make arsenals safe from sparks; arsenals are a metaphor for man's potential for vice and folly which may be easily ignited by tinder boxes—Volpone's feigned illness and Peregrine's feigned *naivete.* Onions, in the second scheme, are to make victims of the plague

(perpetrators of deception) visibly recognizable. It is of course quintessentially ironic that the greatest fool of the play should be the only one to attempt to cure the moral plague of Venice. It is his myopic attempt, moreover, which informs the play's denouement.

If the theme of self-deception is actually the key to the play, as I have suggested, it should be supported in the play's denouement, and so it is, but in a perverse way that is peculiarly Jonson's own. Jonson puts a "snaffle" in the mouths of his critics, showing why vice *cannot* be punished in his "interludes"—it would not truly "instruct to life" as he in the "office of a comic poet" is obliged to do. Self-deception is wilful blindness; it can only be cured by the victim himself. In V.iii Mosca exposes each of the clients in unequivocal terms. Volpone subsequently rubs salt in their wounds, mocking them for having been so easily deceived. Voltore, indeed, confesses to the court once he thinks all is lost. Yet the moment when they learn Volpone still lives they are ready to deceive themselves all over again. In Sir Politic's method, then, lies the only solution: rotten eggs and stinking fish must be thrown at deceivers (V.xii.139–42) and preventative methods must be used to protect men's arsenals. Each of the clients (who served as tinder to the court) is stripped of the role in which he deceived the court. Mosca is to be prevented from deceiving in "the habit of a gentleman of Venice" (V.xii.110–112), and Volpone shall never again feign illness, for he will be *made* ill and infirm in prison. None is punished for his crime: if men's arsenals of evil and folly are in danger of ignition then tinder boxes must be carefully watched.

Through the theme of self-deception we can see that Ben Jonson blotted his lines in *Volpone* most carefully. The play is admirably complex and it seems miraculous that he wrote it in but five weeks. Much injustice has been done him by those who were too quick to condemn what they did not fully understand. However, whether in a reading or in performance few have failed to recognize that the play is a masterpiece. If the theme of self-deception as applied here is new in critical terms, it has always been implicitly understood by audiences. They laugh at the clients' attempts to outwit the fox, the knight's attempts at *savoir-faire,* the mountebank's attempt to be a lover, recognizing that self-deception is the height of human folly.

Source: Dorothy E. Litt, "Unity of Theme in *Volpone,*" in *Bulletin of the New York Public Library,* 1969, Vol. 73, pp. 218–226.

P. H. Davison

In the following essay, Davison argues that although Jonson was inspired by the ancient Greek comodies, his interpretation of them was incorrect.

Although Jonson called *Volpone* ''quick *comoedie*, refined,'' this description has not satisfied critics puzzled by the precise nature of the play. Edward B. Partridge, in his illuminating study of Jonson's major comedies, remarks that confusion as to the nature of *Volpone* suggests that ''Jonson either failed to create anything aesthetically pleasing or created a drama too complex in nature and unique in effect to be encompassed by the traditional categories.'' A play ''which creates such a profound sense of evil . . . seems closer to tragedy than comedy,'' he states, and he refers to T. S. Eliot's dictum that, although ''Jonson's type of personality 'found its relief in something falling under the category of burlesque or farce,' these terms are manifestly inadequate'' for the unique world of *Volpone*. Although satire ''may be the least unsatisfactory term'' for the play, it better describes Jonson's method than ''the aesthetic result.''

Partridge is chiefly concerned with imagery in his study of *Volpone,* and he believes (correctly, I feel) that such a study, although it helps to ''reveal the tone of the play,'' cannot entirely clear up the ''confusion about the kind of drama that *Volpone* is.'' Herford and Simpson speak of *Volpone* as approaching Jonson's ''own grandiose and terrible tragedy of two years before,'' *Sejanus.* T. S. Eliot has pointed out that ''No theory of humours could account for Jonson's best plays,'' and he adds that Volpone and Mosca are not humors. More recently Northrop Frye has suggested that *Volpone* ''is exceptional in being a kind of comic imitation of a tragedy, with the point of Volpone's hybris carefully marked.''

Volpone is a comedy: but a special kind of comedy, the ultimate source of which is to be found in the Old Comedy of Greece.

Jonson was well acquainted with the comedies of Aristophanes, and attention has been drawn to this by Herford and Simpson, among others. They point to the use made of *Plutus* and *The Wasps* in *The Staple of News* and speak of Jonson as nowhere being ''less Elizabethan than in the Aristophanic allegory of the *Poetaster* or *The Staple of News*''; however, they do not feel that Jonson approaches ''the poetic splendour of *The Birds* or *The Clouds* . . . .'' It is to these two plays by Aristophanes that

 THAT JONSON MISUNDERSTOOD ARISTOTLE'S VIEW OF COMEDY IS WELL KNOWN. HE QUOTES ARISTOTLE AS SAYING, 'THE MOVING OF LAUGHTER IS A FAULT IN COMEDIE, A KIND OF TURPITUDE, THAT DEPRAVES SOME PART OF A MANS NATURE WITHOUT A DISEASE,' WHEREAS, AS HERFORD AND SIMPSON POINT OUT IN THEIR NOTE ON THIS PASSAGE, ARISTOTLE STATED THAT 'COMEDY IS AN IMITATION OF CHARACTERS OF A LOWER TYPE.'''

Herford and Simpson believe we must ascribe, in *Cynthia's Revels,* ''both the frank use of mythic or fantastic incident against the canon of Jonsonian realism, and the admission of serious and beautiful lyric poetry (as in Echo's Song) contrary to the rigour of the comic spirit.''

Though it is clear that Jonson was familiar with the comedies of Aristophanes, so far as I am aware his dependence upon Aristophanes has generally been thought to have been restricted to the use of such ''mythic or fantastic incident,'' lyric ''contrary to the rigour of the comic spirit,'' an admiration for the tartness of Aristophanes, and, in general, to ''the salt in the old *comoedy*'':

> AVT. Ha! If all the salt in the old *comoedy*
> Should be so censur'd, or the sharper wit
> Of the bold *satyre,* termed scolding rage,
> What age could then compare with those,
>   for buffons?
> What should be sayd of ARISTOPHANES?
> (*Poetaster,* To the Reader)

We also know that Jonson was acquainted with the Old Comedy by the reference to it by Cordatus when he states that *Everyman Out of His Humour* is ''somewhat like *Vetus Comoedia*.'' Precisely what is meant here by Old Comedy is not certain. Thus Herford and Simpson, while stating their interpretation of the passage as necessarily meaning Greek and Roman comedy (as opposed to old comedy in the native English tradition), also record O. J. Campbell's view that Jonson here meant "the Greek comedy which culminated in the work of Aristophanes."

That Jonson misunderstood Aristotle's view of comedy is well known. He quotes Aristotle as saying, "the moving of laughter is a fault in Comedie, a kind of turpitude, that depraves some part of a mans nature without a disease," whereas, as Herford and Simpson point out in their note on this passage, Aristotle stated that "comedy is an imitation of characters of a lower type." In view of the serious, and to some, the quasi-tragic nature of *Volpone*, Jonson's interpretation of the ancients is significant. Thus his repetition from Heinsius in *Discoveries* of the statement that "The parts of a Comedie are the same with a *Tragedie*, and the end is partly the same. For, they both delight, and teach," suggests a view of the structure of comedy which accords with the argument below, in which the *hybris* of tragedy is equated with the *alazoneia* of Aristophanic comedy, giving in *Volpone* the appearance of the hubristic hero wreaking his own downfall. The greater "seriousness" of *Volpone* as compared with Aristophanic comedy is also explicable in the light of Jonson's view (in his reference to Aristophanes in *Discoveries*) that "jests that are true and naturall, seldome raise laughter, with the beast, the multitude. They love nothing, that is right, and proper. The farther it runs from reason, or possibility with them, the better it is." Here, indeed, we have a theoretical basis for what Herford and Simpson describe as "the frank use of mythic and fantastic incident against the canon of Jonson's realism" in *Cynthia's Revels*.

In *Volpone* one has not only the general indebtedness to ancient comedy as Jonson understood it, and to Aristophanes in particular, but also the employment of the Aristophanic figures of *alazon* and [*bomolochos*]. Pickard-Cambridge points out that

> A considerable part of many plays of Aristophanes consists of scenes in which a person of absurd or extravagant pretensions is derided or made a fool of by a person who plays the buffoon—scenes (to use the convenient Greek terms) between an [*alazon*] and a [*bomolochos*]

The [*alazon*] takes many forms, he states, but the [*bomolochos*] "generally takes one of two forms—the old rustic and the jesting slave." In a footnote, he quotes from paragraph 6 of the *Tractatus Coislinianus*: ["*ethe komodias Ta Te bomolochia Kai Ta eironika Kai Ta Ton alazon on.*]"

This passage is also referred to by F. M. Cornford, who states that "Aristotle seems to have classified the characters in Comedy under three heads: The Buffoon (*bomolochos*), the Ironical type (*eiron*), and the Imposter (*alazon*)." However, he concludes that "in the Old Comedy, 'buffoonery' (*bomolochia*) is only the outer wear of 'Irony,'" and thus there is "over against the Imposter, one character only—the Ironical Buffoon."

Although their precise functions have changed a little (for example, Pickard-Cambridge states that the [*bomolochos*] had "a particular function in the prologue—that of stating the subject of the play, requesting the goodwill of the audience, and attracting their favour by some preliminary jesting"), it is this relationship which underlies *Volpone*: [*alazon*]and [*bomolochos*]: Impostor and Buffoon— or perhaps more aptly, as Cornford suggests, Ironical Buffoon.

Northrop Frye argues for four types making two opposed pairs: "The contest of *eiron* and *alazon* forms the basis of the comic action, and the buffoon and the churl polarize the comic mood." This is not only theoretically accurate, but each type exists individually. However, they overlap and interchange frequently, and although churl and buffoon are appropriately paired, the pairing of *alazon* and *eiron* fails to take into account the buffoonery associated so often with the *eiron*. The distinction may, in part, be a social one—Pickard-Cambridge's two forms of "old rustic and the jesting slave." Thus, Peregrine in *Volpone* may seem (at first) more aptly an *eiron* than a buffoon, whereas Volpone disguised as a mountebank plays the buffoon. However, Peregrine in V.iv. engages in buffoonery, and Volpone is a source of irony. Thus, so far as *Volpone* is concerned, I prefer to set one form—the Ironical Buffoon—against the Impostors.

In the main action, Volpone is the principal Impostor, his downfall being worked by Mosca when he changes his role from that of agent to antagonist. The lesser characters of the main action, the four legacy seekers—Voltore, Corvino, and Corbaccio, and Lady Politic Would-Be—are also Impostors.

In the action associated with Sir Politic Would-Be, he himself is an Impostor, and Peregrine is the Ironical Buffoon who exposes him, by verbal irony, as in Peregrine's comments upon Sir Politic's diary, and then in V.iv, when Peregrine frightens Sir Politic into making himself ridiculous in the tortoise shell, and thus completely disposes of him.

The similarity of this Impostor-Ironical Buffoon relationship in the actions associated with Volpone and Sir Politic is significant for two reasons, one dramatic and the other critical. Jonas A. Barish remarks in his study, "The Double Plot in *Volpone*": "For more than two centuries literary critics have been satisfied to dismiss the subplot of *Volpone* as irrelevant and discordant, because of its lack of overt connection with the main plot." In addition to mimicking their environment and thus performing "the function of burlesque traditional to comic subplots in English drama" (which is Barish's concern), there is also this use of Impostor and Ironical Buffoon, common to both plots, which further unifies *Volpone*. Critically, the use of this concept in both actions tends to confirm that it was Old Comedy which was the source of Jonson's inspiration, for, although Volpone's character is complex, making less obvious the relationship with Old Comedy, in Sir Pol and Peregrine one has, very clearly indeed, the Impostor and Ironical Buffoon of Old Comedy.

There is also another association with Old Comedy in the use of animal names. Edward Partridge has pointed out that *Volpone* is not a beast fable cast in the form of classical comedy, for in *Volpone* "reasonable beings appear as lower animals with the instincts of lower animals." Jonson may well have had in mind the practice of Aristophanes as exemplified in *The Wasps, The Birds,* or *The Frogs.* As has already been mentioned, Jonson speaks in *Discoveries* of "the beast, the multitude."

It will be plain that Jonson, in his use of this relationship of Impostor and Ironical Buffoon, has not done so without adapting it. Though the lesser characters can be seen simply as Impostors, Mosca and Volpone are more complex, especially Volpone. Mosca, in his dual role of agent and antagonist, is both Plautine "managing servant" and Ironical Buffoon. Further, when at the opening of Act III he says, "Successe hath made me wanton," we see the beginning of an action that will lead to Mosca overreaching himself in the manner of an Impostor—seeing himself as the "fine, elegant rascall, that can rise, / And stoope (almost together) like an arrow." The imagery itself suggests the dual function.

Just as there are two aspects to Mosca's character, so there are two aspects to Volpone's. Volpone and Mosca combine to deflate the lesser Impostors in the main action, and, in this capacity, Volpone

acts as Ironical Buffoon. The buffoonery is particularly apparent when, in his desire to participate in the action, he disguises himself as a mountebank (II.ii) and as a Commandadore in V.v to V.viii. The Ironical Buffoon aspect of Volpone's character is especially to be seen in V.vi to V.viii, where Corbaccio, Corvino, and Voltore are mocked. Corbaccio and Voltore specifically refer to their being mocked by this Commandadore in the sixth and seventh scenes of the act, and in V.vii, Volpone (still disguised), jeers at Corvino because he has "let the FOXE laugh at your emptinesse." More subtly, Volpone, as has been so clearly demonstrated by Edward Partridge, is the source of much of the play's irony, and in this the ironical aspect of the Ironical Buffoon is stressed. For example, in I.i, in the perversion of religious imagery in praise of gold, an imagery which "at once creates and passes a judgment on Volpone's religion of gold" creates an "irony which is fundamental to the tone" of the whole play.

Thus, in so far as Volpone (with Mosca) brings about the down-fall of the lesser Impostors, Volpone appears as an Ironical Buffoon in speech and behavior. But this does not entirely explain either play or character, for it is only part of the whole, and it is for this reason that a study of the imagery, so largely ironical, cannot entirely clarify the confusion as to the kind of drama represented in *Volpone* (as Partridge has noted).

What must be taken into account is that, although Volpone is at one level the deflating Ironical Buffoon, he is primarily an Impostor, the most magnificent Impostor of them all. He is so from first to last, but it is only in the fifth act, when he feigns death and his agent turns antagonist, that Impostor gains dominance over Ironical Buffoon.

It is significant that when, in III.vii, Volpone attempts to seduce Celia, we have a temporary change in the tone of the play. At this point, irony and buffoonery are absent. Volpone's imposture of the lover is unchecked. The result is melodramatic overstatement, rather than tragic, an impression most apparent in Bonario's lines when he comes to Celia's rescue: "Forebeare, foule rauisher, libidinous swine, / Free the forc'd lady, or thou dy'st, imposter." How apt is Bonario's calling Volpone "imposter"! The melodramatic nature of this scene illustrates the dramatic effect of a situation in which an Impostor is allowed free rein. It is only with the presence, actual or implied, of the Ironical Buffoon, that comedy can be effected in a play dependent upon this relationship.

Perhaps the most skillful employment of this technique of Old Comedy is the nature of Volpone's [*alazoneia*]—that which causes him to overreach himself. Volpone initiates his own destruction, becoming the victim of his own Ironical Buffoonery. In his pretense of death, he wins his final triumph over the four inheritance seekers (and, simultaneously, he acts the Buffoon as he watches in delight, ''Behind the cortine, on a stoole''). But this final imposture, of death, is both the end of the Ironical Buffoon in Volpone and the cause of his downfall. This he himself realizes:

> To make a snare, for mine owne necke! and run
> My head into it, wilfully! with laughter!
> When I had newly scap't, was free, and cleare!
> Out of mere wantonnesse!
> (Volpone, V.xi.1–4)

Here we have the self-initiated fall, the Ironical Buffoonery (''with laughter''), the overreaching.

Some of the excess of Aristophanic comedy, the savageness of the satire, the farce, and the burlesque, is to be found in *Volpone,* but, in Jonson, one has a greater concern for moral issues than in Aristophanes. As Partridge suggests, ''a critic willing to do some violence to the play'' might see *Volpone* ''as a prophetic vision of the society which capitalism, even in Jonson's day, was creating.'' It requires even greater violence to a play by Aristophanes to say something akin to this even though in *Lysistrata,* for instance, one might perceive the undertones of war. Though Jonson adapts what he takes from the Old Comedy and is more concerned with serious issues, one can see how essential the Old Comedy relationship of Impostor and Ironical Buffoon is to the play: it is this relationship that makes clear the nature of the drama of *Volpone. Volpone* is comedy, but close in tone and certain aspects of its technique to Old Comedy, the comedy of Aristophanes. As Jonson said in his address to the two universities, he had written *Volpone*

> *though not without some lines of example, drawne euen in the ancients themselues, the goings out of whose* comœdies *are not alwaies ioyfull, but oft-times, the bawdes, the seruants, the riuals, yea, and the masters are mulcted: and fitly, it being the office of a* comick-Poet, *to imitate iustice, and instruct to life, as well as puritie of language, or stirre vp gentle affections.*

Source: P. H. Davison, ''*Volpone* and the Old Comedy,'' in *Modern Language Quarterly,* 1963, Vol. 24, pp. 151–157.

SOURCES

Bate, Jonathan, ''The Elizabethans in Italy,'' in *Travel and Drama in Shakespeare's Time,* edited by Jean-Pierre Maquerlot, Cambridge University Press, 1996.

Cohen, Ralph A., ''The Setting of *Volpone,*'' in *Renaissance Papers,* 1978, pp. 64-75.

McPherson, David C., *Shakespeare, Jonson, and the Myth of Venice,* University of Delaware Press, 1990.

FURTHER READING

Ford, Boris, ed., *Seventeenth-Century Britain,* Vol. 4, *The Cambridge Cultural History of Britain,* (Series), Cambridge, 1989.
     This book provides an easy way to understand the history of England in the seventeenth century. The book is divided into separate sections on literature, art, and music. An introductory section provides a historical context.

Herford, C. H., Percy Simpson and Evelyn Simpson, eds., *Ben Jonson,* Oxford, 1925–1952.
     This eleven-volume work includes a biography of Jonson and introductions to each of the plays. This text of the plays is a reprint of the 1616 folio that Jonson printed. There is also some information about the public's reception of the plays and a great deal of information dealing with almost any aspect of Jonson's life or work.

Hill, Christopher, *The Century of Revolution 1603–1714,* Norton, 1961.
     Hill is a well-known author of books which examine the cultural and historical background of English Renaissance literature. Hill has provided an well-organized examination of the economic, religious, and political issues of the seventeenth century. The events that led up to the English Revolution, the Revolution, and the Restoration that followed were crucial incidents that shaped the literature of this period and that which followed.

Hirsh, James E., ed., *New Perspectives on Ben Jonson,* Fairleigh Dickinson University Press, 1997.
     Hirsh has compiled a collection of essays on Jonson's work that reveals many of the current scholarly approaches to examining Jonson's texts.

Kay, David W., *Ben Jonson: A Literary Life,* St. Martin's Press, 1995.
     Kay has provided a concise biography of Jonson's life, which also explores the influences of Jonson's early life, his presence at court, and his relationships with other Renaissance playwrights.

Maclean, Hugh, ed., *Ben Jonson and the Cavalier Poets,* Norton, 1974.
     This text provides a good selection of Jonson's poetry. Because a selection of the poetry of Jonson's

contemporaries is also included, Maclean offers readers an easy way to study and compare the poetry of the period.

Sanders, Julie, ed., *Refashioning Ben Johnson: Gender Politics and the Jonsonian Canon,* St. Martin's Press, 1998.
This text contains a collection of essays by scholars in an examination of Jonson's work within their historical and political context.

The Wild Duck

HENRIK IBSEN

1884

In a letter accompanying the manuscript for *The Wild Duck,* Henrik Ibsen wrote to his publisher, ''This new play in many ways occupies a place of its own among my dramas; the method is in various respects a departure from my earlier one. . . . The critics, will, I hope, find the points; in any case, they will find plenty to quarrel about, plenty to misinterpret.'' Ibsen, however, was disappointed in these early expectations. When the play opened in Scandinavia early in 1885, critics paid relatively little attention to it. The play soon traveled throughout the continent. While a few luminaries commended it—notably the playwright George Bernard Shaw and the poet Rainer Maria Rilke—most early critics found the play incomprehensible and incoherent. Audiences, as well, showed little positive response to *The Wild Duck.*

In ensuing years, however, and as people began to understand both Ibsen's notion of ''tragi-comedy'' as well as his insightful characterization, the play began to develop the fine reputation it still holds today. Now popularly regarded as one of Ibsen's more important works, *The Wild Duck* gains further eminence in its issuance of Ibsen into a new era of writing, one in which symbolism and characterization-as opposed to social realism-gained prominence. With *The Wild Duck,* an already esteemed playwright showed his continued interest in exploring new interests and concerns through his work.

AUTHOR BIOGRAPHY

Ibsen was born in 1828 in a small town in Norway. When he was fifteen years old, Ibsen left his family's home to begin an apprenticeship as an apothecary. Two years later, Ibsen fathered a child with an older housemaid, and he was obligated to provide financial support over the next fifteen years.

In the late 1840s, he began to prepare for university examinations. Once at university in Christiana (present-day Oslo), Ibsen became very involved with journalism. He edited a student paper, contributed articles to another paper, and worked on a satirical journal. He also spent a great deal of time on his writing. He completed and published his first play, *Catiline,* by 1849, and published poetry in a journal. In 1859, his one-act play, *The Warrior's Barrow,* becomes the first of his plays to be staged.

In 1851, when he was only twenty-three, Ibsen was engaged as playwright in residence at the National Theater in Bergen. Over the next several years, the theater company performed a new Ibsen play each year. By the end of the decade, his plays were also being performed at the Norwegian Theater in Christiana, where he assumed duties as the artistic director. In both of these capacities, Ibsen was expected to produce ''national drama,'' which checked his artistic expression. The bankruptcy of the Norwegian Theater left Ibsen free to write for himself.

He was awarded a travel grant by the government, which was only the first of many grants that Ibsen received from the Norwegian government, including an annual stipend. He left Norway for Italy in 1864, and he spent the next twenty-seven years primarily living abroad, only returning to Norway for short visits in 1874 and 1885. Despite his absence from his native country, he remained a well-known figure there. For instance he attended the opening of the Suez Canal as Norway's representative, and in 1873, he was knighted.

With *A Doll's House* (1879), classic Ibsen was born. In his work, Ibsen began the exploration of controversial, social issues. Many of his plays created a furor among European audiences. By the late 1880s, however, Ibsen's work had become more self-analytic and symbolic. Works such as *The Master Builder* (1892) explore an artist's relation to society and contains an autobiographical element.

In 1891, Ibsen returned to Norway to live, and he continued to write plays. On his seventieth birthday, he was honored throughout Scandinavia. Also that year, the first volumes of the collected edition of his works was published in Denmark and Germany. In 1901, he suffered his first stroke. Another stroke two years later left him unable to write or walk. He died in 1906.

PLOT SUMMARY

Act I

Act I opens in Hakon Werle's home. In honor of his son's return after a long absence, he is hosting a dinner party. Gregers Werle has invited his old school friend, Hjalmar Ekdal. The men have not seen each other for more than 15 years, and Gregers learns that in the interim, Hjalmar has married Gina, a former housemaid of the Werles; been set up in a photography studio by Hakon; and had a child, Hedvig. The conversation also reveals Hjalmar's father's past: a business partner of Hakon's, Old Ekdal had been found guilty of illegal tree felling and sentenced to prison. This disgrace ruined the life that he had known, as well as his son's, who had to drop out of college. Now, Hakon generously compensates Old Ekdal for copying work. Gregers notes that his father was ''a kind of Providence for you, ''to which Hjalmar heartily agrees.

The other men who make up the dinner party, associates of Hakon, join Gregers and Hjalmar in the study. As they converse, Old Ekdal is forced to pass through the room to leave the house after picking up his work. Hjalmar looks away, pretending not to see his father.

After the party has ended, Gregers confronts his father about his help to the Ekdal family. Gregers implies that his father was also involved in the crime for which Old Ekdal was imprisoned and makes insinuations about his father's past relationship with Gina. Despite his son's chilliness, Werle offers Gregers a partnership in his business, but Gregers refuses. Werle then reveals that he is planning on marrying his current housemaid, Mrs. Sorby. Gregers declares his intention of leaving his father's house, saying that he now has ''an objective to live for,'' but he does not share this objective with his father.

Act II

Act II opens in the Ekdal's apartment. Gina and Hedvig Ekdal are seated in the photography studio,

Henrik Ibsen

which they also use as a living room. They are awaiting Hjalmar's return. Soon after he comes home, however, Gregers pays a visit. Privately, Hjalmar reveals to Gregers that Hedvig is going blind.

Old Ekdal has already returned home, and he insists that Gregers see the attic, which is filled with chickens, pigeons, rabbits, and a wild duck that Hakon gave to Hedvig. Hakon had shot and injured the wild duck, but his dog retrieved it, still alive, from the bottom of the lake. That evening, over Gina's protestations, Gregers also rents the vacant room in the Ekdal's home. He says he will return the next day.

Act III

Act III takes place the next morning. Gina has just returned from shopping and Hjalmar is retouching photographs. Old Ekdal comes into the studio, wanting Hjalmar to help him move the water trough in the attic. When Hedvig volunteers to take over her father's work, Hjalmar joins his father. While the men are in the attic, Gregers comes in. In the ensuing conversation with Hedvig, he learns that she cannot attend school because of her eyesight, but that she dearly loves her parents and her wild duck. They hear shots coming from the attic, which

is how Gregers learns that the Ekdal men use the attic as a "forest" in which to hunt.

When Hjalmar reenters the studio, he is surprised to see Gregers. He tells Gregers about his invention. He does not describe it, but it will make "Ekdal" a respected name once again. Hjalmar tells Gregers how hard the disgrace has been on his father. Gregers tells Hjalmar that he is something like the wild duck, sunk in darkness. Hjalmar asks Gregers not to talk about "blight and poison" as he only likes to talk about pleasant things.

Then the two downstairs neighbors, Molvik and Relling, come over for lunch. During the lunch, Hakon Werle comes to the Ekdal's home to speak with Gregers. He has figured out his son's plans to "open Hjalmar Ekdal's eyes" and does not want him to do so. He says it will be no favor to Hjalmar, but Gregers is resolved. After Hakon leaves, Gregers invites Hjalmar on a walk.

Act IV

Act IV opens later that afternoon upon Hjalmar's return to his home. He rebuffs his family and speaks angrily. He sends Hedvig out for a walk so he can speak with Gina alone. He asks her the truth about her relationship to Hakon Werle, and she confesses that she once had an affair with him. He rails against his wife, and in the midst of this scene, Gregers enters, ecstatic that the truth has been revealed and that the Ekdal's can now form a "true marriage." Next, Mrs. Sorby comes over with the news that Hakon has already left town but is still available if the Ekdal's need any assistance. As response, Hjalmar declares his intention of repaying Hakon for all the assistance he has provided over the years. Mrs. Sorby reveals that Hakon is going blind and then leaves. Hedvig returns from her walk, carrying a letter that Mrs. Sorby gave her. Hedvig gives her father permission to open the letter, which is from Hakon. The letter bequeaths a monthly stipend to Old Ekdal, which Hedvig will inherit upon her grandfather's death.

Hjalmar sends Hedvig from the room and tears the letter in pieces. When he demands to know whether he or Hakon is Hedvig's father, Gina cannot answer him, for she does not know. Hjalmar declares that he will leave the house for good. Hedvig has overheard the conversation, but Gregers tells her that she can win back her father's love by sacrificing what is most important to her: the wild duck. He suggests that she have her grandfather shoot the duck.

Act V

Act V takes place the next morning. Hjalmar has not returned, but Gregers comes over as does Relling, the downstairs neighbor. Relling tells Gregers that his idealism is mistaken; Hjalmar needs to believe in certain lies in order to live. In fact, Relling encourages these lies. Gregers remains unconvinced, and after Relling leaves, he asks Hedvig if she has shot the duck. She has not, but she goes to her grandfather to ask the best way to do so. Hjalmar returns home, but it is only to get his belongings, for he plans to leave for good. Gina sends Hedvig out of the room, but Hedvig is terribly frightened by her father's thoughtless rejection of her. As her parents argue, Hedvig steals into the attic with the gun. Hjalmar and Gina continue to argue, but Hjalmar consents to sit down and eat breakfast. He contemplates staying for a few days—after all, he and his father have no other place to live. Hjalmar confesses that what keeps him away is Hedvig—maybe she never really loved him. Gregers, meanwhile, has heard noises in the attic. They hear a shot suddenly, and Gregers tells Hjalmar that Hedvig has just shot the wild duck as an act of sacrifice so that her father would love her again. Hjalmar searches around the apartment for Hedvig but cannot find her. He goes into the attic where he finds Hedvig lying on the floor. They fetch Relling, but the doctor declares that she is already dead. In an aside, he tells Gregers that Hedvig killed herself. Gregers believes that at least her death will bring out the nobility in her father, but Relling asserts that Hjalmar will simply use Hedvig's death as a further excuse for wallowing in self-pity and sentimentality.

CHARACTERS

Ekdal

Ekdal (also called Old Ekdal) is Hjalmar's father. Years ago, he was Hakon Werle's partner. Convicted of illegally cutting down trees, Old Ekdal was imprisoned, which led to the complete loss of his fortune, reputation, and military rank. After his release, Ekdal returned to live with his son. He has obtained work copying for his former partner, who remunerates him generously. Old Ekdal lives in a fantasy world. He creates a forest for himself in the attic; the rabbits that populate the forest are the bears he once hunted. He also has a drinking problem.

Gina Ekdal

Gina Ekdal is a hard-working, kind woman. She comes from a lower social class than her husband, which is demonstrated by her lapses in grammar, but she is far more efficient and caring than he is. Not only does she accept the role of taking care of the home and family, she also runs her husband's business. She sincerely loves her husband and tolerates his delusions with good humor. She makes every effort to conceal unpleasant realities from Hjalmar. She is intent on making her family happy. Despite her simple background, Gina is astute and intuitive. For instance, when Gregers wants to rent the room, she recognizes his potential for bringing destruction into her family, and she, not Hjalmar, does not want him to move in. In all facets of her life, Gina demonstrates that her primary goal is to protect her family.

Hedvig Ekdal

Fourteen-year-old Hedvig Ekdal is a sensitive, intelligent girl. Due to her failing eyesight, Hedvig's parents keep her out of school and consequently, she is a bit immature for her age. In other ways, however, she demonstrates remarkable maturity. For instance, when Gregers compares himself to the dog that saved the wild duck, she understands that he is speaking in symbolic terms. Unlike her father and grandfather, she uses the attic to broaden her experiences, not to escape reality. She eagerly reads the books left behind. Also unlike the adults, Hedvig believes in her father, thus when he says he is leaving never to return, she takes this as an absolute. Because she so deeply loves him, she intends to sacrifice her duck, which she also loves, as proof of her boundless affection.

Hjalmar Ekdal

Hjalmar Ekdal lives with his wife and daughter. He runs a photographic business, but his wife does most of the work. Hakon Werle has set him up in the business. He apparently once had more promise, but he was forced to leave school after his father's scandal. When the play opens, Hjalmar is living a fairly happy and contented life. He spends his time hunting in the attic with his father in the "forest" they have created. He clings to his "life-lie": his dreams of inventing a photographic device that will restore the lost glory of his family's name. Despite his persistent talk of this invention, Hjalmar makes no effort to actually construct it, and it exists merely in his fantasies. Those around him recognize this truth, and they humor him, never pointing out the inherent laziness of his life. Despite the fact that he is lazy, self-indulgent, shallow, and egocentric, his daughter loves him dearly and his wife constantly strives to protect him from life's harsh realities, a job that she does quite well until Gregers' appearance. While Hjalmar claims devastation at Hedvig's death, Relling points out that Hjalmar's life will merely continue as before, with yet another added touch of melodrama.

Old Ekdal
See Ekdal

Molvik
Molvik is the other downstairs border. He is an alcoholic student. Dr. Relling provides for him a ''life-lie,'' much as he does for Hjalmar. Relling asserts that Molvik drinks, not because he is an alcoholic, but because a demon takes over and makes him do so.

Dr. Relling
Dr. Relling lives downstairs from the Ekdal's. He is one of the few characters who see the world around him clearly. For instance, he perpetuates Hjalmar's ''life-lie,'' understanding that it is what keeps the man going. He scorns Gregers's claims of creating an ''ideal'' existence and maintains the belief that humans need their illusions in order to live happily. Relling also serves as a general commentator on the other characters' behavior, and as a voice of reason. Thus, when he says that Hjalmar will quickly recover from Hedvig's death, it seems that he speaks the truth.

Mrs. Sorby
Mrs. Sorby is Hakon Werle's housekeeper. A widow, she is also a friend of Gina. She is engaged to Hakon, and after Gregers refuses his overtures, she is sent to the Ekdal's with Hakon's bequest for Old Ekdal and Hedvig.

Gregers Werle
Gregers Werle is Hakon Werle's son. Influenced by his mother, he strongly dislikes his father and has spent the past fifteen years in the north, away from his boyhood home. Upon his return—when he pieces together the truth about Gina and his father and her ensuing marriage to Hjalmar—he decides to enlighten his friend to the truth. He mistakenly believes that Hjalmar and Gina cannot be happy since their marriage is based on a lie. He believes that once the truth is expressed, they will

begin anew. In deciding upon this course of action, Gregers does not take into account the individual personalities involved; he believes that everyone will react the way he would react and is surprised when this turns out not to be the case. Not only does Gregers bring about a dysfunction in the relationship between Hjalmar and Gina, he provides the suggestion that leads to Hedvig's death, whether it is intentional or not. Thus he is implicated in the tragedy that befalls her.

Hakon Werle
Hakon Werle is a wealthy industrialist. He pursued Gina fifteen years ago, and after their affair ended and she was pregnant (most probably with his child), he took upon himself the responsibility for making sure that she and her family were financially cared for. He set up Hjalmar in the photography business, he provides Old Ekdal with a job and pays him handsomely, and his final gesture toward the family is a lifetime bequest for Old Ekdal and for Hedvig. He also reaches out toward his son, offering Gregers a partnership in the business, but Gregers refuses. Toward the end of the play, Mrs. Sorby reveals that Hakon is going blind, and the two are planning on marrying.

THEMES

Truth and Falsehood
Truth and falsehood are major themes in *The Wild Duck.* Gregers is determined that Hjalmar learn the truth about Gina's past and why Hakon Werle has been so helpful to the family. Hjalmar has lived in blissful ignorance, never questioning why Hakon decided to be of such service to him and his family. He leads a contented life and actively seeks to avoid unpleasantness, as he childishly tells Gregers. Gina protects Hjalmar from unpleasant economic realities, truly catering to all his needs, both his physical and emotional ones. Hedvig adores him, never seeing how he makes use of her love. For instance, though he worries about her sight, he lets her do eye-straining work of retouching photographs so he can play in the attic with his father. His life is based on one simple, yet determined falsehood: the photographic device that he will never invent. For Hjalmar, the invention is what Relling calls a ''life-lie''—it enables him to live. Ironically, despite his exuberant protests, Hjalmar is quite able to survive knowing the truth about his wife's past and the parentage of Hedvig. Though he claims that

TOPICS FOR FURTHER STUDY

- Imagine that Hedvig had only injured herself, not killed herself. How do you think the family would react? Do you think Hjalmar would change at all? Would the play still be considered tragic?

- Conduct research to find other dramas that are part comedy, part tragedy. What are some of these plays? What do they have in common with *The Wild Duck*?

- Ibsen has raised feminist issues in plays such as *A Doll's House*, in which the heroine leaves her family for an independent life, and *The Wild Duck*, which touches upon issues of female sexuality. Do you think Ibsen could be considered a feminist writer? Explain your answer.

- The symbolism of the wild duck is a much-discussed topic in the field of literature. What do you think the duck most symbolizes? The entry discusses ways in which the duck represents Hjalmar, Gina, and Gregers. Do you think the duck also represents Hedvig? Explain your answer.

- Some critics have stated that there is no likable character in *The Wild Duck*. Do you agree with this assessment? Explain your answer.

- Conduct research into societal values held by Norwegians toward the turn of the nineteenth century. Based on your findings, do you think the viewpoints and attitudes expressed by the characters are accurate? Why or why not?

- Find out more about Ibsen's works. How would you categorize his body of work? What issues were of greatest concern to him? How do his early plays differ from his later plays?

---

he will leave the family, he makes only a show of carrying out these threats. Hedvig, however, a younger-than-average fourteen-year-old, takes her father at his word. She has not yet learned the pattern of lies that can exist in relationships.

Choices and Consequences

Gregers makes the deliberate choice to reveal his suspicions about Gina's past and Hedvig's paternity to Hjalmar. Gregers justifies his actions through claims to idealism and talk about helping Hjalmar and Gina form a marriage based on truth instead of on lies. In deciding to pursue this course of action, however, whether or not Gregers thought about the consequences is subject to debate. Some critics have suggested that Gregers acts as he does in order to exact revenge on his father. They have even suggested that Gregers deliberately urges Hedvig to suicide since her existence as his half-sister sullies his own identity.

Hedvig's suicide is another example of a choice and consequence. There are two possible interpretations of her action. One school of thought contends that Hedvig, coached by Gregers to sacrifice something that she loves to prove her love to her father, determines that self-sacrifice will make the most stunning gesture. An opposing viewpoint contends that Hedvig decides to kill herself only after hearing her father's scornful comment that Hedvig has been playing him for her own purposes. Regardless of why, Hedvig decides to kill herself, as Relling's scrutiny determines. Aside from her death, her action has the consequence of binding her mother and father—but they had begun that process even before her death—and providing her father further opportunity for self-pity.

Identity

Identity is an important theme because it is Hedvig's possible identity as Hakon's daughter that leads to the tragic ending. Many of the other characters, however, raise the issue of identity. In Hjalmar's eyes, for instance, Gina's identity completely changes upon the revelation of her affair with Hakon. This knowledge causes Hjalmar to regard his wife in a completely different manner, thus, she is no longer the person that he has known for the past fifteen years.

Other characters have actually gone through significant changes in their lifetime. Mrs. Sorby was a housekeeper, but she is about to become the wife of a wealthy industrialist. Hjalmar had been a student, but because of his father's scandal, he dropped out of school. The greatest change in identity, however, is seen in the transformation of Old Ekdal. Formerly Hakon's partner, and thus an industrialist himself, he was found guilty of the crime of illegal tree felling. Sentenced to jail, Ekdal emerged from prison to a completely different lifestyle. Instead of being in charge of a company, he performs copying services for his former partner. Since he no longer has access to the northern forests, he creates a wooded scene for hunting in the attic of the apartment house. This action shows Ekdal's inability to let go of his past life and his pathetic clinging to his former identity.

Deception

Many of the characters practice self-deceit. Ekdal's creation of a forest in which he can hunt is one example of this. He pretends that the rabbits are the great bears he once shot down. He wears his army uniform although he has been stripped of his ranking because of his crime. He sports a brown wig, showing his refusal to accept his aging. Hjalmar also practices deception, particularly in respect to his father. He insists upon calling his father the white-haired old man, despite the toupee, as if that will make him more respectable. He steadfastly and vocally maintains his belief in his invention. This serves an ulterior purpose as well, because it provides justification for letting his wife take over most of the daily tasks of running the photography studio.

In contrast, the Ekdal women are remarkably straightforward. Hedvig believes everything she hears, taking her father's histrionics on a literal level. Gina sees through the deceptions of the members of her family, but she accepts and ignores them. Her deliberate innocence stretches from the harmless—pretending not to know that Old Ekdal is drinking liquor—to the fatal—playing along with Hjalmar's game of leaving the household.

Relling occupies somewhat of a middle ground. He encourages Hjalmar's practice of self-deception because he understands it has a greater purpose. Relling alone has the capability of choosing which truths and lies he will see, which he will reject, and

to which he will react. Such understanding of the deliberate deception affords Relling more control than the other characters.

STYLE

Symbolism

The wild duck is the foremost symbol Ibsen employs. The wild duck has come to live with the family after having been shot by Hakon, which in itself is symbolic. Hakon is the instrument of the duck's downfall, just as he was the instrument of Gina's downfall. Both duck and woman almost came to destruction. In the case of the duck, Hakon's dog saved the creature; in the case of Gina, Hakon's money saved her from disgrace. For Gregers, however, the duck, which became caught amidst the mire and rubbish at the lake bottom, comes to represent the Ekdal family: Gina; Old Ekdal, who according to Hakon is one of those people who "dive to the bottom the moment they get a couple of slugs in their body, and never come to the surface again"; and Hjalmar, who according to Gregers has "something of the wild duck" in him, having mired himself in the dark "poisonous marsh." According to some critics, when Gregers entreats Hedvig to sacrifice the duck, he is encouraging the symbolic destruction of the lie that has poisoned her whole family.

To further the symbolic relationship, Gregers sees himself as the "absurdly clever dog" that saves the duck—or the family, or Hjalmar's life—from the swamp. He determines to save Hjalmar and bring him to a truer existence. In seeing himself as a savior, however, Gregers denies the possibility that the duck—or Hjalmar—might lead a worse existence as a result.

The wild duck is a potent symbol for other characters as well. For Old Ekdal, she represents his past life in the wild, where he was the happiest. For Hjalmar, the duck represents a distraction from his present lifestyle.

Imagery

Sight imagery is important in the play. On a literal level, blindness plays a role in its plot. Hakon is going blind, which is why he needs a wife to care for him. Hedvig is going blind, which ties her parentage to Hakon Werle; but her eyesight is also used as a device to show Hjalmar's general careless-ness of her: he forbids her to read so that she might save her vision, yet when it suits his purposes, he has her do painstaking photographic work.

Yet, as pointed out by Otto Reinert in his essay "Sight Imagery in The Wild Duck," the idea of blindness and sight also plays an important role on a figurative level. Gregers is determined "to open Hjalmar Ekdal's eyes." Gregers declares that Hjalmar "shall see his situation as it is." The import of Gregers's actions is underscored by other commentary in the play. Hakon tells Gregers, "You have seen me with your mother's eyes . . . But you should remember that those eyes were-clouded at time," implying that Gregers's vision of the world is not even a truthful one but one that has been imposed on him—much as he wants to impose his vision on Hjalmar.

Similarly, Hjalmar is blind to the realities of life. He refuses to acknowledge his father at the Werle house, pretending that he "didn't notice" Old Ekdal's passage through the room. Hjalmar's spiritual blindness is further reflected in his belief that he has, in Reinert's words, "superior insight." When he leaves with Gregers on the afternoon he learns about Gina's past, he believes that it is Gregers who is in trouble and needs "a friend's wakeful eyes." Though knowledge of the truth causes him to look on his past as one long blind period, he persists in living in that false world, senselessly blaming Hedvig for her parentage. "I can't stand to look at you," he says, as if the mere vision of her has destructive qualities, yet again, he cannot bear to open his eyes to the truth. As Reinert writes, "Both [Gregers and Hjalmar] are incapable of seeing beneath the surface of facts; both are blind to their own reality."

Tragicomedy

The Wild Duck is at the same time both tragic and comic—a tragicomedy. Its tragic elements derive primarily from the ruin that Gregers's flaw—his compulsive and unrealistic need for the idealis-tic—brings upon the Ekdal household and particu-larly on Hedvig. Single-handedly, Gregers takes a secure family and turns them into an isolated collec-tion of people, none of whom trusts or has confi-dence in the other. Hedvig's tragedy, while insti-gated by Gregers's course of action, stems from her father's renunciation of her. His actions are inevita-ble, for they are based on his rampant egotism. Thus, the mantle of tragic character falls upon him as well.

The play's comedic elements derive from the ludicrous behavior of the characters and their sur-roundings: Hjalmar's insistence on his departure from the family at the same time he allows his wife to serve him breakfast; Old Ekdal's "hunting" amidst the decrepit Christmas trees in the attic; even the scenes involving Hjalmar's reproach of Gina are tinged with the comic. Additionally, Gregers's ide-als, pretentiously shared and out of place in the shabby surroundings, are imbued with a broadly comic and unrealistic dimension.

HISTORICAL CONTEXT

Union With Sweden and the Constitution

Since 1536, Norway had been a province of Denmark, but in the early 1800s, Sweden attacked Denmark. The resulting peace treaty transferred Norway to Sweden. Crown Prince Christian Fred-erik, the nephew of the Danish king, refused to accept this transfer. He initiated an uprising and called for the convention of a national assembly. The delegates wrote and signed a constitution, and elected Christian Frederik king of a free and inde-pendent Norway.

Norway received no support from Europe. Swed-ish troops attacked, and Christian Frederik resigned two weeks later. Sweden accepted Norway's consti-tution, which was amended to reflect the union effective November 1814. A Norwegian govern-ment and the National Assembly, the Storting, would make national policy. Though Norway re-mained an independent nation, it shared Sweden's king and foreign policy.

Norway Becomes a Parliament

Despite the popularity of King Charles John, the popularly elected Storting continued to struggle against the king and his cabinet. In 1833 representa-tives from the farming class formed a majority in the Storting. The so-called Farmer Storting advocated greater local control over local matters. The farmers also forged a relationship with radical urban intel-lectuals, which led to the formation of Norway's first political party, the Liberal party, in 1869. The party's major goal was to introduce a parliamentary system of government to Norway. The Liberals passed three amendments to the constitution—in 1874, 1879, and 1880—that would require the par-ticipation of the king in Storting sessions, but the

COMPARE
&
CONTRAST

- **1880:** The second half of the 19th century is an age of literary greatness in Norway. Along with Ibsen, Bjornstjerne Bjornson was a major writer. By the 1890s, writers such as Gabriel Scot and Knut Hamson are introducing symbolism and neoromanticism into the Norwegian literary world.

  1990s: Today, Norway supports its writers through tax exemptions, monetary grants, and government purchasing for libraries. Norway ranks among the world's leaders in books published per capita. About 5,000 new titles are published each year of which about two thirds are works by Norwegian authors.

- **1870s:** Industrialization begins in Norway. This shift in production causes a national migration to urban areas.

  1990s: In the 1990s, industry contributes about one quarter to the country's gross domestic product and employs about one third of the labor force. Important industries include petroleum and gas production, food products, metals and metal products, machinery, and transport equipment.

- **1880s:** In 1889, Norwegian law changes to require children aged seven to fourteen to attend school. The first compulsory education law had been passed in 1860.

  1990s: In the 1990s, the law requires nine years of basic schooling with a tenth optional year. Mandatory subjects include Norwegian, religion, math, music, physical education, science, and English.

---

king refused to sanction this proposal. Members of the Conservative party, who wanted to strengthen the union between Sweden and Norway, held the majority in the Storting, and they supported the king.

In 1882, the Liberals gained a majority in the Storting. They began an impeachment process and removed the government of the king's appointed prime minister from office in 1884. The king saw no option but to ask the Liberal leader to become the new prime minister of Norway. Parliamentarism was thus established.

An Independent Norway

Toward the end of the 19th century, Sweden and Norway were clashing frequently. The Swedish demanded that the union's prime minister be Swedish, and they did not want to give in to Norway's demands for its own consular service. In March 1905, the prime minister's government decided that the issue had to be settled unilaterally. The Storting passed the new consular law, but the king in Sweden vetoed it. The Norwegian ministers, however, re-fused to countersign the veto. When the king would not accept their resignation, they gave up power to the Storting. The prime minister declared that, in refusing to form a new ministry, the king had left Norway without a government, which was unacceptable according to Norway's constitution. Failure to do his constitution duty, he argued, led to his abdication. The Storting thus declared the dissolution of the union.

Sweden demanded a vote by the Norwegian voters that would show whether the nation as a whole agreed with this action. In August 1905, only 184 Norwegian voters voiced dissenting opinion. A final agreement on the dissolution of the union between Sweden and Norway was made in September. Norway was a free and independent country for the first time since 1397.

Social Changes in Nineteenth Century Norway

Over the course of the century, many Norwegian towns saw enormous growth. For example,

Christiania, which had a population of around 12,000 in 1800, had 228,000 residents 100 years later. New roads and railway lines improved communication and trade between towns. Industry grew dramatically, particularly the timber trade and the textile industry. Whereas at the beginning of the decade, Norway was predominantly an agricultural county, by 1900, about 27 percent of Norwegians relied on industry to make their living.

The specifically peasant culture, known as the *Bondekultur,* had flourished in the seventeenth and eighteenth century, but by the mid-1800s it was in a state of decline. Old stave-churches from the Middle Ages were pulled down; peasant costumes, arts, and crafts were neglected; folktales were forgotten or scorned. A group of scholars and intellectuals wanted to ensure the survival of the Bondekultur. They recorded folktales, ballads, legends, and music for future generations. They researched peasant arts and crafts, customs, beliefs, and values.

In 1851, the Society for Popular Enlightenment was founded by educationalists and intellectuals. This society contributed to a new school law in 1860, which called for the establishment of permanent schools in rural areas. Soon, high schools also began to be constructed in rural areas.

Arts in Late-Nineteenth Century Norway

In the 1870s and 1880s, Norwegian literature began to breakthrough on the European and world scenes with foreign translations of the works of writers such as Ibsen, Bjornstjerne Bjornson, Alexander Kielland, and Jonas Lie. These writers availed themselves of changes in Norwegian society—particularly the rise of industry and the disintegration of old rural society—to explore new themes. Norwegians were themselves interested in the new European literary realism, as represented by writers such as Charles Dickens, Gustave Flaubert, and Ivan Turgenev. Writers were also influenced by the Danish critic Georg Brandes, who demanded the new literature must present problems for debate. Many writers were supportive of the Pan-Scandinavian movement, which called for increased solidarity between the three Scandinavian countries: Sweden, Norway, and Denmark.

By the 1890s, however, Norwegian literature underwent the period of New Romanticism. Writers were turning away from the exploration of the individual's role in society to a probing of the relationship between individuals and their inner lives and psyches. In their later works, Ibsen and his contemporaries had turned their ideas inward, as well, but a new group of writers also emerged in the decade, such as Knut Hamsun who later won the Nobel Prize for literature.

Other important developments were made in the arts. In 1899, the National Theatre opened in Christiania with Bjornson serving as its first director. The 1880s were a turning point in Norwegian painting. Young painters traveled to Paris to learn from the works of painters such as Claude Monet. When they returned home, they developed an indigenous school of painting that concentrated on realistically but vividly depicting Norwegian daily life

CRITICAL OVERVIEW

Ibsen published *The Wild Duck* in 1884, and the following winter, it was produced on stage for the first time. Initially, most critics did not respond to Ibsen's humble setting and characters, his sense of humor, and what they saw as his pretentiousness. While some viewers greatly enjoyed the play, they were, at that time, in the distinct minority. Playwright George Bernard Shaw wrote in 1897 after viewing the play, ''Where shall I find an epithet magnificent enough for *The Wild Duck*!'' He found the play to be ''a profound tragedy,'' yet one that kept the audience ''shaking with laughter . . . at an irresistible comedy.'' The poet Rainer Maria Rilke lauded the poetry of Ibsen's words. ''There was something great, deep, essential,'' he wrote. ''Last Judgement. A finality.''

Summing up the majority opinion of the play, Francis Bull wrote in *Norsk Litteraturhistorie* in 1937 that ''[P]eople had got used to the idea that Ibsen's dramas should engage in controversial issues, and when *The Wild Duck* came out, 11 November 1884, the public was utterly bewildered. Alexander Kielland, quoted in Bull's ''Norsk Litteraturehistories,'' found the book odd and was annoyed by 'these everlasting symbols and hints and crude emphases.' Bjornson, cited in Rilke's Review of *The Wild Duck* in *Selected Letters of Rainer Maria Rilke* ''called the whole play 'disgusting,' and thought its psychological foundation false.'' In the years to come, many critics had a hard time understanding both the play and what Ibsen was

A Phoenix Theatre production of The Wild Duck, *1990.*

trying to accomplish. An 1894 reviewer from *The Athenaeum* wrote, ''The play must be a joke . . . it is a harmless, if not very humourous piece of self-banter, or it is nothing.'' In a review of a series of Ibsen's plays written by Edmond Gosse, quoted in Valency's ''The Flower and the Castle,'' echoed what many had already said about the play: ''This is a very long play, by far the most extended of the series, and is, on the whole, the least interesting to read . . . There is really not a character in the book that inspires confidence or liking . . . There can be no doubt that it is by far the most difficult of Ibsen's for a reader to comprehend.''

Havelock Ellis, a sexual psychologist, wrote in 1890 that *The Wild Duck* was ''the least remarkable of Ibsen's [tragedies]. There is no central personage who absorbs our attention, and no great situation . . . [T]he dramatist's love of symbolism, here centered on the wild duck, becomes obtrusive and disturbing.'' Ellis, however, found redemptive factors in the play—as a satire on ideals and beliefs expressed in Ibsen's earlier plays such as *A Doll's House* and *The Pillars of Society.* He also noted that ''Ibsen approaches in his own manner, without, however, much insistence, the moral aspects of the equality of the sexes.'' More laudatory was W. D. Howells, the American author and literary critic, in a review of

1906. He put forth his analysis of Hjalmar's reaction to the truth, which, in light of the body of criticism available to modern readers, seems rather simplistic: ''inference is that the truth is not for every one always, but may sometimes be a real mischief.'' Howells, however, was one of the first critics to explore the important concept of truth and illusion that Ibsen presented.

In years to come, other critics and scholars analyzed the characters. Psychoanalysts Smith Ely Jelliffe and Louise Brink published their analyses in terms of contemporary psychoanalytic theory in 1919. They found Gregers to be a caricature of ''false blundering therapy'' and believed that he ''whimsically represents'' Ibsen's ''own earlier zeal and fate as a reformer.'' In this analysis, they agreed with Ellis; later critics, such as Hermann J. Weigand and Ronald Gray would concur with this opinion.

''Only gradually,'' wrote D. Keith Peacock in *Reference Guide to World Literature,* ''was Ibsen's play recognized as a painful, but at times ironically comic, comment upon humanity's need for the protection of illusion.'' In the years since its first publication, *The Wild Duck* has come to be viewed as one of Ibsen's masterpieces. Dounia B. Christiani, an Ibsen translator, noted in her preface to a 1968 edition of *The Wild Duck* that while it ''gained early recognition [from literary critics and scholars] as the most masterfully constructed of Ibsen's prose dramas, its innovative combination of farce with tragedy and of realism with symbolism has only rather recently won the sort of appreciation that is based on acute critical analysis.'' More contemporary criticism of *The Wild Duck* has focused on symbolism, imagery, and characterization, and some critics have used the play as an insight into Ibsen's beliefs. The play continues to draw attention, both among students and scholars of literature and drama, as well as theatergoing audiences. When the play was staged in New York in 1986, Robert Brustein commented on the director's focus on the play's theme, ''which is the malignant effect of utopian idealism on those who need illusions in order to survive.''

CRITICISM

Rena Korb

Korb has a master's degree in English literature and creative writing and has written for a wide variety of educational publishers. In the following essay, she discuss the tragic and comic elements in The Wild Duck.

In comparison to current esteem for Henrik Ibsen's *The Wild Duck,* the play was vastly underappreciated upon its initial appearance on the stages of Europe. In Scandinavia, the play was somewhat successful but drew little interest from critics. While its Berlin audience applauded it, the play was booed in Rome, disliked in London, and received with indifference in Paris. The criticism it drew in the first few decades after its publication and performance was, generally, negative. Edmund Gosse wrote in an 1889 collection that it was ''the least interesting'' of Ibsen's plays to date. In years since, however, *The Wild Duck* slowly came to be regarded as one of Ibsen's more important works. Only a few decades after it first appeared in theaters, scholars and critics began to study and better understand the play, and thus appreciate it. As early as 1919, Smith Ely Jeliffe and Louise Brink asserted in *The Psychoanalytic Review* that ''Ibsen's power and genius for touching the finer intimate realities of life close at hand, are perhaps most evident in *The Wild Duck.*''

The play also ushered in the final period of Ibsen's career, signifying his shifting interest from social realism to symbolism and characterization. Ibsen portrays the self-deceiving Ekdal family with psychological insight and compassion. At the same time, his play reaches both the heights of tragedy and comedy. Indeed, Ibsen asserted that he had written a ''tragi-comedy,'' an appraisal that has since been accepted by most scholars. The tragedy was as important as the comedy, Ibsen wrote, otherwise Hedvig's death would become ''incomprehensible.'' Indeed, this incoherence was one of the elements against which many early critics railed. Maurice Valency notes that amidst a backdrop of caricatures and melodramas, ''Only the child suffers.'' Her death is the one tragic note in a ''distinctly comic situation.''

The Wild Duck is, at once, serious and farcical. The characters in particular manifest the comic elements. Old Ekdal charges around the attic, wearing his lieutenant's cap and dirty toupee and shooting pigeons and poultry and pretending that he is shooting bears. The wild duck, confined to the attic, has instead of a lake for swimming and diving, a water trough for splashing. Hjalmar, who has just terrified his daughter and is in the process of leaving his wife, still throws his overcoat on the sofa and complains about ''All these exhausting preparations!''

In Hjalmar Ekdal and Gregers Werle, the opposing elements that make up comedy and tragedy are most clearly demonstrated. Each man strongly maintains his belief and his system of ideals, not realizing that his overwrought and overblown opinions appear ludicrous to onlookers. Hjalmar talks quite earnestly of a photographic device he will invent. ''Sure, of course I'm making progress,'' he answers in response to Gregers's question. ''I grapple every single day with the invention, I'm filled with it . . . But I simply must not be rushed; . . . The inspiration, the intuition—look, when it's ready to come, it will come, and that's all.'' Everyone around him understands this truth, what Relling calls Hjalmar's ''life-lie.''

Hjalmar's foolishness is more comically revealed when he returns home to pack his belongings after his night of drunkenness. He says to Gina, ''I must have my books with me. Where are my books?''

Gina: What books? Hjalmar: My scientific works, naturally—the technical journals I use for my invention. Gina [*looking in the bookcase*]: Is it these here

WHAT DO I READ NEXT?

- Ibsen's *A Doll's House* was first published in 1879 and performed the same year. The play centers on the Helmer family. When an outsider threatens to expose one of Nora Helmer's past acts, Nora's illusions about marriage and loyalty are shattered. This play is an early work portraying female independence.

- Swedish playwright August Strindberg was a contemporary of Ibsen. His play *Miss Julie* is one of his most outstanding works. It centers on Julie, an aristocrat young woman who has a brief affair with her father's valet. In it, Strindberg combines dramatic naturalism with his own conception of psychology. With such works, Strindberg helped develop Expressionist drama in Europe.

- George Bernard Shaw's play *Mrs. Warren's*

Profession (1898) centers on a young woman's discovery that her mother's rise from poverty was through prostitution, and that her mother still holds financial interests in several brothels. Learning these unpleasant truths forces the young woman to reevaluate her relationship with her mother and others.

- Irish playwright John Millington Synge also dealt with unsentimental studies of the character of his people. His 1907 comedy, *The Playboy of the Western World*, like *The Wild Duck*, was initially unpopular with local audiences, but has since won widespread acceptance as a masterpiece. It centers of a young Irishman whose self-reported murder of his father earns him much admiration.

---

that there's no covers on? Hjalmar: Yes, of course. Gina [*puts a pile of unbound volumes on the table*]: Shouldn't I get Hedvig to cut the pages for you?

This exchange eloquently demonstrates how little involvement Hjalmar actually has with his ''project.'' It is only a prop—a distracting toy, even.

In her article ''The Will and Testament of Ibsen,'' Mary McCarthy notes the comical connection between the two men; ''Hjalmar's pretended 'purpose in life' is a sort of parody of Gregers' 'purpose to live for.''' The reverse is true as well; Gregers's belief that he can effect a meaningful difference in other people's lives can be seen as his life-lie. In truth, his interference has no positive purpose and seems to mask his own emptiness more than it fulfills any other function. Gregers has spent the past fifteen years up at ''the works,'' where he found life ''Delightfully lonely.'' Though he had ''Plenty of opportunity to think about all sorts of things,'' he never arrived at any project to which he could devote his life—much in the same vein as Hjalmar and his ''invention.'' The project of revealing the truth about Hakon's involvement with the

Ekdals, however, gives him ''an objective to live for.'' That Gregers should take upon himself the responsibility of opening Hjalmar's eyes is both tragic and comic. His sense of self-importance makes it tragic—he cannot help but try and inflict his ideals on those around him—as does the ultimate outcome his interference has on the family. At the same time, his self-importance, which leads to his ill-conceived plan, is comical, for clearly Gregers has no justification for his actions—truly he seems to enjoy meddling and he has nothing else on which to spend his time. At the end of the play, he mournfully but with acceptance verbalizes his role—what he calls his ''destiny'' in life: ''To be the thirteenth man at the table.''

Unfortunately, the rest of the Ekdal family is as ignorant to the intermingling of seriousness and foolishness—reality and illusion—as are Gregers and Hjalmar. Though Gina Ekdal immediately senses the danger that Gregers poses to her family and to the protected world she has created for Hjalmar, her recognition is based on her dependency on Hakon's economic help, thus she fears losing her reality, not her illusion. She protests letting Gregers rent out their extra room: "But can't you see there's something the matter between them again, since the younger one is moving out? . . . And now maybe Mr. Werle will think you were behind it . . . he could take it out on Grandpa. Suppose he loses the little money he makes working for Graberg." Gina also distrusts Gregers because, unlike her husband who is lost in his own world and concerns, she pays attention to Gregers's words and nuances.

> Gregers: She's going look to like you in time, Mrs. Ekdal. How old might she be now? Gina: Hedvig's just fourteen; it's her birthday the day after tomorrow. Gregers: A big girl for her age. Gina: Yes, she certainly shot up this last year. Gregers: The young ones growing up make us realize how old we ourselves are getting. —How long is it now you've been married? Gina: We've been married already fifteen years-just about. Gregers: Imagine, is it that long! Gina [*becomes attentive; looks at him*]: Yes, that's what it is, all right.

Only Hjalmar's careless interruption ends the flow of conversation, but the exchange gains much significance because it shows Gina's wariness at Gregers's questions. She understands the implications in his unspoken words and takes care to answer him honestly if cagily.

Despite Gina's initial sense of foreboding, she is unable to recognize the depth of the threat he poses, for her focus, as befits her role in life, is on the practical rather than the symbolic and emotional. For instance, she questions Gregers's assertion that he would like to be a clever dog, the "kind that goes in after ducks when they plunge and fasten themselves in the weeds and the tangle in the mud" because she mistakenly interprets his statement literally.

Though she is only a child, Hedvig understands that Gregers speaks symbolically:

> Gina: . . . Wasn't that crazy talk, wanting to be a dog? Hedvig: You know what, Mother—I think he meant something else. Gina: What else could he mean? Hedvig: Oh, I don't know. But it was just as though he meant something different from what he was saying-the whole time. Gina: You think so? Well, it sure was queer though.

Her tragedy, however, arises because she takes words *too* seriously. First, she believes Gregers's words—that sacrificing the wild duck is the best way to demonstrate her love for her father. More importantly, she takes Hjalmar's rejection utterly seriously. When he calls her an intruder, Hedvig grabs the pistol and escapes into the attic. She

> MAURICE VALENCY NOTES THAT AMIDST A BACKDROP OF CARICATURES AND MELODRAMAS, 'ONLY THE CHILD SUFFERS.' HER DEATH IS THE ONE TRAGIC NOTE IN A 'DISTINCTLY COMIC SITUATION.'"

overhears him speak of her "manipulation" of him, rhetorically stating: "If I asked her then: Hedvig, are you willing to turn your back on life for me? [*Laughs scornfully.*] Thanks a lot-you'd soon hear the answer I'd get!" In response and in despair, Hedvig kills herself.

Her parents' reactions further underscore the tragic-comic elements of the play. Upon discovery of Hedvig's body, Gina reacts as would a normal parent. She bursts into tears and cries out, "Oh, my baby! My baby!" Hjalmar, in contrast, describes how Hedvig must have "in terror . . . crept into the attic and died for love of me." He dramatically clenches his hands into fists and berates the heavens. "Oh, Thou above . . . ! If Thou *art* there! Why hast Thou done this thing to me? . . ." In the midst of his overdramatizing, however, the serious undercurrent remains ever apparent, for even at this moment of Hedvig's greatest loss—the loss of her life—Hjalmar cannot see past how it will affect his own life.

Source: Rena Korb, in an essay for *Drama for Students*, Gale, 2001.

Brian Johnston

In the following essay, Johnston discusses the symbolic meaning that lies within The Wild Duck.

In 1906, Rainer Maria Rilke wrote to Clara Rilke about his cultural activities in Paris and noted:

> But the most remarkable part of this very long day was the evening. We saw Ibsen's *Wild Duck* at the Antoine. Excellently rehearsed, with a great deal of care and shaping—marvelous. Of course, by reason of certain differences in temperament, details were distorted, crooked, misunderstood. But the poetry! . . . all its splendour came from the inside and almost to the surface. There was something great, deep, essential. Last Judgement. A finality. And suddenly the hour

was there when Ibsen's majesty deigned to look at me for the first time. A new poet, whom we shall approach by many roads now that I know of one of them. And again someone who is misunderstood in the midst of fame. Someone quite different from what one hears. . . .

That the image of the Last Judgment should flash through Rilke's mind suggests that Ibsen's audacious supertext did well up "from the inside and almost to the surface" as it seems to have done for Robert Raphael too who, in a sensitive account of the play, observed of the strange Ekdal attic and its menagerie:

> Hedvig and her grandfather approach their world with a devotion and ritual akin to religious reverence, for the attic with the duck and other treasures may be considered a metaphor for the Christian paradise: it performs in their lives exactly the same function as does a traditional church for many people. Existing on the top floor of the Ekdal microcosm, the attic is the *summum bonum* in their lives; it provides them, just like heaven, with a world of pure value, a realm of nearly perfect orientation. The Ekdals keep returning to this private religion for sustenance just as people do with any traditional illusion that is sacred to them.

In *The Ibsen Cycle* (1975), I outlined how *The Wild Duck* recreated the Christian phase in the long history of the human spirit explored by Hegel and, I claimed, recovered in Ibsen's own imaginative and independent terms in his cycle of twelve realist plays. *The Wild Duck* inaugurated at the same time the second part of Ibsen's three-part cycle. The sequence in which Hegel acts out the spirit's long travail from the time of the Roman empire through the myth of the Fall and the sacrifice of the "natural world" up to the pre-Enlightenment period of the "sun king" and his court is perhaps the richest in the *Phenomenology*. It is a sequence, like the others in the *Phenomenology,* that has shaped our modern identity and that therefore, if we are fully to know ourselves, must be relived imaginatively by a present act of remembrance. In this essay I want to examine the interplay of competing levels of dramatic metaphor, verbal and visual, in Ibsen's drama: the highly conscious intertextuality of his art—those moments in Ibsen's text when the supertext momentarily wells up through the language of everyday life. A struggle takes place between text and supertext for the play's dominant language, and it is the struggle itself, the way in which the spirit invades and infuses a despiritualized everyday reality, that constitutes a major conflict of the play.

In *The Wild Duck* the struggle is especially rich because of the unusual number of competing voices and visions that contribute to the struggle, with the

messianic (Gregers) and the diabolic (Relling) at the lingual extremes. Gina's language is literal, lapsing into malapropism; old Ekdal's a language of superstition and of the world of nature: "Der er hævn i skogen" ("there's vengeance in the forests"). His son Hjalmar has evolved a sentimentally evasive and self-deluding rhetoric under the promptings of Relling, who himself introduces to the discourse of the household the deceptive language of the "livsløgnen" ("life-lie"). Gregers Werle infuses this lingual brew with a potent language of parable, symbol, and metaphor in the service of what he believes are truths transcending the quotidian world of the senses and at war with the lies of his father and Relling.

The still unformed child consciousness of Hedvig, assailed by these disparate voices, responds to this strange new language of Gregers, a secret language of "på havsens bund" ("the depths of the sea") where "Tiden er altså istå" ("time has stood still") and where the attic might not really be an attic. At the end of Act II Gregers declares he wishes to be "en riktig urimelig flink hund; en slig en, som går tilbunds after vildænder, når de dukker under og bider sig fast i tang og tære nede i mudderet" ("an extraordinarily clever dog. One that goes to the bottom after wild ducks when they dive and bite fast to all the weeds and waste down in the mud"). Gina, the literalist, is merely stupefied by this declared ambition, but Hedvig early on tunes in to Gregers' mode of discourse: "det var ligesom han mente noget andet, end det han sa—hele tiden" ("it was as if he meant something different from what he was saying—all the time"). She detects that Gregers talks in parables, that he inhabits something like a medieval world of marvelous correspondences between the God-created Book of Nature waiting to be interpreted and the human condition, where the history of the wild duck, its wounding and rescue, exist in an allegorical dimension to be decoded for hidden spiritual truth. In one odd passage Relling tells Gregers, "Men De tar så skammelig fejl af de store vidunderfluerne, som De tror at se og høre omkring Dem" ("But you're preposterously wrong about the great marvelous presences you believe you see and hear around you"). I will claim that Gregers' is a quintessentially Christian consciousness and mode of discourse sustained in the play by both its scenography—its overall story and action—and its pervasive imagery. That is, it is by recognizing the congruence of the play's verbal imagery with its scenography, action, and metaphorical topography that a distinctly Christian dimension of the play with its attendant dualisms powerfully emerges.

The scenography of the play is notably vertical: from the heights of Høydal (High Dale) to the "havsens bund" ("depths of the sea")—a macrocosm whose vertical structure is recreated, as Robert Raphael saw, in the microcosm of the Ekdal home, with the attic world above and the realm of Relling and Molvik below. This scenography, which is supplemented by character types, actions, and verbal and visual imagery, supplies the medieval Christian dimension of the play. It is not the only dimension but is the richest source of the play's poetry.

On 12 June 1883 Ibsen announced to his friend Georg Brandes that he was working on the plot of a new dramatic work that was to be *The Wild Duck.* He added, "Jeg går i denne tid og tumler med udkastet til et nyt dramatisk arbejde i 4 akter. Der ansamler sig jo gerne mellem år og dag diverse galskaber i en, og dem vil man gerne have et afløb for" ("At the moment I'm setting about revolving the plot of a new dramatic work in four acts. A variety of wild ideas are inclined to gather together in one's mind, and one needs to find an outlet for them"). The variety of wild ideas ("diverse galskaber") in *The Wild Duck* is of a formidable audacity: as an example to which I shall return later, I will mention the trinity of Father, Son, and Holy Duck.

The realistic story of the play goes as follows: at the time when Merchant (Grosserer) Werle is about to marry his mistress, Mrs. Sørby, his son Gregers is invited to descend from Høydal after a fifteen-year exile and attend a feast in his honor. Gregers invites his old friend Hjalmar Ekdal to join him. Hjalmar is humiliated at the party: Merchant Werle pointedly observes that Hjalmar's presence has meant they were an unlucky thirteen at table; then Hjalmar's incongruously shabby father disturbs the sumptuous feast. Gregers becomes convinced that his father has brought about the Ekdals' fall and also has arranged that Hjalmar should marry the merchant's discarded mistress. He decides to make right his own conscience by revealing the truth of how the Ekdals were betrayed.

When he visits their attic studio and dwelling, he finds them more or less comfortably reconciled to their fallen condition, against which they have compensated by constructing a fantasy world of the attic and its menagerie—an escape from unhappy reality. Here, Gregers encounters an old opponent,

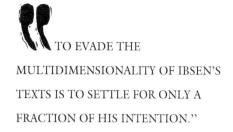

TO EVADE THE MULTIDIMENSIONALITY OF IBSEN'S TEXTS IS TO SETTLE FOR ONLY A FRACTION OF HIS INTENTION."

Dr. Relling, living below the Ekdals with a companion whom Relling describes as "demonisk" ("demonic"). Whereas Gregers believes in bringing saving truth, Relling believes humanity needs "livsløgner" ("life-lies") to survive. . . .

Gregers' truth-bringing creates a crisis in the Ekdal family which, he convinces Hedvig, can be overcome through sacrifice—the sacrifice of what she holds most dear, the wild duck. When the parents believe Hedvig *has* sacrificed the duck, it is important to note, they *are* reconciled, as Gregers predicted. But something goes wrong. Hedvig kills herself. The parents show "noble grief," but Gregers and Relling, resuming their old quarrel, dispute the value of this grief.

This summary of the plot inevitably has left out much, but it covers the main action. However, this action can be retold as much more than a homely domestic tragedy, and I now would like to superimpose upon the realistic story, like an enlarging grid, the story retold from the archetypal dimension.

A Son descends from on high (Høydal) to undo the actions of his Father, whose victims live in a fallen condition of deceit and escapist fantasy. He will free these victims by bringing the Truth, and he uses the imagery of Light to describe this action. He sees this humanity as in the clutches of a Deceiver, living *below* with a demonic companion, indulging in drunken orgies. This fallen family has constructed a miniature landscape and menagerie in the attic which compensates for the lost world of nature, so that the stage is divided, as in familiar Christian iconography, between the humble family in the foreground and a space with animals in the background. The Truth-bringer's action causes great anguish, and, when he urges sacrifice, tragedy ensues. After the catastrophe, the Truth-bringer and the Deceiver resume their dispute over whether humanity can be redeemed. The Son (who does not expect to live long) asserts it is his destiny to be, as if at a perpetual Last Supper, ''at være trettende mand tilbords'' (''thirteenth at table'').

The world of the play is drastically divided between an idea of reality created by the past actions of the Father, powerfully presiding over the fall of the play's chief inhabitants (and abetted by the lies of the Deceiver), and an idea of reality envisaged by the Son, seeking through present actions and through the Truth these inhabitants' redemption. Like the medieval mystery cycles, therefore, *The Wild Duck* is divided between Old Testament (of the Father and Law) and New (of the Son and Salvation).

The second archetypal story runs parallel with the first (''realistic'') one and in fact is the same action looked at from another perspective. (In Ibsen the symbol is always the real seen from another perspective.) Textually, the two stories continually intersect. Each by itself would be inadequate as a drama of human consciousness. The archetypal story alone would have the remote and abstract quality of, say, *The Castle of Perseverance*. The realistic story alone would be as confined and parochial in reference as most modern dramatic realism. The intersection of the two dimensions of action and language creates difficulties both for interpretation and for performance, but they are the difficulties of a major dramatic art and are worth solving. To evade the multidimensionality of Ibsen's texts is to settle for only a fraction of his intention. To cut him down to the size of one's psychological, moral, or political agenda instead of opening oneself up to the immensity of his intention is to create that idea of him—a man ''misunderstood in the midst of fame'' (to recall Rilke's words)—which, in the United States, practically reduces his theatrical output to only two purportedly feminist plays, *A Doll House* and *Hedda Gabler*.

The Wild Duck, as noted above, is the first play of the Cycle's second group, and it inaugurates the profoundly *dualistic* aspect of this second phase of the Cycle. This dualism is visually present on stage in the division, in the Ekdal home, between a foreground space of reluctant work and a background space (the attic) of compensating fantasy—a stage division also present in the Werle household. This dualism continues in the strongly vertical imagery of the play with its extremes of heights and depths, in the social division between the haves and have-nots in the ideological division of Gregers' and Relling's agendas, and so on. How thoroughly Ibsen has *visualized* this dualism can be seen in two

striking uses of an incongruity between character and setting: the shabbily dressed Ekdal emerging to interrupt the sumptuous feast of Grosserer Werle, and the appearance of the splendidly dressed Werle interrupting the shabby feast of the Ekdal home.

I would argue the Ekdals' fantasy attic stands for a realm of the human imagination, of memory of loss which within two-dimensional modernity usually is rendered impotent as fantasy and escapism— e.g., in the trivial diversions of the modern media — but which contains potent hidden, unconscious forces that can awaken and explode into the contemporary world. It is under Gregers' prompting, I believe, that Hedvig awakens these dangerous but liberating powers. That invisible denizen of the attic, the Flying Dutchman, is just such a potent figure of liberating death to the Norwegian girl Senta in Richard Wagner's opera. The Flying Dutchman, I am convinced, is one of the identities of the Stranger from the depths of the sea in *The Lady from the Sea,* a play in which the miniature enclosed landscape of *The Wild Duck*'s attic now explodes, through Ibsen's theatrical magic, into the expansive Romantic scenography of mountains and fjord. The strange symbolism *The Wild Duck* —the secretive realm of the attic, its trees, treasures, and menagerie, with the wild duck at its center—is both new in the Cycle and unique to this play. Such a symbolic or allegorical dimension to art, where the world must be ''read'' as a system of signs to be decoded, is most typical of medieval Christian art. And it is Gregers who reads the world in this way.

Profoundly connected to the Christian themes, action, and imagery of the play is the juxtaposition of the humble and the exalted. This is Ibsen's only play focusing on the ''insulted and injured''—the only play exploring so humble a condition of consciousness. Of all world religions or ideologies, in both its story and its iconography, Christianity above all emphasizes the humble and the homely— in strong contrast to the emphasis on the heroic and the beautiful of the Hellenic tradition, whose recovery was envisaged in the first four plays. Such iconography (encountered in medieval drama) as the stable, the humble family in the foreground, the animals in the background, the angels appearing to the simple shepherds in Palestine, and so on, at the same time is coupled with the most extravagant claims for humanity (for whom specifically the entire cosmos was brought into being) ever made by a religion. Much of this imagery and iconography is repeated in *The Wild Duck.*

The eruptions of Christian themes and imagery are so remarkably frequent when linked with the plot and the characters' situations, conflicts, and actions and with the visual imagery and setting that I cannot see how such a dimension, as an insistent intertextuality, can be denied. In fact, the author of *Brand, Peer Gynt,* and *Emperor and Galilean* creates in the Realist Cycle, with intricate subtlety and delicacy, a multidimensional dramatic work on the most immense scale.

Ibsen's method is an incremental interplay of both visual and verbal suggestion in which the archetypal story gradually seeps through the modern realistic texture, as in the opening scene of the play. That is, instead of creating an overtly Symbolist or allegorical drama, Ibsen infiltrates his supertext into his realistic text little by little. It is only at the close of this incremental process that the full supertext emerges.

In the following excerpts from the play, this incremental process stands revealed. At many points, the allegorical references are self-evident; still, I have noted particular points at which close readings and exact translations clarify the archetypal supertext. I begin with the stage direction describing Merchant Werle's house in Act I. . . .

The opening scene ushers in the first cluster of Christian images—the Fall, hard labor and penance, the descent of the Son, the Last Supper—without disturbing the requirements of the dramatic text to render a plausible modern reality.

Ibsen was being more than unusually disingenuous, I believe, when he assured his publisher, Frederik Hegel, that the play could not "possibly give offense to anyone." The "galskaber" which plays all through the text, as we will see below, is the expression of a creative impulse audacious to the point of genial blasphemy. First there is the Trinity of the Father, Son, and Holy ("velsignede") Duck.

Birds frequently are emblems of spiritual forces. The Holy Ghost traditionally is of course depicted as a dove. Ibsen maintains this avian iconography for the spirit from early in his career to the end. The idealistic lovers of *Love's Comedy* are named after the falcon and swan. The hawk and dove are crucial spiritual emblems in *Brand.* Talking birds accompany Peer's encounter with the Bøyg and with Memnon's statue in *Peer Gynt.* Hilde Wangel in *The Master Builder* is a "rogfuglen" ("bird of prey"). The last words of the Cycle

juxtapose Maia's "Jeg er fri som en fugl! Jeg er fri!" ("I am free as a bird, I am free!") with the words of the Deaconess—"Pax vobiscum!" The idea that a wild duck might be an emblem of the free (wild) spirit, now trapped and tamed, is strongly reinforced by Gregers Werle's own forceful application of this idea.

The Norwegian term for "duck" is "and." The word for "spirit" is "ånd." (The Holy Ghost is "den hellige ånd.") There is only a slight dissimilarity in both the sound and the appearance of the two words. Gregers, the Son, declares he wishes to be an extraordinarily clever dog and save wild ducks who have sunk to the bottom among what Ekdal calls "alt det fandenskab"—"all that devil's mess". To reinforce its archetypal dimension, the wild duck—and its realm, before and after captivity—is presented to Gregers, and to the audience, in the most striking manner.

In Act II, Gregers consoles Old Ekdal for his loss of the natural world, the world of forests and lakes that the wild duck also inhabited. Ekdal, he says, has nothing in the world to connect him to his more free, natural life, and this rouses the old man to reveal the world of the attic and its central denizen. The disclosure of the duck to Gregers—and to the theater audience—is a solemnly reverent, step-by-step revelation paced for maximum effect:

Ekdal (staring astonished at him). Nothing in the world to—!

Gregers. Of course, you've got Hjalmar. But he's got his own family. And a man like you, who's always felt drawn to what is wild and free, is—

Ekdal (Strikes the table). Hjalmar, now he's got to see it!

Hjalmar. But father, is it worth it just now? It's so dark—

Ekdal. Nonsense. There's the moonlight. Come and help me, Hjalmer.

Hedvig. Yes, let's do it, father!

Hjalmar (getting up). Oh, very well.

Gregers (to Gina). What is it?

Gina. You mustn't think it's anything so very special.

(Ekdal and Hjalmar have gone to the rear wall, and each slides one of the double doors aside, Hedvig helping the old man. Gregers remains standing by the sofa. Gina sits unconcerned and sewing. Through the door-opening can be seen a large, long, irregularly shaped attic with recesses and a couple of free-standing stove pipes. There are skylights through which bright moonlight falls on some parts of the room while others remain in deep shadow.)

Ekdal (to Gregers). Come right over here.

Gregers (walks over to him). Just what is it?

Ekdal. Take a look and see. Hm.

Hjalmar (rather embarrassed). All this belongs to father, you understand.

Gregers (at the doorway, looking into the attic). So you keep poultry, Lieutenant Ekdal.

Ekdal. I should think we *do* keep poultry. They've flown up to roost just now. You'll need to see the poultry by daylight.

Hedvig. And then there's—

Ekdal. Shh, shh. Don't say anything just yet.

Gregers. And you keep pigeons, too, I see.

Ekdal. Ah, yes. You could certainly say we keep pigeons! They've got their boxes up there under the rafters. Because pigeons like to roost high up, you know.

Hjalmer. Some are not just ordinary pigeons.

Ekdal. Ordinary! No, you can be sure of that! We have tumblers. And a pair of pouters, as well. But come over here. Can you see that hutch over there by the wall?

Gregers. Yes. What do you use that for?

Ekdal. That's where the rabbits lie at night, young fellow.

Gregers. No! So you've got rabbits as well?

Ekdal. Yes, you can be sure as the devil we've got rabbits. He's asking if we've got rabbits, do you hear, Hjalmar? Hm. But now comes the real thing, just wait. Here it is! Move away, Hedvig. Now come and stand here, just so, and then look down there. Can you see a basket with straw in it?

Gregers. Yes. And I can see a bird lying in it.

Ekdal. Hm.—''a bird''—

Gregers. Isn't it a duck?

Ekdal (offended). Yes, of course it's a duck.

Hjalmar. But what kind of duck, do you suppose?

Hedvig. It's not just any ordinary duck—

Ekdal. Shh!

Gregers. And it isn't a turkish [tyrkisk] duck, either.

Ekdal. No, Mr.—Werle. That's no turkish duck. It's a wild duck [en vildand]. . . .

In the iterations of this identity that follow, the term ''en vildand'' goes through three forms. Ekdal says simply ''en vildand.'' Gregers separates the two parts of the noun and repeats ''En-vild-and,'' emphasizing the strange wild/free aspect. Ekdal finally says ''vildanden,'' which conjoins the article and the two parts of the noun. It would seem that the term has lost its strangeness for the Ekdals, and therefore the duck its challenging identity.

The ensuing story of the duck is told against our *memory* of its moonlit disclosure, like a parable

glossing the strange revelation. The audience is bound to remember, all through the following narration, the strange vision it has just had.

The story of the wild duck (''and'') and its fate is sufficiently poetic to magnify the Ekdals' story—a supertextual enlargement of it that does not compromise its subtextual pathos. The imagery of the lost natural world, presented *visually* in the miniature moonlight disclosure, now *verbally* invades the stage through the dialogue's imagery, serving as a gloss to convey the dimension of the loss. The extent of this loss, and its consequences for the human spirit (''ånd''), will be the theme of the quarrel between the Truth-bringer Gregers and the Deceiver Relling. A broad hint of the messianic connotations of Gregers' identity comes at the conclusion of Act III, which gathers up a cluster of preceding themes:

> *Gregers.* . . . if you once have to carry the cross of being called Gregers [Men når en har det kors på sig, at hede Gregers]—''Gregers'' and then ''Werle'' on top of that! Have you ever heard anything so revolting?
>
> *Hjalmar.* But I don't think that at all.
>
> *Gregers.* Ugh! Isch! I'd like to spit on a fellow with a name like that [a reference to the experience of the original bearer of the Cross]. But once you've borne the Cross of being Gregers Werle in this world the way I have—
>
> *Hjalmar (laughing).* Ha-ha! If you weren't Gregers Werle, what would you like to be?
>
> *Gregers.* If I could choose, I'd like best to be a clever dog.
>
> *Gina.* A dog!
>
> *Hedvig (involuntarily).* Oh no!
>
> *Gregers.* Yes, an extraordinarily clever dog. One that goes to the bottom after wild ducks when they dive and bite fast to all the weeds and waste down in the mud. . . .

Here Gregers has taken over and expanded his father's metaphor about the wounded Ekdals from Act I and has reversed it from adverse Judgment of hopeless loss to an image of Redemption—the New Testament compared to the Old Testament version of the Fall. Ekdal, describing the behavior of the wounded duck, merely reports its natural behavior, but Gregers blends Old Werle's and Old Ekdal's accounts to make a form of prospective parable. This is a language to which Gregers will get Hedvig to respond.

The strangest commentary on the duck's identity and its link with Gregers' messianic action in the play emerges from one of Gina's many malapropisms, occurring at the end of the following conversation about the duck:

> *Hedvig (going to Gregers).* Now you can really see the wild duck.
>
> *Gregers.* I'm looking at it. She's trailing a little in one wing, I think.
>
> *Hjalmar.* Well, that's hardly surprising. That's where she was shot.
>
> *Gregers.* And she's dragging a little on one foot. Isn't that right?
>
> *Hjalmar.* Perhaps just a little bit.
>
> *Hedvig.* You see it was in the foot the dog bit her.
>
> *Hjalmar.* But she's hale and healthy otherwise. And that's really remarkable for one who's had a charge of shot in her body and who's been held in the jaws of a dog—
>
> *Gregers (with a glance at Hedvig).* And has been in the depths of the sea—for so long.
>
> *Hedvig (smiling).* Yes.
>
> *Gina.* That blessed wild duck [Den velsignede vildanden]! There's more than enough crucifying over her [Den gøres der da krusifikser nok for; alternate translation: Enough crucifixes have been made for her]. . . .

Here Gina's comment strays into wild and telling Christian malapropism. The Father has winged the duck, preventing its free flight, whereas the extraordinarily clever dog, whose action the Son wishes to emulate, makes difficult its terrestrial life.

Gregers' messianic identity is further irreverently evoked, I believe, in a very Joycean form of punning "galskab." Relling derisively terms Gregers a "kvakksalver" ("quacksalver"). "Kvakk" not only designates "charlatan": it is also the Germanic word for the cry of a duck. (*OED:* "quack [kwæk] sb. Imitative: cf. Du. *Kwak*, G. *quack*, Sw. *quak* [of ducks or frogs], Icel. *kvak*, twittering of birds.") Although in Dano-Norwegian the word for a duck's cry is "skræpper," the Swedish, German, and Icelandic equivalents are close enough. And what of "salver"? "Salve" and "save" derive from the same Latin root (as "salvation" attests). One entry in the *OED* notes that "salver," "One who salves or heals," is "applied to Christ or the Virgin Mary." Is a "kvakksalver" a charlatan healer or savior of ducks or of souls? Again, it is Gregers who gives himself this dual (and-ånd-salver) identity. When he declares he wishes to be the clever dog who dives to the bottom to save wounded ducks, we, like Hedvig, know he is not discussing canine and avian identities. We know a parable when we hear one.

The play, as noted above, contains some intriguingly parallel and repeated images and actions. The sumptuous feast in the Werle household is paralleled by the humble feast in the Ekdal home. Both feasts are interrupted by an unwanted guest from the "other house," and each intruder is visually incongruous to the alien surroundings. The intrusion of Ekdal into the Werle feast leads to the breakup of the Werle family; the intrusion of Werle (and later Mrs. Sørby) into the Ekdal household leads to the breakup of the Ekdal family. Each intrusion of the Werle household into the Ekdal realm follows the resumption of the old quarrel between Gregers and Relling. This quarrel predates the action of the play, and the last lines of the play imply it will continue as if the two are in eternal conflict. . . .

The first interruption from the Werle household, exacerbating Gregers' quarrel with his father, alienated Hjalmar from his wife; the second will alienate him from his daughter. The Werle realm thus forcefully and destructively intrudes into the subordinate Ekdal realm. Gregers, in Act I, described his father's actions as a "slagmark" ("battlefield") with the "menneskeskæbner" ("smashed human forms" [IV, 243]) strewn all around—a description that implies more than the Ekdals have suffered, lifting the quarrel between Father and Son to a universal conflict, whether the Father is a supreme capitalist power (as is Grosserer) or a celestial one.

In Act V we learn that Hjalmar has temporarily descended into the Relling realm of drunken orgy. His reaction to the experience, once he returns home, is strangely excessive:

> *HJALMAR (talking to himself, half aloud and bitterly, as he empties the table drawer)* You're a scoundrel, Relling!—A villain, that's what you are! Ah, you fiendish tempter! If only I could get someone to get rid of you on the quiet. *(He sets some old letters to one side and discovers the torn piece of paper from the day before. He picks it up and looks at the two pieces, putting them down quickly as Gina enters.)* (IV, 305)

The words Hjalmar uses are "skurk," "keltring," and "kændige forfører," which, denoting "scoundrel," "villain," and "tempter" (forføre is "to tempt or seduce," as in *Genesis* 3.13), clearly suggest Relling's satanic identity. When Gina suggests that Hjalmar temporarily lodge with Relling and Molvik, Hjalmar explodes: "Don't mention the names of those creatures. It's enough to make me lose my appetite just thinking about them. . . . [T]hose two scum, they're capable of every vice". . . .

In a strictly realistic play one would be led to lurid speculation as to what it was that Hjalmar had witnessed between Relling and Molvik below. Here, I believe the intensity of his reaction and its vice and tempter imagery is used to establish Relling's abode as the diabolic location in the world of the play. By now the reader should be aware that neither the messianic nor the diabolic identities in the play carry their solemn traditional valuations.

Gregers counters the diabolic aspect of Relling's influence upon the Ekdal world with his own overstrained messianism. He urges upon Hedvig the supreme spiritual action of the sacrifice of what she loves most. When he suspects her of faltering, he exclaims, ''I can tell by looking at you that it's not fulfilled [fuldbragt],'' employing the same solemn words of Christ that Ibsen uses at other supreme moments in the Cycle (e.g., Hilde Wangel's ''For nu, nu er det fuldbragt!'' [''For now, now it is fulfilled!''] as Solness climbs his tower). Too frequently, Gregers is seen as the villain of the play and Relling its wise therapist adjusting fallen humanity to unhappy reality. This ignores the fact that Gregers' strategy *does* succeed: when Gina and Hjalmar believe Hedvig induced her grandfather to shoot the duck they are reconciled. Nor is it certain that Hedvig's suicide, like her near namesake Hedda's, is only negative. Estrangement and escape from an intolerable world can signal spiritual awakening. The Ekdals could just as well be seen as the victims of the manipulations of Gregers' opponents, Werle and Relling. (The play itself, of course, resists one-sided endorsement of either Gregers or Relling.) When Hedvig retreats from her resolve to sacrifice what she loves most, Gregers will blame the environment in which she grew up:

> *Hedvig.* Last night, at the time, I thought there was something so beautiful about it; but after I'd slept, and thought about it again, I didn't think so much of it.
>
> *Gregers.* No, you can't have grown up here and not have been damaged in some way.
>
> *Hedvig.* I don't care about that. So long as father comes back up here, then—
>
> *Gregers.* Ah, if only you had your eyes opened to what really makes life worth living, if you had the true, joyful, and brave spirit of sacrifice, then you'd see how he'd come back up to you. But I still believe in you, Hedvig. . . .

The play ends on the swift conjunction of the Last Supper and the Devil.

Were we discussing James Joyce's realist textuality, none of this would astonish. It will seem strange to many Ibsenists because of the received ideas about the realistic method devised by Joyce's chosen mentor. The passages above and many others might be seen as coincidences (though so many in one text would be bizarre) were it not for the ways in which they fit the rest of the play's pattern of scene, character-confrontation, plot and story, action, and visual and verbal imagery. Taken together they establish the presence of a huge archetypal story behind the foregrounded modern realist story—a larger, richer, and more imaginative space for the poet to inhabit than the discourse of modernity would seem to permit. It might well be that audiences will not comprehend the references any more than they will detect, for example, multiple parallels and references in *Ulysses* or the elaborate Manichean structure and texture Samuel Beckett self-avowedly built into *Krapp's Last Tape.* The mythopoetic procedure allows the poet imaginatively to grasp and shape his or her world, to make imaginative sense of it. The almost dizzyingly complex conscious intertextuality of *The Master Builder,* for example, lets the dramatist bring his major archetypal forces into aesthetic play, to make his art adequate to his imaginatively apprehended cosmos. This, and not the audience's comfortable and easy comprehension of what is going on, is the major artist's concern. As Ibsen adjured Georg Brandes, ''There actually are moments when the whole history of the world reminds one of a sinking ship; the only thing to do is to save oneself.'' Nevertheless, when the artist employs an elaborate referential system this will give coherence to the art which the audience may enjoy even without understanding exactly what is going on. Though it be *galskab,* yet there's method in it.

I have discovered when teaching the play that students find the presence of Christian archetypes in the text obvious and even insistent, so it is necessary to point out that Ibsen's method actually is subtle enough to have gone undetected. There is a parallel here with T. S. Eliot's use of Euripides' *Alcestis* for the plot of *The Cocktail Party* —a source that Eliot found himself obliged to point out to readers. Once pointed out, it becomes ''obvious.''

A good exercise would be for the reader to take a representative text from an accredited realist dramatist—e.g., Harley Granville-Barker, John Galsworthy, or Arthur Miller—and compare theirs with Ibsen's procedure. The out-and-out realist will be concerned primarily with establishing the everyday plausibility of characters, their situations and their speeches and actions, and not with building up any archetypal dimension: the speech habits will be far less "loaded," extravagant, and histrionic, more univocal, less emphatically idcntifying by repetition (the "claim of idealism," etc.), and, at first sight, more fluid and familiar than Ibsen's method. But any visit to "The Best Plays" of the 1920s, 1930s, 1940s, etc. that received the acclaim of sophisticated reviewers who believed Ibsen "dated" by comparison will find those plays' shelf-life, and that of the reviews, was short indeed, whereas the dialectical architecture of Ibsen's work, his welding together the contemporary and the timeless, has proved triumphantly durable. Certainly these plays are doing odd and unfamiliar things, none more so than *The Wild Duck*. But that is in the nature of a major art.

Ibsen's procedure, then, is to look closely at modern reality to discover its hidden archetypal content. This does not make Ibsen's procedure allegorical, nor are his texts unremittingly archetypal. The text has a dual loyalty: to the realistic and plausible modern story which must be convincingly and movingly rendered by the playwright and performed by the actors, and to the equally imperative archetypal realm—that larger human identity that modernity at all times is in danger of betraying but which for Ibsen justifies human existence.

The astigmatic nature of Ibsen's art is something it has in common with Greek literature from Homer to Euripides, in whose fictional universes events are simultaneously human and divine, local and universal, and where both perspectives are equally insistent, giving to the human condition in Greek epic and drama its extraordinarily numinous quality. It is this quality, I believe, that Ibsen wanted to recover for modern drama. Adrian Poole compares Ibsen's method to the art of Euripides. He points out how it finds an uncanny parallel in what seems to have been Ibsen's actual optical astigmatism and the astigmatism of his art. He quotes from the artist Stephan Sinding who painted the dramatist's portrait and asked Ibsen to remove his spectacles:

> He laid them aside and looked at me. I have never seen two eyes like those. One was large, I might almost say horrible—so it seemed to me—and deeply mystical; the other much smaller, rather pinched up, cold and clear and calmly probing.

Poole notes how this is true of the two aspects of Ibsen's art, "one, as it were, short-sighted, with a keen grasp of the local, immediate and everyday, the other long-sighted, with a view to remote mythic or psychological vistas."

The Wild Duck, while making its modern characters speak the language of modern consciousness, refuses to abet modernity's attempt to erase the mythopoetic/spiritual past from human memory. Our authentic human identity is at stake in this art of *anamnesis* or unforgetting; this is its redemptive purpose, which cannot be served by insisting, in our interpretations, only on the vision of the smaller eye.

Source: Brian Johnston, "'Diverse Galskaber' in Ibsen's The Wild Duck," in *Comparative Drama,* Vol. 30, Spring, 1996, p. 41.

Verna A. Foster

In the following essay, Foster relates The Wild Duck *to modern tragic comedy.*

Tragicomedy is an exceedingly slippery genre that can incorporate the tragic and the comic, the melodramatic and the farcical, the romantic and the satiric in a variety of combinations. It can boast antecedents in Euripidean, Terentian, and medieval drama and cognates in sentimental comedy, the *drame* (serious drama that is neither tragic nor comic), melodrama, savage farce, and so on. But the dramaturgical and emotional fusion of tragic and comic elements to create a distinguishable and theoretically significant new genre, tragicomedy, has developed only twice in the history of drama. Controversial in the Renaissance, tragicomedy has in modern times replaced tragedy itself as the most serious and moving of all dramatic kinds.

In the modern age it is almost impossible to write tragedy, especially within the realistic convention, which emphasizes ordinary human beings from the middle or lower classes speaking unexalted language and possessing failings that often seem more embarrassing than lethal. Any attempt to write tragedy today is likely to produce melodrama instead. But though the dramatic form *tragedy* no longer exists, what is *tragic* in human experience has found its aesthetic home in tragicomedy, where it is simultaneously subverted, protected, and rendered more painful by its peculiar relation with the comic. Ibsen seems to have realized this paradox in writing *The Wild Duck*. As the first modern tragicomedy of any importance, as a tragicomedy written in the realistic convention, and as a paradigm for later tragicomedies, *The Wild Duck* is central to any understanding of this genre—of both the ways in which the modern form shares in the dramaturgy of its Renaissance counterpart and the ways in which it departs from it.

In a scene from a 1979 production of The Wild Duck *at London's Olivier Theatre, Old Ekdal (in uniform) looks on while Dr. Relling, Gina Ekdal, and Hjalmar Ekdal attend to Hedvig Ekdal.*

Ibsen remarked as early as 1875 that his plays were concerned with "the conflict between one's abilities, between what man proposes and what is actually possible, constituting at once both the tragedy and comedy of mankind and of the individual." But in *The Wild Duck* (1884), a self-proclaimed departure from his earlier dramatic method, Ibsen goes further in creating a dramaturgy that more precisely embodies his tragicomic theme and produces in the audience the inextricably mixed tragic and comic responses described by Shaw: "To sit there getting deeper and deeper into that Ekdal home, and getting deeper and deeper into your own life all the time, until you forget that you are in a theatre; to look on with horror and pity at a profound tragedy, shaking with laughter all the time at an irresistible comedy."

Frederick and Lise-Lone Marker argue that in referring to his new method in *The Wild Duck* (in a letter to his publisher, Frederik Hegel) Ibsen includes "the subtle mingling of comedy and seriousness in word, action and visual image" and a "deliberate diffuseness of focus." The play's multiplicity of emotional effects and perspectives derives in part from Ibsen's orchestration of the voices

and attitudes of his ensemble of characters in a manner that was to become characteristic of Chekhov. But the single most important element in Ibsen's tragicomic dramaturgy is his conception of the play's central character, about whose representation he expressed some anxiety in a letter to Hans Schrøder, the head of the Christiania Theater. Ibsen urged that it was extremely important that the actor of Hjalmar Ekdal should in no way create a parody or show any awareness of the comic contradictions in his language and behavior. But this advice does not mean that the audience also should remain unaware of what is ludicrous in Hjalmar. In fact, it is precisely *because* Hjalmar is unconsciously comic that he is also tragic.

Simply put, Hjalmar is a comic character caught in a tragic situation that he does not understand. His circumstances are potentially tragic. He has suffered a loss of social position and honor because of his father's disgrace, and he has been duped into marrying the cast-off, and probably pregnant, mistress of the author of his family's misery. His contribution to the suicide of his beloved daughter is undeniably the stuff of tragedy. Hjalmar certainly sees himself in a tragic light both in the early acts of the play when he tells Gregers that he has ''felt a terrible blow from fate'' and that ''That pistol, there—the one we use to shoot rabbits with — it's played a part in the tragedy of the Ekdals'' and later in his responses to Gregers' revelation about Gina's past and to Hedvig's death. But Ibsen provides the audience with a much more complex view of Hjalmar than Hjalmar has of himself. In the contrast between his idealized self-image as breadwinner, artist, and tragic hero and his actual selfishness and laziness, Hjalmar represents the tragicomic ''conflict between one's aims and one's abilities.'' Using techniques drawn from comic characterization, Ibsen continually subverts Hjalmar's tragic pretensions and thus his status as a tragic protagonist. And yet at the same time it is through his comic qualities that Hjalmar engages the audience's sympathy and is able to elicit a response that incorporates pity and even terror along with laughter. The absurd juxtaposition of the two functions of the pistol, for example, is typical of how Ibsen undercuts Hjalmar's rhetorical presentation of himself as a tragic hero while simultaneously safeguarding what is tragic in his situation against the audience's potential annoyance with his pomposity, lack of self-knowledge, and selfishness.

Throughout the play Ibsen comically underscores the exaggeration and shallow emotional base of Hjalmar's rhetoric by exposing his contradictions and self-deceptions and by playing his self-idealizing protestations against his selfish behavior. In the early acts, for example, Hjalmar variously describes his father's hair as ''white'', ''gray'', and ''silver'' when actually Old Ekdal is almost bald and wears a *''reddish-brown''* wig. His inability to make up his mind about the color of his father's hair in each of his sentimental references to the ''poor old'' man shows that he is thinking more about the effect of what he is saying than about Old Ekdal himself. Hjalmar's rhetorical imprecision becomes a running joke that both undercuts his supposed tragic melancholy and mitigates his self-centeredness. (Later in the play he has to cut himself short in saying that he will not hurt a ''hair'' of the wild duck's head when even he remembers that ducks have feathers.) Similarly, the repeated contradiction between Hjalmar's pretence of self-sacrificing abstemiousness appropriate to his poverty or his fatherhood of a child who is going blind and his willingness immediately thereafter to indulge in ''lovely cool beer'', offered by Hedvig, or a ''crust'' with ''enough butter on'' pits the physical man enamored of his comforts against the spiritual suf-

> THE PLAY'S MULTIPLICITY OF EMOTIONAL EFFECTS AND PERSPECTIVES DERIVES IN PART FROM IBSEN'S ORCHESTRATION OF THE VOICES AND ATTITUDES OF HIS ENSEMBLE OF CHARACTERS IN A MANNER THAT WAS TO BECOME CHARACTERISTIC OF CHEKHOV.''

ferer that he proclaims himself to be. In Act Three Ibsen even edges towards farce in his presentation of Hjalmar's laziness. Hjalmar dithers between helping Old Ekdal in the attic when he thinks he can get away with it and *''hurriedly sitting again''* to work on the photographs whenever he thinks Gina or Hedvig might be watching. Because Hjalmar has no conception of his own selfishness or incompetence (there will be no photographic invention), he remains an essentially comic and thus endearing character. He possesses sufficient charm, after all, to make Gina and Hedvig happy simply by being himself.

But even in the early acts the comedy associated with Hjalmar has a painful edge. His comic gluttony covers over the fact that he has forgotten to bring Hedvig a treat from Werle's dinner party, and his laziness leads him to permit her to touch up the photographs at the expense of her eyes. In the latter part of the play Hjalmar's continuation in the habits we have previously laughed at produces a degree of uncertainty in our response to the sequence of events that leads to Hedvig's death and weakens any sense of tragic inevitability. For example, just as Hjalmar cannot make up his mind about the color of his father's hair, so he proposes a variety of ''sole'' rewards for which, he says, he is working on his invention: to allow his father to wear his military uniform again, to make Hedvig's future secure, to leave Gina a ''prosperous widow'', and to pay back Werle for all the money that the Ekdal family has had from him over the years. Hjalmar hits on this last plan when he realizes that the money Old Ekdal has been paid for copying has probably been payment to Gina as Werle's former mistress. But Hjalmar's determination to repay Werle is the fourth exclusive purpose he has proposed for his work on the invention, and the audience cannot take it very seriously, especially as for Hjalmar the expression of intention is equivalent to the deed itself: ''now I've got that pressing debt off my hands''. (The idea of getting something off one's hands, too, is several times repeated in the play and in this instance carries with it the resonance of earlier comic contexts, as when Gina urges Hjalmar to finish the retouching so that the photographs will be ''off your hands''.) Perhaps the most brilliant use of the reprise of an earlier comic motif occurs in act five as practical Gina uses the lure of bread and butter and hot coffee to persuade Hjalmar to remain in his home a little longer, at least until he can make plans for the future and buy a new hat. Ibsen sets off Hjalmar's clichéd rhetoric against Gina's literal-mindedness, producing, in effect, comic cross-talk:

> HJALMAR I can't shoulder all these burdens in one day.
>
> GINA No, and not when the weather's like it is out. . . .

This cross-talk reinforcing Hjalmar's comic inability to rise to his own rhetoric occurs just minutes before he is called upon to respond to Hedvig's death. In clumsier hands than Ibsen's, Hedvig's death might very well have been melodramatic, especially as the shot is heard exactly on Hjalmar's cue (''Hedvig, are you willing to give up life for me?''). Ibsen, however, preserves what is tragic in Hedvig's death, as in Hjalmar's life, by presenting both as tragicomic. Hedvig's suicide itself, of course, is in no way comic. But it takes place off stage, there is a delay before it is discovered, and what the audience is primarily called upon to respond to is not the death itself but the reaction of the other characters to it, and especially Hjalmar's. Ibsen orchestrates the characters' multiple voices to produce a complex emotional effect. Both Gina's simple language of heartbreak—''Oh, my child, my child!''—and Relling's coldly factual diagnosis are counterpointed with Hjalmar's melodramatic expression of his grief: ''And I drove her from me like an animal! And she crept terrified into the loft and died out of love for me. (*Sobbing.*) Never to make it right again! Never to let her know—! (*Clenching his fists and crying to heaven.*) Oh, you up there—if you *do* exist. Why have you done this to me!''. Hjalmar is deeply moving here, in part because Hedvig's death is an appalling event for the audience as well, but at the same time his characteristically flamboyant and self-regarding rhetoric draws attention away from Hedvig and the weeping Gina and reminds the audience of what is facile in Hjalmar

himself. The focus and mood of the scene are further diffused by Old Ekdal's visionary note (''The woods take revenge''), Gregers' metaphorical contribution (''In the depths of the sea''), and the ''demonic'' Molvik's drunken attempt to assume his priestly function (''The child isn't dead; she sleepeth''), which grotesquely underscores the emptiness of Hjalmar's own rhetoric, especially as Molvik has earlier been set up as a parallel figure to Hjalmar. The conclusion of the sequence is Relling's acerbic response to Molvik: ''Rubbish!''

These multiple voices pull the audience in different directions and block a fully tragic response to Hedvig's death. But what we are left with is something harsher than tragedy because there is no justification of a moral order, no resolution, no closure. Instead the play ends with (in Shaw's term) a discussion between the representatives of a neurotic tragic idealism and a flawed comic skepticism. (Their voices indeed have from the beginning constructed the polarities of Ibsen's tragicomedy.) Gregers wants to believe that ''Hedvig did not die in vain'' and that ''grief freed the greatness'' in Hjalmar. But Relling, more plausibly in view of what we have seen of Hjalmar in the rest of the play, says that within a year Hjalmar will ''souse himself in conceit and self-pity,'' will, in effect, construct for himself another life-lie about '''the child torn too soon from her father's heart'''. Hedvig's death has been rendered absurd, and Shaw is right in saying that Ibsen ''established tragi-comedy as a much deeper and grimmer entertainment than tragedy.''

The importance of the comic elements in Hjalmar's make-up and in the play as a whole can be seen if we look for a moment at the 1983 film adaptation of *The Wild Duck,* in which Liv Ullmann and Jeremy Irons play Gina and Hjalmar. Gone in this version is the comic quality of Hjalmar's (Harold's) contradictions because the film's omissions blunt their immediacy and obscure their frequency. Gone too is the comic exaggeration of Hjalmar's rhetoric. The result is a Hjalmar who is weak and tearful, possessing considerably less charm and vitality than his original. Gina, whose practicality should provide a comic foil to Hjalmar's effusions, becomes instead in the film a sensitive soul, and the comedy of Old Ekdal is similarly lost in pathos. Hedvig dies on screen, and the immediate cut to her funeral entails the omission of most of the responses of the other characters. There is no hyperbolical protestation from Hjalmar and no comment from Relling about his short-lived sorrow. The film ends sombrely enough with Hjalmar's silent grief and

Gina's tentative attempt to comfort him, but it totally lacks the complex discomfort of Ibsen's rough-edged tragicomic irony. Rather, Ibsen's tragicomedy has been transformed into a beautifully acted and moving melodrama because of the excision of most of the comedy.

If it is revealing, therefore, to contrast *The Wild Duck* with melodrama in order to clarify Ibsen's contribution to modern tragicomedy, it is also instructive to distinguish the play from the *drame*. The *drame* originated in the eighteenth century (especially in France under the auspices of Diderot), developed into the social drama of the nineteenth century, and culminated in the early realistic works of Ibsen. The *drame* is essentially realistic in its maturgy, domestic and/or social in its orientation, and focused on a controversial issue of contemporary significance, a "problem" that is aired though not necessarily resolved during the course of the play. Ibsen's earlier realistic plays such as *A Doll's House* and *An Enemy of the People* are, in fact, *drames* that deal with contemporary social problems. But Ibsen stressed that *The Wild Duck* is different in that it "does not concern itself with political or social questions."

The difference, however, does not have to be stated solely in negative terms. Of crucial importance is the play's use of symbolism. Critics have noted in particular Ibsen's new use of a central pervasive symbol that implicates the metaphysical in the mundane: the endlessly suggestive wild duck is metaphorically related to all of the major characters, while the loft full of junk that is like the "depths of the sea" evokes the recesses of the mind. In general, tragicomedy is distinguishable from the *drame* in that it deals with metaphysical rather than social issues, it produces a double vision of human experience, and its emotional effects, to adopt Karl Guthke's useful distinction, "*embrace*" both the tragic and the comic whereas those of the *drame* lie *between* the two polar genres. Nora, for example, calls for neither a tragic nor a comic response; debate over *A Doll's House* tends to deal intellectually with Nora's options rather than concerning itself with the kind of emotional response called for by her plight. Hjalmar, by contrast, evokes both a tragic and a comic response simultaneously; critics ponder what to make of the play rather than what to think about it.

Even Ibsen's use of realistic conventions in *The Wild Duck* can be distinguished from his use of the same techniques in earlier plays. Modern tragicom-edy is distinguished from the *drame* and linked with Renaissance versions of the same genre by its tendency to be in some degree metatheatrical. Metatheatre (or theatrical self-consciousness) is related to tragicomedy's mixed emotional effects, for artifice recognizable to the audience creates distance and thereby blocks without entirely destroying our emotional participation in the characters' experiences. Ibsen's attention to realistic detail in *The Wild Duck* is as great as ever. In a letter to his son, Sigurd, he remarked, "I keep putting in more and more details all the time." And in a letter to Schrøder he said, "In both the ensemble acting and in the stage setting, this play demands truth to nature and a touch of reality in every respect." The dense realistic details in *The Wild Duck* root Ibsen's comic effects in a believable social and psychological context so that the audience cannot dismiss the characters' pain even when we laugh at the way it is communicated (Old Ekdal's drinking, Hjalmar's flowery rhetoric). The audience thus remains to an important degree emotionally engaged with the characters. But though the actors, particularly the actor of Hjalmar, should demonstrate no awareness that some of their lines are funny, as they might if they were acting in a comedy, Ibsen's utilization of comic techniques in a serious drama in itself at times detaches the audience's attention from the characters to the way they are presented. In this respect Ibsen anticipates Brecht's *V-effeckt* by constructing a perspective other than the characters' own from which the audience is required to view them.

The metatheatrical element in Ibsen's dramaturgy in *The Wild Duck* is both embodied and rendered realistic in his self-dramatizing central character. Ibsen motivates Hjalmar's theatricality naturalistically by providing a cultural explanation for it: he was brought up by two idealistic or hysterical maiden aunts (depending on whether we believe Gregers or Relling) and was popular in his youth as one who could declaim other people's lines in an affecting manner. Small wonder that his expression of even the deepest pain is full of rhetorical clichés. Because self-dramatization is second nature to him, the metatheatrical element in Ibsen's presentation of Hjalmar actually feeds into the audience's sympathy for him even as it distances us enough so that we may also laugh at him. Engagement and detachment are held in a particularly fine balance in *The Wild Duck*.

The use of metatheatre to create dramatic distance is an important feature of both modern and

Renaissance tragicomedies. However, the relationship between the two states of tragicomedy has been little understood and sometimes even denied. It is not necessary to posit a genetic connection but rather to observe "family resemblances" between tragicomedies that make it possible, as Alastair Fowler puts it, to discuss "widely divergent works" in terms of generic features of the kind to which they may be supposed to belong. In the case of *The Wild Duck* a fruitful comparison may be made with *Measure for Measure,* one of Shakespeare's so-called "problem plays" that is, like Ibsen's play, better characterized as an ironic tragicomedy.

Renaissance tragicomedy, to be sure, is formally closer to comedy than to tragedy in that it presents difficulties overcome and ends happily. (In the famous formulation of Giambattista Guarini, it presents the "danger but not [the] death" and is governed above all by "the comic order." In *Measure for Measure* the manoeuverings of Duke Vincentio, a metatheatrical figure who in some respects functions as a surrogate dramatist within the play, save Claudio from death and bring about the multiple marriages with which the play ends. Modern tragicomedy is structurally much more diverse than its Renaissance counterpart, but its final effect is often closer to tragedy than to comedy (Hedvig dies in this case), even though the play as a whole may have been more evenly balanced between the two.

However, whether they are ostensibly "comic" or "tragic," the endings of both Renaissance and modern tragicomedies are characterized by ambiguity and discomfort for the audience. Both *Measure for Measure* and *The Wild Duck* ironically subvert the audience's likely generic assumptions about what constitutes a comic or a tragic dénouement. In Shakespeare's play a conventionally happy ending is modified in the direction of tragedy, while in Ibsen's a conventionally tragic ending is modified in the direction of comedy. *Measure for Measure* concludes with a set of arranged marriages whose inappropriateness bodes ill for the unwilling partners in them. Angelo, for example, is compelled to marry the long-suffering Mariana, whom he first abandoned and then had sex with in the belief that she was Isabella; and Isabella, who wished to become a nun, is asked to marry the Duke. At the end of *The Wild Duck* Hedvig's death, as we have seen, evokes from Hjalmar a tragicomic posturing that is little different from his melodramatic manner elsewhere in the play and from Relling a cynical prophecy that Hjalmar's sorrow will be short-lived and

soon comfortably sentimentalized. The discomfort aroused by the endings of both plays is an important part of tragicomedy's aesthetic.

The shared means by which Shakespeare and Ibsen create their tragicomic effects extend to the ways their protagonists combine within themselves tragic and comic possibilities that are represented in purer form by other characters. Duke Vincentio and Hjalmar Ekdal each stands between a tragic idealist (Angelo, Gregers) and a comic skeptic (Lucio, Relling). Vincentio and Hjalmar have self-images that are grotesquely reflected in, respectively, Angelo's self-proclaimed incorruptibility and Gregers' adherence to the "Summons to the Ideal" and undermined by the sardonic commentary of the skeptics as well as by the central characters' own behavior. Hjalmar sees himself as called upon to restore his family's honor but is actually quite comfortable in his reduced circumstances, as Relling is quick to point out. The Duke regards himself as a wise and virtuous ruler, but he gets involved in an unsavory bedtrick and is unable to control either sexual corruption in Vienna or even Lucio's scurrilous attacks on his reputation.

Shakespeare, no less than Ibsen, uses the relations between his three characters to dramatize the tragicomic "conflict between one's aims and one's abilities." The disparity in both plays between aspirations and what is actually accomplished is worked out in terms of the traditional duality of soul and body. Traditionally, the needs of the body have been associated with comedy, while the soul has proved the ground of tragedy. Conflict between the two occurs in other genres, but in tragicomedy the duality is of the essence. In Ibsen's play, as we have seen, the tension between soul and body, tragic and comic, is classically embodied in Hjalmar. In *Measure for Measure* it is represented in the constant subversion of the Duke's moral and spiritual aims by the intransigence of other people's flesh: the sexual corruption of characters such as Pompey, Lucio, and even Angelo and the unwillingness of Claudio and the drunken Barnardine to give up the life of the body and "Be absolute for death" when the Duke, disguised as a friar, urges this spiritual advice upon them. There are times when even the intellectual Duke himself is, like Hjalmar, comically reduced to the physical. He sustains the indignity of hearing himself accused of lechery and drunkenness and finally of being manhandled by Lucio, who pulls off his friar's hood, and with it his spiritual persona, at the end of the play.

Embedded in *Measure for Measure,* and in Renaissance tragicomedy in general, is the optimistic pattern of fall and redemption that characterizes medieval drama. Though Duke Vincentio and Hjalmar Ekdal both have tragicomically inaccurate self-images, the Duke is the more competent of the two and he does have some control over the play's events. As an inherently serious and dignified individual, the Duke could be a tragic figure, but he is placed in a situation that makes him appear comic, and he inhabits a universe that allows second chances, even though nothing is ever quite as the characters would like it to be. The play's inherited comic contours, however, are obscured by its incorporation of psychological and sociological realism. The resulting incongruities complicate and at times subvert the underlying redemptive pattern so that this Renaissance tragicomedy participates also in the dark irony of modern versions of the genre.

The comparison should be made; it should not be stretched too far. Ibsen in *The Wild Duck* negates altogether the possibility of either tragedy or redemption. In attempting to be ''tragic,'' Hjalmar simply underscores the comic basis of his nature. But since he is placed in an irremediable situation, *The Wild Duck* as a whole is a bleaker tragicomedy than *Measure for Measure.* Its dramatic universe appears indifferent to the claims of individuals. If *The Wild Duck* contains any vestige of a redemptive pattern, it lies in Relling's prediction of Hjalmar's recovery from the grief of Hedvig's death. But such consolation is bitter indeed. In its painful confrontations of tragic and comic effects, its presentation of a central character whose comic insufficiency renders his situation the more tragic, and the terrible indeterminacy of its ending, *The Wild Duck* stands as a paradigm for the line of modern tragicomic masterpieces that includes *Uncle Vanya, Juno and the Paycock, A Streetcar Named Desire,* and *Waiting for Godot.* In comparison with *Hamlet* or *King Lear,* a tragicomedy like *Measure for Measure,* disturbing though it often is, may look like comedy. In the modern drama tragicomedy takes the place of tragedy. Hamlet becomes Hjalmar, and Cordelia is driven to Hedvig's pointless suicide.

Source: Verna A. Foster, ''Ibsen's Tragicomedy: The Wild Duck,'' in *Modern Drama,* Vol. 38, Fall, 1995, p. 287.

Robert Brustein

In the following review, Brustein talks about the contemporary remake of The Wild Duck.

At the Arena Stage, Lucian Pintilie's version of Ibsen's *The Wild Duck* is a genuinely new look at the play, which pulls it out of canvas realism into a world of poetic metaphor and savage farce. The opening act in old Werle's house is not altogether promising, but then it's a fearfully difficult piece of exposition (the second act of this five-act play is largely expository too). Pintilie tries to distract our attention from the two servants who provide Ibsen's background material by using strained devices behind a transparent Mylar mirror, including a sumptuous banquet and an anachronistic slide show of vacation photographs, conducted by Mrs. Sorby while the Chamberlains sing ''Harvest Moon.'' (Even in the twenties, the setting of this updated production, Kodak color carousels had not yet been invented.) Here the director appears to be forcing visual interest on a talky drama.

When the scene changes to Hialmar Ekdal's lodgings, however, the play begins to develop a cumulative power. Pintilie's setting is much too spacious to suit the humble means of the Ekdal family—it has the dimensions of a fashionable loft in Soho—while the metal stairway leading to the ''attic'' containing the denizens of Old Ekdal's simulated forest, wild duck included, is high enough to suggest they own the whole piece of real estate, substantial holdings for such impoverished people. (Pintilie is said to have made architectural modifications in the Kreeger in order to accommodate this ambitious design.) Still, the furnishings of this enormous room are gritty enough, including a metal desk and filing cabinet, a clothesline, and a huge arc lamp used for Hialmar's photography. And the squalor is enhanced, despite Gina's heroic efforts to keep the place clean, by eggs periodically splattering on the floor from the atic above.

For all his concern with grandiose environments and visual punctuation, Pintilie keeps us focused on the theme of *The Wild Duck,* which is the malignant effect of utopian idealism om those who need illusions in order to survive. In his effort to lead the Ekdals toward ''a true conjugal union,'' Gregers Werle exposes Gina's adultery with his father, old Werle, and the dubious paternity of their daughter, Hedwig. It is astory that concludes morbidly with Hedwig's suicide, but Ibsen nevertheless realizes it is an occation for ferocious satire, even farce, especially since Gregers (played by Christopher McCann with flatop haircut, Trotsky whiskers, and mealymouthed self-righteousness) is such a priggish wimp and Hialmar (played by Richard Bauer with the flamboyance of a road company

FOR ALL HIS CONCERN WITH GRANDIOSE ENVIRONMENTS AND VISUAL PUNCTUATION, PINTILIE KEEPS US FOCUSED ON THE THEME OF *THE WILD DUCK,* WHICH IS THE MALIGNANT EFFECT OF UTOPIAN IDEALISM OM THOSE WHO NEED ILLUSIONS IN ORDER TO SURVIVE."

version based on a translation by David Westerfer, Pintilie has made the work entirely contemporary and immediate without altering its essential structure. And that, of course, has been the major contribution of our expatriate Rumanian friends to our perception of the classics: to make us see them as fresh works of art rather than anthology pieces or curatorial artifacts. Ciulei, perhaps daunted by the critical atmosphere of New York, has momentarily flagged in his approach; but his protege, Pintilie, has picked up the fallen pennant and waved it proudly aloft.

Source: Robert Brustein "The Wild Duck," (review) in *The New Republic,* Vol., 194, April 14, 1986, p. 27.

Cyrano) such a histrionic poseur. The confusion of styles is precisely what gives the play modernity, and the way the director treats the climax adds postmodern touches as well.

Despite prophetic warnings from Dr. Relling (played with sardonic brilliance by Stanley Anderson, looking like a squashy, whiskey-soaked Anthony Hopkins), Gregers's meddling has destroyed the entire family. While Hialmar vacillates between abandoning the household and completing his breakfast, Hedwig commits suicide in the attic to the accompaniment of screeching barnyard animals. Her body falls to the floor like another splattered egg. The arc light begins to turn in circles around the room. Old Ekdal stands babbling on the stairs. Hialmar, in an orgy of self-pity, shouts hysterically at the ceiling (''How could you do this to me?'') and turns to Gina for comfort. She shrinks at his touch. The spoiled priest Molvig starts praying. Dr. Relling hurls a drink in his face. Relling then drags Gregers the length of the stage to the couch and, shaking him like a puppy, forces his face into the dead body of his victim. Rising, Gregers pulls violently at Relling's nose, Relling pulls Gregers's hair, and with the two locked in a clumsy grapping match, Hedwig's body falls slowly off the couch. Gregers runs from the room, hitting his head on the door frame, as Relling shouts after him, ''Go to hell'' (adding, with a grin, ''See you tomorrow'').

This inspired scene, during which the audience is alternately juggling pathos, laughter, and surprise, is in retrospect the moment toward which the whole production moves, and it redeems whatever casting flaws, longueurs, or directorial excesses occasionally plague it. Using his own free stage

SOURCES

Brustein, Robert, review of *The Wild Duck,* in *The New Republic,* April 14, 1986, p. 27.

Bull, Francis, *Norsk Litteraturehistories,* Volume IV, 1937, pp. 18–19.

Christiani, Dounia B., preface to *The Wild Duck,* translated by Dounia B. Christiani, W. W. Norton & Company, 1968.

Ellis, Havelock, "Ibsen," in *The New Spirit,* 1890.

Howells, W. D., "Henrik Ibsen," in *The North American Review,* Summer, 1906, pp. 1-14.

McCarthy, Mary, "The Will and Testament of Ibsen," in *Sights and Spectacles,* Farrar, Straus & Giroux, 1956, reprinted in *The Wild Duck,* translated by Dounia B. Christiani, W. W. Norton & Company, 1968, pp. 182–189.

Peacock, D. Keith, "The Wild Duck: Overview," in *Reference Guide to World Literature,* 2d ed., edited by Lesley Henderson, St. James Press, 1995.

Reinert, Otto, "Sight Imagery in The Wild Duck," in *Journal of English and Germanic Philology,* Vol. 55, July, 1956, pp. 457–462, reprinted in *The Wild Duck,* translated by Dounia B. Christiani, W. W. Norton & Company, 1968, pp. 177-82.

Rilke, Rainer Maria, review of *The Wild Duck,* in *Selected Letters of Rainer Maria Rilke,* Macmillan and Co., p. 95, reprinted in *The Wild Duck,* translated by Dounia B. Christiani, W. W. Norton & Company, 1968, pp. 216–217.

Shaw, Bernard, review of *The Wild Duck,* in *Our Theatres in the Nineties,* p. 138, reprinted in *The Wild Duck,* translated by Dounia B. Christiani, W. W. Norton & Company, 1968, p. 217.

Smith, Ely Jelliffe, and Louise Brink, "The Wild Duck," in *The Psychoanalytic Review,* October 1919, pp. 357-78.

Valency, Maurice, *The Flower and the Castle,* The Macmillan Company, 1963 pp. 168-76, 379-80, 382-83, reprinted in *The Wild Duck,* translated by Dounia B. Christiani, W. W. Norton & Company, 1968, pp. 199-207.

FURTHER READING

Ferguson, Robert, *Henrik Ibsen,* Richard Cohen Books Ltd., 1996.

> This is a more recent biography of Ibsen.

Henrik Ibsen, edited by Harold Bloom, Chelsea House Publishers, 1998.

> A collection of critical essays on Ibsen's most important works.

Ibsen, Henrik, *The Wild Duck,* translated by Dounia B. Christiani, W. W. Norton & Company, 1968.

> This edition of *The Wild Duck* is annotated with contemporary reviews, scholarly criticism, Ibsen's letters, and suggested sources for the play.

Shafer, Yvonne, *Henrik Ibsen: Life, Work, and Criticism,* York Press, 1985.

> This is a popular, accessible discussion of the influences on Ibsen's work and the scholarly assessment of it.

Glossary of Literary Terms

A

Abstract: Used as a noun, the term refers to a short summary or outline of a longer work. As an adjective applied to writing or literary works, abstract refers to words or phrases that name things not knowable through the five senses. Examples of abstracts include the *Cliffs Notes* summaries of major literary works. Examples of abstract terms or concepts include ''idea,'' ''guilt'' ''honesty,'' and ''loyalty.''

Absurd, Theater of the: See *Theater of the Absurd*

Absurdism: See *Theater of the Absurd*

Act: A major section of a play. Acts are divided into varying numbers of shorter scenes. From ancient times to the nineteenth century plays were generally constructed of five acts, but modern works typically consist of one, two, or three acts. Examples of five-act plays include the works of Sophocles and Shakespeare, while the plays of Arthur Miller commonly have a three-act structure.

Acto: A one-act Chicano theater piece developed out of collective improvisation. *Actos* were performed by members of Luis Valdez's Teatro Campesino in California during the mid-1960s.

Aestheticism: A literary and artistic movement of the nineteenth century. Followers of the movement believed that art should not be mixed with social, political, or moral teaching. The statement ''art for

art's sake'' is a good summary of aestheticism. The movement had its roots in France, but it gained widespread importance in England in the last half of the nineteenth century, where it helped change the Victorian practice of including moral lessons in literature. Oscar Wilde is one of the best-known ''aesthetes'' of the late nineteenth century.

Age of Johnson: The period in English literature between 1750 and 1798, named after the most prominent literary figure of the age, Samuel Johnson. Works written during this time are noted for their emphasis on ''sensibility,'' or emotional quality. These works formed a transition between the rational works of the Age of Reason, or Neoclassical period, and the emphasis on individual feelings and responses of the Romantic period. Significant writers during the Age of Johnson included the novelists Ann Radcliffe and Henry Mackenzie, dramatists Richard Sheridan and Oliver Goldsmith, and poets William Collins and Thomas Gray. Also known as Age of Sensibility

Age of Reason: See *Neoclassicism*

Age of Sensibility: See *Age of Johnson*

Alexandrine Meter: See *Meter*

Allegory: A narrative technique in which characters representing things or abstract ideas are used to convey a message or teach a lesson. Allegory is typically used to teach moral, ethical, or religious lessons but is sometimes used for satiric or political purposes. Examples of allegorical works include Edmund Spenser's *The Faerie Queene* and John Bunyan's *The Pilgrim's Progress.*

Allusion: A refercncc to a familiar literary or historical person or event, used to make an idea more easily understood. For example, describing someone as a ''Romeo'' makes an allusion to William Shakespeare's famous young lover in *Romeo and Juliet.*

Amerind Literature: The writing and oral traditions of Native Americans. Native American literature was originally passed on by word of mouth, so it consisted largely of stories and events that were easily memorized. Amerind prose is often rhythmic like poetry because it was recited to the beat of a ceremonial drum. Examples of Amerind literature include the autobiographical *Black Elk Speaks,* the works of N. Scott Momaday, James Welch, and Craig Lee Strete, and the poetry of Luci Tapahonso.

Analogy: A comparison of two things made to explain something unfamiliar through its similarities to something familiar, or to prove one point based on the acceptedness of another. Similes and metaphors are types of analogies. Analogies often take the form of an extended simile, as in William Blake's aphorism: ''As the caterpillar chooses the fairest leaves to lay her eggs on, so the priest lays his curse on the fairest joys.''

Angry Young Men: A group of British writers of the 1950s whose work expressed bitterness and disillusionment with society. Common to their work is an anti-hero who rebels against a corrupt social order and strives for personal integrity. The term has been used to describe Kingsley Amis, John Osborne, Colin Wilson, John Wain, and others.

Antagonist: The major character in a narrative or drama who works against the hero or protagonist. An example of an evil antagonist is Richard Lovelace in Samuel Richardson's *Clarissa,* while a virtuous antagonist is Macduff in William Shakespeare's *Macbeth.*

Anthropomorphism: The presentation of animals or objects in human shape or with human characteristics. The term is derived from the Greek word for ''human form.'' The fables of Aesop, the animated films of Walt Disney, and Richard Adams's *Watership Down* feature anthropomorphic characters.

Anti-hero: A central character in a work of literature who lacks traditional heroic qualities such as courage, physical prowess, and fortitude. Anti-heros

typically distrust conventional values and are unable to commit themselves to any ideals. They generally feel helpless in a world over which they have no control. Anti-heroes usually accept, and often celebrate, their positions as social outcasts. A well-known anti-hero is Yossarian in Joseph Heller's novel *Catch-22.*

Antimasque: See *Masque*

Antithesis: The antithesis of something is its direct opposite. In literature, the use of antithesis as a figure of speech results in two statements that show a contrast through the balancing of two opposite ideas. Technically, it is the second portion of the statement that is defined as the ''antithesis''; the first portion is the ''thesis.'' An example of antithesis is found in the following portion of Abraham Lincoln's ''Gettysburg Address''; notice the opposition between the verbs ''remember'' and ''forget'' and the phrases ''what we say'' and ''what they did'': ''The world will little note nor long remember what we say here, but it can never forget what they did here.''

Apocrypha: Writings tentatively attributed to an author but not proven or universally accepted to be their works. The term was originally applied to certain books of the Bible that were not considered inspired and so were not included in the ''sacred canon.'' Geoffrey Chaucer, William Shakespeare, Thomas Kyd, Thomas Middleton, and John Marston all have apocrypha. Apocryphal books of the Bible include the Old Testament's Book of Enoch and New Testament's Gospel of Peter.

Apollonian and Dionysian: The two impulses believed to guide authors of dramatic tragedy. The Apollonian impulse is named after Apollo, the Greek god of light and beauty and the symbol of intellectual order. The Dionysian impulse is named after Dionysus, the Greek god of wine and the symbol of the unrestrained forces of nature. The Apollonian impulse is to create a rational, harmonious world, while the Dionysian is to express the irrational forces of personality. Friedrich Nietzche uses these terms in *The Birth of Tragedy* to designate contrasting elements in Greek tragedy.

Apostrophe: A statement, question, or request addressed to an inanimate object or concept or to a nonexistent or absent person. Requests for inspiration from the muses in poetry are examples of apostrophe, as is Marc Antony's address to Caesar's corpse in William Shakespeare's *Julius Caesar:* ''O, pardon me, thou bleeding piece of earth, That I am meek and gentle with these butchers!. . . Woe to the hand that shed this costly blood!. . .''

Archetype: The word archetype is commonly used to describe an original pattern or model from which all other things of the same kind are made. This term was introduced to literary criticism from the psychology of Carl Jung. It expresses Jung's theory that behind every person's ''unconscious,'' or repressed memories of the past, lies the ''collective unconscious'' of the human race: memories of the countless typical experiences of our ancestors. These memories are said to prompt illogical associations that trigger powerful emotions in the reader. Often, the emotional process is primitive, even primordial. Archetypes are the literary images that grow out of the ''collective unconscious.'' They appear in literature as incidents and plots that repeat basic patterns of life. They may also appear as stereotyped characters. Examples of literary archetypes include themes such as birth and death and characters such as the Earth Mother.

Argument: The argument of a work is the author's subject matter or principal idea. Examples of defined ''argument'' portions of works include John Milton's *Arguments* to each of the books of *Paradise Lost* and the ''Argument'' to Robert Herrick's *Hesperides.*

Aristotelian Criticism: Specifically, the method of evaluating and analyzing tragedy formulated by the Greek philosopher Aristotle in his *Poetics.* More generally, the term indicates any form of criticism that follows Aristotle's views. Aristotelian criticism focuses on the form and logical structure of a work, apart from its historical or social context, in contrast to ''Platonic Criticism,'' which stresses the usefulness of art. Adherents of New Criticism including John Crowe Ransom and Cleanth Brooks utilize and value the basic ideas of Aristotelian criticism for textual analysis.

Art for Art's Sake: See *Aestheticism*

Aside: A comment made by a stage performer that is intended to be heard by the audience but supposedly not by other characters. Eugene O'Neill's *Strange Interlude* is an extended use of the aside in modern theater.

Audience: The people for whom a piece of literature is written. Authors usually write with a certain audience in mind, for example, children, members of a religious or ethnic group, or colleagues in a professional field. The term ''audience'' also applies to the people who gather to see or hear any performance, including plays, poetry readings, speeches, and concerts. Jane Austen's parody of the gothic novel, *Northanger Abbey,* was originally intended for (and also pokes fun at) an audience of young and avid female gothic novel readers.

Avant-garde: A French term meaning ''vanguard.'' It is used in literary criticism to describe new writing that rejects traditional approaches to literature in favor of innovations in style or content. Twentieth-century examples of the literary *avant-garde* include the Black Mountain School of poets, the Bloomsbury Group, and the Beat Movement.

B

Ballad: A short poem that tells a simple story and has a repeated refrain. Ballads were originally intended to be sung. Early ballads, known as folk ballads, were passed down through generations, so their authors are often unknown. Later ballads composed by known authors are called literary ballads. An example of an anonymous folk ballad is ''Edward,'' which dates from the Middle Ages. Samuel Taylor Coleridge's ''The Rime of the Ancient Mariner'' and John Keats's ''La Belle Dame sans Merci'' are examples of literary ballads.

Baroque: A term used in literary criticism to describe literature that is complex or ornate in style or diction. Baroque works typically express tension, anxiety, and violent emotion. The term ''Baroque Age'' designates a period in Western European literature beginning in the late sixteenth century and ending about one hundred years later. Works of this period often mirror the qualities of works more generally associated with the label ''baroque'' and sometimes feature elaborate conceits. Examples of Baroque works include John Lyly's *Euphues: The Anatomy of Wit,* Luis de Gongora's *Soledads,* and William Shakespeare's *As You Like It.*

Baroque Age: See *Baroque*

Baroque Period: See *Baroque*

Beat Generation: See *Beat Movement*

Beat Movement: A period featuring a group of American poets and novelists of the 1950s and 1960s—including Jack Kerouac, Allen Ginsberg, Gregory Corso, William S. Burroughs, and Lawrence Ferlinghetti—who rejected established social and literary values. Using such techniques as stream of consciousness writing and jazz-influenced free verse and focusing on unusual or abnormal states of mind—generated by religious ecstasy or the use of drugs—the Beat writers aimed to create works that were unconventional in both form and subject matter. Kerouac's *On the Road* is perhaps the best-known example of a Beat Generation novel, and Ginsberg's *Howl* is a famous collection of Beat poetry.

Black Aesthetic Movement: A period of artistic and literary development among African Americans in the 1960s and early 1970s. This was the first major African-American artistic movement since the Harlem Renaissance and was closely paralleled by the civil rights and black power movements. The black aesthetic writers attempted to produce works of art that would be meaningful to the black masses. Key figures in black aesthetics included one of its founders, poet and playwright Amiri Baraka, formerly known as LeRoi Jones; poet and essayist Haki R. Madhubuti, formerly Don L. Lee; poet and playwright Sonia Sanchez; and dramatist Ed Bullins. Works representative of the Black Aesthetic Movement include Amiri Baraka's play *Dutchman,* a 1964 Obie award-winner; *Black Fire: An Anthology of Afro-American Writing,* edited by Baraka and playwright Larry Neal and published in 1968; and Sonia Sanchez's poetry collection *We a BadddDDD People,* published in 1970. Also known as Black Arts Movement.

Black Arts Movement: See *Black Aesthetic Movement*

Black Comedy: See *Black Humor*

Black Humor: Writing that places grotesque elements side by side with humorous ones in an attempt to shock the reader, forcing him or her to laugh at the horrifying reality of a disordered world. Joseph Heller's novel *Catch-22* is considered a superb example of the use of black humor. Other well-known authors who use black humor include Kurt Vonnegut, Edward Albee, Eugene Ionesco, and Harold Pinter. Also known as Black Comedy.

Blank Verse: Loosely, any unrhymed poetry, but more generally, unrhymed iambic pentameter verse (composed of lines of five two-syllable feet with the first syllable accented, the second unaccented). Blank verse has been used by poets since the Renaissance for its flexibility and its graceful, dignified tone. John Milton's *Paradise Lost* is in blank verse, as are most of William Shakespeare's plays.

Bloomsbury Group: A group of English writers, artists, and intellectuals who held informal artistic and philosophical discussions in Bloomsbury, a district of London, from around 1907 to the early

1930s. The Bloomsbury Group held no uniform philosophical beliefs but did commonly express an aversion to moral prudery and a desire for greater social tolerance. At various times the circle included Virginia Woolf, E. M. Forster, Clive Bell, Lytton Strachey, and John Maynard Keynes.

Bon Mot: A French term meaning "good word." A *bon mot* is a witty remark or clever observation. Charles Lamb and Oscar Wilde are celebrated for their witty *bon mots.* Two examples by Oscar Wilde stand out: (1) "All women become their mothers. That is their tragedy. No man does. That's his." (2) "A man cannot be too careful in the choice of his enemies."

Breath Verse: See *Projective Verse*

Burlesque: Any literary work that uses exaggeration to make its subject appear ridiculous, either by treating a trivial subject with profound seriousness or by treating a dignified subject frivolously. The word "burlesque" may also be used as an adjective, as in "burlesque show," to mean "striptease act." Examples of literary burlesque include the comedies of Aristophanes, Miguel de Cervantes's *Don Quixote,,* Samuel Butler's poem "Hudibras," and John Gay's play *The Beggar's Opera.*

C

Cadence: The natural rhythm of language caused by the alternation of accented and unaccented syllables. Much modern poetry—notably free verse—deliberately manipulates cadence to create complex rhythmic effects. James Macpherson's "Ossian poems" are richly cadenced, as is the poetry of the Symbolists, Walt Whitman, and Amy Lowell.

Caesura: A pause in a line of poetry, usually occurring near the middle. It typically corresponds to a break in the natural rhythm or sense of the line but is sometimes shifted to create special meanings or rhythmic effects. The opening line of Edgar Allan Poe's "The Raven" contains a caesura following "dreary": "Once upon a midnight dreary, while I pondered weak and weary. . . ."

Canzone: A short Italian or Provencal lyric poem, commonly about love and often set to music. The *canzone* has no set form but typically contains five or six stanzas made up of seven to twenty lines of eleven syllables each. A shorter, five- to ten-line "envoy," or concluding stanza, completes the poem. Masters of the *canzone* form include

Petrarch, Dante Alighieri, Torquato Tasso, and Guido Cavalcanti.

Carpe Diem: A Latin term meaning "seize the day." This is a traditional theme of poetry, especially lyrics. A *carpe diem* poem advises the reader or the person it addresses to live for today and enjoy the pleasures of the moment. Two celebrated *carpe diem* poems are Andrew Marvell's "To His Coy Mistress" and Robert Herrick's poem beginning "Gather ye rosebuds while ye may. . . ."

Catharsis: The release or purging of unwanted emotions— specifically fear and pity—brought about by exposure to art. The term was first used by the Greek philosopher Aristotle in his *Poetics* to refer to the desired effect of tragedy on spectators. A famous example of catharsis is realized in Sophocles' *Oedipus Rex,* when Oedipus discovers that his wife, Jacosta, is his own mother and that the stranger he killed on the road was his own father.

Celtic Renaissance: A period of Irish literary and cultural history at the end of the nineteenth century. Followers of the movement aimed to create a romantic vision of Celtic myth and legend. The most significant works of the Celtic Renaissance typically present a dreamy, unreal world, usually in reaction against the reality of contemporary problems. William Butler Yeats's *The Wanderings of Oisin* is among the most significant works of the Celtic Renaissance. Also known as Celtic Twilight.

Celtic Twilight: See *Celtic Renaissance*

Character: Broadly speaking, a person in a literary work. The actions of characters are what constitute the plot of a story, novel, or poem. There are numerous types of characters, ranging from simple, stereotypical figures to intricate, multifaceted ones. In the techniques of anthropomorphism and personification, animals—and even places or things—can assume aspects of character. "Characterization" is the process by which an author creates vivid, believable characters in a work of art. This may be done in a variety of ways, including (1) direct description of the character by the narrator; (2) the direct presentation of the speech, thoughts, or actions of the character; and (3) the responses of other characters to the character. The term "character" also refers to a form originated by the ancient Greek writer Theophrastus that later became popular in the seventeenth and eighteenth centuries. It is a short essay or sketch of a person who prominently displays a specific attribute or quality, such as miserliness or ambition. Notable characters in lit-

erature include Oedipus Rex, Don Quixote de la Mancha, Macbeth, Candide, Hester Prynne, Ebenezer Scrooge, Huckleberry Finn, Jay Gatsby, Scarlett O'Hara, James Bond, and Kunta Kinte.

Characterization: See *Character*

Chorus: In ancient Greek drama, a group of actors who commented on and interpreted the unfolding action on the stage. Initially the chorus was a major component of the presentation, but over time it became less significant, with its numbers reduced and its role eventually limited to commentary between acts. By the sixteenth century the chorus—if employed at all—was typically a single person who provided a prologue and an epilogue and occasionally appeared between acts to introduce or underscore an important event. The chorus in William Shakespeare's *Henry V* functions in this way. Modern dramas rarely feature a chorus, but T. S. Eliot's *Murder in the Cathedral* and Arthur Miller's *A View from the Bridge* are notable exceptions. The Stage Manager in Thornton Wilder's *Our Town* performs a role similar to that of the chorus.

Chronicle: A record of events presented in chronological order. Although the scope and level of detail provided varies greatly among the chronicles surviving from ancient times, some, such as the *Anglo-Saxon Chronicle,* feature vivid descriptions and a lively recounting of events. During the Elizabethan Age, many dramas— appropriately called "chronicle plays"—were based on material from chronicles. Many of William Shakespeare's dramas of English history as well as Christopher Marlowe's *Edward II* are based in part on Raphael Holinshead's *Chronicles of England, Scotland, and Ireland.*

Classical: In its strictest definition in literary criticism, classicism refers to works of ancient Greek or Roman literature. The term may also be used to describe a literary work of recognized importance (a "classic") from any time period or literature that exhibits the traits of classicism. Classical authors from ancient Greek and Roman times include Juvenal and Homer. Examples of later works and authors now described as classical include French literature of the seventeenth century, Western novels of the nineteenth century, and American fiction of the mid-nineteenth century such as that written by James Fenimore Cooper and Mark Twain.

Classicism: A term used in literary criticism to describe critical doctrines that have their roots in ancient Greek and Roman literature, philosophy, and art. Works associated with classicism typically exhibit restraint on the part of the author, unity of design and purpose, clarity, simplicity, logical organization, and respect for tradition. Examples of literary classicism include Cicero's prose, the dramas of Pierre Corneille and Jean Racine, the poetry of John Dryden and Alexander Pope, and the writings of J. W. von Goethe, G. E. Lessing, and T. S. Eliot.

Climax: The turning point in a narrative, the moment when the conflict is at its most intense. Typically, the structure of stories, novels, and plays is one of rising action, in which tension builds to the climax, followed by falling action, in which tension lessens as the story moves to its conclusion. The climax in James Fenimore Cooper's *The Last of the Mohicans* occurs when Magua and his captive Cora are pursued to the edge of a cliff by Uncas. Magua kills Uncas but is subsequently killed by Hawkeye.

Colloquialism: A word, phrase, or form of pronunciation that is acceptable in casual conversation but not in formal, written communication. It is considered more acceptable than slang. An example of colloquialism can be found in Rudyard Kipling's *Barrack-room Ballads:* When 'Omer smote 'is bloomin' lyre He'd 'eard men sing by land and sea; An' what he thought 'e might require 'E went an' took—the same as me!

Comedy: One of two major types of drama, the other being tragedy. Its aim is to amuse, and it typically ends happily. Comedy assumes many forms, such as farce and burlesque, and uses a variety of techniques, from parody to satire. In a restricted sense the term comedy refers only to dramatic presentations, but in general usage it is commonly applied to nondramatic works as well. Examples of comedies range from the plays of Aristophanes, Terrence, and Plautus, Dante Alighieri's *The Divine Comedy,* Francois Rabelais's *Pantagruel* and *Gargantua,* and some of Geoffrey Chaucer's tales and William Shakespeare's plays to Noel Coward's play *Private Lives* and James Thurber's short story "The Secret Life of Walter Mitty."

Comedy of Manners: A play about the manners and conventions of an aristocratic, highly sophisticated society. The characters are usually types rather than individualized personalities, and plot is less important than atmosphere. Such plays were an important aspect of late seventeenth-century English comedy. The comedy of manners was revived in the eighteenth century by Oliver Goldsmith and Richard Brinsley Sheridan, enjoyed a second revival in the late nineteenth century, and has endured

into the twentieth century. Examples of comedies of manners include William Congreve's *The Way of the World* in the late seventeenth century, Oliver Goldsmith's *She Stoops to Conquer* and Richard Brinsley Sheridan's *The School for Scandal* in the eighteenth century, Oscar Wilde's *The Importance of Being Earnest* in the nineteenth century, and W. Somerset Maugham's *The Circle* in the twentieth century.

Comic Relief: The use of humor to lighten the mood of a serious or tragic story, especially in plays. The technique is very common in Elizabethan works, and can be an integral part of the plot or simply a brief event designed to break the tension of the scene. The Gravediggers' scene in William Shakespeare's *Hamlet* is a frequently cited example of comic relief.

Commedia dell'arte: An Italian term meaning "the comedy of guilds" or "the comedy of professional actors." This form of dramatic comedy was popular in Italy during the sixteenth century. Actors were assigned stock roles (such as Pulcinella, the stupid servant, or Pantalone, the old merchant) and given a basic plot to follow, but all dialogue was improvised. The roles were rigidly typed and the plots were formulaic, usually revolving around young lovers who thwarted their elders and attained wealth and happiness. A rigid convention of the *commedia dell'arte* is the periodic intrusion of Harlequin, who interrupts the play with low buffoonery. Peppino de Filippo's *Metamorphoses of a Wandering Minstrel* gave modern audiences an idea of what *commedia dell'arte* may have been like. Various scenarios for *commedia dell'arte* were compiled in Petraccone's *La commedia dell'arte, storia, technica, scenari,* published in 1927.

Complaint: A lyric poem, popular in the Renaissance, in which the speaker expresses sorrow about his or her condition. Typically, the speaker's sadness is caused by an unresponsive lover, but some complaints cite other sources of unhappiness, such as poverty or fate. A commonly cited example is "A Complaint by Night of the Lover Not Beloved" by Henry Howard, Earl of Surrey. Thomas Sackville's "Complaint of Henry, Duke of Buckingham" traces the duke's unhappiness to his ruthless ambition.

Conceit: A clever and fanciful metaphor, usually expressed through elaborate and extended comparison, that presents a striking parallel between two seemingly dissimilar things—for example, elaborately comparing a beautiful woman to an object like a garden or the sun. The conceit was a popular device throughout the Elizabethan Age and Baroque Age and was the principal technique of the seventeenth-century English metaphysical poets. This usage of the word conceit is unrelated to the best-known definition of conceit as an arrogant attitude or behavior. The conceit figures prominently in the works of John Donne, Emily Dickinson, and T. S. Eliot.

Concrete: Concrete is the opposite of abstract, and refers to a thing that actually exists or a description that allows the reader to experience an object or concept with the senses. Henry David Thoreau's *Walden* contains much concrete description of nature and wildlife.

Concrete Poetry: Poetry in which visual elements play a large part in the poetic effect. Punctuation marks, letters, or words are arranged on a page to form a visual design: a cross, for example, or a bumblebee. Max Bill and Eugene Gomringer were among the early practitioners of concrete poetry; Haroldo de Campos and Augusto de Campos are among contemporary authors of concrete poetry.

Confessional Poetry: A form of poetry in which the poet reveals very personal, intimate, sometimes shocking information about himself or herself. Anne Sexton, Sylvia Plath, Robert Lowell, and John Berryman wrote poetry in the confessional vein.

Conflict: The conflict in a work of fiction is the issue to be resolved in the story. It usually occurs between two characters, the protagonist and the antagonist, or between the protagonist and society or the protagonist and himself or herself. Conflict in Theodore Dreiser's novel *Sister Carrie* comes as a result of urban society, while Jack London's short story "To Build a Fire" concerns the protagonist's battle against the cold and himself.

Connotation: The impression that a word gives beyond its defined meaning. Connotations may be universally understood or may be significant only to a certain group. Both "horse" and "steed" denote the same animal, but "steed" has a different connotation, deriving from the chivalrous or romantic narratives in which the word was once often used.

Consonance: Consonance occurs in poetry when words appearing at the ends of two or more verses have similar final consonant sounds but have final vowel sounds that differ, as with "stuff" and "off." Consonance is found in "The curfew tolls the knells of parting day" from Thomas Grey's "An Elegy Written in a Country Church Yard." Also known as Half Rhyme or Slant Rhyme.

Convention: Any widely accepted literary device, style, or form. A soliloquy, in which a character reveals to the audience his or her private thoughts, is an example of a dramatic convention.

Corrido: A Mexican ballad. Examples of *corridos* include "Muerte del afamado Bilito," "La voz de mi conciencia," "Lucio Perez," "La juida," and "Los presos."

Couplet: Two lines of poetry with the same rhyme and meter, often expressing a complete and self-contained thought. The following couplet is from Alexander Pope's "Elegy to the Memory of an Unfortunate Lady": 'Tis Use alone that sanctifies Expense, And Splendour borrows all her rays from Sense.

Criticism: The systematic study and evaluation of literary works, usually based on a specific method or set of principles. An important part of literary studies since ancient times, the practice of criticism has given rise to numerous theories, methods, and "schools," sometimes producing conflicting, even contradictory, interpretations of literature in general as well as of individual works. Even such basic issues as what constitutes a poem or a novel have been the subject of much criticism over the centuries. Seminal texts of literary criticism include Plato's *Republic,* Aristotle's *Poetics,* Sir Philip Sidney's *The Defence of Poesie,* John Dryden's *Of Dramatic Poesie,* and William Wordsworth's "Preface" to the second edition of his *Lyrical Ballads.* Contemporary schools of criticism include deconstruction, feminist, psychoanalytic, poststructuralist, new historicist, postcolonialist, and reader-response.

D

Dactyl: See *Foot*

Dadaism: A protest movement in art and literature founded by Tristan Tzara in 1916. Followers of the movement expressed their outrage at the destruction brought about by World War I by revolting against numerous forms of social convention. The Dadaists presented works marked by calculated madness and flamboyant nonsense. They stressed total freedom of expression, commonly through primitive displays of emotion and illogical, often senseless, poetry. The movement ended shortly after the war, when it was replaced by surrealism. Proponents of Dadaism include Andre Breton, Louis Aragon, Philippe Soupault, and Paul Eluard.

Decadent: See *Decadents*

Decadents: The followers of a nineteenth-century literary movement that had its beginnings in French aestheticism. Decadent literature displays a fascination with perverse and morbid states; a search for novelty and sensation—the ''new thrill''; a preoccupation with mysticism; and a belief in the senselessness of human existence. The movement is closely associated with the doctrine Art for Art's Sake. The term ''decadence'' is sometimes used to denote a decline in the quality of art or literature following a period of greatness. Major French decadents are Charles Baudelaire and Arthur Rimbaud. English decadents include Oscar Wilde, Ernest Dowson, and Frank Harris.

Deconstruction: A method of literary criticism developed by Jacques Derrida and characterized by multiple conflicting interpretations of a given work. Deconstructionists consider the impact of the language of a work and suggest that the true meaning of the work is not necessarily the meaning that the author intended. Jacques Derrida's *De la grammatologie* is the seminal text on deconstructive strategies; among American practitioners of this method of criticism are Paul de Man and J. Hillis Miller.

Deduction: The process of reaching a conclusion through reasoning from general premises to a specific premise. An example of deduction is present in the following syllogism: Premise: All mammals are animals. Premise: All whales are mammals. Conclusion: Therefore, all whales are animals.

Denotation: The definition of a word, apart from the impressions or feelings it creates in the reader. The word ''apartheid'' denotes a political and economic policy of segregation by race, but its connotations— oppression, slavery, inequality—are numerous.

Denouement: A French word meaning ''the unknotting.'' In literary criticism, it denotes the resolution of conflict in fiction or drama. The *denouement* follows the climax and provides an outcome to the primary plot situation as well as an explanation of secondary plot complications. The *denouement* often involves a character's recognition of his or her state of mind or moral condition. A well-known example of *denouement* is the last scene of the play *As You Like It* by William Shakespeare, in which couples are married, an evildoer repents, the identities of two disguised characters are revealed, and a ruler is restored to power. Also known as Falling Action.

Description: Descriptive writing is intended to allow a reader to picture the scene or setting in which the action of a story takes place. The form this description takes often evokes an intended emotional response—a dark, spooky graveyard will evoke fear, and a peaceful, sunny meadow will evoke calmness. An example of a descriptive story is Edgar Allan Poe's *Landor's Cottage,* which offers a detailed depiction of a New York country estate.

Detective Story: A narrative about the solution of a mystery or the identification of a criminal. The conventions of the detective story include the detective's scrupulous use of logic in solving the mystery; incompetent or ineffectual police; a suspect who appears guilty at first but is later proved innocent; and the detective's friend or confidant— often the narrator—whose slowness in interpreting clues emphasizes by contrast the detective's brilliance. Edgar Allan Poe's ''Murders in the Rue Morgue'' is commonly regarded as the earliest example of this type of story. With this work, Poe established many of the conventions of the detective story genre, which are still in practice. Other practitioners of this vast and extremely popular genre include Arthur Conan Doyle, Dashiell Hammett, and Agatha Christie.

Deus ex machina: A Latin term meaning ''god out of a machine.'' In Greek drama, a god was often lowered onto the stage by a mechanism of some kind to rescue the hero or untangle the plot. By extension, the term refers to any artificial device or coincidence used to bring about a convenient and simple solution to a plot. This is a common device in melodramas and includes such fortunate circumstances as the sudden receipt of a legacy to save the family farm or a last-minute stay of execution. The *deus ex machina* invariably rewards the virtuous and punishes evildoers. Examples of *deus ex machina* include King Louis XIV in Jean-Baptiste Moliere's *Tartuffe* and Queen Victoria in *The Pirates of Penzance* by William Gilbert and Arthur Sullivan. Bertolt Brecht parodies the abuse of such devices in the conclusion of his *Threepenny Opera.*

Dialogue: In its widest sense, dialogue is simply conversation between people in a literary work; in its most restricted sense, it refers specifically to the speech of characters in a drama. As a specific literary genre, a ''dialogue'' is a composition in which characters debate an issue or idea. The Greek philosopher Plato frequently expounded his theories in the form of dialogues.

Diction: The selection and arrangement of words in a literary work. Either or both may vary depending on the desired effect. There are four general types of diction: ''formal,'' used in scholarly or lofty writing; ''informal,'' used in relaxed but educated conversation; ''colloquial,'' used in everyday speech; and ''slang,'' containing newly coined words and other terms not accepted in formal usage.

Didactic: A term used to describe works of literature that aim to teach some moral, religious, political, or practical lesson. Although didactic elements are often found in artistically pleasing works, the term ''didactic'' usually refers to literature in which the message is more important than the form. The term may also be used to criticize a work that the critic finds ''overly didactic,'' that is, heavy-handed in its delivery of a lesson. Examples of didactic literature include John Bunyan's *Pilgrim's Progress,* Alexander Pope's *Essay on Criticism,* Jean-Jacques Rousseau's *Emile,* and Elizabeth Inchbald's *Simple Story.*

Dimeter: See *Meter*

Dionysian: See *Apollonian and Dionysian*

Discordia concours: A Latin phrase meaning ''discord in harmony.'' The term was coined by the eighteenth-century English writer Samuel Johnson to describe ''a combination of dissimilar images or discovery of occult resemblances in things apparently unlike.'' Johnson created the expression by reversing a phrase by the Latin poet Horace. The metaphysical poetry of John Donne, Richard Crashaw, Abraham Cowley, George Herbert, and Edward Taylor among others, contains many examples of *discordia concours.* In Donne's ''A Valediction: Forbidding Mourning,'' the poet compares the union of himself with his lover to a draftsman's compass: If they be two, they are two so, As stiff twin compasses are two: Thy soul, the fixed foot, makes no show To move, but doth, if the other do; And though it in the center sit, Yet when the other far doth roam, It leans, and hearkens after it, And grows erect, as that comes home.

Dissonance: A combination of harsh or jarring sounds, especially in poetry. Although such combinations may be accidental, poets sometimes intentionally make them to achieve particular effects. Dissonance is also sometimes used to refer to close but not identical rhymes. When this is the case, the word functions as a synonym for consonance. Robert Browning, Gerard Manley Hopkins, and many other poets have made deliberate use of dissonance.

Doppelganger: A literary technique by which a character is duplicated (usually in the form of an alter ego, though sometimes as a ghostly counterpart) or divided into two distinct, usually opposite personalities. The use of this character device is widespread in nineteenth- and twentieth- century literature, and indicates a growing awareness among authors that the ''self'' is really a composite of many ''selves.'' A well-known story containing a *doppelganger* character is Robert Louis Stevenson's *Dr. Jekyll and Mr. Hyde,* which dramatizes an internal struggle between good and evil. Also known as The Double.

Double Entendre: A corruption of a French phrase meaning ''double meaning.'' The term is used to indicate a word or phrase that is deliberately ambiguous, especially when one of the meanings is risque or improper. An example of a *double entendre* is the Elizabethan usage of the verb ''die,'' which refers both to death and to orgasm.

Double, The: See *Doppelganger*

Draft: Any preliminary version of a written work. An author may write dozens of drafts which are revised to form the final work, or he or she may write only one, with few or no revisions. Dorothy Parker's observation that ''I can't write five words but that I change seven'' humorously indicates the purpose of the draft.

Drama: In its widest sense, a drama is any work designed to be presented by actors on a stage. Similarly, ''drama'' denotes a broad literary genre that includes a variety of forms, from pageant and spectacle to tragedy and comedy, as well as countless types and subtypes. More commonly in modern usage, however, a drama is a work that treats serious subjects and themes but does not aim at the grandeur of tragedy. This use of the term originated with the eighteenth-century French writer Denis Diderot, who used the word *drame* to designate his plays about middle- class life; thus ''drama'' typically features characters of a less exalted stature than those of tragedy. Examples of classical dramas include Menander's comedy *Dyscolus* and Sophocles' tragedy *Oedipus Rex.* Contemporary dramas include Eugene O'Neill's *The Iceman Cometh,* Lillian Hellman's *Little Foxes,* and August Wilson's *Ma Rainey's Black Bottom.*

Dramatic Irony: Occurs when the audience of a play or the reader of a work of literature knows something that a character in the work itself does not know. The irony is in the contrast between the intended meaning of the statements or actions of a character and the additional information understood by the audience. A celebrated example of dramatic irony is in Act V of William Shakespeare's *Romeo and Juliet,* where two young lovers meet their end as a result of a tragic misunderstanding. Here, the audience has full knowledge that Juliet's apparent "death" is merely temporary; she will regain her senses when the mysterious "sleeping potion" she has taken wears off. But Romeo, mistaking Juliet's drug-induced trance for true death, kills himself in grief. Upon awakening, Juliet discovers Romeo's corpse and, in despair, slays herself.

Dramatic Monologue: See *Monologue*

Dramatic Poetry: Any lyric work that employs elements of drama such as dialogue, conflict, or characterization, but excluding works that are intended for stage presentation. A monologue is a form of dramatic poetry.

Dramatis Personae: The characters in a work of literature, particularly a drama. The list of characters printed before the main text of a play or in the program is the *dramatis personae.*

Dream Allegory: See *Dream Vision*

Dream Vision: A literary convention, chiefly of the Middle Ages. In a dream vision a story is presented as a literal dream of the narrator. This device was commonly used to teach moral and religious lessons. Important works of this type are *The Divine Comedy* by Dante Alighieri, *Piers Plowman* by William Langland, and *The Pilgrim's Progress* by John Bunyan. Also known as Dream Allegory.

Dystopia: An imaginary place in a work of fiction where the characters lead dehumanized, fearful lives. Jack London's *The Iron Heel,* Yevgeny Zamyatin's *My,* Aldous Huxley's *Brave New World,* George Orwell's *Nineteen Eighty-four,* and Margaret Atwood's *Handmaid's Tale* portray versions of dystopia.

E

Eclogue: In classical literature, a poem featuring rural themes and structured as a dialogue among shepherds. Eclogues often took specific poetic forms, such as elegies or love poems. Some were written as the soliloquy of a shepherd. In later centuries, "eclogue" came to refer to any poem that was in the pastoral tradition or that had a dialogue or mono-

logue structure. A classical example of an eclogue is Virgil's *Eclogues,* also known as *Bucolics.* Giovanni Boccaccio, Edmund Spenser, Andrew Marvell, Jonathan Swift, and Louis MacNeice also wrote eclogues.

Edwardian: Describes cultural conventions identified with the period of the reign of Edward VII of England (1901-1910). Writers of the Edwardian Age typically displayed a strong reaction against the propriety and conservatism of the Victorian Age. Their work often exhibits distrust of authority in religion, politics, and art and expresses strong doubts about the soundness of conventional values. Writers of this era include George Bernard Shaw, H. G. Wells, and Joseph Conrad.

Edwardian Age: See *Edwardian*

Electra Complex: A daughter's amorous obsession with her father. The term Electra complex comes from the plays of Euripides and Sophocles entitled *Electra,* in which the character Electra drives her brother Orestes to kill their mother and her lover in revenge for the murder of their father.

Elegy: A lyric poem that laments the death of a person or the eventual death of all people. In a conventional elegy, set in a classical world, the poet and subject are spoken of as shepherds. In modern criticism, the word elegy is often used to refer to a poem that is melancholy or mournfully contemplative. John Milton's "Lycidas" and Percy Bysshe Shelley's "Adonais" are two examples of this form.

Elizabethan Age: A period of great economic growth, religious controversy, and nationalism closely associated with the reign of Elizabeth I of England (1558-1603). The Elizabethan Age is considered a part of the general renaissance—that is, the flowering of arts and literature—that took place in Europe during the fourteenth through sixteenth centuries. The era is considered the golden age of English literature. The most important dramas in English and a great deal of lyric poetry were produced during this period, and modern English criticism began around this time. The notable authors of the period—Philip Sidney, Edmund Spenser, Christopher Marlowe, William Shakespeare, Ben Jonson, Francis Bacon, and John Donne—are among the best in all of English literature.

Elizabethan Drama: English comic and tragic plays produced during the Renaissance, or more narrowly, those plays written during the last years of and few years after Queen Elizabeth's reign. William Shakespeare is considered an Elizabethan dramatist in the broader sense, although most of his work was produced during the reign of James I. Examples of Elizabethan comedies include John Lyly's *The Woman in the Moone,* Thomas Dekker's *The Roaring Girl, or, Moll Cut Purse,* and William Shakespeare's *Twelfth Night.* Examples of Elizabethan tragedies include William Shakespeare's *Antony and Cleopatra,* Thomas Kyd's *The Spanish Tragedy,* and John Webster's *The Tragedy of the Duchess of Malfi.*

Empathy: A sense of shared experience, including emotional and physical feelings, with someone or something other than oneself. Empathy is often used to describe the response of a reader to a literary character. An example of an empathic passage is William Shakespeare's description in his narrative poem *Venus and Adonis* of: the snail, whose tender horns being hit, Shrinks backward in his shelly cave with pain. Readers of Gerard Manley Hopkins's *The Windhover* may experience some of the physical sensations evoked in the description of the movement of the falcon.

English Sonnet: See *Sonnet*

Enjambment: The running over of the sense and structure of a line of verse or a couplet into the following verse or couplet. Andrew Marvell's "To His Coy Mistress" is structured as a series of enjambments, as in lines 11-12: "My vegetable love should grow/Vaster than empires and more slow."

Enlightenment, The: An eighteenth-century philosophical movement. It began in France but had a wide impact throughout Europe and America. Thinkers of the Enlightenment valued reason and believed that both the individual and society could achieve a state of perfection. Corresponding to this essentially humanist vision was a resistance to religious authority. Important figures of the Enlightenment were Denis Diderot and Voltaire in France, Edward Gibbon and David Hume in England, and Thomas Paine and Thomas Jefferson in the United States.

Epic: A long narrative poem about the adventures of a hero of great historic or legendary importance. The setting is vast and the action is often given cosmic significance through the intervention of supernatural forces such as gods, angels, or demons. Epics are typically written in a classical style of grand simplicity with elaborate metaphors and allusions that enhance the symbolic importance of a hero's adventures. Some well-known epics are Homer's *Iliad* and *Odyssey,* Virgil's *Aeneid,* and John Milton's *Paradise Lost.*

Epic Simile: See *Homeric Simile*

Epic Theater: A theory of theatrical presentation developed by twentieth-century German playwright Bertolt Brecht. Brecht created a type of drama that the audience could view with complete detachment. He used what he termed "alienation effects" to create an emotional distance between the audience and the action on stage. Among these effects are: short, self-contained scenes that keep the play from building to a cathartic climax; songs that comment on the action; and techniques of acting that prevent the actor from developing an emotional identity with his role. Besides the plays of Bertolt Brecht, other plays that utilize epic theater conventions include those of Georg Buchner, Frank Wedekind, Erwin Piscator, and Leopold Jessner.

Epigram: A saying that makes the speaker's point quickly and concisely. Samuel Taylor Coleridge wrote an epigram that neatly sums up the form: What is an Epigram? A Dwarfish whole, Its body brevity, and wit its soul.

Epilogue: A concluding statement or section of a literary work. In dramas, particularly those of the seventeenth and eighteenth centuries, the epilogue is a closing speech, often in verse, delivered by an actor at the end of a play and spoken directly to the audience. A famous epilogue is Puck's speech at the end of William Shakespeare's *A Midsummer Night's Dream.*

Epiphany: A sudden revelation of truth inspired by a seemingly trivial incident. The term was widely used by James Joyce in his critical writings, and the stories in Joyce's *Dubliners* are commonly called "epiphanies."

Episode: An incident that forms part of a story and is significantly related to it. Episodes may be either self-contained narratives or events that depend on a larger context for their sense and importance. Examples of episodes include the founding of Wilmington, Delaware in Charles Reade's *The Disinherited Heir* and the individual events comprising the picaresque novels and medieval romances.

Episodic Plot: See *Plot*

Epitaph: An inscription on a tomb or tombstone, or a verse written on the occasion of a person's death. Epitaphs may be serious or humorous. Dorothy Parker's epitaph reads, "I told you I was sick."

Epithalamion: A song or poem written to honor and commemorate a marriage ceremony. Famous examples include Edmund Spenser's

''Epithalamion'' and e. e. cummings's ''Epithalamion.'' Also spelled Epithalamium.

Epithalamium: See *Epithalamion*

Epithet: A word or phrase, often disparaging or abusive, that expresses a character trait of someone or something. ''The Napoleon of crime'' is an epithet applied to Professor Moriarty, arch-rival of Sherlock Holmes in Arthur Conan Doyle's series of detective stories.

Exempla: See *Exemplum*

Exemplum: A tale with a moral message. This form of literary sermonizing flourished during the Middle Ages, when *exempla* appeared in collections known as ''example-books.'' The works of Geoffrey Chaucer are full of *exempla*.

Existentialism: A predominantly twentieth-century philosophy concerned with the nature and perception of human existence. There are two major strains of existentialist thought: atheistic and Christian. Followers of atheistic existentialism believe that the individual is alone in a godless universe and that the basic human condition is one of suffering and loneliness. Nevertheless, because there are no fixed values, individuals can create their own characters—indeed, they can shape themselves—through the exercise of free will. The atheistic strain culminates in and is popularly associated with the works of Jean-Paul Sartre. The Christian existentialists, on the other hand, believe that only in God may people find freedom from life's anguish. The two strains hold certain beliefs in common: that existence cannot be fully understood or described through empirical effort; that anguish is a universal element of life; that individuals must bear responsibility for their actions; and that there is no common standard of behavior or perception for religious and ethical matters. Existentialist thought figures prominently in the works of such authors as Eugene Ionesco, Franz Kafka, Fyodor Dostoyevsky, Simone de Beauvoir, Samuel Beckett, and Albert Camus.

Expatriates: See *Expatriatism*

Expatriatism: The practice of leaving one's country to live for an extended period in another country. Literary expatriates include English poets Percy Bysshe Shelley and John Keats in Italy, Polish novelist Joseph Conrad in England, American writers Richard Wright, James Baldwin, Gertrude Stein, and Ernest Hemingway in France, and Trinidadian author Neil Bissondath in Canada.

Exposition: Writing intended to explain the nature of an idea, thing, or theme. Expository writing is often combined with description, narration, or argument. In dramatic writing, the exposition is the introductory material which presents the characters, setting, and tone of the play. An example of dramatic exposition occurs in many nineteenth-century drawing-room comedies in which the butler and the maid open the play with relevant talk about their master and mistress; in composition, exposition relays factual information, as in encyclopedia entries.

Expressionism: An indistinct literary term, originally used to describe an early twentieth-century school of German painting. The term applies to almost any mode of unconventional, highly subjective writing that distorts reality in some way. Advocates of Expressionism include dramatists George Kaiser, Ernst Toller, Luigi Pirandello, Federico Garcia Lorca, Eugene O'Neill, and Elmer Rice; poets George Heym, Ernst Stadler, August Stramm, Gottfried Benn, and Georg Trakl; and novelists Franz Kafka and James Joyce.

Extended Monologue: See *Monologue*

F

Fable: A prose or verse narrative intended to convey a moral. Animals or inanimate objects with human characteristics often serve as characters in fables. A famous fable is Aesop's ''The Tortoise and the Hare.''

Fairy Tales: Short narratives featuring mythical beings such as fairies, elves, and sprites. These tales originally belonged to the folklore of a particular nation or region, such as those collected in Germany by Jacob and Wilhelm Grimm. Two other celebrated writers of fairy tales are Hans Christian Andersen and Rudyard Kipling.

Falling Action: See *Denouement*

Fantasy: A literary form related to mythology and folklore. Fantasy literature is typically set in nonexistent realms and features supernatural beings. Notable examples of fantasy literature are *The Lord of the Rings* by J. R. R. Tolkien and the Gormenghast trilogy by Mervyn Peake.

Farce: A type of comedy characterized by broad humor, outlandish incidents, and often vulgar subject matter. Much of the ''comedy'' in film and television could more accurately be described as farce.

Feet: See *Foot*

Feminine Rhyme: See *Rhyme*

Femme fatale: A French phrase with the literal translation "fatal woman." A *femme fatale* is a sensuous, alluring woman who often leads men into danger or trouble. A classic example of the *femme fatale* is the nameless character in Billy Wilder's *The Seven Year Itch,* portrayed by Marilyn Monroe in the film adaptation.

Fiction: Any story that is the product of imagination rather than a documentation of fact. characters and events in such narratives may be based in real life but their ultimate form and configuration is a creation of the author. Geoffrey Chaucer's *The Canterbury Tales,* Laurence Sterne's *Tristram Shandy,* and Margaret Mitchell's *Gone with the Wind* are examples of fiction.

Figurative Language: A technique in writing in which the author temporarily interrupts the order, construction, or meaning of the writing for a particular effect. This interruption takes the form of one or more figures of speech such as hyperbole, irony, or simile. Figurative language is the opposite of literal language, in which every word is truthful, accurate, and free of exaggeration or embellishment. Examples of figurative language are tropes such as metaphor and rhetorical figures such as apostrophe.

Figures of Speech: Writing that differs from customary conventions for construction, meaning, order, or significance for the purpose of a special meaning or effect. There are two major types of figures of speech: rhetorical figures, which do not make changes in the meaning of the words, and tropes, which do. Types of figures of speech include simile, hyperbole, alliteration, and pun, among many others.

Fin de siecle: A French term meaning "end of the century." The term is used to denote the last decade of the nineteenth century, a transition period when writers and other artists abandoned old conventions and looked for new techniques and objectives. Two writers commonly associated with the *fin de siecle* mindset are Oscar Wilde and George Bernard Shaw.

First Person: See *Point of View*

Flashback: A device used in literature to present action that occurred before the beginning of the story. Flashbacks are often introduced as the dreams or recollections of one or more characters. Flashback techniques are often used in films, where they are typically set off by a gradual changing of one picture to another.

Foil: A character in a work of literature whose physical or psychological qualities contrast strongly with, and therefore highlight, the corresponding qualities of another character. In his Sherlock Holmes stories, Arthur Conan Doyle portrayed Dr. Watson as a man of normal habits and intelligence, making him a foil for the eccentric and wonderfully perceptive Sherlock Holmes.

Folk Ballad: See *Ballad*

Folklore: Traditions and myths preserved in a culture or group of people. Typically, these are passed on by word of mouth in various forms—such as legends, songs, and proverbs— or preserved in customs and ceremonies. This term was first used by W. J. Thoms in 1846. Sir James Frazer's *The Golden Bough* is the record of English folklore; myths about the frontier and the Old South exemplify American folklore.

Folktale: A story originating in oral tradition. Folktales fall into a variety of categories, including legends, ghost stories, fairy tales, fables, and anecdotes based on historical figures and events. Examples of folktales include Giambattista Basile's *The Pentamerone,* which contains the tales of Puss in Boots, Rapunzel, Cinderella, and Beauty and the Beast, and Joel Chandler Harris's Uncle Remus stories, which represent transplanted African folktales and American tales about the characters Mike Fink, Johnny Appleseed, Paul Bunyan, and Pecos Bill.

Foot: The smallest unit of rhythm in a line of poetry. In English-language poetry, a foot is typically one accented syllable combined with one or two unaccented syllables. There are many different types of feet. When the accent is on the second syllable of a two syllable word (con- *tort*), the foot is an "iamb"; the reverse accentual pattern (*tor* -ture) is a "trochee." Other feet that commonly occur in poetry in English are "anapest", two unaccented syllables followed by an accented syllable as in inter-*cept*, and "dactyl", an accented syllable followed by two unaccented syllables as in *su*-i- cide.

Foreshadowing: A device used in literature to create expectation or to set up an explanation of later developments. In Charles Dickens's *Great Expectations,* the graveyard encounter at the beginning of the novel between Pip and the escaped convict Magwitch foreshadows the baleful atmosphere and events that comprise much of the narrative.

Form: The pattern or construction of a work which identifies its genre and distinguishes it from other genres. Examples of forms include the different genres, such as the lyric form or the short story form, and various patterns for poetry, such as the verse form or the stanza form.

Formalism: In literary criticism, the belief that literature should follow prescribed rules of construction, such as those that govern the sonnet form. Examples of formalism are found in the work of the New Critics and structuralists.

Fourteener Meter: See *Meter*

Free Verse: Poetry that lacks regular metrical and rhyme patterns but that tries to capture the cadences of everyday speech. The form allows a poet to exploit a variety of rhythmical effects within a single poem. Free-verse techniques have been widely used in the twentieth century by such writers as Ezra Pound, T. S. Eliot, Carl Sandburg, and William Carlos Williams. Also known as *Vers libre.*

Futurism: A flamboyant literary and artistic movement that developed in France, Italy, and Russia from 1908 through the 1920s. Futurist theater and poetry abandoned traditional literary forms. In their place, followers of the movement attempted to achieve total freedom of expression through bizarre imagery and deformed or newly invented words. The Futurists were self-consciously modern artists who attempted to incorporate the appearances and sounds of modern life into their work. Futurist writers include Filippo Tommaso Marinetti, Wyndham Lewis, Guillaume Apollinaire, Velimir Khlebnikov, and Vladimir Mayakovsky.

G

Genre: A category of literary work. In critical theory, genre may refer to both the content of a given work—tragedy, comedy, pastoral—and to its form, such as poetry, novel, or drama. This term also refers to types of popular literature, as in the genres of science fiction or the detective story.

Genteel Tradition: A term coined by critic George Santayana to describe the literary practice of certain late nineteenth- century American writers, especially New Englanders. Followers of the Genteel Tradition emphasized conventionality in social, religious, moral, and literary standards. Some of the best-known writers of the Genteel Tradition are R. H. Stoddard and Bayard Taylor.

Gilded Age: A period in American history during the 1870s characterized by political corruption and materialism. A number of important novels of social and political criticism were written during this time. Examples of Gilded Age literature include Henry Adams's *Democracy* and F. Marion Crawford's *An American Politician.*

Gothic: See *Gothicism*

Gothicism: In literary criticism, works characterized by a taste for the medieval or morbidly attractive. A gothic novel prominently features elements of horror, the supernatural, gloom, and violence: clanking chains, terror, charnel houses, ghosts, medieval castles, and mysteriously slamming doors. The term ''gothic novel'' is also applied to novels that lack elements of the traditional Gothic setting but that create a similar atmosphere of terror or dread. Mary Shelley's *Frankenstein* is perhaps the best-known English work of this kind.

Gothic Novel: See *Gothicism*

Great Chain of Being: The belief that all things and creatures in nature are organized in a hierarchy from inanimate objects at the bottom to God at the top. This system of belief was popular in the seventeenth and eighteenth centuries. A summary of the concept of the great chain of being can be found in the first epistle of Alexander Pope's *An Essay on Man,* and more recently in Arthur O. Lovejoy's *The Great Chain of Being: A Study of the History of an Idea.*

Grotesque: In literary criticism, the subject matter of a work or a style of expression characterized by exaggeration, deformity, freakishness, and disorder. The grotesque often includes an element of comic absurdity. Early examples of literary grotesque include Francois Rabelais's *Pantagruel* and *Gargantua* and Thomas Nashe's *The Unfortunate Traveller,* while more recent examples can be found in the works of Edgar Allan Poe, Evelyn Waugh, Eudora Welty, Flannery O'Connor, Eugene Ionesco, Gunter Grass, Thomas Mann, Mervyn Peake, and Joseph Heller, among many others.

H

Haiku: The shortest form of Japanese poetry, constructed in three lines of five, seven, and five syllables respectively. The message of a *haiku* poem usually centers on some aspect of spirituality and provokes an emotional response in the reader. Early masters of *haiku* include Basho, Buson,

Kobayashi Issa, and Masaoka Shiki. English writers of *haiku* include the Imagists, notably Ezra Pound, H. D., Amy Lowell, Carl Sandburg, and William Carlos Williams. Also known as *Hokku*.

Half Rhyme: See *Consonance*

Hamartia: In tragedy, the event or act that leads to the hero's or heroine's downfall. This term is often incorrectly used as a synonym for tragic flaw. In Richard Wright's *Native Son,* the act that seals Bigger Thomas's fate is his first impulsive murder.

Harlem Renaissance: The Harlem Renaissance of the 1920s is generally considered the first significant movement of black writers and artists in the United States. During this period, new and established black writers published more fiction and poetry than ever before, the first influential black literary journals were established, and black authors and artists received their first widespread recognition and serious critical appraisal. Among the major writers associated with this period are Claude McKay, Jean Toomer, Countee Cullen, Langston Hughes, Arna Bontemps, Nella Larsen, and Zora Neale Hurston. Works representative of the Harlem Renaissance include Arna Bontemps's poems ''The Return'' and ''Golgotha Is a Mountain,'' Claude McKay's novel *Home to Harlem,* Nella Larsen's novel *Passing,* Langston Hughes's poem ''The Negro Speaks of Rivers,'' and the journals *Crisis* and *Opportunity,* both founded during this period. Also known as Negro Renaissance and New Negro Movement.

Harlequin: A stock character of the *commedia dell'arte* who occasionally interrupted the action with silly antics. Harlequin first appeared on the English stage in John Day's *The Travailes of the Three English Brothers.* The San Francisco Mime Troupe is one of the few modern groups to adapt Harlequin to the needs of contemporary satire.

Hellenism: Imitation of ancient Greek thought or styles. Also, an approach to life that focuses on the growth and development of the intellect. ''Hellenism'' is sometimes used to refer to the belief that reason can be applied to examine all human experience. A cogent discussion of Hellenism can be found in Matthew Arnold's *Culture and Anarchy.*

Heptameter: See *Meter*

Hero/Heroine: The principal sympathetic character (male or female) in a literary work. Heroes and heroines typically exhibit admirable traits: ideal-ism, courage, and integrity, for example. Famous heroes and heroines include Pip in Charles Dickens's *Great Expectations,* the anonymous narrator in Ralph Ellison's *Invisible Man,* and Sethe in Toni Morrison's *Beloved.*

Heroic Couplet: A rhyming couplet written in iambic pentameter (a verse with five iambic feet). The following lines by Alexander Pope are an example: ''Truth guards the Poet, sanctifies the line,/ And makes Immortal, Verse as mean as mine.''

Heroic Line: The meter and length of a line of verse in epic or heroic poetry. This varies by language and time period. For example, in English poetry, the heroic line is iambic pentameter (a verse with five iambic feet); in French, the alexandrine (a verse with six iambic feet); in classical literature, dactylic hexameter (a verse with six dactylic feet).

Heroine: See *Hero/Heroine*

Hexameter: See *Meter*

Historical Criticism: The study of a work based on its impact on the world of the time period in which it was written. Examples of postmodern historical criticism can be found in the work of Michel Foucault, Hayden White, Stephen Greenblatt, and Jonathan Goldberg.

Hokku: See *Haiku*

Holocaust: See *Holocaust Literature*

Holocaust Literature: Literature influenced by or written about the Holocaust of World War II. Such literature includes true stories of survival in concentration camps, escape, and life after the war, as well as fictional works and poetry. Representative works of Holocaust literature include Saul Bellow's *Mr. Sammler's Planet,* Anne Frank's *The Diary of a Young Girl,* Jerzy Kosinski's *The Painted Bird,* Arthur Miller's *Incident at Vichy,* Czeslaw Milosz's *Collected Poems,* William Styron's *Sophie's Choice,* and Art Spiegelman's *Maus.*

Homeric Simile: An elaborate, detailed comparison written as a simile many lines in length. An example of an epic simile from John Milton's *Paradise Lost* follows: Angel Forms, who lay entranced Thick as autumnal leaves that strow the brooks In Vallombrosa, where the Etrurian shades High over-arched embower; or scattered sedge Afloat, when with fierce winds Orion armed Hath vexed the Red-Sea coast, whose waves o'erthrew Busiris and his Memphian chivalry, While with perfidious hatred they pursued The sojourners of

Goshen, who beheld From the safe shore their floating carcasses And broken chariot-wheels. Also known as Epic Simile.

Horatian Satire: See *Satire*

Humanism: A philosophy that places faith in the dignity of humankind and rejects the medieval perception of the individual as a weak, fallen creature. "Humanists" typically believe in the perfectibility of human nature and view reason and education as the means to that end. Humanist thought is represented in the works of Marsilio Ficino, Ludovico Castelvetro, Edmund Spenser, John Milton, Dean John Colet, Desiderius Erasmus, John Dryden, Alexander Pope, Matthew Arnold, and Irving Babbitt.

Humors: Mentions of the humors refer to the ancient Greek theory that a person's health and personality were determined by the balance of four basic fluids in the body: blood, phlegm, yellow bile, and black bile. A dominance of any fluid would cause extremes in behavior. An excess of blood created a sanguine person who was joyful, aggressive, and passionate; a phlegmatic person was shy, fearful, and sluggish; too much yellow bile led to a choleric temperament characterized by impatience, anger, bitterness, and stubbornness; and excessive black bile created melancholy, a state of laziness, gluttony, and lack of motivation. Literary treatment of the humors is exemplified by several characters in Ben Jonson's plays *Every Man in His Humour* and *Every Man out of His Humour.* Also spelled Humours.

Humours: See *Humors*

Hyperbole: In literary criticism, deliberate exaggeration used to achieve an effect. In William Shakespeare's *Macbeth,* Lady Macbeth hyperbolizes when she says, "All the perfumes of Arabia could not sweeten this little hand."

I

Iamb: See *Foot*

Idiom: A word construction or verbal expression closely associated with a given language. For example, in colloquial English the construction "how come" can be used instead of "why" to introduce a question. Similarly, "a piece of cake" is sometimes used to describe a task that is easily done.

Image: A concrete representation of an object or sensory experience. Typically, such a representation helps evoke the feelings associated with the

object or experience itself. Images are either "literal" or "figurative." Literal images are especially concrete and involve little or no extension of the obvious meaning of the words used to express them. Figurative images do not follow the literal meaning of the words exactly. Images in literature are usually visual, but the term "image" can also refer to the representation of any sensory experience. In his poem "The Shepherd's Hour," Paul Verlaine presents the following image: "The Moon is red through horizon's fog;/ In a dancing mist the hazy meadow sleeps." The first line is broadly literal, while the second line involves turns of meaning associated with dancing and sleeping.

Imagery: The array of images in a literary work. Also, figurative language. William Butler Yeats's "The Second Coming" offers a powerful image of encroaching anarchy: Turning and turning in the widening gyre The falcon cannot hear the falconer; Things fall apart. . . .

Imagism: An English and American poetry movement that flourished between 1908 and 1917. The Imagists used precise, clearly presented images in their works. They also used common, everyday speech and aimed for conciseness, concrete imagery, and the creation of new rhythms. Participants in the Imagist movement included Ezra Pound, H. D. (Hilda Doolittle), and Amy Lowell, among others.

In medias res: A Latin term meaning "in the middle of things." It refers to the technique of beginning a story at its midpoint and then using various flashback devices to reveal previous action. This technique originated in such epics as Virgil's *Aeneid.*

Induction: The process of reaching a conclusion by reasoning from specific premises to form a general premise. Also, an introductory portion of a work of literature, especially a play. Geoffrey Chaucer's "Prologue" to the *Canterbury Tales,* Thomas Sackville's "Induction" to *The Mirror of Magistrates,* and the opening scene in William Shakespeare's *The Taming of the Shrew* are examples of inductions to literary works.

Intentional Fallacy: The belief that judgments of a literary work based solely on an author's stated or implied intentions are false and misleading. Critics who believe in the concept of the intentional fallacy typically argue that the work itself is sufficient matter for interpretation, even though they may concede that an author's statement of purpose can be useful. Analysis of William Wordsworth's *Lyri-*

cal Ballads based on the observations about poetry he makes in his "Preface" to the second edition of that work is an example of the intentional fallacy.

Interior Monologue: A narrative technique in which characters' thoughts are revealed in a way that appears to be uncontrolled by the author. The interior monologue typically aims to reveal the inner self of a character. It portrays emotional experiences as they occur at both a conscious and unconscious level. images are often used to represent sensations or emotions. One of the best-known interior monologues in English is the Molly Bloom section at the close of James Joyce's *Ulysses*. The interior monologue is also common in the works of Virginia Woolf.

Internal Rhyme: Rhyme that occurs within a single line of verse. An example is in the opening line of Edgar Allan Poe's "The Raven": "Once upon a midnight dreary, while I pondered weak and weary." Here, "dreary" and "weary" make an internal rhyme.

Irish Literary Renaissance: A late nineteenth- and early twentieth-century movement in Irish literature. Members of the movement aimed to reduce the influence of British culture in Ireland and create an Irish national literature. William Butler Yeats, George Moore, and Sean O'Casey are three of the best-known figures of the movement.

Irony: In literary criticism, the effect of language in which the intended meaning is the opposite of what is stated. The title of Jonathan Swift's "A Modest Proposal" is ironic because what Swift proposes in this essay is cannibalism—hardly "modest."

Italian Sonnet: See *Sonnet*

J

Jacobean Age: The period of the reign of James I of England (1603-1625). The early literature of this period reflected the worldview of the Elizabethan Age, but a darker, more cynical attitude steadily grew in the art and literature of the Jacobean Age. This was an important time for English drama and poetry. Milestones include William Shakespeare's tragedies, tragi-comedies, and sonnets; Ben Jonson's various dramas; and John Donne's metaphysical poetry.

Jargon: Language that is used or understood only by a select group of people. Jargon may refer to terminology used in a certain profession, such as computer jargon, or it may refer to any nonsensical

language that is not understood by most people. Literary examples of jargon are Francois Villon's *Ballades en jargon,* which is composed in the secret language of the *coquillards,* and Anthony Burgess's *A Clockwork Orange,* narrated in the fictional characters' language of "Nadsat."

Juvenalian Satire: See *Satire*

K

Knickerbocker Group: A somewhat indistinct group of New York writers of the first half of the nineteenth century. Members of the group were linked only by location and a common theme: New York life. Two famous members of the Knickerbocker Group were Washington Irving and William Cullen Bryant. The group's name derives from Irving's *Knickerbocker's History of New York.*

L

Lais: See *Lay*

Lay: A song or simple narrative poem. The form originated in medieval France. Early French *lais* were often based on the Celtic legends and other tales sung by Breton minstrels—thus the name of the "Breton lay." In fourteenth-century England, the term "lay" was used to describe short narratives written in imitation of the Breton lays. The most notable of these is Geoffrey Chaucer's "The Minstrel's Tale."

Leitmotiv: See *Motif*

Literal Language: An author uses literal language when he or she writes without exaggerating or embellishing the subject matter and without any tools of figurative language. To say "He ran very quickly down the street" is to use literal language, whereas to say "He ran like a hare down the street" would be using figurative language.

Literary Ballad: See *Ballad*

Literature: Literature is broadly defined as any written or spoken material, but the term most often refers to creative works. Literature includes poetry, drama, fiction, and many kinds of nonfiction writing, as well as oral, dramatic, and broadcast compositions not necessarily preserved in a written format, such as films and television programs.

Lost Generation: A term first used by Gertrude Stein to describe the post-World War I generation of American writers: men and women haunted by a sense of betrayal and emptiness brought about by the destructiveness of the war. The term is commonly applied to Hart Crane, Ernest Hemingway, F. Scott Fitzgerald, and others.

Lyric Poetry: A poem expressing the subjective feelings and personal emotions of the poet. Such poetry is melodic, since it was originally accompanied by a lyre in recitals. Most Western poetry in the twentieth century may be classified as lyrical. Examples of lyric poetry include A. E. Housman's elegy ''To an Athlete Dying Young,'' the odes of Pindar and Horace, Thomas Gray and William Collins, the sonnets of Sir Thomas Wyatt and Sir Philip Sidney, Elizabeth Barrett Browning and Rainer Maria Rilke, and a host of other forms in the poetry of William Blake and Christina Rossetti, among many others.

M

Mannerism: Exaggerated, artificial adherence to a literary manner or style. Also, a popular style of the visual arts of late sixteenth-century Europe that was marked by elongation of the human form and by intentional spatial distortion. Literary works that are self-consciously high-toned and artistic are often said to be ''mannered.'' Authors of such works include Henry James and Gertrude Stein.

Masculine Rhyme: See *Rhyme*

Masque: A lavish and elaborate form of entertainment, often performed in royal courts, that emphasizes song, dance, and costumery. The Renaissance form of the masque grew out of the spectacles of masked figures common in medieval England and Europe. The masque reached its peak of popularity and development in seventeenth-century England, during the reigns of James I and, especially, of Charles I. Ben Jonson, the most significant masque writer, also created the ''antimasque,'' which incorporates elements of humor and the grotesque into the traditional masque and achieved greater dramatic quality. Masque-like interludes appear in Edmund Spenser's *The Faerie Queene* and in William Shakespeare's *The Tempest.* One of the best-known English masques is John Milton's *Comus.*

Measure: The foot, verse, or time sequence used in a literary work, especially a poem. Measure is often used somewhat incorrectly as a synonym for meter.

Melodrama: A play in which the typical plot is a conflict between characters who personify extreme good and evil. Melodramas usually end happily and emphasize sensationalism. Other literary forms that use the same techniques are often labeled ''melodramatic.'' The term was formerly used to describe a combination of drama and music; as such, it was synonymous with ''opera.'' Augustin Daly's *Under the Gaslight* and Dion Boucicault's *The Octoroon, The Colleen Bawn,* and *The Poor of New York* are examples of melodramas. The most popular media for twentieth-century melodramas are motion pictures and television.

Metaphor: A figure of speech that expresses an idea through the image of another object. Metaphors suggest the essence of the first object by identifying it with certain qualities of the second object. An example is ''But soft, what light through yonder window breaks?/ It is the east, and Juliet is the sun'' in William Shakespeare's *Romeo and Juliet.* Here, Juliet, the first object, is identified with qualities of the second object, the sun.

Metaphysical Conceit: See *Conceit*

Metaphysical Poetry: The body of poetry produced by a group of seventeenth-century English writers called the ''Metaphysical Poets.'' The group includes John Donne and Andrew Marvell. The Metaphysical Poets made use of everyday speech, intellectual analysis, and unique imagery. They aimed to portray the ordinary conflicts and contradictions of life. Their poems often took the form of an argument, and many of them emphasize physical and religious love as well as the fleeting nature of life. Elaborate conceits are typical in metaphysical poetry. Marvell's ''To His Coy Mistress'' is a well-known example of a metaphysical poem.

Metaphysical Poets: See *Metaphysical Poetry*

Meter: In literary criticism, the repetition of sound patterns that creates a rhythm in poetry. The patterns are based on the number of syllables and the presence and absence of accents. The unit of rhythm in a line is called a foot. Types of meter are classified according to the number of feet in a line. These are the standard English lines: Monometer, one foot; Dimeter, two feet; Trimeter, three feet; Tetrameter, four feet; Pentameter, five feet; Hexameter, six feet (also called the Alexandrine); Heptameter, seven feet (also called the ''Fourteener'' when the feet are iambic). The most common English meter is the iambic pentameter, in which each line contains ten syllables, or five iambic feet, which individually are composed of an unstressed syllable followed by an accented syllable. Both of the following lines from Alfred, Lord Tennyson's

"Ulysses" are written in iambic pentameter: Made weak by time and fate, but strong in will To strive, to seek, to find, and not to yield.

Mise en scene: The costumes, scenery, and other properties of a drama. Herbert Beerbohm Tree was renowned for the elaborate *mises en scene* of his lavish Shakespearean productions at His Majesty's Theatre between 1897 and 1915.

Modernism: Modern literary practices. Also, the principles of a literary school that lasted from roughly the beginning of the twentieth century until the end of World War II. Modernism is defined by its rejection of the literary conventions of the nineteenth century and by its opposition to conventional morality, taste, traditions, and economic values. Many writers are associated with the concepts of Modernism, including Albert Camus, Marcel Proust, D. H. Lawrence, W. H. Auden, Ernest Hemingway, William Faulkner, William Butler Yeats, Thomas Mann, Tennessee Williams, Eugene O'Neill, and James Joyce.

Monologue: A composition, written or oral, by a single individual. More specifically, a speech given by a single individual in a drama or other public entertainment. It has no set length, although it is usually several or more lines long. An example of an "extended monologue"—that is, a monologue of great length and seriousness—occurs in the one-act, one-character play *The Stronger* by August Strindberg.

Monometer: See *Meter*

Mood: The prevailing emotions of a work or of the author in his or her creation of the work. The mood of a work is not always what might be expected based on its subject matter. The poem "Dover Beach" by Matthew Arnold offers examples of two different moods originating from the same experience: watching the ocean at night. The mood of the first three lines— The sea is calm tonight The tide is full, the moon lies fair Upon the straights. . . . is in sharp contrast to the mood of the last three lines— And we are here as on a darkling plain Swept with confused alarms of struggle and flight, Where ignorant armies clash by night.

Motif: A theme, character type, image, metaphor, or other verbal element that recurs throughout a single work of literature or occurs in a number of different works over a period of time. For example, the various manifestations of the color white in Herman

Melville's *Moby Dick* is a "specific" *motif,* while the trials of star-crossed lovers is a "conventional" *motif* from the literature of all periods. Also known as *Motiv* or *Leitmotiv.*

Motiv: See *Motif*

Muckrakers: An early twentieth-century group of American writers. Typically, their works exposed the wrongdoings of big business and government in the United States. Upton Sinclair's *The Jungle* exemplifies the muckraking novel.

Muses: Nine Greek mythological goddesses, the daughters of Zeus and Mnemosyne (Memory). Each muse patronized a specific area of the liberal arts and sciences. Calliope presided over epic poetry, Clio over history, Erato over love poetry, Euterpe over music or lyric poetry, Melpomene over tragedy, Polyhymnia over hymns to the gods, Terpsichore over dance, Thalia over comedy, and Urania over astronomy. Poets and writers traditionally made appeals to the Muses for inspiration in their work. John Milton invokes the aid of a muse at the beginning of the first book of his *Paradise Lost:* Of Man's First disobedience, and the Fruit of the Forbidden Tree, whose mortal taste Brought Death into the World, and all our woe, With loss of Eden, till one greater Man Restore us, and regain the blissful Seat, Sing Heav'nly Muse, that on the secret top of Oreb, or of Sinai, didst inspire That Shepherd, who first taught the chosen Seed, In the Beginning how the Heav'ns and Earth Rose out of Chaos. . . .

Mystery: See *Suspense*

Myth: An anonymous tale emerging from the traditional beliefs of a culture or social unit. Myths use supernatural explanations for natural phenomena. They may also explain cosmic issues like creation and death. Collections of myths, known as mythologies, are common to all cultures and nations, but the best-known myths belong to the Norse, Roman, and Greek mythologies. A famous myth is the story of Arachne, an arrogant young girl who challenged a goddess, Athena, to a weaving contest; when the girl won, Athena was enraged and turned Arachne into a spider, thus explaining the existence of spiders.

N

Narration: The telling of a series of events, real or invented. A narration may be either a simple narrative, in which the events are recounted chronologically, or a narrative with a plot, in which the account is given in a style reflecting the author's artistic concept of the story. Narration is sometimes used as a synonym for "storyline." The recounting of scary stories around a campfire is a form of narration.

Narrative: A verse or prose accounting of an event or sequence of events, real or invented. The term is also used as an adjective in the sense "method of narration." For example, in literary criticism, the expression "narrative technique" usually refers to the way the author structures and presents his or her story. Narratives range from the shortest accounts of events, as in Julius Caesar's remark, "I came, I saw, I conquered," to the longest historical or biographical works, as in Edward Gibbon's *The Decline and Fall of the Roman Empire,* as well as diaries, travelogues, novels, ballads, epics, short stories, and other fictional forms.

Narrative Poetry: A nondramatic poem in which the author tells a story. Such poems may be of any length or level of complexity. Epics such as *Beowulf* and ballads are forms of narrative poetry.

Narrator: The teller of a story. The narrator may be the author or a character in the story through whom the author speaks. Huckleberry Finn is the narrator of Mark Twain's *The Adventures of Huckleberry Finn.*

Naturalism: A literary movement of the late nineteenth and early twentieth centuries. The movement's major theorist, French novelist Emile Zola, envisioned a type of fiction that would examine human life with the objectivity of scientific inquiry. The Naturalists typically viewed human beings as either the products of "biological determinism," ruled by hereditary instincts and engaged in an endless struggle for survival, or as the products of "socioeconomic determinism," ruled by social and economic forces beyond their control. In their works, the Naturalists generally ignored the highest levels of society and focused on degradation: poverty, alcoholism, prostitution, insanity, and disease. Naturalism influenced authors throughout the world, including Henrik Ibsen and Thomas Hardy. In the United States, in particular, Naturalism had a profound impact. Among the authors who embraced its principles are Theodore Dreiser, Eugene O'Neill, Stephen Crane, Jack London, and Frank Norris.

Negritude: A literary movement based on the concept of a shared cultural bond on the part of black Africans, wherever they may be in the world. It traces its origins to the former French colonies of Africa and the Caribbean. Negritude poets, novelists, and essayists generally stress four points in their writings: One, black alienation from traditional African culture can lead to feelings of inferiority. Two, European colonialism and Western education should be resisted. Three, black Africans should seek to affirm and define their own identity. Four, African culture can and should be reclaimed. Many Negritude writers also claim that blacks can make unique contributions to the world, based on a heightened appreciation of nature, rhythm, and human emotions—aspects of life they say are not so highly valued in the materialistic and rationalistic West. Examples of Negritude literature include the poetry of both Senegalese Leopold Senghor in *Hosties noires* and Martiniquais Aime-Fernand Cesaire in *Return to My Native Land.*

Negro Renaissance: See *Harlem Renaissance*

Neoclassical Period: See *Neoclassicism*

Neoclassicism: In literary criticism, this term refers to the revival of the attitudes and styles of expression of classical literature. It is generally used to describe a period in European history beginning in the late seventeenth century and lasting until about 1800. In its purest form, Neoclassicism marked a return to order, proportion, restraint, logic, accuracy, and decorum. In England, where Neoclassicism perhaps was most popular, it reflected the influence of seventeenth- century French writers, especially dramatists. Neoclassical writers typically reacted against the intensity and enthusiasm of the Renaissance period. They wrote works that appealed to the intellect, using elevated language and classical literary forms such as satire and the ode. Neoclassical works were often governed by the classical goal of instruction. English neoclassicists included Alexander Pope, Jonathan Swift, Joseph Addison, Sir Richard Steele, John Gay, and Matthew Prior; French neoclassicists included Pierre Corneille and Jean-Baptiste Moliere. Also known as Age of Reason.

Neoclassicists: See *Neoclassicism*

New Criticism: A movement in literary criticism, dating from the late 1920s, that stressed close textual analysis in the interpretation of works of literature. The New Critics saw little merit in historical and biographical analysis. Rather, they aimed to examine the text alone, free from the question of how external events—biographical or otherwise—may have helped shape it. This predominantly American school was named "New Criticism" by one of its practitioners, John Crowe Ransom. Other important New Critics included Allen Tate, R. P. Blackmur, Robert Penn Warren, and Cleanth Brooks.

New Negro Movement: See *Harlem Renaissance*

Noble Savage: The idea that primitive man is noble and good but becomes evil and corrupted as he becomes civilized. The concept of the noble savage originated in the Renaissance period but is more closely identified with such later writers as Jean-Jacques Rousseau and Aphra Behn. First described in John Dryden's play *The Conquest of Granada,* the noble savage is portrayed by the various Native Americans in James Fenimore Cooper's "Leatherstocking Tales," by Queequeg, Daggoo, and Tashtego in Herman Melville's *Moby Dick,* and by John the Savage in Aldous Huxley's *Brave New World.*

O

Objective Correlative: An outward set of objects, a situation, or a chain of events corresponding to an inward experience and evoking this experience in the reader. The term frequently appears in modern criticism in discussions of authors' intended effects on the emotional responses of readers. This term was originally used by T. S. Eliot in his 1919 essay "Hamlet."

Objectivity: A quality in writing characterized by the absence of the author's opinion or feeling about the subject matter. Objectivity is an important factor in criticism. The novels of Henry James and, to a certain extent, the poems of John Larkin demonstrate objectivity, and it is central to John Keats's concept of "negative capability." Critical and journalistic writing usually are or attempt to be objective.

Occasional Verse: poetry written on the occasion of a significant historical or personal event. *Vers de societe* is sometimes called occasional verse although it is of a less serious nature. Famous examples of occasional verse include Andrew Marvell's "Horatian Ode upon Cromwell's Return from England," Walt Whitman's "When Lilacs Last in the Dooryard Bloom'd"— written upon the death of Abraham Lincoln—and Edmund Spenser's commemoration of his wedding, "Epithalamion."

Octave: A poem or stanza composed of eight lines. The term octave most often represents the first eight lines of a Petrarchan sonnet. An example of an octave is taken from a translation of a Petrarchan sonnet by Sir Thomas Wyatt: The pillar perisht is whereto I leant, The strongest stay of mine unquiet mind; The like of it no man again can find, From East to West Still seeking though he went. To mind unhap! for hap away hath rent Of all my joy the very

bark and rind; And I, alas, by chance am thus assigned Daily to mourn till death do it relent.

Ode: Name given to an extended lyric poem characterized by exalted emotion and dignified style. An ode usually concerns a single, serious theme. Most odes, but not all, are addressed to an object or individual. Odes are distinguished from other lyric poetic forms by their complex rhythmic and stanzaic patterns. An example of this form is John Keats's "Ode to a Nightingale."

Oedipus Complex: A son's amorous obsession with his mother. The phrase is derived from the story of the ancient Theban hero Oedipus, who unknowingly killed his father and married his mother. Literary occurrences of the Oedipus complex include Andre Gide's *Oedipe* and Jean Cocteau's *La Machine infernale,* as well as the most famous, Sophocles' *Oedipus Rex.*

Omniscience: See *Point of View*

Onomatopoeia: The use of words whose sounds express or suggest their meaning. In its simplest sense, onomatopoeia may be represented by words that mimic the sounds they denote such as "hiss" or "meow." At a more subtle level, the pattern and rhythm of sounds and rhymes of a line or poem may be onomatopoeic. A celebrated example of onomatopoeia is the repetition of the word "bells" in Edgar Allan Poe's poem "The Bells."

Opera: A type of stage performance, usually a drama, in which the dialogue is sung. Classic examples of opera include Giuseppi Verdi's *La traviata,* Giacomo Puccini's *La Boheme,* and Richard Wagner's *Tristan und Isolde.* Major twentieth- century contributors to the form include Richard Strauss and Alban Berg.

Operetta: A usually romantic comic opera. John Gay's *The Beggar's Opera,* Richard Sheridan's *The Duenna,* and numerous works by William Gilbert and Arthur Sullivan are examples of operettas.

Oral Tradition: See *Oral Transmission*

Oral Transmission: A process by which songs, ballads, folklore, and other material are transmitted by word of mouth. The tradition of oral transmission predates the written record systems of literate society. Oral transmission preserves material sometimes over generations, although often with variations. Memory plays a large part in the recitation and preservation of orally transmitted material. Breton lays, French *fabliaux,* national epics (including the Anglo- Saxon *Beowulf,* the Spanish *El Cid,* and the Finnish *Kalevala*), Native American myths and legends, and African folktales told by plantation slaves are examples of orally transmitted literature.

Oration: Formal speaking intended to motivate the listeners to some action or feeling. Such public speaking was much more common before the development of timely printed communication such as newspapers. Famous examples of oration include Abraham Lincoln's "Gettysburg Address" and Dr. Martin Luther King Jr.'s "I Have a Dream" speech.

Ottava Rima: An eight-line stanza of poetry composed in iambic pentameter (a five-foot line in which each foot consists of an unaccented syllable followed by an accented syllable), following the abababcc rhyme scheme. This form has been prominently used by such important English writers as Lord Byron, Henry Wadsworth Longfellow, and W. B. Yeats.

Oxymoron: A phrase combining two contradictory terms. Oxymorons may be intentional or unintentional. The following speech from William Shakespeare's *Romeo and Juliet* uses several oxymorons: Why, then, O brawling love! O loving hate! O anything, of nothing first create! O heavy lightness! serious vanity! Mis-shapen chaos of well-seeming forms! Feather of lead, bright smoke, cold fire, sick health! This love feel I, that feel no love in this.

P

Pantheism: The idea that all things are both a manifestation or revelation of God and a part of God at the same time. Pantheism was a common attitude in the early societies of Egypt, India, and Greece—the term derives from the Greek *pan* meaning "all" and *theos* meaning "deity." It later became a significant part of the Christian faith. William Wordsworth and Ralph Waldo Emerson are among the many writers who have expressed the pantheistic attitude in their works.

Parable: A story intended to teach a moral lesson or answer an ethical question. In the West, the best examples of parables are those of Jesus Christ in the New Testament, notably "The Prodigal Son," but parables also are used in Sufism, rabbinic literature, Hasidism, and Zen Buddhism.

Paradox: A statement that appears illogical or contradictory at first, but may actually point to an underlying truth. "Less is more" is an example of a paradox. Literary examples include Francis Bacon's statement, "The most corrected copies are commonly the least correct," and "All animals are equal, but some animals are more equal than others" from George Orwell's *Animal Farm.*

Parallelism: A method of comparison of two ideas in which each is developed in the same grammatical structure. Ralph Waldo Emerson's "Civilization" contains this example of parallelism: Raphael paints wisdom; Handel sings it, Phidias carves it, Shakespeare writes it, Wren builds it, Columbus sails it, Luther preaches it, Washington arms it, Watt mechanizes it.

Parnassianism: A mid nineteenth-century movement in French literature. Followers of the movement stressed adherence to well-defined artistic forms as a reaction against the often chaotic expression of the artist's ego that dominated the work of the Romantics. The Parnassians also rejected the moral, ethical, and social themes exhibited in the works of French Romantics such as Victor Hugo. The aesthetic doctrines of the Parnassians strongly influenced the later symbolist and decadent movements. Members of the Parnassian school include Leconte de Lisle, Sully Prudhomme, Albert Glatigny, Francois Coppee, and Theodore de Banville.

Parody: In literary criticism, this term refers to an imitation of a serious literary work or the signature style of a particular author in a ridiculous manner. A typical parody adopts the style of the original and applies it to an inappropriate subject for humorous effect. Parody is a form of satire and could be considered the literary equivalent of a caricature or cartoon. Henry Fielding's *Shamela* is a parody of Samuel Richardson's *Pamela.*

Pastoral: A term derived from the Latin word "pastor," meaning shepherd. A pastoral is a literary composition on a rural theme. The conventions of the pastoral were originated by the third-century Greek poet Theocritus, who wrote about the experiences, love affairs, and pastimes of Sicilian shepherds. In a pastoral, characters and language of a courtly nature are often placed in a simple setting. The term pastoral is also used to classify dramas, elegies, and lyrics that exhibit the use of country settings and shepherd characters. Percy Bysshe Shelley's "Adonais" and John Milton's "Lycidas" are two famous examples of pastorals.

Pastorela: The Spanish name for the shepherds play, a folk drama reenacted during the Christmas season. Examples of *pastorelas* include Gomez

Manrique's *Representacion del nacimiento* and the dramas of Lucas Fernandez and Juan del Encina.

Pathetic Fallacy: A term coined by English critic John Ruskin to identify writing that falsely endows nonhuman things with human intentions and feelings, such as ''angry clouds'' and ''sad trees.'' The pathetic fallacy is a required convention in the classical poetic form of the pastoral elegy, and it is used in the modern poetry of T. S. Eliot, Ezra Pound, and the Imagists. Also known as Poetic Fallacy.

Pelado: Literally the ''skinned one'' or shirtless one, he was the stock underdog, sharp-witted picaresque character of Mexican vaudeville and tent shows. The *pelado* is found in such works as Don Catarino's *Los effectos de la crisis* and *Regreso a mi tierra.*

Pen Name: See *Pseudonym*

Pentameter: See *Meter*

Persona: A Latin term meaning ''mask.'' *Personae* are the characters in a fictional work of literature. The *persona* generally functions as a mask through which the author tells a story in a voice other than his or her own. A *persona* is usually either a character in a story who acts as a narrator or an ''implied author,'' a voice created by the author to act as the narrator for himself or herself. *Personae* include the narrator of Geoffrey Chaucer's *Canterbury Tales* and Marlow in Joseph Conrad's *Heart of Darkness.*

Personae: See *Persona*

Personal Point of View: See *Point of View*

Personification: A figure of speech that gives human qualities to abstract ideas, animals, and inanimate objects. William Shakespeare used personification in *Romeo and Juliet* in the lines ''Arise, fair sun, and kill the envious moon,/ Who is already sick and pale with grief.'' Here, the moon is portrayed as being envious, sick, and pale with grief— all markedly human qualities. Also known as *Prosopopoeia.*

Petrarchan Sonnet: See *Sonnet*

Phenomenology: A method of literary criticism based on the belief that things have no existence outside of human consciousness or awareness. Proponents of this theory believe that art is a process that takes place in the mind of the observer as he or she contemplates an object rather than a quality of the object itself. Among phenomenological critics

are Edmund Husserl, George Poulet, Marcel Raymond, and Roman Ingarden.

Picaresque Novel: Episodic fiction depicting the adventures of a roguish central character (''picaro'' is Spanish for ''rogue''). The picaresque hero is commonly a low-born but clever individual who wanders into and out of various affairs of love, danger, and farcical intrigue. These involvements may take place at all social levels and typically present a humorous and wide-ranging satire of a given society. Prominent examples of the picaresque novel are *Don Quixote* by Miguel de Cervantes, *Tom Jones* by Henry Fielding, and *Moll Flanders* by Daniel Defoe.

Plagiarism: Claiming another person's written material as one's own. Plagiarism can take the form of direct, word-for- word copying or the theft of the substance or idea of the work. A student who copies an encyclopedia entry and turns it in as a report for school is guilty of plagiarism.

Platonic Criticism: A form of criticism that stresses an artistic work's usefulness as an agent of social engineering rather than any quality or value of the work itself. Platonic criticism takes as its starting point the ancient Greek philosopher Plato's comments on art in his *Republic.*

Platonism: The embracing of the doctrines of the philosopher Plato, popular among the poets of the Renaissance and the Romantic period. Platonism is more flexible than Aristotelian Criticism and places more emphasis on the supernatural and unknown aspects of life. Platonism is expressed in the love poetry of the Renaissance, the fourth book of Baldassare Castiglione's *The Book of the Courtier,* and the poetry of William Blake, William Wordsworth, Percy Bysshe Shelley, Friedrich Holderlin, William Butler Yeats, and Wallace Stevens.

Play: See *Drama*

Plot: In literary criticism, this term refers to the pattern of events in a narrative or drama. In its simplest sense, the plot guides the author in composing the work and helps the reader follow the work. Typically, plots exhibit causality and unity and have a beginning, a middle, and an end. Sometimes, however, a plot may consist of a series of disconnected events, in which case it is known as an ''episodic plot.'' In his *Aspects of the Novel,* E. M. Forster distinguishes between a story, defined as a ''narrative of events arranged in their time- sequence,'' and plot, which organizes the events to a "sense of causality." This definition closely mirrors Aristotle's discussion of plot in his *Poetics.*

Poem: In its broadest sense, a composition utilizing rhyme, meter, concrete detail, and expressive language to create a literary experience with emotional and aesthetic appeal. Typical poems include sonnets, odes, elegies, *haiku,* ballads, and free verse.

Poet: An author who writes poetry or verse. The term is also used to refer to an artist or writer who has an exceptional gift for expression, imagination, and energy in the making of art in any form. Well-known poets include Horace, Basho, Sir Philip Sidney, Sir Edmund Spenser, John Donne, Andrew Marvell, Alexander Pope, Jonathan Swift, George Gordon, Lord Byron, John Keats, Christina Rossetti, W. H. Auden, Stevie Smith, and Sylvia Plath.

Poetic Fallacy: See *Pathetic Fallacy*

Poetic Justice: An outcome in a literary work, not necessarily a poem, in which the good are rewarded and the evil are punished, especially in ways that particularly fit their virtues or crimes. For example, a murderer may himself be murdered, or a thief will find himself penniless.

Poetic License: Distortions of fact and literary convention made by a writer—not always a poet—for the sake of the effect gained. Poetic license is closely related to the concept of "artistic freedom." An author exercises poetic license by saying that a pile of money "reaches as high as a mountain" when the pile is actually only a foot or two high.

Poetics: This term has two closely related meanings. It denotes (1) an aesthetic theory in literary criticism about the essence of poetry or (2) rules prescribing the proper methods, content, style, or diction of poetry. The term poetics may also refer to theories about literature in general, not just poetry.

Poetry: In its broadest sense, writing that aims to present ideas and evoke an emotional experience in the reader through the use of meter, imagery, connotative and concrete words, and a carefully constructed structure based on rhythmic patterns. Poetry typically relies on words and expressions that have several layers of meaning. It also makes use of the effects of regular rhythm on the ear and may make a strong appeal to the senses through the use of imagery. Edgar Allan Poe's "Annabel Lee" and Walt Whitman's *Leaves of Grass* are famous examples of poetry.

Point of View: The narrative perspective from which a literary work is presented to the reader.

There are four traditional points of view. The "third person omniscient" gives the reader a "godlike" perspective, unrestricted by time or place, from which to see actions and look into the minds of characters. This allows the author to comment openly on characters and events in the work. The "third person" point of view presents the events of the story from outside of any single character's perception, much like the omniscient point of view, but the reader must understand the action as it takes place and without any special insight into characters' minds or motivations. The "first person" or "personal" point of view relates events as they are perceived by a single character. The main character "tells" the story and may offer opinions about the action and characters which differ from those of the author. Much less common than omniscient, third person, and first person is the "second person" point of view, wherein the author tells the story as if it is happening to the reader. James Thurber employs the omniscient point of view in his short story "The Secret Life of Walter Mitty." Ernest Hemingway's "A Clean, Well-Lighted Place" is a short story told from the third person point of view. Mark Twain's novel *Huck Finn* is presented from the first person viewpoint. Jay McInerney's *Bright Lights, Big City* is an example of a novel which uses the second person point of view.

Polemic: A work in which the author takes a stand on a controversial subject, such as abortion or religion. Such works are often extremely argumentative or provocative. Classic examples of polemics include John Milton's *Aeropagitica* and Thomas Paine's *The American Crisis.*

Pornography: Writing intended to provoke feelings of lust in the reader. Such works are often condemned by critics and teachers, but those which can be shown to have literary value are viewed less harshly. Literary works that have been described as pornographic include Ovid's *The Art of Love,* Margaret of Angouleme's *Heptameron,* John Cleland's *Memoirs of a Woman of Pleasure; or, the Life of Fanny Hill,* the anonymous *My Secret Life,* D. H. Lawrence's *Lady Chatterley's Lover,* and Vladimir Nabokov's *Lolita.*

Post-Aesthetic Movement: An artistic response made by African Americans to the black aesthetic movement of the 1960s and early '70s. Writers since that time have adopted a somewhat different tone in their work, with less emphasis placed on the disparity between black and white in the United States. In the words of post-aesthetic authors such as Toni Morrison, John Edgar Wideman, and Kristin Hunter, African Americans are portrayed as looking inward for answers to their own questions, rather than always looking to the outside world. Two well-known examples of works produced as part of the post-aesthetic movement are the Pulitzer Prize-winning novels *The Color Purple* by Alice Walker and *Beloved* by Toni Morrison.

Postmodernism: Writing from the 1960s forward characterized by experimentation and continuing to apply some of the fundamentals of modernism, which included existentialism and alienation. Postmodernists have gone a step further in the rejection of tradition begun with the modernists by also rejecting traditional forms, preferring the anti-novel over the novel and the anti-hero over the hero. Postmodern writers include Alain Robbe-Grillet, Thomas Pynchon, Margaret Drabble, John Fowles, Adolfo Bioy-Casares, and Gabriel Garcia Marquez.

Pre-Raphaelites: A circle of writers and artists in mid nineteenth-century England. Valuing the pre-Renaissance artistic qualities of religious symbolism, lavish pictorialism, and natural sensuousness, the Pre-Raphaelites cultivated a sense of mystery and melancholy that influenced later writers associated with the Symbolist and Decadent movements. The major members of the group include Dante Gabriel Rossetti, Christina Rossetti, Algernon Swinburne, and Walter Pater.

Primitivism: The belief that primitive peoples were nobler and less flawed than civilized peoples because they had not been subjected to the tainting influence of society. Examples of literature espousing primitivism include Aphra Behn's *Oroonoko: Or, The History of the Royal Slave,* Jean-Jacques Rousseau's *Julie ou la Nouvelle Heloise,* Oliver Goldsmith's *The Deserted Village,* the poems of Robert Burns, Herman Melville's stories *Typee, Omoo,* and *Mardi,* many poems of William Butler Yeats and Robert Frost, and William Golding's novel *Lord of the Flies.*

Projective Verse: A form of free verse in which the poet's breathing pattern determines the lines of the poem. Poets who advocate projective verse are against all formal structures in writing, including meter and form. Besides its creators, Robert Creeley, Robert Duncan, and Charles Olson, two other well-known projective verse poets are Denise Levertov and LeRoi Jones (Amiri Baraka). Also known as Breath Verse.

Prologue: An introductory section of a literary work. It often contains information establishing the situation of the characters or presents information about the setting, time period, or action. In drama, the prologue is spoken by a chorus or by one of the principal characters. In the "General Prologue" of *The Canterbury Tales,* Geoffrey Chaucer describes the main characters and establishes the setting and purpose of the work.

Prose: A literary medium that attempts to mirror the language of everyday speech. It is distinguished from poetry by its use of unmetered, unrhymed language consisting of logically related sentences. Prose is usually grouped into paragraphs that form a cohesive whole such as an essay or a novel. Recognized masters of English prose writing include Sir Thomas Malory, William Caxton, Raphael Holinshed, Joseph Addison, Mark Twain, and Ernest Hemingway.

Prosopopoeia: See *Personification*

Protagonist: The central character of a story who serves as a focus for its themes and incidents and as the principal rationale for its development. The protagonist is sometimes referred to in discussions of modern literature as the hero or anti-hero. Well-known protagonists are Hamlet in William Shakespeare's *Hamlet* and Jay Gatsby in F. Scott Fitzgerald's *The Great Gatsby.*

Protest Fiction: Protest fiction has as its primary purpose the protesting of some social injustice, such as racism or discrimination. One example of protest fiction is a series of five novels by Chester Himes, beginning in 1945 with *If He Hollers Let Him Go* and ending in 1955 with *The Primitive.* These works depict the destructive effects of race and gender stereotyping in the context of interracial relationships. Another African American author whose works often revolve around themes of social protest is John Oliver Killens. James Baldwin's essay "Everybody's Protest Novel" generated controversy by attacking the authors of protest fiction.

Proverb: A brief, sage saying that expresses a truth about life in a striking manner. "They are not all cooks who carry long knives" is an example of a proverb.

Pseudonym: A name assumed by a writer, most often intended to prevent his or her identification as the author of a work. Two or more authors may work together under one pseudonym, or an author may use a different name for each genre he or she publishes in. Some publishing companies maintain "house pseudonyms," under which any number of authors may write installations in a series. Some authors also choose a pseudonym over their real names the way an actor may use a stage name. Examples of pseudonyms (with the author's real name in parentheses) include Voltaire (Francois-Marie Arouet), Novalis (Friedrich von Hardenberg), Currer Bell (Charlotte Bronte), Ellis Bell (Emily Bronte), George Eliot (Maryann Evans), Honorio Bustos Donmecq (Adolfo Bioy-Casares and Jorge Luis Borges), and Richard Bachman (Stephen King).

Pun: A play on words that have similar sounds but different meanings. A serious example of the pun is from John Donne's "A Hymne to God the Father": Sweare by thyself, that at my death thy sonne Shall shine as he shines now, and hereto fore; And, having done that, Thou haste done; I fear no more.

Pure Poetry: poetry written without instructional intent or moral purpose that aims only to please a reader by its imagery or musical flow. The term pure poetry is used as the antonym of the term "didacticism." The poetry of Edgar Allan Poe, Stephane Mallarme, Paul Verlaine, Paul Valery, Juan Ramoz Jimenez, and Jorge Guillen offer examples of pure poetry.

Q

Quatrain: A four-line stanza of a poem or an entire poem consisting of four lines. The following quatrain is from Robert Herrick's "To Live Merrily, and to Trust to Good Verses": Round, round, the root do's run; And being ravisht thus, Come, I will drink a Tun To my *Propertius*.

R

Raisonneur: A character in a drama who functions as a spokesperson for the dramatist's views. The *raisonneur* typically observes the play without becoming central to its action. *Raisonneurs* were very common in plays of the nineteenth century.

Realism: A nineteenth-century European literary movement that sought to portray familiar characters, situations, and settings in a realistic manner. This was done primarily by using an objective narrative point of view and through the buildup of accurate detail. The standard for success of any realistic work depends on how faithfully it transfers common experience into fictional forms. The realistic method may be altered or extended, as in stream of consciousness writing, to record highly subjective experience. Seminal authors in the tradition of Realism include Honore de Balzac, Gustave Flaubert, and Henry James.

Refrain: A phrase repeated at intervals throughout a poem. A refrain may appear at the end of each stanza or at less regular intervals. It may be altered slightly at each appearance. Some refrains are nonsense expressions—as with "Nevermore" in Edgar Allan Poe's "The Raven"—that seem to take on a different significance with each use.

Renaissance: The period in European history that marked the end of the Middle Ages. It began in Italy in the late fourteenth century. In broad terms, it is usually seen as spanning the fourteenth, fifteenth, and sixteenth centuries, although it did not reach Great Britain, for example, until the 1480s or so. The Renaissance saw an awakening in almost every sphere of human activity, especially science, philosophy, and the arts. The period is best defined by the emergence of a general philosophy that emphasized the importance of the intellect, the individual, and world affairs. It contrasts strongly with the medieval worldview, characterized by the dominant concerns of faith, the social collective, and spiritual salvation. Prominent writers during the Renaissance include Niccolo Machiavelli and Baldassare Castiglione in Italy, Miguel de Cervantes and Lope de Vega in Spain, Jean Froissart and Francois Rabelais in France, Sir Thomas More and Sir Philip Sidney in England, and Desiderius Erasmus in Holland.

Repartee: Conversation featuring snappy retorts and witticisms. Masters of *repartee* include Sydney Smith, Charles Lamb, and Oscar Wilde. An example is recorded in the meeting of "Beau" Nash and John Wesley: Nash said, "I never make way for a fool," to which Wesley responded, "Don't you? I always do," and stepped aside.

Resolution: The portion of a story following the climax, in which the conflict is resolved. The resolution of Jane Austen's *Northanger Abbey* is neatly summed up in the following sentence: "Henry and Catherine were married, the bells rang and every body smiled."

Restoration: See *Restoration Age*

Restoration Age: A period in English literature beginning with the crowning of Charles II in 1660 and running to about 1700. The era, which was characterized by a reaction against Puritanism, was the first great age of the comedy of manners. The finest literature of the era is typically witty and urbane, and often lewd. Prominent Restoration Age writers include William Congreve, Samuel Pepys, John Dryden, and John Milton.

Revenge Tragedy: A dramatic form popular during the Elizabethan Age, in which the protagonist, directed by the ghost of his murdered father or son, inflicts retaliation upon a powerful villain. Notable features of the revenge tragedy include violence, bizarre criminal acts, intrigue, insanity, a hesitant protagonist, and the use of soliloquy. Thomas Kyd's *Spanish Tragedy* is the first example of revenge tragedy in English, and William Shakespeare's *Hamlet* is perhaps the best. Extreme examples of revenge tragedy, such as John Webster's *The Duchess of Malfi,* are labeled "tragedies of blood." Also known as Tragedy of Blood.

Revista: The Spanish term for a vaudeville musical revue. Examples of *revistas* include Antonio Guzman Aguilera's *Mexico para los mexicanos,* Daniel Vanegas's *Maldito jazz,* and Don Catarino's *Whiskey, morfina y marihuana* and *El desterrado.*

Rhetoric: In literary criticism, this term denotes the art of ethical persuasion. In its strictest sense, rhetoric adheres to various principles developed since classical times for arranging facts and ideas in a clear, persuasive, appealing manner. The term is also used to refer to effective prose in general and theories of or methods for composing effective prose. Classical examples of rhetorics include *The Rhetoric of Aristotle,* Quintillian's *Institutio Oratoria,* and Cicero's *Ad Herennium.*

Rhetorical Question: A question intended to provoke thought, but not an expressed answer, in the reader. It is most commonly used in oratory and other persuasive genres. The following lines from Thomas Gray's "Elegy Written in a Country Churchyard" ask rhetorical questions: Can storied urn or animated bust Back to its mansion call the fleeting breath? Can Honour's voice provoke the silent dust, Or Flattery soothe the dull cold ear of Death?

Rhyme: When used as a noun in literary criticism, this term generally refers to a poem in which words sound identical or very similar and appear in parallel positions in two or more lines. Rhymes are classified into different types according to where they fall in a line or stanza or according to the degree of similarity they exhibit in their spellings and sounds. Some major types of rhyme are "masculine" rhyme, "feminine" rhyme, and "triple" rhyme. In a masculine rhyme, the rhyming sound falls in a single accented syllable, as with "heat"

and "eat." Feminine rhyme is a rhyme of two syllables, one stressed and one unstressed, as with "merry" and "tarry." Triple rhyme matches the sound of the accented syllable and the two unaccented syllables that follow: "narrative" and "declarative." Robert Browning alternates feminine and masculine rhymes in his "Soliloquy of the Spanish Cloister": Gr-r-r—there go, my heart's abhorrence! Water your damned flower-pots, do! If hate killed men, Brother Lawrence, God's blood, would not mine kill you! What? Your myrtle-bush wants trimming? Oh, that rose has prior claims— Needs its leaden vase filled brimming? Hell dry you up with flames! Triple rhymes can be found in Thomas Hood's "Bridge of Sighs," George Gordon Byron's satirical verse, and Ogden Nash's comic poems.

Rhyme Royal: A stanza of seven lines composed in iambic pentameter and rhymed *ababbcc.* The name is said to be a tribute to King James I of Scotland, who made much use of the form in his poetry. Examples of rhyme royal include Geoffrey Chaucer's *The Parlement of Foules,* William Shakespeare's *The Rape of Lucrece,* William Morris's *The Early Paradise,* and John Masefield's *The Widow in the Bye Street.*

Rhyme Scheme: See *Rhyme*

Rhythm: A regular pattern of sound, time intervals, or events occurring in writing, most often and most discernably in poetry. Regular, reliable rhythm is known to be soothing to humans, while interrupted, unpredictable, or rapidly changing rhythm is disturbing. These effects are known to authors, who use them to produce a desired reaction in the reader. An example of a form of irregular rhythm is sprung rhythm poetry; quantitative verse, on the other hand, is very regular in its rhythm.

Rising Action: The part of a drama where the plot becomes increasingly complicated. Rising action leads up to the climax, or turning point, of a drama. The final "chase scene" of an action film is generally the rising action which culminates in the film's climax.

Rococo: A style of European architecture that flourished in the eighteenth century, especially in France. The most notable features of *rococo* are its extensive use of ornamentation and its themes of lightness, gaiety, and intimacy. In literary criticism, the term is often used disparagingly to refer to a decadent or over-ornamental style. Alexander Pope's "The Rape of the Lock" is an example of literary *rococo.*

Roman a clef: A French phrase meaning "novel with a key." It refers to a narrative in which real persons are portrayed under fictitious names. Jack Kerouac, for example, portrayed various real-life beat generation figures under fictitious names in his *On the Road.*

Romance: A broad term, usually denoting a narrative with exotic, exaggerated, often idealized characters, scenes, and themes. Nathaniel Hawthorne called his *The House of the Seven Gables* and *The Marble Faun* romances in order to distinguish them from clearly realistic works.

Romantic Age: See *Romanticism*

Romanticism: This term has two widely accepted meanings. In historical criticism, it refers to a European intellectual and artistic movement of the late eighteenth and early nineteenth centuries that sought greater freedom of personal expression than that allowed by the strict rules of literary form and logic of the eighteenth-century neoclassicists. The Romantics preferred emotional and imaginative expression to rational analysis. They considered the individual to be at the center of all experience and so placed him or her at the center of their art. The Romantics believed that the creative imagination reveals nobler truths—unique feelings and attitudes—than those that could be discovered by logic or by scientific examination. Both the natural world and the state of childhood were important sources for revelations of "eternal truths." "Romanticism" is also used as a general term to refer to a type of sensibility found in all periods of literary history and usually considered to be in opposition to the principles of classicism. In this sense, Romanticism signifies any work or philosophy in which the exotic or dreamlike figure strongly, or that is devoted to individualistic expression, self-analysis, or a pursuit of a higher realm of knowledge than can be discovered by human reason. Prominent Romantics include Jean-Jacques Rousseau, William Wordsworth, John Keats, Lord Byron, and Johann Wolfgang von Goethe.

Romantics: See *Romanticism*

Russian Symbolism: A Russian poetic movement, derived from French symbolism, that flourished between 1894 and 1910. While some Russian Symbolists continued in the French tradition, stressing aestheticism and the importance of suggestion above didactic intent, others saw their craft as a form of mystical worship, and themselves as mediators between the supernatural and the mundane. Russian symbolists include Aleksandr Blok, Vyacheslav Ivanovich Ivanov, Fyodor Sologub, Andrey Bely, Nikolay Gumilyov, and Vladimir Sergeyevich Solovyov.

S

Satire: A work that uses ridicule, humor, and wit to criticize and provoke change in human nature and institutions. There are two major types of satire: "formal" or "direct" satire speaks directly to the reader or to a character in the work; "indirect" satire relies upon the ridiculous behavior of its characters to make its point. Formal satire is further divided into two manners: the "Horatian," which ridicules gently, and the "Juvenalian," which derides its subjects harshly and bitterly. Voltaire's novella *Candide* is an indirect satire. Jonathan Swift's essay "A Modest Proposal" is a Juvenalian satire.

Scansion: The analysis or "scanning" of a poem to determine its meter and often its rhyme scheme. The most common system of scansion uses accents (slanted lines drawn above syllables) to show stressed syllables, breves (curved lines drawn above syllables) to show unstressed syllables, and vertical lines to separate each foot. In the first line of John Keats's *Endymion,* "A thing of beauty is a joy forever:" the word "thing," the first syllable of "beauty," the word "joy," and the second syllable of "forever" are stressed, while the words "A" and "of," the second syllable of "beauty," the word "a," and the first and third syllables of "forever" are unstressed. In the second line: "Its loveliness increases; it will never" a pair of vertical lines separate the foot ending with "increases" and the one beginning with "it."

Scene: A subdivision of an act of a drama, consisting of continuous action taking place at a single time and in a single location. The beginnings and endings of scenes may be indicated by clearing the stage of actors and props or by the entrances and exits of important characters. The first act of William Shakespeare's *Winter's Tale* is comprised of two scenes.

Science Fiction: A type of narrative about or based upon real or imagined scientific theories and technology. Science fiction is often peopled with alien creatures and set on other planets or in different dimensions. Karel Capek's *R.U.R.* is a major work of science fiction.

Second Person: See *Point of View*

Semiotics: The study of how literary forms and conventions affect the meaning of language. Semioticians include Ferdinand de Saussure, Charles Sanders Pierce, Claude Levi-Strauss, Jacques Lacan, Michel Foucault, Jacques Derrida, Roland Barthes, and Julia Kristeva.

Sestet: Any six-line poem or stanza. Examples of the sestet include the last six lines of the Petrarchan sonnet form, the stanza form of Robert Burns's "A Poet's Welcome to his love-begotten Daughter," and the sestina form in W. H. Auden's "Paysage Moralise."

Setting: The time, place, and culture in which the action of a narrative takes place. The elements of setting may include geographic location, characters' physical and mental environments, prevailing cultural attitudes, or the historical time in which the action takes place. Examples of settings include the romanticized Scotland in Sir Walter Scott's "Waverley" novels, the French provincial setting in Gustave Flaubert's *Madame Bovary,* the fictional Wessex country of Thomas Hardy's novels, and the small towns of southern Ontario in Alice Munro's short stories.

Shakespearean Sonnet: See *Sonnet*

Signifying Monkey: A popular trickster figure in black folklore, with hundreds of tales about this character documented since the 19th century. Henry Louis Gates Jr. examines the history of the signifying monkey in *The Signifying Monkey: Towards a Theory of Afro-American Literary Criticism,* published in 1988.

Simile: A comparison, usually using "like" or "as", of two essentially dissimilar things, as in "coffee as cold as ice" or "He sounded like a broken record." The title of Ernest Hemingway's "Hills Like White Elephants" contains a simile.

Slang: A type of informal verbal communication that is generally unacceptable for formal writing. Slang words and phrases are often colorful exaggerations used to emphasize the speaker's point; they may also be shortened versions of an often-used word or phrase. Examples of American slang from the 1990s include "yuppie" (an acronym for Young Urban Professional), "awesome" (for "excellent"), wired (for "nervous" or "excited"), and "chill out" (for relax).

Slant Rhyme: See *Consonance*

Slave Narrative: Autobiographical accounts of American slave life as told by escaped slaves. These

works first appeared during the abolition movement of the 1830s through the 1850s. Olaudah Equiano's *The Interesting Narrative of Olaudah Equiano, or Gustavus Vassa, The African* and Harriet Ann Jacobs's *Incidents in the Life of a Slave Girl* are examples of the slave narrative.

Social Realism: See *Socialist Realism*

Socialist Realism: The Socialist Realism school of literary theory was proposed by Maxim Gorky and established as a dogma by the first Soviet Congress of Writers. It demanded adherence to a communist worldview in works of literature. Its doctrines required an objective viewpoint comprehensible to the working classes and themes of social struggle featuring strong proletarian heroes. A successful work of socialist realism is Nikolay Ostrovsky's *Kak zakalyalas stal* (*How the Steel Was Tempered*). Also known as Social Realism.

Soliloquy: A monologue in a drama used to give the audience information and to develop the speaker's character. It is typically a projection of the speaker's innermost thoughts. Usually delivered while the speaker is alone on stage, a soliloquy is intended to present an illusion of unspoken reflection. A celebrated soliloquy is Hamlet's "To be or not to be" speech in William Shakespeare's *Hamlet.*

Sonnet: A fourteen-line poem, usually composed in iambic pentameter, employing one of several rhyme schemes. There are three major types of sonnets, upon which all other variations of the form are based: the "Petrarchan" or "Italian" sonnet, the "Shakespearean" or "English" sonnet, and the "Spenserian" sonnet. A Petrarchan sonnet consists of an octave rhymed *abbaabba* and a "sestet" rhymed either *cdecde, cdccdc,* or *cdedce.* The octave poses a question or problem, relates a narrative, or puts forth a proposition; the sestet presents a solution to the problem, comments upon the narrative, or applies the proposition put forth in the octave. The Shakespearean sonnet is divided into three quatrains and a couplet rhymed *abab cdcd efef gg.* The couplet provides an epigrammatic comment on the narrative or problem put forth in the quatrains. The Spenserian sonnet uses three quatrains and a couplet like the Shakespearean, but links their three rhyme schemes in this way: *abab bcbc cdcd ee.* The Spenserian sonnet develops its theme in two parts like the Petrarchan, its final six lines resolving a problem, analyzing a narrative, or applying a proposition put forth in its first eight lines. Examples of sonnets can be found in Petrarch's *Canzoniere,* Edmund Spenser's *Amoretti,* Elizabeth Barrett

Browning's *Sonnets from the Portuguese,* Rainer Maria Rilke's *Sonnets to Orpheus,* and Adrienne Rich's poem ''The Insusceptibles.''

Spenserian Sonnet: See *Sonnet*

Spenserian Stanza: A nine-line stanza having eight verses in iambic pentameter, its ninth verse in iambic hexameter, and the rhyme scheme ababbcbcc. This stanza form was first used by Edmund Spenser in his allegorical poem *The Faerie Queene.*

Spondee: In poetry meter, a foot consisting of two long or stressed syllables occurring together. This form is quite rare in English verse, and is usually composed of two monosyllabic words. The first foot in the following line from Robert Burns's ''Green Grow the Rashes'' is an example of a spondee: Green grow the rashes, O

Sprung Rhythm: Versification using a specific number of accented syllables per line but disregarding the number of unaccented syllables that fall in each line, producing an irregular rhythm in the poem. Gerard Manley Hopkins, who coined the term ''sprung rhythm,'' is the most notable practitioner of this technique.

Stanza: A subdivision of a poem consisting of lines grouped together, often in recurring patterns of rhyme, line length, and meter. Stanzas may also serve as units of thought in a poem much like paragraphs in prose. Examples of stanza forms include the quatrain, *terza rima, ottava rima,* Spenserian, and the so-called *In Memoriam* stanza from Alfred, Lord Tennyson's poem by that title. The following is an example of the latter form: Love is and was my lord and king, And in his presence I attend To hear the tidings of my friend, Which every hour his couriers bring.

Stereotype: A stereotype was originally the name for a duplication made during the printing process; this led to its modern definition as a person or thing that is (or is assumed to be) the same as all others of its type. Common stereotypical characters include the absent- minded professor, the nagging wife, the troublemaking teenager, and the kindhearted grandmother.

Stream of Consciousness: A narrative technique for rendering the inward experience of a character. This technique is designed to give the impression of an ever-changing series of thoughts, emotions, images, and memories in the spontaneous and seemingly illogical order that they occur in life. The

textbook example of stream of consciousness is the last section of James Joyce's *Ulysses.*

Structuralism: A twentieth-century movement in literary criticism that examines how literary texts arrive at their meanings, rather than the meanings themselves. There are two major types of structuralist analysis: one examines the way patterns of linguistic structures unify a specific text and emphasize certain elements of that text, and the other interprets the way literary forms and conventions affect the meaning of language itself. Prominent structuralists include Michel Foucault, Roman Jakobson, and Roland Barthes.

Structure: The form taken by a piece of literature. The structure may be made obvious for ease of understanding, as in nonfiction works, or may obscured for artistic purposes, as in some poetry or seemingly ''unstructured'' prose. Examples of common literary structures include the plot of a narrative, the acts and scenes of a drama, and such poetic forms as the Shakespearean sonnet and the Pindaric ode.

Sturm und Drang: A German term meaning ''storm and stress.'' It refers to a German literary movement of the 1770s and 1780s that reacted against the order and rationalism of the enlightenment, focusing instead on the intense experience of extraordinary individuals. Highly romantic, works of this movement, such as Johann Wolfgang von Goethe's *Gotz von Berlichingen,* are typified by realism, rebelliousness, and intense emotionalism.

Style: A writer's distinctive manner of arranging words to suit his or her ideas and purpose in writing. The unique imprint of the author's personality upon his or her writing, style is the product of an author's way of arranging ideas and his or her use of diction, different sentence structures, rhythm, figures of speech, rhetorical principles, and other elements of composition. Styles may be classified according to period (Metaphysical, Augustan, Georgian), individual authors (Chaucerian, Miltonic, Jamesian), level (grand, middle, low, plain), or language (scientific, expository, poetic, journalistic).

Subject: The person, event, or theme at the center of a work of literature. A work may have one or more subjects of each type, with shorter works tending to have fewer and longer works tending to have more. The subjects of James Baldwin's novel *Go Tell It on the Mountain* include the themes of father-son relationships, religious conversion, black life, and sexuality. The subjects of Anne Frank's

Diary of a Young Girl include Anne and her family members as well as World War II, the Holocaust, and the themes of war, isolation, injustice, and racism.

Subjectivity: Writing that expresses the author's personal feelings about his subject, and which may or may not include factual information about the subject. Subjectivity is demonstrated in James Joyce's *Portrait of the Artist as a Young Man,* Samuel Butler's *The Way of All Flesh,* and Thomas Wolfe's *Look Homeward, Angel.*

Subplot: A secondary story in a narrative. A sub-plot may serve as a motivating or complicating force for the main plot of the work, or it may provide emphasis for, or relief from, the main plot. The conflict between the Capulets and the Montagues in William Shakespeare's *Romeo and Juliet* is an example of a subplot.

Surrealism: A term introduced to criticism by Guillaume Apollinaire and later adopted by Andre Breton. It refers to a French literary and artistic movement founded in the 1920s. The Surrealists sought to express unconscious thoughts and feelings in their works. The best-known technique used for achieving this aim was automatic writing— transcriptions of spontaneous outpourings from the unconscious. The Surrealists proposed to unify the contrary levels of conscious and unconscious, dream and reality, objectivity and subjectivity into a new level of ''super-realism.'' Surrealism can be found in the poetry of Paul Eluard, Pierre Reverdy, and Louis Aragon, among others.

Suspense: A literary device in which the author maintains the audience's attention through the build-up of events, the outcome of which will soon be revealed. Suspense in William Shakespeare's *Hamlet* is sustained throughout by the question of whether or not the Prince will achieve what he has been instructed to do and of what he intends to do.

Syllogism: A method of presenting a logical argument. In its most basic form, the syllogism consists of a major premise, a minor premise, and a conclusion. An example of a syllogism is: Major premise: When it snows, the streets get wet. Minor premise: It is snowing. Conclusion: The streets are wet.

Symbol: Something that suggests or stands for something else without losing its original identity. In literature, symbols combine their literal meaning with the suggestion of an abstract concept. Literary symbols are of two types: those that carry complex associations of meaning no matter what their con-texts, and those that derive their suggestive meaning from their functions in specific literary works. Examples of symbols are sunshine suggesting happiness, rain suggesting sorrow, and storm clouds suggesting despair.

Symbolism: This term has two widely accepted meanings. In historical criticism, it denotes an early modernist literary movement initiated in France during the nineteenth century that reacted against the prevailing standards of realism. Writers in this movement aimed to evoke, indirectly and symbolically, an order of being beyond the material world of the five senses. Poetic expression of personal emotion figured strongly in the movement, typically by means of a private set of symbols uniquely identifiable with the individual poet. The principal aim of the Symbolists was to express in words the highly complex feelings that grew out of everyday contact with the world. In a broader sense, the term ''symbolism'' refers to the use of one object to represent another. Early members of the Symbolist movement included the French authors Charles Baudelaire and Arthur Rimbaud; William Butler Yeats, James Joyce, and T. S. Eliot were influenced as the movement moved to Ireland, England, and the United States. Examples of the concept of symbolism include a flag that stands for a nation or movement, or an empty cupboard used to suggest hopelessness, poverty, and despair.

Symbolist: See *Symbolism*

Symbolist Movement: See *Symbolism*

Sympathetic Fallacy: See *Affective Fallacy*

T

Tale: A story told by a narrator with a simple plot and little character development. Tales are usually relatively short and often carry a simple message. Examples of tales can be found in the work of Rudyard Kipling, Somerset Maugham, Saki, Anton Chekhov, Guy de Maupassant, and Armistead Maupin.

Tall Tale: A humorous tale told in a straightforward, credible tone but relating absolutely impossible events or feats of the characters. Such tales were commonly told of frontier adventures during the settlement of the west in the United States. Tall tales have been spun around such legendary heroes as Mike Fink, Paul Bunyan, Davy Crockett, Johnny Appleseed, and Captain Stormalong as well as the real-life William F. Cody and Annie Oakley. Literary use of tall tales can be found in Washington Irving's *History of New York,* Mark Twain's *Life on the Mississippi,* and in the German R. F. Raspe's *Baron Munchausen's Narratives of His Marvellous Travels and Campaigns in Russia.*

Tanka: A form of Japanese poetry similar to *haiku.* A *tanka* is five lines long, with the lines containing five, seven, five, seven, and seven syllables respectively. Skilled *tanka* authors include Ishikawa Takuboku, Masaoka Shiki, Amy Lowell, and Adelaide Crapsey.

Teatro Grottesco: See *Theater of the Grotesque*

Terza Rima: A three-line stanza form in poetry in which the rhymes are made on the last word of each line in the following manner: the first and third lines of the first stanza, then the second line of the first stanza and the first and third lines of the second stanza, and so on with the middle line of any stanza rhyming with the first and third lines of the following stanza. An example of *terza rima* is Percy Bysshe Shelley's ''The Triumph of Love'': As in that trance of wondrous thought I lay This was the tenour of my waking dream. Methought I sate beside a public way Thick strewn with summer dust, and a great stream Of people there was hurrying to and fro Numerous as gnats upon the evening gleam,. . .

Tetrameter: See *Meter*

Textual Criticism: A branch of literary criticism that seeks to establish the authoritative text of a literary work. Textual critics typically compare all known manuscripts or printings of a single work in order to assess the meanings of differences and revisions. This procedure allows them to arrive at a definitive version that (supposedly) corresponds to the author's original intention. Textual criticism was applied during the Renaissance to salvage the classical texts of Greece and Rome, and modern works have been studied, for instance, to undo deliberate correction or censorship, as in the case of novels by Stephen Crane and Theodore Dreiser.

Theater of Cruelty: Term used to denote a group of theatrical techniques designed to eliminate the psychological and emotional distance between actors and audience. This concept, introduced in the 1930s in France, was intended to inspire a more intense theatrical experience than conventional theater allowed. The ''cruelty'' of this dramatic theory signified not sadism but heightened actor/audience involvement in the dramatic event. The theater of

cruelty was theorized by Antonin Artaud in his *Le Theatre et son double (The Theatre and Its Double),* and also appears in the work of Jerzy Grotowski, Jean Genet, Jean Vilar, and Arthur Adamov, among others.

Theater of the Absurd: A post-World War II dramatic trend characterized by radical theatrical innovations. In works influenced by the Theater of the absurd, nontraditional, sometimes grotesque characterizations, plots, and stage sets reveal a meaningless universe in which human values are irrelevant. Existentialist themes of estrangement, absurdity, and futility link many of the works of this movement. The principal writers of the Theater of the Absurd are Samuel Beckett, Eugene Ionesco, Jean Genet, and Harold Pinter.

Theater of the Grotesque: An Italian theatrical movement characterized by plays written around the ironic and macabre aspects of daily life in the World War I era. Theater of the Grotesque was named after the play *The Mask and the Face* by Luigi Chiarelli, which was described as ''a grotesque in three acts.'' The movement influenced the work of Italian dramatist Luigi Pirandello, author of *Right You Are, If You Think You Are.* Also known as *Teatro Grottesco.*

Theme: The main point of a work of literature. The term is used interchangeably with thesis. The theme of William Shakespeare's *Othello*—jealousy—is a common one.

Thesis: A thesis is both an essay and the point argued in the essay. Thesis novels and thesis plays share the quality of containing a thesis which is supported through the action of the story. A master's thesis and a doctoral dissertation are two theses required of graduate students.

Thesis Play: See *Thesis*

Three Unities: See *Unities*

Tone: The author's attitude toward his or her audience may be deduced from the tone of the work. A formal tone may create distance or convey politeness, while an informal tone may encourage a friendly, intimate, or intrusive feeling in the reader. The author's attitude toward his or her subject matter may also be deduced from the tone of the words he or she uses in discussing it. The tone of John F. Kennedy's speech which included the appeal to ''ask not what your country can do for you'' was intended to instill feelings of camaraderie and national pride in listeners.

Tragedy: A drama in prose or poetry about a noble, courageous hero of excellent character who, because of some tragic character flaw or *hamartia*, brings ruin upon him- or herself. Tragedy treats its subjects in a dignified and serious manner, using poetic language to help evoke pity and fear and bring about catharsis, a purging of these emotions. The tragic form was practiced extensively by the ancient Greeks. In the Middle Ages, when classical works were virtually unknown, tragedy came to denote any works about the fall of persons from exalted to low conditions due to any reason: fate, vice, weakness, etc. According to the classical definition of tragedy, such works present the ''pathetic''—that which evokes pity—rather than the tragic. The classical form of tragedy was revived in the sixteenth century; it flourished especially on the Elizabethan stage. In modern times, dramatists have attempted to adapt the form to the needs of modern society by drawing their heroes from the ranks of ordinary men and women and defining the nobility of these heroes in terms of spirit rather than exalted social standing. The greatest classical example of tragedy is Sophocles' *Oedipus Rex*. The ''pathetic'' derivation is exemplified in ''The Monk's Tale'' in Geoffrey Chaucer's *Canterbury Tales*. Notable works produced during the sixteenth century revival include William Shakespeare's *Hamlet, Othello,* and *King Lear*. Modern dramatists working in the tragic tradition include Henrik Ibsen, Arthur Miller, and Eugene O'Neill.

Tragedy of Blood: See *Revenge Tragedy*

Tragic Flaw: In a tragedy, the quality within the hero or heroine which leads to his or her downfall. Examples of the tragic flaw include Othello's jealousy and Hamlet's indecisiveness, although most great tragedies defy such simple interpretation.

Transcendentalism: An American philosophical and religious movement, based in New England from around 1835 until the Civil War. Transcendentalism was a form of American romanticism that had its roots abroad in the works of Thomas Carlyle, Samuel Coleridge, and Johann Wolfgang von Goethe. The Transcendentalists stressed the importance of intuition and subjective experience in communication with God. They rejected religious dogma and texts in favor of mysticism and scientific naturalism. They pursued truths that lie beyond the ''colorless'' realms perceived by reason and the senses and were active social reformers in public education,

women's rights, and the abolition of slavery. Prominent members of the group include Ralph Waldo Emerson and Henry David Thoreau.

Trickster: A character or figure common in Native American and African literature who uses his ingenuity to defeat enemies and escape difficult situations. Tricksters are most often animals, such as the spider, hare, or coyote, although they may take the form of humans as well. Examples of trickster tales include Thomas King's *A Coyote Columbus Story,* Ashley F. Bryan's *The Dancing Granny* and Ishmael Reed's *The Last Days of Louisiana Red*.

Trimeter: See *Meter*

Triple Rhyme: See *Rhyme*

Trochee: See *Foot*

U

Understatement: See *Irony*

Unities: Strict rules of dramatic structure, formulated by Italian and French critics of the Renaissance and based loosely on the principles of drama discussed by Aristotle in his *Poetics*. Foremost among these rules were the three unities of action, time, and place that compelled a dramatist to: (1) construct a single plot with a beginning, middle, and end that details the causal relationships of action and character; (2) restrict the action to the events of a single day; and (3) limit the scene to a single place or city. The unities were observed faithfully by continental European writers until the Romantic Age, but they were never regularly observed in English drama. Modern dramatists are typically more concerned with a unity of impression or emotional effect than with any of the classical unities. The unities are observed in Pierre Corneille's tragedy *Polyeuctes* and Jean-Baptiste Racine's *Phedre*. Also known as Three Unities.

Urban Realism: A branch of realist writing that attempts to accurately reflect the often harsh facts of modern urban existence. Some works by Stephen Crane, Theodore Dreiser, Charles Dickens, Fyodor Dostoyevsky, Emile Zola, Abraham Cahan, and Henry Fuller feature urban realism. Modern examples include Claude Brown's *Manchild in the Promised Land* and Ron Milner's *What the Wine Sellers Buy*.

Utopia: A fictional perfect place, such as ''paradise'' or ''heaven.'' Early literary utopias were included in Plato's *Republic* and Sir Thomas More's

Utopia, while more modern utopias can be found in Samuel Butler's *Erewhon,* Theodor Herzka's *A Visit to Freeland,* and H. G. Wells' *A Modern Utopia.*

Utopian: See *Utopia*

Utopianism: See *Utopia*

V

Verisimilitude: Literally, the appearance of truth. In literary criticism, the term refers to aspects of a work of literature that seem true to the reader. Verisimilitude is achieved in the work of Honore de Balzac, Gustave Flaubert, and Henry James, among other late nineteenth-century realist writers.

Vers de societe: See *Occasional Verse*

Vers libre: See *Free Verse*

Verse: A line of metered language, a line of a poem, or any work written in verse. The following line of verse is from the epic poem *Don Juan* by Lord Byron: ''My way is to begin with the beginning.''

Versification: The writing of verse. Versification may also refer to the meter, rhyme, and other mechanical components of a poem. Composition of a ''Roses are red, violets are blue'' poem to suit an occasion is a common form of versification practiced by students.

Victorian: Refers broadly to the reign of Queen Victoria of England (1837-1901) and to anything with qualities typical of that era. For example, the qualities of smug narrowmindedness, bourgeois materialism, faith in social progress, and priggish morality are often considered Victorian. This stereotype is contradicted by such dramatic intellectual developments as the theories of Charles Darwin, Karl Marx, and Sigmund Freud (which stirred strong debates in England) and the critical attitudes of serious Victorian writers like Charles Dickens and George Eliot. In literature, the Victorian Period was the great age of the English novel, and the latter part of the era saw the rise of movements such as decadence and symbolism. Works of Victorian lit-

erature include the poetry of Robert Browning and Alfred, Lord Tennyson, the criticism of Matthew Arnold and John Ruskin, and the novels of Emily Bronte, William Makepeace Thackeray, and Thomas Hardy. Also known as Victorian Age and Victorian Period.

Victorian Age: See *Victorian*

Victorian Period: See *Victorian*

W

Weltanschauung: A German term referring to a person's worldview or philosophy. Examples of *weltanschauung* include Thomas Hardy's view of the human being as the victim of fate, destiny, or impersonal forces and circumstances, and the disillusioned and laconic cynicism expressed by such poets of the 1930s as W. H. Auden, Sir Stephen Spender, and Sir William Empson.

Weltschmerz: A German term meaning ''world pain.'' It describes a sense of anguish about the nature of existence, usually associated with a melancholy, pessimistic attitude. *Weltschmerz* was expressed in England by George Gordon, Lord Byron in his *Manfred* and *Childe Harold's Pilgrimage,* in France by Viscount de Chateaubriand, Alfred de Vigny, and Alfred de Musset, in Russia by Aleksandr Pushkin and Mikhail Lermontov, in Poland by Juliusz Slowacki, and in America by Nathaniel Hawthorne.

Z

Zarzuela: A type of Spanish operetta. Writers of *zarzuelas* include Lope de Vega and Pedro Calderon.

Zeitgeist: A German term meaning ''spirit of the time.'' It refers to the moral and intellectual trends of a given era. Examples of *zeitgeist* include the preoccupation with the more morbid aspects of dying and death in some Jacobean literature, especially in the works of dramatists Cyril Tourneur and John Webster, and the decadence of the French Symbolists.

Cumulative Author/Title Index

A

Aeschylus
    Prometheus Bound: V5
    Seven Against Thebes: V10
Ajax (Sophocles): V8
Albee, Edward
    Three Tall Women: V8
    Tiny Alice: V10
    Who's Afraid of Virginia
      Woolf?: V3
    The Zoo Story: V2
The Alchemist (Jonson): V4
All My Sons (Miller): V8
American Buffalo (Mamet): V3
Angels in America (Kushner): V5
Anonymous
    Everyman: V7
Anouilh, Jean
    Antigone: V9
    Ring Around the Moon: V10
Antigone (Sophocles): V1
Arcadia (Stoppard): V5
Arden, John
    Serjeant Musgrave's Dance: V9
Aristophanes
    Lysistrata: V10
Ayckbourn, Alan
    A Chorus of Disapproval: V7

B

The Bacchae (Euripides): V6
The Balcony (Genet): V10
The Bald Soprano (Ionesco): V4
Baraka, Amiri
    Dutchman: V3

Barnes, Peter
    The Ruling Class: V6
Barrie, J(ames) M.
    Peter Pan: V7
Barry, Philip
    The Philadelphia Story: V9
The Basic Training of Pavlo Hummel
    (Rabe): V3
Beckett, Samuel
    Krapp's Last Tape: V7
    Waiting for Godot: V2
Behan, Brendan
    The Hostage: V7
The Birthday Party (Pinter): V5
Blood Relations (Pollock): V3
Blood Wedding (García Lorca): V10
Blue Room (Hare): V7
Boesman & Lena (Fugard): V6
Bolt, Robert
    A Man for All Seasons: V2
Bond, Edward
    Lear: V3
    Saved: V8
Brecht, Bertolt
    The Good Person of
      Szechwan: V9
    Mother Courage and Her
      Children: V5
    The Threepenny Opera: V4
Brighton Beach Memoirs
    (Simon): V6
The Browning Version (Rattigan): V8
Buried Child (Shepard): V6
Burn This (Wilson): V4
Bus Stop (Inge): V8

C

Capek, Karel
    R.U.R.: V7
Carballido, Emilio
    I, Too, Speak of the Rose: V4
The Caretaker (Pinter): V7
Cat on a Hot Tin Roof
    (Williams): V3
The Chairs (Ionesco): V9
Chekhov, Anton
    The Cherry Orchard: V1
    The Three Sisters: V10
    Uncle Vanya: V5
The Cherry Orchard (Chekhov): V1
Children of a Lesser God
    (Medoff): V4
The Children's Hour (Hellman): V3
Childress, Alice
    Trouble in Mind: V8
    The Wedding Band: V2
A Chorus of Disapproval
    (Ayckbourn): V7
Christie, Agatha
    The Mousetrap: V2
Come Back, Little Sheba (Inge): V3
Coward, Noel
    Hay Fever: V6
    Private Lives: V3
Crimes of the Heart (Henley): V2
The Crucible (Miller): V3
Cyrano de Bergerac (Rostand): V1

D

Death and the King's Horseman
    (Soyinka): V10

Death and the Maiden
    (Dorfman): V4
Death of a Salesman (Miller): V1
Delaney, Shelagh
    A Taste of Honey: V7
Doctor Faustus (Marlowe): V1
A Doll's House (Ibsen): V1
Dorfman, Ariel
    Death and the Maiden: V4
Dutchman (Baraka): V3

E

Edward II (Marlowe): V5
Electra (Sophocles): V4
The Elephant Man (Pomerance): V9
Eliot, T. S.
    Murder in the Cathedral: V4
The Emperor Jones (O'Neill): V6
Entertaining Mr. Sloane (Orton): V3
Equus (Shaffer): V5
Euripides
    The Bacchae: V6
    Iphigenia in Taurus: V4
    Medea: V1
Everyman (): V7

F

Fences (Wilson): V3
Fiddler on the Roof (Stein): V7
Fierstein, Harvey
    Torch Song Trilogy: V6
Fool for Love (Shepard): V7
for colored girls who have
    considered suicide/when the
    rainbow is enuf (Shange): V2
Ford, John
    'Tis Pity She's a Whore: V7
The Foreigner (Shue): V7
The Front Page (MacArthur): V9
Fugard, Athol
    Boesman & Lena: V6
    ''Master Harold''. . . and the
        Boys: V3
    Sizwe Bansi is Dead: V10
Fuller, Charles H.
    A Soldier's Play: V8
Funnyhouse of a Negro
    (Kennedy): V9

G

García Lorca, Federico
    Blood Wedding: V10
    The House of Bernarda Alba: V4
Genet, Jean
    The Balcony: V10
The Ghost Sonata (Strindberg): V9
Gibson, William
    The Miracle Worker: V2
Glaspell, Susan
    Trifles: V8
The Glass Menagerie (Williams): V1

Glengarry Glen Ross (Mamet): V2
Goldsmith, Oliver
    She Stoops to Conquer: V1
The Good Person of Szechwan
    (Brecht): V9
Gorki, Maxım
    The Lower Depths: V9
Guare, John
    The House of Blue Leaves: V8

H

The Hairy Ape (O'Neill): V4
Hammerstein, Oscar
    The King and I: V1
Hansberry, Lorraine
    A Raisin in the Sun: V2
Hare, David
    Blue Room: V7
    Plenty: V4
Hart, Moss
    Once in a Lifetime: V10
    You Can't Take It with You: V1
Havel, Vaclav
    The Memorandum: V10
Hay Fever (Coward): V6
Hecht, Ben
    The Front Page: V9
Hedda Gabler (Ibsen): V6
The Heidi Chronicles
    (Wasserstein): V5
Hellman, Lillian
    The Children's Hour: V3
    The Little Foxes: V1
Henley, Beth
    Crimes of the Heart: V2
Highway, Tomson
    The Rez Sisters: V2
The Homecoming (Pinter): V3
The Hostage (Behan): V7
Hot L Baltimore (Wilson): V9
The House of Bernarda Alba (Garcia
    Lorca): V4
The House of Blue Leaves
    (Guare): V8
Hughes, Langston
    Mule Bone: V6
Hurston, Zora Neale
    Mule Bone: V6

I

I, Too, Speak of the Rose
    (Carballido): V4
Ibsen, Henrik
    A Doll's House: V1
    Hedda Gabler: V6
    Peer Gynt: V8
    The Wild Duck: V10
The Iceman Cometh (O'Neill): V5
The Importance of Being Earnest
    (Wilde): V4
Inge, William
    Bus Stop: V8

Come Back, Little Sheba: V3
Picnic: V5
Inherit the Wind (Lawrence
    and Lee): V2
Ionesco, Eugene
    The Bald Soprano: V4
Ionesco, Eugène
    The Chairs: V9
Iphigenia in Taurus (Euripides): V4

J

Jarry, Alfred
    Ubu Roi: V8
Jesus Christ Superstar (Webber and
    Rice): V7
Jonson, Ben(jamin)
    The Alchemist: V4
    Volpone: V10

K

Kaufman, George S.
    Once in a Lifetime: V10
    You Can't Take It with You: V1
Kennedy, Adrienne
    Funnyhouse of a Negro: V9
The Kentucky Cycle
    (Schenkkan): V10
The King and I (Hammerstein and
    Rodgers): V1
Kopit, Arthur
    Oh Dad, Poor Dad, Mamma's
        Hung You in the Closet and
        I'm Feelin' So Sad: V7
Krapp's Last Tape (Beckett): V7
Kushner, Tony
    Angels in America: V5

L

Lady Windermere's Fan (Wilde): V9
Lawrence, Jerome
    Inherit the Wind: V2
Lear (Bond): V3
Lee, Robert E.
    Inherit the Wind: V2
The Little Foxes (Hellman): V1
Long Day's Journey into Night
    (O'Neill): V2
Look Back in Anger (Osborne): V4
The Lower Depths (Gorki): V9
Lysistrata (Aristophanes): V10

M

MacArthur, Charles
    The Front Page: V9
Major Barbara (Shaw): V3
Mamet, David
    American Buffalo: V3
    Glengarry Glen Ross: V2
    Speed-the-Plow: V6
Man and Superman (Shaw): V6

A Man for All Seasons (Bolt): V2
Marat/Sade (Weiss): V3
Marlowe, Christopher
    Doctor Faustus: V1
    Edward II: V5
"Master Harold". . . *and the Boys*
    (Fugard): V3
McCullers, Carson
    The Member of the Wedding: V5
Medea (Euripides): V1
Medoff, Mark
    Children of a Lesser God: V4
The Member of the Wedding
    (McCullers): V5
The Memorandum (Havel): V10
Miller, Arthur
    All My Sons: V8
    The Crucible: V3
    Death of a Salesman: V1
The Miracle Worker (Gibson): V2
Miss Julie (Strindberg): V4
A Month in the Country
    (Turgenev): V6
Mother Courage and Her Children
    (Brecht): V5
Mourning Becomes Electra
    (O'Neill): V9
The Mousetrap (Christie): V2
Mule Bone (Hurston and
    Hughes): V6
Murder in the Cathedral (Eliot): V4

N

'night, Mother (Norman): V2
The Night of the Iguana
    (Williams): V7
No Exit (Sartre): V5
Norman, Marsha
    'night, Mother: V2

O

The Odd Couple (Simon): V2
Odets, Clifford
    Waiting for Lefty: V3
Oedipus Rex (Sophocles): V1
*Oh Dad, Poor Dad, Mamma's Hung
    You in the Closet and I'm
    Feelin' So Sad* (Kopit): V7
Once in a Lifetime (Kaufman and
    Hart): V10
O'Neill, Eugene
    The Emperor Jones: V6
    The Hairy Ape: V4
    The Iceman Cometh: V5
    *Long Day's Journey into
        Night*: V2
    Mourning Becomes Electra: V9
Orton, Joe
    Entertaining Mr. Sloane: V3
    What the Butler Saw: V6
Osborne, John
    Look Back in Anger: V4

Our Town (Wilder): V1

P

Peer Gynt (Ibsen): V8
Peter Pan (Barrie): V7
The Philadelphia Story (Barry): V9
The Piano Lesson (Wilson): V7
Picnic (Inge): V5
Pinter, Harold
    The Birthday Party: V5
    The Caretaker: V7
    The Homecoming: V3
Pirandello, Luigi
    *Right You Are, If You Think You
        Are*: V9
    *Six Characters in Search of an
        Author*: V4
Plenty (Hare): V4
Pollock, Sharon
    Blood Relations: V3
Pomerance, Bernard
    The Elephant Man: V9
Private Lives (Coward): V3
Prometheus Bound (Aeschylus): V5
Pygmalion (Shaw): V1

R

R.U.R. (Capek): V7
Rabe, David
    *The Basic Training of Pavlo
        Hummel*: V3
    Streamers: V8
A Raisin in the Sun (Hansberry): V2
Rattigan, Terence
    The Browning Version: V8
The Real Thing (Stoppard): V8
The Rez Sisters (Highway): V2
Rice, Tim
    Jesus Christ Superstar: V7
Right You Are, If You Think You Are
    (Pirandello): V9
Ring Around the Moon
    (Anouilh): V10
Rodgers, Richard
    The King and I: V1
*Rosencrantz and Guildenstern Are
    Dead* (Stoppard): V2
Rostand, Edmond
    Cyrano de Bergerac: V1
The Ruling Class (Barnes): V6

S

Salome (Wilde): V8
Sartre, Jean-Paul
    No Exit: V5
Saved (Bond): V8
Schenkkan, Robert
    The Kentucky Cycle: V10

School for Scandal (Sheridan): V4
Serjeant Musgrave's Dance
    (Arden): V9
Seven Against Thebes
    (Aeschylus): V10
Shaffer, Peter
    Equus: V5
Shange, Ntozake
    *for colored girls who have
        considered suicide/when the
        rainbow is enuf*: V2
Shaw, George Bernard
    Major Barbara: V3
    Man and Superman: V6
    Pygmalion: V1
She Stoops to Conquer
    (Goldsmith): V1
Shepard, Sam
    Buried Child: V6
    Fool for Love: V7
    True West: V3
Sheridan, Richard Brinsley
    School for Scandal: V4
Shue, Larry
    The Foreigner: V7
Simon, Neil
    Brighton Beach Memoirs: V6
    The Odd Couple: V2
*Six Characters in Search of an
    Author* (Pirandello): V4
Sizwe Bansi is Dead (Fugard): V10
The Skin of Our Teeth (Wilder): V4
Smith, Anna Deavere
    Twilight: Los Angeles, 1992: V2
A Soldier's Play (Fuller): V8
Sophocles
    Ajax: V8
    Antigone: V1
    Electra: V4
    Oedipus Rex: V1
Soyinka, Wole
    *Death and the King's
        Horseman*: V10
Speed-the-Plow (Mamet): V6
Stein, Joseph
    Fiddler on the Roof: V7
Stoppard, Tom
    Arcadia: V5
    The Real Thing: V8
    *Rosencrantz and Guildenstern Are
        Dead*: V2
Streamers (Rabe): V8
A Streetcar Named Desire
    (Williams): V1
Strindberg, August
    The Ghost Sonata: V9
    Miss Julie: V4

T

A Taste of Honey (Delaney): V7
The Three Sisters (Chekhov): V10

Three Tall Women (Albee): V8
The Threepenny Opera (Brecht): V4
Tiny Alice (Albee): V10
'Tis Pity She's a Whore (Ford): V7
Torch Song Trilogy (Fierstein): V6
Trifles (Glaspell): V8
Trouble in Mind (Childress): V8
True West (Shepard): V3
Turgenev, Ivan
    A Month in the Country: V6
Twilight: Los Angeles, 1992
        (Smith): V2

U

Ubu Roi (Jarry): V8
Uncle Vanya (Chekhov): V5

V

Valdez, Luis
    Zoot Suit: V5
Vidal, Gore
    Visit to a Small Planet: V2

Visit to a Small Planet (Vidal): V2
Volpone (Jonson): V10

W

Waiting for Godot (Beckett): V2
Waiting for Lefty (Odets): V3
Wasserstein, Wendy
    The Heidi Chronicles: V5
Webber, Andrew Lloyd
    Jesus Christ Superstar: V7
The Wedding Band (Childress): V2
Weiss, Peter
    Marat/Sade: V3
What the Butler Saw (Orton): V6
Who's Afraid of Virginia Woolf?
        (Albee): V3
The Wild Duck (Ibsen): V10
Wilde, Oscar
    *The Importance of Being
        Earnest*: V4
    Lady Windermere's Fan: V9
    Salome: V8

Wilder, Thornton
    Our Town: V1
    The Skin of Our Teeth: V4
Williams, Tennessee
    Cat on a Hot Tin Roof: V3
    The Glass Menagerie: V1
    The Night of the Iguana: V7
    A Streetcar Named Desire: V1
Wilson, August
    Fences: V3
    The Piano Lesson: V7
Wilson, Lanford
    Burn This: V4
    Hot L Baltimore: V9

Y

You Can't Take It with You
        (Kaufman and Hart): V1

Z

The Zoo Story (Albee): V2
Zoot Suit (Valdez): V5

Nationality/Ethnicity Index

Anonymous
  Everyman: V7

African American
Baraka, Amiri
  Dutchman: V3
Childress, Alice
  Trouble in Mind: V8
  The Wedding Band: V2
Fuller, Charles H.
  A Soldier's Play: V8
Hansberry, Lorraine
  A Raisin in the Sun: V2
Hughes, Langston
  Mule Bone: V6
Hurston, Zora Neale
  Mule Bone: V6
Kennedy, Adrienne
  Funnyhouse of a Negro: V9
Shange, Ntozake
  *for colored girls who have
    considered suicide/when the
    rainbow is enuf*: V2
Smith, Anna Deavere
  Twilight: Los Angeles, 1992: V2
Wilson, August
  Fences: V3
  The Piano Lesson: V7

American
Albee, Edward
  Three Tall Women: V8
  Tiny Alice: V10
  *Who's Afraid of Virginia
    Woolf?*: V3

  The Zoo Story: V2
Baraka, Amiri
  Dutchman: V3
Barry, Philip
  The Philadelphia Story: V9
Childress, Alice
  Trouble in Mind: V8
  The Wedding Band: V2
Eliot, T. S.
  Murder in the Cathedral: V4
Fierstein, Harvey
  Torch Song Trilogy: V6
Fuller, Charles H.
  A Soldier's Play: V8
Gibson, William
  The Miracle Worker: V2
Glaspell, Susan
  Trifles: V8
Guare, John
  The House of Blue Leaves: V8
Hammerstein, Oscar
  The King and I: V1
Hansberry, Lorraine
  A Raisin in the Sun: V2
Hart, Moss
  Once in a Lifetime: V10
  You Can't Take It with You: V1
Hecht, Ben
  The Front Page: V9
Hellman, Lillian
  The Children's Hour: V3
  The Little Foxes: V1
Henley, Beth
  Crimes of the Heart: V2
Hurston, Zora Neale
  Mule Bone: V6

Inge, William
  Bus Stop: V8
  Come Back, Little Sheba: V3
  Picnic: V5
Kaufman, George S.
  Once in a Lifetime: V10
  You Can't Take It with You: V1
Kopit, Arthur
  *Oh Dad, Poor Dad, Mamma's
    Hung You in the Closet and
    I'm Feelin' So Sad*: V7
Kushner, Tony
  Angels in America: V5
Lawrence, Jerome
  Inherit the Wind: V2
Lee, Robert E.
  Inherit the Wind: V2
MacArthur, Charles
  The Front Page: V9
Mamet, David
  American Buffalo: V3
  Glengarry Glen Ross: V2
  Speed-the-Plow: V6
McCullers, Carson
  The Member of the Wedding: V5
Medoff, Mark
  Children of a Lesser God: V4
Miller, Arthur
  All My Sons: V8
  The Crucible: V3
  Death of a Salesman: V1
Norman, Marsha
  'night, Mother: V2
Odets, Clifford
  Waiting for Lefty: V3
O'Neill, Eugene
  The Emperor Jones: V6

The Hairy Ape: V4
The Iceman Cometh: V5
*Long Day's Journey into
      Night*: V2
Mourning Becomes Electra: V9
Pomerance, Bernard
      The Elephant Man: V9
Rabe, David
      *The Basic Training of Pavlo
          Hummel*: V3
      Streamers: V8
Rodgers, Richard
      The King and I: V1
Schenkkan, Robert
      The Kentucky Cycle: V10
Shange, Ntozake
      *for colored girls who have
          considered suicide/when the
          rainbow is enuf*: V2
Shepard, Sam
      Buried Child: V6
      Fool for Love: V7
      True West: V3
Shue, Larry
      The Foreigner: V7
Simon, Neil
      Brighton Beach Memoirs: V6
      The Odd Couple: V2
Smith, Anna Deavere
      Twilight: Los Angeles, 1992: V2
Stein, Joseph
      Fiddler on the Roof: V7
Valdez, Luis
      Zoot Suit: V5
Vidal, Gore
      Visit to a Small Planet: V2
Wasserstein, Wendy
      The Heidi Chronicles: V5
Wilder, Thornton
      Our Town: V1
      The Skin of Our Teeth: V4
Williams, Tennessee
      Cat on a Hot Tin Roof: V3
      The Glass Menagerie: V1
      The Night of the Iguana: V7
      A Streetcar Named Desire: V1
Wilson, August
      Fences: V3
      The Piano Lesson: V7
Wilson, Lanford
      Burn This: V4
      Hot L Baltimore: V9

Argentinian

Dorfman, Ariel
      Death and the Maiden: V4

Canadian

Highway, Tomson
      The Rez Sisters: V2
Pollock, Sharon
      Blood Relations: V3

Chilean

Dorfman, Ariel
      Death and the Maiden: V4

Czechoslovakian

Capek, Karel
      R.U.R.: V7
Havel, Vaclav
      The Memorandum: V10

English

Arden, John
      Serjeant Musgrave's Dance: V9
Ayckbourn, Alan
      A Chorus of Disapproval: V7
Barnes, Peter
      The Ruling Class: V6
Bolt, Robert
      A Man for All Seasons: V2
Bond, Edward
      Lear: V3
      Saved: V8
Christie, Agatha
      The Mousetrap: V2
Coward, Noel
      Hay Fever: V6
      Private Lives: V3
Delaney, Shelagh
      A Taste of Honey: V7
Ford, John
      'Tis Pity She's a Whore: V7
Goldsmith, Oliver
      She Stoops to Conquer: V1
Hare, David
      Blue Room: V7
      Plenty: V4
Jonson, Ben(jamin)
      The Alchemist: V4
      Volpone: V10
Marlowe, Christopher
      Doctor Faustus: V1
      Edward II: V5
Orton, Joe
      Entertaining Mr. Sloane: V3
      What the Butler Saw: V6
Osborne, John
      Look Back in Anger: V4
Pinter, Harold
      The Birthday Party: V5
      The Caretaker: V7
      The Homecoming: V3
Rattigan, Terence
      The Browning Version: V8
Rice, Tim
      Jesus Christ Superstar: V7
Shaffer, Peter
      Equus: V5
Stoppard, Tom
      Arcadia: V5
      The Real Thing: V8

*Rosencrantz and Guildenstern Are
      Dead*: V2
Webber, Andrew Lloyd
      Jesus Christ Superstar: V7

French

Anouilh, Jean
      Antigone: V9
      Ring Around the Moon: V10
Genet, Jean
      The Balcony: V10
Jarry, Alfred
      Ubu Roi: V8
Rostand, Edmond
      Cyrano de Bergerac: V1
Sartre, Jean-Paul
      No Exit: V5

German

Brecht, Bertolt
      *The Good Person of
          Szechwan*: V9
      *Mother Courage and Her
          Children*: V5
      The Threepenny Opera: V4
Weiss, Peter
      Marat/Sade: V3

Greek

Aeschylus
      Prometheus Bound: V5
      Seven Against Thebes: V10
Aristophanes
      Lysistrata: V10
Euripides
      The Bacchae: V6
      Iphigenia in Taurus: V4
      Medea: V1
Sophocles
      Ajax: V8
      Antigone: V1
      Electra: V4
      Oedipus Rex: V1

Hispanic

Valdez, Luis
      Zoot Suit: V5

Irish

Beckett, Samuel
      Krapp's Last Tape: V7
      Waiting for Godot: V2
Behan, Brendan
      The Hostage: V7
Shaw, George Bernard
      Major Barbara: V3
      Man and Superman: V6
      Pygmalion: V1

Sheridan, Richard Brinsley
  School for Scandal: V4
Wilde, Oscar
  *The Importance of Being
    Earnest*: V4
  Lady Windermere's Fan: V9
  Salome: V8

Italian

Pirandello, Luigi
  *Right You Are, If You Think You
    Are*: V9
  *Six Characters in Search of an
    Author*: V4

Mexican

Carballido, Emilio
  I, Too, Speak of the Rose: V4

Native Canadian

Highway, Tomson
  The Rez Sisters: V2

Nigerian

Soyinka, Wole
  *Death and the King's
    Horseman*: V10

Norwegian

Ibsen, Henrik
  A Doll's House: V1
  Hedda Gabler: V6
  Peer Gynt: V8
  The Wild Duck: V10

Romanian

Ionesco, Eugene
  The Bald Soprano: V4
Ionesco, Eugène
  The Chairs: V9

Russian

Chekhov, Anton
  The Cherry Orchard: V1
  The Three Sisters: V10
  Uncle Vanya: V5
Gorki, Maxim
  The Lower Depths: V9

Turgenev, Ivan
  A Month in the Country: V6

Scottish

Barrie, J(ames) M.
  Peter Pan: V7

South African

Fugard, Athol
  Boesman & Lena: V6
  *''Master Harold''. . . and the
    Boys*: V3
  Sizwe Bansi is Dead: V10

Spanish

García Lorca, Federico
  Blood Wedding: V10
  The House of Bernarda Alba: V4

Swedish

Strindberg, August
  The Ghost Sonata: V9
  Miss Julie: V4

Subject/Theme Index

*Boldface terms appear as subheads in Themes section.

1920s
    Once in a Lifetime: 151-153
1980s
    The Kentucky Cycle: 90

A

Abandonment
    Lysistrata: 106, 108
    Once in a Lifetime: 160
Abstinence
    Tiny Alice: 283, 287-288
Absurdity
    The Memorandum: 128
Absurdity
    The Memorandum: 123, 128-129,
        132, 137-139
Adultery
    The Three Sisters: 273, 278
Aesthetics
    Sizwe Bansi is Dead: 233,
        236-237
Africa
    The Balcony: 8-9
    Death and the King's Horseman:
        51-52, 56-59, 78
    Seven Against Thebes: 183-185,
        188-190, 194-209, 212-213
    Sizwe Bansi is Dead: 221, 224-
        227, 239-240, 245
Alienation and Loneliness
    The Three Sisters: 253
Alienation
    Sizwe Bansi is Dead: 242, 244

Allegory
    The Memorandum: 139, 141
    Tiny Alice: 288, 290-291
    The Wild Duck: 362-365
Ambiguity
    Sizwe Bansi is Dead: 231, 233
Ambition
    Ring Around the Moon: 177
American Northeast
    Blood Wedding: 36-37
    The Kentucky Cycle: 85, 90
    Once in a Lifetime: 145-
        146, 151-155
American South
    Death and the King's Horseman:
        77-78
    The Kentucky Cycle: 82-85,
        92, 101-102
Angels
    The Kentucky Cycle: 96, 98
Anger and Hatred
    Seven Against Thebes: 186
Anger
    The Kentucky Cycle: 84-85
Apartheid
    Sizwe Bansi is Dead: 223-225,
        231-233, 237-241
Appearance versus Reality
    Ring Around the Moon: 172
Appearance Vs. Reality
    Volpone: 310, 312-314, 337-340
Appearances and Reality
    Volpone: 312
Atonement
    Volpone: 321, 323
    The Wild Duck: 361-364

B

Beauty
    Ring Around the Moon: 178-179
Betrayal and Deception
    The Memorandum: 128
Betrayal
    The Kentucky Cycle: 100
    The Memorandum: 128, 131
Blasphemy
    Seven Against Thebes: 209-211
Bloomsbury Group
    Tiny Alice: 295-297

C

Choice and Fate
    Seven Against Thebes: 186
Choices and Consequences
    The Wild Duck: 351
Christianity
    Blood Wedding: 43, 45, 47
    Death and the King's Horseman:
        55-56
    Tiny Alice: 301
    The Wild Duck: 353, 355-356,
        361-363, 366
City Life
    Sizwe Bansi is Dead: 238,
        240, 244-246
Class Conflict
    Volpone: 312
Classicism
    The Kentucky Cycle: 89
Comedy
    Lysistrata: 104, 108-109, 116
    Once in a Lifetime: 145, 151-
        152, 162-164

Ring Around the Moon: 181-182
Volpone: 314, 316-317, 321-326,
    333-334, 341-344
The Wild Duck: 368-373
Communism
    The Memorandum: 123-124,
        129-131
Courage
    Volpone: 320, 324
Crime and Criminals
    The Balcony: 2, 8, 10
    The Kentucky Cycle: 84-85,
        89, 91
    The Memorandum: 125-126
    Seven Against Thebes: 207-208
    Volpone: 320-321, 324-325
Cruelty
    The Kentucky Cycle: 82-84,
        89-92, 95-97
    Seven Against Thebes: 206-
        207, 210-212
Culture Clash
    *Death and the King's
        Horseman:* 54

D

Dance
    Death and the King's Horseman:
        50-51, 57, 63, 65-66
    Ring Around the Moon: 172-173
    The Three Sisters: 273,
        275, 277-279
Death
    The Balcony: 6
    Blood Wedding: 25
    Seven Against Thebes: 187
Death
    The Balcony: 3-4, 7-8, 17-18
    Blood Wedding: 22, 25-30,
        34-35, 39-47
    Death and the King's Horseman:
        51-55, 58-62, 65-69, 73-
        76, 79-80
    The Kentucky Cycle: 85, 88-
        90, 95, 97-98
    Seven Against Thebes: 185-188,
        199-201, 204-208, 211-
        212, 215
    Sizwe Bansi is Dead: 221-224,
        229-230, 234-235
    The Three Sisters: 247-249,
        257, 266, 269-271, 275, 277
    Tiny Alice: 284-285, 288,
        291, 301-302
    The Wild Duck: 349, 351, 367,
        369-370, 373
Deceit
    Volpone: 307-309, 337, 339-340
Deception
    Volpone: 313
    The Wild Duck: 352

Description
    Blood Wedding: 42, 46-47
    Death and the King's Horseman:
        64-65
    Seven Against Thebes: 195-
        196, 215, 217
Dialogue
    Once in a Lifetime: 152-154
    Ring Around the Moon: 173
    The Three Sisters: 273-275
    Tiny Alice: 299
Disease
    Lysistrata: 110-111
    Volpone: 316-317
Divorce
    Blood Wedding: 33
Drama
    The Balcony: 1, 8-9, 15-16
    Blood Wedding: 27-30, 37-
        38, 42-43
    Death and the King's Horseman:
        56, 58-59, 64-66, 69, 78-79
    The Kentucky Cycle: 90, 92,
        96, 98-101
    Lysistrata: 108-109, 112-113
    The Memorandum: 137, 139, 142
    Once in a Lifetime: 152-
        155, 163-164
    Ring Around the Moon: 180-181
    Seven Against Thebes: 188-190,
        200, 206, 209, 211-213, 217
    Sizwe Bansi is Dead: 230-
        232, 235, 237
    The Three Sisters: 247, 249, 255,
        257-258, 264
    Tiny Alice: 284, 288, 290-
        291, 295-298
    Volpone: 315-317, 322, 324-325,
        341, 343-344
    The Wild Duck: 355-357, 362-
        363, 367-368, 372-373
Dreams and Visions
    Sizwe Bansi is Dead: 233-234,
        240, 242-243, 246
    The Three Sisters: 272-276
Duty and Responsibility
    *Death and the King's
        Horseman:* 55
Duty and Responsibility
    Death and the King's Horseman:
        49-53, 57, 59-62, 79-80

E

Emotions
    Blood Wedding: 27, 38, 42-43
    Death and the King's Horseman:
        57, 62
    The Kentucky Cycle: 88, 100-101
    Ring Around the Moon: 171
    Seven Against Thebes: 186, 190,
        204, 209, 215

Sizwe Bansi is Dead: 239-
    240, 245
The Three Sisters: 254, 258-260,
    263, 278-279
The Wild Duck: 367-371
Envy
    Ring Around the Moon:
        168-169, 173
Epic
    Seven Against Thebes: 215-218
Essay
    Death and the King's Horseman:
        63, 65, 69
Europe
    The Balcony: 1, 8-9
    Blood Wedding: 28-30
    Death and the King's Horseman:
        51-52, 56, 58-59
    Lysistrata: 105-106, 110-115
    The Memorandum: 123, 128-132,
        137, 139, 142
    Ring Around the Moon:
        166, 173-174
    Seven Against Thebes: 188-191,
        214, 216-218
    The Three Sisters: 248-249, 254-
        258, 262-265, 269-270
    Tiny Alice: 295, 298
    Volpone: 307, 309, 313-315, 318-
        322, 326, 332-336, 340
    The Wild Duck: 353-355
Evil
    Death and the King's Horseman:
        64-65, 75
    The Kentucky Cycle: 93-97
    Seven Against Thebes: 211-212
    Tiny Alice: 290-291
    Volpone: 323, 325-326, 330-
        333, 341, 343
    The Wild Duck: 360, 366
Exile
    Death and the King's Horseman:
        56-57
Existentialism
    Sizwe Bansi is Dead: 230-
        233, 236-237
Exploitation
    Sizwe Bansi is Dead: 240-241
Expressionism
    Tiny Alice: 300-302

F

Family
    Sizwe Bansi is Dead: 223
Farce
    Once in a Lifetime: 163-164
Farm and Rural Life
    Blood Wedding: 28-29
    The Kentucky Cycle: 84-85, 91
    Volpone: 314-315
    The Wild Duck: 355

Fate and Chance
　Blood Wedding: 21-22, 27, 30,
　　38-39, 42-45
　Death and the King's Horseman:
　　65-68
　The Memorandum: 137, 141
　Once in a Lifetime: 150-154
　Seven Against Thebes: 184, 186-
　　191, 200-205, 209-212
　Sizwe Bansi is Dead: 234-235
　The Three Sisters: 265-267
Fear and Terror
　Death and the King's Horseman:
　　73, 75-76
　Seven Against Thebes: 190-193,
　　202, 204-206, 209-210, 213
Film
　Once in a Lifetime: 145, 147-148,
　　152-159, 164
Folklore
　The Kentucky Cycle: 98
　Ring Around the Moon: 178
　The Three Sisters: 277-278
Friendship and Loyalty
　Once in a Lifetime: 150

G

Ghost
　Death and the King's Horseman:
　　54, 57, 59
　Sizwe Bansi is Dead: 234, 237
God and Faith
　Tiny Alice: 286
God
　Seven Against Thebes: 187, 190,
　　202-203, 207, 210
　Tiny Alice: 283-288, 292-
　　294, 301-302
Great Depression
　Once in a Lifetime: 151-153
Greed
　Volpone: 313
Greed
　The Kentucky Cycle: 89, 95
　Volpone: 307, 313-314, 322, 324-
　　326, 335-336, 344
Grief and Sorrow
　Blood Wedding: 43, 45-47
　Seven Against Thebes: 184-185,
　　204-205, 209, 212
　The Wild Duck: 370, 372-373
Grotesque
　The Memorandum: 139

H

Happiness and Gaiety
　Death and the King's Horseman:
　　65-66
　The Three Sisters: 266, 268-
　　271, 277-279
　Volpone: 321-324

Hatred
　Death and the King's Horseman:
　　71, 75
　The Kentucky Cycle: 84,
　　91, 94-95
　The Memorandum: 137, 140
　Ring Around the Moon: 176-177
　Seven Against Thebes: 185-186,
　　190, 194-196, 204-207,
　　214-217
　Sizwe Bansi is Dead: 242,
　　244-245
　Tiny Alice: 287
　Volpone: 322, 324, 338, 340
Heritage and Ancestry
　Death and the King's Horseman:
　　50, 53-54, 59
　Seven Against Thebes: 198-200
Heroism
　The Balcony: 15, 17
　Ring Around the Moon: 172-174
　Seven Against Thebes: 187
　Sizwe Bansi is Dead: 231,
　　235, 237
　Volpone: 321-324
History
　The Balcony: 10
　Death and the King's Horseman:
　　70-72, 76, 78
　The Kentucky Cycle: 82, 88,
　　90, 101-103
　The Memorandum: 131
　Once in a Lifetime: 157-159
　The Wild Duck: 366
Homelessness
　Death and the King's Horseman:
　　73, 76-77
Homosexuality
　Tiny Alice: 287, 290, 297
Honor
　Seven Against Thebes: 187
Honor
　Blood Wedding: 43-46
　Death and the King's Horseman:
　　68-69, 74-75
　Seven Against Thebes: 187-188
Hope and Optimism
　Once in a Lifetime: 151
Hope
　Once in a Lifetime: 151
　Sizwe Bansi is Dead: 233-235
　The Three Sisters: 248,
　　250, 253-255
　Volpone: 338
Human Laws versus Divine Laws
　Seven Against Thebes: 187
Humility
　The Wild Duck: 361-362
Humor
　Lysistrata: 104-105, 110, 112,
　　114-115, 119-120
　The Memorandum: 137-139

　Once in a Lifetime: 152,
　　154, 159-164
　The Three Sisters: 264
　Tiny Alice: 303-305
　Volpone: 314, 317, 320, 322-327,
　　331, 338, 340-343
　The Wild Duck: 355-359, 368-373

I

Identity
　The Wild Duck: 351
Illusion and Reality
　The Balcony: 6
　Tiny Alice: 285
Imagery and Symbolism
　The Balcony: 17, 19-20
　Blood Wedding: 29, 33, 35,
　　38-39, 43-47
　Death and the King's Horseman:
　　67-72, 76
　The Memorandum: 137-138
　Ring Around the Moon: 179-180
　Seven Against Thebes: 203-204,
　　209, 211-212
　Sizwe Bansi is Dead: 232, 236
　The Three Sisters: 271
　Tiny Alice: 281, 287, 291,
　　300, 302
　Volpone: 329-330, 335, 339-341
　The Wild Duck: 352-353, 360-364
Imagination
　The Balcony: 2-4, 8
　Death and the King's Horseman:
　　70-72
　Sizwe Bansi is Dead: 235-
　　237, 243, 245
　The Wild Duck: 361-362
Incest
　Seven Against Thebes: 198-200
Individual versus Machine
　The Memorandum: 128
Insanity
　Tiny Alice: 283-287, 291
Irony
　Death and the King's Horseman:
　　64-65, 68-69
　The Memorandum: 137-142
　Sizwe Bansi is Dead: 240-241
　The Three Sisters: 275, 278
　Tiny Alice: 303-305
　Volpone: 324, 338-340, 343
　The Wild Duck: 371-373
Islamism
　Death and the King's Horseman:
　　51, 54, 56, 58

K

Killers and Killing
　The Balcony: 3, 12-13
　Blood Wedding: 25

Death and the King's Horseman:
51-52, 71
The Kentucky Cycle: 83-85,
89, 92-97
Seven Against Thebes: 204-208
Sizwe Bansi is Dead: 232-233
Knowledge
The Memorandum: 124-125, 138

L

Landscape
Blood Wedding: 44-47
The Kentucky Cycle: 88-90
The Wild Duck: 352, 360-363
Law and Order
The Balcony: 3-4, 7-8
Blood Wedding: 21-22, 26-28
The Kentucky Cycle: 88, 90-91
Lysistrata: 106, 108, 112
The Memorandum: 124-126
Seven Against Thebes: 187, 190,
208-210, 213
Sizwe Bansi is Dead: 220-221,
226, 238-245
Tiny Alice: 283-289, 292-
293, 301-302
Volpone: 308-310, 313-314, 319-
320, 325-326, 330-332, 335-
336, 339-340
The Wild Duck: 352-355
Life Cycle
*Death and the King's
Horseman:* 53
Limitations and Opportunities
Sizwe Bansi is Dead: 223
Limitations and Opportunities
Sizwe Bansi is Dead: 223-
225, 240-243
Literary Criticism
Volpone: 343
The Wild Duck: 356-357
Loneliness
Blood Wedding: 43, 47
Sizwe Bansi is Dead: 239,
243, 245
Love and Passion
The Three Sisters: 253
Love and Passion
Blood Wedding: 20-22, 26-27,
31-38, 41-47
The Kentucky Cycle: 95
Lysistrata: 118-120
Ring Around the Moon: 167-
169, 173-182
The Three Sisters: 249, 253-254,
258-261, 266-278
Tiny Alice: 284, 287, 290,
300-302
Volpone: 322-323, 326-327,
337-340
The Wild Duck: 349-351, 368-370

Lower Class
The Three Sisters: 255-257

M

Marriage
Blood Wedding: 20-22, 27, 31-35,
39-41, 44-47
Death and the King's Horseman:
52, 54-55, 61-62, 65-67
Ring Around the Moon:
169, 171, 174
The Three Sisters: 274, 276, 278
Tiny Alice: 284, 287
Masculinity
Lysistrata: 118-120
Sizwe Bansi is Dead: 241,
243, 246
Materialism
Tiny Alice: 301-302
Meaning of Life
The Three Sisters: 253
Mental and Physical Infirmity
Volpone: 336-338
Messianism
The Wild Duck: 360, 364-366
Middle Ages
The Wild Duck: 360-362
Middle Class
Death and the King's Horseman:
70, 72, 74, 77
Ring Around the Moon: 175-177
Sizwe Bansi is Dead: 239-240
Middle East
Ring Around the Moon: 167-169,
172-173, 176-177
Modernism
Blood Wedding: 27, 29
Monarchy
The Balcony: 3-4, 7
Death and the King's Horseman:
49, 51-53, 57, 59-61, 64-65,
73, 75-76, 79-80
Seven Against Thebes: 209,
211-212
Sizwe Bansi is Dead: 233, 236
Volpone: 315-316
The Wild Duck: 354
Money and Economics
The Kentucky Cycle: 84-85, 91
Lysistrata: 105-106, 110-111
Once in a Lifetime: 146-148, 151-
153, 158-159
Ring Around the Moon:
169, 171-178
Sizwe Bansi is Dead: 240-243
Tiny Alice: 282, 284, 286-289
Volpone: 312-315, 327-330
The Wild Duck: 352, 354-355
Monologue
Sizwe Bansi is Dead: 224-227
Mood
The Three Sisters: 262-263

Morality
Volpone: 313
Morals and Morality
Death and the King's Horseman:
63-69, 75
The Kentucky Cycle: 99-101
The Memorandum: 137-142
Seven Against Thebes: 187-
188, 206, 208
Sizwe Bansi is Dead: 231,
234, 236-238
Tiny Alice: 288, 291
Volpone: 307, 314, 316, 320,
322-330, 334-335, 338, 340
The Wild Duck: 361-362
Motherhood
Blood Wedding: 33, 35
Murder
The Kentucky Cycle: 84,
88-91, 95
Seven Against Thebes: 199-200,
207, 209-210
Music
Blood Wedding: 20, 22, 27,
29, 41-47
Death and the King's Horseman:
51, 55, 57, 59, 63, 66
Lysistrata: 104, 106, 109,
112, 118, 120
The Memorandum: 138, 142
Once in a Lifetime: 145, 153
Seven Against Thebes: 204-
205, 208-209
The Three Sisters: 249, 253, 256,
268, 270-274, 277-279
Mystery and Intrigue
Seven Against Thebes: 208-212
Tiny Alice: 290-291
Volpone: 308-309, 314, 320-325
Myths and Legends
Death and the King's Horseman:
70-72
The Kentucky Cycle: 98, 101-102
Ring Around the Moon: 179-180
Seven Against Thebes: 184, 188-
193, 198-199, 203-208,
211, 213, 217

N

Narration
Death and the King's Horseman:
71-72
Once in a Lifetime: 163
Sizwe Bansi is Dead: 232-234
Nature
Blood Wedding: 38-41, 44-45
Seven Against Thebes: 210
Sizwe Bansi is Dead: 238-
241, 244-246
The Three Sisters: 271
Tiny Alice: 286, 290

Volpone: 321, 323, 325-331, 337, 339, 341-344
The Wild Duck: 361, 367, 371, 373
North America
Death and the King's Horseman: 49, 58-59
Once in a Lifetime: 151-153

O

Obedience
Lysistrata: 108
Ode
Seven Against Thebes: 194-196
The Three Sisters: 279
Oedipus Complex
Seven Against Thebes: 183-185, 189-194, 197-199, 202-212
Old Age
Lysistrata: 104-106, 110, 118-120

P

Painting
Blood Wedding: 27
The Wild Duck: 355
Paranormal
Sizwe Bansi is Dead: 233
Parody
Once in a Lifetime: 163-164
Seven Against Thebes: 202-205
Passivity
Sizwe Bansi is Dead: 240-241, 245
Perception
Blood Wedding: 42-45
Volpone: 312
Permanence
Blood Wedding: 31-32
Death and the King's Horseman: 66, 69
Persecution
Sizwe Bansi is Dead: 229, 231, 233, 237
Volpone: 310, 312-315, 323-325, 336-340
The Wild Duck: 366
Perseverance
The Three Sisters: 269-271
Personal Identity
Seven Against Thebes: 199-201
Sizwe Bansi is Dead: 221-223
The Wild Duck: 352, 360, 364-365
Personal Integrity versus Greed
The Kentucky Cycle: 89
Personality Traits
Lysistrata: 109
Seven Against Thebes: 188
Volpone: 314
Personification
Tiny Alice: 292-294
The Wild Duck: 371-372

Philosophical Ideas
Death and the King's Horseman: 62-69, 76
The Memorandum: 136-137, 141-142
Sizwe Bansi is Dead: 234, 236, 244
The Three Sisters: 267-268
Tiny Alice: 295-296, 300, 302
The Wild Duck: 362, 366
Plants
Blood Wedding: 39-40
Plot
The Balcony: 11
The Memorandum: 139, 141
Seven Against Thebes: 188-189
Tiny Alice: 293
Volpone: 307, 310, 313-315, 322-323, 330-331, 337-339
The Wild Duck: 363, 366
Poetry
Blood Wedding: 20, 29-30, 44, 46
Ring Around the Moon: 178-179
Seven Against Thebes: 215-217
Sizwe Bansi is Dead: 240, 242, 244
The Three Sisters: 277-278
Politicians
The Balcony: 3-4, 8
The Memorandum: 130-131, 137-138
Volpone: 338-340
Politics
The Balcony: 1, 8-9
Blood Wedding: 29-30
Death and the King's Horseman: 58, 62-64, 68-77
The Kentucky Cycle: 90-91
Lysistrata: 110-112
The Memorandum: 130, 132, 136-140
Ring Around the Moon: 174
Sizwe Bansi is Dead: 224-226, 232-233, 236-240, 243, 245-246
The Three Sisters: 255-258
Volpone: 309-310, 316-317, 334-335
The Wild Duck: 354
Postcolonialism
Death and the King's Horseman: 77-78
Poverty
Ring Around the Moon: 171-172
Pride
Blood Wedding: 43-44
Prophecy
Seven Against Thebes: 200-201, 205-208, 211-212
Prostitution
The Balcony: 1-4, 7-8, 12-18
Psychology and the Human Mind
Blood Wedding: 38-40

Death and the King's Horseman: 72
Seven Against Thebes: 207
Tiny Alice: 290
The Wild Duck: 355-356, 366-367
Punishment
Seven Against Thebes: 190
Volpone: 312-314, 319-320

R

Race
The Balcony: 18-19
Sizwe Bansi is Dead: 225-227, 232, 234, 239-241, 246
Racism and Prejudice
Sizwe Bansi is Dead: 223-225, 238-239
Rakes, Rogues, and Villains
Volpone: 322, 324-325
Realism
The Three Sisters: 255
Tiny Alice: 300, 302
The Wild Duck: 346, 355, 357
Religion and Religious Thought
Blood Wedding: 42-43
Death and the King's Horseman: 55-56, 62-64
Ring Around the Moon: 180
Seven Against Thebes: 183-184, 187-190, 202-204, 209-211, 214-215
Tiny Alice: 283, 286-289, 292, 294, 301-305
Volpone: 316
The Wild Duck: 360, 362, 365
Revenge
The Kentucky Cycle: 83-84, 89, 94-98, 101
Volpone: 337, 339
Rewriting American History
The Kentucky Cycle: 88
Roman Catholicism
Tiny Alice: 282, 287, 289

S

Saints
The Three Sisters: 273, 277-278
Satire
The Balcony: 15-16
Once in a Lifetime: 151, 154-155, 160, 163-164
Volpone: 322-323
Science and Technology
The Memorandum: 128-129, 136, 139, 142-143
Once in a Lifetime: 148, 153, 158-159
Sentimentality
The Wild Duck: 367, 369-372
Setting
Blood Wedding: 27

The Kentucky Cycle: 85, 89
Seven Against Thebes: 188, 190
Sizwe Bansi is Dead: 220, 224
Volpone: 317-320, 333-336
The Wild Duck: 362-363
Sex
  Lysistrata: 108
Sex and Sexuality
  The Balcony: 1, 4, 11, 13-18
  Death and the King's Horseman:
    65-67
  Lysistrata: 105, 108-120
  Seven Against Thebes: 198, 200
  Tiny Alice: 281, 283, 285, 287-
    288, 303-305
  Volpone: 319-320
Sexual Abuse
  The Kentucky Cycle: 84,
    88, 91, 94-95
Sexuality
  Tiny Alice: 287
Sickness
  Volpone: 307-310, 314-315, 340
Sin
  Death and the King's Horseman:
    66-67
  Seven Against Thebes: 207, 209
  Tiny Alice: 287, 289, 291
  Volpone: 307, 316, 325, 329-332,
    336-337, 342
  The Wild Duck: 372
Slavery
  The Kentucky Cycle: 84, 89, 91
Social Order
  The Balcony: 4, 7
  The Three Sisters: 255-256
Socialism
  Death and the King's Horseman:
    72-77
Soothsayer
  Seven Against Thebes: 205-
    206, 210
Spiritual Leaders
  Seven Against Thebes: 209-211
  Tiny Alice: 288-289
Spirituality
  Seven Against Thebes: 201-203,
    207-208, 211
  The Three Sisters: 269-271
  Tiny Alice: 285-292
Sports and the Sporting Life
  Volpone: 321, 323-325, 338-340
Storms and Weather Conditions
  Blood Wedding: 43, 45-47

Strength and Weakness
  Lysistrata: 108
Structure
  Blood Wedding: 39, 42, 45
  The Kentucky Cycle: 89
  Seven Against Thebes: 200-201
Success and Failure
  Once in a Lifetime: 151
Success and Failure
  Death and the King's Horseman:
    49, 52, 55, 57, 59, 64-67
  Sizwe Bansi is Dead: 240,
    242-243
Suicide
  Death and the King's Horseman:
    49, 51-52, 57, 59, 64, 67,
    69-70, 74-76
Surrealism
  Blood Wedding: 27, 29
Survival
  Sizwe Bansi is Dead: 233-236

T

The American Dream
  The Kentucky Cycle: 88
The Individual versus Society
  Blood Wedding: 26
Time and Change
  Sizwe Bansi is Dead: 231-232
Tone
  Blood Wedding: 45-47
  Volpone: 340-341, 344
Totalitarianism
  The Memorandum: 137, 139-141
Tragedy
  Blood Wedding: 20, 30, 42-43
  Death and the King's Horseman:
    56-58, 63-66, 78-80
  Lysistrata: 109
  Seven Against Thebes: 183, 185,
    187-188, 191
  The Wild Duck: 367-370, 373
Tragicomedy
  The Wild Duck: 367, 370-373
Trust
  Seven Against Thebes: 202-204
Truth and Falsehood
  The Wild Duck: 350

U

Uncertainty
  Death and the King's Horseman:
    64-66

Seven Against Thebes: 209-212
Understanding
  Blood Wedding: 42
  Death and the King's Horseman:
    75-76
  The Wild Duck: 352, 355-356
Upper Class
  The Balcony: 4, 6-7
  Death and the King's Horseman:
    75-77
  Ring Around the Moon: 167, 171-
    173, 176-177
Utopianism
  Death and the King's Horseman:
    71, 74, 76

V

Value of Rituals and Symbols
  The Balcony: 7
Victim and Victimization
  Volpone: 314
Violence
  The Kentucky Cycle: 88

W

War and Peace
  Lysistrata: 108
War, the Military, and Soldier Life
  The Balcony: 8-9
  Death and the King's Horseman:
    56, 58, 63-64, 67, 69
  The Kentucky Cycle: 99-100
  Lysistrata: 105-106, 109-119
  Seven Against Thebes: 187-
    189, 193-212
  The Three Sisters: 249, 253, 255-
    257, 273-274
Wealth versus Poverty
  Ring Around the Moon: 171
Wealth
  Ring Around the Moon: 166-167,
    171-172, 176-180
  Seven Against Thebes: 213
  Volpone: 308-310, 313, 315, 318-
    320, 327-328, 333, 336
Wildlife
  Blood Wedding: 43-44
  The Three Sisters: 271
  Tiny Alice: 287-288
  Volpone: 321-332, 336-340
  The Wild Duck: 349, 352-
    353, 360-366